MAJOR AIRLINES
OF
The World

TWA Trans World Airlines Routes..........
Routes Certificated or Applied For _____
Other Airlines.......................
Copyright by C.S. HAMMOND & Co., N. Y.

TWA
Vacation
Guide
and
WORLD
ATLAS

TWA
Vacation Guide and WORLD ATLAS

compiled for
TRANS WORLD AIRLINES

Published by
C. S. HAMMOND and COMPANY
MAPLEWOOD, N. J.   NEW YORK, N. Y.

ACKNOWLEDGEMENTS

TWA-*Trans World Airlines wishes to gratefully acknowledge the cooperation and help of the many state, federal, provincial and foreign government travel and information offices who have made this book possible by supplying background material and photographs. We are especially indebted to the Organization of American States (The Pan American Union), the National Association of Travel Organizations and the American Geographical Society for the use of their material.*

CONTENTS — MAPS

CONTENTS — VACATION GUIDE ARTICLES

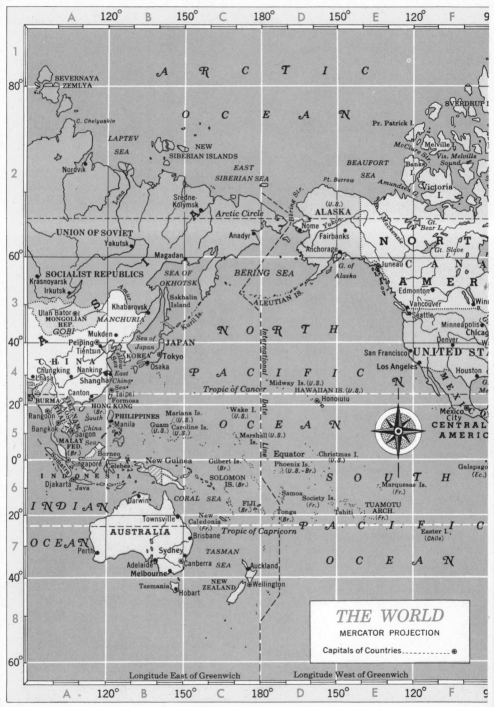

6

THE WORLD

MERCATOR PROJECTION

Capitals of Countries............ ◉

Air-Line Distances in Statute Miles

POLAR PROJECTION
MAP OF
THE WORLD

Copyright by C.S. HAMMOND & CO., N.Y.

SCALE ON MERIDIANS

STATUTE MILES
0 500 1000 1500 2000

Azimuthal Equidistant Projection
Tangent at North Pole

10

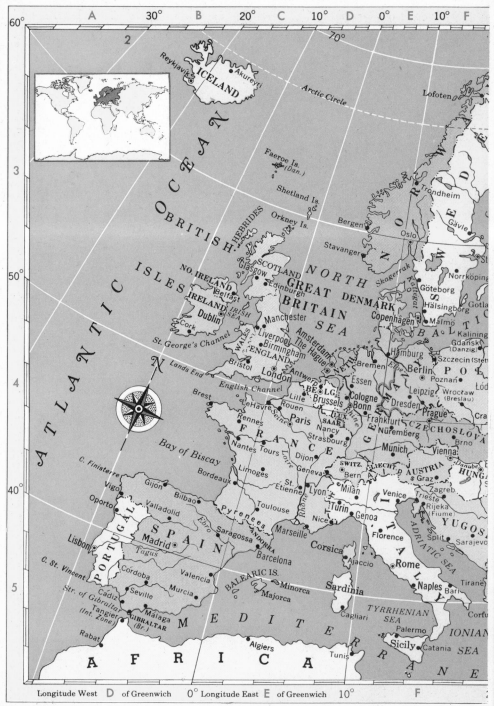

A 30° B 20° C 10° D 0° E 10° F

60°

2

Reykjavik Akureyri
ICELAND

70°

Arctic Circle

Lofoten

NORWAY

Faeroe Is.
(Dan.)

3

Trondheim

Gävle

Shetland Is.

Bergen

Oslo

St

SWEDEN

BRITISH

Orkney Is.

Stavanger

Norrköping

O

Skagerrak

NORTH

Göteborg

Hälsingborg

Gotla

ISLES

HEBRIDES

SCOTLAND

Glasgow Edinburgh

GREAT

DENMARK

Kattegat

Copenhagen

Malmö

BALTIC

50°

NO. IRELAND

Belfast

BRITAIN

SEA

Kalining

IRELAND

IRISH

Dublin

SEA

Manchester

Liverpool The Hague

Amsterdam

Hamburg

Gdansk
(Danzig)

Szczecin (Stet

POL

Cork

WALES

Birmingham

ENGLAND

Antwerp

NETH

Bremen

Elbe

Berlin

St. George's Channel

Bristol

London

Essen

Poznan

Lód

Lands End

BEL. LG.

Cologne

Leipzig

Wroclaw
(Breslau)

N

Brest

Lille
Brussels

Bonn

Dresden

Prague

Cra

English Channel

Rouen

LUX.

Rhine

Frankfurt

GERMANY

CZECHOSLOVA

LeHavre Seine

SAAR

Nürnberg

4

Rennes

Paris

Nancy

Brno

FRANCE

Strasbourg

Munich

Vienna

Nantes Tours

Dijon

Danube

Bay of Biscay

Limoges

Geneva

SWITZ.

Bern

LIECHT.

AUSTRIA

HUNG

C. Finisterre

Bordeaux

St.
Etienne

Lyon

Milan

s Graz

Zagreb

Vigo

Gijon

Rhône

Venice

Trieste

Rijeka
(Fiume)

40°

Oporto

Bilbao

Pyrenees

Toulouse

Nice

Turin

Genoa

YUGOS.

Valladolid

ANDORRA

Marseille

Florence

ADRIATIC SEA

Split

PORTUGAL

SPAIN

Saragossa

Sarajevo

Lisbon

Madrid

Barcelona

Corsica

Rome

Tagus

Ajaccio

ITALY

Córdoba

Valencia

BALEARIC IS.

Sardinia

Naples

Bari

C. St. Vincent

Murcia

Minorca

Tirane

5

Cadiz

Seville

Majorca

Cagliari

TYRRHENIAN

SEA

Corfu

Str. of Gibraltar

Málaga

GIBRALTAR
(Br.)

Palermo

IONIAN

Tangier
(Int. Zone)

M E D I T E R

Sicily

Catania

SEA

Rabat

AFRICA

Algiers

Tunis

RANE

E

ATLANTIC OCEAN

NORTH SEA

BALTIC

Longitude West D of Greenwich 0° Longitude East E of Greenwich 10° F

SHETLAND ISLANDS
Same scale as main map

Unst
Yell
Fetlar
Whalsey
Lerwick
Papa Stour
Foula

Keighley
Preston
Burnley
Bradford
Halifax
Blackburn
Bolton
Huddersfield
Rochdale
Oldham
Blackpool
IRISH SEA
Wigan
St. Helens
Burton
Manchester
Hyde
Stockport
Macclesfield
Southport
Bootle
Wood
Salford
Warrington
Wallasey
Liverpool
Birkenhead
Ellesmere Port
Chester
Crewe
R. Dee

MILES
0 4 8 12 16 20

Lerwick
Fair I.
SHETLAND ISLANDS

Westray
Sanday
Stronsay
Kirkwall
Hoy
Scapa Flow
Pentland Firth
ORKNEY ISLANDS
C. Wrath
Strathy Pt.
Thurso
Wick
Loch Shin
Loch Inver

Dornoch Firth
Tain
Fraserburgh
Dingwall
Invergordon
Elgin
Buckie
Peterhead
Moray Firth
Nairn
Inverurie
Aberdeen
Stornoway
Lewis
Harris
North Minch
Little Minch
the Hebrides
North Uist
South Uist
Barra Isles
Skye
Portree
Mallaig
Rum
Coll
Tiree
Mull
Tobermory
Iona
Gulf of
Firth of Lorne

Inverness
CULLODEN MOOR
Loch Ness
Ballater
Braemar
Blair-Atholl
Pitlochry
Forfar
Glamis
Brechin
Montrose
Arbroath
Dundee
Firth of Tay
St. Andrews
Perth
Auchterarder
Methil
Kirkcaldy
Firth of Forth
Dunfermline
North Berwick
Falkirk
Dunbar
Glasgow
Edinburgh
Berwick-u.-T.
Peebles
Abbotsford
Alnwick
Dryburgh
Galashiels
Blyth
Melrose
Hawick
Annan
Newcastle
South Shields
Gateshead
Sunderland
Durham
Lockerbie
Carlisle
Dumfries
Castle Douglas
Stranraer

Stonehaven

Loch Linnhe
Ben Nevis
4,406
Fort William
Loch Shiel
Caledonian Canal
Oban
Loch Awe
Inveraray
Callander
Loch Lomond
Greenock
Gourock
Paisley
Kilmarnock
Troon
Prestwick
Ayr
Maybole
Girvan

Jura
Islay
Campbeltown
Arran
Firth of Clyde
North Channel
Giant's Causeway
Ballycastle
Coleraine
Limavady
Ballymena
Larne

Matin Head
Malin Head
Tory I.
L. Swilly
Buncrana
Aran I.
Dunglow
Letterkenny
Londonderry

ATLANTIC OCEAN

SHETLAND ISLANDS
Same scale as main map
Kirkcaldy
Alloa
Dunfermline
Firth of Forth
Stirling
Bannockburn
Boness
Falkirk
Musselburgh
R. Forth
Edinburgh
Dumbarton
Clydebank
Forth & Clyde Canal
Airdrie
Glasgow
Coatbridge
Motherwell
Port Glasgow
Clyde
Paisley
Greenock
Rutherglen
Hamilton
Largs
Loch Long

MILES
0 4 8 12 16

GREAT BRITAIN
and
IRELAND

BONNE PROJECTION
Copyright by C.S. HAMMOND & Co., N.Y.

SCALE OF MILES
0 20 40 60 80

SCALE OF KILOMETRES
0 10 20 40 60 80

Capitals of Countries ⊕
Canals ────

14

G E R M A N Y

LUXEMBOURG

S A A R

PROVINCES

NETHERLANDS

1 Drenthe......J 2
2 Friesland......G 1
3 Gelderland......G 3
4 Groningen......J 1
5 Limburg......G 5
6 North Brabant F 4
7 North Holland.E 2
8 Overijssel......H 3
9 Utrecht......F 3
10 Zeeland......C 4
11 South Holland.E 3

BELGIUM

1 Antwerp......E 5
2 Brabant......E 6
3 East Flanders.C 6
4 Hainaut......C 6
5 Liege......G 6
6 Limburg......F 5
7 Luxembourg......F 8
8 Namur......E 7
9 West Flanders B 5

Copyright by C. S. HAMMOND & CO., N. Y.

4535

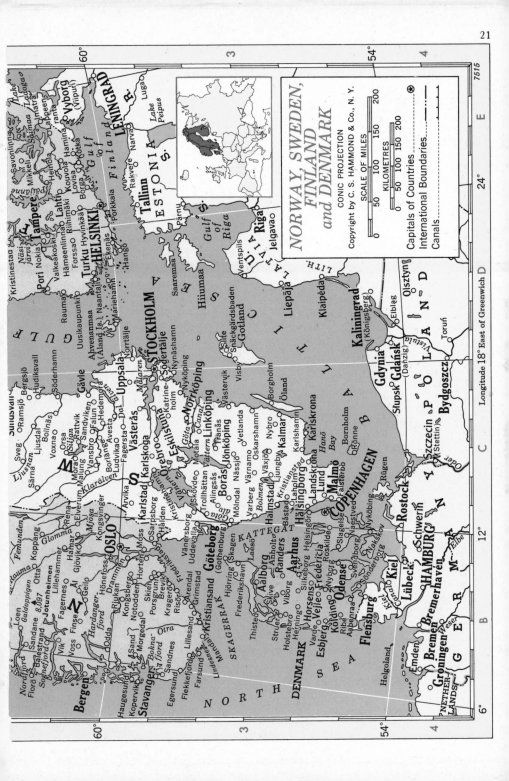

NORWAY, SWEDEN, FINLAND and DENMARK

CONIC PROJECTION

Copyright by C. S. HAMMOND & Co., N. Y.

SCALE OF MILES

| 0 | 50 | 100 | 150 | 200 |

KILOMETRES

| 0 | 50 | 100 | 150 | 200 |

Capitals of Countries ⊛
International Boundaries
Canals

Longitude 18° East of Greenwich

7615

SWITZERLAND AND LIECHTENSTEIN

AUSTRIA CZECHOSLOVAKIA and HUNGARY

CONIC PROJECTION

SCALE OF MILES

0   20   40   60   80   100

SCALE OF KILOMETRES

0   20   40   60   80   100

Capitals of Countries   ⊛

International Boundaries   — · · —

Canals   ——

18°   E   20°   F   22°   G

1

50°

2

48°

3

46°

4

Oder
Odra
Opole
Nysa
Nysa
Jeseník
Vrbno
Raciborz
Gliwice
Sosnowiec
Stalinogród
Vistula
Krnov
Opava
Karviná
Dvorec
Bohumín
Ostrava
Slezská Ostrava
Český Těšín
Frýdek
Hranice
Jablunkov
Nový Jičín
Jablunka
Pass
Nowy
Targ
Dunajec
Nowy Sącz
Sanok
Dukla Pass
stějov
Bečva
Valašské
Meziříčí
Přerov
Čadca
Kroměříž
Vsetín
Námestovo
High
Tatra
Podolínec
Bardejov
Gottwaldov
(Zlín)
Žilina
Orava
Liptov.
Sv. Mikuláš
Beluša
Stalin
(Gerlachouka)
Kežmarok
Sabinov
Stropkov
Humenné
Uherské
Hradiště
Turč.
Sv. Martin
Ružomberok
8,700
Poprad
Spišská Nová Ves
Nové
Město
Trenčín
Korytnica
Low
Tatra
Dobšiná
Prešov
Vranov
Košice
Michalovce
Kúty
Piešťany
Bánovce
Nitra
Handlová
Zvolen
Banská
Bystrica
Brezno
Tisovec
Detva
Smolník
Revúca
Rožňava
Sečovce
Uzhgorod
Latoritsa
Malacky
Hlohovec
Topoľčany
Rimavská
Sobota
Gönci
Sátoraljaújhely
Mukachevo
Trnava
Sered
Nová
Baňa
Banská
Štiavnica
Poltár
Edelény
Sárospatak
Bratislava
Nitra
Hron
Levice
Lučenec
Ipeľ
Sajó
Hernád
Tisza
Kisvárda
Petržalka
Šahy
Salgótarján
Diósgyőr
Tokaj
Šurany
Nové
Zámky
Ipoly
Balassagyarmat
Miskolc
Nyíregyháza
Calovo
Kolárovo
Štúrovo
Pásztó
Matra
3,318
Mező-
kövesd
Polgár
Hajdúnánás
Nagykálló
Nyír-
bátor
Fehérgy-
armat
Lébény
Komárno
Vác
Gyöngyös
Heves
Hajdúböszörmény
Hajdúhadház
Satu-
Mare
Csorna
Győr
Tata
Esztergom
Hatvan
Jászárokszállás
Jászapáti
Balmazújváros
Carei
Kisbér
Varsány
Újpest
BUDAPEST
Rákospalota
Hajdúszoboszló
Debrecen
Pápa
Köröshegy
2,339
Mór
Budafok
Csepel
Soroksár
Nagykáta
Monor
Jászberény
Kunhegyes
Karcag
Madaras
Püspökladány
Nagyléta
Berettyóújfalu
Székesfehérvár
Vál
Ráckeve
Cegléd
Abony
Törökszentmiklós
Kisújszállás
Túrkeve
Crisul
Repede
Veszprém
Adony
Hercegfalva
Kunszent-
miklós
Szolnok
Mezőtúr
Dévaványa
Sebes Körös
Oradea
Bakony
Siófok
Nagykőrös
Gyoma
Mezőberény
Salonta
Balatonfüred
Dunaföldvár
Kecskemét
Szarvas
Békés
Sarkad
Beiuş
Balaton
Tab
Paks
Kiskőrös
Csongrád
Szentes
Békéscsaba
Gyula
Negru
Balatonszentgyörgy
Marcali
Kalocsa
Kiskun-
halas
Kiskunmajsa
Oros-
háza
Crişul
Alb
Şebiş
Tolna
Kistelek
Hódmezővásárhely
agykanizsa
Kaposvár
Szekszárd
Kiskunfélegyháza
Kiskunhalas
Kiskundorozsma
Makó
Battonya
Arad
Lipova
Csurgó
Bátaszék
Baja
Janoshalma
Szeged
Mureşul
Szigetvár
Pécs
Bácsalmás
Barcs
Mohács
Subotica
Senta
Tisa
Drava
Sombor
Kikinda
Jimbolia
Timişoara
Lugoj
Timişul

Greenwich 18°   E   20°   F   22°   G   6535

26

E 2° F 0° G 2° H 4°

Adour
Auch
Castres
Montpellier
Dax
Bayonne
Pau
Tarbes
Toulouse
Béziers
Sète
Santoña
Bermeo
San Sebastián
Irún
Lourdes
Carcassonne
Narbonne
Bilbao
Sestao
Eibar
Tolosa
Foix
G. of Lions
BASQUE
PROV'S
Vitoria
NAVARRE
Peña
Colorada
9,459
ANDORRA
Llivia
Nuria
Perpignan
Estella
Pamplona
Pico de Aneto
11,167
Andorra la Vella
Port-Bou
C. de Creus
Miranda
de Ebro
to.Domingo
Logroño
Tafalla
Aragón
Jaca
Boltaña
Seo de Urgel
Puigcerda
Olot
Figueras
Gulf of Rosas
Calahorra
Uncastillo
Graus
Tremp
Berga
Vich
Gerona
Palafrugell
Alfaro
Tudela
Huesca
Barbastro
Solsona
Manresa
Sabadell
Calella
San Felíu de Guixols
Tarazona
Borja
Sierra de
Moncayo
Saragossa
Balaguer
Lerida
Montserrat 4,064
Igualada
Mataró
Soria
La Almunia
(Zaragoza)
Pina
Fraga
Tarrasa
Badalona
BARCELONA
Almazán
Ateca
Calatayud
Azuara
Ebro
Caspe
Flix
Poblet
Reus
Hospitalet
Sitges
Villanueva y Geltrú
Sigüenza
Daroca
Albalate
Alcañiz
Tarragona
Gulf of
San Jorge
C. de Tortosa
Guadalajara
Monreal
del Campo
Calanda
Tortosa
Amposta
Ulldecona
Vinaroz
Benicarló
Nudo de
Albarracin
6,034
Tereul
Alcora
Cabanes
Cuenca
Cañete
Villarreal
Castellón de la Plana
Chelva
Burriana
Liria
Sagunto
Gulf of
Utiel
Valencia
Torrente
Valencia
Sueca
Alcira
La Roda
Júcar
Oliva
Iviza
(Ibiza)
Tomelloso
Manzanares
Albacete
Ayora
Játiva
Denia
Cabo
de la Nao
Formentera
Ibiza
Almansa
Villena
Alcoy
Infantes
Tobarra
Yecla
Villajoyosa
Yeste
Hellín
Elda
Alicante
Jumilla
Segura
Elche
Calasparra
Cieza
Orihuela
Caravaca
Mula
Murcia
Huéscar
Totana
Alcantarilla
La Unión
Cabo de Palos
Vélez Rubio
Lorca
Cartagena
Baza
Albox
Águilas
Sierra Nevada
Vera
Mojácar
Mulhacén
11,417
Níjar
Almería
Berja
Motril
Adra
C. de
Gata
Alborán
(Spain)

BALEARIC ISLANDS
Minorca
Ciudadela
Alcudia
Bay
Mahón
Inca
Artá
Majorca
Manacor
Palma
Lluchmayor
Cabrera

MAJORCA inset:
Colmenar
Viejo
Algete
Chamartin
de la Rosa
Alcalá
de Henares
MADRID
Carabanchel Bajo
P. Nuevo
Puente
de Vallecas
Leganés
Vallecas
Navalcarnero
Getafe
Arganda
Ciempozuelos
Colmenar
de Oreja
3° 30'

SPAIN and PORTUGAL
CONIC PROJECTION
SCALE OF MILES
0 25 50 75 100 125 150
SCALE OF KILOMETRES
0 25 50 75 100 125 150
Capitals --- ⊛ International Boundaries ----

E Longitude 2° West of F Greenwich 0° Longitude G East of 2° Greenwich H 8535

ITALY

CONIC PROJECTION

SCALE OF MILES

0   20   40   60   80   100   120

SCALE OF KILOMETRES

0   20   40   60   80   100   120

Capitals of Countries ⊗

Regional Capitals ⊙

AFRICA

LAMBERT AZIMUTHAL
EQUAL-AREA PROJECTION

SCALE OF MILES

0 200 400 600 800 1000 1200

SCALE OF KILOMETRES

0 400 800 1200

Capitals .... ⊙

International Boundaries .... ▬▬▬

Canals .... ┅┅┅

Copyright by C. S. HAMMOND & Co., N.Y.

CAPE VERDE ISLANDS
(Ilhas do Cabo Verde)
(PORTUGUESE)

SCALE OF MILES

0 50 100

Boavista
Santo Antão
Porto Grande
São Nicolau
Sal
São Vicente
São Tiago
Fogo
Praia

17° 23° 15°

ATLANTIC OCEAN

Ascension
° (Br.)

St. Helena
° (Br.)

Tropic of Capricorn

Pointe-Noire
Luebo Kongolo
Léopoldville
Cabinda
Matadi
C O N G O
Albertville
L. Kisale
L. Upemba
L. Mweru
Manono
Elisabethville
Jadotville

Luanda
Malange
A N G O L A
Benguela
Nova
Lisboa
Sá da Bandeira
Moçâmedes
C. Frio

SOUTH
WEST
AFRICA
Tsumeb
Windhoek
Lüderitz
Walvis Bay
Port Nolloth

Ujiji
TANGANYIKA
Dodoma
L. Tanganyika

FEDERATION OF
RHODESIA
Broken Hill
Lusaka
Livingstone
Victoria Falls
Zambezi
Bulawayo
Zimbabwe

NYASALAND
Zomba

BECHUANA-
LAND
L. Makarikari
Maun
Serowe
Mafeking

Zanzibar
ZANZIBAR
Tanga
Dar-es-Salaam
Aldabra Is.
Comoro Is.
(Fr.)
Diego-
Suarez
Tamatave
Majunga
Tananarive
Antsirabe
M A D A G A S C A R
Tuléar
C. Ste. Marie

Lindi (Br.)
C. Delgado
Ruvuma
L.
Nyasa
M O Z A M B I Q U E
Nampula
Quelimane
Beira
Inhambane
Limpopo

Mozambique Channel

Salisbury

Mbabane
SWAZI-
LAND
Zululand
Lourenço Marques
Pietermaritzburg
Durban
Basutoland
Ld.
East London

U N I O N   O F
S O U T H   A F R I C A
Pretoria
Johannesburg
Kimberley
Bloemfontein
Orange
Oudtshoorn
Knysna
Port
Elizabeth
Calvinia
Cango
Caves
Capetown
Muizenberg
C. of Good Hope
Plettenberg
Bay
C. Agulhas

INDIAN

OCEAN

Long. West of Greenwich 20° A 10° B 0° C 10° D 20° E 30° F 40° G Long. 50° East H of 60° Greenwich

34

G 55° H 60° J 65° K 70° L 75°

40° 1

CASPIAN SEA

S.S.R.

Tashauz○ Urgench Kyzyl-Kum Desert ○Tashkent Andizhan
Kara-Bogaz-Gol Khiva○ Syr Dar'ya Kokand
S. Kara-Kum Desert Amu ○Bukhara Leninabad Vakhsh CHINA
Krasnovodsk Dar'ya Samarkand Stalin Peak 24,589 SINKIANG
Kizyl-Arvat Chardzhou Stalinabad○ Pamir
Ashkhabad Bayram-Ali Termez Faizabad JAMMU
Atrek Mary○○ Andkhui Mazar-i-Sharif Khanabad Hindu Kush Chitral AND
Bandar Shah○Gurgan Meshed Tus○ Maimana Charikar Khyber Pass Abbottabad
Babulsar Babol R. a.Sabzawar Nishapur Kabul Peshawar Taxila Srinagar
Elburz ▲Demavend 18,603 Kashmar○ Herat Rud Attock Rawalpindi KASHMIR
Rayy Qum Tehran (Teheran) AFGHANISTAN Ghazni Dera Ismail Khan Sialkot Amritsar
Darya-yi-Namak Dasht-i-Kavir Sangar Kalat-i-Ghilzai Lahore
Kashan Shindand Helmand Kandahar Dera Ghazi Khan Multan
Isfahan Tabas Farah Quetta Sutlej Bahawalpur Bikaner
Gavkhaneh Yezd I R A N Zabul Dasht-i-Lut Hamun-i-Helmand Rudbar Chagai Kalat Shikarpur Sukkur Jodhpur
shahr ▲Kuh-i-Dinar 14,030 Namakzar Zahidan Hills Larkana Mohenjo-Daro Nawabshah Thar Desert
Shiraz○ Persepolis Kerman Siahan Nal Bela Hyderabad Udaipur
Kazerun Tashk Sirjan Bam Kharan Kalat Indus Ahmadabad
Bushire Lar Hamun-i-Jaz Murian Iranshahr Tump Turbat Randla Bhavnagar Surat
Mund Bandar 'Abbas Jask Makran Chahbar Gwadar (Oman) Karachi Tatta Rann of Kutch Diu Damão
BAHREIN Manama Lingeh Str. of Hormuz G. of Kutch Porbandar (Port.India) (Port.India)
QATAR Doha Sharja OMAN Muscat Bombay
Abu Dhabi Sohar GULF OF OMAN
TRUCIAL Baraimi Matrah Akhdar
Cancer

A al Khali

RATE SULTANATE OF OMAN Sur Ras al Hadd
Masira ARABIAN SEA

N

THE NEAR EAST
CONIC PROJECTION
SCALE OF MILES
0 100 200 300 400
KILOMETRES
0 100 200 300 400

Capitals of Countries ....⊛
Other Capitals ....◉
International Boundaries —··—
Other Boundaries ——·—

Sauqira Bay
Kuria Muria Is. (Aden)
Dhofar Murbat
Qamr Bay Salala
W. Hadhramaut

Socotra (Aden)

0° G 55° Longitude H East of 60° Greenwich J 65° K 70° 7575

ISRAEL and JORDAN

CYLINDRICAL PROJECTION

SCALE OF MILES

0   5   10   15   20   25

SCALE OF KILOMETRES

0   5   10   15   20   25

Capitals of Countries ⋯⋯⋯⋯ ☆

District Capitals ⋯⋯⋯⋯⋯⋯ △

International Boundaries⋯⋯

District Boundaries⋯⋯⋯⋯

Sub-District Boundaries⋯⋯⋯

Israel is shown according to the terms of the Israeli-Jordanian and Israeli-Egyptian armistice agreements. The districts and sub-districts of the former Palestinian Mandate are shown for reference only and are not the present-day administrative divisions.

A 60° B 70° C 80° D

U. S. S. R.

Sultanabad · Andkhui · Balkh · Kulyab · R. Pamir · Khorog · Yarkand (Soche) · Takla Makan

Qain · Shibarghan · Mazar-i-Sharif · Faizabad · Khanabad · Khorog

Shindand · Kushka · Maimana · Bamian · Hindu Kush · Chitral · Gilgit · Baltit · Karakorum · Karghalik · Moji · Khotan (Hotien) · SINKIANG

Birjand · Herat · Daolat Yar · Charikar · Chilas · K2 (Godwin Austen) 28,250 · Keriya

Farsi · Kabul · Jalalabad · Peshawar · Abbottabad · Attock · JAMMU · Skardu · Muztagh 23,890

Jawain · Farah · Ghazni · Khyber Pass · Kohat · AND KASHMIR · Srinagar · Leh · KU

Zabul · Kandahar · Kalat-i-Ghilzai · Bannu · Dera · Punch · Rudok · Thog · Jalung

Khash · Sangar · Ismail Khan · Sialkot · Jammu · Dharamsala · Chushul · Tashigong · Gartok · Mendong Gomba

Rudbar · Ft. Sandeman · Quetta · Loralai · Lahore · Amritsar · Jullundur · Simla · Laga · Trans-H

Zahidan · Chagai · Nok · Nushki · Sibi · Multan · Ferozepore · Chandigarh · Dehra Dun · Tradom

Khash · Kundi Kharan · Kalat · Rajanpur · Bahawalpur · Ludhiana · Patiala · Ambala · Saharanpur · Almora · Jumla · Mustang

Iranshahr · Siahan · Kalat · Khuzdar · Derabugti · Sutlej · Meerut · Moradabad · Bareilly · Katmandu · PATAN

Panjgur · Mghenjo-Daro · Shikarpur · Bikaner · Churu · New Delhi · Aligarh · Shahjahanpur · Sallyana

Tump · Turbat · Larkana · Sukkur · Khairpur · Jaisalmer · Jaipur · Agra · Lucknow · Faizabad · Gorakhpur · Chapra

Gwadar (Oman) · Bela · Sonmiani · Nawabshah · Jodhpur · Ajmer · Gwalior · Lashkar · Kanpur · Banaras + · Sarnath · Patna

Tropic of Cancer · Karachi · Hyderabad · Mirpur · Jalor · Tonk · Datia · Jhansi · Allahabad · Ganges · Gaya

Nagar Parkar · Sirohi · Udaipur · Neemuch · Kotah · Sironj · Rewa · Daltonganj

Mandvi · Bhuj · Viramgam · Abu · Sanchi · Saugor · Ranchi · How

Jamnagar · Morvi · Ahmadabad · Ujjain · Vindh · Bhopal · Jubbulpore · Chirmiri · Jamshedpur · CALCU

Rajkot · Baroda · Ratlam · Narbada · Chhindwara · Bilaspur

Porbandar · Bhavnagar · Indore · Khandwa · Seoni · Balaghat · Raipur · Sambalpur · Raj · Cutt

Junagadh · Surat · Dhulia · Ellichpur · Bhandara · Bolangir · Bhu

Veraval · Diu (Port. India) · Damao (Port. India) · Navsari · Jalgaon · Akola · Amraoti · Nagpur · Kanker · Russelkonda · Puri

Jamnagar · Yeola · Nasik · Ajanta · Wardha · Yeotmal · Chanda · Jeypore · Chicacole

BOMBAY · Kalyan · Ahmadnagar · Aurangabad · Nanded · Godavari · Jagdalpur · Vizianagaram

ARABIAN SEA · Murud · Poona · Bidh · Nizamabad · Visakhapatnam

Mahabaleshvar · Barsi · Secunderabad · Hanamkonda · Rajahmundry

Ratnagiri · Sholapur · Gulbarga · HYDERABAD · Eluru · Kakinada

Kolhapur · Bijapur · Kistna · Vijayavada · Yanaon

Malvan · GOA (Port. India) · Belgaum · Raichur · Guntur · Masulipatnam

Pangim · Gadag · Hubli · Bellary · Kurnool · Chirala

Karwar · Davangere · Anantapur · Kavali

Kumta · Shimoga · Tumkur · Cuddapah · Nellore

Udipi · Bangalore · Kolar Gold Fields · BE

Mangalore · Chetlat · Mysore · Vellore · Madras

LACCADIVE ISLANDS (India) · Ootacamund · Salem · Mahabalipuram

Kozhikode · Mahe · Kanchipuram · Pondichéry

Kavaratti · Coimbatore · Trichur · Tanjore · Cuddalore · Karikal

Kalpeni · Tiruchirappalli · Madurai · Negapattinam · Jaffna

Alleppey · Periyar L. · Rames-waram

Minicoy · Trivandrum · Tuticorin · CEYLON · Trincomalee

Eight Degree Channel · Tirunelveli · Nagercoil · Gulf of · Anuradhapura · Batticaloa

MALDIVE IS. (Br.) · C. Comorin · Mannar · Sigiriya

Negombo · Colombo · Kandy · Nuwara Eliya · Badulla

Moratuwa · Ratnapura · Galle · Copyright by C. S. H

Longitude D East of

B 70° C

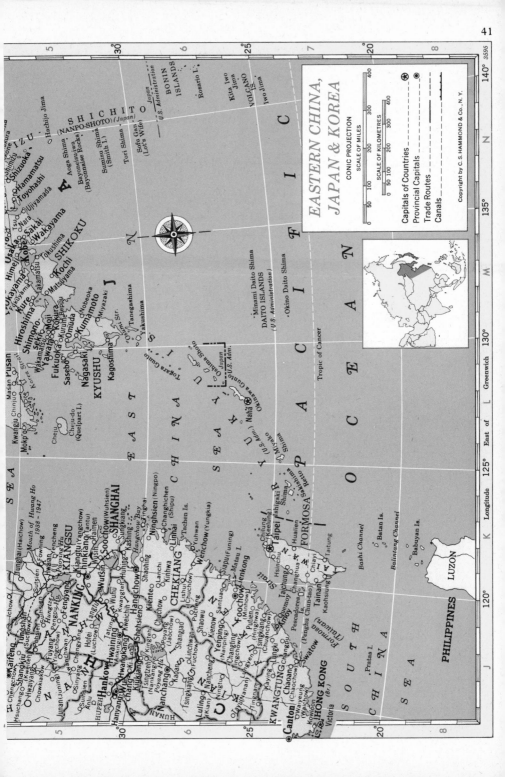

EASTERN CHINA,
JAPAN & KOREA

CONIC PROJECTION

SCALE OF MILES

SCALE OF KILOMETRES

Capitals of Countries
Provincial Capitals
Trade Routes
Canals

Copyright by C. S. HAMMOND & Co., N. Y.

42

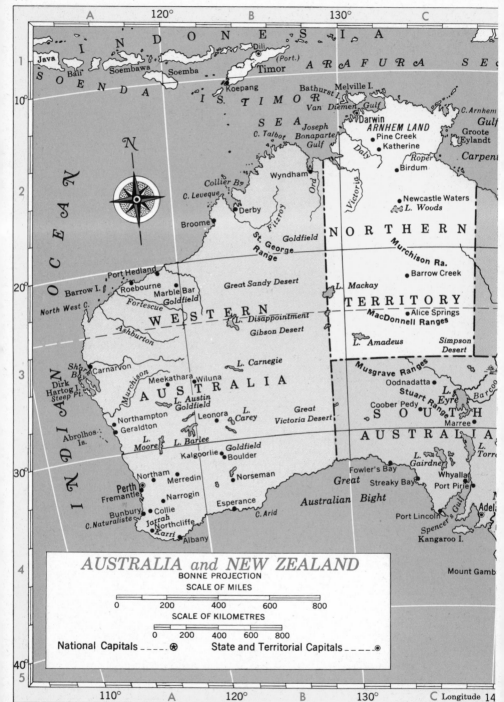

44

A 120° B 130° C

INDONESIA

Java
Bali Soembawa Soemba
SOENDA
Dili
(Port.)
Timor
Koepang
IS. TIMOR
ARAFURA SEA

1

10°

Bathurst I. Melville I.
Van Diemen Gulf
Darwin
ARNHEM LAND
Pine Creek
Katherine
C. Arnhem
Gulf
Groote
Eylandt
Carpen

C. Talbot
Joseph
Bonaparte
Gulf

SEA

Daly
Roper
Birdum

Collier B?
C. Leveque
Wyndham
Ord
Victoria
Newcastle Waters
L. Woods

2

Derby
Fitzroy
Broome
St. George
Goldfield
Range

NORTHERN

Murchison Ra.

20°

Port Hedland
Barrow I.
Roebourne
Marble Bar
Goldfield
Fortescue

Great Sandy Desert

L. Mackay

Barrow Creek

TERRITORY

MacDonnell Ranges
Alice Springs

WESTERN

Ashburton
L. Disappointment
Gibson Desert

L. Amadeus

Simpson
Desert

North West C.

3

Shark
B?
Dirk
Hartog I.
Steep Pt.
Carnarvon
Murchison
Meekathara Wiluna

L. Carnegie

AUSTRALIA

Musgrave Ranges
Oodnadatta
L.
Eyre

Stuart Range
Coober Pedy

SOUTH

Northampton
Geraldton
L. Austin
Goldfield
Leonora
L.
Carey
Great
Victoria Desert

Marree

Abrolhos
Is.
L.
Moore
L. Barlee
Kalgoorlie
Boulder
Goldfield

AUSTRALIA

L.
Gairdner
Whyalla
Port Pirie
L.
Torre

30°

Northam Merredin
Perth
Fremantle
Narrogin
Esperance
Norseman

Great

Fowler's Bay
Streaky Bay

Port Lincoln
Spencer
Gulf
Adel

INDIAN OCEAN

Bunbury Collie
C. Naturaliste Jarrah
Northcliffe
Karri
Albany
C. Arid

Australian Bight

Kangaroo I.

4

Mount Gamb

AUSTRALIA and NEW ZEALAND

BONNE PROJECTION

SCALE OF MILES

0 200 400 600 800

SCALE OF KILOMETRES

0 200 400 600 800

National Capitals ____ ⊗ State and Territorial Capitals ____ ◉

40°

5

110° A 120° B 130° C Longitude 14

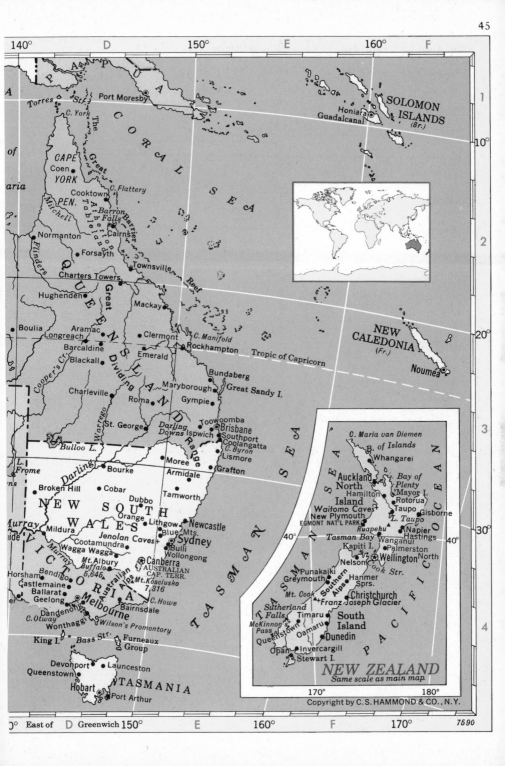

140° D 150° E 160° F

1

P A P U A

Torres Str.
Port Moresby
C. York
The
Mitchell

C O R A L

Honiara
Guadalcanal

**SOLOMON
ISLANDS**
(Br.)

10°

of
aria
?

CAPE
Coen
YORK
PEN.
Cooktown
C. Flattery
Barron
Falls
Barrier
Cairns
Normanton
Forsayth

S E A

Q U E E N S L A N D

Reef

Charters Towers
Hughenden
Mackay

Boulia
Aramac
Longreach
Clermont
C. Manifold
Barcaldine
Emerald
Rockhampton
Blackall

Great
Dividing

Charleville
Bundaberg
Maryborough
Great Sandy I.
Roma
Gympie

Tropic of Capricorn

**NEW
CALEDONIA**
(Fr.)

Noumea

20°

Cooper's Cr.

L.
Frome
ns

Darling
Bourke
Broken Hill
Cobar

St. George
Toowoomba
Darling
Downs
Ispwich
Brisbane
Southport
Coolangatta
C. Byron
Lismore
Grafton

R a n g e

Moree
Armidale

**N E W   S O U T H
W A L E S**

Dubbo
Tamworth
Orange
Lithgow
Newcastle
Mildura
Blue Mts.
Cootamundra
Jenolan Caves
Sydney
Wagga Wagga
Bulli
Wollongong
Mt. Albury
Buffalo,
6,646
Canberra
**AUSTRALIAN
CAP. TERR.**
Mt. Kosciusko
7,316

30°

Murray
aide
V I C T O R I A
Horsham
Murray
Bendigo
Castlemaine
Ballarat
Geelong
Dandenong
Melbourne
C. Otway
Wonthaggi
Wilson's Promontory
Bairnsdale
C. Howe

King I.
Bass Str.
Furneaux
Group

Devonport
Launceston
Queenstown
T A S M A N I A
Hobart
Port Arthur

T A S M A N   S E A

New — inset:

NEW ZEALAND inset:
C. Maria van Diemen
B. of Islands
Whangarei
Auckland
North
Hamilton
Bay of
Plenty
Mayor I.
Rotorua
Island
Waitomo Caves
New Plymouth
Taupo
Gisborne
EGMONT NAT'L PARK
L. Taupo
Ruapehu
Napier
Tasman Bay
Wanganui
Hastings
Kapiti I.
Palmerston
North
Nelson
Wellington
Cook Str.
40°
Punakaiki
Greymouth
Southern
Hanmer
Sprs.
Mt. Cook
Alps
Franz Josef Glacier
Christchurch
Sutherland
Falls
Timaru
South
McKinnon's
Pass
Oamaru
Island
Queenstown
Dunedin
Opan
Invercargill
Stewart I.

P A C I F I C   O C E A N

NEW ZEALAND
Same scale as main map.

170° 180°

0° East of D Greenwich 150° E 160° F 170° 75 90

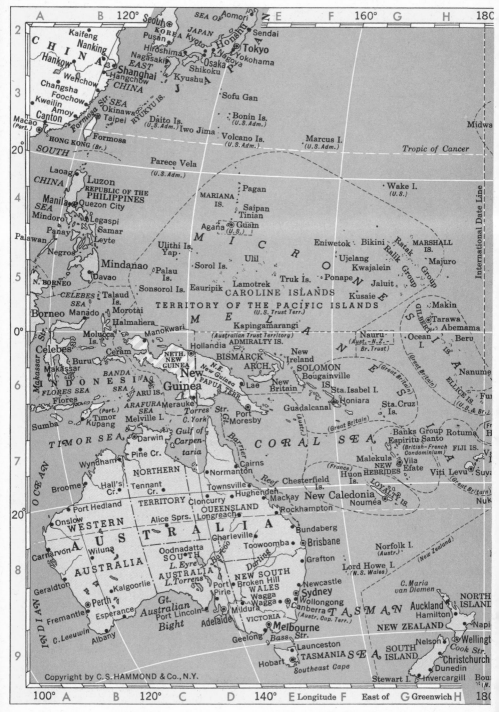

46

A · B · 120° · C · 140° · E · 160° · G · H · 180

SEA OF · Aomori
CHINA · Kaifeng · Seoul · JAPAN · Sendai
Nanking · KOREA · Kyoto · Honshu · Tokyo
Hankow · Pusan · Hiroshima · Nagoya · Yokohama
Changsha · Wenchow · EAST · Nagasaki · Osaka · Shikoku
Foochow · Shanghai · Hangchow · CHINA · Kyushu
Kweilin · Amoy · CHINA · Kyushu
Canton · Formosa Str. · SEA · Sofu Gan
Macao · Okinawa · RYUKYU IS. · Daito Is.
(Port.) · HONG KONG · Taipei · (U.S.Adm.) · Iwo Jima
Formosa · (Br.) · Bonin Is.
SOUTH · (U.S.Adm.)
Volcano Is. · Marcus I.
(U.S.Adm.) · (U.S.Adm.) · Tropic of Cancer
Laoag · Parece Vela
CHINA · Luzon · (U.S.Adm.) · Wake I.
Manila · REPUBLIC OF THE · (U.S.)
Mindoro · PHILIPPINES · Pagan
SEA · Quezon City · MARIANA · Saipan
Palawan · Legaspi · IS. · Tinian
Panay · Samar · Agana · Guam
Negros · Leyte · (U.S.)
Ulithi Is. · M I C R O · Eniwetok · Bikini · MARSHALL
N. BORNEO · Mindanao · Yap · Ratak · IS.
Davao · Sorol Is. · Ulil · Ujelang · Group · Majuro
CELEBES · Palau · Truk Is. · Kwajalein · Ralik
SEA · Talaud · Is. · Lamotrek · Ponape · N · Jaluit · Group
Borneo · Manado · Is. · Sonsorol Is. · Eauripik · CAROLINE ISLANDS · Kusaie · S
Morotai · E
Halmahera · TERRITORY OF THE PACIFIC ISLANDS · Makin
Molucca · Manokwari · (U.S. Trust Terr.) · Tarawa
Celebes · Is. · M E L · Kapingamarangi · Abemama
Buru · Ceram · (Australian Trust Territory) · Nauru · Ocean · Beru
Makassar · ADMIRALTY IS. · (Aust.-N.Z.- · I.
BANDA · NETH. · BISMARCK · Br. Trust) · Nanume
INDONESIA · NEW · New · New · E
FLORES SEA · SEA · GUINEA · N.E. · Ireland · SOLOMON
Flores · ARU IS. · New Guinea · Lae · Bougainville · ELLICE IS.
Sumba · Timor · (Port.) · PAPUA TERR. · Britain · IS. · Sta. Isabel I. · (U.S. & Br.)
Kupang · Merauke · Torres · Port · Guadalcanal · Honiara · Sta. Cruz
ARAFURA · Melville I. · Str. · Moresby · Is.
TIMOR SEA · Darwin · C. York · Banks Group · Rotuma
Gulf of · Espiritu Santo · FIJI IS.
OCEAN · Pine Cr. · Carpen- · Barrier · CORAL SEA · (British-French · Vila
Wyndham · taria · Cairns · Condominium) · Viti Levu · Suva
Broome · Hall's · Tennant · Normanton · Reef · Malekula · Efate
Cr. · NORTHERN · Townsville · Chesterfield · HEBRIDES · Is.
Port Hedland · Cloncurry · Hughenden · Is. · LOYALTY IS.
Onslow · TERRITORY · QUEENSLAND · Longreach · Mackay · New Caledonia
WESTERN · Alice Sprs. · Rockhampton · Nouméa
AUSTRALIA · Bundaberg · Norfolk I.
Carnarvon · Wiluna · Charleville · Brisbane · (Austr.)
SOUTH · Toowoomba · (New Zealand)
Geraldton · AUSTRALIA · Darling · Grafton · Lord Howe I.
Kalgoorlie · L. Eyre · AUSTRALIA · (N.S. Wales)
Perth · L. Torrens · NEW SOUTH · Newcastle · C. Maria
Gt. · Port · Broken Hill · WALES · van Diemen · NORTH
Fremantle · Australian · Pirie · Wagga · Sydney · ISLAND
Esperance · Bight · Port Lincoln · Mildura · Wagga · Wollongong · Auckland
C. Leeuwin · Canberra · TASMAN · Hamilton
Albany · Adelaide · VICTORIA · (Austr. Cap. Terr.) · NEW ZEALAND · Napi
Geelong · Melbourne · SEA · Nelson · Wellingt
Bass Str. · SOUTH · Cook Str.
Launceston · ISLAND · Christchurch
TASMANIA · Dunedin
Copyright by C.S. HAMMOND & Co., N.Y. · Hobart · Southeast Cape · Stewart I. · Invercargill

100° A · B · 120° C · D · 140° E Longitude F · East of G Greenwich H · 180

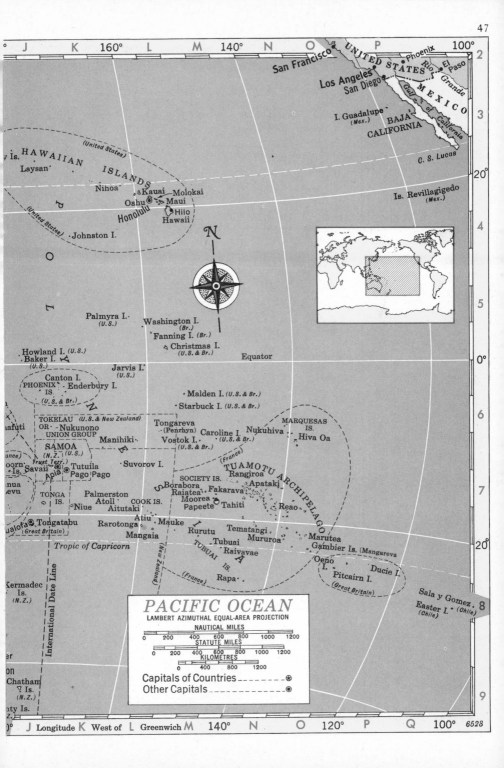

J 160° K L M 140° N O P 100° 2

United States
San Francisco
Los Angeles
San Diego
Phoenix
Rio Grande
El Paso
M E X I C O
Gulf of California
I. Guadalupe (Mex.)
BAJA CALIFORNIA
3
C. S. Lucas
Is. Revillagigedo (Mex.)
20°

y Is.
H A W A I I A N   I S L A N D S
Laysan
(United States)
Nihoa
Kauai Molokai
Oahu Maui
Honolulu Hilo
Hawaii
4

(United States)
Johnston I.

N

5

Palmyra I. (U.S.)
Washington I. (Br.)
Fanning I. (Br.)
Christmas I. (U.S. & Br.)
Equator 0°

Howland I. (U.S.)
Baker I. (U.S.)
Jarvis I. (U.S.)
Canton I.
PHOENIX IS. Enderbury I.
(U.S. & Br.)
Malden I. (U.S. & Br.)
Starbuck I. (U.S. & Br.)
6

aruti
TOKELAU (U.S. & New Zealand)
OR Nukunono
UNION GROUP
Manihiki
SAMOA (N.Z. & U.S.)
ance)
orn
Is.
Savaii
Apia
Tutuila
Pago Pago
nua
evu
TONGA IS.
Palmerston Atoll
Niue COOK IS.
Aitutaki
ualofa Tongatabu
(Great Britain)
Tongareva (Penrhyn)
Vostok I. (U.S. & Br.)
Caroline I. (U.S. & Br.)
Suvorov I.
SOCIETY IS.
Borabora Fakarava
Raiatea
Moorea Tahiti
Papeete
Rarotonga Mauke
Atiu
Mangaia
MARQUESAS IS.
Nukuhiva
Hiva Oa
(France)
TUAMOTU ARCHIPELAGO
Rangiroa Apataki
Reao
Rurutu Tematangi
Tubuai Mururoa
Raivavae
Marutea
Gambier Is. (Mangareva)
7

Tropic of Capricorn
TUBUAI IS.
Rapa
(New Zealand)
(France)
Oeno I.
Pitcairn I.
(Great Britain)
Ducie I.
20°

Kermadec Is. (N.Z.)
International Date Line
er
on
Chatham Is. (N.Z.)
ty Is.
Sala y Gomez (Chile)
Easter I. (Chile)
8

PACIFIC OCEAN
LAMBERT AZIMUTHAL EQUAL-AREA PROJECTION
NAUTICAL MILES
0 200 400 600 800 1000 1200
STATUTE MILES
0 200 400 600 800 1000 1200
KILOMETRES
0 400 800 1200
Capitals of Countries _ _ _ _ _ _ _ ⊛
Other Capitals _ _ _ _ _ _ _ ◉
9

48

8511

SOUTH AMERICA

LAMBERT AZIMUTHAL
EQUAL-AREA PROJECTION

SCALE OF MILES

0 100 200 400 600

SCALE OF KILOMETRES

0 200 400 600

Capitals of Countries ....●

International Boundaries ----·····

Copyright by C.S. HAMMOND & Co., N.Y.

(Map of South America with numerous labeled cities, rivers, and geographic features, including:)

Vitória, Campos, Nitrói, Rio de Janeiro, C. de São Tomé, Cabo Frio, Tropic of Capricorn, Santos, São Paulo, Campinas, Caldas, Petrópolis, Pocos de Caldas, Juiz de Fora, Ribeirão Preto, Paranaguá, Florianópolis, Curitiba, Joinville, Itajaí, Passo Fundo, Caxias do Sul, Pôrto Alegre, Pelotas, Los Patos, Maracaju, Marília, Londrina, Pto. Casado, San Bernardino, Villarica, Falls, San Ignacio, Santa Maria, Bagé, Livramento, Uruguaiana, Concepción, PARAGUAY, Asunción, Capiatá, San Pedro, Encarnación, Posadas, Grande, Salto, URUGUAY, Durazno, Melo, Paysandú, Mercedes, SANTA TERESA NATL PARK, La Coronilla, Rocha, Punta del Este, Montevideo, Jujuy, Rosario de la Frontera, Formosa, Resistencia, Corrientes, Goya, Concordia, Paraná, Colonia Suiza, La Plata, Rio de la Plata, C. San Antonio, Salta, Tucumán, Santiago del Estero, La Rioja, Catamarca, Jesús María, Córdoba, Santa Fe, Rosario, Avellaneda, Buenos Aires, Santa Rosa, Azul, Tandil, Mar del Plata, Tarija, San Juan, Alta Gracia, Villa María, Rio Cuarto, Pampas, Bahía Blanca, Curacó, Tocopilla, Antofagasta, Taltal, Copiapó, La Serena, Ovalle, Aconcagua, Mendoza, San Luis, San Rafael, Neuquén, Colorado, Viedma, G. San Matías, I. San Ambrosio (Chile), I. San Félix (Chile), Más Afuera, Is. Juan Fernández (Chile), Más a Tierra (Chile), Portillo, Valparaíso, Viña del Mar, Santiago, Rancagua, San Carlos, Lake District, Negro, Rio, San Carlos de Bariloche, Pto. Madryn, Chubut, Comodoro Rivadavia, G. San Jorge, C. Tres Puntas, Talca, Chillán, Concepción, Angol, Temuco, Villarica, Valdivia, Puerto Montt, Ancud, I. de Chiloé, ARCHIPIÉLAGO de los CHONOS, Aysen, Buenos Aires, San Julián, Bahía Grande, FALKLAND ISLANDS (Br.), Port Stanley, I. Campana, I. Wellington, I. Madre de Dios, Santa Inés, I. Hoste, Punta Arenas, Gallegos, Tierra del Fuego, Ushuaia, Cape Horn, I. de los Estados, Tropic of Capricorn

Longitude West of Greenwich

A T L A N T I C   O C E A N

P A C I F I C   O C E A N

N

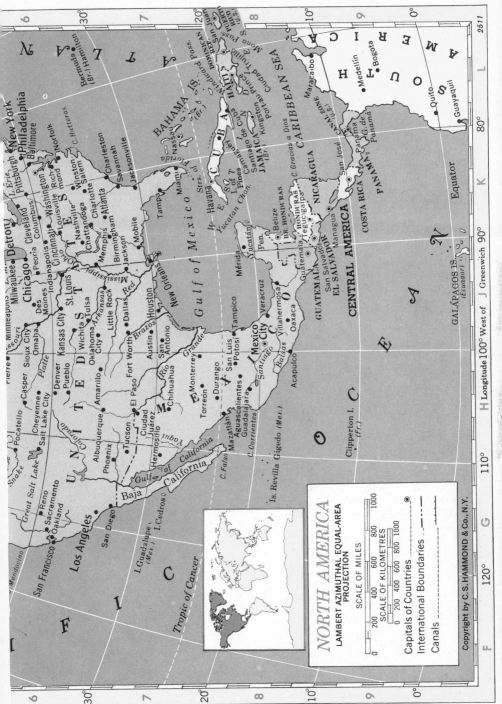

51

NORTH AMERICA
LAMBERT AZIMUTHAL EQUAL-AREA PROJECTION

SCALE OF MILES
0 200 400 600 800 1000

SCALE OF KILOMETRES
0 200 400 600 800 1000

Capitals of Countries
International Boundaries
Canals

CANADA

CONIC PROJECTION

SCALE OF MILES

0 100 200 300 400 500

SCALE OF KILOMETRES

0 100 200 300 400 500

Capitals of Countries _____ ⊛
Provincial Capitals _____ ◉
Canals _ _ _ _ _ _ _ _ _

Copyright by C. S. HAMMOND & Co., N. Y.

53

3520

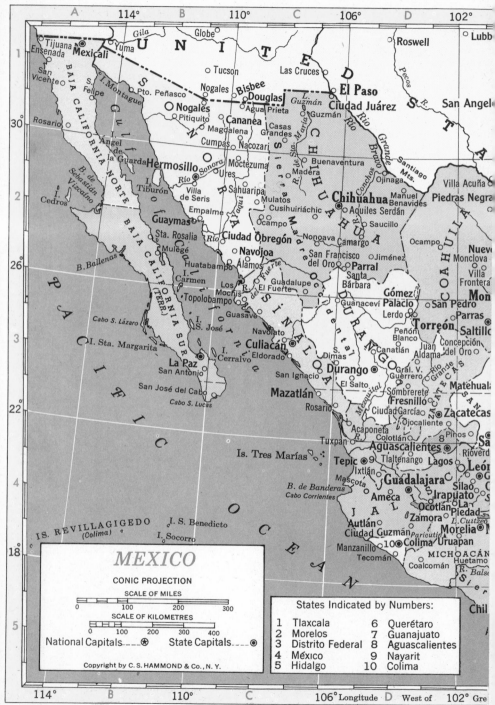

54

MEXICO

CONIC PROJECTION

SCALE OF MILES

0   100   200   300

SCALE OF KILOMETRES

0   100   200   300   400

National Capitals ⊕   State Capitals ⊚

States Indicated by Numbers:

1	Tlaxcala	6 Querétaro
2	Morelos	7 Guanajuato
3	Distrito Federal	8 Aguascalientes
4	México	9 Nayarit
5	Hidalgo	10 Colima

CENTRAL AMERICA

CONIC PROJECTION

SCALE OF MILES

0 25 50   100   150

SCALE OF KILOMETRES

0 25 50   100   150

Capitals of Countries _____⊛
International Boundaries___.___
Canals _____

Copyright by C.S. HAMMOND & Co., N.Y.

A 92°　　　B　　　88°　　　C　　　Longitude

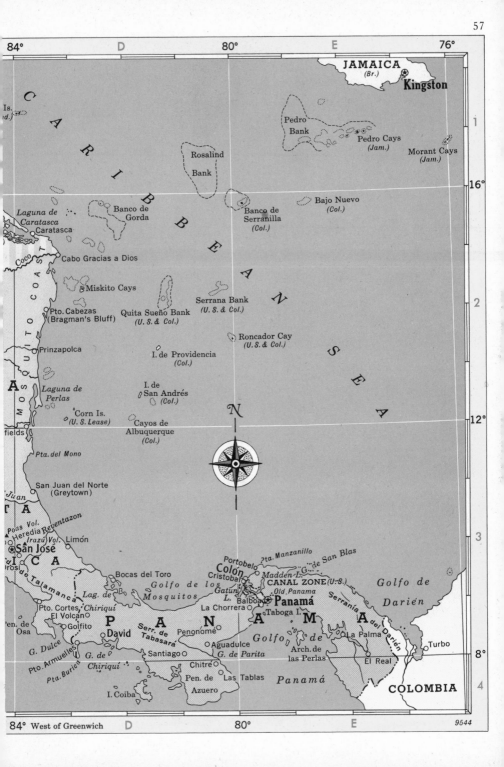

84°   D   80°   E   76°

JAMAICA
(Br.)
✪ **Kingston**

Is.
nd.f)

C A R I B B E A N

Pedro
Bank

Pedro Cays
(Jam.)

Morant Cays
(Jam.)

1

Rosalind

Bank

16°

Bajo Nuevo
(Col.)

Laguna de
Caratasca
Caratasca

Banco de
Gorda

Banco de
Serranilla
(Col.)

Coco

Cabo Gracias a Dios

Miskito Cays

Serrana Bank
(U. S. & Col.)

2

M O S Q U I T O   C O A S T

Pto. Cabezas
(Bragman's Bluff)

Quita Sueño Bank
(U. S. & Col.)

Prinzapolca

Roncador Cay
(U. S. & Col.)

I. de Providencia
(Col.)

A

Laguna de
Perlas

I. de
San Andrés
(Col.)

S E A

Corn Is.
(U. S. Lease)

fields

Cayos de
Albuquerque
(Col.)

12°

N

Pta. del Mono

San Juan del Norte
(Greytown)

Juan

Poas Vol.
Heredia *Reventazon*
(Irazú)Vol. Limón

San José

3

de Talamanca

I C A

Portobelo

Pta. Manzanillo

de San Blas

Bocas del Toro

Colon
Cristobal

Madden L.

Golfo de
Darién

rosi

Gatún

Golfo de los

Mosquitos

L.

Old Panama

Balboa

CANAL ZONE *(U.S.)*

Panamá

Serranía

Pto. Cortes
El Volcan

Lag. de
'Chiriquí

La Chorrera

Taboga I.

del

P A N A

Golfito

David

Serr. de
Tabasará

M

Penonomé

Golfo de

A

de

La Palma

Darién

Turbo

Pen. de
Osa

G. Dulce

G. de

Aguadulce

Arch. de
las Perlas

8°

Pto. Armuelles

Chiriquí

Santiago

G. de Parita

El Real

Pta. Burica

Chitré

Pen. de

Las Tablas

Panamá

COLOMBIA

4

I. Coiba

Azuero

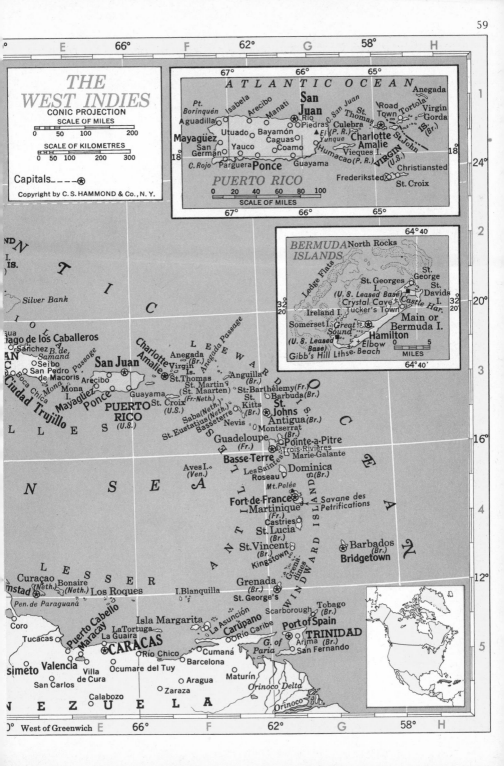

59

THE WEST INDIES

CONIC PROJECTION

SCALE OF MILES

0 50 100 200

SCALE OF KILOMETRES

0 50 100 200 300

Capitals ____⊛

Copyright by C. S. HAMMOND & Co., N. Y.

PUERTO RICO

ATLANTIC OCEAN

Pt. Borinquén
Aguadilla
Isabela
Arecibo
Manati
San Juan
Rio Piedras
C. San Juan
St. Thomas
(U.S.)
Culebra (P. R.)
Road Town
Tortola
Anegada
Virgin Gorda
VIRGIN IS. (Br.)
Mayagüez
Utuado
Bayamón
Caguas
El Yunque
Charlotte Amalie
St. John
San Germán
Yauco
Coamo
Humacao (P. R.)
VIRGIN (U.S.)
Christiansted
C. Rojo
Parguera
Ponce
Guayama
Vieques I.
Frederiksted
St. Croix

18°
24°
67° 66° 65°
1

BERMUDA ISLANDS

North Rocks
Ledge Flats
St. Georges I.
St. George
St. Davids I.
Crystal Cave
Castle Har.
(U. S. Leased Base)
Tucker's Town
Ireland I.
Somerset I.
Great Sound
Main or Bermuda I.
(U. S. Leased Base)
Hamilton
Elbow Beach
Gibb's Hill Lths.

32 20'
32 20'
64° 40'
64° 40'

MILES
0 5

2
20°

ND
N.
IS.

Silver Bank

Santiago de los Caballeros
Sánchez B. de. Samaná
Seibo
San Pedro de Macoris
Boca Chica
Ciudad Trujillo
Mona I.
Mayagüez
Arecibo
Ponce
Guayama
San Juan
Charlotte Amalie
Anegada Virgin Is. (Br.)
St.Thomas
St. Martin (St. Maarten) (Fr.-Neth.)
Anguilla (Br.)
St.Barthélemy (Fr.)
St. Kitts (Br.)
Barbuda (Br.)
Saba (Neth.)
St.Eustatius (Neth.)
Basseterre
Nevis
St. Johns
Antigua (Br.)
Montserrat (Br.)
PUERTO RICO (U.S.)
St. Croix (U.S.)

LEEWARD ISLANDS

Guadeloupe (Fr.)
Pointe-a-Pitre
Trois-Rivières
Marie-Galante
Basse-Terre
Les Saintes
Roseau
Aves I. (Ven.)
Dominica (Br.)
Mt.Pelée
Fort-de-France
Martinique (Fr.)
Savane des Petrifications
Castries
St.Lucia (Br.)
St.Vincent (Br.)
Kingstown
Barbados (Br.)
Bridgetown
Grenadines
Grenada (Br.)
St. George's

WINDWARD ISLANDS

LESSER

Curaçao (Neth.)
Amstad
Bonaire (Neth.)
Los Roques
Pen. de Paraguaná
I.Blanquilla
Coro
Tucacas
Puerto Cabello
Maracay
La Guaira
Isla Margarita
La Asunción
La Tortuga
Río Chico
CARACAS
Cumaná
Barcelona
simeto
Valencia
Villa de Cura
San Carlos
Ocumare del Tuy
Aragua
Zaraza
Maturín
Calabozo

Carúpano
Río Caribe
Scarborough
Tobago (Br.)
Port of Spain
TRINIDAD
Arima (Br.)
G. of Paria
San Fernando

Orinoco Delta
Orinoco

VENEZUELA

ANTILLES
CARIBBEAN SEA

16°
12°

West of Greenwich

66° 62° 58°
E F G H

UNITED STATES
Western Part
POLYCONIC PROJECTION
SCALE OF MILES
0   50   100   200   300
SCALE OF KILOMETRES
0 50 100   200   300
See United States Eastern Part for legend.

FLAGS OF LEADING NATIONS

ARGENTINA

CUBA

NORWAY

THAILAND

AUSTRALIA

CZECHOSLOVAKIA

IRAN

PAKISTAN

TURKEY

AUSTRIA

DENMARK

IRELAND

PERU

UNION OF SOUTH AFRICA

BELGIUM

EGYPT

ISRAEL

PHILIPPINES

U. S. S. R.

BRAZIL

FINLAND

ITALY

POLAND

UNITED KINGDOM

CANADA

FRANCE

JAPAN

PORTUGAL

UNITED STATES

CEYLON

GERMANY (Western)

KOREA (South)

SAUDI ARABIA

URUGUAY

CHILE

GREECE

MEXICO

SPAIN

VENEZUELA

CHINA (Nationalist)

INDIA

NETHERLANDS

SWEDEN

VIETNAM

COLOMBIA

INDONESIA

NEW ZEALAND

SWITZERLAND

YUGOSLAVIA

Introduction to The Vacation Guide

We hope this vacation guide will help to make your travels more interesting and enjoyable: In selecting the places to describe, we have tried to give you a cross section of each country, highlights of the many attractions you will find. Of course, you will enjoy making your own discoveries.

The information on customs given in the tables is for U. S. citizens only; passport regulations and currency rates change from time to time, and your travel agent will always have the latest information. As English is spoken in most of the larger cities of the world, we have omitted information on language. However, it is always advisable to take along a handbook of useful terms and a slight knowledge of the local language is a big advantage.

Wherever you go, whether you travel by real or imaginary Skyliner, we wish you —

HAPPY LANDINGS!

Great Britain and Ireland

LAND OF TRADITION

Great Britain is a land in which the past is always becoming the present, in which history is inescapably part of the picture of today, and thus it is that Great Britain has become a storehouse of treasures that are both the work of nature and work of man. Her people, like Americans, are a heterogeneous race, evolving from Britons, Angles, Saxons, Danes and Normans; each region has developed local characteristics so that you find "the canny Scot, the austere North countryman, the lively Cockney and the talkative Welshman." You will find that they are a conservative race, hesitant to accept changes, but you will also find them a warm-hearted race, anxious to extend visitors a warm and genuine welcome. Great Britain is small, at no time are you more than a hundred miles away from the sea, and her highways and railroads are unexcelled. You may reach any section without an unduly long journey and the varying wealth of beauty in the British scene unfolding on either side will constantly delight you — her cities, little thatched cottages, ancient ruins, magnificent castles all surrounded in scenic beauty.

THE EMERALD ISLE

The storied "Emerald Isle," comprising Northern Ireland and the Republic of Ireland, is famed throughout the world for its verdant beauty. For generations poets have sung of its green hills and rugged coasts. From the hills the mists roll down across the countryside, and with the clear cool air helps to give Ireland its special greenness — an Emerald Isle indeed! Here you may meet on any country road the old jaunting carts in use today as they have been for centuries, see the ivied ruins of ancient castles and picturesque cottages along the wayside. Ireland presents its many scenic charms, as beautiful today as it has been through the centuries. Here, too, you will find a warm-hearted people proud of their land and happy to welcome the visitor.

FOOD AND DRINK

No trip to Britain is complete without a visit to a pub, short for public house. Pubs are many and various, defying classification. There are, however, two kinds to look for — the really ancient and the traditional "gin palace" with its monumental brass rails and fittings and its wealth of decorated glass in doors, windows and mirrors. You may drink mild or bitter beer, or you may prefer a glass of half and half; there is a great variety of beers and ales. Be sure to sample what was probably the beer that Shakespeare drank. This comes from a small brewery at Stratford-on-Avon and is called Flower's Bitter; it is very strong. Irish whisky and Scotch, of course are popular, though not as high proof as sold in the U. S. Gin, too, is popular and the dark, strong Guinness stout.

Outside the large cities, which of course have their share of restaurants with a continental cuisine, the fare is comparatively plain, not being embellished with spicy sauces or exotic ingredients. Here one gets his game, venison, fowl and seafood *au naturel,* and it will prove a delightful change. Try roast beef and Yorkshire pudding. Ireland is famous for delicious prawns, lobsters, oysters and smoked salmon, and also for the unique Gaelic coffee. This beguiling potion consists of sugar, coffee, Irish whisky and thick cream. Tea is an institution which may consist of a complete supper, simple bread and butter, hot scones or crumpets, or a variety of biscuits (cookies).

SPORTS

The British of all classes are enthusiastic about sports. They love to shoot, to participate in games, to ride horses and bet on horse races and to fish. The great spectator sports are football (soccer and rugby) in the autumn and winter, cricket in the spring and summer and both flat-racing and steeplechasing. Hunting in England is restricted to fox-hunting on horseback. Not so in Scotland, where bird and game are excellent. Good fishing, especially for salmon, is found throughout Great Britain. Tennis is played all over and golf and water sports facilities are unexcelled.

The Irish also love sports of all kinds and here, too, you will find the best in hunting, fishing, golf and water sports. Trout fishing is particularly good, beginning in May when the trout and fisherman both go mad; the trout mesmerized by the May-Fly, the fisherman, by the trout. Hurling is Ireland's baseball and is a thrilling game to watch. Gaelic football and hand-

Houses of Parliament in London from Westminster Bridge
TWA-Trans World Airlines

ball are typical Irish games. Flat racing and steeplechasing are almost equally popular in Ireland, and are equally exciting.

IN AND AROUND LONDON

Present-day London is one of the biggest cities in the world (pop. 8,346,137), so big that it comprises a county in itself (the County of London) and is sometimes called Greater London. The oldest part of London is known as the City of London and is the nucleus around which this sprawling metropolis grew. The "City," as Londoners call it, is small, only about one square mile, but it has a history that reaches back to Roman times and its people and institutions have shaped the world's destinies for a thousand years.

Thoughts of London remind one of the famous Dr. Samuel Johnson who dominated the intellectual life of his day from Fleet Street (London's newspaper row), which is the link that joins the historic City to the more residential, but no less historic, West End. The visitor seeing the sights of London will pass by Gough Square, where the Doctor lived; the old Cheshire Cheese Inn, where he dined; and St. Clement Danes Church where he worshipped and where his statue stands beside the ruins of that once beautiful Wren Church. It was the good Doctor who said, "Why, Sir, you find no man, at all intellectual, who is willing to leave London. No, Sir, when a man is tired of London, he is tired of life; for their is in London all that life can afford." Be that as it may, it is certainly true that there is so much to see and do in London that no one visit is sufficient to "do" the city properly. Below are just a few of the many places you will not want to miss.

The Tower of London has not seen the whole of London's history, but it has indeed seen most of it. This great Norman castle stands today almost unaltered since the days when Gundulf built it in 1078 for William the Conqueror, and chose its site in an angle of the Roman Wall which was already a thousand years old. Portions of this wall can still be seen within the precincts of the Tower. The Tower guards, the famous "Beefeaters," still wear their colorful scarlet, black and gold uniforms. Armor, relics of executions and a fine early Norman chapel are in the White Tower. The Wakefield Tower houses the Crown Jewels, a dazzling and historic collection. Not far from the Tower is St. Paul's Cathedral, the greatest work of Sir Christopher Wren, which stands on the site of the original one destroyed in the fire of 1666. Many famous people are buried here, including Wren himself, Nelson, Wellington and Florence Nightingale. Nearby is London Bridge from where you can watch below the busy scene of ships unloading in the Pool, a reach of the Port of London. At the southern end of the bridge is Southwark Cathedral, parts of which date from 1207, with its Harvard Chapel, a memorial to the founder of Harvard University. Near the other end of the Bridge is the seething maelstrom of the City's business heart, Threadneedle Street, Throgmorton Street, Lombard Street and Cornhill where are the temples of finance. Here are also the Bank of England which was incorporated under Royal Charter in 1694 to raise money for the war against Louis XIV (a military guard has been mounted at night since the Gordon Riots of 1780); Mansion House, the official residence of the Lord Mayors of London, built in 1739; the Royal Exchange, with its golden grasshopper perched on the top. Petticoat Lane (Mid-

HIGHLIGHT MAP OF LONDON ENGLAND

❶ Foreign Office
❷ 10 Downing Street
❸ Horse Guards
❹ Admiralty
❺ War Office
❻ United Service Mus.
❼ New Scotland Yard
❽ College of Arms
❾ Cleopatra's Needle
❿ Covent Garden
⓫ National Gallery
⓬ Houses of Parliament & Westminster Hall
⓭ Gough Square
⓮ Cheshire Cheese Inn
⓯ St. Clement Danes Ch.
⓰ Royal Exchange
⓱ Central Criminal Court
⓲ Hyde Park Corner

MAP SHOWS MAJOR STREETS

© C. S. HAMMOND & CO., N. Y.

68

dlesex Street) is a fascinating open-air street market in the City where one can buy antiques, curios and second-hand goods of all descriptions. On Queen Victoria Street is the College of Arms or College of Heralds which deals with matters relating to heraldry. The building was presented to the college by Queen Mary in 1555 and was reconstructed after the Great Fire. The Guildhall, on Gresham Street, is the home of one of the great Livery Companies, or medieval trade guilds, of the City of London. The Staple Inn, Holborn, dates from 1586 and is of interest as the only remaining example of domestic Tudor architecture in London. Close by is the Central Criminal Court, known as "Old Bailey," standing on the site of Newgate Prison.

The most historic building in the West End is Westminster Abbey, which contains more historical treasures than any other building in Britain. Built in the year 800, it was originally used as a royal mausoleum and until the time of George II only the kings of England were buried here. Of particular interest is the Chapel of Henry VII, built in 1503, the finest Perpendicular building in Britain. The fan-tracery vaulting of the roof is indescribably beautiful. Many famous statesmen, authors and other public figures have been "given the Abbey" at their deaths. Don't miss the Poet's Corner where are buried such famous men as Chaucer and Spenser. The Coronation Chair is in Edward the Confessor's Chapel. Across the roadway from the Abbey is the Palace of Westminster, the official name for the Houses of Parliament. These buildings stand on one of the oldest sites in London. The only original building still in existence, Westminster Hall was built in 1097. Westminster Hall possesses a magnificent hammer-beam roof which was built by Richard II in 1399. It has looked down upon many famous and tragic scenes: the trial of Essex; the trial of Guy Fawkes, who planned to blow up the Houses of Parliament in 1605, and who has been remembered annually and almost affectionately ever since with fireworks and bonfires on November 5th; and the trial in 1649 of Charles I, who stubbornly denied the legality of the court which tried him. A rather charming insight into British nature is provided by this incident: Recently when the roof of the Hall was being repaired for war damage, the timber used was cut from the same estate as the original timber and from trees that were standing when the original timber was cut. When Parliament is sitting a flag flies from Victoria Tower by day; by night a light burns in the clock tower. The clock is known as Big Ben, although in fact this name is more properly given to the great bell which strikes the hours. Running due north from Parliament, in a straight line to Trafalgar Square, is the broad thoroughfare known as Whitehall. Here flourishes the machinery of government, the Home Office, the Treasury, the War Office, the Admiralty and other government departments, each one housed in its own majestic and rather pompous palace. On the west side of Whitehall, the Horse Guards is the scene of an interesting ceremony, the mounting of the guard, which takes place every morning at 11:00. Leading off Whitehall is famous little Downing Street, where at Number 10 resides the Prime Minister. Near the corner is the Cenotaph, the nation's memorial to the dead of two world wars. On Trafalgar Square is the National Gallery which has an excellent collection of all the great masters. Among the many outstanding pictures are Holbein's "Duchess of Milan" and Velasquez' "Robely Venus." From Trafalgar Square, the Mall leads to Buckingham Palace, the London home of Her Majesty the Queen. The Royal Standard flies from the mast when the Queen is in residence. On days of national rejoicing, Londoners assemble in thousands at the Palace gates, cheering and awaiting Her Majesty's appearance on the balcony of the center window. The Palace was built by the Duke of Buckingham in 1703 and was first used as a royal residence by Queen Victoria. A dramatic sight is the changing of the guard. Times are posted on the Palace gates. Nearby is St. James's Palace, a mellow, red brick, Tudor building which is the official residence of the court. Originally a hospital, the building was converted by Henry VIII into a hunting lodge for himself and Anne Boleyn. The Palace was used as a royal residence after 1698 when the Palace of Whitehall was burnt down. Charles I took leave of his children here before his execution and Charles II, James II, Mary II and George IV were born here. St. James St. which links the Palace grounds with Piccadilly is the street of clubs. Here is the Carlton, Brooks's, White's, Boodle's and many others whose names are familiar. Piccadilly is the focal point of London and it contains everything. Here are the shops, hotels, restaurants, art galleries, clubs and residences. At one end is Piccadilly Circus where flower girls sell their bouquets under the guardian statue of Eros, and at the other end is Hyde Park Corner. At this corner stands Apsley House, the first Duke of Wellington's home which is traditionally known as No. 1 London. It now houses the National Wellington Museum. Across Hyde Park, at Oxford Street, is Marble Arch. Originally built as a "triumphal arch" entrance to Buckingham Palace, the Arch was found to be too narrow for the State Coach and was erected at its present position close to the site of the old Tyburn gallows. Hyde Park is a favorite place of Londoners who love to watch the ducks swimming in the Serpentine or stop and listen to the harangues of the soap box orators. At one end of the park is Kensington Gardens and Kensington Palace. The palace was bought by William III for whom Wren built the South Wing. Queen Victoria and Queen Mary were both born here. The State apartments may be visited on weekends and the London Museum is also housed here. Nearby is the Natural History Museum with its great collection of animals and plants, and the Victoria and Albert Museum which has an excellent collection of fine and applied art and historic costumes. Here too is the Science Museum. Across the city is Regent's Park with one of the world's largest collection of animals, birds and reptiles. A children's corner provides pony rides and a large collection of domestic animals and pets. The magnificent series of terraces surrounding the park is a fine example of Regency architecture. Near here, on Marylebone Road, is Madame Tussaud's, the famous waxworks museum which contains effigies in authentic costume and setting of famous and notorious characters of history and modern times. Its Chamber of Horrors is celebrated.

On the south bank of the Thames is the Royal Festival Hall with its marvelous acoustics. It is a permanent memorial to the 1951 South Bank Exhibition. The nearby Telekinema now houses the National Film Institute film club. Close by is County Hall, the imposing headquarters of the London County Council. Lambeth Palace, the Imperial War Museum and the Old Vic are also on the south side of the Thames, near Waterloo Station. Across the Thames, opposite the Festival Hall, stands Cleopatra's Needle. This Egyptian obelisk stood in front of the Temple of the Sun at Heliopolis about 3,500 years ago. It was towed to England by sea in 1877 after being abandoned and subsequently recovered during a storm in the Bay of Biscay.

Among the many notable galleries and museums in London, the British Museum is one of the most interesting. The history of many civilizations is illustrated here through exhibits of their arts and crafts. Proud possessor of one of the finest collections in the world, the museum contains an unrivaled collection of Assyrian, Babylonian, Egyptian, Greek and Roman antiquities. Among the prize exhibits are the Elgin Marbles, an original copy of the Magna Carta, the *Codex Sinaiticus,* and the Rosetta Stone. Tate Gallery, Millbank, is another fine museum and is the modern branch of the National Gallery. It has a fine sculpture gallery and a comprehensive collection of Turner's paintings. Among the modern painters represented are Sargent, Legros, Van Gogh, Matisse, Cézanne and Sisley. The National Portrait Gallery displays contemporary portraits of the men and women who have made British history over the last four or five centuries. Another notable museum is the Wallace Collection which offers eighteenth century French fine and applied arts, old masters, sculpture, furniture, ceramics and armor.

No one would visit London without browsing through some of her famous shops. There are two main shopping areas, the West End, comprising the areas around Oxford Street, Regent Street and Piccadilly, and the Kensington area, composed of Knightsbridge, Brompton Road and Kensington High Street. These are the areas of the big department stores and of hundreds of small specialist shops. In the West End, Bond Street has shops that are famous the world over — jewelers, perfumers, art and antique shops, hairdressers and all kinds of exclusive shops for women. For men, what is perhaps the most famous men's tailoring center in the world, Savile Row and nearby streets, lies between Bond Street and Regent

71

A rainy night in Soho, London's Greenwich Village
British Information Services

Street. In Piccadilly is **Simpson's,** famous for Daks slacks and suits, and **Fortnum and Mason's** a "must" for anyone interested in exotic food delicacies. Nearby, in Brompton Road, is **Harrods** another world-famous department store, worth a visit by the tourist who wishes to experience the plush calm and almost clerical dignity of a store with over 100 years of trading knowledge. Aside from the smart shops, there are the open-air markets, for which London is famous. The best known of all is the **Caledonian Market** in Bermondsey where bargains can be had in antiques, silver, glass, china, etc. Close to Piccadilly Circus is **Berwick Street market** where there is always a brisk trade in fruit, vegetables and clothing. An interesting early-morning experience is a visit to the big wholesale markets of **Billingsgate, Covent Garden** and **Smithfield** which are the principal distribution centers of London's food supply. If you have time, you should attend an auction at one of the famous auction rooms like **Christie's** or **Sotheby's.**

London is famous for, among other things, the high standard of its legitimate theater, and you will find hit shows there the year round. A particularly delightful custom at the theater is the serving of tea or coffee at your seat during intermission. Before or after the theater there are a great number of delightful restaurants and clubs where you may enjoy the best in wining and dining. **Soho** is the diner's Greenwich Village of London, and **Mayfair** is his Manhattan. Both are popular. If you are looking for continental food, personal attention and intimate atmosphere, then you should go to one of the Soho restaurants. On the other hand, if you wish to eat with the fashionable set, you should choose one of the Mayfair restaurants where music, dancing, cocktail bars and lounges add to the amenities of the dining room.

During your visit, be sure to visit **Battersea Park,** the largest of the many parks of London. It boasts of growing all the flowers mentioned by Shakespeare and contains the Festival Gardens, a happy combination of pastoral fantasy and fun-fair concocted for the 1951 Festival of Britain.

INTERESTING PLACES AROUND LONDON

Within easy reach of London are a number of places of historic and other interest. Within 25 miles is WINDSOR CASTLE, an incredibly vast castle which has been the chief residence of British sovereigns for 850 years. It was to this fairy-tale castle, overlooking the Thames, that Shakespeare was summoned by Queen Elizabeth who requested of him a play with more about Falstaff. "Merry Wives of Windsor" was the resulting play. Here in St. George's Chapel, an outstanding example of Perpendicular architecture, repose the bodies of many English kings, including that of Charles I. The castle contains valuable paintings and furniture. Of particular interest are the Albert Memorial Chapel and the Horse Shoe Cloisters . . . . On the opposite bank of the Thames is the ancient and famous Eton College, founded in 1440 by Henry VI and containing a magnificent group of buildings known as School Yard. . . . Near here is STOKE POGES with the cemetery which was the scene of Gray's Elegy. . . . Downstream and near EGHAM is the island where King John put his seal to the Magna Carta in 1215. . . . Upstream from Windsor is MAIDENHEAD which affords punting on the Thames and, in the evening, dinner and dancing in the open air. . . . Situated on a particularly beautiful stretch of the Thames Valley is HENLEY-ON-THAMES, a quiet and attractive country town famous for its regattas. . . . Fifteen miles from London is HAMPTON COURT PALACE which was built by Cardinal Wolsey in 1515 and reluctantly handed over to Henry VIII ten years later. The old part is in excellent repair and the Palace contains most of the original paintings of court favorites by Sir Peter Lely. Many of the ceilings are by Verrio and much of the woodwork is by Grinling Gibbons. The gardens are beautiful and a visit to the Palace makes an ideal summer afternoon trip. Entrance is by the Trophy Gate leading to the fine Great Gatehouse (part of Wolsey's original building) and into the Clock Court, named after an astronomical clock constructed for Henry VIII. The State Rooms which were designed by Wren for William III, house many famous paintings, notably of the Italian school. The Great Kitchen contains interesting old cooking utensils and facilities. Some fine tapestries may be seen in the Great Hall. In the William III Orangery are the Mantegna tempera paintings of the Triumph of Julius Caesar. In the Gardens are the Great Vine, planted in 1768, the Maze and the famous Chestnut Avenue. . . . Not far from here is HAM HOUSE, built in 1610, formerly the property of the Duke of Lauderdale, a member of the famous "Cabal" Ministry. This house contains a unique collection of Stuart furniture. . . . At RICHMOND the view of the Thames from the top of Richmond Hill opposite the famous Roebuck Hotel is one of the finest in southern England. Here also is the historic Sheen Palace. . . . SYON HOUSE at Brentford is the historic home of the Dukes of Northumberland and is noted for its magnificent Adam interior, its State rooms, period furniture and paintings. . . . Across the Thames from Syon House are the lovely Kew Gardens which contain the famous botanical museum. . . . Also on the outskirts of London, is KEN WOOD, Hampstead, commanding a view of the city from the northern heights. A bequest of the late Lord Iveagh, this mansion is maintained as a typical country home of an eighteenth century gentleman. It has a fine Adam interior and contains an excel-

lent collection of paintings, including works of Reynolds, Romney, Raeburn and Hoppner, in addition to a self-portrait of Rembrandt.

THE SOUTHEAST OF ENGLAND

This section is the gateway to Great Britain and is rich in historical interest, romantic legends and quaint customs. It is also the playground of holiday-makers.

The county of Kent is a land of fragrant orchards, of hops and green grass, of moats and of ancient, red brick, timbered houses, a land where spring arrives gracefully and transforms the countryside into a land of great beauty. Observing the happy character of this land today, one can hardly realize what an apprehensive feeling must have dominated it during the days of 1940 when the hard-pressed British Expeditionary Forces returned to the towns of Ramsgate, Dover, Folkestone, etc. . . . CANTERBURY is the see of the Primate of All England and contains one of the loveliest and most ancient cathedrals in England. It was in this cathedral that Archbishop à Becket was murdered in 1170 on the steps to the altar. Here rests the body of the Black Prince, hero of the Battle of Poitiers, in his great effigy tomb. Fine examples of Roman mosaic pavements were discovered in the town during the clean-up of the bomb damage caused by reprisal raids during the last war. . . . Of the many inland places of interest in Kent, TUNBRIDGE WELLS is one of the most famous watering-places in England. Its chalybeate springs have been noted since 1606 and were known to Macaulay, Thackeray and Meredith. Of particular interest here is the Pantiles, a 17th century colonnaded row of shops. . . . Nearby are two of the most beautiful houses in England: Penhurst Place, the superb 14th century, ancestral home of Lord de L'Isle and Dudley; and Knole, an ancient and famous house which covers five acres and is filled with treasures of every kind. Both are open to the public. . . . ROCHESTER, on the Medway River, is one of the historic routes from Dover to London and is dominated by its great Norman castle. The castle keep, with walls twelve feet thick, is a masterpiece of Norman military architecture. Rochester's Norman Cathedral possesses a particularly fine recessed doorway and beautiful carved woodwork. This place was beloved by Dickens and it was at nearby Gad's Hill where he spent his last years. . . . Along the Kentish coast are a procession of popular seaside resorts. **HERNE BAY**, with seven miles of sea-front and excellent facilities, is an ideal seaside center from which to explore Kent and Canterbury. . . . Below are **MARGATE**, popular since 1850 and **BROADSTAIRS**, a favorite of Dickens, which offers picturesque promenades, beautiful gardens, golf, tennis, cricket, bowls, concerts and dancing. . . . Nearby **RAMSGATE** specializes in sea fishing and yachting. . . . South is **DEAL**, scene of the landing of Julius Caesar in 55 B.C., an unrivaled center from which to enjoy a golfing holiday. Championship courses in the area are Sandwich, Deal, Cinque Ports and Walmer Castle. The ill-famed **Goodwin Sands**, marked by lightships and exposed at low tide, lie seven

made England his. The site of the battle is some seven miles inland, where the **Battle Abbey** now stands. The altar is said to stand on the spot where the Conqueror pitched his tent and ate his supper, with the English dead around him. . . . To the west is **EASTBOURNE** which lies at the foot of the lovely, rolling, turf-covered South Downs. Near this popular resort are several attractions, including the **Long Man of Wilmington**, a figure cut out by removing the turf from the face of the chalk downs and **Beachy Head**, a magnificent headland which drops a sheer 575 feet into the sea below. . . . Further along is **SEAFORD**, a charming little bathing and golfing resort and **BRIGHTON**, the "prince of seaside resorts," which provides every form of entertainment and distraction for the holiday-maker in a

A typical English country village
British Information Services

miles out to sea. . . . Below Deal is **DOVER**, a gay, charming town. Dover, chief of the ancient Cinque Ports, has always been in the front line of English history, and never was this more true than during the second world war. In the grounds of the formidable **Dover Castle** on the heights overlooking the town, is the oldest standing building in England, the **Pharos** or lighthouse which guided the Roman supply ships into the harbor. . . . A few miles away is **FOLKESTONE**, associated, as Dover is, with crossings to the Continent. It attracts many visitors with its racecourse, concerts and extensive gardens fronting the sea, from which one can see the coast of France on a clear day.

In **Sussex**, **HASTINGS** is famous as a holiday resort and as the place where in 1066 William the Conqueror, Duke of Normandy, defeated King Harold and

setting graced by the best in Regency architecture. George IV "created" Brighton as a resort and a constant reminder of him stands in the center of the town. It is his incredible pleasure **Pavilion**, an architectural extravaganza played on an Indo-Chino-Moorish theme. . . . In **Hampshire County**, **PORTSMOUTH** (233,464) is England's largest navy yard and **SOUTHSEA** is a sunny and popular resort. Both give access to many fascinating sightseeing trips—Porchester Castle, Arundel Castle, Netley Abbey and Beaulieu Abbey and to the delightful **Isle of Wight** across the waters of the Solent. This is the big yachting center of England and is one of the most picturesque coastal islands.

THE SOUTHWEST COUNTRY

In Wiltshire is England's most important prehistoric monument, **Stonehenge**, the world-famous circle of vast neolithic stones standing on Salisbury Plain, where thousands of soldiers have found their military legs. . . . To the south is SALISBURY, with its magnificent cathedral. . . . Near the sea in Southampton is New Forest, a densely wooded, 93,000-acre tract which was formerly the royal hunting ground of William the Conqueror and is now the home of wild ponies. . . . EXETER is the county town of Devon and is picturesquely situated on the banks of the river Exe. Although severely damaged during the war, its chief glory, the cathedral, still stands. Adjoining it is the Old Close which contains some interesting old houses. In Rougemont Grounds may be seen the remains of the ancient city walls and of Rougemont Castle, erected by William the Conqueror. . . . At the mouth of the Exe is EXMOUTH, an attractive bathing resort with a good golf course and lovely gardens. . . . From Exmouth one may travel to Plymouth via the route through the open moorland of Dartmoor, a very scenic drive, or take the coastal road via the famous and equally beautiful resorts of TORQUAY and DARTMOUTH. . . . PLYMOUTH (208,985), always near the heart of English history, is where Sir Francis Drake finished his game of bowls on the Hoe before setting sail to rout the Spanish Armada. Here is also where the Pilgrim Fathers set sail for the New World on the Mayflower in 1620. Being one of the chief seaports of the country, Plymouth was badly damaged during the last war, but with characteristic courage, her people have set to work to rebuild their pleasant, historic town. To sit on the Hoe and watch the diversity of shipping in the sound is a favorite summer pastime. . . . Across the river Tamar is the county of Cornwall, England's most westernmost toe. It is a land of legends, ancient history and of quaint customs; it is a land of cromlechs, dolmens and prehistoric circles. Remarkable among these landmarks obtruding from the past is the Trevethy Stone in the Looe Valley. There is an amazing similarity between Cornwall and Brittany on the west coast of France, a similarity which is extended to the astonishing resemblance between Mont St. Michel and St. Michael's Mount standing in Mounts Bay near PENZANCE. The latter is an excellent headquarters from which to explore the Lands End district and from here boats may be taken to the

Scilly Islands. . . . The coasts of Cornwall are rugged and the scenery is bold and picturesque. Snug harbors and charming little seaside towns, where early spring brings bright flowers long before they bloom in any other part of England, provide everything needed for a happy, sunny vactionland. . . . Northeast of Cornwall, in Somerset, is BATH, the most celebrated of English spas. The Romans discovered the medicinal hot springs here in A.D. 44 and established an elaborate system of baths which today form the best preserved and most important Roman relics in Great Britain. During the eighteenth century it became a rendezvous of society who came to see not only the many visiting royalty, but also to see Beau Nash, the Master of Ceremonies. Bath is a planned city and its beauty is attributable to the ablest architects of the eighteenth century. It possesses a marked individuality which is at once recognized by the visitor who sees for the first time the architectural miracle of its crescents and classical buildings.

WALES

Although it has been 700 years since England and Wales became part of the same kingdom, the Welsh have managed to retain their own individuality and their own language.

In the south NEWPORT, although it is one of the main commercial ports, has an ancient history. Its castle, of which only a portion remains, dates from the close of the eleventh century. Three miles northeast of the town, at CAERLEON, are the remains of a Roman settlement that was the headquarters of the second Augustan Legion. The valley of the River Usk, which flows into the sea at Newport, vies with that of the Wye in the scenery which it has to offer. Close to its source the river flows past BRECON where a ruined castle and the ancient priory church of St. John, now a cathedral, may be seen. To the east are the Black Mountains, a tract of wild and open country. To the south are the Brecon Beacons, a country dear to the hearts of hikers. . . . Between Newport and Swansea are many places of interest and beauty. Caerphily Castle to the north of Cardiff is the largest and most remarkable of the castles Edward I built in Wales. BRIDGEND also has its ruined castle, and in its neighborhood are Ewenny Priory, Coychurch and Coyty. . . . SWANSEA stands at the entrance to the Gower Penin-

The old Welsh town of Llangollen nestles between the hills on banks of the River Dee
British Information Services

sula, an attractive stretch of wild and wooded country with a picturesque and irregular seacoast. . . . KIDWELLY and CARMARTHEN, each with its ruined castle, lie to the west. In the main street of Carmarthen is a carefully preserved oak tree upon which, according to local legend, the welfare of the town depends. . . . Inland and to the north the country becomes mountainous and more picturesque. Steep hills intersected by green and fertile valleys, narrowing as they ascend the heights, lakes and wooded slopes, heather and rock abound. The coastline is rugged and in many places precipitous. It is the haunt of all kinds of sea birds and of the gray seal. . . . One of the most popular seaside resorts in Wales is ABERYSTWYTH, where the visitor will find much to attract him. There are many sporting facilities, and, owing to its situation halfway up the coast of Wales, Aberystwyth makes an excellent headquarters from which to explore the countryside. . . . The visitor should not miss the beautiful Elan Valley in the neighboring county of Radnor. Here a chain of lakes, some natural and some caused by the flooding of the valleys, have made of the countryside a very picturesque Welsh Lake District. . . . Wales is noted for its fine castles. Most of these were built by Edward I (1272-1307) during his subjugation of the country. Harlech, close to Caernarvon and Conway at either end of the Menai Straits, which separate the Isle of Angelesey from the mainland, are among the best known. CAERNARVON is an excellent base from which to make excursions into the mountainous region known as Snowdonia. The ascent of Snowdon, the highest mountain in England and Wales, can be made by

rail from Llanberis. At the summit is a hotel. . . . On the north coast of Wales are several seaside resorts which are much frequented by holiday-makers. LLANDUDNO, attractively situated in Orme's Bay, and COLWYN BAY are resorts where scenery, safe bathing and many entertainments may be found. ABERGELE, RHYL and PRESTATYN are other holiday resorts which have many attractions to offer the visitor. . . . Of inland holiday resorts LLANGOLLEN, on the river Dee, is famed for its salmon fishing. The surrounding country offers many beautiful walks.

THE MIDLANDS

England is always remembered by visitors for her lavish green countryside with its lovely trees, green grass and neat hedgerows; and nowhere is the countryside more typical than in the Midlands. Strangely enough, this is also the manufacturing center, with such industrial cities as Birmingham, Coventry and Wolverhampton. . . . BIRMINGHAM (1,112,340), the industrial heart of Warwick, boasts of being able to make anything from "a pin to a power-press." The city does not lack for cultural interests; the city possesses a modern university, a library which contains the biggest collection of Shakespearean books in the world and a museum which contains one of the most important collections outside London. . . . To the east are the pasture lands of the East Midlands, the grass country and light soil so dear to fox hunters. The very best hunting country is in the area surrounding Kettering, Melton Mowbray and Grantham. . . . Northwest of Birmingham, in Staffordshire, WOLVERHAMPTON is a well-planned city that manages to retain a pleasant residential air, in spite of being a busy industrial center. . . . Nearby is CANNOCK, famous for its coal and Cannock Chase, a stretch of delightful moorland. . . . Also nearby is LICHFIELD, known for its red sandstone cathedral (one of the smallest, yet most graceful cathedrals in England) and its associations with the venerable Dr. Johnson. The lexicographer's birthplace is now a Johnson museum. . . . Southeast of Birmingham is COVENTRY (258,211), through which Lady Godiva is reputed to have ridden naked to save the townspeople from oppressive taxes levied by her husband. Today the city is the center of the automobile and cycle industry. . . . Southwest is romantic WARWICK, which contains some of the finest half-timbered architecture to be found in England and the magnificent Warwick Castle which stands four square and majestic on the banks of the river Avon. This is the greatest of British baronial castles and contains many well-known pictures and a fine collection of armor, including a helmet worn by Cromwell. . . . Adjoining Warwick is LEAMINGTON (the famous Royal Leamington Spa), a resort which makes an ideal center for exploring the neighboring countryside. . . . Nearby, at the northern extremity of the lovely Cotswold Hills, and on the banks of the lazy-flowing Avon, is STRATFORD-UPON-AVON. This charming, historic town was the birthplace of Shakespeare and his home now houses the Shakespeare Museum and Library. Holy Trinity Church contains Shakespeare's tomb, on which is a doggerel inscription, attributed to the poet, threatening the would-be disturber of his bones. The Shakespeare Memorial Theater, in which the Shakespeare Festival takes place each year, is a modern building, built with funds subscribed in Britain and the United States. It is equipped with all the most up-to-date theatrical contrivances. Nearby is the charming flower-surrounded cottage of Anne Hathaway. . . . South of Stratford-upon-Avon lie the Cotswold Hills, generally known as the Cotswolds. Here all the buildings and roofs are made of the local honey-colored stone and the buildings represent the best of the graceful domestic Tudor architecture. The villages of Burford, Bibury, Chipping Camden, Chipping Norton, Chipping Sodbury, Broadway and Moreton-in-Marsh, to mention a few, are splendid examples of the Cotswold scene.

. . . East of the Cotswolds, the ancient city of OXFORD is a happy combination of probably the most beautiful university city in the world and a thriving industrial town with one of Europe's largest automobile assembly plants. High Street or The High is an unforgettable sight with the beautiful Oxford college buildings lining either side. The colleges, twenty-one in all, are from 400 to 500 years old, and many have remarkably lovely gardens which sparkle like jewels in their somber setting of ancient lichen-covered walls. Of particular note is Magdalen with its beautifully proportioned tower and graceful bridge spanning the River Cherwell and its garden which has been tended almost since before history was written. . . . Nearby is Woodstock with Blenheim Palace, birthplace of Winston Churchill and home of the Duke of Marlborough, a major point of interest. . . . To the north is BANBURY of nursery rhyme fame, from which can be visited Sulgrave Manor, ancestral home of the Washington family, which houses the Washington Museum containing many relics of the first president of the United States.

EAST ANGLIA

Between the Wash and the Estuary of the Thames is a country of fertile plains, steeped in history and legend. This is East Anglia, originally a powerful Anglo-Saxon Kingdom and subsequently an Earldom of England. Today it is a rich grain and stock-raising region and has important fisheries.

CAMBRIDGE, as all the world knows, is where the scholastic youth of England, or at least such as have not gone to Oxford and other universities, is trained to face a competitive world. The colleges of Cambridge are an architectural feat whose glory is King's College Chapel, a superb Perpendicular building, perfect alike within and without. The visitor should make a point of seeing "The Backs," which are the backs of the colleges and their gardens running down to the river Cam. On a fine day in spring there is no lovelier scene. . . . Nearby NEWMARKET has been the center of flat-racing since the days of Charles II and you may see hundreds of horses being trained each day on Newmarket Heath. There are two race-courses in the town. . . . One of the great landmarks of this region is Ely Cathedral, in ELY, which takes its name rather unromantically from the eels which used to abound in the surrounding marshes. Its most notable feature is the graceful, Gothic central octagon which has been described as the most beautiful design in all Gothic architecture. . . . Fifty miles north of here is **NORWICH**, the beautiful county town of Norfolk. The two most notable features of Norwich are the **cathedral** and the **castle**. The **castle**, erected in the twelfth century, was refaced in 1840 and has now an undeniably modern appearance. After doing duty as the county prison for five centuries it now houses the **Norfolk museum**, which contains some fine examples of the Norfolk school of painting by Cotman and others. The **cathedral** is an impressive Norman building with a fine spire and beautiful flying buttresses. The **Norfolk Broads** may be explored from Norwich by boat. These delightful, flower-fringed, shallow lagoons and lakes are connected by streams and form a favorite yachting and vacation center. . . . All along the coast of East Anglia are delightful seaside resorts with such famous names as Great Yarmouth, Gorleston, Cromer, Sheringham and Hunstanton. Hunstanton, in the north, is a convenient place from which to visit **Sandringham**, the country home of Her Majesty, The Queen, and the famous **Huntstanton** and **Hokkham Halls**.

THE NORTH OF ENGLAND

There is no part of England that offers so much contrast, such variety of scenery and interest, as the north of England. In the county of Yorkshire alone one may pass, within the distance of an afternoon's walk, from flat pastureland where cows stand hock-deep in good grazing to lonely moorland heights where the curlew's mournful cry echoes among the rocks. The north of England can claim even to have a language, or at least an accent of its own, one that is becoming more and more the standby of every aspirant to vaudeville renown, the accent of Yorkshire and Lancashire.

Yorkshire is divided into three Ridings, North, East and West. **YORK,** one of the most beautiful and historic towns in all England, is situated on the spot where the three Ridings meet. It contains so much to see that the visitor may just as well forget his timetable. An idea of the atmosphere of York may be gained from the fact that the curfew is still rung there and has been since William the Conqueror first ordered that fires should be covered at night as a precaution against accident. The best view of the massive and magnificent **Minster** is to be had from the **walls** which encircle the town. The **Minster** (England's largest medieval cathedral) was founded before history was written, and has existed in its present outward form since the year 1474, when a building program of 250 years was completed. Don't miss the many quaint side-streets which, in many cases, possess the oddest of names and retain much of their medieval character. . . . Other places you will want to visit in Yorkshire include the cathedral town of **RIPON** with the famous ruins of **Fountains Abbey**, **HELMSLEY** which is an excellent center from which to see the **Yorkshire moors** and the superb Cistercian ruin of **Rievaulx Abbey**, **HARROGATE**, a beautiful spa with a 200-acre garden, **SCARBOROUGH**, the ultimate in seaside resorts and **WHITBY**, famous for its salmon, its Abbey, its picturesque streets and quaint houses and its amusement parks and other entertainments. . .

Anne Hathaway's charming, flower-encircled cottage, Stratford-on-Avon
British Information Services

To the north is the county of **Durham** and the city of **DURHAM,** an architectural treasure. Durham's Norman **cathedral** and ancient castle, standing formidable on their great base of rock overlooking the river Wear are sights which should not be missed. Durham's university is one of the oldest in England. . . . Further north is Northumberland which possesses on the river Tyne one of the most famous shipbuilding districts in the wrold which centers around **NEWCASTLE** (291,723). North of here is the rugged Border Country. A remarkable ancient monument is **Hadrian's Wall** which dates back two thousand years and runs across hill and dale from one side of England to the other, from Wallsend on the Tyne to Bowness on the Solway. . . . On the other side of England, across the Pennine Hills, is **CHESTER,** county town of Cheshire, with a medieval air thoroughly in keeping with its ancient history. The **Chester rows,** or galleries, fronting the first floors of the timbered Tudor buildings in the four main streets, are a famous feature of the town. The city walls form a complete circle and have survived intact to this day. In many parts of the town and around the cathedral are to be found delightful examples of what might be described as fairytale gingerbread architecture. . . . Passing northwards we come to the **LAKE DISTRICT,** the name given to a district of mountains and lakes in the counties of Westmoreland, Cumberland and Lancashire, although Cumberland has the largest portion of it. There are eleven lakes in all, of which the largest is **Windermere.** Though the highest peak in the district is no more than 3,000 feet high, the scenery is really impressive and has been the inspiration of many poets. Wordsworth lived at **Grasmere;** so did Coleridge. Shelley had a cottage at **Keswick.** There are many organized tours of the lakes, one of the finest being the drive from **Keswick** to **Buttermere,** past the lovely **valley of Borrowdale,** over the **Honiston pass** and back through **Newlands.** The rock-climbing in the Lake District can be a real challenge.

Scotland

Scotland is the land of romance. The rugged outlines of the highlands are the same today as they were 10,000 years ago. The red deer roam over the same hills. The salmon ascend the same rivers. The grouse fly over the same moors. Scotland has its own dress and its own music, and these, too, seem to have grown with and become part of the Scottish scene. All this is not to say, that Scotland is behind the times. **GLASGOW** (1,089,555), on the River Clyde, is a thriving commercial center in which almost every manufacture in Great Britain is represented. Its shipbuilding yards on both banks of the river as far down as Greenock are world famous. Ships from every part of the world enter and clear at its docks. Glasgow is the most important seaport in Scotland and the second largest city in the United Kingdom. Not to be missed within the city are the **cathedral,** a fine Gothic structure, and the ornamental **park at Kelvingrove.** The park contains the **art gallery** and **museum** which contains many fine examples of the great masters, including Rembrandt, Rubens, Titian, Botticelli and others. On the north side of the park is the **University of Glasgow,** founded in 1450, whose school of engineering has established a standard that is universally acknowledged. The city has a fine new **zoo,** opened in 1947. A short journey out of Glasgow lie the red ruins of **Bothwell Castle,** the finest example of thirteenth century architecture in Scotland. . . . At **EDINBURGH** (466,770), the Castle stands high on its rock, dominating the beautiful city below. The old town is built on the sloping ridge that descends from the rock to the palace of Holyrood one mile away. The **Castle** dates from the seventh century and is famed for its association with the great names of Scottish history: Robert Bruce, the Earl of Douglas, Mary, Queen of Scots and Charles Stuart. The **Scottish War Memorial** for those who fell in 1914-1918 is a shrine and gallery of honor built on Castle Rock and is certainly one of the most beautiful memorials in the world. On the various panels, windows and friezes which decorate the memorial no detail of service was forgotten, and even mice and carrier pigeons appear among the reliefs. **Holyrood Palace,** the residence for six years of Mary, Queen of Scots, is a sixteenth century building in the French style. Visit Queen Mary's apartments where John Knox had his historic interview with the Queen, and the picture gallery, which houses over 100 portraits

Edinburgh's great castle overlooks Princes Street with its
line of double-deck trams
British Information Services

of Scottish kings. There you can trace
Scotland's history back to its very beginnings. The Palace lies at the foot of Arthur's Seat at the far end of the Royal
Mile, which route embraces the old High
Street. Parallel with the High Street and
separated from it by Princes Street Gardens is the more modern and famous
Princes Street — one of the most beautiful
streets in the world. This is the main
thoroughfare and shopping center of Edinburgh, and here, among other things, you
may see the graceful monument to Sir
Walter Scott, John Knox's house and, close
by, Scotland's National Gallery. The famous "Edinburgh Festival" of music,
ballet and drama which perpetuates the
city's long association with the arts, is
held every year from mid-August to the
beginning of September.

South of Edinburgh is typical Border
Country — hills and wooded slopes with
compact little Border towns lying in sheltered valleys, through which run swift,
impatient streams. This is the country
so loved by Sir Walter Scott and you
may visit the lovely home where he
lived in ABBOTSFORD. The house and
grounds contain many memorials of him
and interesting relics collected by him. . . .
Nearby are the abbey ruins of Melrose
and Dryburgh. It was the monks at Melrose Abbey that, through their skillful
manipulation of wool, paved the way for
the growth of the important woolen industry in the Border Country. The heart of
the Scottish hero, Robert Bruce, lies buried
beneath the high altar of the abbey. . . .
Nearby Dryburgh Abbey is the burial
place of Scott. The abbey is a picturesque
ruin charmingly situated in a loop of the
River Tweed. . . . Up the valley of the

Teviot is HAWICK, a modern town with
a thriving woolen industry and an ancient
history. The "Riding of the Marches," a
custom observed each year here, celebrates
the defeat of a body of English soldiers by
the men of Hawick at Hornshole in 1514
after the Battle of Flodden. Hermitage
Castle is one of the oldest standing baronial
buildings in Scotland. . . . PEEBLES is
an industrial center and also an attractive
holiday resort which has many historical
associations. The Tweed, on which it is
located, and other neighboring rivers offer
excellent fishing. . . . To the north, on the
coast, is DUNBAR famous for its history
and good golf. Dunbar saw the hurried
embarkation of Edward II in 1314 after
his defeat at Bannockburn; it also saw the
elopement of Mary, Queen of Scots, with
the unprincipled Bothwell. Today it is a
popular holiday resort with a most unusual sea-water swimming pool in a
delightful natural setting. . . . Nearby
NORTH BERWICK, famous for golf, is
another fashionable resort. Bass Rock, a
precipitous pile that rises 350 feet from
the sea, stands a mile off-shore and is a
nesting colony for gannets. . . . In the
southwest corner of the Lowlands lies
Galloway, a county of high moorland
and twisting valleys. This region is often
neglected by the tourist and is well worth
a visit. DUMFRIES, where Robert Burns
is buried, is the gateway to this area and
many delightful excursions may be made
from here. Lincluden Abbey, Caerlaverock
Castle, the charmingly named Sweetheart
Abbey and Argigland, the birthplace of
Paul Jones, who was gardener, pirate,
admiral and founder of the American navy,
are all within easy reach. . . . Westward,
on the coast is the pleasant holiday resort

of GIRVAN and AYR, famous as the center of the Burns country. . . . At ALLOWAY, on the outskirts of Ayr, is the cottage where the poet was born; in the center of the town is the Auld Brig, a Burns landmark which for five hundred years was the only bridge in the town; two and a half miles from Ayr is the Brig o' Doon which will be remembered in connection with Tam o' Shanter's wild ride on his mare, Meg. Close to the bridge is the Burns Monument, which takes the inappropriate form of a Grecian temple, in which are preserved the bibles exchanged between Burns and Highland Mary, Jean Armour's wedding ring, and many other Burns relics. . . . PRESTWICK, immediately north of Ayr, possesses one of the world's best international airports, is also a noted holiday resort. . . . It is a short journey north from Glasgow to STIRLING, the gateway to the highlands where the English and Scottish nobility journey for the grouse shooting which begins on August 12th and lasts until December 10th. Near Stirling is another impressive castle dating from the fourteenth century and now adapted to the requirements of a modern barracks. . . . At BANNOCKBURN, one mile away, the battle of that name was fought in the year 1314. The battle opened with single combat between the Scottish King Robert the Bruce, mounted on a shaggy pony and armed only with an axe, and the fully appointed English knight, Sir Henry de Bohin. The latter was split in half. . . . Go west from Stirling into the lovely Trossach country, the setting for the romantic episodes of "The Lady of the Lake" as well as for some of the dramatic scenes of "Rob Roy." Here a chain of lochs, set in the midst of imposing hills, runs from Callander in the east to the head of Loch Lomond in the west. Thence the road runs past Loch Awe, through the precipitous Brander Pass to OBAN on the coast, which is not only an excellent center from which to explore the western highalnds, but also one from which to visit the islands — MULL, where wild goat are to be found; the tiny IONA where St. Columba landed with fifteen missionaries in the year 563 and founded a monastery (in the burial ground lies Duncan, victim of Macbeth); and the island of SKYE. This island, wild, lonely and still primitive, is dominated by the granite rocks of the giant Cuilins. The wet and misty climate produces weird atmospheric effects. Islanders will direct you to PORTREE, where Bonnie Prince Charlie took his leave of Flora Macdonald. . . . A short trip by steamer will take the visitor to the outer HEBRIDES where the islanders still speak Gaelic. He will find Lewis with its standing stones marking the graves of ancient warriors; Harris, home of Harris tweed; and North and South Uist. . . . From Skye the visitor may return by way of MALLAIG and take the road or railway past Loch Eil or Loch Eilt to FORT WILLIAM, which stands on the Caledonian Canal at the foot of Ben Nevis, the highest mountain in Great Britain. . . . Visit INVERNESS, the capital of the highlands where, in the third week of September, you may see the Northern Meeting of the clans who gather there for the highland games. Do not miss this event if you wish to see the full splendor of highland dress, the national sports and the music and dancing of Scotland at their best. . . . Northwest of Inverness are the wildest and loveliest parts of the highlands. Here is the home of the red deer, the haunt of the wild cat and the nests of the golden eagle. To walk through this lonely, unchanged country is an experience never to be forgotten. . . . Just east of Inverness is Culloden Moor where, in the battle of that name in 1746, the last hopes of the Jacobites for the return of the house of Stuart were finally crushed. . . . Loch Ness is one of the largest and deepest lochs in Scotland. Never more than a mile wide it is twenty-four miles long and in places 900 feet deep. The water has never been known to freeze. Throughout its length the loch offers on either hand changing scenery of hill and woodland typical of the beauty of the highlands. . . Between Inverness and Perth to the south are some of the greatest fishing grounds in Scotland. The road leads past the Cairngorm Mountains through the Grampians and runs beside the Spey, one of the greatest of all Scottish salmon rivers, through Kingussie, thence to Blair Atholl and Pitlochry on the Tummel, also famed for salmon, and finally to Dunkeld and Perth, between which are some of the most famous salmon pools of the river Tay. . . . An alternate route from Inverness to Perth, more interesting to the non-fisherman perhaps, follows the coast as far as ABERDEEN, a city built of granite. This is the chief city of northern Scotland and is also a pleasant resort with an excellent beach. . . . From here the road follows the valley of the Dee, another famous salmon river. Here, high up in the mountains, is Balmoral Castle, the Scottish home of the Queen; Invercauld House, where the head of the Farquharson clan lived, and Braemar Castle, a miniature Scottish castle perfect in every detail. At the nearby mountain resort of BRAEMAR is held the annual Royal Highland Games. . . . From Braemar the road winds upwards, past the Devil's Elbow, and then falls through Glen Shee and out to the coast and DUNDEE, of marmalade fame. This is the fourth largest Scottish city and is a prosperous manufacturing and ship-building center. . . . Near Dundee is Glamis Castle, parts of which date from the eleventh

the west. There are many hundreds more and the visitor may be assured that wherever he happens to be in Scotland he will have a first-class course within reasonable distance.

Ireland

DUBLIN (523,183) is a city full of history, tragic and glorious, with haunting memories of great patriots, statesmen, scientists and scholars. It is a rare mixture of ancient and modern and is beautifully situated on Dublin Bay in the broad valley of the River Liffey, with the granite domes of the Wicklow Hills sheltering it on the south. You will see here many examples of the Georgian style in spacious squares, streets and fine buildings. On Custom

On Inn's Quay, Dublin, stands the impressive Four Courts with its colonnade of Corinthian columns
British Information Services

century. One of the finest and most picturesque of Scottish castles, it is the seat of the Queen Mother's family. . . . Below Dundee is PERTH, called the "Fair City." It is charmingly situated on the right bank of the Tay and is famed not only for its associations with Scott's novel "The Fair Maid of Perth," but also for the fine old church of St. John dating from 1126. . . . To those who are thinking of a golfing holiday, Scotland, which is the home of golf, has so many good courses to offer that it would be difficult to know where to start. Gleneagles, at Auchterarder, near Perth, and St. Andrews, the headquarters of golf, on the east coast of Fife, are courses which will be familiar, at least by name, to all players of the game. Other famous courses are North Berwick and Muirfield in the east; Turnberry, Prestwick and Troon in

House Quay stands the Custom House, a noble Georgian architectural piece, which was burned down during the Rising of Easter Week, 1916, but has been excellently restored. In contrast, nearby is the most impressive of Dublin's modern buildings, the huge glass-fronted Aras Mhic Dhiarmada or MacDermott Building which houses the bus station. Visit Trinity College, founded 1591; its library contains 500,000 volumes and over 2,000 manuscripts, including the world-famous Book of Kells. Nearby is an interesting group of buildings opposite the lovely St. Stephen's Green: The National Museum with a fine Natural History and Irish antiquities collection; the National Library; Leinster House which houses the Parliament and the National Gallery of Art offering an exceptionally good selection of the Old Mas-

MAP OF DUBLIN

ters. Nearby is the impressive **Bank of Ireland,** formerly the Parliament House, which has no windows. The 13th century **Dublin Castle** houses various official departments along with the lovely Church of the **Most Holy Trinity** which was formerly the royal chapel. Close by is **Christ Church Cathedral** which has a beautiful interior and many interesting historical items. A few blocks from here is **St. Patrick's Cathedral** where Jonathan Swift was Dean from 1713 to 1745 and where he is buried. Other interesting churches are: **St. Audoen's,** with a fine peal of six bells which were cast in 1423 and are the oldest in Ireland; **St. Michan's,** dating from the 17th century, where you may see in the vaults bodies which have lain for centuries without signs of decomposition, and St. **Werburgh's,** where lies the body of Lord Edward Fitzgerald. Visit **Mansion House** and the **General Post Office,** headquarters of the Irish Volunteers in the 1916 Insurrection. **O'Connell Street,** Dublin's finest thoroughfare, is a broad avenue with a striking alignment of statues. Here you will find the **Nelson Pillar,** from the top of which you get a panoramic view of the city. On **Parnell Square,** the **Municipal Gallery of Modern Art** occupies one of Dublin's finest Georgian houses. To the south O'Connell runs into **Grafton Street,** Dublin's most fashionable shopping center. The **Four Courts** is a magnificent structure designed by James Gandon in the 18th century. At Ballsbridge the **Royal Dublin Society** has its splendid show grounds where the **Spring Show** is held each May and the **International Horse Show** is held each August. A visit to **Guinness's Brewery** will be an interesting experience. **Phoenix Park** is famous for its **People's Gardens.** Here also is the **Zoo** with its famous **lions,** the American Embassy, the Papal Nunciature, the Arus an Uachtarain (The President's Residence) and the **Racecourse.** In **Croke Park** you will see hurling at its best.

THE REST OF LEINSTER

Domed granite mountains, wooded valleys, deep glens, clear lakes and streams, moorland and bog and picturesque villages characterize the scene. All may be visited easily from Dublin. Just south of Dublin is the big yachting center of **DUN LAOGHAIRE, BRAY,** popular resort, and **KILLINEY** with its beautiful bay rivaling that of Naples. . . . An hour's drive south takes you through bold passes and glens of richly wooded beauty into the **Wicklow Mountains,** "The Garden of Ireland," with vast expanses of purple heath and golden furze. While here visit **AVOCA,** "The Meeting of the Waters," about which

Thomas Moore created the poem, and **GLENDALOUGH** (Glen of two Lakes), a summer resort of great beauty. The "Seven Churches" here, primitive ecclesiastical stonework at least a thousand years old, are associated with St. Kevin and the beginnings of Christianity in Ireland. . . . See the picturesque old fishing town of **WEXFORD** with its narrow, winding streets. Each year Wexford stages a Festival of Music and Ballet which is exceptional. Nearby is the Norman **Johnstown Castle**. . . . **KILKENNY** is a city steeped in Ireland's history. From the nearby quarries it receives the title of "The Marble City." See the **Cathedral of St. Canice**, with its beautiful central tower and the **Tholsel**, or **tollhouse**, with its curious clock tower and front arcade. . . . Between Dublin and Kildare is the famous **Curragh**, where some of the best racing stock on earth is produced. . . . In the Royal County of **Meath** is **TARA**, site chosen by the High Kings of Ireland for their palaces. Here you can explore the beautiful **Valley of the Boyne**, famous as a battlesite and as a trout and salmon fishing region. . . . The counties of **Westmeath** and **Longford** abound in beautiful lakes and streams, including the **Shannon** in the center of Ireland. This area is dear to the hearts of sportsmen and sightseers alike. **MULLINGAR**, with its fine **Cathedral**, **LONGFORD**, a quaint market town, or **ATHLONE** on the Shannon make good headquarters from which to explore this beautiful country. . . . On the coast is the smallest county of Leinster, **Louth**. **DUNDALK**, its thriving industrial town, is convenient to a number of interesting spots: **Carlingford Lough**, renowned for its beauty; **Blackrock**, with good beaches; **Greenore**, excellent seafishing; **Drogheda**, an old and interesting seaport-industrial town on the Boyne, with **St. Peter's Church**, in which is the well preserved head of Ireland's martyr-saint, **Blessed Oliver Plunket**.

ULSTER

Ulster is a delightful combination of rugged mountains, intensively cultivated farms, great and small lakes and cities whose products are sold the world over. . . . **BELFAST** (443,670), second largest city of Ireland is an industrial center with the greatest shipyards, tobacco factory, rope factory and linen factories in the world. The city is situated in surroundings of great natural beauty at the head of Belfast Lough. The glens of Antrim, the vast expanses of Lough Neagh, the pretty farms of County Down and the blue waters of the Irish Sea are close at hand. Around **Donegall Square**, focal point of the city, you will find the **Linen Hall Library** and the **City Hall**. **Donegall Place** and **Royal Avenue**, off the Square, are the main shopping streets. Here you will see the famous Belfast linen displayed for sale. Visit **Queens University**, the nearby **Art Gallery and Museum** situated in beautiful botanical gardens and the **Parliament Buildings** in **Stormont Park**, all of which are on the outskirts of the city. Visit **Cavehill** and view the city from its beautiful park and visit the **zoo** at Bellevue. Don't miss a trip to the shipyards. . . . From Belfast you can explore the Antrim coast and the famous and beautiful rugged **Glens of Antrim**. Coastal towns to visit include: **CARRICKFERGUS**, famous for its salt mines; **LARNE**, port for trips to Stranraer; **BALLYCASTLE**, a resort with the fantastic **Giant's Causeway** and **PORTRUSH**, a golfing and seaside resort with fine beaches. Inland, see **ANTRIM**, with a Round Tower dating from the 10th century; **Lough Neigh**, largest lake in Ireland; **BALLYCLARE**, noted for good linens and **LISBURN**, in the valley of the Lagan, with the **Maze Race Course**. . . . County Down is rich agricultural country which combines low soft hills with the stark beauty of the **Mountains of Mourne** as they sweep down to the sea. Along the coast are the fine resorts **Bangor**, **Donaghadee** and **Warrenpoint** in the south, backed by the mountains. . . . Visit historic **DOWNPATRICK** and nearby **Inch Abbey** at the end of **Strangford Lough**. Visit **BANBRIDGE**, on the River Bann, famous in song and as a golfing and fishing center. . . . See **NEWCASTLE** at the foot of **Slieve Donard**, a sports center with a fine beach and easy access to the **Mournes** and **ARDGLASS**, famous for its herring. . . . County Armagh is a gentle county, noted for its apple orchards. Visit **ARMAGH**, the Ecclesiastical capital of Ireland, and its magnificent **Cathedral** on a hilltop overlooking the town. . . . **PORTADOWN** is a quiet town, where sports of all types are found in plenty and where you can buy good linen or pottery. The flower nurseries here are famous for their exquisite roses, including the newly perfected **blue rose**. . . . Derry is a county of many contrasts with much to attract tourists. Near good salmon and trout fishing, LONDONDERRY is an historical city where may be seen parts of the old city walls. Don't miss a visit to the Guildhall and to Ship Quay Street. See the Cathedral at the top of Gt. James' St. . . . Visit COLERAINE, famous for its linen and whiskey and PORTSTEWART, a resort noted for its safe beaches and coves. . . . Inland, Tyrone County is a mosaic of mountains, glen, river and lake, dominated by the Sperrin Mountains. DUNGANNON, once the stronghold of the O'Neill Clan and now a bustling center for the linen industry and a first-class base for sport, offers golf, fishing and horse-racing. . . . OMAGH, too, offers good fishing and golf and makes a convenient center for touring the beautiful valleys among the Sperrin Mountains. . . . Other attractive towns include STRABANE, COOKSTOWN, POMEROY and BENBURB, where the historic Battle of 1646 was fought and victory achieved by Owen Roe O'Neill. . . . County Fermanagh has some of the most wonderful lake scenery in Ireland. ENNISKILLEN is the link between Upper and Lower Lough Erne and has an interesting Castle and Cathedral. Near here is Devenish Island with one of the finest round towers in Ireland. . . . Visit BELLEEK, famous for its lovely, delicate china and pottery and GARRISON on the shores of Lough Melvin, famous for its "Sonaghan" and "Gillaroo" trout. . . . In the western part of the county are a number of interesting caves to explore. . . . County Cavan consists mainly of undulating pastoral land dotted with many mineral springs. Everywhere you will see cattle grazing and acre upon acre of potatoes.

The town of CAVAN, with its interesting modern cathedral, is well-situated in the center of good hunting, shooting and fishing country. . . . Perhaps the most beautiful area of Cavan lies around VIRGINIA, with the lovely Lake of Ramor nearby, where you may swim, fish or boat. . . . Monaghan is a county of small hills, high hedges, twisting roads and a myriad of beautiful lakes. Here you will love the ancient market town of MONAGHAN, CASTLEBLAYNEY, another market town, with its famous Hope Castle and CLONES, famous for its crochet lace and 11th-century cross in the market place. . . . CARRICKMACROSS is the home of the precious Carrickmacross lace. . . . The beauty of County Donegal is known the world over. Blue skies, high mountains, golden beaches, frowning cliffs give it an atmosphere all its own. An attractive holiday center is the seaside resort BUNDORAN, with its fine, sunny climate. . . . In the middle of Lough Derg is a tiny island where thousands of pilgrims go each year to St. Patrick's Purgatory to fast and do penitence. . . . The "wee" neat town of DONEGAL is scenically situated at the head of Donegal Bay. It boasts of the imposing ruins of Donegal Castle, the old stronghold of the O'Donnell Clan, Donegal Abbey and a striking modern Church of the Four Masters. . . . High on the banks of the River Erne, BALLYSHANNON is a popular seaside resort. . . . Southwestern Donegal is where the Donegal tweed industry centers and cottage industries and crafts abound. Two main centers are KILCAR and ARDARA. . . . North of Dungloe the fabulous country called The Rosses is as unspoiled now as a thousand years ago. Here is a combina-

Giant's Causeway, great stepping stones of basalt caused by the cooling of a lava flow
British Information Services

tion of wild heather, strewn mountains peppered with unusual rocks, across which streams jump, struggle and gurgle the song of the Highlands of Donegal. And here flourishes the Gaelic tongue. . . . Near MILFORD, one of the best fishing areas, you can visit Golan Loop and The Fairy Glen. . . . The Inishowen Peninsula, between Loughs Swilly and Foyle contains a number of delightful holiday resorts. Along the coast are excellent, safe beaches. . . . To the south are the twin towns BALLYBOFEY and STRANORLAR astride the River Finn, both famous for salmon fishing par excellence.

CONNACHT

Connacht comprises a region of vast expanses of bogland, bare mountains, steep cliffs and beautiful lakes. In County Galway, you must see the ancient city of GALWAY on famed Galway Bay. Here you can see the Spanish Arch and Spanish Parade, Lynch's Castle, where you will learn the derivation of the word lynching, Eyre Square with its charming little statue of Padraic O'Conaire, one of Ireland's best-loved writers, marking the town's center, and the Church of St. Nicholas, where Columbus prayed before setting out for America. One of Ireland's great natural phenomena occur at the Salmon Weir Bridge where thousands of salmon pause on their journey to the vast stretches of Lough Corrib. If you are here in July, don't miss the Galway Races, a major social event. . . . From Galway steamers will take you to picturesque Aran Islands, locale of Flaherty's fascinating documentary film, "Man of Aran." . . . Island-dotted Lough Corrib affords the best trout fishing. . . . West of Galway is the fabulous wild, mountainous region, Connemara, dominated by the "Twelve Pins," a stretch of land whose scenery changes with every shower and ray of sunshine. Northeast of this area is Joyce's Country, a paradise for hikers and climbers, famous for its picturesque mountain scenery. . . . Other places to visit in Galway are Tuam, with its Cathedral and Cross of Tuam; Ballinasloe, famous for its October Horse and Cattle Fair and as a resort, and Gort, with its leaning round tower and queer caves with underground streams. . . . County Mayo is an area of small farms and more magnificent mountain and Atlantic scenery. . . . Connected to the mainland by a narrow bridge is the artist's haven and the

nation's playground, Achill Island with its ocean air and its vast stretches of silvery strand lying between towering cliffs. Here nature is at its grandest; the seaward cliff face drops two thousand feet sheerly into ocean depths and though the strong winds blow, there is no bitterness in their blast. . . . On beautiful Clew Bay, the town of WESTPORT has a Continental air, its rows of lime trees lining the Mall by the river. . . . Nearby is Croagh Patrick, the lofty peak St. Patrick is said to have climbed that he might banish all snakes and venomous things from Ireland forever into the wide ocean. . . . Throughout the county are excellent fishing waters, including Lough Conn, with its famous "Gillmoor" trout, and Lough Mask, where the trout are large and fight gamely. . . . Other towns of interest include Cong, with its Cross of Cong, one of Ireland's greatest Christian antiquities and Knock, renowned as the scene of an Apparition of the Blessed Virgin. . . . County Sligo is another beautiful sea-side county with a lake district that rivals Killarney. SLIGO is a busy and important market town and is a good center for exploring the Northwest of Ireland. . . . Nearby is Lough Gill with the small island of Innisfree mentioned by Yeats in his "The Lake Isle of Innisfree" and the Caves of Kesh. . . . STRANDHILL is a pleasant resort on the coast and, if you are a golfer, you should not miss the championship course at ROSSES POINT. . . . See Ballymote, with the remains of the Franciscan Friary and the castle built in 1300. . . . Two lakes set in great beauty are Lough Gara, and wind and rain-swept Lough Talt in the Ox Mountains, a good fishing lake. . . . County Leitrim has sent many of its sons and daughters to the U. S. It is a region of quiet and pleasant scenery, good hunting and fishing. Visit CARRICK-ON-SHANNON, a good center for hunting, shooting, tennis, fishing and other sports. . . . Lough Melvin is the native home of the "Gillaroo" and "Sonaghan" trout, both real "fightin' fish." . . . County Roscommon is an inland county which produces potatoes and has excellent cattle and sheep grazing land. In an abbey on an island in Lough Key, situated in scenic grandeur, is where were written the "Annals of Lough Cé" which now repose in the Trinity library in Dublin. . . . In ROSCOMMON see the Castle built in 1268 and the Cistern Abbey built in 1257. . . . BOYLE,

Atop its massive limestone base, the Rock of Cashel is a familiar landmark of Tipperary

Irish Tourist Bureau

a thriving town nestled at the foot of the Curlew Hills, is proud possessor of a Cisterian abbey built in 1161.

MUNSTER

Occupying the southwest of Ireland, Munster Province contains some of Ireland's greatest beauty spots. In the city of CORK, on the majestic River Lee, you will not want to miss Shandon Church with its famous bells, the modernistic church of Christ the King, the very beautiful Franciscan Church, famous for its murals, and the Cork Public Museum. . . . Six miles from Cork is BLARNEY CASTLE, where you may hang by the ankles and kiss the famous Blarney Stone. . . . On the coast are many attractive spots: BALLYCOTTON, famous for deep-sea angling; CROSSHAVEN, yachting, swimming and fishing center; YOUGHAL, with its fine beach and COURTMACSHERRY, with fine sea and river bathing and fishing. . . . Characteristic of West Cork, which couples some of the most beautiful scenery of Ireland with a glorious Atlantic coast line, is Glengarriff, with beauty beyond words. Here you find a mild climate, sub-tropical vegetation and the wonderful Garnish Island, featuring a delightful Italian garden. . . . County Kerry is probably the most beautiful part of Ireland. The towering hills, the wild Atlantic coast and the lush loveliness of Lakes of Killarney, make a visit to Kerry a "must." Make KILLARNEY with its lovely Cathedral of St. Patrick, your base for sightseeing and starting place for the fascinating "Ring of Kerry," an enchanting tour. You will see PUCK FAIR, where the Goat is crowned each August; DERRYNANE, birthplace of the Irish Liberator, Daniel O'Connell; PARKNASILLA, a beautiful resort, and Windy Gap which will give you one of the most spectacular views in Ireland. Visit DINGLE amidst rugged beauty and pre-historic ruins. Off-shore are the Blasket Islands. See TRALEE, capital of "The Kingdom," and BALLYBUNION, a popular resort with good golfing. . . . County Limerick and County Clare offer more typical Irish scenery with many lakes for good fishing and hunting and scattered ruins of old castles and abbeys. Here is famous Shannon Airport, where you can buy souvenirs, and the modern, bustling city of LIMERICK, with well-preserved Georgian buildings. See King John's Castle, the Treaty Stone and St. Mary's Cathedral. . . . From ENNIS you can tour the unique region of West Clare with the awesome Cliffs of Moher. . . . County Tipperary, famous in song, is rich, undulating, pastoral country. Visit TIPPERARY and CASHEL, famous for the prominent Rock of Cashel, where the Irish Kings were crowned. . . . Visit the Glen of Aherlow, a remarkable defile near Tipperary. . . . In County Waterford visit the city of WATERFORD, famous for its glassware; the nearby seaside resort of TRAMORE, with good bathing and the annual Tramore Races; CAPPOQUIN, on the southern slope of the Knockmealdown Mountains where you can visit Mount Mellary Abbey; Dungarvan, Ardmore and Lismore, interesting small towns.

France

PARIS AND FRANCE

Synonymous with gaiety, good food for gastronomes, gorgeous gowns, grapes for wine, all the good things in life, has a unique appeal to the traveler. From lovely Paris, "City of Light," to Normandy and Brittany, land of Calvados and strawberries, to the quaint Basque country in the Pyrenees, to Strasbourg, of *pâté-de-foi-gras* fame, to the swank resorts of the Riviera, the people, customs, scenery — all are equally charming. Go to France to see Paris but don't forget to see as much as possible of the rest of France.

SMOOTH HIGHWAYS INTO THE PAST

While reveling in the enjoyment of her material pleasures, you will, as every visitor to this traditional land of liberty and fraternity, permanently enrich your own life with the heritage of Europe recorded in France's historic palaces, magnificent museums and Gothic cathedrals and storied past. Each region is easily accessible by smooth highways and national and local bus and rail service provide inexpensive travel. The people of each region still cherish their ancient customs and rituals and, especially on "fete" days, their colorful native dress. In Alsace, on the least provocation, gay processions march along the streets accompanied by shouts, bells, drums, bugles and flags flying high. In Normandy still can be seen processions of the "Charitons," dressed in their silver and gold embroidered costumes, escorted by bell-ringers and standard bearers. Women of Brittany still wear their charming lace caps and the men, their native suits. Everywhere past and present suffuse, making a delightful land and people.

DINE AND WINE WITH ABANDON

The art of preparing delectable dishes is instinctive with the French. Nowhere else in the world can be found the variety and mouth-watering goodness of their concoctions, from the "Cordon bleu" restaurants to the smallest of provincial inns. Good food deserves good wine and the wine of France is superb. To say nothing of her beautiful liqueurs. Let your "host" guide you in selecting typical local dishes and suggesting which wine to serve with each course, and by all means, forget diets and eat to your heart's content. Subtlety in the use of spices is the keynote of the French cuisine. However, the food is never spicy in the "hot" sense of the word, except for an occasional speciality. Chicken (*poulet, poularde*) and duck (*canard*) prepared in 1001 ways, according to the region, is always delicious. Shell fish specialities like *moules marinère* (mussels steeped in white wine), *crayfish bisque, crevettes* (shrimp) and, as a matter of fact, all fish dishes look and taste so good, even non-fish eaters find themselves savoring each morsel. Desserts in each region are intriguing. There seems an unending variety of little cakes, filled or not with some delicious cream, souffles, tarts, *crepes* (those delicious little pancakes flavored with different liqueurs), and fruit, fresh or preserved, served in any of the luscious flavored liqueurs. And with dessert comes the *fromage* (cheese) of which there is also an unending variety, a type to suit every taste. France is the home of such famous cheeses as Roquefort, Brie, Camembert and many others. One could go on forever, but let it suffice that you will heartily enjoy eating your way through France.

PARIS

This fabulous city (pop. 2,820,534) not only serves as the epitome of glamor, it has been a focal point of culture as well. For centuries generation after generation of people from all over the world have gravitated to Paris as the center of Western Civilization. In Paris, history, poetry and art sit on every doorstep, set the backdrop for everyday living. The ancient winding streets, the sidewalk cafes, the fine shops, the lovely public gardens and parks, the scintillating crowds, combine to make the city an endless panorama of human warmth and culture.

Sightseeing tours can be arranged by bus or car through the American Express or your travel agent. In summer, little excursion boats, "bateaux-mouches," make two-hour trips up and down the Seine starting at the Pont de Solferino. There is a restaurant and bar on board.

In the heart of the city, the ISLANDS OF THE SEINE. Ile de la Cité is the cradle of Paris and site of famous Cathedral of Notre Dame, begun in 1163 and finished 200 years later. Also on this island, that masterpiece of Gothic art, La Ste. Chapelle, built as a shrine by St.-Louis; the Conciergerie where Marie-Antoinette, Madame Dubarry and ultimately Danton and Robespierre were imprisoned during the Revolution; the **Palais de Justice** which contains relics of the earliest Capetian monarchs; the lovely **Flower Market**, and on Sundays the **Bird Market**. **Ile St.-Louis**, developed by Louis XIII is notable for its 17th and 18th century houses. The two most famous are the **Hotel de Lauzun** on the **Quai d'Anjou**, dating from 1657, where Théophile Gautier and Baudelaire lived and the **Hotel Lambert**, dating from 1640. Daumier worked for many years at No. 9 Quai d'Anjou.

LEFT BANK OF THE SEINE

From the Cité, Pont Michel leads to Blvd. St. Michel, main street of the **LATIN QUARTER,** and for generations the haunt of students. Off Blvd. St. Michel on Rue St. Severin, the Church of St. Severin, dating from the 13th century, combines early Gothic and late Renaissance architecture. Near by, **St. Julien le Pauvre,** one of the oldest churches, dating from the 12th century, has an acacia in the garden brought from America in 1600, believed to be the oldest tree in Paris. Streets behind the church are old and picturesque. **Cluny Museum,** on Blvd. St. Germain, was built in the 14th century and is one of the few medieval buildings still standing in Paris. It houses a rare and valuable collection of medieval art and crafts. Nearby is the **Sorbonne,** perhaps the most influential and greatest school of liberal arts in Europe. On Place Marcelin Berthelot, is the **College de France,** founded by François I in opposition to the Sorbonne. **St. Etienne du Mont,** Place Ste. Geneviève, contains the shrine of the Patron Saint of Paris, St. Geneviève. Opposite, the **Pantheon,** built in her honor in the 18th century in the form of a Greek cross houses the tombs of Voltaire, Rousseau, Victor Hugo and Zola.

East of the center of the city, at the Quai St. Bernard, **Jardin des Plantes** covers 75 acres and contains a zoo, botanical garden and a museum of natural history. During the German siege of 1870 hungry Parisians broke in and ate some of the animals here. Opposite the park, on Rue Geoffroy, is **La Mosquée,** a Moroccan mosque built after the first world war, and surrounded by the North African quarter. On Rue Monge, also near the gardens, are the ruins of the old Roman theater,

Horse-drawn fiacres provide a delightful way of seeing the Arch. of Triumph and other sights of Paris
French Govt. Tourist Office

HIGHLIGHT MAP OF
PARIS
FRANCE

MAP SHOWS MAJOR STREETS
© C. S. HAMMOND & Co., N.Y.

1. Mus. d'Art Moderne
2. Pal. de Glace
3. Auto Club
4. Min. de la Marine
5. Mus. Cernuschi
6. Bourse
7. Pl. des Victoires
8. Banque de France
9. Ecole Centrale
10. Thea. Châtelet
11. Thea. Sarah Bernhardt
12. Tour St. Jacques
13. Hôtel de Ville
14. Pal. de Justice
15. Hôtel des Monnaies
16. Bouffes-Parisiens
17. Colonne de Juillet
18. Opéra
19. Opéra-Comique
20. Pont de Solférino
21. Sorbonne
22. St. Julien le Pauvre
23. Place d'Italie
Q.= Quai   R.= Rue

To Le Bourget Airport

To Fontainebleau & Orly Airport

To Cité Univ. & Parc Montsouris

To Hippodrome de Longchamp

To Versailles

To Cimetière de Picpus

To Bois de Vincennes

ST. ANTOINE

MARAIS

MONTMARTRE

LES BATIGNOLLES

AUTEUIL

Lutetia Arena, destroyed in the year 280.

Gobelins Tapestry Factory, 42 Ave. des Gobelins, with its museum of tapestries old and modern, was established as a state monopoly by Louis XIV's mercantilist minister Colbert. Parc Montsouris, with a fine view of the city, contains a cascadefed lake and a replica of the Palace of the Bey of Tunis which is an observatory. Opposite the park on Blvd. Jourdan is the Cité Universitaire, a village of student housing units built after World War I and reflecting the national architecture of the various countries whose students live there. Off Ave. Denfert-Rochereau is the Observatory originally built by Perrault in the 17th century. Through its great telescope the Moon and Mars were first photographed. Five intricate clocks combine to establish the official French time. The Catacombs, 2 Place Denfert-Rochereau, the huge, eery underground cemetery were originally quarries dating to Roman times. (Be sure to take along a flashlight.) Nearby is the Cemetery of Montparnasse which contains the tombs of Saint-Saens, Saint-Beuve, Baudelaire, De Maupassant and Dumont d'Urville.

From the western end of the Ile de la Cité Pont-Neuf, the oldest bridge in Paris, built in 1578, leads to the SAINT GERMAIN QUARTER. On Quai Conti, near the bridge, stands the Institut de France where the five French Academies meet. This sprawling edifice with its domed roof was built in the 17th century by Le Vau. Next door is the French mint or Hotel des Monnaies. Close by is Ecole des Beaux Arts, scene of the annual wild Art Students' Ball. The gallery displays works of Fragonard, David, Ingres, etc. At Rue Bonaparte and Place St. Germain des Près stands St. Germain des Près, oldest church in Paris. Its Roman transept, tower and nave date from the 11th century. Nearby the 17th century Church of St. Sulpice is famous for its Delacroix murals. Surrounded by its beautiful and popular gardens Luxembourg Palace and Museum was built by Marie de Médicis in 1620. The museum contains contemporary painting and sculpture.

Pont Alexandre III which connects the Esplanade des Invalides with the Champs-Elysées, was built for the exhibition in 1900 and is the largest and most elaborate bridge in Paris. Approached by its imposing, tree-lined esplanade, Les Invalides, the tomb of Emperor Napoleon, with its golden dome is an impressive sight. The sarcophagus of red granite, presented by Czar Nicolas of Russia, rests in the crypt directly under the great dome and surrounded by trophies, flags and commemorative bas-reliefs. The dome was built by Mansard in 1706 for the Eglise des Invalides. The Hotel des Invalides, founded by Louis XIV as an old soldiers' home, houses the very important museum of the Army. Next to the tomb of Napoleon is the Church of St.-Louis des Invalides, decorated with French regimental flags and statues of great soldiers and many souvenirs of Napoleon. Across the Blvd. des Invalides is Hotel Biron (Rodin Museum), a beautiful house which represents the best of the pretentious 18th century houses of the Blvd. St. Germain. It houses the works of the famous sculptor. Opposite the Place de la Concorde is the Palais Bourbon or Chambre des Deputés where the National Assembly sits. Near Les Invalides is Ecole Militaire, one of the greatest works of the architect Gabriel, where Napoleon was commissioned. The Champ de Mars, originally market gardens and later a Revolutionary meeting place, has for the past hundred years been the site of many world exhibitions. It leads to the Eiffel Tower which was built in 1887 for a world exhibition. Elevators ascend to the top and there are restaurants on the first and second landings which command a magnificent view of the city.

RIGHT BANK OF THE SEINE

Opposite Notre Dame, the magnificent Hotel de Ville, City Hall of Paris, stands on the site where public executions took place until 1832. The interior and the inner courts are equally handsome. Next door, the Church of St. Gervais and St. Protais is a 16th century edifice remarkable for the height of its interior. Nearby is the Tour St. Jacques which dates back to the Carolingian kings. Up the Rue des Archives from the Hotel de Ville is the Palais des Archives (National Archives) housed in the old Hotel de Soubise. The surrounding area is called the Marais Quarter, one of the oldest sections in Paris and once a swamp. Here still stand a number of houses from the Renaissance, including the Musée Carnavelet which is the historical museum of the city of Paris. The apartment of Madame de Sévigné, a one-time tenant is still preserved in it.

"Winged Victory," one of the many priceless exhibits in the Louvre

French Govt. Tourist Office

Near by is the Place des Vosges, a large square around which lived many noble families in the time of Henry IV and of Louis XIV. The buildings here represent the best in Paris architecture. Where Victor Hugo lived at No. 6 is a small commemorative museum. On the Rue St. Antoine, main thoroughfare running through the Marais, are a number of curious and interesting old houses and churches, including the Church of St. Paul-St. Louis, Hotel de Mayenne, the Hotel Sully, and the Temple de Ste. Marie. The avenue ends at the Place de la Bastille, site of the old prison destroyed by the mob on July 14th, 1789. In the center of the square is the Column of Juillet with its symbol of liberty, erected by Louis Philippe in 1840 commemorating the revolution of 1830.

At a little distance from the Bastille, is the Cemetery of Pere Lachaise which encloses many tombs of celebrated Frenchmen, including De Musset, Rossini, Haussmann, Baudry, Chopin, Rosa Bonheur, Balzac and others. South of this is the small, historic Picpus Cemetery where Lafayette is buried. Still further south is the Bois

de Vincennes, with the biggest zoo in Paris. The Chateau de Vincennes, built in the 14th century, was long a royal residence and then a prison. The Grand Condé, Fouquet, Diderot, Mirabeau and the Duc d'Enghien were all imprisoned here. It was General Gamelin's headquarters at the beginning of World War II. During the German Occupation many French Resistance workers were tortured to death here.

The handsome Blvd. de Sebastopol leads from the Seine to Blvd. St. Martin where stand two impressive arched gates, Porte St. Denis and Porte St. Martin which commemorate Louis XIV's victories on the Rhine and the taking of Besançon. Nearby is the Conservatory of Arts and Crafts which houses among other things Bleriot's plane, Daguerre's camera and some of the first automobiles. Don't miss the great market place near here, Les Halles, named "the belly of Paris" by Zola. Especially visit the flower stalls and cheese market, and you must have onion soup at one of the restaurants in the area. About 5:30 A.M. is the best time, when all the food is on display like precious jewels.

On the Rue du Louvre, **La Bourse** is a complète madhouse during stock-exchange hours. Built in 1899, it is supposedly a model of the temple of Vespasian in Rome. The **Bibliothèque Nationale**, 58 Rue de Richelieu, was originally Cardinal Mazarin's palace which he reputedly won in a game of cards. It contains one of the finest collections of books and engravings in the world, including one of the first printings from the Gutenberg press. Don't miss the manuscript room and the medals and antiquities room. Across the Rue de Petits Champs is the **Palais Royal** where Louis XIV lived as a boy. This is historically one of the most interesting buildings in Paris. At the south end corner is the **Comédie Française**. Close by is the church of St. **Germain l'Auxerrois**, dating to the 12th century with facade from the 15th and 16th centuries. Note the main door, 13th century, and the 15th century porch. It was from here the signal rang out for the massacre of the Huguenots on the Feast of St. Bartholomew in 1572. Across the Rue de Rivoli is the **Louvre**, the world's most famous art museum. Built originally by Philippe Auguste as a fortress, it was converted to a palace by Charles V and then completely rebuilt by Francis I from plans by Pierre Lescot. Henry IV, Louis XIII and Louis XIV made further additions and Napoleon I and Napoleon III continued the work which had been discontinued when Louis XIV moved to his fabulous Versailles Palace. This is the home of the "Mona Lisa," the "Venus de Milo," the "Winged Victory of Samothrace" and major collections of every school of painting and sculpture. Make a point of going some Friday night when the sculpture galleries are especially illuminated. A most appropriate setting for this magnificent *musée* is the **Jardin de Tuileries**, the most beautiful gardens in Paris. This one-time public garbage heap was first transformed by Catherine de Médicis and later developed by the famed gardener, Le Notre. Close by **The Madeleine** contains many beautiful paintings of the life of Mary Madgalen and fine vari-colored, marble statuary. Its organ is one of the finest in Paris and the church music here is excellent. A must! Pay an early morning visit to the flower market at the Madeleine. In the center of the

Place Vendôme stands a tall column, an imitation of Trajan's column, topped by a statue of Napoleon in his imperial garb. The ornamental frieze of the column depicts scenes from the campaign of 1805. From here the **Rue de la Paix**, of dress-making and jewel shop fame, leads to the **Opera**, designed by Charles Garnier. The *pièce de résistance* here is the magnificent grand staircase. Almost as striking is the mirrored foyer.

From the Madeleine, the **Grand Boulevards** form a semicircle outlining the "old city." To really get the feel of Paris life, take a mid-afternoon stroll along these tree-lined, thirty-yard-wide avenues. Or better still, enjoy a drink at one of the sidewalk cafes and watch Paris flow by.

MONTMARTRE

The heights of Montmartre have played a major part in the military history of the city. Atop the summit of the Butte, **Sacré-Coeur**, with its shining dome dominates the "City of Light." This basilica affords an unmatched view of Paris. In the **Cemetery of Montmartre** are tombs of a long line of famous Frenchmen, including Zola, Stendhal, Gautier, Berlioz, Offenbach and many others. Visit the **Place du Tertre**, center of the colorful village life of Montmartre and see the **waxworks** at the **Musée Grevin**, 10 Blvd. Montmartre.

Back in the heart of the city is **Place de la Concorde**, a magnificent square which was the site of bloody "Madame Guillotine" during the Revolution and almost 3,000 heads fell to her knife. The **Obelisk of Luxor**, a solid piece of red granite, rises some ninety feet high between the fountains in the center of the square. The palaces on the Rue Royale side, now **Hotel Crillon** and the **Ministry of Marine**, were designed by Gabriel. At the entrance to Champs Elysées, leading up to the Etoile, are the celebrated statuary horses of Marly. On the northeast corner is the **American Embassy**. The **Champs Elysées** forms a small park adjacent to the Concorde and then continues as a broad avenue to the Etoile. Probably the most frequented street in Paris, it rather resembles a permanent Easter Parade. On the south side of the Champs Elysées, on either side of the Pont Alexandre III are the **Petit** and the **Grand Palais**. The former houses the fine art exhibitions of the city of Paris and the latter is the exhibition hall where special shows are held throughout the year. On the north side, actually in the Rue Faubourg St. Honoré, is the **Palais de l'Elysée**, the residence of the President of France. The **Arc de Triomphe de l'Etoile** is a huge monument honoring the French army. It stands at the junction of twelve avenues which form the **Etoile** or **Star**. Sculpturing on the monument commemorates Napoléon's victories. Under the arch rest the ashes of the French Unknown Soldier, marked by an eternal flame, first lighted in 1920. The view of Paris from the top of the arch is magnificent. From the Etoile, the Ave. Kléber leads to the

ber of interesting statuary tributes to famous writers and composers. At the western end of the city is the **Bois de Boulogne**. This great forest-park has several lakes, a cascade and the **Longchamp racecourse** as well as a small **zoo** (the Jardin Zoologique d'Acclimation), a paradise for children.

To really feel you belong, sip an aperitif at a sidewalk cafe around six in the evening at the **Rond-Point des Champs-Elysées** or at the **Place Clichy** or **Place Pigalle** and have your after dinner coffee and liqueur at one of the cafes in the

The exquisite Hall of Mirrors at Versailles
French Govt. Tourist Office

Palais de Chaillot where the United Nations sat in 1948 and in 1951-52. It includes a theatre, a concert hall, the fine **Museum of Man**, a museum of ships, a museum of French statuary, a museum of French folk art and the Aquarium. Near by is the **Museum of Modern Art** and the **Musée Guimet** with an excellent collection of Asiatic art.

Paris is noted for its lovely squares, gardens and parks. A particularly pleasant one is the **Parc Monceau**. Originally laid out as a fantasy, it is now laid out in formal English style and is adorned with a num-

Blvd. St. Germain or **Blvd. St. Michel**.

IN THE ENVIRONS OF PARIS

VERSAILLES, nine miles southwest of Paris, is the vast, magnificent palace of Louis XIV surrounded by its park with probably the most beautiful gardens in the world. In the park are the **Grand and Petit Trianons**, pavilions built for the pleasures of Louis XIV, Madame Du Barry and later, Marie Antoinette. Visit the **Museum**, the fabulous **Hall of Mirrors** where the Peace Treaty was signed in World War I, the **Royal Suites** and Marie Antoinette's charming **hamlet**. The great fountains are turned on the first Sunday of each month from May to September. On the way to Versailles, don't miss a visit to the porcelain factory and museum at SEVRES. . . . RAMBOUILLET, thirty-five miles southwest of Paris, in the forest of Yveline, is the summer residence of the President of France. Francis I died here. The forest, intersected by valleys and lakes, is one of the loveliest of the Ile de France. . . . Still further is CHARTRES, fifty miles southwest of Paris, with its famous cathedral, the finest Gothic cathedral in the world. Its statuary and stained-glass windows are superb.

Another great palace, FONTAINE-BLEAU, sits in the heart of a vast forest twenty-five miles southeast of Paris. It dates to the 12th century and is full of memories of the court. Louis XIII was born here. Since Philippe-Auguste the kings of France have all added to it through the works of such great artists as da Vinci, Cellini and the noted gardener, Le Notre. A favorite residence of Napoleon, the striking interior decorations and Empire style furniture, the throne room, the abdication room all seem to be shrouded still with his personality. The horse-hoof staircase in the great courtyard was the scene of his farewell to the old guard in 1814. . . . Also deep in the forest of Fontainebleau is the village of BARBIZON which gave its name to the 19th century school of painting. Millet, Rousseau, Corot, Troyon and Dupré all lived here. Near here Millet painted his celebrated "Angelus."

Northwest of Paris is ST.-GERMAIN-EN-LAYE. The original chateau was built by Louis IX, but the rebuilding of Francis I has left only the chapel of the first building. Louis XIII lived here and Louis XIV was born here. In the palace is a wonderful museum of Gallo-Roman antiquities. The surrounding forest is a favorite holiday spot for Parisians. . . . On the way to St. Germain visit MALMAISON, residence of the Empress Josephine which houses a museum of Napoleonic mementoes.

SAINT DENIS, six miles northeast of Paris, is the burial place of the French Kings and is filled with statuary and carving representing the entire sweep of French history to the death of Louis XVIII. All that remains of the original abbey, built by Dagobert, Pepin and Charlemagne is the crypt. The porch and two towers date from the reconstruction of the Abbot Suger in the 12th century. The rest dates from the time of St. Louis, in the 13th century. . . . Twenty miles northeast of Paris, CHANTILLY is famous for the estate of the Constable de Montmorency which became the property of Prince de Condé in the 16th century. It contains a fine park designed by Le Notre and a chateau restored by the Duc d'Aumale in the 19th century. In the library is the famous medieval illuminated manuscript, the "Grandes Heures de Duc de Berry." This is the birthplace of the luscious *Creme Chantilly* or "whipped cream." . . . Further northeast is SENLIS with its 12th century cathedral and ruins of an old Roman fortress and the Roman wall around the town. . . . Fifty miles northeast, in another great forest, the town of COMPIEGNE was the scene of the capture of Joan of Arc and where she was sold to the British for trial and burning as a witch. Here is an old Renaissance town-hall and a stately chateau built by Gabriel. It was here the Armistice was signed in 1918 and again when Hitler forced the French to sign in 1940.

At MEAUX, twenty-five miles east of Paris, is a beautiful 12th century cathedral. Its tower gives a good view of the field of the first Battle of the Marne in 1914. . . . Of particular interest to Americans is CHATEAU THIERRY, fifty miles east of Paris, which was the center of the battle-fields of World War I. Near here is the American cemetery.

EASTERN FRANCE AND ALSACE

Picturesque little villages with peaked rooftops surmounted by the traditional stork nests nestle in deep valleys and thick forests. The scenery is eye-filling, the local inns are famous for their excellent food and Alsatian wines and the people are charming, friendly and colorfully costumed.

On the way to Nancy see VERDUN, dramatic symbol of World War I, and visit the forts and the Memorial. If possible, take a side trip to the fortified city of METZ which has many 13th to 15th century houses and the 13th century cathedral of St. Etienne. . . . On to NANCY (pop. 120,484), city of King Stanislas. Visit the Town Hall, the Duke's Palace and, by all means, the Place Stanislas with its imposing wrought iron gates. . . . Near by more battlefields of World War I can

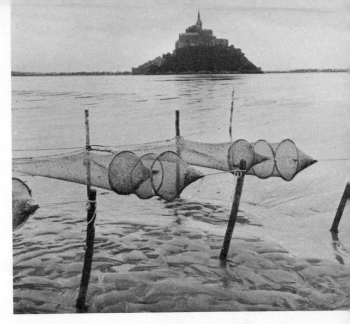

Mont Saint Michel, the great abbey on a rock in the sea, with fish traps drying in the foreground
French Govt. Tourist Office

be visited. . . . STRASBOURG (pop. 193,-353), beautiful, artistic capital city of Alsace, is interesting for its 11th century Gothic cathedral and its famous clock with moving figures, for the Church of St. Thomas where the Maréchal de Saxe is buried and the museum-palace of the Dukes of Rohan. The old districts have many quaint houses such as the Kammerzell, a beautiful 16th century Alsatian house, now an excellent restaurant.

The trip through the Vosges below Strasbourg is most delightful. . . . At COLMAR visit the Musée d'Unterlinden. . . . Continue through the 15th century village of OBERNAI to pictureque and historic hilltop of Ste. Odile, to the HOHWALD and the castle of Hoch Koenigsbourg which offers a panoramic view. . . . Near here are a number of quaint villages, including SELESTAT, RIBEAUVILLE and ORBEY, all famous for their vintage wines and good food. . . . GERARDMER, in the lake district, is famous for its cheese and as a resort. . . . Also in the Vosges is one of France's most beautiful spas, VITTEL. . . . Near here is the village of DOMREMY where Joan of Arc was born in 1412.

THE CHAMPAGNE COUNTRY

This is the country roughly limited by the triangle formed by Epernay on the south, Chalons-sur-Marne on the east and Reims on the north, and from which, say the French, must come all the wine that bears this name.

In REIMS (pop. 114,682) is the famous and magnificent 13th century Cathedral with its exquisite rose window, the Fine Arts Museum and the nearby Fort de la Pompelle. Spend an afternoon at one of the famous champagne cellars, Pommery for instance. . . . In EPERNAY it is worth while to see the caves of Moet et Chandon, a favorite place of Napoleon's. . . . Near Epernay, on the hill, is the lovely village of HAUTVILLIERS with its ancient abbey. Here tradition says, the happy monk Dom Perignon discovered in about 1700 the wonderful secret of bubbling champagne.

NORMANDY AND BRITTANY

This region compares favorably with any other in Europe for tourist appeal. The haunt of artists and writers, these provinces have a unique beauty. The people and the land have grown together in complete harmony. Quaint market towns, brightly colored regional costumes, rough hewn houses, colorful fishing ports, attractive farmsteads, green forests, rocky isles, sand beaches and the tang of salt air all combine to make a tourist paradise. Steeped in history, the region also boasts of many shrines, feudal castles, abbeys and medieval monuments and some of the most beautiful cathedrals in France. Incidentally, one can travel here for very little, especially in Brittany where hotels and pensions average from four to five dollars a day including food. And the food is always good.

First of the Norman cathedral towns is the capital, ROUEN (pop. 113,062), called by Victor Hugo "the hundred-spired town," but sadly damaged in World War II. See the cathedral with its remarkable tower or "lantern," the churches of St. Ouen and St. Maclou, the museums, the medieval Hotel de Bourgheroulde, the Gros-Horloge and the market place where Joan of Arc was burned. . . . West of Rouen on the coast are the fashionable resort towns of TROUVILLE and DEAUVILLE, either being an excellent place to week-end from Paris. But have a reservation; they're crowded in the summer months. . . . CAEN was the scene of the fierce battle in the summer of 1944 when the Allied Armies broke out of the beachhead. The grim walls of its abbeys epitomized the simplicity and severity of true Norman architecture. See the Church of St. Peter, the Abbey of St. Etienne, the Convent of the Trinity, and the Hotel d'Escoville. Local buses make trips to St. Laurent sur Mer, the U. S. Army cemetery on the bluffs overlooking Omaha Beach, to Vierville and Pte. du Hoe which was captured by means of rope ladders fired up the cliffs by rockets and to Utah Beach. . . . South of Caen, FALAISE is the castle town where William the Conqueror was born. . . . In BAYEUX see the superb 11th century, Norman Gothic Cathedral of Notre Dame and the famous 160-foot tapestry describing the conquest of England by William the Conqueror. The tapestry is on display in the old Episcopal Residence and is one of the most remarkable historical souvenirs extant. . . . To the southwest is ST.-LO, destroyed in June 1944, and COUTANCES with its fine Cathedral, one of the best examples of Norman architecture. Its octagonal tower or lantern is perhaps the finest of its kind in France. . . . At AVRANCHES you will get a wonderful view of Mont Saint Michel, one of the most inspiring monuments of all times. Mont Saint Michel, the great abbey on the rock in the sea, between Normandy and Brittany, is one of the great sights of the world. The huge rock, jutting 256 feet high out of the sea, is engirdled at the base with medieval turreted walls. Behind the walls the buildings of the village are scattered on three levels at the base of the rock. The lovely Gothic abbey crowns the very pinnacle, a gilded statue of St. Michael poised above

the entire structure. Visit the Abbey, the museums and be sure to take a walk around the ramparts. . . . On the northern coast of Brittany ST.-MALO is an interesting walled fishing port, from where Jacques Cartier sailed to discover the St. Lawrence. See the castle of Anne of Brittany and the ramparts. . . . Across the river Rance is DINARD, most popular resort of this "Emerald Coast." . . . Other towns in northern Brittany include the beautiful resorts of ST. LUNAIRE, ST. BRIAC and ST. CAST, ST. BRIEUC, the old fishing harbor of PAIMPOL, TREGUIER, birthplace of St. Yves, a small town with a medieval aspect and a cathedral which combines Gothic and Roman style, LANNION and MORLAIX.

Between Lannion and Brest is the most picturesque part of Brittany, dotted with massive granite churches with open belfries, quaint shrines and ancient monuments and customs that set the Bretons apart from the rest of France and reflect their Celtic origin and Druidical religious past. Remarkable are the religious ceremonies or Pardons (the French Tourist Bureau will give you the dates and places they occur).

From the seaport of BREST, almost completely devastated in World War II, you pass through PLOUGASTEL-DAOULAS, famous for its strawberries, on the way to QUIMPER, from where we get that charming ware decorated with figures and motifs of Breton design. Market day here is a most colorful sight. Visit the Cathedral. . . . Near by are the fishing harbors of CONCARNEAU, sardine fishing center. . . . To the east is QUIMPERLE, and the old fortress town of HENNEBONT with its interesting Breton museum. . . . At CARNAC are the famous prehistoric dolmens and menhirs, like Stonehenge in England. . . . AURAY is the shrine of Brittany and is famous for the Pardon of Ste. Anne d'Auray held every year on the 25th and 26th of July. . . . From the picturesque fishing port of QUIBERON, you can take a ferry to the beautiful island of Belle-Ile-en-Mer with its giant lighthouse. . . . VANNES has an excellent museum of Celtic and Roman antiquities, a 13th century cathedral and interesting medieval ramparts. From here trips may be taken by excursion boat to offshore islands, or by car or train to the old walled city of GUERANDE with its many towers and gates. . . . To the north of Vannes lies JOSSELIN, one of the most interesting castles in Brittany. . . . RENNES was the capital of the old duchy of Brittany in the middle ages and is still the intellectual capital of Brittany. It has many museums, a modern Cathedral, 17th century Palais de Justice and an impressive town hall in Louis XV style. . . . VITRE is another interesting castle town in the area.

THE LOIRE VALLEY

The district of the wonderful Chateaus of the Loire lies roughly between Orleans and Chinon, comprising the old provinces of Touraine and Anjou. Touraine, still called the "Garden of France," was the favorite playground of French Kings in the 15th and 16th centuries, and together with Anjou offers the tourist an unending variety of fabulous castles ranging in styles from medieval to refined Renaissance.

In ORLEANS, liberated by Joan of Arc in 1429, see the cathedral and the Statue to Joan in the center of the city. . . . Nine miles from Blois is CHAMBORD, largest of the provincial castles and a favorite residence of Francis I, noted for

its spiral staircase. . . . Nearby is CHEVERNY with its beautiful gardens, built by Louis XIII. . . . BLOIS is an interesting old city and its magnificent Renaissance castle overlooking the river recalls the pomp and pleasures of Francis I, and such ladies as Louise of Savoy, Diane de Poitiers, Catherine de Médicis and the girl who was later Mary, Queen of Scots. . . . Between Blois and Tours are the castles of CHAUMONT and AMBOISE and VOUVRAY, famous for its sparkling wines. . . . TOURS is an attractive city connected with its suburbs by a lovely stone bridge across the Loire. See the Cathedral with its stained glass windows and fine facade, the 15th century square lined with gabled houses and the basilica where St. Martin is buried. . . . In the vicinity of Tours visit the castles of CHENONCEAUX, straddling the river Cher, AZAY-LE-RIDEAU, VILLANDRY, CHINON and LOCHES where cruel Louis XI tortured his victims and watched them swing from the trees of the orchard. Here he kept his unfortunate cardinal, La Balue, in a cage which permitted him neither to stand nor lie down. Above the torture chamber is the peep-hole where Louis

Springtime in Normandy
French Govt. Tourist Office

watched the activities below. . . . In FONTEVRAULT see the tombs of the Plantagenets in the chapel of the famous abbey built in the 12th century. . . . SAUMUR is another castle town with also the well-known French cavalry school, well worth a visit. . . . ANGERS offers the Gothic Cathedral, the massive pentagon-shaped castle of King Rene and the world-known collection of tapestries of the Apocalypse. . . . Among the numerous other famous castles in the Loire Valley are LANGEAIS, LUYNES, PLESSIS-LES-TOURS, SULLY, USSÉ and VALENCAY.

VENDEE, VIENNE, THE CHARENTE

Below the Loire is a rich and pleasant countryside stretching down to the vineyards of Bordeaux. Although not as exciting tourist-wise as some other parts of France, the area is historically important and there are a number of interesting places to visit.

POITIERS was the site of the victory of the English under the Black Prince in the Hundred Years' War. The 13th century cathedral was built by Eleanor of Aquitaine and is a perfect example of Romanesque style. See the ancient Baptistry of St. Jean, the 11th century church of Ste. Radegonde and the two museums. . . . Nearby is the site where Clovis defeated Alaric and his barbarian horde in 507 and where Charles Martel stopped the Saracen invasion in 732. . . . The historic seaport of LA ROCHELLE was the stronghold of the Huguenots. Its great watch tower and gate date from the 13th century. Of interest are its grim medieval towers, particularly the Tour St. Nicholas. . . . COGNAC, along the lovely river Charente, and the neighboring town of JARNAC produce the great brandy of France. COGNAC is interesting as the birthplace of Francis I and for the chateaux-cum-warehouses of the famous manufacturers such as Hennessy, Martell and Otard, situated in the very castle of Francis I . . . JARNAC, noted for Bisquit and Courvoisier, has a replica of the Louvre's Pavillon de Flore, now the main office of Courvoisier. Trips through the distilleries can be made. . . . ANGOULEME, home of Marguérite de Valois, sits on a high hill and is notable for the Byzantine touch of the architecture of its Cathedral of St. Pierre. BORDEAUX (pop. 250,306), in the heart of the world's finest wine growing district, is a city of fine restaurants. This busy port is an attractive city with a number of fine 18th century buildings, a Cathedral and several important museums. . . . Villages near by notable for their wines are PESSAC for Graves; BLANQUEFORT and SOULAC for Médoc; BARSAC for Sauterne; and CADILLAC for St. Emilion.

BASQUE COUNTRY

Below the lake-dotted, thick, pine forests of Landes lies the country of the Basques. Here are found still preserved the picturesque customs, festivals, games and dances of a very ancient and interesting civilization.

Beautiful BIARRITZ, on the Basque coast, is one of the most elegant of the French bathing resorts with two casinos, night clubs and large hotels. . . . South of Biarritz are the beach resorts of GUETHARY, ST. JEAN DE LUZ and HENDAYE, on the border between France and Spain. From here you can cross the border to IRUN or SAN-SEBASTIAN. . . . Just north of Biarritz are the resorts of HOSSEGOR and CHIBERTA which is famous for its excellent golf course. . . . Next door to Biarritz is the cathedral city of BAYONNE with an historic old castle. . . . To really see the Basques, go inland to some of the villages and towns like USTERRITZ, MAULEON or ST.-JEAN-PIED-DE-PORT. Incidentally, there is wonderful fishing to be had near ST.-JEAN-PIED-DE-PORT, and also there are frequent exhibitions of the Basque national sport, pelote, a version of Jai Alai.

THE PYRENEES REGION

This is a land of bracing climate and cloudless skies, high valleys and lofty forest-clad mountains with snow and glaciers, forests and torrents, upland villages and castle-topped crags, watering-places and winter sports resorts.

PAU, in the heart of Gascony, is a major winter resort with its famous terrace affording a magnificent view of the mountains, its castle where Henry IV was born and its excellent wine and pate de foi gras. From this vicinity came a number of France's great warriors, including Jean de la Valette, d'Artagnan of the Three Musketeers and General Foch. . . . Miraculous LOURDES, where Bernadette saw Our Lady in 1858, attracts thousands of pilgrims each year who flock to the basilica erected above Bernadette's grotto. . . . Near by are resorts of CAUTERETS and

Pelote is the "national" game
of the Basques
French Govt. Tourist Office

GAVARNIE, and to the north, TARBES. This is the start of the most beautiful part of the Pyrenees. . . . The road to LUCHON crosses the Col d'Aspin, a pass 4500 feet in altitude, goes through BAREGES, well-known for its waters, past the impressive Cirque de Gavarnie (mule trips can be taken to the Cirque), via the Tourmalet pass (6600 ft.) and on down the valley to the "Queen of the Pyrenees," LUCHON. . . . Near here are two other major resorts, BAGNERES DE BIGORRE and SUPER-BAGNERES, a summer-winter resort. . . . On to ST. GIRONS, LABOUICHE, known for its underground river, and the picturesque city of FOIX, over the Puymaurens Pass to LATOUR-DE-CAROL, a quaint little town and gateway to the romantic little principality of ANDORRA. . . . FONT-ROMEU, 6000 feet altitude, is the loveliest of summer resorts. . . . After the fortress of VILLEFRANCHE DE CON-FLENT, built entirely of pink marble is PRADES, famous for its music festival where Pablo Casals was persuaded to play again. . . . After Prades is the entry to the LANGUEDOC, past the peak of Perthus. . . . Below Perthus, on the coast, are the colorful fishing villages of BANYLUS and COLLIOURE. . . . Northward are PER-PIGNAN, with its turreted fortress and CARCASSONE, that masterpiece of medieval military architecture. The guides here are excellent and in the masonry you can trace the city's fascinating history from the time it was a Roman camp. Northwest is TOULOUSE (217,667), capital of the Languedoc and rich in art treasures with its church of St. Sernin, the most beautiful Romanesque church in France, and a fine collection of sculpture in the Musée des Augustins. While in Toulouse,

try some cassoulet, that famous local specialty made of lamb, pork, goose, onions, garlic and haricot beans, combined to make the most terrific thick stew you ever ate. . . . Northeast is ALBI, the "red city," scene of the bloody purging of the Albigesian heretics by Simon de Montfort. Blood is still suggested by the color of the construction stone of the whole city and of its extraordinary Cathedral of Ste.-Cecile. See the old quarters and monuments of mixed Roman and Gothic styles.

THE RHONE VALLEY

Provence has had a long and eventful history and one can still see in its cities founded by the Romans a number of the Old World's most impressive monuments. The terrain here is quite varied and the scenery delightful. Fertile valleys and plains dotted with vineyards, orchards, olive groves and gorgeous flowers, and, on the coast, the blue, blue sea and lush tropical foliage. Travel here is also a gastronomic delight. From here we get all those wonderful dishes a la Provencal, characterized by the zesty garlic and or tomatoes. Provencales are intensely traditional and their folklore, exceptionally colorful and gay.

ORANGE boasts of its Roman theater and curious Arch of Triumph. . . . The richest, gayest, biggest city of the Valley, AVIGNON is where Pope Clement V came to set up his court in the time of the quarrels over the Papacy in the 14th century. The famous Palace of the Popes, the papal residence until Gregory XI returned to Rome in 1403, still stands with its great towers and arches. The famous bridge, Pont d'Avignon of the song, had originally 22 arches, of which only 3 remain. . . . The lords of the redoubtable

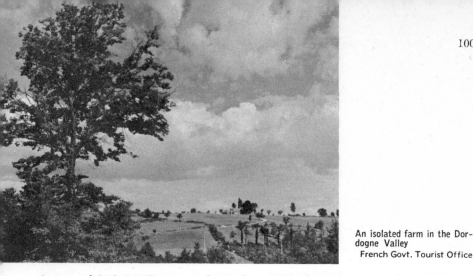

An isolated farm in the Dordogne Valley
French Govt. Tourist Office

fortress of **LES BAUX** were undisputed masters of Provence for years, and the medieval ruins are a tourist curiosity. Bauxite was first discovered here. . . . At the city of **ARLES**, with its relics of the Greek settlement five centuries before Christ, was found the famous Venus now in the Louvre. Visit the **Cloister of St. Trophime** and the two **museums of art**, pagan and Christian. . . . To the northwest lies the great monument to the Romans, **NIMES**, founded by Augustus. The most important relics are the great **Arena** where bullfights take place several times a year, the **Temple of Diana** which dates from before Christ, the **Maison Carée**, an Augustan temple, and the **Jardin de la Fontaine**. Near by is the **Pont du Gard**, a Roman acqueduct built in 19 B.C. . . . Southwest of Nimes is the winegrowing and University city of **MONTPELLIER** and near it some wonderful scenery, particularly the mountain village of **ST. GUILHELM-LE-DESERT**, favorite of painters. . . . **CAMARGUE**, the little island in the Rhone delta is a fascinating little world of its own. Local cowboys, called "guardians," herd cattle and small white horses in ranch-style. Their costumes and those of the women are most picturesque. **STE. MARIES DE LA MER** is the chief center and is the shrine of the Gypsies. . . . Southeast of Avignon is **AIX-EN-PROVENCE**, capital of the scholarly king known as René the Good. AIX has an interesting **cathedral**, the **Cloister of St. Sauveur** and a museum of **tapestries**. . . . Also near Avignon is **CHATEAU-NEUF-DU-PAPE**, famous for its fine red wines. . . . In MARSEILLE (pop. 605,-

577), the great port, is the **Cathedral of Norte Dame**, the **Chateau d'If**, where the Count of Monte Cristo was imprisoned and of course the **Bouillabaisse**, that incomparable fish soup made of fish peculiar only to the Marseille area.

AUVERGNE AND THE DORDOGNE

In the heart of the Massif Central, **AUVERGNE** is a country of volcanic origin. At the bottom of ancient craters lie translucent lakes surrounded by the dark-blue-green conifers, and everywhere the black lava points up the colorful villages and towns. To the south the turbulent Tarn River winds through an impressive gorge. This region is known as the cradle of French architecture and on all sides are castles and magnificent churches with graceful outlines and primitive sculpture, among the best examples of Romanesque art.

LE PUY clusters around four great volcanic rocks. Long a pilgrimage center and an Episcopal see since the 6th century, the village boasts of a fine **cathedral**, old **baptistry** and a number of fine Romanesque and Gothic buildings. St. **Michel**, perched atop a needle rock, is one of the most photographed churches in Europe. . . . **CLERMONT-FERRAND**, capital of Auvergne, includes the medieval hill town of **MONTFERRAND** with a number of fine old houses. The Church of **Notre Dame du Port** is an enormous pile constructed of lava. . . . South of here, **MONT-DORE** at the foot of the Sancy Mountain is in the heart of the Massif Central and is well-known for its **dead volcanoes** and many **thermal resorts**. From here one can take excursions to the surrounding lakes.

Perhaps the most beautiful valley of the country, the **DORDOGNE** holds much to fascinate the traveler.— the ever-present castles, ancient towns, the famous pre-historic caves built in rocks overhanging the river, hilltop villages, natural chasms and other natural phenomena, all of equal interest.

ROCAMADOUR is a tiny village, long a place of pilgrimage, perched atop sheer cliffs. . . . Not far from here is **Padirac**, a naturally formed **deep chasm**. . . . Near **SARLAT**, **a pate de foi gras-** and truffle-canning center were discovered the **caves of Lascaux** with extraordinary wall paintings suggesting Picasso. . . . **PERI-GUEUX**, noted for rich art treasures and gastronomic delights, has the wonderful 12th century **Cathedral of St. Front**, perched high on a hill above the town and river, and an interesting museum of pre-historic relics. North of Périgueux is **LIMOGES**, capital of the Limousin and center of fine porcelain manufacture. Visits may be made to the large factories and there is a **ceramics museum** in the city. This was the birthplace of Renoir and the art gallery displays a number of his works. . . . Near here is the village of **ORADOUR-SUR-GLANE**, whose inhabitants were massacred by the Germans on June 10th, 1944. The French Government has made the village into a shrine, leaving everything as it was, including the piles of human cinders.

THE RIVIERA

No one needs to be told how beautiful is this "Cote d'Azur" with its white sand, blue sea and dazzling sunshine. An ideal vacation spot, the Mediterranean Coast offers everything from the charm of small villages to the excitement of large cities. Here is a gourmet's heaven and a water-sports fan's haven.

East of Toulon, the twisting coastal road runs along the rugged base of the Esterel Massif from **ST. TROPEZ** with its little white villas roofed with red tiles, through **ST. MAXIME** and **ST. RAPHAEL** to **CANNES**, the social capital, with its famous **Promenade de la Croisette**. . . . From Cannes the road leads to the chi-chi **JUAN-LES-PINS** and **CAP D'ANTIBES**. Along here gambling casinos, luxury hotels, smart bars, yachts, bikinis and underwater fishing are some of the delights to be expected. Hollywood's favorite **Hotel du Cap** or **Eden Roc** is perched on the top of a small peninsula and is noted for its small pool around which are sunned some very expensive bodies. In the old fortified town of **ANTIBES** is the **Grimaldi Museum**, to which Picasso has contributed greatly. . . . To the east is NICE (pop. 208,453) with its two casinos, big hotels, parks, shops and **Promenade des Anglais**, and also its old port, like an Italian town with narrow, twisting, climbing streets, noises and rich smells. Highlight of the Nice winter season (though the Riviera is now an all-year-round resort) is the famous **Mardi-Gras** festival, which leave the street cleaners face to face with staggering piles of flowers and confetti. . . . East of Nice the fabled **Corniche Drive** over the Turbie leads past **VILLEFRANCHE, CAP FERRAT** and **BEAULIEU** to **MONTE CARLO** in the romantic little principality of **MONACO**, with its own palace, courts, mint and police. Monaco exists on the gambling revenue of its gingerbread casino, but two of its principal interests are the splendid views from all parts of the massive rocks on which it is perched and the wonderful **Oceanographic Museum**. . . . Eastward is **MENTON** and its **Bridge of St. Louis** and SAN REMO on the Italian Riviera.

In the background of the Riviera is Upper Provence, a wild mountainous district of deep gorges in the foothills of the Alps with many hill towns of ancient stone that changes color with the light. Near Cannes is **GRASSE**, the perfume capital of France. . . . On the cliffs above the Cannes is **VALLAURIS** where Picasso has his atélier and where Rita Hayworth and Aly Khan were married. . . . In **VENCE** is the lovely chapel of **St. Dominique** decorated by Matisse. Between Cap Ferrat and Monaco is the fortified town of **EZE**, clinging to a sheer cliffside.

THE ALPS

The principal mountain region of France is that of the Alps, stretching from just above the Riviera through Savoy and Lake Geneva to the Jura. The Iserian Road across the French Alps is one of the most scenic and highest in Europe. Rivalling the world-famous peaks of Switzerland and Austria, these mountains have popular centers for climbing and skiing and many are only a couple of hours away from the Mediterranean. One can ski all day and, after a not-too-long drive, dine and dance at night in the snug warmth of the Riviera. Spas and watering places

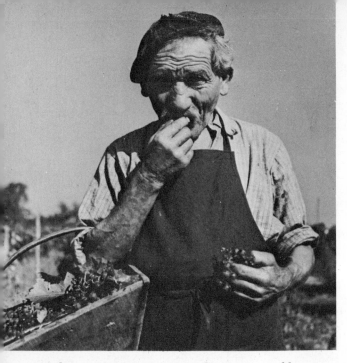

Harvest in the Bordeaux wine country
French Govt. Tourist Office

in these mountains are among the most popular in France.

Three of the principal spas are AIX-LES-BAINS, on beautiful Lake Bourget, ANNECY, with its long lake, and EVIAN on Lake Geneva. All have excellent facilities for sports and other recreation.

To list all ski resorts would be impossible in this limited space and the French Tourist Bureau can better tell you details concerning transportation, reservations, etc. Here we list only the major areas around which there are resorts with good facilities. In the MONT BLANC REGION are Mégève, Chamonix, Les Houches, St. Gervais, Les Contamines, Morzine and Las Clusaz.... In the SAVOY REGION, Val d'Isère, Courcheval, Les Allues and Valloire are popular centers. ... DAUPHINE REGION includes Alpe d'Huez and Villard-de-Lans. . . . The HAUTES ALPES REGION, Briançon, Serre Chevalier and Montgenevre. . . . In the RIVIERA REGION, Auron, Beuil and Valberg. . . . in the PYRENEES REGION are Font-Romeu and Barages.

LAND OF WINE

BURGUNDY. This ancient and historic province whose powerful dukes rivalled the kings of France, stretches roughly from LYON in the south to VEZELAY in the north and today is most notable for the delights of its vines and its kitchens. The noble wines include Chablis, Pouilly, Chambertin and Pommard.

At CLUNY is one of the most remarkable architectural and historic monuments of the region, the Abbey of Cluny, once the intellectual center of the Christian world. . . . In BEAUNE are the celebrated hospitals run by the monks. The most interesting is the Hotel Dieu, founded by Rollin in 1443, which preserves the aspects of the Middle Ages in its decor, uniforms and furnishings, its beds and utensils and its fascinating pharmacy. The Hotel Dieu is rich from its vineyards in Savigny, Meursault, Pommard and Volnay.... The charming town of VEZELAY, with its many medieval reminders, is celebrated as the resting-place of the bones of Mary Magdalene in the tremendous Romanesque Basilica of the Magdalène. . . . In the village of ST.-PERE-SOUS-VEZELAY is a fine Gothic church. . . . Other cities and towns of interest in Burgundy include DIJON, interesting for its old Palace of the Dukes of Burgundy, its fine museum and other fine buildings, MACON, AUTUN and SAULIEU. . . . North of Vezelay lies the Cote d'Or and its great vineyards. In AUXERRE and in SENS are remarkable Gothic cathedrals, both of which are named St. Etienne. SENS is at the limits of the Ile de France, the "Chateau Country" adjacent to Paris.

The Low Countries

GATEWAY TO EUROPE

The small constitutional monarchies of the Benelux countries — Belgium, Luxembourg and the Netherlands — provide opportunities for all kinds of holiday pleasure compressed into one vacation of sheer delight, for from the quaint to the cultural or the medieval to the modern is just a matter of minutes in these diminutive countries. Sturdy dykes, twirling windmills, colorful floral mosaics, quaint costumes, hoary traditions, strange customs, feudal castles, picturesque villages, peaceful parks, fragrant woods, lazy streams, busy canals, surging rivers, resurrected cities, thriving towns are there for the seeing. But most of all, they are famous for the magnificent museums and art galleries featuring their own great masters like Rembrandt, Vermeer, the Van Eycks and many others; their dramatic history—some of the fiercest fighting of World War II took place here — and glorious scenery, from Holland's renowned tulip land to the wild, rugged country of Luxembourg's Ardennes. Last but by no means least, these indomitable, hard-working peoples will welcome you with a heartfelt friendliness unsurpassed in any other part of the globe.

MANY TONGUES

The language of the Netherlands is, of course, Dutch, while the two national languages of Belgium are French and Flemish. The Grand Duchy of Luxembourg is a bilingual or even a trilingual country. Luxembourgish, a West Frankish idiom, is the everyday language spoken by all classes of the population, although German and, more particularly, French are the official languages. However, the people all over these three countries have a good knowledge of English.

FOOD SPECIALTIES

Everyone knows about the famous Dutch cheeses, and their fish dishes are almost equally well-known. Many of the world's best varieties of cheese are to be found throughout Belgium, too. However, the Belgian food specialties vary in different sections. The following meats and fish are featured: *carbonades flamandes* (braised beef, Flemish style) in all the Flemish towns; *fricadelles Bruxelloises* (small, thin braised steaks garnished with braised endives); *fritures d'anguilles et anguilles au vert* (fried eels, and eels, Belgian style, with shredded herbs, oil and vinegar) at Boitsfort near Brussels; *moules et frites* (mussels and French-fried potatoes) in the lowlands, but especially in Brussels, except in May and June; *poulets de Bruxelles* (chicken, Brussels style); *jambon d'Ardenne* (smoked ham); *waterzoeie de poisson et de poulet* (fish or chicken stews) at Antwerp and at Ghent; *tartines Flamandes au Jambon* (Flemish pastries with ham); *boudins* (sausages) at festivals and fairs and *lapin aux pruneaux* (rabbit with prunes) in Flanders. The famous Belgian tarts and pastries are Brussels wafers; siska wafers at Knokke; cheese tarts at Wavre, Mons and Brussels; rice tarts everywhere; rice and macaroon tarts at Liege, Verviers and vicinity and sugar tarts in the Walloon sections. Delicious Belgian cakes and biscuits, which may be exported, include: *noeuds de Bruges; kletskoppen de Bruges; boterletters* at Antwerp; almond breads; Greek breads; *bernardins; speculoos;* shortcake at Brussels and most other cities; *cramique* (a sweet brioche bread without raisins), also a Brussels specialty and mocha cakes at Ghent. Belgium is a large producer of standard beers, and there are some special varieties particularly identified with the country, in general of a heavy type and quite strong. Gastronomical specialties of Luxembourg include black pudding and sausages; mashed potatoes and horse-radish; smoked pork and broad beans; Ardennes ham, cooked and uncooked; jellied suckling pig; *gras-double*, Luxembourg fashion; sauerkraut and boiled potatoes; cooked cheese; *les pensées brouillées* (special pastries of the carnival season) and from April to September, trout and crawfish, Luxembourg fashion, and pike of the Sure, Moselle and Our. Brewing is a very old Luxembourg industry and the favorite drinks include Luxembourg beer, Luxembourg Moselle Wines, black currant wine of the Chateau de Beaufort and non-alcoholic grape juice.

Belgium

ART AND FOLKLORE

BRUSSELS (pop. 1,299,295), or *Broeksele* (habitation near to the marsh),

A lovely, peaceful canal scene
in the old city of Bruges
Official Belg. Tourist Bureau

capital of Belgium, was originally founded in the seventh century. A halt for merchants became a *marche* (market), where the Grand Place now stands. This was the cradle of Brussels. Although the incomparable Grand Place actually dates from the end of the seventeenth century, when it was reconstructed after the bombardment of 1695 by Louis XIV, most of the unique buildings grouped around it date from the fifteenth century. The Hôtel de Ville (Town Hall) is a beautiful example of Gothic architecture remarkable for its style, paintings and tapestries. Other buildings facing the famous square are the elaborate Maison du Roi (King's House), now housing the collections of the Communal Museum, and the Maisons des Corporations (Guild Houses) — reminders of the medieval craftsmen's guilds. The Porte de Hal (Hal Gate), with its collection of weapons and armor, is the last vestige of the old second town wall. At one end of the historic Parc de Bruxelles is the Louis XVI style Palais de la Nation, where Parliament sits. Across the park is the Louis XV style Palais du Roi (King's Palace) and on a third side the remarkable Palais des Beaux Arts, one of the finest concert halls in Europe. A few doors away are the Musée d'Art Ancien, showing paintings by such masters as Ingres, Delacroix, Van Eyck, Memling, Breughel the Elder and the Younger, Rubens, Teniers, Rembrandt and Vermeer van Delft, and sculpture including works by Rodin and Constantin Meunier; the Musée d'Art Moderne, containing canvases by Stevens, Rik Wauters, Courbet, Matisse and others, and the Bibliothèque Royale, with its beautiful collection of manuscripts. Eglise Notre-Dame des Victoires, south of these, is a masterpiece of later Gothic work. On its east side is the Place du Petit Sablon, surrounded by a splendid wrought-iron grill with varied designs. Forty-eight small columns each carry a statue by Dillens representing sixteenth-century trades. In the background are statues of the Counts of Egmont and Hornes, together with famous Belgians of the sixteenth century. Nearby is the Musée Instrumental du Conservatoire Royal de Musique, including more than 4,000 ancient and modern instruments. Across the Place Poelaert is the Palais de Justice, whose dome, fired by the Germans in 1944, has been reconstructed. In the northeastern part of the city is the Colonne du Congrès (Congress Column), commemorating Belgian independence, with the tomb of the Unknown Soldier, and Collegiale des SS. Michel et Gudule, the most important church in Brussels and one of the most beautiful Gothic cathedrals in Europe, representing several centuries work. With spendid stained-glass windows by Vernard van Orley, it contains a remarkable monument of the Duke of Merode and paintings by Rubens, Coxie, Van Orley and Nevez. Near the Grand Place is the popular Manneken-Pis Fountain, first mention of which is found in a document dating from 1452. Tours may be taken southwards to the green tide of the Forêt de Soignes, the most beautiful beech wood of Europe and the epic battlefield at the village of Waterloo; or northwestward to Hekelgem, where visitors to the small cabarets may watch artists reproducing well-known pictures with vividly colored sand. . . . GHENT (166,096), "city of flowers," is a textile production center and the second port in Belgium, connected to the North Sea by a first-rate ship canal twenty miles long. The "Vrijdagmarkt" (Friday Market) was the city forum of the Middle Ages. It was here that, on the occasion of their "Joyous Entry," Counts of Flanders took the oath to maintain the privileges of the city and the county. Near the market is the big wrought-iron gun belonging to the Burgundian period and popularly known as "Dulle Griet" (Mad Meg), which is seventeen feet long, weighs sixteen tons and "fired" stone balls weighing nearly 700-weight. Across the Leie (Lys) is one of the richest museums of Belgium, the Folklore Museum, containing a large collection commemorating the customs and traditions of the Flemish people. Nearby is the formidable Castle of the Counts, built in 1180 by Philip of Alsace, Count of Flanders and Vermandois. A striking reminder of feudal life, with its vast halls, underground rooms and collection of instruments of torture, this imposing fortress is one of the main centers of interest in the country. Grouped around St. Jorishof (St. George's Court) are the Middle Ages manorial residence, named Achtersikkel (literally: after-sickle) for its first owners, the Van der Sickelen, now the Royal Conservatoire of Music; the Belfry and 52-bell carillon, symbol of civic freedom, whose museum houses a collection of ancient bells; the Cloth Hall, built in 1425, meeting place of the Assizes, presided over by the *Halleheren* or gentlemen of the hall, for solving disputes connected with the wool and cloth trades; and the huge, quadrilaterally shaped, part-Gothic and part-Renaissance Town Hall, characterized by the various classical orders of the columns (Doric, Ionic and Corinthian) and the vastness of its rooms, each with its own history. A few doors east is St. Bavon Cathedral, comprising three distinct parts belonging to different periods. This cathedral contains magnificent pictures, among them the incomparable masterpiece of Jan and Hubert Van Eyck, the "Adoration of the Mystic Lamb" (1432). The Van Eyck brothers, who were born at Maeseyck, included their own portraits in the panel of the Just Judges. No church is so closely linked to the life and history of the city as St. Nicholas Church, with its famous oak choir

stalls and its imprints of various ages and styles, although the oldest parts, in Romanesque, date from the beginning of the thirteenth century. Nearby on the Leie (Lys), are the Graslei (Quay of Herbs) Trade and Merchant Guild Houses, including the House of the Corporation of Free Boatmen, considered a masterpiece of the last period of Gothic style, and the "Spijker" (c. 1200), one of the finest specimens of Romanesque civic buildings. The Rabot, or small fortress, on the west side, a fine example of Middle Ages martial architecture, quite unaccountably escaped the destruction by which Charles V struck the entire defense system in 1540. The small Beguinage, a picturesque town within the city, is a vestige of religious life in the Middle Ages, where hundreds of beguines, or secular nuns, still wearing the ancient Flemish headdress, occupy quaint cottages or larger communal homes. The annual procession, marked by a carpet of natural flowers, on the 15th of August, Assumption Day, is well worth seeing. . . . Once a textile center and a great seaport, BRUGES, northwest of Ghent, is famed for its exquisite handmade lace, its network of placid canals, its steeply gabled old houses and its carillon in the town hall, where regular concerts are given by the carillonneurs. On the first Monday after May 2nd, the town holds the famous Procession of the Holy Blood, depicting the principal scenes from the Old and New Testaments. At the end of the procession comes the little decorated gold casket containing the drop of Holy Blood brought back from the Crusades by Thierry d'Alsace in 1150. . . . Belgium's sandy coastline is dotted with beach resorts. One of the best is KNOKKE ZOUTE, "the garden of the North Sea." Besides the two excellent courses at the Royal Zoute Golf Club and fifty tennis courts, visitors enjoy horseback riding in the pine woods and "land yachting" on the beach. . . . The great eighteenth-century painter, Peter Paul Rubens, who is buried in St. Jacques Church, dominates the artistic heritage of ANTWERP (784,313). His canvases may be seen in the Royal Art Museum, the Plantin-Moretus Museum and Notre Dame Cathedral, and his home is open to visitors. Also, take an excursion on the Schelde, the Tamise, the Doel and the Albert Canal. . . . LIEGE (156,208), a university, industrial and commercial center, is also a town of art and an old capital, containing many fine museums. Cesar Franck, sometimes called the founder of modern French instrumental composition, was born in Liege in 1822. Visitors will enjoy the trip south to Val St. Lambert, long a glass-blowing center, whose crystal works are housed in an ancient abbey. . . . So famous is the watering place at SPA, southeast of Liege, near the skiing area of Belgium, that the name "spa" has become a general term in the English language for a mineral-water resort. . . . The old tourist city of DINANT-SURMEUSE, city of the copper beaters, is dominated by a gaunt but attractive citadel. The hammered-copper craft has survived here since the thirteenth century, although the artisans now have to be supplied with copper from the Belgian Congo. . . . In the southeast corner of Belgium is the pretty town of BASTOGNE, focal point of the famous December, 1944, Battle of Ardennes. An unusual vast monument has been erected at the place called "Mardasson" in memory of the heroic resistance of the American soldiers during the offensive. Here also are the interesting Museum of the Ardennes Offensive and "La Cave," old headquarters of the American general, MacAuliffe.

Luxembourg

FEUDAL CHARM

LUXEMBOURG, thousand-year-old capital of the Grand-Duchy, was, for many centuries, one of the most powerful fortresses in the world. Although dismantled, many remains have been preserved, particularly the ancient fortifications of the Citadel of St. Esprit, now transformed into charming parks with pleasant walks, especially picturesque around the lower town, including a network of underground passages and shelters or casemates hewn from the solid rock. The Grand Ducal Palace, residence of H. R. H. Grand Duchess Charlotte, was built in the sixteenth and eighteenth centuries, the older part in a remarkable Renaissance style. On the same square is the state's most outstanding church, the Cathedral of Notre Dame, with magnificent Renaissance sculptures (1613-1618) and a crypt containing the tomb of John the Blind, King of Bohemia and Count of Luxembourg. A few blocks

southwest is the massive, stone-arched Pont Adolphe, one of the city's 65 bridges. The famous Promenade de la Corniche, unique in Europe, and the elegant Spanish Turrets are also of great interest. At the military cemetery of Hamm, 7,000 American soldiers of the rugged Third Army are buried, with their commander, General George S. Patton, Jr., among them. In the southwestern mining district, whose tall modern furnaces and rolling mills are open to visitors, is the neo-Gothic church of Dudelange, containing paintings by Dom. Lang, one of the greatest painters of the Grand-Duchy. Esch-sur-Alzette, district center, has a gorgeous park with a famous rose garden, noted for the extensive views over the three countries of France, Belgium and Luxembourg. At the frontier between Luxembourg and Lorraine are the modern, well-known thermal springs of Mondorf-les-Bains. The Moselle valley region in the east is an important vine-growing and wine-producing area, and the river provides fine fishing for ablet, bream, pike, redeye and perch. At any one of the pleasant little towns you may visit the noted wine cellars, like the Caves St. Martin at Remich. North of Luxembourg city are many small villages in idyllic settings, including Junglinster, well-known for the tombstones of the knights of Linster and the romantic manor of the neighboring bourglinster; Mersch, surrounded by gentle hills covered with beech- and fir-tree woods, whose church has a portal of real architectural curiosity; Ansembourg, having a magnificent feudal castle dating from the twelfth century, with a modern manor built in 1639, and Tuntange, with a church known for a Pieta of exceptional beauty. . . . ECHTERNACH, an important holiday center, is the northeastern gateway to the Miller's Dale. Its old patrician houses with their pointed gables, its narrow streets and alleys and its ancient ramparts have kept alive the atmosphere of a medieval town. The ancient Benedictine abbey, founded in the seventh century by St. Willibrord, consists of four wings, each 210 feet long, built round a large square inner couryard, and includes a crypt dating from the Merovingian period (eighth century), with vaults adorned with frescoes painted about 1100. Equally famous is the fine park with its elegant Louis XV pavilion. Miller's Dale also includes Berdorf, in a region abounding in impressive and quaint sandstone **cliff formations**. . . The uplands of the Ardennes in the north is another popular and picturesque holiday area, where the hunting is especially famous. Old, romantic **VIANDEN** was built in the ninth century on the banks of the Our, in scenery of wild grandeur. The formidable, thirteenth-century **castle**, one of the largest feudal fortresses of the continent, is a real architectural jewel unequalled on this side of the Rhine. During Victor Hugo's exile from France, this famous poet lived for a time in Vianden in a **house** now preserved as a museum. Old-world uses and customs are preserved in the **Folklore Museum**, featuring fine old furniture. The imposing ruins of **Bourscheid Castle**, an important medieval fortress between the Rhine and the Meuse, rise on a steep hill 450 feet above the spectacular valley of the Sur. West of Vianden, the small market town of **Esch-sur-Sure**, enshrined between steep crags and almost completely surrounded by the Sure, with its houses clustering round a rocky promontory, is dominated by the ruins of its massive castle and by the forbidding rocks which drop sheer into the river. The beautiful **church in Troisvierges**, in the extreme north, is well-known for its remarkable high altar.

The Netherlands

PICTURE-BOOK COUNTRY

Resurrected **ROTTERDAM** (pop. 646,248) is the second city of the Netherlands and one of the largest seaports in Western Europe. Much of the center was destroyed by bombing in 1940 but like the Phoenix, a fine new city is rapidly emerging from the ruins. The oldest section, **Delfshaven** (literally "port of Delft"), part of Rotterdam since 1389, is the place from which Pilgrim Fathers embarked for America on the *Speedwell* in 1620. Their departure is memorialized in the adjoining **church**, where their last service before embarkation was held. The two sections of the city on either side of the Maas are linked by the magnificent new **Maastunnel**, first Dutch river tunnel and a splendid example of engineering skill, with the land on the left bank forming the 750-acre **Waalhaven**, largest artificial basin in the world. At the center of the city are the gleaming new buildings, including the impressive **Town Hall**. Nearby are the **statue** of the famous philosopher and great scientist, Desiderius Erasmus, born in Rotterdam in 1469, and Ossip Zadkine's memorial statue, "Ruined City," expressing the sentiments felt on seeing the destruction. The **Boymans Museum** has rich collections of paintings, sculpture, drawings and prints. . . . Southeast at **DORDRECHT**, where many famous painters have lived, is the **Grote Kerk** (**Great Church**) with its massive, uncompleted, dark-rose tower and sixteenth-century choir stalls by Jan Terwen. . . . **GOUDA**, east of Rotterdam, is a busy market town whose name is a household word with cheese-lovers all over the world. Its Gothic-style, cathedral-like **Town Hall** is of extraordinary grace and its St. **Janskerk** has 31 wonderful stained-glass windows with 2,412 magnificent panels. The lovely **Weighing-house** by the cheese market is unusual. Go to **Oudewater**

Enchanting Luxembourg,
city of bridges
Office Natl. du Tourisme,
Luxembourg

and be weighed on the medieval Witches Scales and after the traditional test, get the certificate proving you are not a sorcerer. . . . Between Rotterdam and The Hague is the lovely pottery city of DELFT, noted as the town of Vermeer. It still retains the amosphere and character of a seventeeth-century town, because its spacious market square and quiet, tree-shaded canals are lined with picturesque old houses. "Het Prinsenhof" Municipal Museum, a former fifteenth-century monastery, was once the home of William the Silent, Prince of Orange, the Father of the Netherlands, and within its walls he was assassinated in 1584. His tomb, along with the rulers of the House of Orange, is in the Nieuwe Kerk. . . . 's-GRAVENHAGE, or THE HAGUE, seat of the government, is renowned for the dignified charm of its Gothic and Renaissance architecture, its fine avenues and lovely parks and gardens. The name is derived from *Haghe* (hunting grounds) where *Graaf* (Count) Floris IV of Holland built a stronghold as early as 1229. This stronghold is the Binnenhof (Inner Court) with its majestic, gabled Ridderzaal (Hall of the Knights), built in 1280, Upper House (1652) and Lower House (1777) of the Dutch Parliament, some characterful gates and other government buildings. On the third Tuesday of September, the imposing and colorful opening of Parliament takes place, the only pomp and ceremony associated with the Dutch Royal House, when Queen Juliana and her retinue, accompanied by gala-dressed escort, rides in the Golden Coach pulled by eight ebony horses through the city. Adjoining the Binnenhof is "Mauritshuis" Art Gallery, a seventeenth-century palace, with its celebrated collection of old masters, including Rembrandt, Vermeer and Potter. The recently constructed Peace Palace, surrounded by a monumental iron fence and containing valuable gifts from many countries, is where the International Court of Justice sits. Scheveningen, seaside suburb of The Hague, combines the attractions of an old-world fishing village and a cosmopolitan holiday resort, largest and most fashionable in the country. A special magnet for music-lovers is the annual Holland Festival held from mid-June to mid-July, with outstanding organizations like the Hague Residentie Orchestra and the Netherlands Bach Society. . . . North of The Hague is LEIDEN, birthplace of

Rembrandt. Its famous university was founded by William the Silent in 1574 as a reward for the heroism with which the townspeople had successfully resisted a prolonged siege by the Spanish invaders. Distinguished St. Peter's Church retains many memories of the Pilgrim Fathers. Visits can be made to the bulb fields extending northward, producing in the springtime a colorful symphony of incredible loveliness. . . . Among the most attractive towns is HAARLEM (156,856), just west of Amsterdam, ancient residence of the Counts of Holland. Music lovers will be entranced by the 200-year-old baroque pipe organ, still one of the finest in the world, which was played by both Mozart and Handel, in the impressive Grote Kerk (Church of St. Bavo) overlooking the market place. The outstanding attraction, however, is the "Frans Hals" Art Gallery, containing an unrivaled collection of paintings by that great master. Near here, in Spaarndam, is the monument commemorating the legendary boy with his finger in the dyke, symbolizing the traditional courage of the Dutch in their ceaseless struggle against the sea. . . . Busy AMSTERDAM (803,847), capital of the Netherlands, is a remarkable city whose growth can be traced in the concentric semicircles, like the rings of a tree trunk, of its main canals, along which stand proud patrician dwellings built by the merchant princes of the sixteenth and seventeenth centuries. The outer suburbs, on the other hand, are famous for their strikingly modernistic architecture and planning. A real cultural center, this city offers such. magnificent displays as the world-famous collection of masterpieces of the Dutch school, including Rembrandt's renowned "Night Watch," at the "Rijksmuseum" (Netherlands National Gallery); "Rembrandthuis" Art Gallery, the artist's home from 1639 to 1658, and concerts by the celebrated Concertgebouw Orchestra. Heart of the capital is the greatly admired Royal Palace, originally built as the town hall. Don't miss the quaint fishing village of Volendam and the companion island of Marken, where the inhabitants still wear the colorful local costume; the flower auctions at Aalsmeer and the famous bastions at Naarden. . . . Off the coast at DEN HELDER, the naval base, is the Isle of Texel, a bird-lover's paradise, with one of the finest beaches in

Europe. To the east is the impressive **Afsluitdijk,** the phenomenal 18-mile-long enclosing dam that cuts off the Zuyder Zee from the North Sea. . . . On the other side of IJsselmeer is Friesland, whose indomitable, independent inhabitants speak a language entirely their own, more similar to English than Dutch. The impressive, leaning **Oldehove Tower** has been **LEEU-WARDEN'S** architectural landmark for four hundred years. The art treasures assembled in the **Frisian Museum** (antiquarian and historical) make it particularly noteworthy. **Popta Slot,** in Marssum, is a typical sixteenth-century Frisian castle. Oher places of interest in the area are the **Franeker Planetarium,** constructed by a local wool comber in the latter part of the eighteenth century, and the former flourishing port of **Hindeloopen,** now known for its curious painted furniture. . . . The delightful region of woods and moorland surrounding **ASSEN** has some striking archeological landmarks known locally as **"Hunnebedden"** or **"Giants' Beds,"** tumuli raised by the Germanic tribes who lived in this region over 4,000 years ago. In **Drenthe Provincial Museum** are many relics of these early inhabitants. . . . The unusual village of **GIETHOORN,** a little east of Noordoostpolder (North East Polder), is widely known as the "Venice of the North" because the streets are canals, with the old tree-shaded houses linked by high, narrow wooden bridges. . . . In the eastern part of Overijssel province, one of the oldest inhabited areas in Western Europe whose customs date from pre-Christian times, is **ENSCHEDE.** The Town Hall is admired for its modern design, while the **Twenthe Museum** possesses a choice collection of primitives. At nearby **Oldenzaal** is the striking, twelfth-century Church of St. Plechelmus. . . . Rural **ZUT-PHEN,** with is ramparts and fortifications and winding streets, possesses many buildings surviving from the Middle Ages. Most important are the **Drogenaps Tower** and the **Grote Kerk,** with its collection of medieval books and manuscripts chained to the reading desks in the original manner. . . . A favorite holiday ground is the region around **HOOGE VELUWE NATIONAL PARK,** whose chief attraction is the **Kroller-Muller Art Gallery** at Otterlo, containing the largest collection in the world — over two hundred — of works by Vincent Van Gogh. . . . In **ARNHEM,** on the park's southern edge, are a unique assemblage of old Dutch windmills, houses and other relics of Holland's rural culture, carefully re-erected at the **Netherlands Open-Air Folklore Museum.** . . . As is to be expected of a frontier stronghold existing since Roman times, **NIJMEGEN** (106,523), city of Charlemagne, has many old buildings, despite the fact that it suffered considerable destruction during World War II. The oldest of these is the **Valkhof,** a ruined castle built by the Emperor Charlemagne in the eighth century. . . . The oldest fortified town in the Netherlands, **MAA-STRICHT,** in the southernmost region, has endured no less than nineteen sieges in the course of its stormy history. St. Petersberg, originating from the limestone quarries worked here since Roman times, has 400 miles of underground caves and passages, with its unique art gallery painted on the white limestone walls and its mammoth pillared autograph book signed by the great and small of the past ten centuries. The U. S. Military Cemetery at **Margraten,** for American soldiers who died in World War II, contains almost 20,000 graves, all of which have been adopted by Dutch families in the vicinity who keep them covered with flowers. . . . 's-HER-TOGENBOSCH, also known as **BOIS-LE-DUC,** is famous for its truly great poem in stone, the **Cathedral of St. John,** built in the fifteenth century, a marvelous example of the purest flamboyant Gothic style. . . . The canals traversing the heart of **UTRECHT** (185,246), situated right in the middle of Holland, are rather remarkable, with their wharves and cellars below the streets on either side. The fourteenth-century **Cathedral Tower,** a perfect specimen of medieval architecture, is the highest tower in Holland (332 feet), commanding a magnificent view extending as far as the IJsselmeer. In the surrounding countryside are numerous fine chateaux set in delightful woodlands, most notable being the **De Haar Castle** at Haarzuilens, with its thick walls, steep roofs and many pointed towers coming straight from the pages of a fairy tale. . . . **MIDDELBURG,** principal town on Walcheren, the southwest island which is rapidly recovering from the devasting floods of February, 1953, has a handsome **Town Hall** with richly ornamented façade and the **Kloveniersdoelen,** a former military hospital in Flemish Renaissance style.

Germany

CULTURE AND ROMANCE

Germany, the land of beauty and achievement, rich in the inspiration of an historic background and centuries of Western culture, and abounding in the hospitality which has been an outstanding characteristic of all Germanic peoples, from the very earliest times, is ideal for tourists. This country has always been celebrated for the cultivation of the fine arts and especially in music and drama are the German people heirs to a great tradition. Of course, Germany's intellectual and educational life is world-famous, as are her valuable contributions to scientific research. You will enjoy seeing her many historic cities, famous health resorts and spas, the proud castles and tranquil villages — and, of course, the beautiful Rhine. For as Mark Twain said, Germany is a land of infinite variety, and without doubt, you too will find it so.

COFFEEHOUSES, BEER HALLS AND WINE CELLARS

The following are typical German specialities: *labskaus* (cured pork, mashed potatoes and, sometimes, herring, served with poached egg and pickled cucumber), a traditional sailors' dish popular throughout the coastal districts; *rundstück warm* (slice of bread or roll covered with slice of hot pork and gravy) and *pannfisch* (mixture of roast potatoes and fried fish), both Hamburg specialities; *braunkohl mit pinkel* (kale with cured pork chop, smoked bacon, smoked sausage and sausage with the addition of groats and served with roast potatoes), popular in Bremen and Oldenburg; chicken stew and roast goose, specialities of Bremen and Hamburg respectively, but known throughout the coastal region; eel soup, popular in Hamburg and other North German towns; *heidschnuckenbraten* (roast lamb), speciality of the Lüneburg heath; black rye bread and pumpernickel, Bremen and Oldenburg specialities, and all fish and shellfish, including oysters, lobsters and cockles. The Germans are renowned for their delicious pastries, especially butter cake and *bremer klaben* (rich Christmas cake with plenty of raisins and candied peel). Hearty eaters will also appreciate the pleasures of good drinking. The Germans are connoisseurs both of wines and beers. The country is mainly known for the light, dry white wines produced along the Rhine and Moselle valleys. The Rhine wines are the Rheingaus — generally conceded to excel any white wine produced anywhere — Rheinhessens and Palatinates. The Moselle wines have long had a reputation for healthfulness. The Roman poet Ausonius wrote more than 2,000 years ago that the Moselles were "balsam for the shattered nerves of modern man." Most famous of all the tasty German beers are the Bavarian beers. Hanover is the home of the *lütje lage* (a glass of beer and a glass of "corn brandy"), known in Hamburg under the name of *lütt un lütt*. Flensburg is associated with Jamaica rum which, with hot water and sugar, makes the grog popular everywhere in North Germany. Popular specialities are also "tea punch" in North Friesland and "egg grog" in Helgoland, which, like the ordinary grog, is appreciated even on a hot summer day. Strong coffee is a favorite beverage all over Germany, while tea with candy (*kluntjes*) and cream is an East Frisian speciality.

COUNTRY OF THE RHINE

Through the heart of Europe flows the Rhine — the river that Walt Whitman called the most beautiful in the world and whose praise great men have sung in poetry and prose. The cradles of European culture north of the Alps stood along its shores, where great cathedrals in cities dating back to long before the Christian era, storied castles and romantic ruins speak eloquently of the glorious past. The vital artery of Europe, it is the classical route for travel. The cultural and economic center of the Lower Rhine where it flows into the Netherlands is **KLEVE**, scene of the Lohengrin saga. Picturesquely situated on an old Rhine island is **Kalkar**, a popular spot for artists, with the interesting **Church of St. Nicholas**, containing the world-famous art productions, like the wood-carved altars, of the Kalkar School. . . . **ESSEN**, (pop. 605,411) near where the Ruhr River flows into the Rhine, is the 1,100-year-old economic center of the Ruhr area, still a delightful scenic attraction. An ancient architectural monument, built in 796, is the **Essen-Werden Abbey Church**. . . . South of the Ruhr stretches the Bergische Land, with its black-and-white frame houses and its dikes damming up the

Raesfeld Castle in Westphalia, like the many other castles in Germany, presents a fascinating portrait of life of the past
German Tourist Info. Office

water to form picturesque lakes. In the largest town of the Bergische Land, WUP-PERTAL, (363,224) is a unique suspension railway over the Wupper River. South of here is the health resort of Wiehl, in an area of dahlia cultivation. The Wiehl Stalagmite and Stalactite Caves are in the vicinity of Homburg Castle. The magnificent Bergische Cathedral in Altenberg, a treasure of Gothic architecture, nestles on the side of a hill near the well-known summer resort of Odenthal. There is a very unusual and interesting collection at the Röntgen Museum, the German radiography museum, in nearby Remscheid. . . . Back on the Rhine is DUSSELDORF, (500,516) well-known center of art and fashion, the principal city of the Rhenish-Westphalian district, sometimes called the "Paris of Germany." The shops are among the best, especially those on the elegant Königsallee. The city also has one of the best academies of art and art museums in the country. The nearby silk town of Krefeld (171,875) still boasts of the fascinating old moated castle of Linn. München-Gladbach, center of the German cloth industry, has important monuments of architecture, like the 1,000-year-old Minster and baroque Town Hall. Those who wish to re-live medieval times will find that time has in fact passed by Zons, the medieval frontier fortress and toll station of the archbishops of Cologne, between Düsseldorf and Cologne. The town fortifications are completely preserved, including the Customs Tower. . . . Center of the Rhineland is the cathedral city of COLOGNE, (594,941). Founded in 38 B. C., it was the Colonia Agrippina of the Romans, and is now known as the city of fairs. The most famous landmark is, of course, the

Cologne Cathedral, whose renowned twin 515-foot spires were spared by the bombings of World War II. Taking hundreds of years to build — it was founded in 1248 and completed in 1880 — it is the result of many architects' plans. It is also noteworthy for its outstanding stained-glass paintings and sculptures of the Middle Ages, including Stephan Lochner's "The Three Magi," and valuable ecclesiastical vessels. Other outstanding churches are the Church of the Apostles, an important example of late Romanesque architecture, and St. Maria im Capitol, with its famous wooden doors. Cologne, naturally, is also famous for Eau de Cologne, called locally Kölnisch Wasser, which has been made here since the seventeenth century. . . . Between Cologne and Bonn is the garden city of BRUHL. It is worth a visit to see the rococo Castle of Augustusburg, the summer residence of elector Clemens August and now used for official functions by the West German government, with its famous staircase by Balthasar Neumann and rococo gardens. . . . Near the juncture of the frontiers of Germany, Belgium and the Netherlands, AACHEN (129,811) is a well-known spa having the warmest springs in central Europe. During the Middle Ages, 32 kings and emperors were crowned in the massive Imperial Cathedral, which has the marble coronation throne of Charlemagne. The famous Imperial Hall is in the Town Hall. . . . Still further upstream is the old liberal university town of BONN (115,394), booming capital of the Federal Republic, now crowded with civil servants and foreign embassy staffs. Two buildings, one modern, the other several centuries old, are of special interest: the new Bundeshaus (Parliament

House) and the old house where Ludwig van Beethoven was born in 1770. The house and its furnishings have been restored in the manner of the years when the noted composer was alive. Music-lovers will be further interested to know that the Old Cemetery contains the graves of Robert and Clara Schumann, and that the city holds an annual Beethoven Festival in May. From Bonn there opens a fine panoramic view of the picturesque Siebengebirge (Seven Mountains), site of the Nibelungen legends, between the Sieg valley and Westerwald Hills, forming the northernmost wine-growing district of Europe. Drachenfels (Dragon's Crag), which boasts of more visitors than any other mountain in Europe, is the legendary home of the dragon that Siegfried slew, and the red wine made from grapes grown on its slopes is called Dragon's Blood. The famous medieval pottery town, Siegburg, is built around a high hill on which is located the Michaelsberg, an old Benedictine abbey founded in 1064. On the opposite bank of the river, where Bonn is, the Eifel Hills, Germany's largest red-wine belt, reach from the Lower Rhine to the Moselle. Great forests, dikes and the so-called "Maare" — somber lakes filling the craters of long-dead volcanoes — are characteristic of this rugged woodland district. Monschau, an idyllic eighteenth-century town in which life goes on unperturbed by modern changes, is a romantic frontier town of old half-timbered houses in the narrow valley of the Ruhr and at the foot of the mighty castle of the former Lords of Jülich and the Palatinate. Here are fine mansions of the clothmakers, one of which, the "Red House," is a museum. In the wintertime, this is a popular sleighing and skiing center. A little south of Bonn is historic Remagen, unforgettable for many American ex-GI's because this is the spot where the U. S. Ninth Armored Division found a bridge undestroyed in 1945 and swarmed across the natural barrier to the German heartland. The bridge which shortened the war is gone — it finally collapsed after thousands of U. S. soldiers had crossed it — but there are an old Roman road and a Roman gate.
. . . KOBLENZ is a former Roman city situated where the Moselle flows into the Rhine. On the east bank lie the mighty eleventh-century fortress of Ehrenbreitstein, a fortified place since it was a Roman camp. . . . Still further upstream, nestled between the heights of the Hunsrueck and the Taunus Hills, begins the most romantic stretch of the Rhine valley. Here is BOPPARD, the wine-growing town of old-world charm. High above the roofs rises the Cathedral, built in the twelfth and thirteenth centuries, with its vigorous and noble Romanic forms and a choir showing the transition to the new style. An idyllic mountain railway will take you over deep gorges to the heights of the Hunsrueck ranges, to the large and magnificent town forest. Above nearby St. Goar are the ruins of Rheinfels Castle, once one of the strongest fortresses along the river. On a rock on the right bank of the Rhine, in a cut where the river is at its narrowest point, is where the legendary blonde maiden — the Lorelei — sat and sang to lure the river boats to destruction. The Pfalzgrafenstein, a stone structure sitting in the middle of the river below Bacharach, was built by a local count in the fourteenth century as a toll gate, where he simply stretched a chain across the river and didn't let a boat through until the captain paid up. It has only one entrance, a door so high above the water that a visitor had to climb a ladder to get in. Friends of the Rhenish white wines will not fail to visit Rüdesheim where, legend says, Charlemagne brought the first grape vines. The medieval Bromserburg Tower has a wine museum telling the story of the long cultivation of the grape along the Rhine. Above the town is the Niederwald Denkmal ("Watch on the Rhine"), a monument erected by Chancellor Bismarck in 1871. . . . MAINZ, where Johann Gutenberg invented the printing press, is famed also for its wines and for its Mardi Gras festival, the Carnival. The Gutenberg Museum commemorates the invention of modern printing. In Winkel is the oldest stone house in Germany, built in 850. . . . West of Mainz, near the outlet of the Saar into the Moselle, is TRIER, a veritable open-air museum where all epochs are represented since the time of ancient Rome, when this was the largest city north of the Alps. . . . Across the river from Mainz, where the Main flows into the Rhine, is WIESBADEN (220,741). The Romans first discovered the health-giving quality of its mineral springs and it has been one of Europe's leading spas ever since. At the

**MAP OF
FRANKFURT**

HIGHLIGHT MAP OF
FRANKFURT
GERMANY

MAP SHOWS MAJOR STREETS
© C. S. HAMMOND & Co., N.Y.

1. St. Leonhard's Church
2. Goethehaus
3. Römerberg
4. St. Nicolai Church
5. Dom (Cath. of St. Bartholomew)
6. St. Catherine's Church
7. Mun. & Univ. Library
8. Grosses Haus (New Thea.)
9. Beethoven Monument
10. Senckenberg Nat'l Hist. Mus.
11. Saalhof
12. Am Hauptbahnhof
H.= Hotel

Kaiser Friedrich baths is the Roman Arch, built about 300 A. D., a good example of Roman architecture. The **International May Festival** presents some of the best opera, ballet and theater to be seen on the continent. In addition to music there are tennis and golf tournaments and race meetings. . . . "Were anyone to ask me if I could think of a place more befitting my birth, more suitable to my conception as a citizen and more agreeable to my poetic feelings, I could name no other town but Frankfurt am Main." Thus wrote Goethe on September 28, 1824, fifty years after he had left his native town. **FRANKFURT** (532,037), the old Imperial City, continues to be a city full of life, an economic center, an international meeting place and a stronghold of culture and science. The **Goethehaus**, where Frankfurt's greatest son was born, fell a victim to the war but has now been reconstructed with all its furnishings, which had been removed before the bombings. For more that 500 years the venerable **City Hall** (rebuilt in 1952) on the **Römer** (**Roman Hill**) flanked the famous market square. This building with its **Kaisersaal** and the **Prince Electors Chamber** was the scene of the coronation banquets, traditional three-day festivals during which oxen were roasted whole and wine was served free. The "fest" has been revived and is held each summer. Near the Römer, along the river, are two famous old churches: the **Cathedral**, scene of the election of German emperors since 1356 and of their coronation from 1562 to 1792, with a red-sandstone tower from which a magnificent panorama is open to view, and St. **Leonhard's Church**, founded in 1219 by Emperor Frederick II, "Redbeard." A little north is the round-roofed, red-sandstone **Paulskirche** (St. Paul's Church), landmark of German democracy and unity since it is famous in history as the scene of the first German National Assembly in 1848. Downstream on the opposite bank is the **Städel Art Institute and Gallery**, displaying masterpieces dating from all periods of European art, including such outstanding paintings as Jan van Eyck's "Madonna de Lucca." **Senckenberg Natural History Museum** is world-renowned as a research center, with collections including prehistoric animals of exceptional size and rarity, and the **Zoologischer Garten** (**The Zoo**) is the richest zoo in Germany. Further out, trim little towns and a chain of world-known health resorts spread way up to the blue heights of the Taunus Hills, like famous **Bad Homburg**, one of the most beautiful spas in Germany. Long the favorite watering place for European royalty, it was here that King Edward VII of Great Britain had the Homburg hat designed. The **Kurpark** contains a **Russian chapel** and a **Siamese temple**, built by Czar Nicholas II of Russia and King Chulalongkorn of Siam. . . . Between the Nahe and the Rhine, the Palatinate, the districts of Rhenish Hesse and Rhenish Palatinate, are a hiker's paradise. **WORMS**, with its ancient **cathedral** and impressive **Luther Memorial**, is a "must" in every Rhineland itinerary. . . . Upstream on the Neckar, which flows into the great river, is **HEIDELBERG** (116,488), Germany's oldest university town, with its historical stone bridge and the most spectacular **castle** in Germany. This magnificent castle was reduced to ruins in the wars of the 1600's, but the parts still standing span about 700 years. The courtyard forms the stage for the annual summer drama and music festival, while in the castle is a famous wine cask, the **Heidelberger Tun**, so big a stairway is required to get to the top. On the same hill above the castle is the **König-stuhl** (King's Chair), which looks down on the beautiful Neckar valley from 2,000 feet up. **Heidelberg University**, Germany's oldest, was the setting for "The Student Prince" and some of the beer-and-wurst places portrayed in the operetta are still there, like the **Red Ox** and the **Goldener Hecht**, still serving students, as they have done for hundreds of years, in oak-panelled rooms covered with pictures and mementos of long-ago student life.

PICTURESQUE WOODS AND MOUNTAINS

The Black Forest, the woodcarving center, which runs along the east bank of the Rhine from Karlsruhe south to the Swiss border, isn't all forest anymore — there are a lot of cultivated fields — but it's one of the popular summer resort areas. **BADEN-BADEN**, with its matchless position in a lovely valley amid the forest and its unique walks — which may truly be said to be the most beautiful in the world — is the plushiest resort center in the area. The Romans used to bathe in its radioactive chloride hot springs, and kings, queens and the wealthy have been doing it ever since. There are horseback riding, golf (on Germany's best course), a season of horse racing, good music and the Casino.

THE BODENSEE

South of the Black Forest is a resort lake, Lake Constance, bordering Germany,

Switzerland and Austria, a highly popular vacation area with the Germans and the warmest part of the country. **CON-STANCE**, on the lake, dates from the early days of pile settlements. A princely jewel of medieval beauty, it was an episcopal see for fifteen centuries and in 1415 was the seat of the famous council which sentenced John Huss to be burned at the stake. Points of interest include the **Merchants' Hall** by the lake, erected in 1380, containing the great Council Chamber where the conclave of cardinals met; the **Town Hall**, with its magnificent Renaissance Court, and many fine old **patrician houses.**

THE ROMANTIC WAY

In this region between the Main and the Alps, **WURZBURG**, known as the Rococo City, has the handsome, Renaissance-style **residence of the** former **Prince-Bishops**, a splendid example of the jubilant and joyous architecture of Balthasar Neumann. The vestibule in the middle of the building is a masterpiece of architecture and an admirable setting for the great **Mozart Festival** held here every June. . . . **ROTHENBURG** is a dream picture of medieval times as it rises high above the valley of the Tauber. The picturesque old streets and lanes, quaint towers, Gothic churches, Renaissance halls and well-preserved ramparts present a vivid picture of the old days of chivalry and knighthood. Every street, every house, even every stone of Rothenburg can tell its tale. Each year, in front of the **Town Hall**, one of the most exquisite in Germany, is performed the historical play entitled "*Der Meistertrunk.*". . . At the line of demarcation between the scenery of Franconia and that of Swabia, two landmarks adorn the Rieskessel with its waving fields of corn and austere-looking village churches: the "**Ipf,**" a striking tablelike mountain and the "**Daniel,**" a secular tower structure of St. George's Church in **NORDLINGEN**. Even to this day, the cry of the watchman can be heard at night echoing across the narrow streets and alleys from the top of the "Daniel." At the beginning of autumn the horse-loving peasants of the Ries meet here for the **Scharlachrennen** (Scarlet Race) on the **Kaiserwiesen**, which has become the finest venue for riding tournaments and contests in southern Germany. . . . **AUGSBURG** (185,177), the 2,000-year-old town between the Lech and Werlach Rivers, welcomes the visitor with an impressive picture of what was once the "German world-city of the Middle Ages." The **Maximilianstrasse**, with its fine Renaissance **fountains**, monumental **Town Hall** and the **Perlachturm**, is indeed regal in appearance. The **Rote Tor (Red Gate)** to the south of the town, with its walls, moats and bridge, provides the setting for Augsburg's famous open-air festival of drama and opera. From here the road that leads into the delightful scenery of the Allgäu mountains is the ancient Roman Via Claudia, the historical route from Germany to the south. . . . The Romanticists on the royal throne of Bavaria planned the castles of **Neuschwanstein** and **Hohenschwangau**, two of the finest castles in Germany, setting them on the summits of steep rocks in

winter playground of the Bavarian Alps. The "German Beer Hall" is a Bavarian, and particularly a Munich, institution. The **"Oktoberfest"** in the fall is one of Germany's gayest festivals. . . . **OBERAMMERGAU** is a woodcarving center nine out of ten years, but on the tenth year it is the home of the world's most famous pageant, the **Passion Play**. This ancient religious play was instituted in the year 1634 as a thank offering on the part of the pious little community for having been delivered from the plague then raging over Europe. . . . The jewel of the German Alps and a little market town of old-world character, **BERCHTESGADEN**, now a winter-and-summer resort for American military personnel in Germany, was Hitler's favorite hideout, but his Eagle's Nest has been destroyed. The skiing is very

Skier's dreamland — the emerald-studded, gleaming-white landscape of Bavaria
German Tourist Info. Office

the mountainous district. With the storybook Neuschwanstein Castle, built from 1869-1886 in imitation of a medieval castle, King Ludwig II, patron and friend of Richard Wagner, intended to revive the world of Lohengrin and Tannhauser.

THE BAVARIAN ALPS

MUNICH (830,795) is a city with a great many historical associations — past and present. For centuries it was the capital of an independent kingdom, Bavaria. Then it was the birthplace of Nazidom. Now it is the most important city of southern Germany and the gateway to the

good — lifts are available — and nearby is the Königssee, one of the most beautiful of mountian lakes. . . . **GARMISCH-PARTENKIRCHEN** is the leading winter-sports center, as well as a health resort, with complete facilities. Mountain railways run to the top of the **Zugspitze**, highest mountain in Germany and the most celebrated peak in the Bavarian Alps. At the end of January comes the **International Winter Sports Week**. Another resort center is ancient **Mittenwald**, famous for violins.

OLD HANSEATIC TOWNS

The architecture of the North German

Lowlands has quite a style of its own owing to the use of various types of brickwork for structural and decorative purposes. Another outstanding feature is the numerous half-timbered houses, many of them truly magnificent specimens. The life of the people is determined both by the essentially rural character of the land and the coast with its ports and trading centers. Far out to sea stands the red rock of HELGOLAND, well-known landmark and now once again a popular resort. . . Along the coast of the North Sea stretches the chain of the EAST and NORTH FRISIAN ISLANDS, all of them popular seaside resorts, each with its own special character. . . . At FLENSBURG (102,832), on the Danish border, is the old Northern Gate, built in 1595, the "Gateway to Scandinavia." Other unique features of the town are the pharmacy dating from 1604 and the Old Flensburg House, with its fine interior. . . . KIEL (254,449) is identified in most people's minds with the North Sea Canal (Kiel Canal), for which it forms the eastern end. St. Nicholas' Church has a notable crucifix and a bronze font of the fourteenth century. There are collections of works by Schleswig-Holstein painters dating from the seventeenth century in the Hall of Art and unusual items in the Theatrical Museum. There are many seaside resorts on the shores of the Baltic between Kiel and Lübeck, some very fashionable and others quiet and remote. . . . The former Hanseatic town and presently flourishing port of LUBECK (238,-276) is generally regarded as the most beautiful town of northern Germany. In the Middle Ages, it was head of the League and its ancient buildings, lofty towers and old gabled houses furnish a vivid picture of its old prosperity when its proud burgesses held undisputed supremacy over the Baltic. The massive Holsten Gate at the entrance to the old quarters is a fifteenth-century medieval fortified gateway now housing a museum. Not far away is the splendid St. Mary's Church, one of the most admirable examples of low-German brick architecture and also one of the best specimens of early-Gothic in Germany. The combination of old and new in Lübeck extends into the arts where, for example, the fourteenth-century St. Catherine's Church has modern-style sculptures by Barlach, and St. Anne's Museum features arts and crafts going

back to the thirteenth century, while Behn House exhibits modern paintings and sculptures. Lübeck's outer suburb of Travemünde is a popular seaside resort with a fine fishing harbor. The nearby town of Eutin is the birthplace of the illustrious Carl Maria von Weber, notable composer of "Freischütz," "Oberon" and other operas. One of the oldest edifices in Romanesque brick architecture is the beautifully situated Cathedral, founded in 1154, and the oldest North German church built of unhewn stone is St. George's Church, both in Ratzeburg, south of Lübeck. At Mölln — as the legend has it — is the tombstone of Tyll Eulenspiegel, the famous German jester. . . . Germany's largest port and second largest city is the free Hanseatic city of HAMBURG (1,605,606). The protective commercial treaty it concluded with Lübeck in 1241 marks the beginning of the powerful Hanseatic League. However, the disastrous fire of 1842, which destroyed about a third of the inner city, accounts for the lack of historic buildings, although in the Palmaille are gorgeous residential houses of the Empire period. The city is built on ground just above water level and, . therefore, its buildings rest on millions of pilings, and there are many old canals ("Fleete"). The centers of city life are the imposing Town Hall — held above ground by several thousand pilings — with its fine interior and the Exchange, the first in Europe, founded in 1558. The old sailors' district of St. Pauli is the nightlife area, containing both low-class dives and high-class cafes. The noted Chile House is a twentieth-century office building. Don't miss the boat trip around the harbor, an interesting and pleasant experience. In addition to its commercial importance, Hamburg is also a cultural center with its Hall of Art displaying European art from 1400 to today, the Opera House and musical aggregations of the caliber of the Hamburg Symphony Orchestra and the Altona Choral Academy Choir. . . . Southeast of Hamburg is LUNEBURG, another former powerful Hanseatic town and now a spa and tourist center, situated in beautiful, lonely heath country. The town is predominantly late-Gothic in character, with old brick patrician houses of the fourteenth to sixteenth centuries. . . . In quiet, aristocratic CELLE, southwest of Lüneburg, are old houses of the sixteenth and seventeenth centuries and the **Ducal Palace**, built by Italian architects in the seventeenth century, with a magnificent baroque interior, fine chapel and the oldest court theater. . . . Another free Hanse town is Germany's oldest port city, **BREMEN** (444,549). In the historical records, it appears for the first time under the reign of Charlemagne. A leading member of the League, it became a free city in 1646 and in 1949 joined the German Federal Republic. In the center of the old **market place** is the **Roland Statue** (1404), landmark of the city, and flanking it are the noted Gothic **Town Hall**, built one year later, with a Renaissance façade and the oldest German "**Ratskeller**," and the Romanesque-Gothic **Cathedral** (1043), underneath which is the famous **Lead Cellar** containing several mummified bodies. The **Boettcherstrasse**, not far from the market place, has been reconstructed in the old Bremen style by leading artists and the ancient fortifications are now delightful **promenades**. A city noted for its monuments, Bremen's outstanding memorial is a sculptured group representing the "**Bremen Street Musicians**." The **Hall of Art** has a notable collection of 200,000 engravings.

"THE MOST INTERESTING TOWN IN THE WORLD "

That is how journalists have described **BERLIN** (3,350,785). During the past few years, this city has become a symbol of freedom and, at the same time, a gateway connecting the West and the East. Berlin has survived all its vicissitudes because of the character of its inhabitants who combine a keen sense of humor with quick-wittedness and broadmindedness. It is easily accessible from Western Germany by air. Since the division of Berlin into sectors, the new **Schöneberg Rathaus** has become the seat of the Senate of Berlin and the political center of the city. The famous **Freedom Bell**, replica of the Liberty Bell and a gift from the American people in recognition of the bravery of the Berliners during the Russian blockade, hanging in the mighty tower, rings daily at noon. Near the main airfield, **Tempelhof**, is another memento of the blockade — a symbolic "**bridge**" dedicated by the people of Berlin to the Allied airmen who were killed during the airlift. A stroll down **Kurfuerstendamm**, the wide avenue in the center of Berlin, takes you past Berlin's most fashionable and elegant shops, past the cafes with their sidewalk gardens and past the bookshops, all having the same international flavor as the passers-by. Two night clubs deserving special comment are the elegant **Resi** and the **Badewanne** (Bathtub), popular among jazz fans. This amazing street runs near **Potsdamer Platz**, with the "Three-Sector Corner" and the 200-year-old gate, the **Brandenburger Tor**, now the dividing point between West and East Berlin. Also near the street is the **Tiergarten**, one of the world's most famous parks, containing the **Berlin Zoo**. Berlin's most famous landmark of all, though, is the **Funkturm** (Radio Tower), from whose restaurant at the top you may enjoy a magnificent view of the city while feasting on a tasty meal. This tower is in the **Messe-Gelände** (Fair Grounds), which also has terrace gardens and twelve exhibition halls. Since the war, this determined city has regained its former position as an international intellectual center, and visitors whose interests are on the cultural side will be entranced with the opportunities offered here. The modern reconstructed **Schiller Theater** in Charlottenburg is once more playing a leading role in theatrical life, along with the small, well-known **Schlosspark Theater** in Steglitz, the **Renaissance Theater** and others. That Berlin has once more become an important music center is not strange, since its people have always had a deep understanding and love of music. Today, musical Berlin is rich with brilliant opera premiers and memorable concerts by the **Berlin Philharmonic Orchestra** the **Staedtische Oper** and the **RIAS Symphony Orchestra**. Among the summer highlights are the traditional concerts given in the courtyard of the former hunting lodge of the old **Jagdschloss Grünewald**. This castle also contains a collection of precious seventeenth-century Dutch paintings. When George Kolbe, the eminent sculptor, died in 1947, the numerous works he left behind were retained in his secluded house and this has now been opened to the public. A new museum quarter is centered around the richly endowed **Ethnological Museum and Schloss Charlottenburg**, country residence of the Kings of Prussia, with its costly historic rooms and famous mausoleum of Queen Louise, is renowned for its modern art. Or, if you prefer sports, you may visit the **Sportpalast**, the Olympic Stadium, the beach at **Lake Wannsee** or the famous **Avus automobile race tracks**.

Scandinavia

INIMITABLE HOSPITALITY

Although separate countries, each with its own special attractions, Denmark, Norway, Sweden and Finland make up a unit difficult for the traveler to separate. The indescribable beauty of lakes and woodland, ultra-modern architecture in ancient cities studded with historic monuments and reminders of bygone centuries, gently rolling plains ringed by massive mountains and fjords, and the high quality industrial products and wondrous handicrafts may be peculiar to one country only, yet a part of all four.

Of course, Scandinavia is a notable winter-sports area, where fine skiing is enjoyed even in the spring and summer in the arctic north. Perhaps not so well-known, though, is the fact that this whole area provides excellent fishing, marvelous swimming from extensive beaches of immaculate white sand and superb sailing.

American travelers will experience a particular kinship with these peoples, because of the very qualities which distinguish them from some other peoples of the world — the exquisite modern architecture, the high standard of living and the democratic social and political systems. So justly proud of their contributions to contemporary living, these Scandinavians also possess the one final attribute to make everyone's visit the truly unforgettable experience — their unmatched friendliness and hospitality.

GOOD FOOD

And lots of it — is another Scandinavian specialty. Although the traditional cold table or *smorgasbord* (*koldtbord* in Norwegian) is not as common since the war as it once was in Sweden, the big center table, groaning with good things, is still to be found, and in Norway it is still famous for its variety of dishes such as smoked salmon, fresh lobster and Norwegian shrimp. The other food feature common to most Scandinavian countries but extra-special in Denmark is the open-faced sandwich (*smorrebrod* in Danish, *smorbrod* in Norwegian), consisting of a thin slice of buttered bread, heaped with products from farm and sea in hundreds of combinations. Other taste delights in Denmark include the famed Danish pastry, tempting desserts, beer, akvavit and cherry liqueur, while in Norway, venison, ptarmigan in cream sauce, wild raspberries, cloudberries and brown trout are outstanding. As a matter of fact, in all these countries the fruits and berries are out of this world, and there is a variety of tasty sea food.

Denmark

LAND OF HANS CHRISTIAN ANDERSEN

Friendly and hospitable COPEN-HAGEN (pop. 768,105) was considered the capital of Denmark from 1416 on. Christiansborg Palace, on the island of Slotsholmen, is the seat of the Rigsdag (Parliament). Under the palace may be seen the remains of the original palace built by Bishop Absolon in 1167 and the prisoners' Blue Tower. King Frederik's residence is the rococo Amalienborg Palace and the Royal Guard — in full dress of scarlet and blue on festival days — marches through the center of the city every forenoon when the King is in residence to take over the watch at the palace. The beautiful Renaissance Rosenborg Castle is now a museum containing treasures of the Danish Royal Family, including the Crown Jewels and Royal Regalia. One of Christian IV's finest Renaissance buildings is the richly decorated Stock Exchange, with its noteworthy spire. Grundtvig Church, of yellow stone, was inspired by the lovely simplicity of the Danish village church and the symmetry of a church organ. Some other points of interest include the National Museum; the Citadel; the classical Church of Our Lady, with its cold, austere, barrel-vaulted interior; the Round Tower, now used as an observatory; the Zoological Gardens; Our Savior's Church, whose spire is characterized by an open-air spiral staircase; and many other museums and art galleries. You may also visit the famous Carlsberg Breweries. Looking out to sea from Langelinie, a favorite promenade, is "The Little Mermaid," Hans Andersen's renowned character, immortalized in bronze. Christianshavn, on the island of Amager, is perhaps the part of Copenhagen with the greatest number of quaint old houses. In the heart of the city is the famed Tivoli, fairy-garden amusement park, with its Boy Guards, Pantomime Theatre, Corps de Ballet, Symphony Orchestra and illuminated fountains. The well-known **Royal Danish Ballet** performs in season at the **Royal Theatre**.... In northern Zealand are **Kronberg Castle** at **ELSINORE**, scene of Shakespeare's *Hamlet*, where the Hamlet Festival is held the middle of July, and at **HILLEROD**, **Frederiksborg Castle**, with an interesting banquet hall and chapel.... West of the capital is **ROSKILDE**, the medieval capital, where the ancient, twin-spired **Cathedral**, founded in 1170, contains forty of Denmark's royal tombs.... At **RINGSTED** is St. Bendt (St. Benedict) **Abbey Church**, dating from the twelfth century, the finest Roman brick church in Scandinavia.... Near **SLAGELSE**, farther west, is the unique Viking stockade stronghold of **Trelleborg**, built in the year 1000, which in the wintertime garrisoned 1000 warriors.... Nearly all types of Danish scenery are to be seen on Funen Island, the "garden of Denmark," with its idyllic half-timbered country cottages and beautiful manor houses and castles. **ODENSE** (100,940), third largest town in Denmark, is the native town of Hans Christian Andersen, beloved author of oft-told fairy tales, and his **birthplace** is now a museum. Beautiful **St. Canute's Cathedral**, an edifice of great effect, has a richly carved, brilliantly gilded altar piece and a remarkable pulpit. The **Old Funen Village** comprises seventeen old farm houses and dwellings collected from all parts of the island.... In east Jutland is the quaint, little town of **CHRISTIANSFELD** that still bears the stamp of the Moravians who settled here in 1773. The famous honey cake **bakery** still remains, and the **churchyard**, "God's acre," is extraordinary.... Across the moor is **RIBE**, Denmark's old-

est medieval town, more than 1100 years old, noted for its narrow streets and incredibly low houses with storks nesting on the roofs. The impressive **Cathedral** was built about 1130.... Near **VEJLE**, on the east coast, is the **Jellinge Stone**, raised a thousand years ago, with inscription in runic letters, over King Gorm and his Queen Thyra. It contains the first graven image of Christ found in the North.... **SILKEBORG** is a comparatively modern town in the lake district, the fisherman's Eldorado, of Jutland. All through the summer months the **river steamers** maintain frequent service through the lakes, stopping at all points of interest.... Denmark's second largest city is **AARHUS** (116,167). Here, in the splendid **Botanical Gardens**, an old provincial town has been revived picturing life in a Danish town right back to the sixteenth century, with ancient houses of historical value collected from the whole of Denmark. Historical plays are performed here, too. Every week organ concerts are held in **St. Clemens' Cathedral**, the longest church in Scandinavia. Visitors also like the strikingly modern **Town Hall** and **University of Aarhus** and the nine miles of bathing beaches encircling the town. ... Across the Bay of Aarhus, on the peninsula of Mols, is the fairy-tale town of **EBELTOFT** with the smallest **town hall** in the world, and the watchman singing his songs every night.... **AALBORG** is the gay city of northern Jutland. At the town center is **Jens Bangs Stenhus**, Scandinavia's biggest and best-preserved private edifice from the Renaissance period, built by a wealthy seventeenth-century merchant, and **Sct. Budolfi Kirke** (St.

"The Little Mermaid," charmingly situated at the entrance of the port of Copenhagen
Danish Tourist Commission

Scandinavia

Botolph's Church), with its unusual spire, rich furnishings and medieval mural paintings. Tours may be taken through the world-renowned Aalborg Akvavit (snaps) distilleries. A favorite with all is luxurious Kilden Restaurant. . . . From here one can visit the vacation spot of REBILD NATIONAL PARK, where an inspiring and picturesque observance of American Independence Day is held every year. . . . Moens Klint, on the east coast of the ISLAND OF MOEN is famed as a beauty spot because of the curiously formed white chalk cliffs rising steeply from the sea. . . . In the Baltic, southeast of Copenhagen, is the holiday island of BORNHOLM, a veritable bather's paradise with its long stretches of sandy beach and miles of sand dunes. Its historic round churches at one time served as fortresses.

Norway

FJORD JOURNEY

Bounded on three sides by forest-clad hills stretching for miles and on the fourth by the fjord, Norway's capital of OSLO (pop. 417,238) enjoys a marvelous setting. Lovely Akershus Castle, with its slender medieval towers, was first built in 1300, then rebuilt by King Christian IV, who replaced the ponderous fortress style with a more elegant structure. It is now used for important state occasions. The new, twin-towered Rådhuset (City Hall) has been lavishly decorated by Norway's leading artists and contains the world's largest oil painting. On Bygdoy peninsula are some of the outstanding attractions: the remarkable Viking Ships, all found near the Oslo fjord; the Polar exploration ship *Fram*, which has been further north and south than any other ship in the world, used on expeditions by Nansen, Sverdrup and Amundsen; the big, pyramid-shaped building housing the *Fram*, constructed on the same plan as the old Viking boathouses; the Kon-Tiki Museum, with the well-known 1947 raft which traveled close to 5,000 miles across the Pacific, and the large, open-air Norwegian Folk Museum, containing 150 old wooden buildings from various parts of Norway. Frogner Park contains the controversial collection of sculptures by Gustav Vigeland, who worked for over thirty years creating this world of human beings and animals. The

Nationaltheatret (National Theater) is above all the theater of the great Norwegian dramatist, Henrik Ibsen. A lift will take you up to the skier's mecca, Holmenkollen ski-jumping hill, at the top of which is the world's first Ski Museum. . . . If you wish to spend a vacation sea bathing, sea fishing or boating, you will find no more ideal spot in the whole country than the south coast, called the "Norwegian Riviera." The popular seacoast resorts include KRISTIANSAND, with its beautiful cathedral and twelfth-century Oddernes church, and ARENDAL, with the sea on the front doorstep, whose Town Hall is a superb piece of architecture. . . . MORGEDAL, the "Cradle of Skiing" in the country called the "Home of Skiing," is a fine mountain village in Telemark — a name evoking thoughts not only of skiing but of poetry and ancient peasant culture. . . . KONGSBERG, Norway's silver - mining town, is another popular Telemark resort. A visit to the mines is a unique experience. . . . Charming STAVANGER is in the "Fjord Country," an ideal holiday district. The twelfth-century cathedral, one of the most beautiful stone churches in Norway, has a pulpit with magnificent wood carvings. Venerable Kongsgaard School was used in the olden days as a residence for the king. Tours may be made of the Canning Industry School, only one of its kind in Scandinavia, and one of the large canning factories. A great tourist attraction is the steamer trip into the peculiar Lyse fjord, with Pulpit Rock, completely flat on top but rising 1,970 feet above the fjord. . . . During the years of Norway's greatness, BERGEN (110,424), also in the west-coast "Fjord Country," was virtually capital of the country for close on a century and a half (1164-1299) and at an early date became one of the important outposts of the Hanseatic League, vividly recalled by "Gamle Bergen" (Old Bergen), the Bryggen (Quays), Fantoft Stave Church and the Hanseatic Museum. The Bergen Festival, held in early June, includes intimate and orchestral concerts in Edvard Grieg's home, "Troldhaugen," and plays and folk pageants in the medieval castle of Bergenhus. The countryside is ideal for hiking and from the seven mountains surrounding the town there are magnificent views of the sea and land for miles around, especially from the top of Mount Floyen (1,040 feet). Not least of the

From the Lofoten Fisheries in Norway, largest cod fisheries in the world
Norwegian Natl. Travel Off.

town's attractions is the hustle and bustle of its picturesque streets, and the famous fish market as a focal point. As a matter of fact, the city has a well-merited reputation for its sea-food cuisine. Trips may be made via the Bergen Railway to famous ski and trout-fishing resorts like Al, Finse and Voss. . . . BALESTRAND is one of the leading holiday centers, situated on a promontory in the Sogne fjord. . . . GEIR-ANGER, one of the outstanding beauty spots of Norway, nestles at the head of the narrow Geiranger fjord with the graceful "Seven Sisters" and "Bridal Veil" waterfalls. . . . Bombed and entirely burned out in 1940, MOLDE, the "Town of Roses" on the Romsdal fjord, has been rebuilt, and is a center for fishing, swimming or mountain climbing. . . . Friendly little LILLEHAMMER, facing Lake Mjosa, is one of Norway's finest holiday resorts in the Gudbrandsdal valley north of Oslo, where national costume is still worn at work and play. The climate is particularly healthy and refreshing. . . . A favorite with visitors is TRONDHEIM, famous for its wide streets, but whose chief attraction is the magnificent Nidaros Cathedral, one of the proudest architectural treasures of the North. The kings of Norway are crowned in this cathedral. Close to this imposing Gothic edifice, which dates from the twelfth century, lies the 1,000-year-old Archbishop's palace. The old Governor's Residence (Stiftsgården), built in 1770, and now used as a Royal Palace, is Norway's largest timber building. . . . North Norway, consisting of the three counties of Nordland, Troms and Finmark, is situated almost entirely within the Arctic Circle. This is the home of those nomadic, reindeer-tending Lapps and the

"Land of the Midnight Sun," where the traveler enjoys a profusion of blazing color and light such as no other scenery can offer. Perhaps the most outstanding holiday journey one can undertake is the wonderful twelve-day cruise by modern express steamer from Bergen or Trondheim along the entire coast past North Cape to Kirhenes and back. TROMSO, the "Capital of the Arctic," on an island, has a grand view of ice-covered mountains. Visitors may see in the sound the giant German battleship Tirpitz, sunk by the R. A. F. in 1944.

Sweden

CONTEMPORARY LIVING

On the west coast of Sweden, GOTH-ENBURG'S (pop., 353,991) modern public buildings are outstanding examples of contemporary Swedish architecture, and the Art Gallery and Röhss Museum of Industrial Art contain exceptional collections. One of the most popular in Northern Europe, Liseberg Amusement Park has good restaurants, a music hall and theaters, in addition to the usual carnival attractions. Trädgårdsföreningen is perhaps the most beautiful of the many parks and the flowers in the Botanical Gardens are magnificent. Concert House, featuring an excellent symphony orchestra, is renowned for its particularly good acoustics. A favorite attraction is the three-day trip to Stockholm on the charming Göta Canal, through 400 miles of beautiful countryside. . . . To the north is the playground for those who love briny water and hot sun. Here are the finest sailing waters in Sweden and the annual international regattas at MARSTRAND are the festive climax of the yachting season. The cod fishing, too, is marvelous. . . . To the south is the popular west-coast resort of HALMSTAD, which prides itself on a famous fountain, "Europa and the Bull," by the contemporary sculptor Carl Milles. The beautiful medieval St. Nicolai Church, with its interesting sepulchral tablets, is noteworthy, while the Town Hall is an excellent example of modern architecture and construction. . . . BASTAD, an exclusive vacation center, is the site of major tennis and golf tournaments. . . . Located on the narrowest part of the sound between Sweden and Denmark, where some of the best tuna fishing in the world is to be found, HALSINGBORG (71,718) has had great importance for years. Kärnan, the central bastion in the medieval castle, the most remarkable relic of its kind in Scandinavia, still dominates the city scene, and once was a meeting place for the princes and potentates of much of Europe. The thirteenth-century Maria Church has exquisite old furnishings. Popular nearby vacation spots are Ramlösa Spa, Mölle, Torekov and the island Hallands Väderö, a national park with unusual flora and a wealth of birds. . . . MALMÖ (pop., 192,498), across from Copenhagen, Denmark, is one of the oldest cities in this part of the world. Malmöhus Castle. built from 1434-1542, was once a powerful fortress and during its long history has served as a prison, restaurant and now museum. City Theater is generally regarded as the most modern in Europe. . . . The university town of LUND is the cultural center of the fertile southern region and well-known for Scandinavia's finest Romanesque cathedral dating from the early twelfth century, which contains a number of valuable treasures from the Middle Ages, including a giant astronomical clock. . . . The impressive, fortified Kalmar Castle of immense strength, at KALMAR on the southeast coast, the oldest parts of which date from the twelfth century, was once known as "the Lock and Key of Sweden." . . . Almost without exception, the people on the island of OLAND, across the sound from Kalmar, have relatives in the United States, and former U. S. residents are to be found throughout the island. In addition to historical finds going back to the Stone Age, Oland has the greatest concentration in the world of little, old-fashioned windmills,

and its strange beauty has a special appeal for painters. . . . STOCKHOLM (745,936), the capital, praised for its unique beauty, has been called the "Venice of the North." The Old Town, on an island in the turbulent outlet of Lake Mälaren into the Baltic, still retains its quaint medieval character, with its narrow meandering lanes and ancient pastel-tinted buildings, palaces and churches. Mirrored in the surrounding waters are the buildings which make the city famous: the Town Hall, widely considered the most impressive contemporary building in northern Europe; the Royal Palace, an eighteenth-century, neo-classical architectural masterpiece; the thirteenth-century Great Church, adjoining the palace, still the scene of royal ceremonies; Ridderholm Church, sometimes called the "Swedish Pantheon" because it contains the tombs of most of the kings and other great men; the impressive specimens of modern church architecture — Högalid and Engelbrekt Churches — and the magnificent Nordiska Museum. On an island in Lake Malaren is Drottningholm Palace, dating from 1662, justly famous for its formal gardens and its 1765 court theater, the only one left intact in the world. Performances here form the core of the annual Stockholm Festival of Music, Ballet and Drama, held early each June. Distinguished representatives of the scientific and literary world gather in Stockholm every December to participate in the glittering Nobel Festival, when the coveted Nobel Prize awards are made by the King. With more than 10,000 islands, the Stockholm Archipelago presents one of the world's most unusual seascapes, a paradise for swimming, fishing and sailing. The two principal centers are Saltsjöbaden and Sandhamn where big regattas take place. . . . Off the east coast of Sweden is the fabulous, legendary island of GOTLAND, the "Pearl of the Baltic." Visby's stately City Wall frustrated the attempts of many invaders, and Bulverket, the remains of another pre-historic fortification, built on poles over a shallow lake, is unlike anything elsewhere. Picture stones from the pre-Viking era are also unique. Each summer a Miracle Play is performed in the ruins of St. Nicholas' Church, Visby. Some 200,000 migratory sea birds roost on small Stora Karlsö island each spring and the semi-wild "russ" horse, a small, ancient species, is found in no other place but Gotland. On the coast is the famous resort of Snäckgärdsbaden.... Picturesque UPPSALA, north of Stockholm, with Sweden's largest university and finest Gothic cathedral, is pervaded with an air of cultural repose. Uppsala Cathedral, whose 400-foot twin spires are equal to its entire length, contains a veritable treasure of textiles and silver and gold objects. On a hill commanding the town, is the sixteenth-century Uppsala Castle, scene of many great historical events, but of the town's prehistoric political importance as a stronghold of the heathen chieftains, nothing now remains but the gigantic burial mounds. A good time to visit here is on Walpurgis Night, the last day in April, when the Uppsala University students stage their traditional welcome to spring. . . . The province of

Circle, the Midnight Sun never sets for forty days and nights — a country of rolling mountains, of endless plains where nomadic Lapps still graze their reindeer herds, of waterfalls, glaciers and rivers. In up-to-date KIRUNA, about 100 miles north of the Artic Circle, is a most remarkable church, built of wood on an architectural theme drawn from the design of a Lapp hut. . . . ABISKO and RIKSGRANSEN are resorts in this area.

Finland

LAND OF LAKES

Heart of HELSINKI (pop. 363,834), the lively, modern capital of Finland, is Senate Square, or the Great Square. Since most of the buildings surrounding it were

Typical view of provocative Oland, isle of wind and sunshine
Swedish Natl. Travel Office

Dalarna has long been a popular vacation region. To a great extent the local people still wear their colorful national costumes and have preserved many old customs. MORA, on long, romantic Lake Siljan, is the goal of the big event of the skiing season, the 55-mile competition over the route once taken by King Gustav Vasa. . . . RATTVIK is the site of the unique church boat race in July, in which teams compete in the long, multi-oared boats used to take the lakeside villagers to church....Equally popular in winter and summer among skiers, fishermen and hunters is the beautiful, invigorating Swedish mountain range stretching north from Dalarna, including the holiday centers of STORLIEN, FJALLNAS and VALADALEN. . . . More and more people are discovering the strange and unusual beauty of that vast snow-capped region where, north of the Arctic

designed in the early nineteenth century by the same architect, the whole square forms a remarkably homogeneous and attractive sight. Architecturally it is Empire, with its neoclassical slanting roofs over bright-colored buildings. The north side is dominated by the magnificent Great Church of Helsinki, with its beautiful columns and minarets, while the old Helsinki University Building is on the western side. The only exception to these Empire buildings is the mansard-roofed Sederholm Residence, built in 1750. On Mannerheim Road, the main boulevard, is the impressive, modern Eduskuntatalo (Parliament House) of red Finnish granite and the Kansallismuseo (National Museum), with its tower, incorporating the facades of a palace, a castle and a church. Just off this road is the railway square, with the famous Rautatie Asema (Rail-

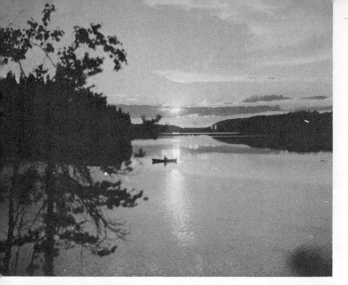

Just one of the thousand scenes of serene beauty in Finland's lakeland
"Finland-Travel"

way Station), one of the most beautiful public buildings in Finland; Ateneum Art Gallery and Kansallisteatteri (National Theater). The Mannerheim Museo, a conspicuous yellow wooden house, was the home of C. G. Mannerheim, Marshall of Finland, and is now preserved as a museum with all his trophies and relics. Since the Finns are great sports-loving people, there are a number of stadiums in the capital, but the most important is Olympic Stadium, built for the 1952 Olympic Games. The top balcony of the stadium tower commands a wide view of the city, coastal islands and dense forests of the interior. Suomenlinna, the Gibraltar of the North, is a group of fortified islands with ramparts protecting the approaches to Helsinki. This island fortress has had a long and stirring history, and the special atmosphere of former centuries can be felt even today. Visitors should also make the trip to Korkeasaari Island Zoo, rich in northern fauna. Seurasaari island, with its open-air museum and a village made up of original old wooden farm buildings from various districts, is a fine natural park and a popular swimming place. Folk dancing and an open-air theater take place during the summer. The most famous of all Helsinki festivals is the Sibelius Festival, held in early June in the Festival Hall of Helsinki University, in honor of Jean Sibelius, Finland's native son and the world's greatest living composer. . . . The tourist cannot help being struck by the profusion of lakes in Finland, and no one should miss taking a cruise through one of the important watercourses on a white passenger steamer. In this way, travel to AULANKO NATIONAL PARK, the number one lake resort near Hämeenlinna, Sibelius' native town. Here you can enjoy the excellent beach, a traditional *sauna* (Finnish steambath) or a restful afternoon by the idyllic swan lake. Hattula church, dating from 1250, is one of the medieval memorials in the vicinity. . . . On the Gulf of Finland, east of Helsinki, lies the town of PORVOO (BORGA), where the first Finnish Diet was summoned by Czar Alexander I, Grand Duke of Finland, in 1809. The town picture has the authentic stamp of the Middle Ages—winding streets, knoblike hills and narrow lanes — and towerless Porvoo Church is one of the largest medieval stone churches. However, from the small market square in front of the old town hall — now a museum — is a typical eighteenth century view. And the nineteenth century spirit is preserved in the home of J. L. Runeberg, national poet and creator of the national anthem. . . . Former capital TURKU (101,239), second largest city in Finland, dating back to about 1150, grew up round its famous Cathedral. Its archipelago is considered the most beautiful in the country, and the Turku Castle an outstanding landmark. . . . Unique experiences are provided by a thrilling rapid-shooting trip in the north, demonstrations by lumberjacks of their hazardous skills in several log-rolling contests or a trip to KILPISJARVI, in the heart of the vast, barren arctic expanse north of the Arctic Circle, where herds of reindeer are tended by colorfully costumed Lapps.

Switzerland

CROSSROADS OF EUROPE

Matchless scenery, centuries-old towns and traditions and the proud cultural heritage of the world's oldest republic have led travelers to Switzerland for generations. The rigid Swiss national standards of hospitality, superb cuisine, cleanliness and honesty appeal particularly to Americans and enable them to enjoy the details of living while they enjoy abundant scenic and historic charms. The scenery, which usually causes visiting writers to resort to the adjective "incomparable," is an ideal backdrop for the unlimited sport and recreation facilities found throughout the country. Of course, the really outstanding sports are mountaineering and skiing, for which this tiny republic has had a matchless reputation for generations, since fifty 13,000-footers, the most challenging peaks of the entire Alpine region, sparkle skyward in Switzerland's Alpine rampart. Beauty, hospitality, health, sport — and education — make this not only the favorite location for all kinds of international conferences, but also the favorite vacation area for people of all nations.

LINGUISTIC TALENT

In the north and east German is spoken by the natives. It's French in the southwest, Italian in the south and a centuries-old language derived from Latin called Romansch in some valleys in the southeast. But to the traveler, English is the universal tongue in Switzerland. Most educated people speak English.

CULINARY SPECIALTIES

French, German and Italian influences predominate in regions where those languages are spoken, so each region has its specialties: *fondue* and *raclette* (melted cheese dishes) in the French section; sausages, roasts and fried potatoes (*rösti*), in the German section; air-dried beef (*bündnerfleisch*) and ham, sliced paper thin, in the Grisons; Italian specialties in the Ticino. Swiss pastries and desserts are world-famed. Swiss wines are excellent, especially when ordered in the region where the grapes are grown — always ask for the local wine. Swiss wines, unlike French, are best when new, and in general, white wines are preferred. Swiss brandies are delicious, but highly potent, with Marc, Kirsch, Pflümli most popular. Swiss beer, too, is excellent.

LAND OF WILLIAM TELL, SYMBOL OF FREEDOM

The lovely, unique capital of the Swiss Confederation, BERN (pop., 146,-499) goes back to the first half of the twelfth century, when a small settlement formed around the Nydegg castle on a narrow peninsula in the river Aare. Throughout the centuries, the Bernese have devoted every care to keeping it as it was built in the Middle Ages. with the result that Bern is one of the best-preserved medieval cities in Europe and one of the loveliest adornments of the continent. Known throughout the world as Bern's greatest attraction is the figure-play on the clock tower, one of the main towers of the wall. Between 1526 and 1530, in this very same tower, Caspar Brunner made this remarkable clock, as well as the astronomical clock next to the figure-play. On the striking of the hour, the different figures on the gilded face are set in motion: the rooster crows; Father Time turns his hourglass, counting the hours with his mouth and scepter; the lion turns his head to watch him; a circle of bears moves around merrily; the jester rings his bell; and high up in the turret, the Knight of Thann, clad in golden armor, strikes out the hours with his hammer. On the cobblestone street in front of the unusual clock tower is the historical, sixteenth-century Zähringer Fountain. Since the medieval towns enjoyed a rather limited supply, water was provided by the fountains in the streets and public squares. These fountains became the most popular meeting places of the citizens, thus playing a doubly important role in their lives. Artistically designed, the fourteen in Bern are still an adornment to the old streets of the town. Another famous fountain, the Anna Seiler Fountain — built in honor of the woman who, in 1342, bequeathed her fortune to the town for the founding of a hospital — is located in front of what was the main tower of the city wall and the western gateway to the town. By the middle of the thirteenth century, not 100 years after the building of the walls, the town had developed so that it spread beyond these limits and from then on this tower was the prison tower. The colorful Ensign Fountain faces the imposing facade of the Town Hall, late Gothic in style, with an impressively styled interior. Standing majestically on the hill overlooking the river is the massive, domed **Houses of Parliament,** from whose southern **Promenade** is a splendid view of the snow-covered Alps. The other dominating building is the **Cathedral,** started in 1421 and completed in 1893, where concerts are given on summer evenings. This Gothic-style, stone church, with its imposing spire, has many lovely details, including the choir stalls, the stained-glass windows and the vivid sculpture of the Last Judgment over the main portal. Twice a week, on a street leading to the Cathedral, the butter, cheese and meat **market** is held, the right of the country people to hold this market going back almost 200 years. Since the national costume is still worn in many places in the Canton of Bern, these country people, dressed in their rich outfits, make a particularly inviting appearance. The climax, though, is the **Onion Market,** held on the fourth Monday in November, when the

dancing and other entertainments continue until early morning and dishes with onions as the main ingredient and cheese cakes are consumed. As a matter of fact, the Bernese appreciate all good food and the town is renowned throughout Switzerland for its excellent specialties: "Bernerplatte," consisting of sauerkraut in winter and green beans in summer, together with a rich choice of smoked meats, bacon and sausages; cheese dishes; trout, prepared in many different ways; Bernese wine (Schafiser) from the Lake of Biel and Bernese gingerbread. As is expected of a capital, Bern possesses several fine museums and particularly worthy of attention is the **Historical Museum,** containing among its most valuable treasures the tapestries and other booty captured from the Burgundians at the battle of Murten in 1476. The most striking feature of Bern's medieval architecture are the **arcades,** the arched-in pavements on both sides of the streets from which the visitor can enjoy the shop windows with their luxurious and tempting displays. A stroll through the town beneath these arcades can very well be combined with a visit to the **bear pits,** whose existence can be traced as far back as the fifteenth century. Since it is popularly believed that the name of the city is derived from the German word for bear (*Bären*), this animal is portrayed on the Bernese coat of arms and bears of all shapes and sizes, made of metal, stone, wood and — very popular ones indeed — of chocolate and gingerbread, are to be found all over the city. . . . From time immemorial the Lake Geneva district, in the southwestern corner of the country has

MAP OF
GENEVA

been a focal point of international routes, since it is almost the core of the network of valleys crisscrossing the Alpine heart of Europe. Still in the hub of things, GENEVA (145,473) is today the "international city" *par excellence*. Although the crest of the hill on which the old quarters now rise — clustering around the very beautiful St. Peter's Cathedral — offered an ideal strategic position for primitive tribes, Geneva was insignificant throughout the Middle Ages until John Calvin, the ardent French champion of the Reformed Faith, sought a haven here from persecution in his own country. Making it the citadel of his new faith — commemorated today by the impressive Reformation Monument — Calvin's arrival in 1536 attracted to the city the famous scholars, pilgrims and travelers of his time. Geneva's reputation as a world center was confirmed upon her designation as seat of the former League of Nations and, later, European headquarters of the United Nations. The large, white United Nations Palace is in Ariana Park, facing the enchanting Mont Blanc, and the International Labor Office, in its splendid setting, lies beyond the Quai du Mont-Blanc. Tall, French-style buildings and innumerable sidewalk cafes lend Geneva a cosmopolitan air and even the most casual visitor has a sense of being right in the center of things. Consistent with its international role, the University, a renowned seat of learning, includes an unusual School of Interpreters, where linguists are trained for world organizations. Another interesting building, the Town Hall has a very original Renaissance courtyard and several handsome halls. No visitor should miss taking a cruise around Lake Geneva on one of the distinctive steamers. . . . The northwestern shores of the lake are known as the La Côte district, where the vine has been cultivated for centuries. Most famous of these white vintages are perhaps the Fechy and Tartegnin, crisply cool and rather heady. Center of the La Côte wine production and an active yachting and sailing center as well is MORGES, known for its charming Grape Harvest Festival. Of remarkable interest is the small parish Church of St. Sulpice, built before 1200 by monks of Cluny Abbey in Burgundy, one of the very few surviving Romanesque structures in Switzerland. . . . LAUSANNE (106,807), centrally situated on the south-facing Swiss shore of Lake

Geneva, has achieved unique newspaper fame as the "City of Kings," for a surprising number of royal personages — both reigning and "ex" — have chosen to take up residence here. It also enjoys international repute as an educational and medical center. Built on three hills, the highest of which is crowned by the old quarter and the fine Cathedral of Norte-Dame, an excellent example of Burgundian Gothic architecture, Lausanne is a city of steep streets and stairways. Unique in modern Switzerland is the watchman who, every evening at 8:30, climbs the 236 steps of the cathedral tower and keeps watch over the city all night, calling the hours at the four corners of the tower. The Federal High Court of Appeal, a very fine example of modern architecture, forms a pleasant contrast with the nearby "Château" of Mon-Repos, headquarters of the International Olympic Committee. A most delightful excursion is the trip to picturesque Gruyères, center of a rich dairy farming country and home of the famous cheese, a perfect gem of a medieval fortified "burg," rising high on a rocky crag at the foot of an old tenth-century castle whose story is a strange intermingling of fact and legend. . . . To the east of Lausanne lies the Lavaux district, the steeply terraced vineyards producing excellent white wines, which are consumed on the home market, mostly open and as an "aperitif," although they also serve as excellent companions to the local specialty: fried filets of lake perch. At the end of this district is quiet and lovely CULLY, a haunt of painters. . . . MONTREUX ranks among the most famous year-round resorts in the world. The view from the flat, tablelike summit of Rochers de Naye is superb, extending over the whole of Lake Geneva, while it also provides excellent skiing. Montreux' celebrated Chillon Castle is one of Europe's famed beauty spots and its walls, lapped by the waters of the lake, have inspired romantic hearts and great poets. The origin of the castle is lost in the dawn of history, but it was Peter, Duke of Savoy, known as the "Little Charlemagne," who made Chillon as we know it today, probably with the help of English military architects from the court of the Plantagenets. The impressive stronghold was used chiefly as a defence and a prison and its courtyard is replete with gloomy memories, since it witnessed numberless execu-

High alpine pasture along Trübsee mountain lake above Engelberg

tions over the centuries, from the countless Jews who were put to death there in 1348 to the 27 "witches" in 1613. Most famous of Chillon's prisoners was Francis Bonivard, Prior of St. Victor Abbey in Geneva and hero of Byron's poem, "The Prisoner of Chillon." The **Musée du Vieux-Montreux** in one of the ancient buildings of the town, a former convent of the eleventh century, has collections and manuscripts on the history of the district. The thirteenth-century **Church of St. Légier-La-Chiésaz** is a fine example of pure Roman architecture. The nearby quiet market town of **Vevey**, site of John Jacques Rousseau's sentimental best-seller of 1763, *La Nouvelle Heloise,* has one of the most modern beaches in the country and is the site of the twelfth-century **Temple de St. Martin,** noted for the grace of its lines and the remarkable windows by the painter Bieler. Culinary specialties of the entire Lake Geneva region include *fondue,* the cheese dish of Western Switzerland which promotes conviviality and good fellowship; *raclette* (cheese melted on the hoop before an open fire and served with potatoes, pickled onions and gherkins) and country-cured sausages (*saucissons*) and ham. . . . Between the lakes of Brienz and Thun, in the Bernese Oberland, lies **INTERLAKEN,** magnificent center for hiking, lake bathing and skiing in the Jungfrau region. The little village of **Brienz,** at which Byron stayed, is famous as a center of woodcarving. At **Jungfraujoch** you may go Ice-skating in the famous ice palace. . . . Queen of high-Alpine resorts is **ZERMATT,** at the foot of the majestic Matterhorn and surrounded by the awe-inspir-

ing giants of the Alps. Under the shelter of Matterhorn's proud summit, this town, key to the region in which have been accomplished the most daring exploits of the pioneers of the Alps, developed until it has now become the "metropolis" of mountineering. Take the famous **open-air railway** up to the peaks to Rotenboden in the Gronergrat or the new **chair lift,** which has a ski-lift extension during the winter, to Sunnegga. . . . In southeastern Switzerland on Lake Maggiore, **LOCARNO'S** mild climate, beautiful surroundings and historic past make it a resort of world-wide repute. The picturesque arcades and attractive shops of the **Piazza Grande** are evidence of the purely Lombard character of the magnificent garden city. The **Sanctuary of the Madonna del Sasso,** which looks down on the town from the brink of a rocky terrace, is one of the architectural jewels of a town rich in splendid buildings and artistic treasures. **Locarno Castle,** of medieval, massive construction and marvelous frescoes, is now an archeological museum. A yearly event is the **International Film Festival,** which transforms Locarno into a meeting place for producers, film stars and journalists. Last, but not least, the beach is famous for its fine sands. . . . Southwest of Locarno on Lake Maggiore is **ASCONA,** originally a fishing village, with picturesque corners, romantic little inns and shady arcades. Bohemian, intellectual and elegant life, art expositions and schools give Ascona and the cafes on the *Piazza* or in the *borgo* (ancient part of the town) a special lively touch. . . . To the southwest lies the romantic village of **BRISSAGO,** on the shore of this eternally peaceful lake. In character the town is essentially Italian, as shown by the historical parish church with its avenue of century-old cypresses and also by a classical early-seventeenth-century chapel, the Madonna del Ponte. . . . At LUGANO, a classic health resort, the art-lover will find many treasures in the collection of paintings — generally regarded as one of the most valuable in Europe — in the Villa Favorita in Castagnola, including among others works by Rubens, Dürer, Titian, Velasquez, Gainsborough and Rembrandt. The notable art collection in the Villa Vallone in the picturesque village of Morcote contains valuable examples of Rumanian folk art and the Vela Museum at Ligornetto has works of the famous sculptor, Vincenzo Vela. . . . With its countless sunny holiday resorts and numerous spas, several of which have been in use since the time of the Romans, the Canton of the Grisons is characterized by an extraordinary profusion of woods and forests rising from the warm southern valleys up to the glaciers and regions of everlasting snow. At the climatic mountain spa of ST. MORITZ the mild southern and the invigorating nordic climate meet. . . . Charmingly situated in northeast Switzerland, between the Lake of Constance and the mountain chain of the Santis, ST. GALLEN, one of the greatest centers of the linen trade, ranks among the prettiest towns in the country. The origin of the town dates back over 1300 years, when the Irish missionary Gallus built his cell here, and to this very day St. Gallen remains the guardian of cultural treasures a thousand years old, represented in the world-renowned Abbey Library, called the finest rococo interior in Europe. The present Cathedral, built 1756-1767, is acknowledged to be one of the masterpieces of baroque architecture. . . . On the Lake of Lucerne — the lake Victor Hugo called "the miracle of Switzerland" — the town of LUCERNE has an atmosphere all its own. Here is the region where Swiss democracy was born and the spirit of the town centers around the deep love of peace and freedom that is so typically Swiss. A top-flight cosmopolitan holiday resort, it still retains all the charm and fascination of the romantic Middle Ages. All travelers will agree with Mark Twain who saw Lucerne as "a fascinating city; with its picturesquely situated hills, its many gables, towers, turrets and bay windows; and with its old gray city wall, peeping out here and there . . . a delightful sight." The famous Lion Monument, on the northern edge, is considered one of the most popular memorials in the world. Commemorating the courage and fidelity of a Swiss regiment that took part in the defense of the Tuileries in Paris in 1792, the "Lion of Lucerne" was designed by the Danish sculptor Bertel Thorwaldsen and carved in a sandstone cliff. Next to the Lion Monument is Lucerne's Glacier Garden, a series of potholes worn in the sandstone bed of an ancient glacier. Here, too, is the Richard Wagner Museum, filled with mementoes of Wagner's residence here, valuable original scores, manuscripts and a collection of old musical instruments. Among the historical points of interest are the covered Chapel Bridge with Water Tower, dating from 1333, and the well-preserved Old Fortifications and Musegg Towers, dating from 1350-1408. Over 500 years ago Lucerne was already noted for its Easter and Passion plays; since 1938 the tradition has found its modern counterpart in the annual Summer Music Festival. Extremely rewarding

Bremgarten, a gem of ancient architecture
Swiss Natl. Tourist Office

scenic excursions can be made to the tops of nearby mountains — the Pilatus, the Rigi and the Stanserhorn. While here you may also obtain some of the exclusive, engraved glassware produced by the skilled designers and craftsmen of Lucerne. . . . BRUNNEN is situated on one of the loveliest bays of the lake, where the country is rich in history. This is the country of William Tell, with many reminders of this romantic, legendary figure, including Tell's Monument and Chapel and the natural monument to F. Schiller, author of the play, *William Tell.* In Rütli Meadow, overlooking the lake, birthplace of Switzerland, representatives of three neighboring valleys met and took the oath that formed the Swiss Confederation in 1291 for the purpose of self-defense against a common foe. On December 9, 1315, representatives of the same highlanders, newly victorious over Louis of Bavaria, met at Kapelle Brunnen and renewed the Everlasting League. The Archives hous-

ing the Charter of Confederation are also located here. This charming town is an ideal center for lake bathing and fishing and for rambles in the mountain. . . . ZURICH (390,020), the metropolis and garden city of Lake Zurich, enjoys a rich cultural life and beautiful scenery. The magnificently decorated shop windows, the picturesque lanes of the Old Town and the lakeside gardens make strolling about it a delight. The most important places of interest are grouped together on both sides of the Limmat River in the center of town, including the Grossmünster, largest Romanesque church in Switzerland, begun about 1100 A. D.; the historic guild houses; the Fraumünster, cloister founded in 853 by Ludwig the German, with Paul Bodmer frescoes representing legends of the city of Zurich; St. Peter's Church, with the largest clock dial in Europe, and a little farther from the others, the Swiss National Museum, with an historical exhibition of the development of Swiss art and culture and valuable collections of paintings, sculpture, stained glass and old state rooms. . . . On the northwestern border, on the Rhine River, is the city of BASEL (183,543), whose Art Museum has an outstanding collection of Holbeins. . . . Between Austria and Switzerland, along the right bank of the Rhine River, is the German-speaking sovereign principality and constitutional monarchy of LIECHTENSTEIN, fourth smallest independent state in Europe. A mountain country, except in the western part, where VADUZ, the capital and chief city is located, its chief industries are farming, stock raising, weaving and woodcarving.

HIGHLIGHT MAP OF
ZÜRICH
SWITZERLAND
MAP SHOWS MAJOR STREETS
© C. S. HAMMOND & Co., N.Y.

MAP OF
ZURICH

Austria

MUSIC AND DANCING

Music and dancing, gaiety and wine, ancient castles and mountain scenery — these things mean Austria, land of emperors and dukes, of song and sport. Vienna, enchanting city on the magic Danube, home of the waltz and the thrilling Viennese opera. The sunny vineyards of Lower Austria and the Burgenland, producing the excellent, tasty Austrian wines. The famed **Tyrol** and **Carinthia**, with their magnificent alpine scenery the mecca of expert mountain climbers and skiers. Salzburg and Gastein valley, of picturesque, colorful folk costumes and dancing, center of the fashionable, sometimes exclusive, health-resort spas with their healing medicinal springs. And all set in the background of old medieval towns, regal palaces and ancient customs. From all these intrinsic features, the well-known "Austrian atmosphere" has resulted and is forever being renewed through the jovial open-heartedness of the people, their recognized musical endowment and their hospitable nature. It is this incomparable "Austrian atmosphere" that holds every visitor in its spell.

CHURCH FESTIVALS

Every Austrian village in the summer offers some particular entertainment, especially on Saturdays and Sundays. You will see some of the most beautiful costumes on "Corpus Christi Day" in June and on "Assumption Day" in August. Beginning in mid-summer and into fall, Austrian villages celebrate "Kirtag," that is the combined anniversary of the consecrating of the church and the Harvest Festival. The dates are set locally and announced only a few weeks before taking place.

FROM TYROL TO VIENNA

Climbing a turreted hill above Lake Constance (Bodensee) at the far western end of Austria is **BREGENZ**, a city antedating Rome. Even the medieval city gate and city walls are still there. The cable car swinging up the **Pfänder** offers a view across the gabled roofs to the old town and the flowery esplanade of the lake to the shores. An enchanting **boat trip** on Lake Constance (Bodensee) at night and an excursion to the **Bregenz Forest**, with its charming villages and peasant costumes dating from another age, are favorites with visitors . . . **FELDKIRCH**, south of Bregenz, is a medieval town boasting **arcades**, **old gates** and fragments of antique walls. The **castle** is seven centuries old but the quality of the wine, the singing and dancing have never been better. . . . To the east is **ST. ANTON**, a pretty alpine dorf famed for its bracing air, many pleasant walks and the tinkling, jangling passage through its main street, morning and evening, of herds of cows and goats. The **zither players, singers and dancers** here are of the best. . . . The historical center of culture and the main junction of the Tyrol, the province world-famous for its beautiful scenery, is **INNSBRUCK**, a Gothic city set on the Inn River at the foot of the majestic Nordkette Range. The **Hofkirche** contains the tomb of Maximilian I, the most elaborate tomb ever erected for a Christian king, and the **Tyrólean Folk Art Museum** has the world's best collection of folk art, costumes, etc. During the summer, native Tyrolean dancing is performed nightly at the **Hotel Maria Theresia**. Innsbruck's **palace** and **gardens** and the **Goldenes Dachl** (Golden Roof) inn are also of great interest. Excursions may be made from here to Berwang, a small remote village nestled in the mountains of the **Ausserfern** district, which is exceptionally rich in Alpine flora; the **Achensee**, Tyrol's highest alpine lake and near the 13th century **Tratzberg Castle**, site of imperial hunting parties in centuries gone by; **Neustift**, considered Austria's most typical alpine village, and the all-year skiing areas in the **Austrian Alps**. . . . Located southeast of Innsbruck at the end of the Ziller Valley, **MAYRHOFEN** is a center of weekly **peasant costume festivals** on Saturday and Sunday from mid-June through mid-September, with the gigantic annual festival taking place on the last Sunday in July. This beautiful alpine village is also famous for its spring flowers. . . . Closer to the eastern border of Tyrol province is **KITZBUHEL**, a medieval town now one of the country's most fashionable resorts during both summer and winter. If it's a gay night-life the visitor is seeking, this is an ideal place to go, since this town is famous for its "Tyrolean evenings." A cable car rises from here to the top of the **Hahnenkamm** . . . Continuing east, **LOFER**, an enchanting fairy-tale-like village, is very well-known for its beautiful alpine flowers. The **Hotel Brau** is decorated in typical modern peasant style by Austria's most famous contemporary architect, Clemens Holzmeister. . . . From the typical lake resort and mountain town of ZELL AM SEE excursions may be made to the **Krimml Water Falls**, the highest falls in Europe. . . . South of Salzburg is the ancient city of HALLEIN with the salt mines (open to visitors) at Dürrnberg. . . . Many-towered SALZ-BURG, one of Europe's most beautiful cities, is at all times bursting with music, history and natural charm. It is famous as the **birthplace of Mozart**, whose home may be visited, and for the **Salzburg Festival**, which starts annually in late July and terminates at the end of August, attracting many eminent musicians, conductors and music connoisseurs from all over the world. The **Abbey and Church of St. Peter**, with its fourth century catacombs, and many other **baroque and Renaissance churches** are also worthy of attention. The twelfth-century fortress-castle of **Hohensalzburg** is one of the best preserved examples of this type of architecture, and includes a park, museum and an excellent view of the city. Other palaces here are the **Mirabell Palace and Gardens** and the **Hellbrunn Castle**, with its famous water works. Delightful excursions can be made to Austria's highest mountain, the **Grossglockner**; the famous town of St. **Wolfgang** with "The White Horse Inn" of operetta fame; **Liechtenstein Gorge** and the village of **Oberndorf**, where **Silent Night, Holy Night** was composed . . . Between Salzburg and Linz is the SALZKAMMERGUT lake district — a treasure house of well-known holiday spots — romantic, poetic, lovely. Nestling between the mountains and hills, dozens of lakes, both great and small, reflect all the loveliness of this blessed landscape. One of the most daring cable lifts in Europe lays bare the unrivalled panorama from the **Feuerkogel**, while the new gondola railway from **Obertraun** opens up the secretive fairy-story world of the **Dachstein Giant Ice Caves** . . . At LINZ white steamers ply back and forth to Passau along the **Danube**, Austria's river of fate with her legendary shores, whose scenery changes from clear views over cosy villages to thick, green forest, through farming country, spacious and fruitful . . . Farther down the Danube, beyond the

wine country, is the fabulous, colorful city of VIENNA — romantic, historical, gay — in her lovely surroundings. Music is the visiting card of the lovely waltz city on the Danube and a stay amidst the lively, carefree life and cultural tradition becomes an unforgettable experience. Here are the **Cathedral of St. Stephen's**, one of the oldest and finest churches in the Catholic world, and the **Capuchin Church**, with the burial crypt of the Hapsburg emperors. Here are the many palaces, including the **Hofburg Castle** and the **Schönbrunn Castle**, with its magnificent coach collection. Here are the great art collections in the **National Galleries**. Here is the joy of taking a ride in a Fiaker around the **Ringstrasse** or eating a meal of the famous Vienna cuisine. And no one should miss at least one evening at the **opera** or at a **Heuriger**, a typical Viennese wine-garden. This city also has a world-renowned **Vienna Music Festival**, held during the month of June . . . In EISENSTADT, south of Vienna on the Leitha mountains, the **Haydn Mausoleum** and the **castle of Esterházy** are the two often visited chief cultural and historical attractions. Castles from the Middle Ages, such as **Forchtenstein**, **Schlaining** and **Güssing**, or **Bernstein castle**, now an exclusive pension, all have most interesting collections and are the stage for historical pageant plays. The immense **Neusiedler Lake**, the only lake on a plain on the continent, in the midst of the famous wine villages, is a popular resort throughout the year. Eisenstadt is in the Burgenland, secretive, ancient border country on the edge of the Hungarian plains . . . GRAZ, the old provincial capital of Styria, called the "Green Land" because of the wealth of beautiful woodlands, has on display the world's largest collection of **medieval armor** — enough to outfit 30,000 men and horses — a fascinating reminder of the many years of development and the deep-rooted traditions of these Austrian people and cities. **Eggenberg Castle**, a lovely baroque hunting castle; **Lur Grotto**, the world's largest alpine caverns, as well as the **city parks** are other attractions . . . At ADMONT, northwest of Graz at the entrance of the wild, romantic climbing country of the Gesäuse mountains, is an ancient **Benedictine abbey**, whose priceless library contains more than 120,000 volumes . . . A little west of here is ALT-AUSSEE, a quaint village with an unfor-

133

The swanky mountain spa of
Badgastein
Austrian State Tourist Dept.

gettable view across the lake into the
Dachstein Glacier . . . Close by is HALL-
STATT, one of Europe's most picturesque
lake villages, located near the site of the
lake dwellers settlement, which gave its
name to the pre-historic Hallstatt Age.
On June 9th the "Feast of Corpus Christi,"
one of the most elaborate Austrian feasts,
is celebrated with a lake procession, and
weekly peasant costume festivals are held
every Saturday and Sunday. Visitors should
not fail to have lunch on the lake shore
and to visit the local museum, with its
choice collection of relics and implements
dating back to the Ice Age . . . VILLACH,
near the point where the borders of Austria, Yugoslavia and Italy join, contains
an interesting Old Quarter and the Para-
celsus House. The "Villach Kirtag Festival" takes place on the first weekend in
August. Visits can be made to the twelfth-
century Cathedral at Gurk; the walled
town, of the Middle Ages; Friesach, whose
townspeople stage plays in the castle during the summer; Europe's best preserved
medieval fortress-castle at Hochosterwitz,
where on the first Sunday in September
the "Kirtag feast" is held in the keep and
courtyard, and the pre-historic excavations at Magdalensberg. Popular nearby
lake resorts include Velden, Pörtschach
and Maria Wörth . . . SPITTAL, with its
Renaissance castle and horse market and
fine park, is very near Villach. It is a gathering point for mountain climbers, who go
by chair lift to the mountain village of
Mallnitz, starting place for high alpine
tours, and a center for swimmers, who enjoy the Weissensee, one of the most lovely
and warmest lakes of the Carinthian Lake

Plateau . . . Between Mallnitz and Böckstein, the Tauern tunnel runs right through
the mighty barrier of the High Tauern
and joins the holiday centers of Carinthia
with the Gastein valley, whose world famous radioactive healing springs have
been recently enhanced by the amazing
cure results of the Böckstein tunnels. In
the elegant hotels and pensions of BAD-
GASTEIN, Europe's most fashionable spa,
and BAD HOFGASTEIN there are about
6000 beds available . . . Neither amateur
nor professional photographers will want
to overlook HEILIGENBLUT, considered
the most photogenic and most beautifully
located alpine village on the continent.
Situated at the foot of the Grossglockner,
it is the home of a famous climbing school.
Franz-Josef-Haus may be seen by driving
up the Grossglockner High Alpine road
. . . South of Heiligenblut is the pretty
little city of LIENZ. Utterly destroyed on
the last day of the war, its central square,
which boasts a pink castle, pale blue
houses, arcades, lacy wrought-iron balconies, has been restored completely. The
Castle Bruck has a distinguished Roman
collection, a splendid Egger-Lienz, De-
fregger Collection of paintings, a restaurant and a pretty view. The "Heimat-
werke" collection is a must, for East Tyrolean craftsmanship, which is unique, can
be seen and purchased there. Lienz Lake
Tristach is excellent for swimming. Interesting excursions include those to the
famed Roman excavation at Aguntum and
to Hinterbichl in the Virgen Valley, home
of the Vienna Choir Boys. A sunset in the
Lienz Dolomites is an unforgettable experience.

Spain

THE LURE OF SPAIN

No single adjective will suffice to describe a country as vast and varied as Spain. Within a few hours a tourist may be transported from regions of perpetual snow in the north to the radiant, sun-drenched provinces in the south. Spain has had a colorful past, and her traditions lend a uniqueness to the character of her people. Winter, spring, summer or fall, all seasons enhance some part of Spain — a land, in fact, with limitless interest for all. But more than this, you will discover that, unlike any other European country, a tour through Spain will impart a mystical experience which will last a lifetime. Spaniards call it being touched by *el alma de Espana* — the soul of Spain!

THE ROMANS CALLED IT HISPANIA

Spain's past is a tale of conquests and reconquests. Originally populated by a primitive race known as Iberians it was later a province of the Roman Empire and governed by Roman pro-consuls. After the decline of the Empire it was overrun by Vandals (Andalusia) and Germanic invaders known as Visigoths. In 711 A.D. Moslems from Africa swarmed up through the south at Gibraltar to occupy parts of Spain for nearly 800 years. The struggle between Christian and Moor continued until the famous monarchs, Ferdinand and Isabel, supplanted the last crescent with the cross in 1492.

BLOOD AND SAND

The great form of entertainment for the Spaniard is the bullfight. Almost every town has its own bull ring. The bullfighters — *toreros* — may become national idols just as ball players attain national renown in our country. Bullfights are usually held on Sunday afternoons (in Madrid and Barcelona they are held on Thursdays also). The bullfight is like a three-act drama. The first act brings on the *picadores* who ride into the arena and thrust steel-tipped shafts into the bull to weary him by loss of blood. During the second act the *banderilleros* exhaust the animal further by placing barbed darts in his shoulder. In the last act the *torero* seeks to tire the bull by having it chase his *muleta* (red cloak) which is manipulated with skill and grace. When the bull is sufficiently infuriated, the kill is attempted which consists of a clean thrust into the back of the neck and downward into the heart. The bull is dragged off by a mule team to the sound of a stirring march while a new bull is released into the ring to begin the drama anew. Six bulls are usually killed in a single afternoon. Some of the best bull rings are located in Barcelona, Seville and Madrid.

DINNERS AT 9:00

Good food and incomparable wines are the glories of Spain. Lunches are served from 2:00 to 4:00. Dinners are never prepared before 9:00 P.M. If you like new delicacies, Spanish food will enthrall you — Spanish dishes are not highly spiced, though well seasoned. A national dish is *cocido,* a stew made with meat, vegetables and garbanzos (chick peas). *Arroz con pollo* (chicken with rice) will delight the palate. *Paella* is the typical dish of Valencia, consisting of fried rice, shellfish, chicken, fish and meat, all deliciously combined. *Caldo* is the national soup of Spain — if soups can attain such distinction! It must be tried at least once. The wines, of course, are as fabulous as they are original in this land of grapes. You may sip the liquid radiance of a sherry from Jerez de la Frontera, from where the name sherry is derived, or you may savor the rich white wine of Málaga. In any case, you will observe that the drink of Spain is her native sherry and that there is a sherry to suit every taste. Sherries are typed according to taste and bouquet, **fino, amontillado,** or **oloroso.**

THE CITIES OF SPAIN

In the center of Spain the capital, **MADRID** (1,618,435), has hotels to satisfy all tastes and purses scattered throughout the city. A well-built town with attractive avenues such as the **Gran Vía** (Avenida José Antonio), the Broadway of Madrid, make walking through the environs an adventure at every step. See the Statue of Cervantes, Spain's great writer. From **Puerta del Sol,** the old gateway of the city that faces the sun, runs the Carréra de San Jerónimo, the street of fashionable shops. Along this thoroughfare may be seen the **Cortes** (Spanish parliament) built during the reign of Isabel II. If you take the **Calle de Alcalá,** Madrid's street of processions, you will not want to miss the **Academia de Bellas Artes** with its fine collection of works by Zurburán,

MAP OF
MADRID

Mengs and Goya. Further down is the **Plaza de Independencia** and the **Puerta de Alcalá,** a monument erected in the honor of Charles III. The **Prado Museum** with paintings by such masters as El Greco, Goya, Velasquez and Murillo are worth the visit to Madrid alone. A trip to **El Rastro** is a must. Here every type of merchandise is sold amid the constant hubbub of bargaining. The bull ring, **Plaza de Toros,** is the setting for exciting exhibitions of the national sport of Spain. (The season is from April to October.) Another memorable sight is **El Retiro Park.** Originally started as a luxurious palace for the English wife of Philip II, the park itself contains the statues of many of Spain's proud monarchs. The **University** and the **Royal Palace** are interesting attractions. The latter is a fine example of 15th century style with elaborate tapestries and beautiful gardens. This was the residence of Alfonso XIII, king of Spain, and has been left undisturbed since his voluntary exile in 1931. Many historic figures have made the trip to Madrid, one doing so involuntarily. It was no one less than Francis I of France who was held captive in a tower at the **Casa de Lujanes** by Charles V. . . . Within an hour's drive from the center of Madrid, about 30 miles, is the **Escorial** built by Philip II in 1563 and completed 21 years later. Constructed as a house of prayer and a sepulchre for Philip and his family, it contains a large monastery, a palace and a library which houses some of the rarest books in the world. . . . Also within a short distance from the capital

is **ALCALA DE HENARES,** birthplace of such notable figures as Cervantes, creator of the immemorable Don Quixote, and Catherine of Aragón, first wife of much-married Henry VIII of England. Here too, was founded by Cardinal Cisneros, great statesman and cleric of Spain, the **University of Madrid,** now located in the city proper. Visit the **Palace of the Archbishops of Toledo** and the **archives.** By all means enjoy a "comida" at the **Hosteria del Estudiante.** It is a typical 15th century inn; note the huge fireplace, goatskin wine containers and old trappings from the horses of caballeros, as well as the beauty of the interior courtyard with its quaint wall. . . . Former capital of Spain, **TOLEDO** is a city of art, history and romance where El Greco lived. Built by the Moors and recognized as the center of medieval learning, it is today the see of the primate of Spain. Among its notable landmarks are the **Cathedral of Toledo,** the **Moorish Bridge** spanning the Tagus River and the Alcázar, once the residence of the Cid, Spain's national hero, and site of the bitter struggle during the Civil War. . . . South of Toledo is CIUDAD REAL, (La Mancha), in whose vicinity you may retrace the journeys of Don Quixote and his faithful squire Sancho Panza where they tilted with windmills and made illusion of reality. . . . AVILA and SEGOVIA are laid in scenic richness. At Segovia, famed for its early Roman history, is one of the finest Roman aqueducts which is still in use. The Suloaga Ceramic Museum has one of the finest exhibits in Spain. Visit the "Segovia Alcázar" (fortress) most typical castle in Spain. Built by Alfonso VI, it has recently been restored. . . . LA GRANJA nearby is a splendid 18th century, French-style palace with magnificent gardens and splashing fountains. . . . AVILA is noted for its medieval wall, the finest example of its kind. It is still in a good state of repair, turrets and all. Visit the Cathedral and the Monastery of Santo Tomás. . . . The great plains of the province of CASTILE, broken here and there by tall sierras or lofty battlements of ancient castles, contains many quaint old towns, some over a thousand years old, such as AYLLON, SIGUENZA, TORDESILLAS and SORIA. It is in this last city that the splendid red of burnt earth dominates stones, bricks and landscape alike. It is truly the "Red City of Spain." . . . SARAGOSSA is a very old city which became famous for the extraordinary defense by its inhabitants against Napoleon. Since then it has been growing, and today it is a progressive and busy town. Visit the El Pilar church where the flags of all the American countries hang from the walls, as well as silver lamps offered to the Holy Virgin by devotees from all over the world.

NORTHERN SPAIN

The northern boundaries of Spain are formed partly by the massive chain of the Pyrenees and the beautiful Bay of Biscay. To the south of these natural barriers is a great land of rolling slopes and cool forests. Basques, Asturians and Galicians inhabit this area, still preserving their regional customs, dialects (the Basques have a language unrelated to any other tongue on earth), and their colorful, picturesque native dress. In this region, the foothills around SANTANDER and ASTURIAS are not easily forgotten. Bear, wild boar, wolf and deer live in the thickets which abound in this section. Also to be found here are the cave paintings

of ALTAMIRA, some of the earliest drawings made by the hand of man. . . . Close by SAN SEBASTIAN and BILBAO are some of the finest golf courses in the world. The Picos de Europa are a mountain-climber's paradise and the inland roads are excellent for cycling. Pelota, a regional game, is played with great skill by almost every villager in these provinces. . . . GALICIA is situated in the northwest corner of the Spanish peninsula. Inland from the surf that crashes with unrestrained fury against the cliffs of Cape Finisterre, is a gentle land of pine trees, heather and vineyards. The *rias* or bays of VIGO and PONTEVEDRA bear a striking resemblance to the fiords of Norway. The *Gallegos* or natives of this northern province still display their Celtic origins. Dressed in short skirts and beret and making music upon the ancient "gaita" (bagpipe), one would think that the hardy Scot had by some strange accident drifted from his northern home. . . . Halfway between PONTEVEDRA and LA CORUNA is SANTIAGO DE COMPOSTELA, shrine of Spain's apostle and patron saint, St. James. During the Middle Ages a steady flow of pilgrims journeyed over the Pyrenees and along the "French Road" to visit the hallowed sepulchre. Thus it was that along the way many of Spain's monasteries grew in size and reputation as they offered rest and food to the weary traveler. The city contains the famous Portico of Glory, a masterpiece of Romanesque art. The whole province of Galicia is celebrated for its delectable seafood — its lobsters, crabs, shellfish, prawns and shrimp are unrivaled for their delicate flavor. . . . In the northeast the visitor has three attractions to choose from: BARCELONA, SITGES and COSTA BRAVA. The first is a great city, second largest (1,280,179) in Spain. Here you can see an exact model of the Santa María in which Columbus discovered the New World. The Rambla, a wide avenue, displays its curious merchandise such as dogs, mice, birds and guinea pigs every morning. A sight to behold is La Sagrada Familia, "a mystic poem worked in stone." The edifice contains shells from the Philippines, angels playing trumpets, biblical scenes, animals and birds, all worked in colored stone. At night pay a visit to the Molino Theater where rank amateurs compete for theatrical fame, (admission price is the purchase of a drink;

Thousands thrill to the matador's skill in Madrid
TWA-Trans World Airlines

a knowledge of Spanish is unnecessary, perhaps an obstacle to the enjoyment of the jokes and songs of the players.) Be sure to visit **Pueblo Español** where each province of Spain is represented in typical style, and the annual **gigantic fair** here, of international interest, are spectacles not to be missed. . . . SITGES is the charming seaside resort of the area with a balmy all-year-round climate. . . . **COSTA BRAVA** (the Catalonian coast) has the loveliest summer climate in the country. Here pine trees grow even upon bare rocks surrounded by cork, almond and olive trees. The crystal-clear water reflects an amazing variety of hues. . . . Roman ruins at **TARRAGONA**, great Gothic monasteries at **POBLET**, green-velvet valleys of **ARAN**, winter sports at **NURIA** are made more unforgettable by a friendly people, the Catalonians, who drink their red wine from odd-shaped beakers and know how to cook. . . . Further down the coast is **VALENCIA**, city of the Cid whose glory is still preserved in epic and legend.

In **ANDALUSIA**, Spain's plastic beauty dazzles the eye. Its very name suggests magic, mystery and Moorish castles. From her cities the great figures of the Age of Discovery and Exploration embarked upon their voyages to find what lay beyond "the end of the world." Orange grooves, white-washed villages, bull-fighters, gypsies and the swirl of many-colored skirts blend themselves together to form a vision of chromatic splendor. For two thousand years different civilizations have left their imprint on the Andalusian soil.

SEVILLE (376,627) is enchanted: Countless scenes delight the eye and everywhere the atmosphere is redolent of the clinging aroma of orange blossoms from her world-famous groves. The slim elegance of the **Statue of the Giralda** (the figure of a woman representing Faith mounted atop the bell tower of the Cathedral) which moves like a weathervane in the slightest breeze, and the sweet fragrance from the nearby **Patio de los Naranjos** (orange groves) will remind the visitor that he has arrived in the land of Bizet's Carmen. The **Cathedral** here is magnificent and is one of the finest examples of Gothic architecture in the world. The **Santa Cruz section** is the Spain of the foreigner's imagination with its narrow tiled streets, patios and grilled windows through which a young *senorita* might be wooed to the accompaniment of a plaintive guitar. Christopher Columbus is entombed here and a library contains documents written in the discoverer's own handwriting. . . . The graceful columns of the magnificent **Mosque** at CORDOBA and the splendor of the formidable **Alhambra**, the fortress-palace in GRANADA, typify the geometrically beautiful Moorish architecture found throughout Andalusia. . . . Within a few miles from Granada is the **SIERRA NEVADA**, second highest range in Europe, where winter-sports facilities are excellent. These lofty mountains are but a few hours away from the sunny Mediterranean coast, making it possible to ski in the morning and bathe in the warm sea in the afternoon. . . . To the southwest is MÁLAGA, land of the famous grape. The Mediterranean coast from Málaga to Gibraltar enjoys a climate almost unequalled in the whole of Europe. This is due not only to its position on the southernmost top of the Continent, but to the protection by various chains of mountains from the northern winter-cold winds and summer-hot breezes that blow from the high Spanish plateau or tableland. The waters of the Mediterranean, warm enough to bathe in winter, are also pleasantly cool in summer. The sun shines on this coast almost constantly and the bathing is ideal, even in the hottest weather. Sword-fishing here is a favorite sport. . . . Inland, near RONDA, the sportsman may practice stalking the Spanish ibex, one of the finest game animals in the world. Ronda itself is one of the most unusual small towns in Spain. Famous as one of the last strongholds of the Moors, you find much Moorish architecture; also what is said to be the oldest bull ring in Spain. There is the former house of the "cid" or Moorish King of the area built on the side of a steep rocky cliff. You enter from street level and keep going down flight after flight, reaching the garden at the lower level and finally a door from which stone steps take you down to the bath at water level. The river which flows through the town provides a crossing for traffic. The city seems to be practically isolated from the rest of the world. . . . GIBRALTAR, the "Gates of Hercules," offers an imposing sight of a familiar Mediterranean landmark.

VACATION ISLANDS

The BALEARIC ISLES of Minorca, Ibiza and Majorca afford a change from the irregular features of the mainland. Peaceful coves, gnarled olive trees and towering cliffs provide the setting where a visitor may do nothing but drink in all the serenity of the Mediterranean atmosphere.

Majorca, the largest island, offers many attractions to the visitor. At Valldemosa you can see the room where George Sand and Chopin spent the winter of 1838 and the piano he used. Note the simple beauty of the Monastery with its drawbridge, secret door and lively flower-adorned patio. Watch the native dancers who dance with their hearts as well as with their feet. . . . Motor to ARTA and visit the caves where you will marvel at the beauty of nature and forget the outside world, listening to the beautiful music played by a string orchestra from a small rowboat. The beautiful coloring in the stalactites and stalagmites is highlighted by an unusual lighting effect. It's like a glimpse of another world. You'll leave feeling better in mind and refreshed in soul. . . . PALMA is an idyllic spot, overlooking the blue bay with its Cathedral spires reaching heavenward, little boats moored in the bay, fishermen coming and going and the blue, blue sky overhead. Nearby is an imposing castle on a hill overlooking the city, the Castillo de Bellver which makes an interesting side trip.

Gossip at the village well in rural Portugal
TWA-Trans World Airlines

Portugal

LAND OF SUNNY LEISURE

If you visit Portugal you will like the serious, warm-hearted people who have a friendly welcome for all who come to their shores. It is a land where the visitor may enjoy charming landscapes and curious old towns without ever being aware of the passage of time. Most of the people are farmers and live a life of simplicity rounded out by hard work. The northern half of Portugal is mountainous and the southern half, flat with some hilly regions; the climate is mild, for the most part, and springtime in Portugal is an enchanting season when the countryside is brilliantly covered by a rainbow of colored flowers.

AN EVENTFUL PAST

In many ways Portugal's history is like that of Spain of which it once formed a part. Rome brought Christianity and the Latin tongue; the Moors influenced architecture, music and mingled their blood with that of the local inhabitants. During the struggle with the Moors a national spirit began to emerge. A young French noble, Henry of Lorraine, was granted the "county of Portugal" by the Spanish Alfonso VI as a reward for his military services. The "county" was extended, and by 1140 Portugal had become a separate kingdom. Later King John I married a daughter of England's John of Gaunt. The Treaty of Windsor, concluded at this time between Portugal and England, is still in force and makes England Portugal's oldest ally. The fifteenth century was the Golden Age of Portugal's history. Inspired by Prince Henry, the Navigator, Portuguese mariners embarked upon their famous voyages. Names like Diaz, Cabral, Da Gama and Magellan testify to Portuguese leadership in the Age of Discovery. A new route to India, discovery of Brazil and the circumnavigation of the globe mark the zenith of power that Portugal had achieved in the civilized world. In 1580 Portugal was placed under Spanish rule, but sixty years later independence was regained, although some of her oversea possessions were lost.

THE BULL SURVIVES

The bullfight in Portugal is different from that in Spain. Some Portuguese bullfighters demonstrate their skill on horseback, others on foot, but in either case the bull is never killed in Portugal. Whatever your interest in bullfights is, you will find other opportunities for giving expression to your sporting instinct. If you like fishing, the rivers of the northern provinces are recommended. Resorts in the south afford good swimming, tennis and golf. Winter sports, such as skiing, are held each January and February in the Serra da Estrêla in central Portugal, the country's highest mountain range. Soccer games, the favorite spectator sport, are played every Sunday from October to July at the huge National Stadium in the outskirts of Lisbon.

GENEROUS MEALS

The Portuguese meal is served for the person with a big appetite. Four or five courses are standard — sometimes more! You can't go wrong on fish or seafood. The Portuguese are also fond of sweets and among their favorite desserts are *arroz doce* (sweet rice) and *ovos moles* (sweetened eggs). Also try *porco a Alentejana* (cubes of braised pork served with clams in their shell). *Dobrada* is also tasty and consists of tripe, prepared with white beans and sausages and served in a heavy cream sauce. There are hundreds of wines to choose from, including Madeira, of course, before the meal and port as the finishing touch. *Vinhos da casa* come with the meal and are likely to be very good. Portuguese rosé wines are among the best in the world and go well with any dish. Mateus Rosé is the most popular.

THROUGH CITY AND TOWN

LISBON (pop. 790,434) is a noble and gracious city rising tier upon tier above the ship-studded water of the Tagus River. It is a city of pastel-colored houses, broad, tree-lined avenues and narrow, winding streets. The center of the city is marked by Rossio Square and the Praça de Restauradores, which leads to the Avenida da Liberdade, a magnificent, tree-lined thoroughfare. This avenue leads to the Park Edward VII with its famous Estufa Fria (greenhouse) made of green slatted wood which allows tropical plants to bloom in an agreeable temperature. Always cool, it is a delightful place to visit on a hot afternoon. Splashing fountains, fish ponds, crystal-clear streams and meandering stone paths add to the beauty of the flowers and plants. Sightseers in Lisbon shouldn't miss the Tower of Belém on the edge of the Tagus which marked the land-

**MAP OF
LISBON**

HIGHLIGHT MAP OF
**LISBON
PORTUGAL**

❶ Praça do Comércio
   (D. José I Mon.)
❷ Ministérios
❸ Arsenal da Marinha
❹ Bank of Portugal
❺ Mus. of Contemporary Art
❻ Teat. Nac. D. Maria II
❼ S. Roque Ch. & Mus.
❽ Teat. Nac. S. Carlos
❾ Inst. Superior Técnico
❿ Conceição Velha Ch.
⓫ P. dos Restauradores
⓬ S. Domingos Ch.
P.= Praça   R.= Rua   H.= Hotel

MAP SHOWS
MAJOR STREETS

C. S. HAMMOND & Co., N.Y.

ing-point of Vasco da Gama after his venturesome expedition to India in 1498. Nearby is the **Jeronimos Monastery** where many of Portugal's kings, queens and heroes are buried. Both of these buildings, the tower and the monastery, are built in Manueline style, a type of architecture influenced by the Age of Discovery and consisting of intricate decoration and nautical symbols such as globes, twisted cables and the Templar cross which was displayed on the sails of early sailing ships. Also of interest near here is the **Coach Museum** which contains one of the best collections of state coaches in the world. Other outstanding sights are the **Royal Palace** (the **Castle of St. George**) which majestically crowns the main hill of the city and affords a magnificent panoramic view of the city and the Tagus; the **National Museum of Ancient Art** with the most complete and valuable collection of Portuguese arts and the **Zoo** with one of Europe's finest collections of animals and lovely gardens.

Nightlife is rather restrained here. Friends usually gather in cafes to indulge in pleasant conversation over small cups of strong coffee. The *Fado* Cafes may afford a new experience. The *fado* is a nostalgic ballad sung to evoke sorrowful sentiments. It is usually improvised by the singer who is accompanied by two guitars — one Spanish and one Portuguese. Most night clubs are found in the **Bairro Alto**, the old part of the city, and in the **Alfama**, where the old Moorish buildings still line winding streets. More enlightening perhaps is the

Port Wine Institute with its amazing list of hundreds of varieties of Port.

South of Lisbon is **SETUBAL**, center of Portugal's all-important sardine industry. Near here are a number of picturesque fishing villages and in Setubal are two interesting 16th century churches. . . . West of the capital on the seacoast is **ESTORIL**, a luxurious seaside resort and winter playground with a very popular **casino**. Popular as a home of ex-kings, it is attractively laid out with masses of flower beds. Take a short walk to **CASCAIS**, a colorful fishing town where each weekday evening a fish auction is held and the bidding is in reverse, in Dutch fashion. Famous also is the **Boca do Inferno**, a huge cave carved out by the sea, into which the waves rush with a deafening roar. . . . A little further up the coast is the resort-fishing village of **ERICEIRA** with an interesting old fort. . . . About twenty miles from Lisbon is **SINTRA**, site of the Royal Palace and Pena Castle perched atop one of the peaks from where you get a magnificent view of land and sea.

Nearby are the famous gardens of Mont-serrate, laid out by a wealthy Englishman in the last century, one of the finest gardens in Europe. . . . On the way to Sintra is QUELUZ with its great palace, the "Versailles of Portugal." Its formal gardens and park with little lakes and fountains are lovely and the interior is beautiful. . . . North of Sintra is MAFRA with its rather fascinatingly ugly monastery-palace. This vast edifice has no less than 5,200 doors and 2,500 windows and required 45,000 workers to build it. Its church towers house over 100 bells which may be heard fifteen miles away. . . . OBIDOS is a fascinating town contained within the crene-lated ramparts of its enormous Moorish fortress. . . . The great church at ALCO-BACA, one of the finest examples of Cistercian art in Europe, has the Cloister of Silence and huge monastic kitchens. The tomb here contains the remains of Portu-gal's immortal lovers, Dom Pedro and Inez de Castro. . . . Ten miles northeast is BATALHA containing the Church of Santa Maria, Portugal's "Westminister Abbey." Here lies John of Gaunt's daughter, English wife of John I of Portugal. The latter's son, Prince Henry, the Navigator, also lies buried here. . . . To the east is FA-TIMA, "The Lourdes of Portugal," one of the best known Catholic shrines in the world. Huge numbers of visitors gather and camp here on the 13th of each month from May to October to commemorate the appearance of Mary as reported by three Portuguese children in 1917. . . . Nearby is NAZARE with its fishing boats curiously painted and shaped like melon rinds. Most typical of Portuguese fishing ports, its in-habitants may be seen wearing their color-ful "Scottish" plaids. . . . Southeast is EVORA, inhabited by Phoenician, Iberian, Roman and Moor. The Roman Temple of Diana may be seen here as well as the Convent of São Francisco which contains the Chapel of Bones, a structure whose walls are lined with human remains. . . . Further north is COIMBRA with its fa-mous University (one of the oldest in Europe) and the only university in Portu-gal. The old Cathedral is reputed to be the finest example of Romanesque architecture in the Iberian Peninsula. . . . A little north of here is BUSSACO with its famous hotel converted from a former palace and its incredible park with trees of every kind and age including genuine Cedars of Le-banon. . . . Also near Coimbra is LUSO, a spa with well-known alkaline springs. . . . FIGUERA DA FOZ, thirty miles out-side the university city, has a beautiful ocean beach with fine hotels and casino. . . . To the north is VISEU, said to have been founded in 500 BC, and a splendid place to sightsee and "take it easy." Here are many fine palaces, a cathedral and a museum which possesses an excellent col-lection of Portuguese primitives. . . . OPORTO (284,842), to the north, is the country's business and financial center and is also a lively, noisy and bustling port, known for its artistically decorated cafes and its extraordinary Church of São Francisco. The church contains one of the most unusual collections of wood decora-tions to be found anywhere. This city is internationally known for its wine industry and has wine lodges where Port is tasted, blended and bottled. . . . Nearby is the pleasant resort of OFIR and, a little fur-ther, GUIMARAES, former capital and of great historic and architectural interest. . . . VIANA DO CASTELO is a beautiful coastal town in the north near the Spanish border. It is well known as a great lace-making center. . . . In the southernmost tip of Portugal are FARO and PRAIA DA ROCHA in the "Kingdom of Algarve," a strip of northern Africa which has wan-dered up to Portugal, ideal winter resorts with excellent swimming and fishing.

THE AZORES AND MADEIRA

The AZORES consist of nine islands having a temperate climate, although often rather damp and misty. They are well suited for raising grapes, oranges and pine-apples. Interesting places to visit are Ponta Delgada and Furnas with its thermal springs on São Miguel Island. The island's volcanic origin makes it quite scenic. . . . At MADEIRA, in a climate of eternal spring, one can lead a lazy existence and watch the sparkling sea. In some districts there are vineyards which produce the famous Maderia wine. This is really an enchanted land with incomparable moun-tain scenery and lush, tropical growth. The hotels here are adept at making life effort-less and pleasant. Funchal, the capital, lies in a perfect setting overlooking the sea with mountains on three sides in the back-ground. Visitors will enjoy every aspect of the town, the busy narrow streets, pic-turesque squares, the colorful market and the lovely town park.

Italy

LAND OF SEAS AND MOUNTAINS

Italy is one of the oldest countries in Europe. Her influence on European and world history has been enormous and enduring. Her influence in architecture, sculpture and drama, all the arts and sciences has affected their development the world over, beginning with the ancient Roman Empire before the Christian era, and then, after a lull, the reawakening in the Renaissance. This lovely land, washed by three seas and traversed by magical mountains, offers her visitors not only the finest in art treasures and historical monuments but a gay and charming modern world also. In Rome, Florence, Venice, Capri and the Riviera life is gay and sophisticated, with dining and dancing under the stars, sunning and swimming in luxurious surroundings. There is entertainment to suit every taste whether it be trying your luck in the casinos or simply relaxing and watching life around you. The Italian, and there are two distinct racial types (the northern fair-complexioned and the southern dark-complexioned), has a penchant for individualism which is expressed in everything he does, be it building a house just a little different from his neighbor's or running his business the way he chooses. The Italian is also a romantic and believes happiness is achieved by the sheer joy of living, breathing, sleeping and waking. He loves good music, good food, good wine and the other pleasures of life. Being a warm-hearted people, they welcome the visitor and will gladly, if given the chance, help him to fully enjoy his visit in their sunny land.

THINGS TO DO

A great part of Italy's charm to visitors is that there is always something to see, hear or do. In Italy, everybody goes to the opera and if you are there during the six months season, January through June, you will, too. In addition to La Scala, all the big cities have quality performances. In summer too, there is music. Outdoor concerts are most popular and in Rome and Venice especially the music is excellent. Italy is a Catholic country and it seems that hardly a day passes that there is not a feast or spectacle somewhere in the country, whether it be a local patron saint's day or a national religious day, such as Epiphany, Feast of St. Joseph, Corpus Christi, Feast of Sts. Peter and Paul or Feast of the Assumption. The celebrations are always colorful and well worth going out of the way to see. Sports of all kinds are ever popular, with automobile racing being probably the most exciting. Horse races, dog races and polo matches draw large audiences. The Italian national sport is *calcio* (soccer). Of course, mountain climbing, skiing and other mountain sports are at their best here, as are water sports, including sailing and under-water hunting. Tennis and golf are also popular, with courts and courses invariably set in picturesque surroundings, more often than not in view of the beautiful sea with a backdrop of snow-capped peaks. Another favorite pastime is cycling. A great event is the Grand Tour of Italy, which occurs in June and is followed with excited interest by all Italians.

ITALIAN FOOD IS TASTY

There are good restaurants in every city. From the big city cafes to the tiny, informal little restaurants in small villages, you will find food of high quality served with wine of equal goodness. The food is a bit starchy, perhaps, but you are on holiday, so forget your diet and enjoy the many tasty dishes. A few of the local specialties include *Carciofi alla Romana* (artichokes seasoned with special herbs and boiled in oil), *Cannelloni* (rolls of pastry, filled with meat and savory, covered with cheese, bechamel and tomato sauce), *Cotoletta alla Bolognese* (a Milanese veal cutlet garnished with melted cheese and covered with a tomato sauce), *Ossobuco* (veal cut across the marrow bone and served with a thick sauce and rice or green peas and mashed potatoes) or *Prosciutto con Fichi o Melone* (ham served with melon or fresh figs). Veal is the favorite Italian meat and is prepared in numerous ways, always good. Eggplant and artichokes are also favorites and equally good. Fish is excellent and there is a great variety. Be sure to try *zuppa de pesce* (a very spicy soup made with a large variety of seafood), especially good in Venice and Genoa. Cheeses play an important role in the Italian cuisine. There is a large selection of soft cheeses such as ricotta, fonina, robiolina, mozzarella, stracchino and bel paese; and of hard cheeses such as provolone, groviera and parmi-

143

The great Triumphal Arch of Constantine in Rome, one of the best-preserved ancient monuments
TWA-Trans World Airlines

giano. The spicy gorgonzola mixed with butter and eaten with pears is something to remember. Favorite dessert is fresh fruit, but there are a number of mouth-watering, rich little pastries such as *Mille Foglie* (creampuff), *Sainte Honoree* (chocolate and vanilla whipped cream tart) or *Zuppa Inglese* (cream pie soaked in liqueur and covered with a thick layer of whipped cream).

The vineyards of Italy produce more wine than any other country except France. From the north come the best red table wines, Barolo and Chianti being the two best known. The vineyards which produce Barolo are in Piedmont within a strictly limited district called Le Langhe, which comprises the vineyards of Barolo and a few adjoining parishes. Chianti is the wine of the vineyards of Radda, Castellina and Gaiole, three parishes known as Chianti Ferrese, in the province of Siena. Although Chianti is usually a red wine, there is now a little white Chianti made. There are also a number of good white wines, both dry and sweet, produced. Italians always drink wine with their meals and even in small restaurants you will find an adequate selection for each course. Among other Italian liquors are Brandy, Grappa, Strega and Maraschino. Vermouth forms the basis for a variety of aperitifs.

ROME (1,657,588), "The Eternal City," belongs not only to Italy but to the world. If you see only one Italian city, let it be Rome and plan to spend at least three days, for that is about the minimum time required to see just the most important sights. Many believe that in no other city in the world is there so much to interest the student or sightseer.

A good place to begin your tour is from **Via Veneto**, the most elegant street in Rome and where the U. S. Embassy and Consulate are located. It leads to the

Villa Umberto or Villa Borghese, a magnificent seventeenth century park which belonged to the Borghese family. The **Pincio Terrace**, across the park, affords a fine view of the city. Nearby the church of **Trinità dei Monti** overlooks the **Piazza di Spagna**, a lovely square with colorful flower stalls on the lower steps. This is one of the most romantic spots in Rome. Nearby is the house where John Keats died. From the square runs **Via Condotti**, the shopping street comparable to the Rue de la Paix in Paris or Fifth Avenue in New York. Across the Tiber via the **Cavour Bridge** is the **Palace of Justice** and the **Castel Sant' Angelo**, the massive round tower built in AD 235 by Hadrian as a mausoleum for himself and his successors. Through the years the tomb has undergone many changes, being used as a fortress, the seat of Conclaves and even the refuge for popes when Rome was under attack.

Close by is **VATICAN CITY** and the **Basilica of St. Peter**, the greatest Christian church, built by the Emperor Constantine in AD 324 close to Nero's Circus and over the Tomb of the Prince of Apostles. Recent excavations have produced evidence of the presence of the tomb of St. Peter, the first Pope, in the crypt. Before the church is an immense square surrounded by an elliptical colonnade, erected by Bernini, consisting of four rows of 284 columns. An Egyptian obelisk rises in the center of the Piazza and on each side is a fountain. In 1506 restoration of the church was started after designs by Bramante, and later carried on by the most celebrated architects of their day, including San Gallo, Peruzzi and Raphael. Michelangelo, who designed the magnificent dome, died before it was completed and his successor, Della Porta, took over. The façade is by Maderna. The new basilica was consecrated by Pope Urban VIII in 1626. It is

144

impossible to describe the beauty and grandeur of St. Peter's or the emotion it creates in all who visit it and its stores of priceless works of art. Among the various buildings from different periods which comprise the **Vatican Palace** are the very important **Vatican Museums** which include the Collection of Antiquities, the Library, the Borgia Apartments, the Rooms of Raphael, the **Sistine Chapel**, with Michelangelo's famous alfrescos of "The Last Judgment" and "The Creation of the World," and the Picture Gallery. Assembled here are more treasures than in any other of the great empires of the world. Next to St. Peter's the most famous of the medieval churches in Rome are the other three major basilicas built in the fourth century: St. **John Lateran, Santa Maria Maggiore** and St. **Paul without-the-Walls.**

Still on the west side of the Tiber, at the top of the **Gianicolo** or **Janiculum,** the beautiful promenade which leads through the former park of the Villa Corsini, is the great **monument to Garibaldi.** The surrounding terraces afford the finest panoramic views of the whole city. Across the Tiber the **Corso Vittorio Emanuele** leads past the church of St. **Andrea Della Valle,** with the largest dome in Rome after St. Peter's, and the sixteenth century **Church of Jesus.** Beyond the church is the **Piazza Venezia** dominated by the colossal **Monument to King Victor Emanuel II** which also contains the tomb of the Unknown Soldier. Also in this square is the **Palazzo Venezia,** which was erected in about 1445 for Cardinal Pietra Barbo who, as Pope Paul II, used the building as a residence. Many popes lived here in succeeding years, and it was the official seat of Mussolini during the Fascist regime. A flight of steps leads to the **Campidoglio** or **Capitol** (on one of the seven hills upon which Rome was built). In the center of the square rises the bronze equestrian Statue of **Marcus Aurelius.** In the background is the **City Hall,** flanked by the **Palazzo Conservatori** and the **Museo Capitolino,** designed by Michelangelo. Close by is the **Roman Forum** with its suggestive group of monuments, the Arch of Septimus, the Temple of Saturn, Trajan's column, the house of the Vestals, etc., which when studied seem to fall into a pattern and show you what this busy center of ancient Rome must have been like. Here it was that the large public meetings and games

were held, and the famous triumphal processions of Rome's emperors and generals, returning from conquest, passed along a winding street, called the Sacred Way, which ran through the Forum. Above the Forum is the **Palatine,** another of the seven hills and, according to legend, where Romulus traced the boundaries of the first city of Rome. Here still stand many colossal remains of the palaces, temples, stadia, and gardens built first for the wealthy private citizens and, later under Augustus, for the Emperor on this pleasant hill. Near here is the **Colosseum,** probably the most symbolic structure reminiscent of ancient Rome. Started by Vespasian and finished by his son, Titus, in AD 80, it was used for gladiatorial combats and had a seating capacity of 500,000. Here Christians were slaughtered for sport, and gladiators battled against lions or fought each other to the death. Sometimes the arena was flooded for mock naval battles. It is particularly effective when seen at night when the moon is full. The **Arch of Constantine,** standing nearby, is one of the best preserved ancient monuments. It was erected to commemorate the victory of Constantine over Maxentius in the Battle of Ponte Milvio, which was fought in AD 312. Another attraction nearby are the **Baths of Caracalla,** the most luxurious and sumptuous bathing establishment of the old world which accommodated 1,600 persons at one time. The building also contained libraries, reading rooms, a stadium, a gymnasium and dining rooms. World-famous open-air opera performances are now given in the ruins during the summer months. Beyond the baths, outside the ancient Roman wall is the **Old Appian Way,** built in 312 BC, once the most important of Roman Consular roads. On each side of the cypress-lined road may be seen ruins of the superb old tombs that lined the road. At the beginning of the Appian Way are the **catacombs,** which embody the oldest and most sacred Christian memories. This vast labyrinth of subterranean galleries is where the early Christians buried their dead and also where they hid during the persecutions.

In the center of the city is the **Pantheon,** the best preserved monument of ancient Rome. Here is where all the Roman gods were worshiped; it has been used as a church continuously for more than 2,000 years. Built in 27 BC by Marcus

Agrippa to celebrate the victory over Antony and Cleopatra, it was completely rebuilt by Hadrian and dedicated to the pagan gods. It was restored by Septimus Severus and Caracalla in AD 202 and was finally consecrated as a Christian church in AD 609. It now contains the tombs of the Kings of Italy. In the center of the **Piazza Colonna,** the heart of the city, rises the **Column of Marcus Aurelius.** Near here is the fabulous **Fountain of Trevi** with its remarkable figures and innumerable jets and cascades. If you throw a coin into the fountain you will be sure to return to Rome. Close by is the **Quirinal,** the former Royal Palace and now the residence of the President of the Republic.

These are but a few of the wonderful sights awaiting you in Rome. In addition to things to see and do in the city itself, there is much of interest in the outskirts. You should also visit the bathing resort of **Ostia** (the Lido of Rome), **Ostia Antica** with its ruins of an ancient port, the fashionable beach of **Fregene** which is surrounded by a lovely pine woods, **Tivoli,** the pleasure resort of the Romans, famous for the beautiful waterfalls formed by the Aniene River, and **Villa d'Este,** the magnificent villa built in 1549.

ROUND ABOUT THE COUNTRY

Most visitors to Italy concentrate on touring her lovely cities with possibly a stop on the Riviera or Capri. However, for those who have the time to tarry awhile, there are picturesque little out of the way villages and towns and incomparable mountain and maritime scenery. As a matter of fact the mountains which form the backbone of Italy seem to rival the sea in providing spectacles as magnificent as any in the world.

In the south of Italy is **NAPLES** (1,-011,919), noted for its pleasant sunny climate and disposition, the beauty of its bay and the overpowering majesty of its towering volcanic hills. Although damaged during the last war, there are still many beautiful buildings to see. Sightseeing highlights include the magnificent 17th century **Royal Palace** built by Fontana for Pope Sixtus V, the colorful **public gardens** and, of course, the **San Carlo Opera House.** The **National Museum** has a magnificent collection of Greek and Roman masterpieces. **Castel Dell'Ovo,** in the bay and reached by a bridge, has a fascinating legend about the derivation of its name. Virgil, considered a sorcerer in the middle ages is supposed to have put a newly laid sea serpent egg into an iron cage, and by magic the egg was transformed into a castle. Visit the **Cathedral** with the famous **Chapel of S. Gennaro,** patron of the city. One of the most popular Neopolitan churches is **Santa Maria di Piedigrotta** where every year in September takes place a picturesque festival which brings throngs of visitors to the city. **Santa Lucia** is the smart quarter of the town with many hotels and palaces located on the **Via Partenope,** the beautiful sea drive that affords a fine view of the lovely Bay of Naples. At the small harbor here are a number of delightful restaurants serving the tasty Neopolitan dishes.

GAY, SUNNY, COLORFUL CAPRI AND ENCHANTING ISCHIA

Long a honeymoon and vacation paradise, **CAPRI** is easily accessible by boat from both Naples and Sorrento. A day spent here will be a delight never forgotten. Most of all you will enjoy the boat trip to the famous **Grotta Azurra,** a walk to the point where you can view the **Faraglioni,** the famous rocks jutting out of the water, a drive to the village of **Anacapri,** a visit to **Villa Jovis,** one of the palaces built by the Roman Emperors Augustus and Tiberius, and a visit to **Villa San Michele** built on the ruins of an ancient Roman villa by the author of *The Story of Michele,* Axel Munthe. Though highly commercialized, this enchanting island has lost none of its charm in 2,000 years and its natural beauties remain unspoiled. In the center of Capri is the characteristic "Piazetta" crowded with open-air cafes where all the tourists sit for hours sipping drinks while the natives sit on the steps of the church that overlooks the square.

Guarding the northwestern entrance to the beautiful Bay of Naples is the island of **ISCHIA,** noted for its mineral springs and beautiful, everchanging scenery. **Mount Epomeo** towers 2,589 feet high in the center of the island. The port of **Porto d'Ischia** consists of a small perfectly sheltered port surrounded by white oriental-looking houses, steep, narrow streets, villas, gardens and beautiful pine woods. From here the road leads to **Casamicciola,** famous for its mineral radio-active waters. The beach here is especially fine and slopes gently into the sea. All over the island there are lovely walks and an excellent twenty-mile long road circles the island, offering magnificent panoramas. Excellent local wines are to be had, including the fine scented Epomeo.

ENVIRONS OF NAPLES

East of Naples is **Mount Vesuvius** and the ruins of **POMPEII.** A visit here is an absolute must. The story told by the ruins will be hard to believe even after you see them. Excavations into this silent city reveal a way of life cut off almost instantly, but preserved in stone since 79 AD, by Vesuvius' first recorded eruption. Visit the **Amphitheater,** the **Foro,** the various temples, the streets and the houses with magnificent mural paintings predominantly in **Pompeian** red.

affording views of magnificent scenery and picturesque villages.

SICILY

PALERMO (483,777), located at the foot of **Mount Pellegrino,** is a most beautiful city. Norman art treasures are still preserved there. The most important monuments are: the **Cathedral, Palazzo dei re Normanni** (of Arabian origin and restored by the Norman kings), the **Cappella Palatina** (richly decorated with twelfth century mosaics), the **Norman Cathedral of Monreale** (its walls are entirely covered with inlaid marble and mosaics and the cloister is adorned with 200 twin columns), the church of **San Giovanni Degli Eremiti** (of oriental style and famous for its thirteenth century clois-

Naples is justly proud of her
beautiful bay
TWA-Trans World Airlines

SORRENTO, south of Naples, noted as a shopping center and for fine swimming, perches on a high cliff with its houses hidden in parks, orange and palm groves and gardens. Below is the intensely blue sea and the fine beach. . . . **POSITANO** is another picturesque town nearby made famous by the many artists who live here. Dazzling white houses contrast with the clusters of green trees descending towards the sea. Quaint, narrow little streets lead to the beach. . . . **AMALFI** whose name recalls memories of bygone days and the powerful Italian seafaring republic, is an ideal weekend spot. It has an interesting **Norman Cathedral.** The exquisite **Amalfi Drive,** running along the coast is a marvelous road, sometimes winding its way through green valleys, sometimes running along the edge of the sea,

ter), the **Palazzo Zisa** (in Moslem style) and the magnificent villas and parks with their tropical plants. . . . About seven miles away is **MONDELLO,** the beach of Palermo, which offers good bathing facilities. . . . On the Ionian Sea, **TAORMINA,** enhanced by gorgeous villas and gardens full of rare plants, and pervaded with the scent of orange blossoms, is the most popular winter and summer resort in Sicily. It is situated on a promontory about 300 yards above sea level and gives a magnificent view of the snow-capped volcano, Mount Etna, in the background. There are many monuments worth visiting, including the **Greek Theater,** which stands on the summit of a hill, the fifteenth century **Palazzo Corvaia,** the **Palazzo Santo Stefano,** the **Cathedral** with the seventh century fountain, and the medieval castle.

. . . Further along is **CATANIA** (297,531), rich in art treasures. The bathing resort here, **La Plaja,** is especially good and is picturesquely set in a thick pine grove.

North of Rome, in the center of Italy, is the beautiful green region of Umbria with its large **Lake Trasimeno. PERUGIA,** its capital, has long been a cultural center and is famous for its **Italian University of Foreigners,** founded in 1307. . . . Nearby is **ASSISI,** the native town of St. Francis. It is a picturesque town and has maintained intact its medieval aspect. The **Basilica,** composed of two churches built one above the other, contains the tomb of St. Francis. . . . West of Perugia, in Tuscany, is another charming medieval town, **SIENA.** Here the famous **Palio** takes place every year (July 2nd and August 16th), attracting tourists from all parts of the world. The Palio is a fifteenth century pageant in which the seventeen boroughs of the town are represented. In the museum here is a magnificent collection of Italian primitive paintings. . . . North of Siena is beautiful **FLORENCE** (376,383); cradle of the Renaissance. It flourished under the Medicis in the 1400's and almost every building in the old part of the city has claim to recognition as a Renaissance shrine. This was the "home town" of Dante, Petrarch, Bocaccio and Galileo and many of Michelangelo's sculptures and Raphael's paintings may still be admired in Florence, each on the spot where it was created. A good place to start sight-seeing is the **Piazza del Duomo** (Cathedral Square). On the same square you can visit the great **Cathedral of S. Maria del Fiore** and admire the splendid dome created by Brunelleschi. Adjoining is the Gothic **bell tower** or **Campanile,** designed by Giotto. Opposite the cathedral is the **Battistero of San Giovanni,** famed for its Ghiberti doors. Other celebrated churches are **Santa Croce,** where Galileo, Michelangelo, Foscolo, Alfieri, Canova and many other great Italians are buried; **Santa Maria Novella** (thirteenth century) with its charming cloisters; **S. Lorenzo,** one of the masterpieces of Filippo Brunelleschi, and **S. Miniato al Monte,** located on a hill which gives a view of the whole city of Florence. The **Piazza della Signoria** is another interesting square which is in effect an outdoor museum, dominated by the tower of the thirteenth century **Palazzo Vecchio** which can be seen from almost anywhere in the city. The outside of this palace is stern and forbidding, but the interior is magnificent. Directly opposite this palace's main entrance is the **Porch of the Lancers,** which contains many wonderful groups of statuary, including "The Rape of the Sabines" and "Hercules Slaying the Centaur." Toward the Arno is another palace, the **Palazzo Uffizi,** which now contains the National Library, State Archives and one of the world's most famous art galleries. A corridor running from the Uffizi to the **Pitti Palace** (with another famous museum) crosses the Arno, over the **Ponte Vecchio,** the last of six bridges that once crossed that river into Florence. It is more than a bridge; it's a market place and a cluster of little shops offering all manner of wares in silver, leather, cloth and other skillfully fabricated materials. Near here you should visit the **straw market** where tourists and natives bargain for lovely goods in linen, straw and leather. You should also visit the **Giardino di Boboli,** the lovely garden with its amphitheater where some of the celebrated performances of the **Maggio Musicale** take place during the months of May and June. Nearby is the famous **Michelangelo Square** atop a hill giving a marvelous view of this beautiful historic city of Florence. . . . In the outskirts of Florence is **FIESOLE** which is famous for its fantastic, rich villas. Situated on a high hill, it gives a panoramic view of Florence and the whole surrounding Arno Valley.

Westward is **LEGHORN** (140,722), the seaport of Florence and site of the **Italian Naval Academy.** Although war damage has left little of historic interest, a visit to **Montenero Sanctuary** is worth while. . . . A half-hour away is PISA with its famous **Leaning Tower** and superb **Cathedral.** . . . About twelve miles northeast of Pisa is the old walled town of LUCCA, often overlooked by tourists. A drive to Lucca is well worth while because it gives you a view of the fertile Italian countryside. In Lucca itself you will see the town's picturesque narrow streets. . . . Northwest of Pisa the bustling port of **GENOA** (680,563), is a fascinating mixture of the medieval and the modern. The old section, with is narrow winding streets, stairs and bridges hemmed in by buildings dating from the Middle Ages, is the most interesting part. Genoa is also a Riviera city and is famous for its surrounding country. Among the many beautiful palaces are the **Palazzo Doria, Palazzo Reale, Palazzo dei Dogi** and the **Palazzo Rosso**. Don't forget to see the **Cathedral of S. Lorenzo** and the **House of Christopher Columbus**.

THE ITALIAN RIVIERA

All three seas of Italy have their individual beauty and characteristic coasts, but the blue of the water seems bluer and the white of the sand seems whiter on the Riviera. Like the adjoining French Riviera, it offers every possible facility for a seaside holiday, from modest little villages to pretentious villas. **SAN REMO** is one of the more fashionable resorts with an excellent climate all year round. It has a vast range of amusements, including the Casino, dog shows, motorcycle races and flower carnivals. San Remo is noted for its beautiful flower market. . . . Not far from San Remo is **ALASSIO**, situated at the center of a bay and surrounded by green hills dotted with luxurious villas. It has a lovely sandy beach, a casino and tennis club. . . . On the coast below Genoa **SANTA MARGHERITA LIGURE** is another ideal resort. Here you will enjoy both a rocky and sandy beach. . . . A little further below Genoa, **RAPALLO** is a favorite with both Italians and foreigners. Here festivals, golf tournaments, regattas, horse races, art exhibitions and shows take place all year round. . . . Next is **PORTOFINO**. Situated in a very small bay, it is one of the most picturesque and charming towns of the Riviera and is famous for its underwater fishing. Portofino attracts a very cosmopolitan society of artists, movie stars, aristocrats and industrialists, although it is a typical fisherman's village.

. . . Further below is **VIAREGGIO**, an elegant, modern resort with smart cafes, shops, bars and restaurants. At Carnival time it is especially gay and colorful.

TURIN AND MILAN

TURIN (712,596), became the first capital of the Italian kingdom in 1861. Testifying to this period of greatness are the city's monuments: The **Palazzo Madama**, which was the seat of the first Italian Senate, the **Royal Palace** and the **Carignano Palace**, where the proclamation of the kingdom of Italy took place. On the hill near the city is the **Basilica of Superga**, where many members of the royal family of Savoy are buried. Turin is mainly an industrial city. The Fiat Corporation's factories are here, together with famous distilleries and chocolate factories. . . . West of Turin is **SESTRIERE** in the Cottian Alps. Because of its magnificent snow fields this is one of the leading winter resorts in Europe, beloved by every type of skier. It is also favored in the summer with a dry healthy climate. . . . East of Turin is **MILAN** (1,268,994). A most important industrial, commercial and financial center, it is a bustling city where "time is money." Second only to Rome in population, it is also a center of culture and intellectual life. First among the art treasures is the **Duomo**, the vast Gothic cathedral, completely constructed in white marble. Started in the fourteenth century and finished in the nineteenth, it rises 355 feet from the ground. Its spire carries a gilded statue of the Virgin Mary, known as the Madonnina. Nearby is the **La Scala**, the world's most famous opera house. Churches you should visit are: the **Basilica of Saint Ambrogio**, founded in the fourth

A romantic ride on the Grand Canal in Venice
TWA-Trans World Airlines

century by St. Ambrogio, Patron of Milan; S. Maria Delle Grazie, where the world-famed "Last Supper" by Leonardo da Vinci can be seen, and the Basilica of San Satiro with its beautiful Baptistery and many others. An outstanding monument is the fourteenth century Castello Sforzesco, which was the residence of the Lords of Milan. Beyond the castle is the park and the Arco Della Pace, erected by Napoleon. Among the museums and galleries you should visit are the Brera Picture Gallery with its valuable paintings and the Ambrosiana Library and Gallery. A most important International Trade Fair is held every year in Milan during the month of April. Countries from all over the world participate. Milan also offers many sport attractions, including the San Siro Hippodrome, the Sport Palace and the Ice Palace. In the vicinity of Milan is the beautiful and romantic lake region with its summer and winter resorts in the foothills of the Alps.

ITALY'S LAKES

The lake region displays amazing scenic contrasts. Luxurious hotels and magnificent villas, built amidst subtropical vegetation, line the lake shores. Rising in the background are dark green hills which gradually merge into rocky mountains covered with snow. These beautiful lakes are either on or very near the Italian-Swiss border. LAKE COMO, just two hours away from Milan, offers many attractions. During the season, April to October, there are yachting races, fashion shows, concerts and of course, tennis and water sports. The town of COMO is well known for its silk industry, one of the finest in the world. Important monuments include the eleventh-century Cathedral, with its Gothic façade and the ancient Palazzo del Broletto. In the surroundings there are many beautiful villas such as the Villa Olmo. . . . CERNOBBIO is probably the most popular and fashionable spring and fall resort on the lake. The small town is linked to Como by boat and streetcar. . . . A favorite center for excursions and sports is BELLAGIO, situated on a promontory in the center of the lake. . . . East of Como is LAKE GARDA, another beautiful and popular resort area, with the tourist centers of GARDONE RIVIERA, where the poet Gabriele D'Annunzio lived, and SIRMIONE, famous for its hyperthermal sulphurous waters. Both are ideal for a vacation or for a long rest. . . . On LAKE MAGGIORE, west of Como, STRESA is the finest climatic resort. The season opens in April and ends in September, which is generally the best month of the year to visit the lakes. Famous for its mountain excursions, walks, swimming and fishing.

ITALY'S MOUNTAINS

The mountains are everywhere in Italy, forming the backbone of this peninsular country and then running across the northern "top" of the country like the crossbar on a "T." Rounded, green-covered mountains, bald, rocky hillocks, regal, snow-capped peaks — all types of mountain scenery can be found in this beautiful land. Mountain climbing is a favorite Italian pastime and the skiing grounds are among the finest in Europe. In northern Italy some of the popular skiing resorts are SESTRIERE (described under Turin), MADONNA DI CAMPIGLIO, SAN MARTINO DI CASTROZZA and SELVA DI GARDENA. CORTINA AMPEZZO, known as the "Queen of the Dolomites," rises 4,015 feet above sea level and can be reached by motor coach from Milan and Venice or by train from Rome, Milan and Venice. Situated in the picturesque Ampezzo Valley and surrounded by the stately Dolomites, Cortina is a great international tourist center during the summer and winter months. There are two aerial cable cars to Mount Pocol (over 5,000 feet high) and Mount Faloria (6,954 feet high), and several chairlifts. Automobile races, tennis and golf tournaments, mountain climbing, fishing, shooting, skiing, skating and bobsledding provide plenty of excitement for vacationists and tourists.

THE QUEEN OF THE ADRIATIC

VENICE (316,228), is one of the most unusual cities in the world and traditionally one of the most romantic. Its geographical position, great historical past and incomparable art treasures are the main reasons for its universal fame. Nevertheless, this paragon of cities got off to a rather unromantic start. In the year 425, Attila the Hun drove the people of northern Italy from their homes and literally out into the Adriatic, where they found refuge on a few bare and dismal islands. Settlements, increasing in number, were built up there. As time passed, the security of their isolation enabled the Venetians to become prosperous and powerful. By the end of the seventh century, Venice had become an independent state and her ruler, or doge, one of the strong men of Europe.

Venice today is built on and around about 120 small islands, close together, in the middle of a great lagoon about a mile and a half from the sea. It is cut up by 150 canals and tied together by 400 bridges. The only means of transportation is by foot on the few very narrow streets or in the characteristic gondolas, boats, motor boats and waterborne streetcars (Vaporetto). The most famous bridges are the **Rialto** and the **Ponte dei Sospiri** (Bridge of Sighs). You will want to see the **Piazza di San Marco**, Venice's only large square, paved with marble. Colonnades and arcades enclose this square on three sides and on the fourth is the **Church Campanile of San Marco**, a marvelous example of Byzantine architecture. Across the square is the **Torre dell' Orologio** and its clock. Two giant bronze Moors strike the hours with sledge-hammers on a large bell. They have been doing it ever since 1497. Not far from the square is the **Palazzo dei Dogi**. A must, of course, is a ride along the **Grand Canal** with its two miles of historic buildings, principally palaces and churches. Robert Browning died in the **Palazzo Rezzonico**. Lord Byron wrote part of "Don Juan" in the **Palazzo Mocenigo**, and Richard Wagner composed the great second act of "Tristan and Isolde" in one of the Palazzi Mocenigo. Each year, in July the traditional **Regata of the Sposalizio de Mare** (Marriage of the Sea) takes place on the Grand Canal. Other palaces along the Canal include the stupendous Gothic Ca' D'Oro, the Ca' Foscari and the Ca' Pesaro. See also the church of **Santa Maria della Salute**, built as an expression of thanks for the end of the plague in 1630. One of the most enjoyable pastimes is a walk through the crowded and narrow alleys, over the arched bridges and into the curious shops of the artisans.

When you've had your fill of the treasures in art and architecture, visit the **Lido**. This beautiful stretch of beach runs along a shoestring island that divides the Venice lagoon from the open sea. It is the most fashionable seaside bathing resort in Italy, attracting a cosmopolitan crowd from all over the world. Here, too, are the **Palazzo Municipale** with the world famous **Casino** and the **Palazzo del Cinema**, where the International Film Festival

is held in September each year. The season is from May through September.

Famous islands in the vicinity are: **MURANO,** a village on five small islands, is world renowned for its centuries-old glass blowing art. Marvelous masterpieces of this work in blown glass from the fourteenth to eighteenth century are exhibited in the **Museo Vetrario**. Nearby, the sixteenth century church of **San Pietro Martire** contains paintings by Giovanni Bellini, Tintoretto and Veronese. **TORCELLO,** a small village in the lonely lagoon, was once an important town and still preserves some of its notable medieval monuments. These include the Church of S. **Fosca,** an octagonal building of the eleventh century and the Cathedral erected during the ninth and the eleventh centuries. **BURANO** is a famous island where the most exquisite laces are made.

Southwest of Venice is one of the oldest and most interesting cities of Italy, **BOLOGNA** (339,195). The **University of Bologna**, founded in 1088, is the oldest in Europe and one of the greatest in the world. The city retains a medieval aspect with its arcaded streets, two remarkable **leaning towers** and hundreds of impressive buildings and churches, all rich in art treasures. Among the many interesting buildings are the **Palace of King Enzo,** the 13th century **Church of San Francisco,** the **Fine Arts Museum** with a fine collection of paintings by Francia, Reni and Domenichino, the **Observatory** and the medieval town hall. Bologna is equally famous for its culinary art. Here, in the restaurants and hotels is found some of the best food in the whole of Italy. . . . A fascinating side trip from Bologna, or from Florence, is a visit to the tiny republic of **SAN MARINO,** atop a mountain in the Apennines. The capital, built on precipitous Mount Titano is a quaint, old-fashioned town with crooked streets built of cobblestones. San Marino is the oldest republic in the world and her people preserve the customs of their ancestors of the 15th century. **Postage stamps** are perhaps her greatest claim to fame and the country does a brisk trade with collectors. . . . Nearby, on the Adriatic is lovely **RIMINI,** second only to the Lido of Venice as a popular Adriatic resort. Beach and sea here are excellent, as are hotel accommodations, and it is a great cosmopolitan favorite.

Greece

BIRTHPLACE OF WESTERN CIVILIZATION

Located in the main stream of civilization, Greece has witnessed from time immemorial the clash of men and ideas and the encounters of armies and of cultures. Birthplace of democracy, she has stood for centuries in the defense of Western civilization from the onslaughts of despotism and tyranny. Determined by Greek thought, by the character of the people and the geographical position of the country, its history stretches back more than 4,000 years. It is a fascinating story of great achievement in the face of recurrent adversity. All of modern Greece is a visual history of European civilization, with the grandeur of the world's greatest art treasures scattered across the land, making the entire country an immense exhibition of art. You may follow the evolution of art through the ages, step by step, from the earliest Minoan Period in Crete to the classical period, which produced such masterpieces as the Parthenon, and later to the Christian era when magnificent Byzantine art flourished. Cradle of civilization and birthplace of the gods, land of legend and beauty which has inspired centuries of art and the essence of philosophy, Greece welcomes the world.

NATIONAL DISHES AND DRINKS

Many Greek specialties may be obtained in the "tavernas," or restaurants of a local character. Among the best are *souvlakia* (lamb or pork on skewers) and *dolmathakia* (rice and meat in vine leaves). There are numerous excellent Greek table wines, including sweet dessert wines like "Mavrodaphni," "Samos" and "Santorini," and there are several good brands of Greek brandy. "Retsinato" and "Kokinelli" are national wines flavored with resin, which are served in the "tavernas." Fish has also been an important food in Greece for centuries.

LAND OF MYTH AND MAGIC

The stage for the greatest artistic and political achievements in all history is mighty ATHENS (pop. 565,084), birthplace of the thought and philosophy underlying the entire structure of Western civilization. Socrates, Plato, Aristotle — the role of masterful thinkers who made their homes in this amazing city is almost unbelievable. To no other do the people of the entire world owe such a rich and meaningful heritage. It was here that the human intellect was first unshackled and the principle of individual freedom brought to birth. But Athens stands for more than progress; she represents the highest pinnacle of attainment in the human aspiration toward the beautiful. Outlined against the sky, overlooking Athens, stands the majestic Acropolis, with its Parthenon, built in the fifth century B. C., a landmark of extraordinary beauty, grandeur and monumental power, a timeless citadel of a most dynamic period in the history of mankind. The mellow-golden marble Parthenon, temple of the Virgin Goddess Athena, with its massive grace, built by the artist Phidias and the architect Ictinus, is the most majestic of all man's architectural achievements and the visitor can return again and again — viewing it from moonlight to bright noon sunshine — and be overwhelmed each time by unsurpassed beauties not seen before. Here, in this building, is the noblest realization of an ideal of perfect symmetry and proportion — of absolute simplicity without rigid stiffness, of imposing grandeur without heaviness, while a perfect dignity and propriety were expressed in every detail. At the entrance to the Acropolis is the great Propylaea, built by Mnesicles, another stately building of the Periclean Age, flanked by the little Temple of Niki. Of a little later age is the Erechtheum, a very rich example of Ionic style, with the famous Caryatid porch on its north side. There was also a wealth of sculptured ornamentation used on this wonderful hill, and many precious fragments of the work of unknown artists of the highest rank are sheltered in the small Acropolis Museum, supplying an invaluable record of early Attic art. A good notion of the theater in Roman times is given by the Theater of Dionysos, on the south slope of the Acropolis, where the great Attic dramas were first performed, and the nearby ancient Odeon of Herodes Atticus, where classic tragedies are still presented. The National Archeological Museum is particularly noted for works of archaic art. This fabulous city, though, is not lost in her glorious past, but adds still more to her accomplishments as the capital of modern Greece. Facing the Tomb of the Unknown Soldier and bounded by the attractive

**MAP OF
ATHENS**

HIGHLIGHT MAP OF
ATHENS
GREECE

LEOF. ALEXANDRAS

❶ Parthenon
❷ Acropolis
❸ Erechtheum
❹ Acropolis Museum
❺ Propylaea
❻ Portico of Eumenes
❼ St. Nicodemus Ch.
❽ Pl. Syntagmatos
(Constitution Sq.)
Pl. = Square
H. = Hotel
Leof. = Avenue

© C. S. HAMMOND & Co., N. Y. *To Ellinikon Airport* MAP SHOWS MAJOR STREETS

National Garden is the strikingly simple **Parliament Building (Old Palace)**, where the Chamber of Deputies meets. The guard of honor at the **Royal Palace**, on another side of the National Garden, is the fighting **Evzone Legion**, famed in legend and song, who wear the traditional Greek "Foustanella." Greek youth shares the pride of earlier generations in the tradition of athletic competition, so one of the attractions of the capital is the annual **Pan-Hellenic Games**, as well as other athletic events held in the magnificent, marble **Stadium of Athens**. Still a center of exciting artistic expression, it presents for the art-lover of today performances by the influential **Greek National Theater** and the annual **Pan-Hellenic Exhibition of Fine Arts**. Northeast of Athens is the **Marathon Mound**, collective tomb of the Athenian soldiers killed in the famous battle against the Persians in 490 B. C. The Byzantine **monastery** of nearby **Daphni** is a finely conceived monument of one period in the long history of Greece: the eleventh century A. D. Representing a moment of supreme inspiration, the famous mosaics in this magnificent edifice are of singular and powerful beauty. . . . On the isthmus linking Peloponissos with mainland Greece is **CORINTH**, with the old paved streets and fountains, made familiar by Paul's sermons and the Epistles to the Corinthians. The ancient city was dominated by the impressive height of **Acro-Corinth**, on which much of the formidable system of ancient fortifications still stands. The walls of the nearby ancient

Citadel of Mycenae, built about the fourteenth century B. C., look down upon the fertile valley below. Agamemnon, known to us through Homer's *Iliad*, ruled here. The entrance to the citadel is by the famous **gate** over which are sculptured two colossal lions — the earliest work of sculpture extant upon Greek soil. It is now clear that a prehistoric civilization was widely spread over the Aegean Islands as well as Greece proper, flourishing for several thousands of years, and that the race disappeared, being superseded by the incoming Greeks. Mycenae is but a late manifestation of this civilization that radiated from Crete in the remote past, a civilization whose greatness was hinted at by the Athenian legend of King Minos and the human tribute exacted by him from primitive Athens. Many of the great "beehive" **tombs** have been found in a royal **cemetery** of the seventeenth century B. C. **Epidaurus**, east of Mycenae, is typical of a shrine of healing. Invalids from all parts came to be healed by the Divine Physician, Ascelpios. You can make out not only the

The Acropolis and the Parthenon, world's greatest architectural masterpiece
Royal Greek Embassy

temples and **altars** of the shrine, but also the **hall** in which the patients slept. The 2,000-year-old **Theater of Epidaurus,** said by Pausanias to be the most beautiful in Greece, attracts eager throngs whenever concerts or dramas are given. . . . Near Sparta, with the site of the **Temple of Artemis Orthis** at which the Spartan youth were scourged, in southern Peloponissos, is **MYSTRA,** once a flourishing Byzantine stronghold and cultural center. Within its small area survives a millenium of magnificent Byzantine glory and splendor. . . . **OLYMPIA,** center of the worship of Zeus and scene of the Olympic Games, is situated in a fertile valley in northwest Peloponissos. The foundations and many of the columns of the **Temples of Zeus and of Hera** are visible. There may also be seen the **gymnasium** where the competitors trained, the **porticos** for the shelter of visitors and the **administrative buildings,** as well as the **stadium** in which the contests took place. This festival, held every fourth year, was the Olympian cycle used by the Greeks for the dating of historical events. On a separate terrace are a number of **treasuries** of the different Greek states. The sculpture from all these buildings is in the **museum,** containing the pediments

and other sculptures from the Temple of Zeus, second only as architectural sculpture to that of the Parthenon, and the two original masterpieces: the Hermes of Praxitiles, with its clear expression of manly vigor in its prime, and the Victory of Paeonios, still expressing the perfect ideal of graceful poise. . . . On the spur of Mt. Parnassus on the mainland, at the little village of **DELPHI,** the famous oracle of Apollo had been situated from very ancient times. The temple and other buildings are placed on a succession of terraces and it is now possible to walk up the inclined zigzag of the sacred way, on its ancient pavement, past some of the buildings. Above the great **Temple of Apollo,** seat of the Delphic oracle, is the finely preserved **Theater of Delphi,** where classic tragedies are still performed, and high above all, a stadium was laid out for racing and other contests. The festival at Delphi, called the Pythia, was held at intervals of four years, alternating with the Olympic Games. In the contests, competitors from the whole Greek world contended for the simple prize of laurel which made life-long heroes of the victors. In the **museum** are the remains of the architecture and temple sculpture, with some very fine statues including the bronze charioteer made for the princes of Syracuse. Just beyond the precinct is the impressive gorge out of which flows the Castalian spring. . . . Known as the "monasteries in the air," the monasteries of **METEORA** in Thessaly were built on pillarlike rocks of great height before the fourteenth century A. D. Of the 23 monasteries originally built with almost incredible difficulties, five are still in use. . . . The seven Ionian Islands are like gems rising out of the blue sea and Kerkyra or Corfu is the loveliest and most splendid of them all. It has a luxuriant vegetation, among which orchards and olive groves abound. The attractive town of **KERKYRA**, capital of the island, surnamed by the Byzantines "the

beauty. **MYKONOS** is the most picturesque of Aegean Islands and most fashionable bathing resort in the Eastern Mediterranean. . . . The mythical birthplace of Apollo and Artemis is **DELOS**, famous sanctuary island of ancient Greece, featuring the primitive **cave-temple of the god** and **rich houses** with magnificent mosaics. . . . **SANTORINI**, or **THERA**, is the island with an underwater volcano, one of the strangest natural phenomena of the world, into the crater of which ships can sail. . . . Mythical birthplace of Zeus, chief of Olympian deities and god of hospitality, is **CRETE**, the "Great Greek Island" famous alike for its history and its natural beauty. Detailed evidence of the way of life of a civilization going back

The chorus of Hecuba (Euripides) at the ancient theater of Epidaurus
Dimitrios Harissiadis, Athens

town with two summits," is one of the most picturesque in the country, with its narrow, shaded streets characteristic of the seventeenth and eighteenth centuries. Of the many fine churches, the richest in Byzantine paintings and silver is **Saint Spyridon Church**, near the famous Esplanade. Besides containing many other interesting monuments and providing many marvelous views, Corfu is also a popular resort, because of the fine seashore and the coastal waters abounding with fish, being especially renowned for lobster fishing. . . . The celebrated Isles of Greece, immortalized in the classic stanzas of Lord Byron, are pearls set by nature in the beautiful Grecian Seas, scenes of indescribable

more than 3,000 years B. C., known as the Minoan period, is to be found in the **Palace of Knossos. The Herakleion Museum** houses a spendid collection of the remains of this wonderful culture. The island's combination of mountain, plain and sea, of luxuriant fertility and of barrenness is characteristically Greek. . . . The resort island of **RHODES**, largest and most beautiful of the Dodecanese, is known as the "Isle of Roses." One-time home of the Knights of St. John, it possesses unique Greek **antiquities** and impressive **medieval remains**, the wonderful and brilliant **Petaloudes (Valley of Butterflies)** and an up-to-date fashionable and popular spa at **Kallithea.**

French North Africa

ISLAM MAGIC AND ANCIENT RUINS

You who want your journey to take you away from the daily round of duties and over-familiar sights, go to North Africa. You will make a journey through history, from Phoenician Carthage to Roman Timgad, to shades of Byzantium at Tebessa and the creations of Arabo-Berber civilization — Fes, Tlemcen and the holy city of Kairouan. Geographically the variety is just as great. There are the magnificent, warm Atlantic and Mediterranean beaches and the coast roads winding high above the sea; the gorges and crests of the Atlas mountains whose scenic beauty cannot fail to arrest even the most fervent mountaineer; the oases and the Sahara, a spectacle of overpowering grandeur and simplicity. Gleaming white, serene, mysterious, intense, scintillating, curious, traditional — all this, and more, are Morocco, Algeria and Tunisia. Everywhere, from Marrakech to Tunis and from Algiers to Mogador, the sun, the sky and the sea contribute to the creation of so fascinating a scene that even before leaving it you will feel the pangs of nostalgia.

EASTERN COSTUME

On the streets, some women in North Africa still hide beneath the all-enveloping, cloaklike robe called *djellaba* and mysterious veil. Otherwise, in the home, they wear an overdress of rich material, called a *foquia,* above another magnificent full-length gown called *kaftan,* with embroidered slippers on their feet. The Berber women and men also wear colorful, flowing robes, whose designs indicate the specific tribe from which they come.

MOROCCAN MANNERS

In Morocco, only Mohammedans may enter the mosques; other people are prohibited from doing so and this prohibition sometimes even extends to the immediate surroundings of the mosque. The Medersas or Mohammedan colleges may, on the other hand, be visited and they give a very good idea of Mohammedan religious architecture.

ORIENTAL FEASTS

Oranges of all kinds, including mandarins coming straight to the table from nearby groves, translucent dates called "fingers of light" in Arabic and other fruit are fitting dessert to a meal of mutton or chicken *couscous* in an appetizing sauce, or perhaps, a dish known as *mechoui du sud* (a sheep roasted whole over a wood fire and served with melted butter). Mint tea is the national beverage of the North Africans and along with mint tea or Moorish coffee served in small cups, they serve Arab sweetmeats, including "golden fritters," *zlabias* with honey, "gazelles' horns" sprinkled with sugar and *rahat-lokoum* (Turkish delight) perfumed with rose or lemon.

SKIRTING THE SAHARA

The economic capital and national port of Morocco is CASABLANCA (pop. 551,322). Here in a queer but interesting melting pot including Europeans, Maghrebines, Levantines and Americans, veiled Arab women, wearing flowing robes, are seen frequenting the enormous, strikingly modern Orthlieb swimming pool, the world's second largest. . . . A little beyond Cape Blanc, the happy fishing ground of lobster-catchers, looms up the old, clean, quiet Portuguese town of MAZAGAN. The remains of the citadel, which the Portuguese began in 1506 and held until 1769, give it a warlike air, while the thick-walled sea gate, the old *darses* or harbor basins, the massiveness and color of the bastions looking out to sea recall to a great extent Lorrain's seascapes. The imposing, gloomy armory adds to the town's picturesqueness. Once the first port in Morocco, Mazagan still has its beach, about three miles long, the finest and most attractive in the country, its casino built on piles, one of the most up-to-date markets, mild winters and cool summers — a perfect spot for relaxation and rest. . . . SAFI, famed for its sardines and pottery, is now the second port of Morocco, but still retains the picturesqueness of the very old trading stations. After going to the wave-splashed Chateau de Mer (sea castle) and loitering on the Potters' Hill, you will enjoy a rest in the Place du Rbat, in the heart of the city, where lanes and impasses form an isle of quiet provincial life. As in the *ksours* in the south, some of these little streets are kinds of tunnels cut out in the high walls of the houses. A change of scenery is afforded by the drive past the black earth of the plains of the Abda-Ahmar and the steep, bare coast to Cape Cantin, the Soloeis of the ancients. . . . Seen from a distance, MOGADOR, white and gleam-

Street in Algiers' mysterious Kasbah
TWA-Trans World Airlines

ing, seems to float upon the waters. There are few spots affording such strikingly contrasting views. On the one hand the Atlantic; on the other, the woods; between them the dazzling, peaceful waters of the little port, romantic islets and a jewel of a town, iridescent in the filmy mist. This town, built in 1765 after the plans of one Cornut, a captive in Morocco, used to be a privateers' hideout. The **fortress, Portuguese bridge** and the **old port** provide vivid recollections of its romantic, adventurous past. The **Purpurariae** is where Juba II set up the dyeworks which supplied Rome with the most-sought-after purple. In the semiarid country to the east, pert little dark-coated goats graze high in the branches of argan trees, often climbing as high as twenty feet to reach the light-green, olivelike fruit. . . . With so little rain it is scarcely ever troublesome and a temperate climate of remarkable regularity, **AGADIR**, called the "Gate to the South," is probably the finest seaside resort in Morocco. For a glimpse of real Arab village life, visit **Tiznit**, a walled desert town, with the **old mosque** and the peaceful **holy spring**. Goulimine, further south, is the home of the famous "blue men." The faces, hands and wrists of the men of this tribe have a bluish tinge from the dyed robes they have worn since centuries back. . . . MARRAKECH (238,436), the great Berber capital and to Moroccans the "city of earthly delights," is a huge oasis at the foot of the snow-clad Atlas peaks. Each Thursday the great *souk* is held out-

side the city walls when the people of the countryside and the caravans of camel traders come to barter with each other. Within the city walls, the center of activity is the public square of **Djemaa el Fna**, where entertainers attract the inhabitants during the long hours of the night. In this city where each section carries one kind of goods, most fascinating is the **Street of the Dyers**, north of the square, where vivid skeins of newly dyed wool drips from walls and bamboo poles slung from roof to roof across the street. Vying in appeal is another attractive section, the aromatic **spice market**. Near the square is the world-famous **Koutoubia Mosque** with its tall minaret. The lovely **Menara Gardens** are outside the *medina*. . . . The intellectual and cultural capital is beautiful **FES** (200,946), founded more than 1,100 years ago, really three cities. The brightly decorated arch of **Bab Bou Jeloud** is the gateway to Fès el Bali (Fès the Old), where cobbled lanes, so narrow the pedestrian may touch both sides at once, twist between walled courtyards. Within the old city is the **tomb of Moulay Idriss II**, one of Morocco's holiest shrines. The narrow **Bab Moulay Idriss**, the **Alley of Sanctuary**, is the passageway where thieves, murderers or political refugees are traditionally safe from arrest. Heart of the city is the 1,000-year-old **Karaouine University**, a scholastic center for the whole world of Islam. The nearby town of **Azrou** is a popular winter-sports area. The holy city of **Moulay Idriss** is so sacred to Moslems that no Christian or Jew may spend the night there, although you may visit it during the day. . . . MEKNES (159,811), west of Fès, is a trading and business center, with hustle and bustle not found in the other ancient cities of Morocco. It was the incredible "Black Sultan" of the Alaouites, Moulay Ismail, who made it famous. Picking it as his capital in 1672, he wanted to ·make the city a rival of Versailles by building palaces and government buildings of enormous size. . . . RABAT (161,461), the white and green Shereefian capital, is on the coast. The French Resident General lives here in a magnificent home surrounded by beautifully tended formal gardens. Gates decorated with the finest art open through the ramparts of the "Victory Camp" of the Almohade sultans, a camp of soldier-monks trained for holy war. The part of this haven overhanging the meandering river of Bou Regreg bears the golden ruins of the Hassan Tower. The quarters of the seafront offer the spectacle of a very different town from the smiling Rabat of villas and gardens. The tawny Kasbah of the Oudaias, the color of the rock it stands upon and the oldest part of the city, is a miniature city in itself. Built in the twelfth century as the equivalent of an English feudal castle, the Kasbah now shelters artisans and craftsmen who keep alive the old handcrafts passed down from generation to generation. Farther inland is the stately, yet delicate ruin of Merinide necropolis of Chellah, built, it is thought, on the site of the Carthaginian and Roman trading stations. . . . In Algeria, near the western border, is the attractive town of TLEMCEN, with its lovely scenery of green orchards and the fine remains of the early Spanish period. Neighboring Bou-Medine contains the ruins of the thirteenth-century mosque Mansoura with its imposing walls and famous minaret. . . . Between Tlemcen and Oran is SIDI BEL ABBES, birthplace of the French Foreign Legion, with its renowned military museum devoted to the history and feats of arms of this crack force, where the First Regiment of the Legion is stationed. . . . ALGIERS (266,165), the largest town in Algeria and the majestic capital, is the residence of the Governor General, seat of the Algerian Assembly and a large, busy, prosperous port. Outstanding views of the city's famous bay may be obtained from the balcony of Saint-Raphaël, the basilica of Notre-Dame d'Afrique and the upper end of the Kasbah. A progressive, modern city, Algiers has luxurious shops in its newer section. In the picturesque seaside region west of the city are the Roman ruins at incomparable Tipasa, including La Grande Basilique Chrétienne (Tomb of the Christians), one of the most beautiful archeological sites on the Mediterranean; and the Roman ruins and valuable collection in the museum at Cherchell, formerly Cesaree, the capital of an artist king before becoming the capital of a Roman province. In the Kabylia, country of the Berbers and of the impressive Djurdjura mountain range, are curious hill-top villages whose inhabitants jealously guard their ancient way of life. . . . Southeast is BISKRA, a luxuriant oasis and an ideal winter resort as well as a spa and health resort. . . . CONSTANTINE, formerly known as Cirta and dating from Phoenician times, having been a fortress which held out against numerous sieges, is extremely pleasant and attractive, built on a steep rock bordering the Rhummel canyon. Because of its unique position there are many bridges in the town, especially spectacular being the suspension bridge of Sidi M'Cid. Do not miss taking a walk through the famous Rhummel Gorges. Beyond the thick forest groves northeast of the city is Bône, with its beaches, plains, orchards, orange groves and Roman ruins. Algeria has given birth to many famous men, but at their head is to be found St. Augustin, the most illustrious of the fathers of the Christian church, who was born at Thagaste and became bishop of Hippo Regius near Bône. It was in this town that he made his famous sermons and wrote those works which contributed so profoundly to the development of Christian civilization in the West. South of the city, Timgad, a striking example of Roman colonization in Numidia and equal in importance to Pompeii, and Lambèse, its neighbor, are among the most interesting military cities of the Roman world preserved to us. . . . Not far from the border of Tunisia are the Roman ruins at TEBESSA, whose Temple of Minerva is the most remarkable relic of pagan religion in North Africa. The basilica here, over-shadowed by the memory of the great St. Augustin, is the greatest and best-preserved of the Christian monuments. . . .

The two important routes across the Sahara connecting North Africa with Central Africa are the HOGGAR ROUTE and the TANEZROUFT ROUTE, and if you want to have a really rare experience, these vast stretches of unforgettable, attractive country can be crossed without any particular danger. The Hoggar route travels through such places as Ghardaïa, the quaint capital of the very barren region of M'Zab; the magnificent gorges of Arak and In Guezzam, with its many prehistoric remains. The Tanezrouft route goes through the oasis of Beni Ounif, whose neighboring oasis of Figuig has 200,000 palm trees and curious fortified villages; the desert of

Musée du Bardo. The attractive village of Sidi Bou Said, facing the sea, overlooks the ruins of Carthage. The Church of Africa, of which the seat was at Carthage, furnished numerous martyrs, including Felicity, Perpetue and Cyprian, and many great and wise men, including Augustin and Tertullian. The ruins of the Basilica of St. Cyprian, at the foot of the red rocks of Sidi Bou Said, offer an entirely unique spectacle. Here, too, is the small, compact St. Louis Chapel, raised to shelter the remains of the French king who died at Carthage of the plague in 1270 A. D., after arriving here at the head of the Eighth Crusade. . . . One of the most

The Cathedral in ancient Carthage, city of Hannibal
TWA-Trans World Airlines

Tanezrouft, "the land of thirst," and the Savannah vegetation near Aguelhoc to Gao in Niger. . . . TUNIS (364,593), the capital of Tunisia, comprises the modern city set out like a chessboard and the Mohammedan quarter, with a very special Oriental character. The position of the town, sheltered by the bay, is most attractive and its fine mosques and colorful markets are famous. Covered by the dust of Tunisia, the vestiges of the first beginnings of the Christian church in this country have come down to us more intact than in any other country, and notable collections from these remains are in the

revered centers of religion in Islam is the holy town of KAIROUAN, south of Tunis. The twelve-centuries-old Grand Mosque is the principal one in North Africa. . . . Situated in barren surroundings nearby is the gigantic amphitheater of El Djem, one of the most impressive Roman buildings in Africa. . . . On the coast is the important fishing village of SFAX, whose Mohammedan part of town is still protected by imposing fortified ramparts. . . . Further down the coast is the lovely bathing resort of DJERBA, celebrated for its climate, the industrious activity of its inhabitants and its Hebrew remains, unique in the world.

Egypt

6,000 YEARS OLD

This ancient African country was a tourists' delight centuries before many other lands were even discovered—attracting tourists with the very same magnetic power luring visitors here today. The pyramids were a source of wonder even in Biblical times; the exuberant cosmopolitanism combined with Oriental mystery of the cities brought pleasure seekers from afar; the healthy climate brought its quota of distinguished personages and the regions of the Upper Nile, with its unequalled examples of age-old artistry and skill, seized the imaginations of romantic travelers. The story of Egyptian civilization is a long one, since from the dawn of recorded history there has been a civilization in the Nile valley, contributing not only learning and inspiration to other countries but exotic pleasure and relaxation to happy visitors from all corners of the globe.

THE NIGHTS OF RAMADAN

Travelers particularly will enjoy visiting Egypt during the Arabic month of Ramadan, the Moslem month of fasting, held during the spring. During this traditional season of remembrance, initiated by the Procession of the Ro'ya and the children's march through the streets, while swinging colored lanterns and chanting traditional songs, the minarets of the mosques are encircled throughout the night by their rings of twinkling lights. Ramadan was chosen as the month of fasting because, according to legend, this is the time the first revelations came to the Prophet Mohammed. From dawn to sunset no food or drink whatsoever may be consumed. To sustain the faster throughout the day, a light repast is taken shortly before dawn and in the small hours of the night, there may be heard the rhythmic beating of a *tablah* (drum), as down the street comes the "Masahharati," awakening the fasters by name for their "Sohoor," as this little meal is called. It generally consists of light foods such as yoghurt, a special kind of beans, fruit and thirst-quenching drinks. At sunset there is nothing more welcome than a glass of *Amar-el-Din,* a delicious and nourishing drink made from sheets of dried apricots, and many people like to break their fast with this. Soon after come the sounds of youthful voices and the sight of swinging lanterns as the children gather together to sing the songs of Ramadan. In some households there are lanterns hanging over the doorways and inside can be heard the chanting of the Koran, and perhaps a glimpse may be caught of a room full of guests, making their Ramadan calls, listening to the chanting and eating the nuts and sweetmeats offered during this month. In some of the older coffeehouses there are recitals from the Arab romances by a minstrel, accompanied on the *rababa,* a small stringed instrument played like the cello. The sunset breakfast, the evenings of pleasant companionship, the songs and the chanting, the lanterns and the lighted minarets — all this makes of Ramadan a happy and a well-loved time.

THE NEW OLD LAND

ALEXANDRIA (925,081), Egypt's second city, is not only a vast Mediterranean port but also a delightful seaside resort, with endless stretches of golden sands and perfect bathing beaches. The very name conjures up the great panorama of its history, which began in 332 B. C., when Alexander the Great entered Egypt with his victorious armies and overcame the Persian rulers. From the small strategically placed fishing village called Rakotis which he selected, this seaport grew to serve for over 1,000 years as the capital of Egypt. Two of the main streets of ancient Alexandria, present-day Fouad Street and Nebi Daniel Street, were then as now the centers of the commercial, cultural and political life of the city. After Alexander's death, the Ptolemaic Dynasty founded here the famous library and museum, attracting the greatest philosophers and scientists of the ancient world. The ruins of the library, the most important of ancient times, are all that remain. Several necropolises of the Hellenistic era have been excavated and those of Mustapha Pasha, Chatby and Anfoushy, together with the Catacombs of Kom El-Chougafa, are particularly interesting, with their wall paintings, collections of funeral furniture and scenes from ancient mythology. The old lighthouse, built during the time of Ptolemy II in 280 B. C. on the Island of Pharos and counted one of the Seven Wonders of the World, was destroyed by earthquake in 1375. The lighthouse which took its place stands at Ras-el-Tine in the western part of the city. Not far from the catacombs is another famous landmark: "Pompey's Pillar." This great column, erected in honor of the Emperor Diocletian in about 297 A. D. and standing some 88 feet high, is made of a beautiful red granite, polished into an exquisite style, while the foundation is made of blocks taken from more ancient buildings, all with their respective inscriptions. A great deal of the story of ancient Alexandria may be pieced together in the **Greco-Roman Museum**, containing a wonderful collection of sculptures, sarcophagi, mummies, jewelry, coins and figurines, including the famous "Tanagras." In the western part of the city is the vast **Montaza Palace** of ex-King Farouk, with its great corridors, sumptuously furnished rooms and atmosphere of unrestrained luxury, surrounded by the magnificent park, formal gardens and pavilions. The fine **Abu el-Abbas el-Morsi Mosque**, dating from the thirteenth century, has exquisite arabesque decorations, wall mosaics, wood engravings and teakwood pulpit. The splendid **Corniche**, which runs along the seafront, leads to the famous, gay suburb of **El Raml** or **Ramleh**, called the Egyptian Riviera. Some of its twelve beaches, particularly those at **Stanley Bay** and **Sidi Bishr**, challenge comparison with the smartest bathing resorts in the world. Excursions include **Abukir**, now a delightful fishing village, site of the ancient city of Canope, where Nelson fought Napoleon; **Rosetta**, a medieval town at one of the mouths of the Nile; and the desert cemetery at **El Alamein**, west of Alexandria, where in 1942 General Montgomery outmaneuvered Rommel's Panzers and annihilated the

Afrika Korps. . . . In 969 A. D. General Gohar invaded the region of **CAIRO** (2,-100,506) with his Arabs and laid the foundations of the capital. This new city was influenced by Heliopolis, on the right shore of the Nile, and Memphis, on the plateau of Giza, on the river's left bank. In Cairo is an entire throbbing and bustling section of the medieval East with its own history and folklore, its own culture and customs, its own philosophy and its own Arabian Nights atmosphere. In this section of covered alleyways, known as the "Mousky," is the famous colorful bazaar of **Khan El Khalili**. Just across the street from one entrance to the Mousky is the great **El Azhar Mosque** and university, religious and educational fountainhead of the entire Moslem world and the oldest university in existence. Founded in 970 A. D. by Gohar, this mosque, whose name means "splendid mosque," with its pure gold ceiling and large columns of gleaming purple and blue tiles, is the greatest work of the Fatimid Dynasty. Here were preserved Muslim science and Arabic language and literature during the dark ages which followed; it is still the greatest center for Muslim culture today. One of the most important monuments in Egypt is the **Mosque of Ahmad ibn Tuln**, built in the ninth century. Of an oblong-shape design, it is notable for the beauty and splendor of its arrangement. It was here in this mosque in 1296 that Prince Hussam El Din, having been charged with the murder of Sultan El Ashraf Khalil, took sanctuary for a whole year. Not far away is the **Sultan Hassan Mosque**, considered by many as the finest example of Arabic architecture

Cairo's bazaars are treasure chests of intricate native art
TWA-Trans World Airlines

in the world, built during the fourteenth century in the Mameluke period with stones from the pyramids. This massive edifice, with its exquisite proportions, has daring minarets, including the highest in Cairo; a masterful arch ornamented of marble and gold; sumptuous, decorated golden and bronze doors; unique latticed windows and the oldest *kursi* (reading stand) found in Egypt, a masterpiece of fine cabinet-making. Opposite is the Citadel, built in the twelfth and thirteen centuries on one of the slopes of Al Mokattam Mount, from where it commands a wonderful panorama of the city of Cairo and, beyond it, the Pyramids and the Sphinx on the west bank of the Nile. Conspicuous for the sheer beauty of its architectural design is Mohammed Ali Mosque, standing in the middle of the Citadel, with its huge dome, alabaster-faced walls and its delicately slender minarets. In the center of Cairo, on the right bank of the Nile, stands the large, square, white Museum of Egyptian Antiquities, or the Egyptian Museum. After 84 years of existence, this museum houses the richest existing collection of antiquities. All archeological ages from prehistoric times to the Roman Empire are there represented by specimens of unique value. Three groups of particular beauty and interest are a unique collection of wondrously preserved mummies of different dynasties; the statuary of the Age of the Pyramids (the 28th to 24th centuries B. C.), including the statue of Chephren, a masterpiece of striking vigor; and a precious collection of relics illustrating all ages of Pharaonic history, with the royal trappings of Tutankhamon, a treasure trove so priceless and beautiful that there are those whose sole reason for visiting Egypt is to see it. Situated near the museum is the sprawling House of Parliament and east of it is Abdin Palace, Farouk's stupendous palace, now a museum. The Museum of Islamic Art, still farther east, contains the world's most precious and comprehensive collections of Muslim art, including a priceless exhibition of earthenware water jugs and filters and the most beautiful specimens of the Mamelukes. The Desert Institute at Heliopolis, on the eastern desert outskirts of Cairo, founded for the scientific study of the desert and its development, contains sections showing the different desert plants and animals in their natural habitat. The

Opera House, next to the beautiful Azbakiya Garden, on Ibrahim Pasha Square or Opera Square, the "Times Square" of Cairo, was built for the celebration of the Suez Canal's opening, when "Aida," commissioned especially for this event, was to be given. However, since Verdi did not complete this notable opera in time, "Rigoletto" was performed instead. Other nighttime entertainment is available at fascinating dancing halls like the Casino Tararin (Kit-Kat) and the Casino Sheherazad with their exotic, elusive perfumes of musk and sandalwood permeating the air, Oriental music and dancers reviving the Arabian Nights and clever gally-gally men displaying their magic tricks. And for the sportsmen, there is the outstanding Gezira Sporting Club on Gezira Island in the Nile. In the suburbs are an endless variety of attractions. Of course, the most important and most famous are those stupendous monuments at Giza: the Pyramids and Sphinx. Occupying the center of the vista is the mysterious figure of the Sphinx, with its head of a man and its body of a beast, lying at the edge of the desert. At its right, a rocky cliff, pierced with tombs, serves as the pedestal to the imposing mass of the Cheops Pyramid, or Great Pyramid, one of the wonders of the world. The Chephren Pyramid, or Second Pyramid, somewhat smaller than that of Cheops, serves as a background to the Sphinx, while the third famous pyramid, that of Mycerinus, is beyond the horizon. These colossal monuments to the great period of Egyptian history were constructed during the Fourth Dynasty, between 2680 and 2560 B.C., and their construction remains a mystery even now. For centuries and centuries, men have gazed with awe at these mighty and wonderful manifestations of the power of ancient Egypt. If possible, visit them several times, by moonlight as well as sunlight, for a complete satisfaction of their majestic attraction, and by all means, take the trip the traditional way — by camel. Adjacent to the Giza pyramids are rows of "mastaba" tombs in which are buried the relatives of the king and the courtiers who formed the official class of the strong central government. At Sakkara, every visitor stands in admiration before the remains of the buildings around the Step Pyramid, by far the most important monument existing on the face of the earth from that date, the Third

Egypt's life line—the Nile
TWA-Trans World Airlines

Dynasty (2780-2680 B.C.). In the midst of that vast enclosure towers the great stepped structure, the first attempt towards the building of a pyramid. Before the time of King Zoser, who was buried in the Step Pyramid, the kings were interred in the huge, rectangular mastabas. The architect Imhotep, the great genius considered in later periods as a God of Medicine, added one mastaba on top of another, each decreasing in size, until the whole building assumed something of a pyramidal form. In **Old Cairo** are many Christian monuments and memorials of the Coptic Church of Egypt, one of the oldest churches in Christianity, whose members are now racially the purest representatives of the ancient Egyptians. Included are the centuries-old **sycamore tree** under which the Holy Family is said to have taken refuge during its flight into Egypt from Herod; the cave in the crypt of the church of **St. Sergins (Abou Serga Church)** where, according to legend, they dwelled; **El Mouallakah, or Suspended Coptic Church,** with its masterful column of icons, its door of inlaid ivory and its beautifully decorated marble; and the **Coptic Museum.**...
Upstream on the Nile River, the ancient route through Egypt, is **FAYOUM**, the garden of Egypt, in one of the richest and most beautiful of all the provinces of Egypt. Surrounded on three sides by the Libyan desert, it is separated from it on the north by salty **Lake Karoun**, the Sacred

Lake or Lake Moeris of the ancients, made by the Pharaohs an aristocratic residential area. The uneven ground here, unique in the country, gives rise to some beautiful scenery, passing through great palm groves and orchards of orange trees and mandarin trees. The lake is popular with fishermen for its excellent soles and enormous sea mullets. South of the lake is the **Pyramid of Illahun,** tomb of Senusert III. From this pyramid came the beautiful jewelry of the princesses, in particular the royal diadem, speaking highly of the skill and taste of the ancient goldsmiths. A beautiful and picturesque excursion through date forests and beside waterfalls and gardens takes you to the **Pyramid of Hawara,** tomb of Amenemhat, founder of the Twelfth Dynasty, who began an ambitious project for turning Lake Moeris into a vast reservoir. To the south of the pyramid sretches the funerary temple known as the **Labyrinth,** without doubt the most important and most complicated of discovered funerary temples, made up of twelve covered courtyards, in two stories of 1,500 rooms each, forming an infinity of winding turns and false exits. The tombs of these rulers of the Middle Kingdom are scattered along the valley of the Nile, with the most celebrated those of the princes at **Beni Hassan,** renowned for their rich paintings. King Amenhotep IV, who later called himself Akhenaton, of the Eighteenth Dynasty (1567-1320 B.C.), built a

new capital on the site of **Tell el-Amarna.**
Here are the remains of his palaces and
temples, as well as the houses, villas and
tombs of his courtiers. . . . At LUXOR
and **KARNAK,** two villages further up
the Nile, was the ancient city of Thebes,
of which Homer said "that only the grains
of sand outnumbered the wealth enclosed
within Thebes and its hundred gates."
The wealth of the Sudan and the Asiatic
countries poured into Thebes, and the
Court of Pharaoh was the meeting place
of the envoys of all the then known
world, who flocked to the capital of the
Empire to offer their homage to the King,
present their tribute and express their loyalty to Egypt. These mighty monuments
speak highly of the great power, skill and
engineering ability of the Egyptians. On
the right bank of the mighty river is the
Luxor Temple, the **Karnak Temple** and
the **"Avenue of the Sphinxes,"** connecting
the two temples. This fabulous, two-and-
one-half-mile-long avenue, the greatest
thoroughfare of ancient Thebes, built by
King Amenhotep III, was of overwhelming
grandeur, lined by marble temples, palaces, obelisks encased in gleaming metal
and on either side, rows of ram-headed
sphinxes, each with a statue of the Pharaoh
between its paws. On the opposite bank
are the sepulchral temples of **Thotmes** at
Deir-el-Bahari, one of the most remarkable
monuments of Egyptian architecture; of
Set I and **Rameses II** at **Qurna** and of
Rameses III at **Medinet Habu.** The Great
Hypostyle Hall at Karnak and the stupendous **Memnon statues** are also representa-
tive of the majesty and daring of ancient
Egypt. The **Valley of the Kings** contain
the royal sepulchres of tombs of the New
Kingdom (1567-1090 B. C.), veritable
subterranean mansions, or a series of corridors and chambers hewn in the rock,
some of which go more than hundreds of
feet deep, the innermost of which contains the granite sarcophagus with the
golden coffin of the ruler, all decorated
with splendid bas-reliefs illustrating the
funerary beliefs prevailing during that
epoch. Some four hundred **private tombs,**
believed to belong to the nobility, are
terraced on the desert hill at Qurna. . . .
Halfway between Luxor and Aswan is
EDFU. Here is the **Temple of Horus,** from
the Ptolemaic Period (332-30 B. C.), with
its mighty pylon towers, one of the best
preserved in all Egypt. Taking 180 years

to complete, it is one of their real masterpieces, reflecting both the traditional
Pharaonic architecture and a moderation of
Greek lines. . . . The last stop on the Nile
is at **ASWAN,** famous for its modern and
ancient archtecture, as well as being popular as a health resort because of its magnificent dry, warm climate. The modern
masterpiece is the splendid, mile-and-a-
half-long Aswan Dam, which has added
over a million and a half acres of land to
cultivation. It is in fact this dam which
was responsible for the submerging of the
beautiful island of **Philae.** The **Temple of
Isis** built there dates from the Pharaonic
era down through the Ptolemaic and
Roman periods. When the sluice gates are
opened between July and October and the
water recedes, you may still visit this mysterious and magic home of the "Lady of
Enchantment," but in winter only the
pylons of the temples are to be seen in the
middle of a vast expanse of water. From
the famous **Aswan granite quarries** many
of the most noted obelisks and statues of
ancient Egypt originated, and these
quarries are still being actively worked in
much the same manner as they were thousands of years ago. . . . The traveler who
wishes to really see all of Egypt should
visit the OASIS OF AMUN at SIWA, most
delightful and most luxuriant of Egypt's
oases, in the endless sands of the Libyan
desert in the northwest. Throughout conquests, religious upheavals and successive
dominations by Alexander the Great, the
Romans, Christian monks and the Arabs,
the isolated population of Siwa has retained its own individual character, making
a living vestige of a people who otherwise
belong now only to history. At the beginning of the route leading to the oasis there
is situated, on a rise in the ground, a sort
of citadel. As the caravan approaches,
what at first appeared to be one great
building divides itself up into a series of
old but solid fortifications and some
extremely picturesque **houses.** The houses
are, in fact, crowded together one on top
of the other in tiers, thus forming a town
of eight stories. At the **Temple of Amun,**
the ruins of which lie not far away from
the spring of Cleopatra, was found the
famous oracle of Jupiter-Amun, consulted
by Alexander in 331 B. C. His visit left
such a great impression that when he was
in Asia he sent messengers to consult the
priests of Siwa before any important step.

Central Africa

THE HEART OF THE CONTINENT

The African continent is to most Americans a land of mystery. No longer remote and inaccessible, but still suffused with the spirit of the frontier, Africa is now available to the modern tourist. You will see strange landscapes, exceptionally interesting animal life and exquisite flora in the most enchanting settings. You will be entranced by Africa's great variety of interest, ranging from scenes of breathtaking beauty to the traditions of the ancient folklore of the natives. You will see such thrilling sights as the dances of the giant Watusis and the homes of the mysterious Pygmy people. And you will never forget your first sight of game in the magnificent national parks, the great wildlife sanctuaries of the world. For the serious hunter, the non-conformist seeking the really rare and unusual and the traveler looking for a remote, serene vacation, the savage beauty of Africa, its fascinating charm and picturesque people insure a never-to-be-forgotten time of your life.

PRIMITIVE, MYSTERIOUS WONDERLAND

After visiting the colorful market, serene La Parc de Bock, the impressive Albert the First Monument, the native quarters and the "Corniches," from which there are superb views of the city, in LEOPOLDVILLE, capital of the Belgian Congo, you may take a steamer up the Congo River or Lualaba River, famed in story and song, to STANLEYVILLE, in the central part of the country. One of the oldest towns in the Congo, it was founded by the English explorer Sir Henry Morton Stanley, of Stanley and Livingstone fame, in 1883. Considered the most typical of all Congo towns, it is today the center of communciations, not only of the Belgian Congo, but of the whole of central Africa. The town even boasts a fine, large Stanleyville Cathedral. It is a good starting point for hunting parties venturing into the interior and because of the picturesque Wagenia Fisheries near the Seventh Cataract of the river's rapids and the impressive Tshopo Falls, also a favorite tourist center. The native quarters are fascinating, as are the nearby Arabicized negro village and other villages like Wamba, where you may be fortunate enough to see a Mabudu dance; Niangara, with the artistically decorated native courthouse, and Gangala na Bodio, where you will watch the trained elephants working. Unusual scenic attractions include the Elephants' Way, the Wanie Rukula landscape and the Mount Hoyo caves near Irumu. . . . Another popular excursion steamer sails through the beautiful scenery between KONGOLO and ELISABETHVILLE, on the Congo's most picturesque sector, the last navigable part of its upper reaches. On board the Prince Leopold life is pleasant and restful. At the numerous calling places where fuel is taken in, travelers may land and mix with the natives in their exceptionally picturesque and charming environment. The peaceful river flows through the famous Kisale Lake, with its luxuriant vegetation of lotus flowers, water lilies and papyrus, and skirts along the Upemba Lake, whose shores attract many herds of elephants. At Elisabethville, where visitors enjoy many of the amenities of a European town, are famous copper smelting sheds and one of the best appointed and up-to-date native townships, where many different tribes can be seen. . . . ALBERTVILLE, built by the Arab slave traders as a port for slaves, is on the shore of Lake Tanganyika, deepest lake in Africa, and has many picturesque villages in the neighborhood. A fascinating excursion can be made through the desolate jungle and high into the mountains to the Luvua River and then through dense flat bush country to Manono, where huge open tin mines employ the most modern machinery. From Albertville clean and well-appointed steamers leave for trips on the lake, with a stop at Kigoma, on the east shore in Tanganyika, for a short drive to Ujiji, largest purely native city in east Africa, originally a center of the slave trade and the place where Stanley found Livingstone. . . . North of Lake Tanganyika is BUKAVU, on beautiful Lake Kivu. This attractive town is a fine place to enjoy a restful visit by the shores of the lake or to tour Ruanda-Urundi. The lake, situated 5,200 feet above sea level, surrounded by green mountains and containing many wooded islands, is reminiscent of Switzerland. To the north is Katana, with a large native market, and to the south is the Ruzizi valley, with coffee and cinchona plantations. A lovely mountain road leads into Ruanda, where the giant Watusi tribe lives as overlords of the smaller Bantu natives, including the villages of **Nyanza**, where the King of Ruanda resides, and **Kabgayi**, where the White Fathers mission is located. On the northern shores of Lake Kivu is **Kisenyi**, at the foot of the **Virunga Volcanoes**, one of which is still active and makes a "pillar of smoke by day and a pillar of fire by night." A road passes right over the lava flows of 1912, 1938 and 1948. Here the Watusis perform their colorful native dances, the most spectacular in Africa. . . . **RUINDI CAMP** is in **Albert National Park**, a fully protected nature reserve covering some 2,022,500 acres and offering a great variety of remarkable sites

is the **QUEEN ELIZABETH GAME PARK**, the newest and one of the most interesting game reserves in Africa, especially famous for its elephants, although buffalo and hippos also abound and even some lions are found. The game may be seen feeding and watering on the banks of the river. Tours include the **Salt Lake** at Katwe and the fisheries on **Lake Edward**. . . . **FORT PORTAL**, capital of the native kingdom of Toro, is situated in the foothills of the snow-covered Mountains of the Moon. The area of **Bundabugyio**, situated on the Semliki Flats, is famous for crocodiles and is also the center of the

A familiar scene along the placid Congo
Quentin Keynes of Gendreau

and innumerable specimens of a fauna which has almost disappeared from most districts of the Congo. From here you may visit **Rutshuru Falls**, see elephants, hippos and buffalo, as well as pelican and other waterfowl, and drive through **gorilla country** and **bamboo** and **podocarpus forests**. . . . There are Pygmy villages near **BENI**, a small market town on the edge of the Ituri Forest, and **fine walks** in the neighborhood of lovely **MUTWANGA**, on the slopes of the beautiful Ruwénzori Mountains, whose native name means "Mountains of the Moon." The **American Mission** in Mutwanga is well worth a visit. . . . On the Ruwenzori slopes in Uganda

Carnegie Yellow Fever Research Institute. . . . From **BUTIABA** on Lake Albert, a launch sails up the Nile, through a truly tropical setting containing all types of game, to the foot of beautiful **Murchison Falls**. From the top of the falls is a magnificent view of the Victoria Nile. . . . **KAMPALA**, situated like Rome on seven hills, near Lake Victoria, is the commercial capital of Uganda and the native capital of Buganda. Here is the **Tomb of Mutesa I**, former Kabaka (ruler) of the Baganda, a Bantu tribe. Even when the Europeans reached the territory, the Baganda, one of the most powerful of the tribes in eastern Africa, were an organized

The main cascade only of the great, magnificent Victoria Falls

Philip Gendreau

and comparatively civilized people, with developed political organizations above the average in Africa. The old fort may still be seen on **Old Kampala Hill,** and both the **Anglican** and **Roman Catholic Cathedrals** are spectacularly situated on the tops of hills. Other places of interest include the **House of the Kabaka,** the **Makerere University College** and the unique **Uganda Museum.** In the rolling Uganda country to the north of Kampala, an export crop of cotton is grown by well-to-do native farmers in long white robes. . . . The incomparable country in western Kenya between **KERICHO,** in a beautiful area of tea plantations, and **NAIROBI** includes the spectacular Rift valley, splitting Africa from south to north, and numerous lakes covered by thousands of flamingos. At Nairobi, the capital, are the **Coryndon Memorial Museum,** with its distinguished collections, and the attractive, modern **Parliament Building.** This town also continues in importance as an outfitting center for African big-game *safaris.* The extremely popular **Nairobi National Park** contains up to thirty species of game, including lion, hippo, giraffe, cheetah and an abundance of antelope and some of the smaller carnivora. One of the most important sites in the world from an archeological point of view is **Olor-**

gesailie, the only known "living-site" of hand-ax men, dating from approximately 200,000 years ago. . . . The world-famed spectacle attracting most African visitors is the mighty, indescribable **VICTORIA FALLS,** on the Zambezi River, at the northwestern border of Southern and Northern Rhodesia. This is the world's greatest waterfall, twice as high and twice as wide as Niagara. As their discoverer, David Livingstone, remarked in his diary, "It is rather a hopeless task to endeavour to convey an idea of it in words, since, as was remarked on the spot, an accomplished painter, even by a number of views, could but impart a faint impression of the glorious scene." The flood waters come down during April, May and June and the Victoria Falls then are at their best, except that the dazzlingly white mass of spray fills the chasm and towers hundreds of feet into the blue sky, and veils the splendor of the falls to some extent. Take the **Dawn Patrol Flight** and the **trip by boat** up the river to Kandahar Island. . . . In the eastern part of Southern Rhodesia are the **ZIMBABWE RUINS,** ruined fortress city of unknown origin that continues to puzzle scientists. Some say that it was built by the Queen of Sheba, but other scientists claim it was the Empire of Monomatapa.

Union of South Africa

ROOTS IN GOLD AND DIAMONDS

As truly fabulous as the tales written about it, the Union of South Africa is a modern, progressive country whose cities, carved against the wild, untamed background of mountain and jungle, have their roots in gold and diamonds, and perhaps wealth yet undisturbed by the centuries. The flora and fauna of the country is fabulous and the coasts and mountains offer superlative scenic beauty. But the most provocative feature of this land is her native tribes; their colorful dress, amazing dances, ornate finery and their willingness to perform for a moderate *bansela* (tip) make a visit to their kraals (villages) a delight.

WHITE WINE AND LOBSTER TAILS

Richly endowed with basic food staples, fruit and cattle, the Union's cuisine is superb. Fish and shellfish, including the famous lobster tails and rock oysters, are delicious. The variety of fruits is legend; try the delicate Hanepoot grapes or the *spaanspek* or muskmelon, served iced with a syrup made of brown sugar, cinnamon and a dash of the native liqueur called van der Hum. A great delicacy in the Cape Province is penguin eggs. Most typical food is the *braaivleis*, or barbecue, meat roasted over an open fire. The Union produces its own fine wines and brandies, comparable in flavor to their European counterparts.

AROUND THE COUNTRY

Cape Province, the land of flowers, vineyards, great forests, wild coasts and historic homes, is the seat of the Union's legislative capital and most famous seaport, CAPETOWN. Beloved by seamen of all ages and countries, Capetown is called the "Tavern of the Seven Seas." Built beneath and around wondrous Table Mountain, it is beautifully situated facing the bay. Two of the oldest and most historical buildings in the city are the Dutch Reformed Church, containing a magnificent pulpit carved by Anton Anreith, whose work adorns many Old Cape buildings, and the solidly built Old Supreme Court, a monument to the builders of an earlier age. Visit the Houses of Parliament, St. George's Cathedral, headquarters of the Anglican Church, and Government House. No one should miss the famous Gardens, a botanist's paradise, whose seeds were planted by the Dutch East India Company and whose shrubs and trees were brought from every country on earth. The central walk of the gardens leads to the South African Museum, world-famous for its plaster casts of Bushman and Hottentots, the Cape's two aboriginal tribes. Nearby is the striking National Art Gallery, housing the private old-masters collection of Sir Alfred Beit, as well as a fine group of paintings by South African moderns. Ten minutes drive from the city is the lower station of the aerial cableway to the top of Table Mountain. From here one gets a panoramic view of the Cape Peninsula. Near Capetown is the "Groote Schuur" (the Great Barn) where Cecil Rhodes lived and which houses all his treasures. Be sure to take the Marine Drive around the Cape of Good Hope and see all the charming resorts on the coast, including world-famous Muizenberg. Another must is a visit to the National Botanic Gardens at Kirstenbosch. . . . Driving toward the east one travels through miles of fertile, flower-covered countryside. Here is the famous and incredibly beautiful stretch of coast line known as the Garden Route, running from Capetown to Plettenberg Bay skirting the Outeniqua and Tzitzikama Mountains. Along this route you can visit the Ostrich Farm at Oudtshoorn, the fabulous Cango Caves, Wilderness, a gem among resorts, and the famous cliffs called Knysna Heads. This coast is dotted with delightful holiday centers with excellent facilities for swimming, boating, camping and fishing. An interesting excursion into the rolling hills inland brings you to the land of the two million Bantu, called the "Red Blanket People" because of their unique robes. . . . At KIMBERLY, the diamond center of South Africa, one can still visit the Big Hole, where diamond mining began. Although it is no longer in operation there are several other nearby mines which can be visited. . . . Natal, land of the mighty Drakensberg and the hamlets of the Zulus, is hemmed by sub-tropical beaches and wonderful surf. DURBAN is a modern city of imposing buildings and wide tree-lined avenues. Here European civilization has come to terms with the African, for Zulus may be seen walking the streets dressed in the height of European fashion or colorfully arrayed in tribal dress. Durban has developed as a national playground. Its personality is expressed in its fine race courses, tennis courts, bowling greens, golf courses and modern theaters. Its harbors are a yachtman's paradise and the resorts strung out along the coast make this area the Union's "Riviera.". . . Northwest of Durban are the scenic roads which lead to the **Drakensberg (Dragon's Mountain)**. No part of South Africa is more varied or profuse in beauty and legend. The roads climb into the kraals of the Zulu tribes and past the caves of the Bushmen. Between May and August the peaks and higher slopes of the Drakensberg are snow-covered; in summer they are carpeted with a host of brilliant veld flowers. There are numerous resorts and the bracing climate encourages one to enjoy the excellent variety of sports, climbing, riding, fishing for trout, swimming. . . . To the northeast, in the heart of Zululand, is **HLUHLUWE**, the great game preserve where you can see the rare white rhinos lumbering about, as well as zebra, giraffe, impala, warthog and other wild beasts. . . . **Transvaal**, that land of gold, big game and dynamic, rich skyscraper cities, lies to the northwest of the Drakensberg. Through its interior runs a spinal column of gold. Built over this column is the fabulous city of **JOHANNESBURG**. Perhaps the single greatest symbol of progress is Johannesburg's tallest building, **Escom House**, a vast glass and concrete structure which dominates its surroundings like a watch tower. A tour of the city must include a visit to a gold

mine to see the precious metal being extracted 8,000 feet below the surface and to see the thrilling African tribal dances of the native mine workers. They perform in the mine compounds, beating their shields and tossing their high headdresses, while they thump the earth with their bare feet to the throbbing music of the "kaffir pianos," huge wooden xylophones. . . . To the north is **PRETORIA**, the Union's beautiful capital, with its magnificent **Union Buildings** and flowering jacaranda trees which rival the cherry trees in Washington, D.C. . . . Northeast of the capital is **Kruger National Park**, the world's largest wildlife sanctuary. Here, in this great 8,000 square-mile-tract of Bushveld untouched by civilization except for modern tourist camps, one sees the amazing variety of animals native to South Africa wandering at large. . . . The Orange Free State is a province of prairies, waving grain, sheep and cattle. Its lovely capital, **BLOEMFONTEIN** ("Fountain of Flowers"), lies in the heart of the boundless veld. From Naval Hill in the center of the city, site of the Lamont Hussey Observatory of Michigan University and the Franklin Game Reserve, one gets a magnificent panoramic view of the surrounding undulating farmlands and flat-topped hills, or *koppies*. Among the city's many elegant buildings the historic, classical **Raadzaal** and Union's impressive **Court of Appeals** stand out. Nearby is another important **Observatory** at **Mazelspoort**, the Boyden Southern Station of Harvard University, most important one in the Southern Hemisphere.

The Premier mine near Pretoria has produced more diamonds than any other mine in the Union

Philip Gendreau

Turkey

LINK OF TWO CONTINENTS

A panorama of seven thousand years of human history — of varying cultures and civilizations — the like of which no other land has experienced, is revealed in every corner of modern Turkey. Dating back to the fourth millennium before the Christian era, people of the paleolithic period, and those of the Age of Caverns, lived on these highlands and along the coast. Then came the Hittites, Lydians, Phrygians, Carians, Dorians, Aeolians, Ionians, Commerians, Bithynians, Persians, Greeks, Romans, Byzantines, Danishmends, Seljuks and finally the Ottoman Turks, who established themselves after the beginning of the fourteenth century. Today, the splendid reminders of this old-world romance, combined with the new-world culture of the modern, Westernized Turkish Republic create an intriguingly unique country — a bridge, both geographically and culturally, between East and West, as well as a bridge to the remote civilizations of the ancient past.

GOURMETS OF THE NEAR EAST

Turkey has always had the reputation of a paradise of good living and gastronomy. A famous old Turkish proverb says, "The spirit gets into a man with the food he eats." For many centuries, the delights of Turkish cooking have enchanted the palate of Westerners visiting the country and Americans generally take with zest to *boreks* (a special preparation of pastry dough with cheese or chopped-meat filling) and *cerkes tavugu* (chicken prepared with a special walnut and red-pepper sauce). You must not miss the *shish kebab* with rice (*pilâv*) and if you prefer vegetables, another specialty is stuffed eggplant (*zeytin yagli patlican dolmasi*) and green peppers (*biber dolmasi*). Besides its great variety, the main characteristic of Turkish cuisine is that, contrary to the Oriental cuisines, it makes a very moderate use of spices such as pepper. However, in fashionable restaurants of Istanbul and Ankara, the food is of both Turkish and French cuisine. Fresh fish from the Bosphorus are served to suit every palate. Fresh fruit in season comes from all parts of Turkey: strawberries from the Arnavutköy hills (Bosphorus) and from the old Heralion; honeylip figs and raisins from Izmir; big luscious peaches from Bursa; savory pears from Ankara; oranges, tangerines and grapefruit from the Mediterranean coast and sweet melons and watermelons from all parts of the country. The famous Anatolian wine used to adorn the tables of Roman emperors. There are good liqueurs made from genuine fruits and plenty of *raki,* the national drink, distilled from grapes, flavored with anise and drunk as an aperitif. A formal dinner in Turkey begins with *raki* and is occasionally accompanied by various hors d'oeuvres. There is, of course, the famous Turkish coffee, served in a demitasse, strong and if desired, without sugar. The important place occupied by coffee in Turkish life is best illustrated by an old Turkish proverb: "A cup of coffee commits one to forty years of friendship."

ANCIENT GLAMOUR

For glamour, few cities can compare with the thrilling city of ISTANBUL (pop. 1,000,022), the ancient Constantinople, whose name alone conjures up fabulous visions of Eastern glory and might. Situated at the entrance of the Bosphorus, linking the sea of Marmara to the Black Sea, it is the only city in the world astride two continents: Asia on the east and Europe on the west. Two bridges, Galata and Atatürk, over the Golden Horn, famous estuary of the Bosphorus, link the two main districts: Old Istanbul and Beyoğlu, both on the European side. Old Istanbul is crowded with Byzantine monuments, most prominent being Saint Sophia, world-famous basilica built in the sixth century by Justinian and one of the supreme religious structures in the world. Converted into a mosque after the conquest, it now has been made into a museum. The interior, adorned with magnificent mosaics and the most beautiful specimens of Arabic calligraphy, is unsurpassed for artistic beauty and originality. Nearby Topkapi Saray (Old Saraglio) is the ancient dwelling of the Ottoman sultans, from which the great empire was ruled for centuries. Consisting of several structures set in a vast garden with a breathtaking view, it includes the harem quarters and a museum, housing among other items the magnificent golden throne of Shah Ismail, an incomparable collection of Chinese porcelain and an elaborately carved marble sarcophagus. Istanbul is the "city of 500 mosques," all built during the Ottoman period. Most prominent is the Mosque of Sultan Ahmed, one of the most beautiful, better known as the "Blue Mosque" from the magnificent blue tiles adorning the interior. Biggest, most gorgeous and best-situated, being visible from all parts, is the Mosque of Süleymaniye, known as the Magnificent, most famous of the Ottoman sultans. Built in 1550-1557 by Koca Sinan, master of Turkish architecture, it has among many marvels of its interior amazing acoustics. The city once had scores of cisterns and the most outstanding of those still in existence is Yerebatan Sarnici (Sunken Cistern or Sunken Palace), largest of all Byzantine cisterns and the only one containing water. Built 1400 years ago, it has 336 columns still standing; a boat trip around the columns is a most interesting experience. Fountains constitute one of the most typically beautiful features of Istanbul, for in the Moslem faith, helping a weary passer-by to quench his thirst is a pious act. The famous decorated Fountain of Ahmet III, built in 1712, is one of the best specimens of Turkish rococo style. At the Beyoglu end of Galata Bridge is Galata Kulesi (Tower), one of the landmarks of Istanbul, said to have been built under the Emperor Zeno in the fifth century. In Beyoglu is Istiklâl Caddesi (Avenue of Independence), most fashionable and interesting avenue of the city, leading to Taksim Meydam (Taksim Square), hub of its Westernism, with the imposing Memorial of the War of Independence in the center. On the European side of the Bosphorus is the immense Palace of Dolmabahçe,

whose splendors surpass all imagination. Built in 1853 by Sultan Abdülmecit, the architectural style is mixed, being the work of both Turkish and European architects, with acres of marble, luxurious furniture and interior decorations abounding in porphyry, crystal and other precious materials. Occupying the slope from the top of a hill down to sea level on the same shore are the three main fortresses and eighteen minor ones of Rumelihisar, a castle of Mehmet II. On the Asiatic shore is the white marble Beylerbeyi Sarayi (Palace of Beylerbey), one of the most elegant in the city. All these sumptuous sights along the Bosphorus may be enjoyed on one of the delightful boat rides on its waters. . . . Research seems to have proven that ANKARA (286,781), the capital since 1923 and a modern metropolis with large boulevards and all kinds of European-style buildings, has been inhabited since paleolithic and neolithic time. However, some archeologists believe that it was first built by the Hittites, who had founded a powerful empire in Anatolia 2,000 years before the Christian era. In 278-277 B. C. the Galatians, having invaded the region, made the city their capital, Galatia, and laid the foundations of the present-day Citadel. During the Byzantine period, the walls halfway to the top were built, and several restorations and reconstructions followed in the Seljuk and Ottoman periods. The Galatians also built the Temple of Augustus, although it was originally dedicated to Men, a Galatian divinity. No museum in the world contains so full and rich a collection of Hittite works as the Museum of Archaeology of Ankara. Most

A reminder of Istanbul's Ottoman past is the outstanding Blue Mosque
Turkish Information Office

remarkable of all is the Mausoleum of Kemel Atatürk, founder and first president of the Turkish Republic. Just finished in 1953, it contains three main parts: the mausoleum, the promenade leading to a vast ceremonial court and dependent buildings, all adorned with statues and towers. . . . KAYSERI, "the city of mausoleums" southeast of Ankara, reached the climax of its prosperity under the Seljuk Turks, when it became one of their capitals, and it swarms with their monuments, all of great value. Döner Kümbet, or the Turning Mausoleum, dating from the twelfth century, is a masterpiece of Seljuk art. Near Urgüp are the fairy chimneys in wonderful Göreme, the "Petrified Valley," with its fantastic and peculiar-shaped rocks transformed both by nature and man into chapels and tombs. The exact history of these monastic colonies is unknown, but it is certain from the dates carved everywhere that many a Byzantine sybarite must have gone here for repose during his last days. Tokali Kilise (The Church with the Buckle), biggest in the valley, contains almost-intact liturgical furniture and walls adorned chronologically with scenes from the New Testament. . . . Founded in 301 B. C., HATAY or ANTAKYA (ancient Antioch) on the River Asî (Orontes) was the capital of Syria and for centuries one of the principal cities of the world. Caesar and Augustus did much for her prosperity, hence the important ruins dating from the Roman era: aqueducts, catacombs and a great portion of the walls with towers and gates. It was in Antioch that the apostles held their first meeting before they set out to conquer the Roman world and there can still be seen the grotto or the church of St. Peter, housing the first Christian church. Antakya Museum is the richest in the world for Roman mosaics, a great number of which adorned the houses of Roman officials living here from the third to the fifth centuries. . . . In KONYA, northwest of Antakya, Karatay Kolege (Medrese), with its remarkable gate in Seljuk style, is famous for the black and blue mosaics covering its dome and walls. The elaborate gate and nearby minaret of Ince Minare, built as a university in 1265-7, are masterpieces of Seljuk stone-cutting art. An outstanding feature is the Museum of Islamic Art, formerly the quarters for the order of Whirling Dervishes or Mevlevî, consisting of a hall where the ritual dance took place

and the adjacent mausoleum housing the tomb of Mevlâna Celâleddin, the Rumî, mystic poet, philosopher and founder of the order. The hall is crowded with relics, including a thousand-year-old hand-written Koran, beautifully illuminated volumes of Rumî's famous *Mathnabi* and *Divan-i Kabir,* invaluable 700-year-old rugs and gorgeous velvet and textiles of the sixteenth century. . . . On the southern coast is ANTALYA, favorite with sportsmen, with miles of sandy beaches on the blue Mediterranean, snow-capped mountains within easy reach and abundant fish and game in the region. At the Theater of Aspendos (15,000 seats), ancient amphitheater, you may watch, during the Antalya Festival, a performance of Shakespeare's *Romeo and Juliet* or some other famous drama. In Alanya, the 700-year-old Seljuk Tersane (Shipyard) is in service even today. . . . IZMIR (230,508), known for nearly 3,000 years as "the first city of the Eastern Mediterranean," is the second port of Turkey and center of a rich agricultural area. Kadife Kale (The Velvet Castle) overlooks the city and commands a breathtaking view of the bay. The walls and towers on the hill were originally built during the reign of Alexander the Great, with traces of additional construction and repairs made during the Ottoman period. The ancient Agora, dating from the second century B. C., is still the market place of Izmir. With its three-story construction, it surpasses agoras elsewhere, which never exceeded two stories. The two Caravanserais of Kizlar Ağasi Hani (sixteenth century) and Cakaloğlu Hani (eighteenth century) are historic inns where caravans coming from the East, bringing silks and spices from India and the Orient on their way to Europe, found rest and food. Hisaronu and its environs is well-known for its open-air cafes and hawkers selling Oriental treasures. Excavations have unearthed some remains of the glorious city of Seljuk or Ephesus, including the 2,000-year-old Grand Theater (24,500 seats), where a whisper carries to the other side of the arena. According to popular tradition, the Church of St. John is the burial place of the apostle and the Shrine of the Virgin Mary is the house where she spent the last days of her life. Drives to these sites take you through enchanting country of meandering streams, silvery olive groves and picturesque small

Some of the amazing rock formations in the "Petrified Valley," a geological wonder
Turkish Information Office

towns. . . . One of Turkey's most popular resort cities is BURSA (100,007), a city essentially Turkish, where everything — even the atmosphere — belongs to the past. Biggest mosque in Bursa is Uli Cami (Great Mosque), a great rectangle covered with twenty cupolas. However, two world-famous monuments considered the most magnificent specimens of early Turkish-Ottoman art at its highest are Yeşil Cami (Green Mosque) and Yeşil Türbe (Green Mausoleum) containing the tomb of its builder, Mehmet I. Masterpiece of the mosque is the Mihrat (altar), a jewel of ceramic art. These monuments received their names from their decorations of greenish tiles, made by a secret process lost for centuries, and those adorning the octagonal mausoleum are especially remarkable. To its unchallenged merit as an historic and artistic city, Bursa adds that of a famous spa and most visitors to the city go primarily to visit these thermal baths. Oldest and most famous, dating largely from the fourteenth century, is Eski Kaplica (Old Spa). Bursa is situated at the foot of a huge mountain called Uludağ, a three-fold attraction as a summer resort, an alpinistic center and a winter-sports area, where the streams and lakes abound in trout and the forest with wild game. A delightful trip can be made to Karacabey Harasi (Ranch of Karacabey), where pure Arab horses are bred. Do not leave Bursa without visiting the Biçakcilar (Covered Bazaar), where hand-made Turkish hunting knives and the best Turkish towels and silks are sold, since the city has been famous for its silks from time immemorial.

Syria, Lebanon and Cyprus

KEY TO THE NEAR EAST

Located at the eastern edge of the Mediterranean, in the heart of the Middle East, Syria's and Lebanon's central geographic position has made them, since the dawn of history, the highway of nations and the goal of empire builders. In ancient times, when the camel was the principal means of land transport, the great caravans of commerce passed through here, and Damascus, enchanting oasis on the edge of the desert, was the leading international trading post, whose possession was considered essential to the security of all the great empires of the past. Everywhere the traveler goes he will encounter evidences of succeeding civilizations, as the whole history of the human race unfolds before him. Today more than ever, Damascus is the meeting place of world travelers and traders and from a military point of view, still the vital pivot of the entire area. While preserving the ancient relics of the mighty civilizations of long ago, Syria and Lebanon confidently look ahead to even greater glories in the future.

ISLAND BASTION

Another valuable gateway to the Near East is the beautiful island of Cyprus. Although chiefly famous for its strategic importance, its vigorous, irregular scenery, its many sandy beaches, its rare old ruins and its quiet, calm country and port life make it ideal for those seeking a remote, lazy vacation on the exquisite, shining Mediterranean.

FRUITS OF DAMASCUS

Rivers springing from sources in the mountains make their way through lovely valleys, turning wide surroundings into big oases. It is therefore not surprising that apricots, cherries, peaches, grapes, apples, pears and other fruits are particularly delicious and abundant here.

DESERT OASES AND A LOVELY ISLAND

Located at the foot of the snow-capped peaks of Anti-Lebanon, DAMASCUS (291,157), Syria's capital since time immemorial, is a luxuriant oasis in striking contrast with the desert surrounding it. In fact, it was this contrast which was said to have caused the Prophet Mohammed to decline to enter this garden city, explaining that no man is entitled to enter paradise twice. To the Arabs and the entire world of Islam it is the cradle of Islamic culture and the symbol if Islamic glory. Damascus is not only the oldest inhabited city in the world, but is also the oldest existing capital. It was a great and flourishing capital city in Biblical times and figures prominently in the wars of Egypt and Babylon. Within the old city is the House of Judas, where Paul stayed, plus the home of Ananias, the disciple at Damascus, and "the street which is called Straight." (Acts IX:10-11). A busy, cobblestoned street, which in Biblical times possessed a colonnade, traces of which have been discovered, it is one of the longest in Damascus and one of the major souk (bazaar) or business streets. Because of the variety of the wares displayed, a visit to these souks — an important magnetic charm of the city — constitutes a new and thrilling experience an American will long remember. Near the eastern terminus of the street called Straight is Bab Kysan, St. Paul's Gate or window in the wall, where "the disciples took him by night, and let him down by the wall in a basket." (Acts IX:25). A few blocks north of the street in the center of the old city is the magnificent Omayad Mosque, ranking in sanctity with the mosques of Mecca and Medina. On the site of this mosque a Roman temple dedicated to Jupiter stood. This temple, of which two monolithic columns still stand, was destroyed by the Emperor Theodosius I (379-395 A. D.), who erected in its place a basilica dedicated to St. John the Baptist. After the Arab conquests of the seventh century, the church was simultaneously used for both Christian and Arab worship. However, in 708 A. D. the basilica was converted by the Caliph El Walid into a mosque, which he lavishly and magnificently adorned. Burned and pillaged on several occasions since, it has each time been restored, now including fine stained-glass windows, costly marble pavements and a minaret which is a masterpiece of the Arabian-Egyptian style. Adjoining the mosque is the handsome tomb of Saladin, the Moslem leader who finally defeated the Crusaders and restored the Holy Land to the Moslems. Across the way is the old El Azem Palace, one of the most beautiful in Damascus, constructed of alternate tiers of black and yellow stones. West of this section is another area of interest where the Sultan Suleyman Mosque with its twin minarets, the modern Syrian University and the Damascus Museum are located. . . . Located in an oasis in the heart of the Syrian desert, 1,300 feet above sea level, PALMYRA, ancient Tadmor, was for centuries an important caravan station on the route from Damascus to Baghdad, attaining the height of its prosperity in the third century under the famous Queen Zenobia, part-Greek and part-Arab, whose armies, defying the power of Rome, occupied all of the eastern part of the Roman Empire, including Egypt, until the city was finally destroyed by Emperor Aurelian in 273 A. D. On the east side of the ruined city is the Corinthian-style Temple of Baal, with a court over 650 feet wide. Only the lower parts of the temple walls and the massive gate remain standing, but the elaborate niches which contained the figures of the gods can still be seen. The Monumental Arch Building, originally consisting of two great arches, still has one arch standing. Also of interest are the Tetrapylon, a huge monolith of granite speckled with blue; the small Funeral Temple and the Necropolis, containing the richly decorated "tomb of the three brothers." . . . West of Palmyra is quaint, old HOMS (100,142), or ancient Emesa, now a clean market town. There is a large and beautiful mosque, dating back only to the last century, but of an elegant architectural style. . . . Ancient HAMA, "the Melodious City," nestling among great willows and poplars on the banks of the Orontes River, has hundreds of rare, fascinating, huge primitive chain pumps or water wheels, called *norias*, in-cessantly creaking, turning and pumping water for the city. The handsome Great Mosque, formerly a Christian church, has remarkably fine minarets and the Beit el Azm Palace is famed for its courts and its eighteenth-century paintings. . . . Near the northern border is interesting ALEPPO (324,899), Syria's largest and most picturesque city, already a renowned city in the days of Nineveh and Babylon and capital of a great kingdom 2,000 years before Christ, possessing a character of its own that has been preserved through countless generations. On a hill in the middle of town, surrounded by a deep moat, is the Citadel, a magnificent example of Arab military engineering, dating back to the thirteenth century. Even the ancient city wall, with the Gates of Antioch, El Hadid (Iron Gate) and Quinnesrine, is still almost wholly intact. You will also enjoy a walk within the walls, through the unique arched *souks* and a stop at one of the picturesque *khans* or ancient caravan inns, like the fine Khan el Wazir or Khan es Saboun. After visiting the busy, noisy markets, you will enjoy a few quiet hours at the Dallal Palace, containing some exquisite woodwork and a beautiful courtyard with fountains; the great Mosque of Zacharia, with the most beautiful minaret in Syria, dating from 1290, or the Aleppo Museum, with its rare treasures. At St. Simeon are the imposing ruins of a Byzantine fort in a picturesque setting and the great Basilica of St. Simeon, one of the largest churches in the entire Near East, built in the Syria-Roman style popular in the Antioch region. . . . The ancient port

Because irrigation is imperative in Lebanon, even primitive methods are better than none

Philip Gendreau

city of **LATAKIA,** founded by the Greeks over 2,000 years ago, has played a prominent part in history. Today it is the center of the mysterious Nosairia sect, found only in this region. Near the town is the ancient storied **Castle of Sahion,** once an impregnable stronghold. Taken and held for many years by the Crusaders, it was finally reconquered by the Arabs under Saladin. Triangular in shape, it contains Byzantine, Frankish and Arabic work. . . . Further south along the coast is **TARTUS.** In 1099 the city was occupied by the Crusaders, who fortified it and made it a great stronghold. Right on the sea is the **castle of the Knight Templar.** Here, too, the Crusaders built a great **cathedral** in the twelfth century, whose western façade has a pointed and richly ornamented portal. A lovely boat ride will take you to the charming little island of **Ruad,** a quaint fishing center. Perhaps the most majestic relic of the Crusades is the great castle of the Hospitalers, the **Krak des Chevaliers,** dominating the Homs Pass and hence the main inland Damascus-Aleppo road and also the port of Tripoli on the Mediterranean. Called by the Arabs *"Jamrat el Franji"* (Frankish Firebrand), this fortress, besides being an almost impregnable stronghold, is one of the most beautiful architectural gems of the Middle Ages.

LEBANON

BEIRUT (177,780), capital and chief port of Lebanon, was an early center of Christianity and a great seat of learning during the Roman Empire. It still contains some notable universities, especially the famous **American University,** founded by a Presbyterian missionary in 1866, and the **Université Saint-Joseph,** founded by French Jesuits in 1843, one of the most important cultural and scientific centers in the Near East, having played a primary role in the revival of Arabic literature. The city, too, is well-known for its association with the legend of St. George and the Dragon, for it was here in the bay that he is supposed to have killed the monster. Despite its long history and ancient glory, there are no buildings of note in today's city, because it was leveled by earthquake in the sixth century and the buildings were apparently not rebuilt. The Roman ruins of **Baalbek,** "City of the Sun," are the country's most popular attraction. Most important are those of the **Acropolis,** including the **Propylaea,** with its richly ornamented walls; the large **Court of the Altar;** the **Great Temple of Jupiter,** marked by the six magnificent yellow-stone columns over sixty feet high, and the exquisitely decorated **Temple of Bacchus,** one of the best-preserved and most beautiful antique buildings in this area. Between Beirut and Baalbek, you will travel through the famous Cedars of Lebanon, which went into the construction

Biblical scenes recur on the street called Straight

Philip Gendreau

of the temple of Solomon. The Lebanon Mountains, rising to more than 10,000 feet, with many attractive summer resorts, are popular with both skiers and hunters.

CYPRUS

Cyprus is an island in the eastern Mediterranean, lying sixty miles west of Lebanon, with an area less than half that of Wales. The coastline is indented and rocky, but interspersed are long, sandy beaches, accounting for its main attraction for people from other lands, since the bathing all along the coast is excellent. NICOSIA, the capital, lies several miles south of the center of the northern coast. An important monument within the walls is the Mosque of St. Sophia, built in the thirteenth century as a church. The younger Orthodox Cathedral is famous for its frescoes. Outside the walls, the Cyprus

. . . FAMAGUSTA, on the east coast, is another medieval walled city, whose fortifications contain Othello's Tower. A few miles north is the Late Bronze Age city site at Engomi, one of the island's richest archaeological sites. Identified as the capital of the Kingdom of Alasia, which enjoyed diplomatic relations with Egypt and the Hittite Empire in the fifteenth and fourteenth centuries B. C., even the grid street plan has been established. A number of intact tombs, containing valuable vases and gold objects, have also been discovered. The cathedral at Famagusta and the Castle of Kantara, farther to the north, are beautiful examples of medieval architecture. . . . At LIMASSOL, an important port on the southern coast, is the chapel where Richard Coeur de Lion is believed to have been married in 1191. On the

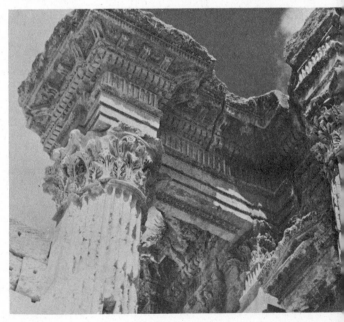

Surpassing even the Parthenon in the detailed lacelike carving are the columns of the Temple of Bacchus
Philip Gendreau

Museum displays valuable collections of antique pottery, jewelry and coins, among many others. . . . In the beautiful rugged scenery of the north coast is KYRENIA, a popular summer resort. Guarding the harbor from the crest of the high hill at the pass through the mountains is the twelfth-century St. Hilarion Castle. To the east is the wonderful Bellapais Abbey, one of the finest examples of Gothic architecture in the Levant, and the Castle of Buffavento.

nearby acropolis of Curium is a large bath complex of the fourth century A. D., including a series of subterranean rock-cut cisterns. The adjoining Roman Theater has masonry of fine quality. The Apollo Sanctuary is west of the acropolis. . . . PAPHOS, on the west coast, where Sergius Paulus, the Roman governor, was converted to Christianity by Paul, is rich in Roman, Byzantine and later ruins, and also has a medieval port.

Iran

LAND OF OMAR KHAYYAM

Iran is the new name for ancient Persia, one of the first great empires, land of Cyrus the Great and Darius, which 2500 years ago, extended from India and the borders of Mongolia to Egypt and the Danube. Persians based their brilliant civilization upon arts and traditions old as the pyramids and throughout the lands conquered by them they spread and developed culture. Evidence of her glories fill museums the world over. Her sculpture, pottery, carpets and miniatures, her gardens and her poetry have inspired ensuing generations and civilizations and so her glorious heritage remains. Today the country, reduced in power and size as a result of a series of disastrous wars, faces a bright new future, revitalized by large-scale social, industrial and economic reforms. The cities of modern Iran, improved by great new buildings and broad avenues, carefully preserve their original charm and historic monuments. The Iranian people are intelligent, friendly and hospitable. In the cities the houses are surrounded by the inevitable walled garden, bright with flowers, and the cafes are filled with chattering groups of friends who spend hours sipping tea or arrack. In the mountains nomadic tribes herd goats and fat-tailed sheep and practice their ancient arts. They supply the scattered farm villages with hides and cheese and supply the bazaars with their beautiful handicrafts.

SHERBETS TO PILAUS

Rice and lamb, of course, are eaten everywhere. There is an unending variety of rice dishes, pilaus; one favorite is chicken, rice, nuts and dates deliciously combined; another is a mixture of fish, chopped fresh dill and other herbs and rice. Kabob, skewered pieces of lamb roasted over coals, is delicious; often it is served with a sauce concocted from various tangy spices and fruit juice. Cucumbers and fruits are served with almost every meal. Persian melons are world famous and there are a number of different varieties, all equally delicious. Sherbets originated in Iran and are still quite popular. They are made from all citrus fruits, but the most delicious and refreshing is one made from the grenade or pomegranate.

AROUND THE COUNTRY

TEHERAN (pop. 600,000), located on a fertile plain south of the Elburz Mountains, is the political, industrial and cultural center of Iran. Although the southern part is typically Oriental with a jumble of narrow, winding streets, the northern part is well planned, with broad tree-lined avenues and many beautiful buildings, many of which are of Western style decorated in traditional Iranian motif. In the center is the spacious Maidan Sipah, a square around which are a number of fine modern government buildings. See the Gulistan Palace (Rose Garden) with the elaborate Persian Peacock Throne, decorated with rubies, pearls and emeralds, which was brought by the Nadir Shah as a trophy of his march to Delhi in 1739. In the western part of the city is where the Shah resides in his modern Marble Palace, surrounded by stately grounds and flanked by the Senate and the residence of the Prime Minister. Visit the impressive National Bank and see the Crown Jewels on display there and see the Sepahsalar Mosque. In the eastern part of the city is another square, the Maidan Baharestan, a popular gathering place. Facing it is the very majestic Majlis or Parliament. Don't miss the fascinating Bazaar where you can buy an amazing variety of exotic Oriental treasures. . . . In the foothills of the Elburz Mountains, north of Teheran, are a number of pleasant summer resorts overlooked by snow-capped Mount Demavend. The evergreen forests here offer good hunting and unforgettable walks and rides in the woods. On the snowy slopes winter sports are popular. . . . Across the mountains on the Caspian Sea are two fine, modern seaside resorts, RAMSAR, with its beautiful gardens and casino and BABULSAR, famous for its caviar. . . . South of Teheran are the ruins of ancient Rayy, a pilgrimage center, with the mausoleum of the late Reza Shah (it was he who instigated the reforms which have so greatly helped the Iranian people and their historic land) and the beautiful golden-domed shrine of the ninth-century saint, Shah Abdul Azim. . . . Other major pilgrimage centers are QUM, a little further south, with its exquisite Shrine of Fatima, which also has a dome of gold and stands as a great landmark both day and night, its light shining afar, and **MESHED**, the Holy City, in the northeast, with its tremendous **Shrine of Imam Reza**, brother of Fatima, and the 8th Imam of the Shiites. Nearby are the **ruins of ancient Tus**, burial place of Persia's great poet, Firdausi; a little further away is **NISHAPUR** with its magnificent tomb of Omar Khayyam. . . . In the southeast is **KERMAN**, famous for the nearby ruins of **Ardeshir and Dokhtar forts** which date from the third century. Within the walled city is a great 11th-century mosque. . . . **SHIRAZ**, in the southwest, has many fine mosques, including one of the largest in Iran and has many beautiful gardens. See the bazaar and the **blue-tiled dome of the mausoleum of Shah Chiragh**. Visit the **tombs of Saki and Hafiz**, two of Persia's immortal poets of the 13th and 14th centuries. From Shiraz comes the best of wines produced in the country. . . . Just north of Shiraz, at the extraordinary **Ruins of Persepolis**, you are plunged into the atmosphere of the first world empire. Here are seen remains of the palaces with great staircases, halls and columns and rock tombs of Persian Kings, including that of Darius. . . . To the north **ISFAHAN** (200,000) retains the charm and glamour of the time of the great Shah Abbas, the early seventeenth century, displayed in its blue-domed mosques and royal palaces. The vast square, **Maidan-i-Shah**, in the center of the city, encloses magnificent rose and jasmine gardens. Facing the square are

the **Masjid-i-Shah** or Royal Mosque, built in the late 1600's, an outstanding example of Persian architecture, and the great blue-domed **Lutfallah Mosque**. Countless shops in the bazaar and along the avenues turn out the fascinating handicrafts native to the city. Don't miss the historic, colonnaded **Safavid Bridge**. . . . If you like the smell of oil and the busy hustle and bustle of modern life, make a side trip to **ABADAN**. You'll spend the day seeing the largest oil refinery in the world and at night you can enjoy a cool boat ride on the river and moonlight fishing. . . . Southwest of Isfahan is the ancient town of **SUSA**, scene of the biblical story of Esther. Around 500 B. C. Susa was the winter home of the Achaemenian kings and excavations have disclosed ruins of the ancient palace, treasure house and citadel. . . . Another historic city, **HAMADAN**, the ancient Ectabana, capital of Media, has a number of ancient monuments, including the supposed tombs of Esther and Mordecai, the tomb of the mystical poet Baba Tahir, the tenth-century stone Parthian lion, and the beautiful new stone Mausoleum of Avicenna, the great Persian philosopher. . . . **TABRIZ** (260,000), second largest city of Iran is the trade center for the northwest. Tabriz, famous for its beautiful rugs, has several times been razed by earthquakes and there are few historic buildings here. However, there are a number of lovely mosques and the bazaars are filled with many fascinating articles.

Reliefs from the Apadana Stairway at the amazing ruins of Persepolis
Oriental Inst., Univ. Chicago

Iraq

MESOPOTAMIA—"LAND BETWEEN RIVERS"

With the establishment of the Kingdom of Iraq in 1921, Iraq regained her status as a political entity — a status lost in 1258 as a result of the Mongol invasions. Throughout the land a strange variety of monuments testify to its illustrious past, representing a succession of widely different periods in her long history, along the ageless waters of the Tigris and Euphrates, within whose coils, tradition says, the Garden of Eden was found and lost. Ur, Babylon, Nineveh, Samarra — the glory, wealth and learning of these amazing capitals of mighty empires resounds through the ages. And today, Iraq is advancing again toward its old-time fame but, this time, because of its great deposits of vital oil, is looking ahead, planning a new and fuller life for all.

THE PEOPLE

Many of the vicissitudes through which the country has, at various times, passed are reflected in one or another of the modern Iraqi people. About four-fifths of the population are Moslem Arabs. The tribal system, to which almost the whole population outside the cities is subject, may be considered a heritage from Arabia. Apart from the marsh tribes in the south, tending their buffaloes from canoes, there are Bedouin tribes, nomadic pastors of camels, sheep and horses; cultivator tribes near the rivers and semi-settled, semi-nomadic tribes, whose behavior varies with the climate. Every stage in tribal development from the desert nomad to the cultivator can be observed, and it is interesting to note how few of his tribal characteristics the *fallah* has lost in his transition from the desert to the town. In the cities the racial blending is more subtle and complicated. The races include Kurds, Indo-Iranian by extraction, of the Islamic religion but with a language of their own, whose families are characterized by the strongest possible feudal sense, a rigorous code of honor and considerable freedom of the women; Christians, mostly living in the Mosul district; Jews, the majority of whom live in Baghdad, and many others like the Yezidis, Turcomans and Shebeks.

LOCAL CUSTOMS

Arab tribesmen dress in long shirts made of gray sheeting or unbleached gray cloth, while the women generally wear black *abas* or cloaks made of wool, goat hair or imported silk, although in urban centers, many men wear European clothes. Rice, bread, dates and meat comprise the chief diet of the laboring class.

LAND OF THE "ARABIAN NIGHTS"

Capital and largest city of Iraq is romantic BAGHDAD (364,049), on the Tigris River. Although begun in 762 A. D., by the beginning of this century it had shrunk to the dimensions of a small Arab market town with twisting lanes and rickety houses. With the birth of the new state after World War I, the capital has been transformed. From its fringes, flower-lined boulevards lead to distant suburbs along the riverbank, where private residences are seen, standing in pleasant gardens and adapting the local brickwork to the requirements of climatic extremes. Among the notable modern buildings is the impressive, dignified Royal Mausoleum, tomb of King Faisal I, founder of the modern state. Outstanding examples of the traditional Arab ornamentation adapted to the functional character of a modern building is the group including the City Hall and Opera House, as well as buildings like the White Palace, or Government Guest House, the Ministry of Defense and the Royal Bilat, the official palace of the court. Although in the old days Baghdad was the polished, luxurious capital of mighty Near East empires, standing alone as the rival of Byzantium, the only architectural remains are the famous college building of Al-Mustansir Billah, called the Mustansiriyah, the restored Abbasid Palace in the citadel, now housing fine collections of Arab antiquities, and the medieval city gate, known as Bab al Wastani, rebuilt as a Museum of Arms. Certain of its mosques, though, notably that which covers the tombs of the two Imams at Khadimein, make up in the richness of their ornament for what they lack in antiquity. The Iraqi National Museum has many priceless works of art of early Mesopotamian culture. The circumstances of tribal life and other characteristics of the country have enabled Iraq to become the largest breeder of Arab horses in the world. Thus, horse racing and polo have become the most popular sports. The most prominent feature of capital cities of the

181

Small barges called "belem"
paint a picturesque fore-
ground for the Maquan
Mosque in Baghdad
Philip Gendreau

Kassites, who had defeated the Hittites, was always the great temple-tower or *ziggurat*, at the summit of which the central shrine was built. At Aqer Quf, near Baghdad, the denuded remains of this great structure rears up against the sky like an eerie Tower of Babel. Here, too, are the **Treasure Chamber** and vaulted **wine cellar** of King Kurigalzu with its Kassite inscriptions. Dating from the time of the Abbasid Caliphs in the eighth century A. D. is the astonishing mushroom city of **Samarra**, northwest of Baghdad, whose mosques and mansions once spread over twenty miles along the river. Still standing are the walls of two enormous "Friday Mosques," with strange, spiral minarets recalling the Babylonian *ziggurats,* and the great central archway of the caliphs' palace. Below Baghdad is the famous **Arch of Ctesiphon,** built between 226-636 A. D. by a Sasanian king, recog-

nized as the greatest span of any similar brick structure in the world. West of the picturesque holy city of Karbela is the fortified palace called **Al 'Ukhaidir,** built in the early years of Islam by some eccentric Arab potentate. Its buttressed enclosure wall and many of its stone-vaulted chambers remain almost intact, forming an astonishing landmark in the waterless desert. . . . At **KUT,** downstream on the Tigris, is one of the numerous barrages constructed to bring water to idle lands. Nearby are the ruins of the fabulous city of **Babylon,** the Babylon of Nebuchadnezzar, one of the Chaldeans who ruled from 606-539 B. C., nothing being left of the older city of Hammurabi. . . . In the north, near **MOSUL** (203,273), is the old capital of **Nineveh,** moved there in 720 B. C. during the period of the powerful Empire of Assyria, when this city greatly surpassed old Babylon in wealth and magnificence.

Ctesiphon, great wonder arch
of the East
Philip Gendreau

Saudi Arabia

MYRRH, FRANKINCENSE, OIL

Not many travelers from Western countries visited Saudi Arabia before the discovery of its rich oil fields in the 1930's, yet it is an ancient land, as many ruins throughout the country prove. The frankincense and myrrh of the Biblical "Three Kings" could have come from Arabia, as it was an important product of the southern part of the country. . . . Government concessions given to oil and mining companies have brought modern roads, communication and transportation facilities to take the place of the camel and the donkey, although the motor car has not yet eliminated the former as a means of travel for Bedouins and other nomads of the desert, or the motor truck, the latter as a beast of burden. Arabia's cities are crowded places; their crooked streets are beehives of activi-

ARABIAN BANQUET

Arabs are hospitable; coffee is served on every and any occasion. A typical formal banquet has a whole roast sheep as its main course — served on a huge platter with rice and raisins; dishes of soup, stews, chicken, vegetables, fruit and candies are placed around the platter. After coffee, at the end of the meal, small cups of sweetened tea, flavored with mint, are served. Today, Western-style foods are more likely to make up a menu for foreign visitors. Friday is the Moslem Sabbath, and the month of Ramadan is their lenten season.

ABOUT THE CITIES

MECCA, about 40 miles from the Red Sea and one of Saudi Arabia's two capitals, is the famous Holy City of the Moslem world. Every Moslem's desire is to make

A Bedouin and his camel stand in strange contrast to the modern background of the drilling rig

Philip Gendreau

ty. The country has vast deserts dotted with oases, the largest being **HOFUF**, east of Riyadh. It has seven immense springs and a population of more than 100,000. The walled city of Hofuf has a Governor's palace, a mosque, market place and numerous residences, whose flat roofs are used as sleeping quarters.

SPORTS-LOVING PEOPLE

Arabs love sports. Fishing is largely commercial but "dhows" and dugout canoes with sails go out from Red Sea and Persia-Gulf ports; Arab guides know where the different varieties of fish can be found. Horse racing on beautiful Arabian steeds is the "Sport of Kings"; football and baseball have become popular and hunting with falcons is still done, but not extensively.

a pilgrimage to this birthplace of the Prophet Mohammed at least once during his lifetime, but non-Moslems may not enter the Holy City. . . . **MEDINA** is the burial place of the Prophet and non-Moslems are also excluded from this second sacred city. . . . **JIDDA**, on the Red Sea, is about 40 miles west of Mecca and a main stopping place for pilgrims to the Holy City. It has a busy airport outside the city. . . . **RIYADH**, in the eastern central part of Saudi Arabia, is the political capital with the royal palace dominating the city. . . . **DHAHRAN**, near the Persian Gulf, is a new city, built by the Arabian-American Oil Co. to house its personnel and their families. It has a hospital, modern stores and the first motion picture theater built in Saudi Arabia.

Jordan

ANCIENT AND HOLY GROUND

Jordan (until recent times the major portion of ancient Palestine) and the River Jordan are familiar and revered names to Hebrews, Moslems and Christians the world over. The founders and leaders of the world's three great faiths knew its cities and pilgrims down through the ages have come to visit its shrines. The Christian especially considers the River Jordan a hallowed stream, for Christ waded into its waters to be baptized by John the Baptist. Many sacred songs have been written about the river and its banks. About half of the river's 200 winding miles run through Jordan to its outlet in the Dead Sea. A major portion of Jordan is desert, peopled by Bedouins who raise goats and sheep. Wealth is still rated by these nomadic tribes in the number of camels a man owns, but a modern automobile, standing outside his black tent, is no longer a rare sight. A large part of the Arab world is fast adopting Western ideas and methods.

ABOUT THE CITIES

AMMAN (pop. 150,000), the Philadelphia of Bible times, is the capital of Jordan — an interesting and fast-growing modern city. Arabic-type homes rise on its hillsides; its main streets are filled with buses and passenger cars and are lined with shops, restaurants and business establishments. In contrast to its modernity are its historic ruins giving visitors who view them an idea of ancient Philadelphia. . . . JERUSALEM (170,000), southwest of Amman, is partly in Israel and partly in Jordan, the latter part being called the "Old City." It is truly the Holy City for within its walls are most of the shrines of the Holy Land. The Moslem Mosque of the 7th century, The Dome of the Rock, is built over a rock 58 feet long by 44 feet wide, covering an abyss. Moslems, Christians and Jews each have their own traditions for holding the Rock in reverence. The Church of the Holy Sepulchre is the sacred shrine of Christianity. What is left of Solomon's Wall is known as the "Wailing Place of the Jews" who began the custom of coming here in the Middle Ages to mourn the loss of Jerusalem. Outside the city's walls are the Garden of Gethsemane and the Mount of Olives. . . . BETHLEHEM, to the southwest, has the Church of the Nativity as the sacred shrine of Christendom. It is believed to have been erected on the spot where stood the stable in which Christ was born. . . . JERICHO, near the Dead Sea, and about 800 feet below sea level, is in a farming area — Jordan's arable area is not large but its fertile fields produce substantial crops of grain, tobacco, vegetables and fruits. This is the modern Jericho, but not far away the ruins of ancient Jericho are being brought to light. After the first Jericho had been ruined in battle another was built over it. A part of a wall believed to be Joshua's famous wall has been uncovered. . . . EL KERAK, also a very old city, has, in addition to interesting ruins, an enormous 12th-century castle built by the Crusaders. . . . PETRA, in the south, ancient in pre-historic times, was an important and prosperous Christian town until destroyed in the 12th century. It is known today for its colorful ruins, which were discovered in the early part of the 19th century. It is called "The Rock City," for palaces, temples, tombs and an amphitheater carved out of stratified rock have been found, probably the most amazing ruins in all Jordan. . . . JERASH in the north, the Gerosa of Biblical days, was a large and prosperous town in the early centuries of the Christian era, but became a deserted town in the 12th century. Its ruins attract many tourists.

The lovely Church of the Nativity is built over the grotto where Christ is believed to have been born in Bethlehem
TWA-Trans World Airlines

Israel

LAND OF THE BIBLE

Israel, one of the youngest countries in the world, is a pulsating, modern country, but it is also a link with ancient traditions. The long-sought Jewish homeland, it is the mecca for the Christian pilgrim, as well as the Moslem, who wishes to see the land where his religion was born and tread the same dusty paths, lush valleys and legendary mountains that knew the step of the prophets and seers of old. The redeemed soil of Israel is again a wonderland of exotic plants and delicate wild flowers, of luscious fields and unrivaled orchards. Here East and West meet and the pages of the Bible become reality.

HUMAN KALEIDOSCOPE

Although roughly the size of New Jersey, the heritage of myriad civilizations lives on in Israel — a fascinating paradox of a land which is one nation and, simultaneously, a dazzling kaleidoscope of different national cultures — for 85% of her citizens were born elsewhere and the old customs and old costumes remain. Therefore, although Hebrew is the official language, Yiddish is very common and English is spoken everywhere. Most road signs are in Hebrew, Arabic and French and signs in hotels and interesting sites are also in English.

MILK AND HONEY

From sunny, hillside vineyards come the luscious grapes which are pressed into Israel's famed wines. Jaffa oranges are received joyously all over, and the orange and the grapefruit make the country's national drink "Mitz." In the sub-tropical Jordan Valley clusters of bananas and dates grow, while large watermelons and syrupy sweet figs, exotic guavas, juicy mangoes, all grown in the lovely Galilee, soon find their way to the tables of Jerusalem, Tel Aviv and Haifa. Apples and luscious plums, too, from the orchards of the Sharon Valley and the "Sabra," the wild prickly pear, complete the fruit fare of Israel. The Galilee is also famous for its ancient, gnarled olive groves.

YESTERDAY, TODAY AND TOMORROW

3,000-year-old JERUSALEM (120,-000) the Eternal, city of David, has been revered as the Holy City in the hearts and minds of men. Within her precincts were nurtured the world's greatest monotheistic religions and her ancient stones have formed a backdrop to some of the greatest dramas on the stage of history. On Mount Zion, one of the most holy places, are David's Tomb, believed to be where the Church of the Dormition is now situated, and the Cenacle, site of the last supper and first meeting place of the city's early Christians. Another ancient site is Romema, the camp of the Roman 10th legion which destroyed the temple. Bezalel Museum contains antiquities of Israel and the Government Archaeological Museum specializes in archaeological objects found in the country. Typical of Israel's many well-preserved mosaics is the famous Byzantine floor at Beth Guvrin in the Judean foothills. The nearby picturesque village of Ain Karim is venerated by the Christians as the birthplace of John the Baptist. Jerusalem is a modern city, too, with interesting new buildings in addition to the historical ones, including the imposing Convention Center, scene of exhibitions and festivals. No one visiting Israel today should miss seeing one of the new collective settlements like nearby Ramat Rahel. . . . The gay, teeming seaside metropolis of TEL AVIV has merged with aged, oriental JAFFA to form a single city (330,000), cultural center of the country as well as the largest city. The Municipal Museum contains modern works of art, mostly by Jewish painters, and Bialik House Museum serves also as a library devoted to Jewish poetry. Theatrical companies with headquarters in Tel Aviv include "Habimah," oldest theatrical company in the country, specializing in classical tragedies and comedies, and "Chamber Theatre," composed mainly of young actors, performing mostly translated drama in a lighter vein. The renowned Israel Philharmonic Orchestra and many chamber music groups give performances regularly. The gay "Adloyada" is the culmination of Purim carnival time, celebrating the rescue of the Jews by Esther in the time of King Ahasuerus, replete with fancy-dress parades, masked balls and dancing in the streets. . . . Between Tel Aviv and Haifa are the seaside resorts of NETANYA, with its diamond cutting and polishing factories, and the nineteen-centuries-old port of CAES-AREA, built by Herod the Great and capital of Roman governors. . . . Israel's

185

Modern Dizengoff Square in
Tel Aviv's residential section
Israel Govt. Tourist Office

main port, **HAIFA** (122,000), is the location of famed **Mount Carmel**. From the Carmel's breezy summit, the prophets Elijah and Elisha denounced the heathen priests of Ba'al. Today, the slopes house the **major church of the Carmelite order** and the **World Faith Center**, with its gold and marble Temple of Justice. Mount Carmel's greatest attraction, besides its huge wonderland of parks, gardens and forests, is its breath-taking view encompassing **Acre Bay**, the nearby beaches and resorts, the snow-capped mountains of Lebanon, the saffron hills of Galilee and the green-carpeted Valley of Zebulun. . . . The northern guardian of the Zebulun Valley is **AKO or ACRE**, one of the most ancient cities in the Holy Land. Surviving successive Egyptian, Canaanite, Phoenician, Hellenistic, Arab, Crusader and Turkish occupations, its massive battlemented walls withstood the onslaught of Napoleon. Here the Crusader **citadel, Mosque of Jezzar Pasha, old port** and Arab **market** are high lights of any tour. A famous bathing spot is Acre's **"Purple Beach,"** so named because there the Phoenicians manufactured their famous purple dyes. . . . In the northern highlands of Israel is the lofty summer resort of **TSEFAT or SAFED**, mysterious, shadowy, beautiful, where the towering sages of Judaism who explored the depths of Kabala walked through the town's narrow streets 400 years ago, in contrast with today's **Artists Lane**, gathering place of surrealists, impressionists and other modern artists. Visible from the heights of Safed is a gleaming, harp-shaped body of water almost 700 feet below sea level — the **Sea of Galilee** or **Lake Tiberias**. One of the world's oldest spas, whose medicinal hot springs have been an attraction for 2,000 years, its gentle waters also bring swimmers and sailors there throughout the year. On the north shore are the **Mount of the Beati-** tudes, upon the slopes of which Jesus preached the Sermon on the Mount, and **Capernaum or Kefar Nahum**, with the ruins of the synagogue where Christ is believed to have taught, and also containing a synagogue of the second or third century. On the west shore is the country's most famous thermal resort, **Tiberias**. Celebrated near the shores is **Nebi Shueib**, festival to honor the Druze patron saint Jethro, father-in-law of Moses, when brightly dressed Druze dance their wild Debka and perform their famous fantasia. . . . Every Christian pilgrim to the Holy Land visits **NAZARETH**, the boyhood home of Jesus. Built on the traditional site of this home is the twentieth-century **Church of the Workshop of St. Joseph**. Here, according to legend, at the **Virgin's Well**, is where the Angel Gabriel first appeared to Mary. . . . The Romans and the Crusaders battled at **MEGIDDO**, southwest of Nazareth, the Biblical Armageddon where you may still visit the stables of King Solomon and venture into a bygone world of temples, high places, fortresses and garrison buildings. . . . The Negev mountains constitute a fascinating world in themselves — of highly variegated shapes, of all colors of the rainbow, of peaks and canyons twisted and contorted by the giant hand of nature. The Negev is no less renowned for its two seas: the Dead Sea, containing water saturated with salt, and the Red Sea, teaming with tropical fish and corals. The capital of the Negev is Abraham's city of **BEERSHEBA** and the southern boundary is **EILAT**, on the clear, cobalt gulf. Among the sandy wastes roam Bedouin tribesmen, desert warriors whose hospitality is legend. Here, too, is **EIN GEDDI**, where David sought refuge from Saul's anger; Biblical **SEDOM or SODOM**, the lowest point on the face of the earth, and **ETZION GABER**, where King Solomon mined his copper.

India and Pakistan

NEW NATIONS—AGE-OLD ROOTS

The two new republics of southern Asia — India and Pakistan — present a picture so varied and a culture so diffuse that to attempt to describe adequately their many fascinating facets would be an impossible task. Even the land ranges from the great extremes of the towering snow-clad peaks in the undulating Himalayan range, through the beautiful, breathtaking Kaghan, Indus, Kashmir or Kulu valleys and the vast plains, plateaus and fertile fields of the Punjab or Central India, to the barren, sandy, desert wastes of Sind and the dark, mysterious jungles of East Bengal and Malabar. The people, too, are just as diverse as their scenic background, including in the rich racial mosaic the tall, fair Kashmir, the enterprising Punjabi, the chivalrous Rajput, the rugged Pathan, the artistic Bengali and the quick-witted Tamilian. Consequently, most of the world's great religions are also represented, with Buddhism, Jainism and Sikhism, Christianity and Zoroastrianism adding their own particular flavors to the predominant faiths of Hinduism in India and Mohammedanism in Pakistan. This variegated pattern stems from the influences of the many strange, multifarious peoples who have swept into the land, introducing their own cultures upon that highly developed civilization already existing here over 4,000 years ago. Thus, the ancient traditions, picturesque customs and manners and great artistic achievements combine in a scene found in no other region on earth.

ART OF DANCING

Indian classical dance is a highly perfected art, in which the movements of eyes, neck and arms, the grace and beauty of sculpturesque poses and the pattern of sound and cadence woven by the feet constitute a rhythmic whole. In its classical forms, rhythm, music and gesture are fused to convey a single impression. These find purest expression in *Bharata Natyam* — pure dance, not a dance drama — the traditional style prevalent in South India. The artist is usually a woman and the dancing is done to traditional Carnatic music. *Abhinaya* is one aspect of the dance wherein the dancer interprets a song, especially the emotion and mood of it, by means of facial expressions and sensitive gestures. Today the Indian ballet is represented mainly by three dance forms: the *Kathakali, Kathak* and *Manipuri. Kathakali,* originating from Malabar, is a highly developed pantomimic dance in which classical, medieval and modern strands have been harmonized into a unique science of histrionics. Literally the word means "story play," enacted through movements of the body, gestures, artistic mime and music. This is usually performed by men, since it calls for virile movements of the body, with the dancers wearing heavy make-up in bright colors, voluminous costumes and much jewelry. *Kathak,* of North India, is more lyrical and less dramatic than *Kathakali,* with the dance rendering episodes from the *Radha Krishna* legend in pantomimic form. Although retaining Hindu themes and sentiments, courtly and foreign influences are noticeable in the fleeting footwork and swift movements of the body. Each dance is set to a traditional melody and the movements of the dancer tell the story. In contrast to the classical *Kathakali* and the sophisticated *Kathak,* the *Manipuri* dance is a folk ballet of the east.

ASIAN DELICACIES

Pakistanis are fond of food that is spicy and well-flavored. Among the tasty dishes are a variety of curries and pilaus, especially cooked meat or fish with rice, *kebabs* (fried or broiled meat), *shami kebabs* (fried meat cakes), *kofta* (meat balls), *murgh-i-Mussalam* (stuffed fried chicken) and *shahi tukre* (sweetbreads cooked in milk and honey). The Punjab, where citrus fruits grow in great profusion, is noted for its fruit drinks.

INDIA, VARIED AND INTERESTING

BOMBAY (2,839,270) is a modern, cosmopolitan, commercial city. Centered around the Flora Fountain, the very hub of Bombay's busy life, are the High Courts and the Secretariat, both in the Venetian Gothic style; the Prince of Wales Museum; Jehangir Art Gallery, containing modern Indian paintings and sculpture, and the domed Gateway of India, based on the 16th-century Gujerat style. In the evening, the center of interest is the city's splendid promenade by the sea, the Marine Drive, to which sophisticated ladies, elegantly dressed in *saris,* lend color and gaiety. On Malabar Hill, from the Hanging Gardens, is a panoramic view of the

The exquisite, delicate Derva Rota or Ra Kherigar Palace, with its breathtaking view, at Junagad

Philip Gendreau

city and colorful **Chowpatty** beach. Near the gardens are the **Parsi Towers of Silence,** where the dead are exposed to the elements. Across the beautiful harbor is the island of **Elephanta,** with its famous caves. **Ganesh Gupta,** the main cave, is one of the earliest examples of a Brahmanical temple, dating back to the 8th century A. D. The Buddhist cave temples near **Ajanta,** some of which are 2,000 years old, lie in a narrow gorge and form a stupendous cave-picture gallery unique in the history of art. . . . Southeast of Bombay is **BIJAPUR,** splendid capital of a powerful 16th-century Muslim state, whose architecture combines grandeur and grace, as well as ornamentation. Its finest building is **Gol Gumbaz,** mausoleum of Sultan Muhammed Adil Shah, with its enormous dome, second largest in the world. . . . At **SANCHI,** site of extensive Buddhist remains, is the imposing **Great Stupa,** a solid dome of sandstone with profusely carved gateways. . . . Rich in historic associations and architectural beauty, **GWALIOR** is the site of **Gwalior Fort,** about two miles long and 2,700 feet wide. Six massive gateways of elaborate design lead to the fort, while within is the splendid **Manmandir Palace,** one of the best specimens of Hindu architecture. . . . Strategically situated on the Yamuna River, **DELHI** (914,790) has always been the gateway to the rich Gangetic plains, in addition to commanding the roads to all parts of India. Planned by Sir Edward Lutyens and Sir Herbert Baker, the modern city of **NEW DELHI** (276,314) was formally opened in 1931. A refreshing feature is the long, tree-lined road, ablaze

in spring with flaming *gulmohur,* yellow laburnum and mellow, cool jacaranda and margosa. According to Fergusson, "the most magnificent palace in the East or perhaps in the world" was the **Red Fort,** with its graceful ramparts. The marble hall, **Diwan-i-Khas (Hall of Private Audience),** with its graceful arches and flower-inlaid piers, has been immortalized by the Persian couplet inscribed in letters of gold on its walls: "If there be a paradise on earth. It is this, it is this, none but this!" Opposite is **Jama Masjid,** biggest and most beautiful mosque in India, also erected by the Emperor Shah Jahan. Built of red sandstone and white marble, its three striped, bulbous domes and two tall and slender minarets are characteristic of Mughal architecture. Inside the ruined fort of **Purana Qila** is the **Qila-i-Kuhna Masjid (Sher Shah's Mosque),** an excellent example of Indo-Afghan architecture with the pointed arch, a Muslim feature, combined with brackets essentially Hindu in style. The first great example of Mughal architecture is the beautifully proportioned, impressive **tomb of Emperor Humayun,** built in 1565 of red sandstone with a central dome of white marble. On the road to **Humayun's tomb** is that of **Isa Khan,** built in 1547, the "last true example of the Lodi style of architecture," main features of which are an octagonal building with an enclosing veranda and a hemispherical dome surrounded by eight smaller domes. Commanding a panoramic view of Delhi from the south is the 5-story **Qutb Minar,** highest stone tower in India, completed in about 1190. Around **Princes' Park,** west of Purana Qila, stand the mansions of the Maharajas of the former princely states. Still further west are the modern government buildings including the palatial red-and-white sandstone **Rashtrapati Bhavan,** official residence of the President of the Republic, and the fascinating circular **Parliament Building,** encircled with an open colonnade. **Jantar Mantar,** the observatory erected in 1725 by Maharaja Jaisingh II of Jaipur, the great astronomer-king, contains six huge masonry instruments to study the celestial bodies. . . . The Western Himalayas offer many interesting hill resorts, chiefly **SIMLA,** formerly the summer capital of India, known for its splendid view and fine walks. . . . Further downstream on the Yamuna is **AGRA** (375,665), city of the **Taj Mahal,** known throughout the world for its pierced marble work and beauty of proportion. . . . The most ancient and holy city of India, **BANARAS,** (341,811) array of shrines, temples and palaces rise in several tiers from the bank of the Ganges River. At nearby **Sarnath,** Buddha delivered his "first sermon," expounding the four Noble Truths. The famous **Asoka Pillar,** whose lion capital has been adopted by the Republic of India as the state emblem, stands here. . . . **CALCUTTA** (2,-548,677) is the largest city in India and second only to London in the Commonwealth. Residents spend most of their leisure time either at **Dkakuria Lakes** or the **Maidan,** where there are golf courses, football fields and the Brigade Ground for ceremonial parades. The **monument to Sir David Ochterlony,** at the northern end of the Maidan, is of Eastern design with a rare combination of an Egyptian base, a Syrian column and a dome, with its metal cupola, that is typically Turkish. At the southern end of the Maidan is the finest building in Bengal — the **Victoria Memorial** — an enormous, symmetrical pile of white marble. A rich storehouse of Indian history, it contains pictures and engravings of Indian scenery besides a fine collection of Persian manuscripts. Near the Circular Canal are the famous **Jain Temples,** four in number, the most important being dedicated to Shree Shree Sheetalnathji, tenth of the 24 Jain deities. On the other side of the Hooghly River are the **Botanical Gardens,** a great attraction because of the 170-year-old **Great Banyan Tree,** more than 1,000 feet in circumference and 88 feet high, capable of sheltering three regi-

ments of soldiers under its branches. . . . Of the 7,000 temples once located in **BHUBANESHWAR,** on the eastern coast, not more than 100 now remain. Exquisitely carved, they are amongst the oldest in India and exhibit a variety of architectural styles of about ten centuries ago. . . . Center of the sunny south, seat of an ancient civilization, **MADRAS** (1,416,056) even today retains an old-world charm. Nucleus of the English establishment was **Fort St. George,** completed in 1653, and within it is **St. Mary's Church,** reputed to be the oldest English church in Asia, with its handsome marble tablets. The wide sea-front **Marina** is reputed to be the second-best beach in the world, while lining it are the Moorish-style **Chepauk Palace;** the imposing, sixteenth-century, Italian-renaissance-style **Presidency College** and the modern-Gothic **San Thome Cathedral,** with its beautiful stained-glass windows. Among the temples in Madras, most striking is the **Kapaleeswarar Koil** in Mylapore, "the abode of peacocks." This temple has the characteristic towering pylon, known as *gopuram,* typical of Dravidian architecture. Behind the temple is a large sacred tank surrounded by flights of steps on the four sides, where devotees may be seen at all times of day, bathing and cleansing themselves before worship. Across the Adyar River are the headquarters of the **Theosophical Society,** an expansive estate of appealing beauty, offering cool, quiet shelter under the huge banyan tree on the grounds or in the well-equipped library with its rare collection of palm-leaf manuscripts and ancient books dating back a thousand years. Music forms an integral part of life in South India, which has a rich heritage in this fine art. **Carnatic** music, as this classical type is called, has been kept alive by a long line of artists, quite a few of whom live in Madras, and the cultural life of the city is one busy, stimulating round of concerts and dance recitals, particularly during the Christmas season. . . . A pleasant seaside resort south of Madras is **MAHABALIPURAN,** also known as the Seven Pagodas. The first foundations of Dravidian architecture in India were laid by the ancient Pallava dynasty, who ruled the territory now known as the Madras State during the sixth to eighth centuries A.D. In this small village are the earliest remnants of their monolithic temples, figures and carvings, unique

A richly adorned court elephant delivers guests at a durbar, or reception, in Bharatpur, during "Holi," the Hindu spring festival
Screen Traveler, Gendreau

in conception and masterly in execution, all hewn out of the rocks, most important being the **Five Rathas**, the bas-relief on a huge rock popularly known as **Arjuna's Penance**, the **Mahishasura Mandapam**, the **Krishna Mandapam** and the **Shore Temples**. . . . MADURAI (361,781), further south, has always been a seat of Tamil learning and culture. Its many religious festivals, celebrated with elaborate ritual and pageantry, have earned for it the name of the "City of Festivals." The pillars of the ornate **Meenakshi Temple**, built in the seventeenth century, produce varying notes when tapped. . . . On an island near the extreme southeastern limit of the peninsula, amidst wavy palms and glistening sands, stands **RAMESWARAM**, one of the most sacred places of the Hindus. Its temple, the finest example of South Indian architecture, is famous for its 4,000-foot-long pillared corridor. . . . OOTACA-MUND, is a pleasant resort in the Nilgiri Hills, noted for their tropical charm. Dense jungles, deep ravines, peaceful lagoons, gliding snake-boats and palm-fringed shore form the smiling land of Malabar, southwest of these hills. Here the jungles abound in wild beasts, which the visitor may see in the game sanctuary skirting the shores of **Periyar Lake**.

KASHMIR

Nestling in the bosom of the Himalayas lies the valley of Kashmir — the tourists' paradise — where hunters, anglers, lovers of hiking and trekking all find their delight. SRINAGAR (207,787) lies along the banks of the Jhelum, its waters crossed by seven bridges, and near **Dal Lake**, surrounded by the lovely pleasure gardens laid out by the Mughal emperors. . . . For the vigorous traveler, **GILGIT AGENCY** offers excellent mountain climbing, fishing and skiing facilities.

PAKISTAN—WORLD'S LARGEST MUSLIM NATION

KARACHI (1,009,438) in West Pakistan, capital of the country and its chief port, is one of the most prosperous cities of the East. A spaciously laid out modern metropolis of broad throughfares and fine buildings, its longest road, **Bunder Road**, with narrow crowded bazaars, is the biggest business and shopping district. In the heart of the city, near the Bunder Road, are two of the city's finest modern buildings: the **Chief Court** and the **Parliamentary Building**. All foreign dignitaries and missions never fail to visit the tomb of **Quaid-i-Azam Mohammad Ali Jinnah**, founder and first Governor General of Pakistan. Sports enthusiasts will be especially pleased with the fine **race course**, whose Quaid-i-Azam's Gold Cup race, on May 13th, is the racing classic and one of the top social events of the season. . . . At **TATTA**, fifteenth-century capital of the Sammas Rajputs, the Moghul architecture and mosaic tilework decoration reached the acme of artistry. Its greatest monument is the **mosque** begun by Emperor Shah Jahan in 1647, whose main dome has exquisite mosaics of white and blue set in a blaze of bright colors. Among an astonishing array of Muslim tombs along the **Makli ridge** is the **tomb of Mirza Jani Beg**, the last of the Tarkhan rulers, with richly carved surface tracery on the enclosure walls. In contrast, Tatta is also extremely popular with hunters, for the surrounding country abounds with game, including partridge, grouse, snipe, hog and bear. . . . Around the year 3,000 B. C. the Indus Valley Civilization flourished along the banks of the mighty Indus River, in the stretch of territory extending from the Arabian Sea to the Himalayan foothills. Center of this great human endeavor was **MOHENJO-DARO,** the Mound of the Dead, northeast of Karachi. These ruins include the **citadel,** containing a remarkable series of structures, with its massive fortifications. A similar city, but not so spectacular, is at Harappa in the Punjab. . . . An entirely different place is **SUKKUR,** a flourishing market town and site of the world-famed, mile-long **Sukkur Barrage,** longest dam in the world. Close by is the large, single-span **Sukkur Railway Bridge,** built in 1887, one of the first cantilever railway bridges ever constructed. . . . The delightful town of **QUETTA,** at the foot of the Murdar mountain, is an ideal summer resort, with a magnificent climate, sunny yet bracing. . . . The remarkable **Nur Mahal,** once the State Palace, is located in **BAHAWALPUR,** in the eastern section, a town noted for its delicate pottery and fine embroidery work. . . . Testifying to the creative excellence of Muslim craftsmen of the Moghul age are many ancient buildings, mosques and mausoleums in the historic city of **MULTAN** (190,122), a town of considerable antiquity in the Punjab. The city is, additionally, the only place in the subcontinent where important monuments of the early Arab or pre-Moghul era still remain. Outstanding among the **five famous tombs** of the twelfth to fourteenth centuries is the **tomb of Rukni-Alam,** built between 1320 and 1324. The **old fort** near the city is well worth a visit. . . . **LAHORE** (849,476) is a gay, charming and hospitable city — center of Pakistan's cultural and academic life. Modernity glows in a setting of ancient history, as lining the vast avenue of the **Mall** are buildings like the massive building of the **Punjab University,** oldest and largest in the land, and the office of the "**Civil and Military Gazette,**" where Rudyard Kipling worked. Down the road from the office is the huge, unserviceable cannon known to the literary world as **Kim's Gun.** Away from the hum of business, Lahore relaxes in the vast pleasure grounds of the famous **Shalimar Gardens,** built by Shah Jahan, the fifth Moghul

emperor, in 1637. Water flows gracefully over three terraces through an artificial channel studded with fountains. The pure marble cascade is embedded with tiny shelves for lamps, so at night when the lamps are lit, the water shines and glistens in the hues of flickering flames. Shah Jahan, creator of the Taj Mahal in memory of his beautiful queen, also built in Lahore one of the first mausoleums of the East — the **tomb of the Emperor Jahangir** — in memory of his father. Rising above the banks of the Ravi River, the red-sandstone mausoleum is surrounded by the spacious **Dilkusha Garden. Badshahi Mosque,** built in 1673 by Aurangzeb, the last of the great Moghul emperors, is another memorable monument. Reputedly the largest in the world, designed on the model of the Al Walid Mosque in Mecca, the Badshahi Mosque has an ascetic grandeur and magnificence all its own, with its towering red minarets, vast steps and three superb domes of gleaming white marble. Other attractive mosques are the elegant **Sonehri or Golden Mosque,** a structure of exquisite symmetry of form and size, and gracing the animated bustle of the **Kashmiri Bazaar, Wazir Khan's mosque,** a building of superb beauty and elegance, embellished with arabesque paintings, vivid lacquered tiles and inlaid pottery. Facing the Badshahi Mosque is the famous **Shahi Quila (Imperial Fort),** the site of which dates from the twelfth century. **Shah Burj Darwaza,** the main entrance, is a typical Moghul gateway, grand in conception and beautiful in the detail of its execution. In the palace area are the **Shish Mahal (Palace of Mirrors),** decorated with scintillating mosaics of glass and small convex mirrors of different colors, and the exquisite and costly marble, curvilinear-roofed pavilion known as **Naulakha.** Between the mosque and the fort is the **Hazuri Bagh,** an exquisite marble pavilion containing the remains of Dr. Muhammad Iqbal, the great poet-philosopher who first conceived of the sovereign state of Pakistan. . . . The **salt mines at ATTOCK,** a small town lying on the border between the Punjab and North West Frontier Province, are among the wonders of the world — hundreds of feet of thick seams form lovely caverns of rock salt, resplendent in gleams of flickering light. . . . Another favorite hill station is **ABBOTTABAD** in the midst of the most lovely scenery, where snow-clad mountains gaze down on a panorama of pine-strewn hills, rivers, fields of gold and vivid green and little villages hanging precariously on the hill crests. This is an excellent starting point to tour the **Kaghan Valley**, a region of breathtaking beauty offering pleasant shooting and very good trout fishing. . . . To the north is **TAXILA**, with extensive **remains of three** distinct cities dating from about 190 to 85 B. C. The **Buddhist stupas** and the monasteries at **Mohra Moradu** and **Jaulian** are the best-preserved monuments of their kind in Pakistan. The **Zoroastrian temple**, constructed in the Scytho-Parthian epoch, is another magnificent architectural specimen. . . . The rugged hill country of the Khyber Pass is the land of warriors who carry their rifles as nonchalantly as the

symbolizing the Pathans' fanatical devotion to Islam, and the fortress of **Jamrud**, at the end of the thirty-mile-long pass. . . . DACCA (411,279), the capital of East Pakistan with a touch of medievalism, possesses a number of intriguing historical remains from Moghul times, including the huge **Lal Bagh Fort**, the **Burra** and **Chota Katras** (**Gateways**) and over a thousand mosques. It also has many fine modern buildings like the outstanding **High Court** and famous **Dacca University**. Travelers are always pleasantly pleased, too, with the city's fresh, verdant look of thick bamboo clumps and palm grooves relieved by splashes of vividly colored flowering trees. Through the surrounding fertile countryside flow the mightiest rivers of the East — the Ganges, the Brahmaputra and the

Gorgeous Shalamar Gardens
in Lahore
Consular Div., Govt. Pakistan

Westerner does his umbrella, although at the same time, hospitality to the stranger still remains the age-old and inviolate custom. **PESHAWAR** (151,776) is the center of this frontier tribal country, home of the tall, bearded and large-boned Pathan, of the Afridi and of the Khattak sword dance. A picturesque city, it also remains an important center of trade between Afghanistan and Pakistan and its **Bijori Gate Bazaar** is even yet the meeting place of caravans from many countries. In keeping with its long history, the city's **Museum** has a rich collection of the Gandhara sculptures and Buddhist relics. Ten miles from Peshawar begins the historic **Khyber Pass**. This roof-top highway winds down the entire course of history. Lying aloft the highway is the famous **Ali Masjid Mosque**,

Meghna — and up and down these rivers stream comfortable **boats** from which may be obtained excellent views of the land of jute, rice, coconut and tea. . . . **SUNDARBANS**, a forest region in the southwest corner of East Bengal, is the haunt of the famous Royal Bengal tiger and, consequently, a mecca for international sportsmen. . . . A rewarding experience for the really hardy and adventurous visitor is a trip to the wild and unexplored **CHITTAGONG HILL TRACTS**, the habitat of primitive tribes of Mongolian extraction who build their houses high on stilts, where the rivers team with fish, the jungle is ablaze with color and innumerable species of wildlife — elephant, tiger, leopard, rhinoceros, bison, deer, python — haunt its shaded depths.

Ceylon

LANKA: "THE RESPLENDENT"

The charm and fertility of the island of Ceylon has been its bane as well as its blessing. Separated from the continent of India by only a narrow strip of sea and standing athwart the highway along which caravels of East and West quested for commerce or conquest, the island has throughout the centuries attracted the stranger from across the seas. Still blessed with a fertile soil, pleasant climate, magnificent scenery and central position, Ceylon retains today its magnetic pull for peoples of other lands.

BLOOD LINES

The Sinhalese comprise roughly two-thirds of Ceylon's population, tracing their descent from the earliest Aryan settlers, who intermarried freely with the indigenous inhabitants. From very early times they have had a distinct language, which was at first an Aryan dialect written in the Brahmi script. The majority profess the Buddhist religion, although there is a considerable minority which is Christian. Buddhism, brought to Ceylon from north India, exercised a vital influence on the life of the people, shaping their culture and civilization and providing a focus for their national unity. Up in the extreme north and away in the east, remote from the turmoil and strife of the heart of the Sinhalese Kingdom but affected by the many centuries of association and conflict with the peoples of South India, a new physical type settled down and developed a separate race-consciousness, culminating today in the group called Ceylon Tamils. Heirs to a civilization claiming an antiquity beyond the Aryan, they speak a language which is recognized as the oldest, richest and most highly organized of the Dravidian group.

FOLK ART

The Golden Age of Sinhala folk arts was the Kandyan age of Ceylon history, with the system of service tenure ensuring the economic self-sufficiency of the artisan. Today, among the most colorful of the folk arts are the masks of Ceylon, the artistic expression of the folk mind, as distinguished from the "fine arts," the art of the sophisticated. Ceylon masks are of two categories: those used in the ritual dances, the *Yak Natun,* and those featured in the *Kolam.* In the ritual dances, the myths and legends of the past are vigorously danced out to the singing of the deeds of the supernatural. In the *Kolam,* the popular masquerade of the south, actors don masks suited to the several roles and disguised by the masks, short episodes are enacted giving free scope for the comic. The art of the Ceylon mask ranks among the highest expressions of the art of simple folk.

CINNAMON ISLE

COLOMBO (424,816), modern capital of Ceylon, is a world-famous port, with luxurious shops, pleasant parks, exotic temples and crowded, colorful bazaars where the East holds sway. The thriving city once offered protection to the trading vessels of the Arabs, Egyptians, Greeks and Romans, and later to the ships of the Portuguese, Dutch and English. Adjoining stately Queen's House, residence of the Governor-General, is Gordon Gardens, site of an old Dutch church where the last Sinhalese king of Kotte was buried, now a miniature park containing a huge rock, relic of the Portuguese occupation, on which is carved the arms of the King of Portugal. In picturesque Victoria Park are birds of bright plumage, flowers of brilliant hues and leafy bowers, including the Madara tree, rarest in Ceylon, whose bark is poisonous and whose wood is said to be an effective charm against wild elephants; balsawood trees, yielding the lightest wood in the world, and magnificent collections of orchids. Of striking architectural beauty, with its great white dome and pillared façade, is the Town Hall. On a hill near Main Street is Wolvendaal Church, a fine cruciform built in 1749 in Doric style, containing many memorials of Dutch rule. In Kochchikadde and Sea Street are shrines sacred to Hinduism, with artistically carved stone pillars and exteriors a mass of grotesque figures, images and symbols, expressions of the age-old art of India. During the Dutch regime, cinnamon was cultivated in a number of gardens outside the city. This is now the fashionable residential quarter. A few miles out from town is the famous Buddhsit temple of Kelaniya, a masterpiece of oriental temple construction, held in greatest veneration. Frescoes of exquisite beauty and color adorn the walls. . . . Drowsy, flower-fragrant, set amidst the picturesque hills, KANDY is the famous and beautiful mountain stronghold that was the last part of Ceylon to fall into foreign hands. Heart of the town is the **Dalada Maligaqa (Temple of the Tooth)**, enclosed by an ornamental stone wall and a moat. The **Pattirippuwa (Octagon)** was at one time a British military prison and is now a library containing a valuable collection of rare old palm-leaf manuscripts. Most striking features of the temple are the many images of Buddha; the elaborate door inlaid with silver and ivory, with two pairs of elephants' tusks on either side, at the entrance to the sanctuary containing the silver-gilt, bell-shaped shrine protecting the Sacred Tooth; and the six inner shrines ornamented with precious stones. Next door is the **Audience Hall**, with its excellent wall plates and rich carvings on the satinwood pillars. It was here that Ceylon's independence was celebrated in 1948. Kandy's chief glory is the lake, said to have been made by Sri Wickrama Raja Sinha, the last king of Kandy. The famous **Kandy Perahera** is held in August, when richly caparisoned elephants, tom-tom beaters, Kandyan dancers and chieftains in jeweled costumes walking in stately procession combine to make this the most glamorous pageant in the East.

At **Peradeniya** are the famous **Royal Botanical Gardens**, containing among their unequalled luxuriance of exotic vegetation a spice collection and the stately Palm Avenue, one of the world's finest collections of palms. . . . Nestling in the bosom of the mountains, **NUWARA ELIYA**, with its fine invigorating air and picturesque scenery, is a most charming spot. There are attractions to gratify every taste — wild rugged heights and peaceful plains, cataracts and babbling brooks, golf on one of the finest courses in the East, trout fishing and mountaineering. A few miles out are the noted **Hakgala Gardens**, with giant tree ferns, sunken rose gardens and ornamental creeks. . . . The stupendous domes of dagobas loom large and a 2,000-year-old history unfurls as the visitor approaches the holy city of **ANURADHAPURA**, for 1,400 years the capital of Ceylon. Devanampiya Tissa, who reigned during the third century B. C., founded the monastery called **Isurumuniya**, in a setting at once picturesque and peaceful. A white dagoba gleams amidst the green foilage and reflections are cast in the still blue waters, while sculptures of supreme beauty, such as the panel of "Lovers," enhance this ancient rock temple. King Dutugemunu,

There are many highly decorative Moslem mosques in Colombo
TWA-Trans World Airlines

Kandyan dancing girls playing the pantheru, a ring-
shaped instrument with brass
cymbals
Ceylon Dept. of Information

most celebrated ruler, conquered the Drav-idians who held Ceylon in thrall, and the period of freedom that followed was marked by the renaissance of art. The greatest work undertaken by him was the **Ruanveliseya**, of enormous proportions, with its white dome and gilded spire. A masterpiece of architecture and a striking memorial to the artistic genius of the Sinhalese race, it is the most celebrated dagoba in Ceylon, being regarded by all as a monument of peculiar sanctity. Largest building is the **Elephant Stables**, whose columns are of such an unusual height that the appellation is quite fitting. In these ancient edifices, the entrance received sculptural embellishments and most characteristic of these were the stone slabs with rounded tops, called guardstones, bearing anthropomorphic representations of serpent deities (Nagas). The moonstone, a semi-circular slab, with its characteristic feature of a procession of animals, is also peculiar to Sinhalese architecture. Considered the best of its kind and chiselled with extreme grace is that at the **Queen's Pavilion**. Rivalling the Roman baths are the splendid stone tanks called *pokunas*, most prominent of which is the **Kuttam pokuna** of the Abhayagiri area.

. . . The enormous mass of granite, forming the rock of **SIGIRIYA** (Lion Rock) rises abruptly, with beetling brows and precipitous sides, to a height of some 600 feet above the surrounding plain. In the fifth century A. D. King Kassapa transformed it into the most impregnable fortress in ancient Ceylon. Oldest and best-preserved of the ancient paintings in the country, in a cavity on the western face of this rock, are portraits of 21 ladies, the only secular pictures known to ancient Ceylon art. That they are the work of a master painter or painters, opinion is agreed, but experts will never tire of wondering who they are, what they are up to, why and wherefore they were created. At the summit of the rock, where Kassapa had his palace, is a carefully planned **drainage system** for the palace, massive **ramparts** even now over thirty feet high and a great **moat**. . . . Ceylon has supplied precious stones to the world since the earliest days and at **RATNAPURA**, city of gems, primitive, quaint gem mines may be seen, where the working methods have remained unchanged throughout the centuries. Also center of a busy planting district, the charm of the hilly slopes is enhanced by tea and rubber plantations.

Japan

GEM OF THE PACIFIC

No longer a remote country, veiled and untouched by the main currents of the world, and one of the few Eastern countries still open to visitors, Japan is the goal of those with a taste for the mysterious, alluring Orient, for she is fascinating in endless ways. Her land is rich in lofty peaks, verdant plateaus, picturesque cascades, sapphire lakes and health-giving hot springs. Life in Japan is no less colorful, with festivals that hăve been preserved through the ages, arts that are redolent of her long cultural history and amusements brimming with exotic charm. Those who feel the magnetism of the mellow Oriental civilization happily will fall completely under the spell of this intoxicating land.

JAPANESE FESTIVALS

To every Japanese the New Year is the festival of festivals. Every house front is decorated with the *kado matsu*, a pair of decorative stands of pine twigs and bamboo stalks, all symbolic of good luck. Friends and relatives come to say their New Year greeting and are served two specialties: *otoso*, sweetened Japanese wine, and *zoni*, a soup containing rice cakes and vegetables. The most popular amusements are battledore and shuttlecock by the girls, kiteflying by the boys and card games, called *karuta*, unique to Japan, by everybody. Generally speaking, the festivals held in Tokyo and southwestern Japan are more animated than those of Kyoto and its surrounding provinces, which have a more ancient origin and are more dignified, but not in the least lacking in color and charm.

EXOTIC DRESS

On social and ceremonial occasions, especially during the New Year season, the long-sleeved, elaborately patterned *kimono* of the Japanese women comes into prominence. As in the case of the *obi*, the sash which holds the *kimono* together, there are various unwritten laws governing the colors and designs of the *kimono* to be used for different occasions.

EASTERN FOODS

Sukiyaki and *tempura* are the two names in Japanese cooking that are gaining international fame with the epicure. The former is a tasty preparation of thin slices of choice meat and vegetables, cooked in sweetened soya sauce, and the latter consists of fresh prawns and fish in season deep-fried in the finest vegetable oil. Japanese wine, called *sake,* is made from rice, and is drunk hot. Japanese beer is regarded by many as being among the best in the world. Japanese green tea is drunk not only at meal times but throughout the day at frequent intervals, and it is customary in the home to serve tea to a visitor regardless of the time of day.

ORIENTAL ISLANDS

Situated on the Sumida River, TOKYO (pop. 5,385,071), the capital since 1869, is roughly divided into two quarters: the educational and residental uptown and the commercial and industrial downtown. Marunouchi, the most Westernized section, is the hub of the commercial activities, while Ginza, with many top-ranking stores, restaurants and theaters, is probably the busiest shopping street in the country. One of the most beautiful sights in Tokyo when viewed from across the spacious Palace Plaza is the Nijubashi, or "Double Bridge," forming the main entrance to the Imperial Palace, across one of the series of picturesque moats surrounding the palace grounds. A short distance from the palace is the imposing, gleaming white granite National Diet Building, with its massive central tower. In Ueno Park, the city's largest, is the Tokyo National Museum, displaying art treasures of old Japan. Rikugien Garden, the most interesting of several landscape gardens, dates back to the early eighteenth century and represents a typical landscape garden of feudal days. Of the many cultural legacies preserved through generations, two forms of stage art have been particularly favored, the Kabuki drama and the highly stylized Noh play. Both have unique qualities: The Kabuki charms one with colorful costumes and settings, classic music and female roles played by male actors, while the Noh moves one with its simplicity, elegance, purity and quiet, created by a combination of recitation of its literary texts, classic music and symbolic movement of players. These players usually perform at the capital. Of the many festivals held in Tokyo, two of the most popular are the Sanja Festival in May, when many portable shrines are paraded through the streets while performances of the

Higashi Honganji Temple

1 Japan Travel Bureau
2 Marunouchi Hotel
3 Hotel Tokyo
4 Hotel Teito
5 New Marunouchi Bldg.
6 Yashima Hotel
7 Marunouchi Bldg.
8 Mitsubishi Bldg. (Am. Emb.)
9 Tokyo Sta. Hotel
10 Ch. of Commerce
11 Tokyo Kaikan Bldg.
12 Imperial Hotel
13 Min. of Agr. & Forestry
14 Nikkatsu Hotel
15 Hattorio Bldg. (Tokyo P.X.)

Ueno
Nat'l Mus.
Tokyo Lib.
Fine Arts Gallery
Tokyo Univ. of Fine Arts
Zoo
Ueno Science Mus.
Park
To Asakusa Park
Umaya Br.
To Chiba

Kuramae Br.
Doai Hosp.
Earthquake Mem. Hall

Tokyo Univ.

Tokyo U. Hosp.
Yushimatenjin Shrine
Matsuzakaya Dept. Store

To Karakuen Gardens

GINZA STREET

AKIHABARA

SUMIDA

Kanda Myojin Shrine

Ryogoku Br.
Memorial Hall

RIVER

SURUGADAI
Y.W.C.A.
Nicolai Cathedral
Transportation Mus.
Meiji Univ.
Chuo Univ.
OGAWAMACHI

Hamacho Park
Meijiza Thea.

JIMBOCHO
OGAWA-MACHI
Univ. Club

KANDA

YOSHI-CHO
Suitengu Shrine

Foreign Lang. Univ.
Meteor. Observatory
Mitsui Bldg.

OTE-MACHI
Tokyo Seimi Bldg.
Mitsukoshi Dept. Store & Thea.
Stock Exch.
Shirokiya Dept. Store

Tekko Bldg.
Min. of Transport.
Tokyo R.R. Sta.
NIHONBASHI
Takashimaya Dept. Store

Kaijo Bldg.

MAP SHOWS MAJOR STREETS

Imperial
Palace

MARUNOUCHI
N.Y.K. Bldg.
Meiji Bldg.
Central P.O.

KYO-BASHI

HIGHLIGHT MAP OF
TOKYO
JAPAN

Double Br.
Dai Ichi Bldg.
Tokyo Met. Off.
Foreign Trade Mus.

YURAKUCHO
Nippon Thea.
GINZA STREET
Matsuya Dept. Store
St. Luke's Hosp.

Met. Police Dept.
Sanshin Bldg.
Hibiya Imperial Thea.
Ernie Pyle Thea.
TWA
Mitsukoshi Dept. Store
Kabuzika Thea.

To Akasaka Det. Palace
Supreme Court
Park
GINZA
Matsuzakaya Dept. Store
Shinbashi Enbujo Thea.
Tokyo Thea.
Nishi-Honganji Temple

Kasumigaseki Det. Palace
Kachidoki Br.

Diet Bldg.
Kojimachi Park
Peer's Club
Min. of Education
NHK Bldg. (Radio Tokyo)
Min. of For. Affairs
Tsukiji Hosp.

Prime Minister's Res.
SHIMBASHI
To Yokohama

Central Wholesale Market

To Meiji Shrine
To Shiba Park
Atago Hill
Hama Detached Palace

Okura's Mus.
© C. S. HAMMOND & Co., N. Y.

dengaku dance and the *binzasara* add to the gaiety, and the **Tori-no-Ichi** (**Cock Fair**) in November, when the *kumade,* or decorated bamboo rakes, a symbol of good luck, is sold. The most famous of all, however, are the "Cherry Dances" of the **Azuma Odori**, with the lovely dancers dressed in colorful kimonos, given during the cherry blossom time in April at the Shimbashi Embujo Theater. Of the native Japanese sports having a special appeal to foreign visitors, foremost are **Judo** (called also **Jujitsu**) and Sumo. Those interested in the former are advised to visit **Kodokan Hall**. Championship tournaments of **Sumo**, the traditional Japanese wrestling, usually performed by giant professionals, are held in January, May and September. The **Outer Garden of Meiji Shrine** has in its area the **Memorial Picture Gallery** and various sports facilities, including a baseball diamond, track and field stadium, gymnasium and swimming pool. ... **NIKKO NATIONAL PARK**, north of Tokyo, is noted for its wonderful harmony of natural beauty and artistic splendor. The high light is **Toshogu Shrine**, built in 1636, one of the greatest monuments in the history of Japanese architecture, with its striking, richly decorated **Yomeimon Gate** and vermilion-painted, crescent-moon-shaped **Sacred Bridge**. Here also are **Lake Chuzenji**, a favorite for yachting, boating and trout fishing, and its **Kegon Waterfall**, probably the most famous cataract in Japan. In the winter, the wind turns the water into a cluster of gigantic, lacelike icicles. ... West of Tokyo is the quiet seaside resort of **KAMAKURA**. Perhaps best-known of its many historic mementoes is **Diabutsu** (**Great Buddha**), a superb bronze image measuring 42 feet in height and cast in 1252 standing in the grounds of the Kotokuin Temple. Although smaller than the Buddha in Nara, as a work of art it is considered far superior. The **Hachiman Shrine**, founded in 1063, has two museums: the new **Art Museum** and the **Kamakura Kokuhokan** (**Municipal Art Museum of Kamakura**), housing many rare art objects of the time when this city was the seat of government (1185-1336). ... **HAKONE**, farther west, forms the southern part of the **Fuji-Hakone National Park**. A popular mountain and hot-spring resort, it has a superb view across Lake Hakone to Mt. Fuji, the highest mountain in Japan. Despite its great

height, Fuji is not a difficult peak to scale and attracts hordes of climbers during the summer. ... Glittering cloisonne ware are the prize of **NAGOYA** (1,030,635), industrial center of central Japan. Nearby **Ise-Shima National Park** is known for the **Mikimoto pearl farms** in Ago Bay, as well as for its attractive beach scenery. The **Japan Alps** and **Joshin-etsu National Parks** offer pleasure to mountaineers and skiers throughout the year. ... For about five months from the beginning of May, the unique **cormorant fishing** is to be seen on the Nagara River at **GIFU** (211,845). Every moonless night the flotilla of fishing boats glides down the river under the light of blazing torches, while teams of clever birds, held with strings by master fishermen, busily duck and dive and come up every few minutes with their catch of "ayu," a troutlike fish. Each cormorant wears a ring around the base of its neck so that it may not swallow any except very small fish. ... The capital of the country for more than ten centuries (794-1869), **KYOTO** (1,101,854), often called Japan's art center, is a city rich in historic association and legendary lore. **Nijo Detached Palace**, or **Nijo Castle,** originally belonged to the Tokugawa Shoguns and the grandeur of its decoration and embellishments is in striking contrast to the simplicity of the **Old Imperial Palace**. An embellishment in red lacquer is added to the beauty of **Heian Shrine**, with its beautiful garden of cherry trees, azaleas and irises. Other celebrated Buddhist fanes are the magnificent **Higashi** and **Nishi Honganji Temples**, both splendid examples of Japanese Buddhist architecture, and **Sanjusangendo**, also called the "Hall of Thousand Buddhas," an elongated temple constructed during the thirteenth century. Originally built as the country villa of a shogun, **Ginkakuji** (**Silver Pavilion**) has an elegant landscape garden and a ceremonial tearoom. Kyoto is also a city of festivals and colorful fetes, some gay and others solemn and mystical, including the distinctive **Miyako Odori** ("Cherry Dances") at the Kaburenjo Theater. Other fascinating festivals are the "Aci Matsuri" (Hollyhock Festival) in May, a procession led by an imperial messenger and his suite in full court costume and said to trace its origin back to the sixth century, and the "Mibu Kyogen" in April, consisting of a number of pantomime farces originating in the thirteenth century However, the **Gion Festival** in July, dating back to the ninth century, is the largest and gayest celebration and one of the country's best-known, with its parades of ornamental floats. . . . NARA, south of Kyoto, was the cradle of Japanese art, crafts and literature. Its **Nara Park**, largest in the country, is a natural woodland where tame deer roam at will. At the foot of Mt. Mikasa is **Kasuga Shrine**, reached along an avenue of antique stone lanterns. The shrine buildings, painted a bright vermilion and hung with some 1,000 metal lanterns, are celebrated for their classic architecture and enchanting setting. **Horyuji Temple**, consisting of a cluster of buildings, each a flawless masterpiece in

strongest castles in the country. **Nakanoshima** is the civic center, while **Sennichimae** and **Dotombori** are the pleasure quarters and **Shinsaibashi-suji** is the busiest shopping street. At the **Banraku Theater**, only one of its kind in Japan, are presented the celebrated Japanese puppet plays, employing the unique "Three-man Puppetry," each of the principal puppets being operated by three manipulators, producing amazing lifelike movements. The spring **Sumo** tournament takes place at the Prefectural Gymnasium. From here the visitor should take the steamer trip through the romantic **Inland Sea,** a scenic, island-studded waterway between Honshu Island and the islands of Shikoku and Kyushu. . . . A vivid reminder of Japan's

The unique Itsukushima Shrine on Miyajima
Japan Tourist Assn.

its respective style of architecture, and housing a wealth of priceless objects of art, is the oldest existing temple in Japan and probably the most antique wooden structure in the world, since it traces its founding to the year 607. Another attraction is **Todaiji Temple**, noted for its big bell and colossal bronze Daibutsu, at 53 feet high the largest of its kind in the world, completed in 749 after repeated trials in casting. . . . The second largest city in Japan is OSAKA (1,956,136). An important center of domestic and foreign commerce from the very early days of Japanese history, Osaka's position was further strengthened when in 1584 Toyotomi Hideyoshi had his residential **Osaka Castle** built here, one of the grandest and

grandeur in the feudal days is the stately donjon of **Egret Castle,** with its white walls and gracefully curving lines, at HIMEJI (212,100), northwest of Osaka. . . . In HIROSHIMA (285,712), where the atomic bomb exploded on August 6, 1945, stands the **Peace Tower.** Miyajima (Shrine Island), scenic gem of the Inland Sea, is noted chiefly for the **Itsukushima Shrine,** whose buildings are connected by corridors or galleries stretching out over the sea, so that at high tide the whole edifice seems to be floating on the surface of the sea. The "torii" gate of the shrine, made of camphor wood and over fifty feet high, rises out of the sea nearly 200 yards from the shore. . . . One of the best-known hotsprings resorts is BEPPU, on the eastern

Cormorant fishing—a fascinating, nighttime spectacle
on the Nagara River
Japan Tourist Assn.

coast of Kyushu, the southernmost island. Featured here are hot sand baths on the beach, where people half bury themselves in the sand soaked with hot-spring water gushing out from below. In the suburbs are numerous "Hells," including boiling ponds of hot-spring water, and bubbling mud.... An exotic port city is NAGASAKI (241,-805), at the western extremity of Kyushu. The Uraba Mansion located here is associated with *Madame Butterfly.* Unzen National Park, across the bay, is an internationally renowned summer resort. Among Nagasaki's many outstanding festivals is the October Okunchi Festival, when many colorful dances of Chinese origin are performed, of which the *Ja Odori,* or Dragon Dance, is the best. . . . SENDAI (341,685), north of Tokyo, is the cultural center of northern Honshu. Well-known scenic attractions are Matsushima ("Pine Islands"), a great number of islands, each covered with aged, gnarled pine trees, dotting Matsushima Bay. At nearby Mt. Zao, an ideal ground for skiing, may be seen the "silver thaw," the weird spectacle of rows upon rows of trees coated with

scintillating ice, standing like statues in the snow. A rural country from of old, the district still preserves a number of quaint customs and colorful events. Of these the "Tanabata Matsuri" or Star Festival is best-known for its gorgeous pageantry, when the whole city becomes alive with colored decorations of various designs. In the "Nomaoi Matsuri," or Horse Festival, held in July on the Hibarigahara Plain at Haranomachi, south of Sendai, gallant horsemen in ancient armor demonstrate their skill. . . . SAPPORO (313,850) is the center of Hokkaido, the northernmost island. At Sankakuyama are many ski jumps, among which the "Okura schanze" is one of the best in the Orient. . . . SHIKOTSU-TOYA NATIONAL PARK includes Lake Toya, abounding in salmon trout and crabs, and Jozankei Spa, with excellent skiing slopes in the surrounding mountains . . . The small village of SHIRAOI, near Sapporo, is in the Ainu district, where these aborigines of Japan, now found only in Hokkaido, live in accordance with their old customs and manners.

Hong Kong and Singapore

TWO FABULOUS, EXCITING CITIES

Hong Kong and Singapore, two of the most colorful, if not *the* most colorful ports in the world, both lie on islands off the Asian mainland, the one off China, the other off the southern tip of the Malay Peninsula. They are the Occident's gateways to the East and the Orient's gateways to the West. Malays, Chinese, Indians, Pakistanis and Europeans, Muslims, Buddhists and Christians live side by side in peace and goodwill. With justice are these free ports called melting pots of East and West.

AND A VARIED MENU, TOO

With their cosmopolitan populations, Hong Kong and Singapore have, perhaps, the most varied collection of exotic foods in the world. In both cities, a visitor has the opportunity of enjoying a variety of Chinese dishes — and the best. The Chinese people are well-versed in good eating and Chinese food, particularly Cantonese dishes, is probably the best in the world. Cantonese food has been supplemented by Peking, Tientsin, Shanghai, Szechwan and Fukien dishes, including bird's nests, savory soups, shark's fins, stuffed chicken and an almost bewildering list of other delicacies. For the unconventional who like to go "slumming," Hokien Street in Singapore, at night with its brightly lit stalls along the sides of the street, provides the most delightful Hokien Mee (noodles boiled and flavored with prawns, vegetables and spices in a tasty bowl of soup). *Satay* (pieces of skewered meat, grilled with spice) is spoken of with relish among the various communities in Singapore. It is eaten with rice cakes, cucumber and peanut curry.

BAY WINDOW OF THE ORIENT

Formerly a notorious retreat for smugglers and pirates, since the British took it over as a free port HONG KONG (1,857,000) has become one of the world's greatest harbors and entrepôts. Indeed a beautiful place, its gorgeous scenery compares favorably with the loveliest in the world. Take the cable car of the Peak Tram in Garden Road for a distinctive ride almost vertically up to Victoria Peak, the top of the island. You may catch a distant glimpse of Macao, the friendly Portuguese possession forty miles south, while northwards in the distance is the forbidden territory of Communist China. Down at Causeway Bay is the famous home and gardens of the late Aw Boon Haw, the Tiger Balm King, including the peculiar, crude impressions of the Chinese Nirvana. Here are the colony's only authentically duplicated pagoda and some of the weirdest pictures of "heaven" and "hell" ever devised. Lovely Botanic Gardens, fronting Government House, are laid out in formal English style, with sloping lawns. The Anglican Cathedral in Garden Road, nearby shopping district in the central part of town, and "Cat" (Catchick) Street are part of the old and the new. In Cat Street, they say, you pick up unearthly bargains and reports persist of famous antiques now adorning museums in London, Paris and New York having been acquired here for a few cents. Along Island Road, circumscribing the entire island, colorful vistas unfold one after another and you marvel at the kaleidescope as it shifts from the formal European to the distinctively Chinese. In the bay, at the fascinating fishing village of Aberdeen, are the famous floating restaurants serving a variety of sea food, which, still alive, are shown the diner before going into the pot. Repulse Bay is dramatized by the baronial mansion of Eucliff. Designed as a miniature Versailles and replete with rich furnishings and oils by European masters, from the outside Eucliff looks rambling, so caused, according to hearsay, by a superstition of the owner that death would overtake him the moment he stopped building. In fact, he died during the Japanese occupation, when building materials were not available. Stanley has its old fort, its tiny village and its fleet of fishing junks. Shek-O, nestling at the bottom of a hill, is one of the island's loveliest spots, with a marvelous beach. The mainland of Kowloon — particularly around the Peninsula Hotel — is famous for its modern shops, theaters and restaurants. In the Tin Hau Temple at Shamshuipe is the famous Dragon Mother. Supposed to have originated 200 years before our era, at the time of the First Emperor, the one who built the Great Wall, she was said to have been a fishing girl by the name of Wang, who caught an eight-claw fish she called the "dragon." The emperor sent for the girl to become one of his concubines, but the dragon thwarted all his attempts to get hold of her, and when she died she was buried with honors and a temple raised to her memory. In the temple, the Dragon Mother sits in state in her shrine, the paper-dressed figures in front of her are the 60 years of the Chinese cycle, of which 1955 was the 32nd. The rural towns of **Taipo, Unlong** and **Shatin,** in the New Territories beyond Kowloon, are notable for the old-world nature of their temples, streets and environment, where you get the feeling of looking at China itself, an emotion impos-

structures around it, its architecture is typically Moorish, its roofline ornamented with minarets and its walls featuring unusual designs. Singapore's famous **Change Alley,** a motley collection of roadside stalls linking the same two places, still retains its glamour and the reputation as a bargain hunter's mecca. Across the Singapore River, in front of the **Victoria Memorial Hall and Theatre,** is the **statue of Sir Thomas Stamford Raffles,** who founded the city in 1819. The outlet of the river presents a picturesque scene, with its odd craft —

Street scene in Hong Kong, featuring the rickshaw, taxi of the Orient
Philip Gendreau

sible of being conjured up in the cosmopolitan urbanity of the island itself. Finally, there is **Tai-O,** on the tip of Lantao Island, a town built on stilts and mostly inhabited by fishermen. The **Taoist Temple** in the hills above, reached only after a two-hour trek, is so far away from the clamor of civilization that the wind whistling through the trees sounds like a jet in turmoil.

"THE LION CITY"

In **SINGAPORE** (940,824), between Collyer Quay and **Raffles Place,** the city's business heart, is the striking **Arcade.** With its quaint color scheme of pale green and yellow contrasting oddly with the other

sampans (rowboats), tongkangs (lighters), twakows (small cargo-boats) and launches — and a background of buildings of typically Chinese-architecture. In the grounds of majestic **St. Andrew's Cathedral** one can, with luck, watch snake-charmers at work and itinerant Indians displaying feats of juggling and "magic" or have their future told by turbaned fortune-tellers. **Mariaman Kovil** is a typical South Indian Hindu temple, whose archway and roof are profusely decorated with groups of animals and human figures carved and painted in marvelous colors. Cheek-by-jowl with the temple is **Pagoda Street,** otherwise known as the "junkman's paradise." On Tank

Native barges on the colorful Singapore River
Screen Traveler, Gendreau

Road is the **Chettiar Temple**, place of worship of the Hindus, figuring largely in the celebrations connected with the **Thaipusam Festival**, when devotees suffer self-inflicted tortures as part of vows they make and as a propitiation for sins. **Chinatown**, in New Bridge Road, is a crowded, teeming area, full of strange merchandise. From the windows flutter the family washes — not on strings, but strung out on long bamboo poles, looking for all the world like an array of multicolored banners. At night, the air is filled with the babel of Chinese dialects, mingled with the crash and thunder of gongs and cymbals accompanying the clicking of wooden sticks and the piping of flutes. One of the Tiger Balm King's famous residences is **Haw Par Villa**, of unusual design and architecture. An elaborately designed archway marks its entrance and the roadway leading to the villa is flanked by porcelain dragons, grotesquely-shaped trees and uniquely-fashioned rocks. The grounds have a miniature Chinese garden. Buddhist rites may be witnessed at the **Buddhist Temple** off Rangoon Road, which includes the 300-ton, hand-fashioned Buddha and the subterranean room beneath the Buddha's seat where the caretaker-priest spends part of his day in silent meditation. Most interesting of all Chinese temples in Singapore is the **Monkey God Temple or Soon Thian Keng Temple**. The monkey is worshiped by Buddhists because of the service he gave the Chinese monk, Hsuan Tsang, during the latter's journey to India to fetch the sacred scriptures. Every Sunday morning, a medium paints his face white and red, puts on a monkey-skin robe and colorful headdress and goes into a trance, during which he cuts his tongue with a sword, smearing the blood on bits of yellow paper. These are then taken home by devotees, burned and the ashes eaten as medicine. One of the "musts" is that gourmet's paradise in Orchard Road — **Prince's** — with an atmosphere restful and luxurious. The "orang laut" or sea men, the inhabitants of Singapore when Raffles landed, are scattered in small communities at **Kallang Pulai River** and **Pulau Brani**, many living in thatched huts built on stilts above the water. Don't miss **Johore Bahru**, across the causeway linking the colony with the mainland, including the palatial **Bakit Serene**, residence of the Sultan of Johore, and the famous waterfall of **Kota Tinggi**.

Burma

LAND OF PAGODAS

BURMA is often called the "Golden Land" and with good reason — all over the country the dominant features of any scene are gold-encrusted pagodas. On hilltops and valleys, in cities and villages, the tinkling temple bells are heard. The majority of Burmese people are Buddhists and devoted to their religion; almost all festivals, and there are many, are based on religion, even though often observed as social holidays. Burmese theater entertainment falls into four categories. The leading dramas are based on Buddhist tradition — stories of Buddha's birth, his life and the lives of ancient kings. They portray every phase of human emotion and usually end on a tragic note. Then there is a type of musical comedy, without actual plot, with jokes and dances comprising the entertainment. Still another theatrical art is a form of ballet — group dancing with singing. The marionette show is also popular; and often consists of a long play. . . . To see the real Burma, one must travel through the rural areas where 85% of the Burmese people live. While its cities are business, educational and cultural centers, Burma is a country of villages. . . . In Upper Burma is Lake Inle, a beautiful body of water 12 miles long — the largest lake in the country. Here you can see the unique manner in which the famous "leg-rowers" propel their boats.

RANGOON (pop. 737,079), Burma's capital, is considered one of the finest cities in the East. It has two beautiful lakes, Kandawgyi and Inya; on the shores of the latter, part of the University of Rangoon is located, whose campus is the largest in the East. Rangoon also has the largest and most famous Buddhist shrine in the world, the Shwedagon Pagoda, dating back 2,500 years, and, in the exact center of the city, is 2,250-year old picturesque Sule Pagoda, housing ancient Buddhist relics. The City Hall is of architectural interest. . . . MANDALAY is not an old city but has been described as one of the most alluring. It is noted for its wooden architecture with the monasteries presenting the finer examples. . . . MOULMEIN is a scenic port, protected from the sea by Bilugyun Island and picturesquely situated on the Salween River. . . . PAGAN, on the east bank of the Irrawaddy, south of Mandalay, draws pilgrims who venerate the pagodas and shrines laid waste in battle in the 13th century. The ruins cover several miles.

Rice terraces form interesting geometric formations in the interior of Burma
Philip Gendreau

Thailand

OXCARTS TO AIRPLANES

Thailand is one of the most fascinating countries to visit, for it has much to interest the traveler. Ornate temple spires beautify the skyline, and the gentle ringing of tiny bells form a pleasing background. It has cultural traditions several centuries old. The music differs from the Western style, but the dances are graceful and expressive; girls are trained in this art from childhood. In the decoration of silver arti-

Outdoor sports have become very popular.

BANGKOK (pop. 750,000), capital of Thailand, situated on the left bank of the Chao Phraya River, is a busy city, with modern transportation facilities and an important airport. It is also a colorful city, its people largely Buddhists, as the 400 Buddhist temples in the city testify. The life of the Buddhist is completely centered around his religion; most young men become monks for short periods, usually

The Hindu Temple of Dawn, with its intricate decoration, in Bangkok
TWA-Trans World Airlines

cles the Siamese craftsman is unexcelled. . . . Oxcarts were one of the chief methods of transportation not so long ago. Today planes and railways have largely supplanted the oxcart and elephant, as means of travel. However, river traffic is still important, and families live their entire lives on small craft floating on the waters of the country. In some rural areas elephants are still trained for heavy work; in the cities modern household appliances are obtainable. Missionaries introduced Western educational systems, medicine and modern methods in other fields. . . . In foods, rice and fish are chief staples; fruits and vegetables are plentiful and in the larger cities many well-known brands of canned goods are available. . . . In sports, Thailand's many rivers and its location on the Gulf of Siam offer opportunities for fresh- and salt-water fishing.

three months; they wear yellow robes and beg for their food — the yellow raiment singling them out as worthy of alms. The canals, which cut through the city, are full of activity. Farmer's wives in sampans bring their fruits and vegetables and sell them to customers at the waters' edge. . . . For other sightseeing there are royal palaces, the royal temple of Wat Phra Kaeo a National Library and a Museum; Wat Benjamabopit is a beautiful spireless temple built of marble with glazed tile roofs — unique among the temples of Bangkok.

AYUTTHAYA, north of Bangkok on an island at the mouth of the Pa Sak River and a former capital, has interesting ruins. Destroyed in battle in the 18th century were a royal palace, several temples and pagodas. They are among the few relics left of Thailand's earlier times.

Indonesia

THE NECKLACE OF THE EQUATOR

Geographically, Indonesia is made up of the largest island group in the world, extending for well over 3,000 miles between the continents of Asia and Australia. Because it is situated across the equator, it has no "seasons" as we do — only wet and dry. But in spite of its tropical position, only a part of the land area suffers the sweltering heat usually associated with the equator. In the people, as well as the land, there is much diversity. In parts of the islands very ancient customs and traditions exist which seem to take one back to the days of the wild tribe, to magic and witchcraft; then above that layer is the gentle animism of the Hindu period. Mohammedanism has also contributed a great share in molding the life and attitudes of the Indonesian. Successive invasions down the centuries and the seas which separate each island have produced different physical types, a number of languages and a great variation of customs, dress and folklore. Indonesian scenery will be unforgettable with its volcanic mountains rising from the land, its temples of ancient grace and solemnity, its thriving cities and its blending of the old and the modern.

TAPE AND GOUDEK

Each city of Indonesia has its particular dish. Around the Bandung area *tapé,* the product of a ferment made from rice and applied to the cassava root, is considered a delicacy by the Javanese. Also, when ripe, the *tapé* is toasted until the outside of the pulpy mass is crackly and brown, at which time it is glazed with butter and has the appearance of gingerbread. Another delicacy is a type of gold fish (unlike our household variety). In Djokjakarta the famous dish is *goudek,* a vegetable dish spiced with red peppers and seasoned with herbs, moistened with cocoanut milk and completed by the addition of hard-boiled eggs. It is usually sold in the street by a vendor. *Krupuk* is a typically Indonesian food. Made from rice, wheat or cassava flour mixed with some savory ingredient, such as powdered fish, it is steamed, dried and then baked. It is eaten as a crunchy sort of cracker.

A GLIMPSE OF THE CITIES

DJAKARTA, capital of the Republic of Indonesia, is located on the island of Java. The city has a population of about two million and is the center of government as well as of transportation and communication. Means of transportation are varied and include trolley cars, electric trains, taxis, buses and trucks, as well as horse-drawn carts and professional porters who carry your market purchases in baskets slung to the back or on shoulder-poles. In fact, Djakarta takes on the aspect of many Western cities: There is the inevitable line-up of modern cars in traffic jams; jeeps bang into burly trucks; girls wear the latest fashions and are concerned with cosmetics; hungry office-workers lick ice-cream cones. Milk, bread, papers, in fact, everything, is delivered to your door on bicycles by peddlers with whom you must bargain like mad before you get a reasonable price. One of the sights of Djakarta is the *betjak,* the foot-pedalled tricycle-taxis in which you sit as though you were in a chair on wheels. The city has many first-class hotels, theaters and boarding houses. There is a small but interesting zoo and an aquarium down on the coast. Djakarta's Museum has been well known to visitors for many years and contains some remarkable records and relics of Indonesia's ancient cultures. Some relics of old are to be found, however, in the city itself. There is the Amsterdam Gate of white-washed brick of evident Dutch architecture. Nearby is the Sacred Cannon which still has the reputation for magical powers among some Indonesians. There are still many canals in Djakarta, and in the older sections of the town you will find old diamond-paned windows with swinging shutters on old white-washed and gabled houses which look out over the canals — a bit of 16th-century Holland set in the Orient. Also in this section is the old town hall dating from 1710 and the remains of a church built around 1695 where the sermons were preached in Portuguese for the benefit of the immigrants from Malaya. Also in the old section is the Chinese quarter in the Glodok area with its quaintly-built houses crowded over broad streets and old canals. . . . To the southeast of the capital is BANDUNG, a recognized holiday and tourist resort because of its magnificent scenery and cool climate. Besides the city itself, there are a half-dozen smaller towns in the area which are almost equally attractive for

Batak villages, with these strange peaked huts, are seen in Sumatra
Screen Traveler, Gendreau

holiday-makers. Bandung is known for its clean, tree-lined streets, its parks and gardens and the rapidity of its development. It is the only city in all Indonesia with a local bus service whose drivers and conductors are all women and girls. It prides itself as an educational center and includes the Technical Faculty of the Indonesian University as well as the Bosscha Observatory, the best equipped in Indonesia. Bandung is known as the "Paris of Java" not only for its modes and clothes-conscious people but because the inhabitants of this region display that light-hearted gaiety so often ascribed to Parisiennes. As for Bandung modes — they are legion. The batiks are brightly colored and the flowered jackets the women wear are as original as they are gay and exotic. . . . Near the southern coast is DJOKJA-KARTA, former capital of the Republic. "Jogji," as it is familiarly called, is not a big city — you can walk across its greatest extent in a couple of hours. One long main street links the northern part with the southern part where the ruins of the old Water Palace lie and where the Kraton (Royal House) is situated, whose buildings exhibit some of the most beautiful examples of Javanese interior decoration to be found anywhere. Here large courtyards are shaded by great trees. The public buildings and reception halls of the Kraton have exquisitely carved, painted and gilded wooden pillars and cross beams, polished tile floors and an atmosphere of great peace and charm about them. Trees have been planted here on all occasions of celebration, such as the birth of an heir to the throne or in other times of national rejoicing. The principal shopping center of the city is down the main street, but markets are scattered in different areas and small shops abound. The quarters of

the second Royal House of Djokjakarta, Paku Alam, lie to the east of the city's center. . . . Traveling northwest across Java one comes to MAGELANG. Here is located the great Hindu-Javanese Temple of Borobudur, recovered from the depths of tropical growth. The temple stands on a rise of ground backed by jagged hills. This wonderful stone edifice with its galleries of meditating Buddhas is a masterpiece of masonry, hoary with great age and sanctified by a man's past endeavor to be at one with the everlasting. . . . An interesting trip is one taken to BALI, off the eastern tip of Java. Here is an island of Hindu culture where flourish Asiatic mammals, birds and insects not found on the larger islands. This is the homeland of the much publicized dancers still practicing an art steeped in ancient Hindu tradition. Being so small an island, with plenty of winds to cool it, it is balmy and pleasant most of the year. Arts and crafts are the principal activities of the island's population. Fine pottery, gold and silver ornaments and engraving in wood, stone and metal are arts in which the Balinese craftsmen are adept. . . . To get an "all around" impression of Indonesia, a trip to SULAWESI (CELEBES) should be made. This queer-looking island is mostly mountainous with placid waters and land-locked bays. The city of MAKASSAR lies on the western side of the tip of the southern peninsula. Here you will find the old trading quarter dating back to the 17th century. Other parts of the city are dotted with squares and fortresses reminiscent of Dutch colonial days. Makassar's markets are bright with gay colors and hand-woven baskets of lovely shapes. Rattan, palm leaf and other pliable materials are woven into innumerable articles and have a charm which is irresistible to the curiosity seeker.

The Philippines

EAST MEETS WEST

An Occidental culture in an Oriental setting on tropical islands of great beauty, makes a visit to the Republic of the Philippines something to always remember. The Spanish discoverer, Ferdinand Magellan landed on the island of Cebu in 1521, claimed the archipelago for Spain and named it for his Spanish King, Philip II. Magellan found here a mixed race, with a culture largely Malayan, whose history dated back to very early times. Spain ruled the Philippines for almost four centuries, during which time Christianity and Spanish culture became firmly established. Spain ceded the islands to the United States in 1898 and rapid advances in education were made during that regime. A Commonwealth form of government was set up in 1935, and the Republic of the Philippines became an independent nation in 1946. . . . Filipinos are a literate people; many converse in Spanish and Tagalog (the national language) and English is spoken, or understood, almost everywhere in the principal islands. A "Filipino" may belong to any one of more than 40 ethnological groups, but the Filipinos themselves prefer to be classed as Malays.

The Philippine archipelago consists of more than 7,000 islands, rich in scenic beauty; nearly 900 of them are inhabited. Forest-covered mountains come down to the sea and waterfalls, wide fertile valleys, coastal plains, navigable rivers, bays and gulfs, white beaches and palm-shaded villages offer a pleasing panorama to the traveler arriving by sea. Inter-island boats maintain regular schedules, and traveling by air between most cities is easy and convenient. There are also many fine roads for the motorist to enjoy; the visitor from the West will find facilities resembling those at home. In most cities American and Continental cuisine of fine quality prevails, and there are many restaurants specializing in Oriental dishes. *Lechon* (roast pig served the Filipino way) is a great favorite; sea foods and native-style curried chicken are much in demand.

AROUND THE ISLAND

LUZON, in the north, is the largest and most important island of the Philippines, yet the primitive and the modern lie very close together; primitive Negritos, who still hunt with bows and arrows, live within 50 miles of cosmopolitan Manila. In northern Luzon the fertile fields in the Cagayan Valley produce the tobacco rolled into the famous Manila cigars and cigarettes. Guided tours of these vast fields include a visit to the factories. . . . MANILA, in southern Luzon is the metropolis of the Philippines. With a population of over a million, it is the largest commercial, industrial, cultural and social center of the nation. Almost destroyed in World War II, a large part of Manila has been restored; modern buildings have been designed and splendid parks and avenues have been laid out with the beautification of the city in mind. Manila is located on the Pasig River where the river enters Manila Bay — the finest harbor of the Orient. . . . Dewey Boulevard skirts the shores of the bay and is lined with modern hotels, restaurants and spacious homes. To Luneta Park, facing the bay, go the people for an afternoon's stroll in the bracing air, and, in the evening, to watch the glorious sunsets. . . . Westward, across the bay, is the Bataan peninsula and, nearby, the island of Corregidor, famous battlegrounds in World War II. Tours are conducted for visitors. . . . INTRAMUROS, called the "Walled City," was laid out by the Spanish explorer, Legaspi, in 1571, and designated by him the capital of the archipelago. In 1590 a wall was built around the city, and this section of Manila remained for centuries a fine example of a Spanish medieval town, as well as the first capital of the nation. This historic "Walled City" was shelled to almost a rubble heap during World War II, but some portions of the old wall remained standing, as did a few buildings. . . . The Church of Saint Augustine was not badly damaged. It is the oldest stone church in the Philippines — a massive structure begun in 1599 and completed in 1606. . . . Fort Santiago, another stone structure built in 1592, is of interest. In its gruesome dungeons Filipino prisoners were condemned to torture and death. It was used as an internment camp during World War II. . . . Beyond Intramuros, Modern Manila, in spite of its Western ways, has an Oriental flavor. The Escolta shopping district displays in its attractive stores imported items from the West and Philippine products. . . . You will want to see Rizal Avenue's arched sidewalks crowded with people, and to visit the **Yangco** and **Central Markets**. . . . **San Sebastian Church** of Gothic style is the first prefab steel structure in the world. The sections were brought from Belgium and erected in 1891 — also one of the few buildings to have escaped destruction in World War II. The oldest educational institution in the Philippines is the **University of Santo Tomas**, built in 1611. Several. thousand Allied nationals were imprisoned here during World War II. For the sportslover visiting Manila there is golf, tennis, fishing, or watching horse races, cock fights or movies. To watch the Basque game of jai alai being played, is exciting; it is one of the fastest of all games. . . . Manila can also offer the visitor a gay night life with fine entertainment, excellent food and dancing to the music of good orchestras. Filipinos, besides being a friendly people, are musical and love to dance. Some hotels, restaurants and night clubs are air-conditioned. . . . **QUEZON CITY** (107,977), north of Manila, has been the capital of the Republic of the Philippines since 1948. The city was named for Manuel L. Quezon, first President of the Commonwealth, who desired to build a new and more beautiful capital. . . . **TAGAYTAY CITY**, south of Manila, can give you an idea of how the Swiss Alps would look in the tropics: sun-clad instead of snowclad. The city is located on a ridge overlooking **Lake Taal** with **Taal volcano** rising from the center of the lake — probably the lowest volcano in the world. From the heights of the city the view is magnificent. The drive from Manila is through Luzon's rustic scenery: nipa houses, rice fields, salt beds, orchards and cocoanut plantations. . . . **BAGUIO**, the "City of Pines," some 130 miles north of Manila, lies 5,000 feet above sea level in wooded mountains. It

is an ideal vacation resort with good hotels, golf courses and other attractions. . . . In this vicinity are the famous **Rice Terraces** which wind more than a thousand miles around steep mountainsides. Experts consider them to be a greater engineering feat than the Pyramids of Egypt; they are an awe-inspiring sight. The Igorots built these step-like terraces over a period of 1,500 years. . . . The market place in Baguio is usually crowded with Igorots and other primitive people, selling their native handicrafts. . . . **LAS PINAS**, a quaint town within easy motoring distance of Manila, has in its church an organ made entirely of bamboo wood over 100 years ago — possibly the only one of its kind in the world. . . . A trip up the **Pasig River** to **Laguna Province** provides an interesting view of life along its shores. . . . A thrilling experience is a visit to **Pagsanjan Falls**, where skilled boatmen — two to a canoe — take you up to the falls and "shoot the rapids." . . . From **LEGASPI**, a busy city in a cocoanut-producing area, the traveler may drive to several scenic spots: **Tiwi Hot Springs**, **Bato Lake** and the **Kagsawa ruins**. . . . High on **Mt. Mayon** volcano is **The Rest House**. Wild strawberries growing in the volcanic soil make this a popular place to visit.

VISAYAS is the name given to the central group of islands between Luzon and Mindanao, the larger ones being **CEBU**, **NEGROS**, **PANAY**, **LEYTE** and **BOHOL**. . . . **CEBU**, on the island of Cebu, is a beautiful city. In 1565 Legaspi founded a Spanish settlement on the site of Magellan's landing in 1521. Still to be seen is a **Cross**, believed to have been planted by the discoverer's own hand, marking the spot where he placed the flag of discovery. . . . A launch trip to nearby **Mactan Island** is a popular excursion. A

Rural scene in the Philippines
Shell photo from Philippine
Association

St. Joseph's, principal Catholic church of Bacolod
Shell Photo., Philippine Assn.

monument stands on the site where Magellan was killed by a native chief. . . . In the church of **San Agustin** is a doll-like image said to have been given to a local chief by Magellan; it has been venerated as **"Santo Niño"** (Holy Child) for four centuries. . . . Cebu's cosmopolitan life blends well. There are golf and tennis clubs and an open-air night club has a natural swimming pool. . . . **BACOLOD**, on **NEGROS ISLAND**, is in a large sugar-producing area. Guided tours may be taken through immense fields of sugar cane and the larger mills. A prosperous city, it has beautiful parks, wide boulevards and palatial homes. . . . **ILOILO**, on the island of **PANAY**, also enjoys prosperity from the sugar industry. However, it is especially noted for its "pina cloth," fine, silk-like material made from the fibres of a certain type of pineapple plant, native to this region, and woven into wearing apparel. . . . **Villa Beach** is a popular resort a few miles west. . . . **MINDANAO**, the second largest island in the Philippine archipelago, is the most southerly of the principal islands. . . . **ZAMBOANGA**, one of its chief cities, is a charming place to visit. Hanging gardens rise above lily ponds and fountains; boulevards wind through cocoanut groves and rice fields; orchids grow in profusion in the hills, filling the air with their fragrance. Zamboanga is the home of the **Moros**, who are not a race but a Mohammedan people living much as their ancestors did in villages built on bamboo stilts. Their colorful attire and their handicrafts make a visit to the **Mohammedan areas** of Mindanao a "must". . . . A trip to **TALUKSANGAY** will give you the interesting experience of seeing a primitive Moro ceremonial dance, held in the **Mohammedan Mosque**. . . . A trip to historic **Fort Pilar** and beautiful **Pasonanca Park** would be interesting. The gaily colored sails of the Moro's fishing boats, called **vintas**, dotting the seas, add their charm to picturesque Zamboanga. . . . **DAVAO** has a beauty typical of the South Seas, yet it is an important seaport and is the center of a large abaca growing area. Abaca is a tough-fibred hemp from which Manila rope is made. The plantations are well worth visiting. . . . West of Davao lies **Mt. Apo**, the Philippine's highest mountain (9,690 feet), easily seen from the city on clear days. . . . Around the town of **DEL MONTE** are large pineapple plantations and a canning plant where visitors are welcome. . . . There are other interesting places to visit on the island of Mindanao: **Lanao Lake** in the province of **LANAO**, where Moro communities surround the lake; **BUKIDNON** province, a pineapple plantation area and **COTABATO** province where native Moro villages are the attraction. Moros are skilled pearl divers and fishermen; beautiful pearls and brightly colored fish are for sale in the native markets, and their metal work and coral jewelry are much in demand.

On the island of **JOLO**, south of Mindanao, Moros form a large part of the population. Here lived the Sultan of Sulu, once the ruler of the Philippine Mohammedans. Travelers, who come to this southern island, would find a visit to **Sulu's Mosque** very interesting. . . . The islands of **LEYTE, MINDORO, SAMAR** and **PALAWAN** are mountainous, thickly forested and have much of scenic interest to the visitor.

The Philippine islands form a compact group and are considered by many to be the most fertile tropical islands in the world. Less than 50 miles off the coast of northern Mindanao is the greatest ocean depth on this planet. Mt. Everest could be completely submerged in this "deep."

Australia

"DOWN UNDER "

Australia is a young, vigorous country of rugged individualism. As many American GI's found out during the last war, the people of our two countries are very much alike, and Americans visiting this friendly nation will feel right at home. In a land of sunshine and temperate climate, these people are outdoor-minded and sports-loving. Although noted for its many extensive beaches, the snowfields in the Australian Alps are larger even than Switzerland's. Especially fascinating to the visitor are the strange animals and plants common only to this small continent, like the well-known kangaroo; the koala, the original "Teddy bear"; the mixed-up platypus and the dingo, or wild dog; the speedy emu; the highly popular kookaburra, often known as the "laughing jackass," and the bird-world's greatest mimic —the lyre bird; the gum tree (eucalyptus), in some places towering higher than the California redwoods; the freak bottle tree (baobab), which stores water in its trunk, and the jarrah, one of the world's hardest woods. Another distinctive feature of the country is the approximately 50,000 aborigines living in the far north, in Central Australia or on reservations. One of the most primitive peoples in existence and the oldest living species of man, they live the life of the Stone Age. Nevertheless, they have made one notable contribution to world civilization—the boomerang, their deadly weapon now beloved as a toy by many a young boy on the other side of the globe. Aborigines are remarkably proficient trackers and superb bushmen and, despite the backwardness of most of the tribes, many have attracted attention even in professional fields, most recently in the art field. In other words, if you want a vacation of the familiar mixed with the exotic, go to Australia.

ABOUT FOOD

Passion fruit is an Australian specialty; no fruit salad is served without it and it is used in icings and fillings as well. However, if you want to sample the real national dish, order crayfish or steak and fried eggs. And if you feel really daring, try the kangaroo-tail soup or crocodile steak served by some of the private clubs. Also the Australian dark beer and dry wines are excellent.

ROUND A CONTINENT

SYDNEY, the oldest and largest of Australia's cities and the third city of the British Commonwealth, is the chief port of the wool, dairy, wheat and heavy-industry state of New South Wales and has what Captain Phillip, who brought the first settlers here in 1788, described as "the finest harbour in the world," dominated by the great arch of the Harbour Bridge. Within a radius of fifteen miles from the heart of the city are at least 27 ocean and bay beaches, including the world-famous Manly, Bondi and Coogee beaches. The Australian Jockey Club Carnival, which includes the race for the Sydney Cup, is held during Easter week. Down toward the harbor is the city's picturesque corner of old buildings and winding streets, which follow the exact paths of the country's first cattle wagons. Music lovers will want to attend the concerts of the Sydney Symphony Orchestra, one of the world's finest, and all tourists enjoy a visit to Taronga Park Zoo. The city's gastronomic specialty is rock oysters, considered by many to be the best in the world. Although its pace is never frenetic, Sydney's tempo does resemble that of the American way of life more than that of any other Australian city. From here, you may take tours to GRAFTON, where in late October and early November the Jacaranda Festival provides one of the country's most colorful spectacles; through the coastal, bush and river panoramas of Bulli Pass and National Park and the majestic scenery of the Blue Mountains and Jenolan Caves and to Mt. Kosciusko (7,328 feet) in the Australian Alps, the continent's highest peak, for skiing from June to October, trout fishing from November to April or mountain-climbing any time during the year . . . Southwest of Sydney is CANBERRA, the garden city and capital of Australia, located in a broad valley in the foothills of the Australian Alps. A planned, model city, built from the design of Walter Burley Griffin, an architect from Chicago, its wide, sweeping avenues, brilliant gardens and modern buildings give a magnificent setting to the nation's Parliament. The big, low Parliament House, with its uncluttered, dignified lines, the fortress-like Australian War Memorial Museum, the Governor-General's and Prime-Minister's residences and the other public buildings are Canberra's main attractions. . . . MELBOURNE, the second largest city and first in business and finance, has a quiet dignity that makes it as distinctive from Sydney as Boston from New York. Here, on the first Tuesday in November, you may witness an Australian institution, the Melbourne Cup race at beautiful Flemington Racecourse, the greatest event on the country's horse-racing calendar. In late September the final matches of the Australian Rules season — the Australian national football game — provide football thrills. For the more intellectually inclined, there are open-air concerts in the lovely Botanical Gardens and the great art collection of the National Gallery of Victoria, one of the most richly endowed galleries in the world. Tours may be taken by road to the Dandenong Ranges, for the fern gullies and bush, and by paddle-boat or motor coach along the Murray River, the country's largest, beginning in the Australian Alps and continuing 1500 miles down to the sandpits and rolling breakers off the southern coast. . . . In the northeast part of the state of Victoria is Mount Buffalo National Park, where some of the best trout fishing in the whole Commonwealth can be had, and including the fine skiing grounds at Mount Buffalo. . . . HOBART, on the island of Tasmania, the heart-shaped pendant to Australia known as the Island State or the Apple Isle, is backed by one of the most beautiful settings of any city. Besides this spectacular setting on the Derwent River, overshadowed by towering Mount Wellington, its winding, hilly streets, old narrow byways of the convict days and the small docks used by the fishing fleets all con-

tribute to its intriguing character. A trip from Hobart to Port Arthur, on the densely wooded Tasman Peninsula, will take you past a wild rugged coast to the ruins of what was the most famous of Australia's penal settlements. . . . The capital city of South Australia, famed for its wheat and fine wines, is ADELAIDE, called the "city of churches." Backed by the Mount Lofty Ranges, the city proper is separated from the suburbs by an attractive "green belt" of more than 1,700 acres of park, garden and sport grounds. There are also several excellent beaches, such as Victor Harbour, and exciting deep-sea fishing in the waters of Spencer Gulf. Here in the heart of the wine country, at Barbossa Valley, visitors may take part in the Barbossa Harvest Festival. Another interesting trip may be taken to Mount Gambier, where an extinct volcano has formed four wonderful lakes. Adelaide's Museum and Art Gallery houses a notable collection of Australian art. . . . Inland is the unique town of COOBER PEDY, which because of the continual heat is built beneath the surface of the earth. Its opal mines are renowned. . . . At the isolated settlement of ALICE SPRINGS, in the heart of the lonely, sparsely settled lands of the interior, are vast aboriginal reservations, the haunts of buffalo and crocodiles. . . . The famous Golden Mile, richest strip of land in the world, is in the desert city of KALGOORLIE, Australia's most productive gold-bearing region. . . . PERTH, the largest city on the west coast, is the center of the timber and mineral area. With more sunshine than any other city in the country, it is famous for the gay, varicolored wildflowers, like the green and red kangaroo paw, that carpet the surrounding

Wool droving on Kanembla Sheep Station, near Holbrook in Australia, one of the world's greatest wool-producing countries
Philip Gendreau

hills in the spring. The **University of Western Australia** was the first free university in the British Empire. From here visits can be made to the tall timber area, specifically the **Karri** and **Jarrah forests**, in Australia's southwest corner and the fascinating and extensive caves in the **Yallinup district**. . . . North of Perth is the all-year-round seaside resort of **GERALDTON** . . . Forty miles offshore in the Indian Ocean are the **ABROLHOS ISLANDS**, the southernmost coral isles in the world, where swimming enthusiasts are attracted by the **beaches** and **warm, clear water** and gourmets by the outstanding **sea food**. . . . Still farther up the coast is **BROOME**, home port for the pearl luggers of the Indian Ocean. . . . **DARWIN**, in the northern cattle-raising region, is one of the world's last frontier towns, reminiscent of the unsophisticated towns of the old American Wild West. Here are found some of the world's real adventurers: the pearl divers of the Arafura Sea, the crocodile hunters of Arnhem Land and the gold prospectors from the lonely inland. This town is also the favorite with big-game hunters, since from Darwin experienced Northern Territory guides conduct **shooting parties** in search of buffalo and crocodiles. . . . The railroad trip from **CAIRNS**, Queensland's northernmost port, to the **Atherton Tableland** provides many awe-inspiring views as the train slowly climbs up round the mountainside from the coastal plains below, with its bright tropical foliage and yellow and green cane-

fields. The **Barron Falls**, although not as magnificent as some of the world's other famous falls, are just as beautiful as the others and are one of the continent's greatest sights. . . . Dotted with gardens bright with tropical flowers and shrubs and enjoying a climate that is the envy of the rest of Australia, **BRISBANE**, capital of the sugar-cane state of Queensland, is a city noted for its **friendliness** and **gorgeous scenery**. Although not a city of outstanding buildings, the **City Hall** is magnificent. The rolling **Darling Downs** are a richly productive growing region. Visits may be made to **Lone Pine Fauna Preserve** and the tropical fruit farms at **Oasis Tourist Gardens** and **Redlands**. The south coast beaches, especially **Southport**, **Surfers' Paradise** and **Coolangatta**, are favorites with vacationers. . . . One of the world's major scenic attractions is the **GREAT BARRIER REEF**, the mighty coral formation fringing Australia's east coast for 1,200 miles. **Brilliant coral** lies just below the surface of the sea and the water between the white-beached, palm-fringed islands teem with strange **tropical fish**, making this an ideal region for a lazy carefree vacation, especially for naturalists, anglers and sightseers. . . . **NORFOLK ISLAND**, an Australian possession 930 miles east of the continent, is being developed as a tourist resort, since it has an equable climate and fine scenery. Many of the island's inhabitants are descendants of the mutineers of the renowned ship *Bounty*.

New Zealand

HOME OF THE MAORI

A mountainous country, New Zealand is halfway between the Equator and the South Pole. Attractions for visitors from across the seas include the art and culture of the Maori — the Polynesian people who established themselves here six or seven centuries ago and now share the rights, privileges and responsibilities of citizenship with the New Zealanders of European descent — the beauty and grandeur of the country's magnificent scenery; and the fine sports activities. There are hundreds of miles of sandy beaches, good climbing, skiing and skating, rivers well-stocked with

salmon and trout, and good shooting, especially for deer.

DINING

New Zealand cooking is typically British and since mutton is quite plentiful, there are many dishes featuring it. All kinds of sea food are available in delicious dishes.

FISHING, SKIING AND MOUNTAIN CLIMBING

New Zealand cooking is typically **LAND** (329,193), has a main harbor, the **Waitemata**, which carries more yachts and pleasure craft than any other city of its size in the world. The fine **Auckland War Memorial Museum**, with its classical columns and multitudinous gardens, has an

An avalanche slides off the Caroline icefall on the face of Mt. Cook
New Zealand Embassy

excellent Maori collection. Rightly regarded as one of the sights of the dominion is the **Waipoua Kauri Forest**, on the Northern Wairoa River, containing many magnificent groups of kauri trees. This giant kauri pine is the dominion's best-known and most useful timber tree, although, unfortunately, extensive exploitation in the past has left few remaining stands. Big-game fishing attracts many to the east coast of North Island, especially off **Mayor Island** and the **Bay of Islands**, where swordfish, black and striped marlin, mako and kingfish are caught in record weights. . . . There is probably no spa in the world so rich in mineral springs, pools and geysers as **ROTORUA** and the thermal wonderland area of **Wakarewarewa**, a land of spurting steam, bubbling water and boiling mud. This is also a center of Maori population, where the artistic villages and colorful customs of these proud, kind, intelligent people may be observed at first hand. Housewives will especially enjoy the fantastic, easy cooking technique of the Maori women, which merely consists of suspending the food in the boiling, steaming streams. In addition, this is one of the country's most popular fishing areas, notably for the famed New Zealand rainbow and brown trout. In the Rotorua district hundreds of thousands of acres of pine trees have been planted, creating the awe-inspiring **Kaiangaroa State Forest**, largest man-made forest in the world. A nearby scenic wonder is the **Waitomo Caves**, with their unique **Glow-Worm Grot-**

to. . . . On **Lake Taupo**, largest lake in New Zealand, which is noted for its rainbow trout, the town of **TAUPO** is the center of another popular fishing region. Greatest of all New Zealand national parks is famous **Tongariro National Park**, just south of the lake. Here, three mighty volcanic cones — Tóngariro, Ngauruhoe and Ruapehu — of which Naguruhoe is given to periodic outbursts of a spectacular but harmless nature, dominate an area given to the government by Te Heu Heu Tukino, paramount chief of the Ngati-Tuwharetoa Tribe, by whom these volcanoes were regarded as guardian deities. The weird thermal activity of the region is seen particularly at Ngauruhoe's active crater and on the slopes of the shattered peak of Tongariro, where the Ketetahi hot springs present the appearance of a regular inferno. On the slopes of Ruapehu are splendid skiing grounds. . . . **WELLINGTON** (133,-414), the capital, is at the southern tip of the North Island. It has a large and attractive harbor — in this case set in a natural amphitheater of steep hills. Besides the fine baroque **Parliament Buildings**, the **National Art Gallery** and the **Dominion Museum**, with an extensive Maori art collection, are located here. Its **Alexander Turnbull Library** is one of the best historical reference libraries in the world, with a notable collection of early editions and manuscripts. Standing off the west-coast beaches of **Paraparaumu** and **Waikanae** is a fragment of original New Zealand **Kapti Island**, one-time haunt of lawless whalers and traders, of pirates, murderers and head-hunters. Now a sanctuary of recovered nature, the luxuriant, evergreen bush, with its dense undergrowth of shrubs, vines, ferns and giant tree-ferns, is slowly extending to cover the island and the forest is once again alive with native birds like the kiwi and the weka, which cannot fly; the musical bellbird and tui; the alert and friendly fantail; the kaka, green and brown parrot of the forest, and the kea, or mountain parrot. A wide variety of trees and shrubs, ranging from those associated with the low country to rare mountain and subalpine species, may be found in **Egmont National Park,** encompassing the beautiful lone peak of Mount Egmont, rising sheer from the rich, fertile plains on the west coast of North Island. A true volcanic peak built up over a long period of time into one of the most perfectly shaped mountains in the world, it is a favorite with skiers. . . . With its parks, tree-lined avenues, street names and imposing **Cathedral, CHRISTCHURCH** (174,221), the city of the plains, nearly halfway down the east coast of the South Island, is regarded as the most English of New Zealand cities. It is laid out in neat, straight lines on the plains, with the grassy-banked Avon River breaking the geometric pattern as it wanders through the city. It has public gardens peerless in New Zealand and many fine private gardens. Alpine climbers speak in high praise of the climbing in the region of **Tasman Park,** including the great Tasman Glacier, largest in the dominion with a total length of over eighteen miles and an average width of one mile and a quarter, considered by ski experts to provide one of the finest skiing grounds in the world; majestic Mount Cook and a number of other lofty peaks and extensive glaciers. Unique among famous glaciers are the two nearby great rivers of ice, **Franz Josef Glacier** and **Fox Glacier,** which, born among the snow and ice fields of the Southern Alpine Chain, descend through dense forest for the major part of their journey. Giant piles of stone pancakes — rock formations and caves — are stacked high along the west coast at **Punakaiki,** near **Greymouth.** Close by, the sea rushes with great force into a famous blowhole between rocky barriers, sending up waterspouts sometimes 150 feet into the air. . . . **HANMER SPRINGS,** north of Christchurch, is a popular spa and **TIMARU,** south of Christchurch, is a favorite seaside resort. . . . **DUNEDIN,** farther down the coast, was founded under the auspices of the Free Kirk of Scotland and has strong associations with Edinburgh, whose Celtic name it bears. Besides a wide range of industries, it has the **University of Otego** and many fine churches. Sea food is inexpensive and good and the city is enviably near the oyster beds at Stewart Island. **St. Kilda** and **St. Clair** are fine, long, sweeping beaches. . . . From South Island's chief tourist center of **QUEENSTOWN,** west of Dunedin, visitors go skiing on famous **Coronet Peak** and fishing in snow-fed rivers, providing fine salmon catches, as well as rainbow and brown trout. Largest, grandest and wildest of New Zealand's parks is **Fiordland National Park,** encompassing the Southern Fiords in the extreme southwest, having no counterpart elsewhere in the world. So wildly broken is this fiord country, it was not until 1888 that Quintin McKinnon, an intrepid explorer who had long searched for some way through the maze of huge canyons and mountain walls, discovered after many attempts the one passable saddle, later named in his honor **McKinnon's Pass,** and the doorway to fiordland was finally unlocked. The canyons through which this **Milford Track** trail, called the "World's Wonder Walk," winds its way are huge chasms among sheer walls of the mountain, chiseled and sculptured from the solid rock by glacier ice of some prehistoric era. Now, in strange contrast to the manner of their making, a fairy forest of trees, shrubs, ferns and hanging mosses, marking the dramatic change to subtropical conditions, fills these gorges and climbs high among the clefts and crevices surrounding them. **Sutherland Falls,** near Milford Sound, is the highest waterfall in the Southern Hemisphere. . . . Fast becoming one of the country's favorite resorts is little **OBAN** on Stewart Island, known to the Maori as "Rakiura," or "Isle of the Glowing Skies," one of the great scenic attractions of the dominion. Clothed in dense forests, with hundreds of delightful bays and havens, this lovely isle has a remarkably mild climate throughout the year. **Port William** was a favorite anchorage for old whaling ships, while **Paterson Inlet** is a base for the modern Antarctic-bound whalers.

Hawaii

PACIFIC PARADISE

Eons ago a series of eruptions began in a 2000-mile cleft on the floor of the Pacific Ocean. Thus was born the chain of volcanic mountains which now form the enchanting **HAWAIIAN ISLANDS**. It took many centuries for the lava flows to build these mountains to a maximum height of 32,000 feet — **Mauna Kea** on the island of Hawaii is 14,000 feet above sea level and 18,000 feet below; the highest peak in the islands. It took more centuries for the bald peaks to become covered with soil and seeds brought by the sea from other lands; rain and sun helped these early plantings to develop into the luxuriant foliage of today. A visit to these beautiful islands is a traveler's delight — no passports, no language difficulties, the comforts of home in the tourist centers — all this in exotic settings differing in character on each island. You will be soothed by Hawaiian music (Polynesian chants, blended with hymns of the early missionaries; form the basis of modern Hawaiian music), and entranced by girls dancing the hula. The real hula is a very graceful dance — the hands tell the story and the hips and feet provide the rhythm. Many customs of the Polynesians have been carried down through the ages in spite of the Western way of life in modern Hawaii.

FOOD

One of the high spots of a visit to Hawaii is to attend a *luau* (feast). This typically Hawaiian entertainment has become famous. Pigs, roasted in a pit with potatoes and fish wrapped in ti leaves, are served with shellfish, fresh pineapple, cocoanut pudding and other South Sea side dishes, at ti-leaf covered tables decorated with brilliant flowers. During the feast you listen to Hawaiian music and watch the hula dancers. Another famous dish is *poi*, a starchy pudding made from taro root pounded into a paste and allowed to ferment. Chicken cooked with taro leaves in cocoanut milk is also popular.

SPORTS

For recreation water sports lead the field; surfboard riding, the sport of Hawaiian kings, has been popular for centuries; a trip in an outrigger canoe is fun; deep-sea and spear fishing furnishes exhilarating sport. Baseball, basketball and football are seasonal sports. Each fall, in addition to conventional football, a barefoot football game is played — punts by shoeless experts average 50 yeards or more. Each spring well-known polo stars come to play night games with island teams.

AROUND THE ISLANDS

The island of **HAWAII** is the largest of the Hawaiian chain and, geologically, the youngest. Its two active volcanoes, **Mauna Loa**, nearly 14,000 feet high, and **Kilauea**, form the nucleus of the part of Hawaiian National Park located on Hawaii island, a wonderland of Nature's creation. You can drive through the Park over a good road, bordered with giant ferns — some rising to a height of 40 feet — to a plateau from which you may safely watch the boiling lava in Kilauea's main crater. The drama of the building of the Hawaiian Islands unfolds before you when watching an eruption. . . . **HILO**, on the east coast, is the orchid center of the island. These exquisite and fragrant flowers are everywhere — they border lawns, are woven into leis and are shipped all over the world. Large sugar plantations surround Hilo and a drive to visit them is interesting. . . . You might also want to see the black beach at Kalapana — the black "sand" is powdered lava. . . . **Puna Warm Springs**, ringed with ferns, has its waters warmed by volcanic heat. . . . A drive from Hilo to **KONA** on the west coast takes you through one of the fascinating scenic areas of the world. The first Christian church was established at Kona in 1820 by the first misisonaries who came from New England in clipper ships. The summer palace of Hawaiian royalty is open to visitors and a monument marks the spot where Captain Cook was killed. . . . **HONAUNAU** is an ancient "City of Refuge" for hunted men. The foundations of a temple believed to have been built in the 12th century to mark the site of ancient pagan rites, have been restored. Kona attracts vacationists because of its restful "Old Hawaiian" atmosphere. . . . **MAUI**, second largest of the Hawaiian Islands, has, in its part of Hawaiian National Park, a dormant volcano for its chief attraction — **Haleakala**, "House of the Sun." Legend says the god Maui stood on the summit of the mountain, trapped the Sun and extracted his promise to slow his pace over the land. Afterward, the mountain exploded creating the world's largest crater, 21 miles around the rim and 3000 feet deep; most visitors plan to get there early enough to see the changing colors of dawn bursting over the crater's rim. You watch in awesome silence as the sun appears and the glorious spectacle makes you understand why the primitive people of the island called the mountain "The House of the Sun.". . . On Maui are many lovely valleys, but the loveliest is **Iao Valley**; its walls, rising to a height of 4000 feet, form an amphitheater around a 1200-feet spire of rock called "The Needle.". . . The **HANA** district is also a very scenic area — rushing mountain streams, cascades, waterfalls, exotic plants and trees, all under a clear, intensely blue sky, make a panorama to delight the eye. . . . You arrive on Maui near **WAILUKU**, on the western side of the island; from there a short plane trip, or a drive through ever-changing scenery, will bring you to HANA. The comfort of a fine hotel awaits you, while the unhurried life of old Hawaii is about you. . . . **OAHU** is the third largest of the Hawaiian Islands. Oahu means "Gathering Place" and the name is still appropriate. It is the chief center for all the islands and the "cross-

roads of the Pacific.". . . **HONOLULU** (pop. 248,034), largest city and capital of the Territory, is an age-old port and the gateway to all Hawaii; its airport is one of the busiest in the world. It is probably the only city in the world where steamer and plane arrivals and departures are, traditionally, colorful occasions. Symbolic of the warm friendliness of island people is the **aloha** greeting with the placing of a **lei** (wreath) around the shoulders of each passenger. **Aloha** means friendship, good fellowship, love, and people submit courtesouly to this expression of "hail" or "farewell.". . . There is much to see in beautiful Honolulu; the Bishop Museum has a wonderful collection of Polynesian relics; the **Academy of Art** has interesting displays; you may drive through the campus of the **University of Hawaii** and the throne room at **Iolani Palace**, a former royal residence, is open to visitors. An interesting drive from Honolulu takes you to **Pearl Harbor, Schofield Barracks** and **Hickam Field**, places where history was made on December 7, 1941. Beautifully laid out in the long-dormant crater of Punchbowl volcano is the **Pacific National Memorial Cemetery**, where rest the dead

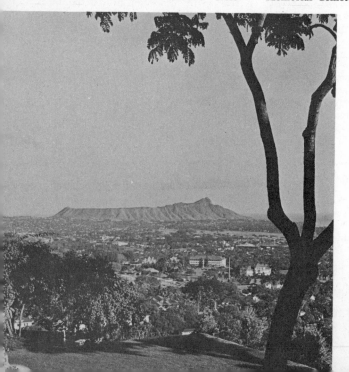

Lure of Hawaii—panoramic view of famous Diamond Head from Makiki heights back of Honolulu
Hawaii Visitors Bureau

In front of the Judiciary building in Honolulu's civic center stands this statue of Kamehameha, renowned ruler of Hawaii
Hawaii Visitors Bureau

from the Pacific area of World War II. . . . South of Honolulu is famous **Waikiki Beach** and the equally famous Hawaiian landmark, **Diamond Head**, an extinct volcano, the legendary home of Pele, the goddess of fire. . . . Some seven miles from Honolulu is **Nuuanu Pali**, a pass at the head of Nuuanu Valley. The beauty of this valley is unequalled anywhere in the islands; the north face is a sheer rocky cliff, in places 2000 feet high. . . . **KAUAI**, fourth in size of the Hawaiian chain, is, geologically, the oldest of the group — the first to appear above sea level. Some clear traces of pre-historic people have been found on this island. An interesting place to visit is the first sugar plantation started in 1836 and still in operation. Kauai was the first island to be protected by cannon mounted on bastions. . . . The scenry is unsurpassed in beauty; on a leisurely drive around the northern coast you pass wide golden beaches bordered with palm trees and separated from each other by headlands and streams. In Hanalei Valley rice paddies are cultivated as in ancient days; the luxuriant foliage on the slopes and a blue half-moon bay are a scenic delight. The eerie **Haena Caves** are

interesting. . . . Along the southern shore of the island you can visit the **Spouting Horn**, a geyser-like spectacle caused by the surf shooting through cavernous rocks and making a weird noise at each "eruption.". . . **Waimea Canyon** is also one of the beauty spots of the islands; its huge cliffs, deep gorges and soft colors, change constantly in the sunshine — a truly inspiring sight. At Kalalau Lookout one sees the complete grandeur of the canyon with the view of Kolalau Valley. . . . **MOLOKAI** "The Friendly Isle," is fifth in size of the Hawaiian group. For the traveler who wishes to get away from the strenuous life of the modern cities, Molokai offers the ideal vacation land. The scenery is delightful and some place names fascinating, such as Puu Peelua, Hill of the Caterpillar God or Puu Mano, Hill of the Shark God. Some of the best game fishing in the Pacific is found in the waters off Molokai. Hunting is by special arrangement with ranchers and the Territorial Board of Agriculture and Forestry, for deer, goats and game birds. You can play pasture golf or tennis, go crabbing or clamming, ride horseback Western style or just relax and drink in Hawaiian sunshine and peace.

Fiji Islands

CROSSROADS OF THE SOUTH PACIFIC

Of all the Pacific territories, the one with probably the brightest future is the British Crown Colony of Fiji, an archipelago including over 300 islands varying greatly in size and occupying a central position in the southwestern Pacific. About a hundred of them are inhabited, while many others are used by the Fijians either for the planting of food or for temporary residence during the turtle-fishing season. All the larger islands are of volcanic origin, but activity has long ceased. In general, these volcanic islands are rugged, with sharp peaks and crags overlooking steep-sided valleys, but there are also wide areas of rich alluvial land, for most of the rivers have built extensive deltas. Of the smaller

panied by a choir of squatting Fijian men and women — part singing is a distinctive feature of the vocal music in Fiji — or often women alone. The tall, lithe dancing women dress in cotton robes extending from neck to ankle, while the singers wear colored cotton *sulus,* cotton camisoles and necklets of leaves and flowers. The men joining in the *meke* wear kilts of broad, long, green or yellow leaves, with anklets and perhaps necklets of leaves, and paint their faces black, resembling masks.

KAVA DRINKING

Kava, or yaqona, drinking, one of the most ancient and honored customs among the Polynesians, is the backbone of almost all ceremonial and social occasions in Fiji, Samoa and Tonga. It is associated with

A native Fijian village near Suva

Philip Gendreau

islands, a surprising number are formed wholly or partly of limestone. Coral reefs surround practically all the islands, some being fringing reefs, attached to the land, others, barrier reefs standing some distance offshore with lagoons of calm water between. Extraordinarily rich and remarkably healthy, Fiji is a delightful Pacific-islands world of beauty, color and charm, where the people still are unspoiled and life goes on much as it did a hundred years ago, setting a splendid example for the rest of the world as a place where many people of different races live peacefully and happily together.

EXQUISITE GRACE AND HARMONY

Fijian dancing, or *meke,* is a matchless harmony of time and motion, accom-

most of the religious and state functions because by this device the supremacy of the head chief and the status of all the lesser chiefs is recognized and acknowledged, and they, in turn, through the same means show their loyalty and allegiance to the British government in the person of the governor. In the old days, the kava-drinking ceremony also invoked the aid of the chief's ancestor before a battle was fought. Although kava is quite harmless, it is a little shocking at first taste, since it is a concoction made from the root of the pepper tree, but nevertheless, no one dare refuse the offer of a bowl.

IN A TURQUOISE SEA

SUVA, principal town and capital of the colony, is stituated in southeastern

One of the alluring beach scenes typical of the South Pacific islands
Philip Gendreau

Viti Levu, on a peninsula fronting a spacious harbor on the one side and a seaplane base on the other. Today, the rugged mountain peaks that capture the visitor's eye as his ship passes through the narrow passage in the reef admitting him into Suva Bay no longer harbor cruelty and treachery, but a magnificent race of men who have proved their loyalty and courage and take their place honorably with the races making up the British Commonwealth of Nations. In fact, Tamavua Heights is now the town's lovely residential area. A little more than one hundred years ago, however, the Fijian village of Suva, which means "a mound of earth, a landmark," stood on the site of Government House and the Botanical Gardens. Near the main entrance to the gardens stood the largest building in the village, the bure-ni-kalou, a temple of the local spirit-deity. The Fiji Museum, founded in 1902, is now located in a fine new building in the Botanical Gardens and houses among its many exhibits a great variety of Fijian artifacts and a Solomon Islands' collection. The sport of skin diving and underwater fishing is gaining many supporters in the Fijis and there are now two clubs, with plenty of available equipment, catering to adherents. Apart from the sport of stalking your own fish, there are numerous coral formations along the reefs that provide an ever-changing pattern of color and grace. From tiny, inch-long, blue, green, striped, dappled or other myriad-patterned midgets to giant "oqo," or barracuda, who also occasionally weave their way between the coral heads, there's an aquarium at your fingertips. Another exciting sport, popular from March through October, is turtle fishing — fishing with your bare hands. Choose a fine sunny day with the seas

reasonably calm and cruise along the reef about a hundred yards out in deep water, and you may even catch a turtle weighing up to seven or eight hundred pounds. The reward is a fine shell as a trophy and lots of good turtle steaks for broiling and soup. If you are lucky enough to be in Fiji when there is a race meeting at Ba, on the northwestern side of Viti Levu, make a special point of attending. The horses are not quite top-class thoroughbreds, but that adds to the fun. There is an excellent open-air pool in the city, yachting flourishes under the auspices of the Royal Suva Yacht Club, rugby games and other athletic events are held at the Fiji Amateur Sports Association's grounds at Buckhurst Park and fishing, particularly trolling and spear fishing, are popular, especially at Tailevu and Navua. The hill resort of Vunindawa is good for fresh-water fishing, as well as trips on horseback. A favorite excursion is the fascinating drive through the ever-changing scenery along Transinsular Road, visiting the sugar plantations around Nausori; the very rich Tavua gold fields; Nandarivatu, a popular resort in the northern mountains; more sugar plantations and mills near Ba and Lautoka; and Singatoka, which means "the sun departs thence," on the southwestern tip of the island, with the most perfect climate in Viti Levu. Little inter-island steamers cruise to Ovalau, rich in historical associations centered around the old capital of the colony, Levuka, set on the side of the island's steeply sloping hills and still an important distribution port and an educational center; Taveuni, well-styled the "Garden of Fiji" because of its deep rich soil and highly developed plantations; the coastal ports like Labasa on Vanua Levu, second largest island, and Rotuma, a coral jewel.

Venezuela

COUNTRY OF MODERN DISCOVERY

This land of oil and iron is also a land of orchids and diamonds, of snowy Andean peaks and emerald jungles, of the mighty Orinoco and the world's highest waterfall. Much of its splendid, rugged scenery is being explored today for the first time, while its wealth of resources is still being discovered and developed, for the "Age of Discovery" in Venezuela is far from over. But this country is more than mere geography and resources. It is people — nearly 5 million of them. Some are sophisticated city dwellers whose ancestors founded the larger cities during colonial days; others are farmers who cultivate the fertile mountain valleys; some are *llaneros* (cowboys) who ride the plains tending their herds and who dance the *joropo*, Venezuela's national dance; some are oil workers of Negro descent and still others are immigrants from Europe. The people and the land combine to create a country of much material and social development, a country which looks back on a proud cultural heritage and forward to a future filled with limitless possibilities.

HOME OF THE GREAT LIBERATOR

Venezuela's past properly begins with the name of Alonso de Ojeda who, in 1499, sailed into Lake Maracaibo, where, seeing Indian pile-dwellings over the water, he named the land Venezuela (Little Venice). To colonize a part of this land, Charles V of Spain granted a contract to a German firm, the Welsers, and while they accomplished valuable explorations, they so antagonized Spanish authorities that the contract was terminated. Venezuela later became part of the Viceroyalty of New Granada. Early in the 19th century when Napoleon had overrun Spain, attempts were made to secure independence. It was at this time that Simón Bolívar, a native of Caracas, rose to prominence as the "Great Liberator" of South America. Nowhere can you go in Venezuela without meeting reminders of the greatest of her native sons. There is scarcely a town which does not have a statute of the Liberator in the center of its plaza. So if you would like to enrich your trip, take a good biography of Bolívar with you and become acquainted with the "George Washington" of South America and his native land.

PLATOS TIPICOS

Each section of the country has its own traditional dish, but the national dish is *hallaca*, a sort of boiled pie with a corn-meal cover and filled with meat and a dozen other ingredients. Other unusual dishes include *pastel de Maracay* (turtle meat potpie) and *pabellón* (rice, meat and fried bananas). Try some of Venezuela's fruit—chirmoyas, zapotes and granadillas. All coffee lovers will enjoy Venezuela's products as well as its flavorful chocolate.

EXTRA CURRICULAR ACTIVITIES

In Caracas you can play golf and tennis, swim in the pools of various clubs, ride horseback and bowl. The beach resorts of Macuto, near La Guaira, offer surf bathing and deep-sea fishing. Other excellent beaches are Catia de la Mar, Choroni and Margarita Island. Big-game hunting is good in the Guiana Highlands as well as in the *llanos* of Guárico State, where the jaguar lives along with land tortoise, deer, fox and tapir. The rivers which wind through the country are stocked with eels, stinging ray and fighting fish which make delicious eating. Here too, in the lagoons inhabited by brightly-plumed herons, the huntsman will find a large specie of Moscovy duck often weighing as much as 20 pounds.

TOURING THE COUNTRY

LA GUAIRA is the country's principal port dramatically situated along a narrow strip of Caribbean coast. This ancient city, founded in 1589, rises from the harbor on terraced ledges hewn from rock, with La Silla Peak rising behind it. This city is connected to the capital by the Autopista, an amazing superhighway which cost about 7 million dollars per mile, and is a masterpiece of engineering. . . . The capital, CARACAS (pop. 487,903) comprises two distinct sections: the ancient town, with its baroque style of architecture, and the new city, composed of modern suburbs spreading into the surrounding hillsides. All the great landmarks of Caracas are retained in the "historic quadrilateral," covering 12 blocks in the town's center. This Spanish colonial "city of red-tiled roofs" contains an abundance of charm and interest. Most of the attractions are within a few blocks of the Plaza Bolívar. Paved with mosaic and shaded by arched trees, it is a favorite gathering place. On the east side of the Plaza is a colonial cathedral which displays within its interior paintings by such masters as Rubens and Murillo. The **Palace of Justice,** facing the plaza, stands on the site where the Declaration of Independence was signed in 1811. The **Church of San Francisco** is the oldest and most interesting in the city with an altar lavishly carved and covered with gold. Nearby is the **Bolivarian Museum** where many relics of the Liberator are kept. Especially interesting is a medallion with a miniature of George Washington and a lock of his hair which was sent to Bolívar by the Washington family. The **Casa Natal,** where Bolívar was born, is an aristocratic colonial home which has been made into a national shrine. The **National Pantheon** contains the remains of Bolívar. Behind the tomb rises a great white marble likeness of him At the side of the tomb are memorials to the great historic figures of Miranda and Sucre. In the suburbs is located the impressive ultramodern **University City.** The stadia here are large enough to accommodate the Olympic Games. **Miraflores Palace** is the presidential residence. Nearby is **Calvary Hill** from whose crest an excellent view of the city and valley may be had. You can see bullfights in season at the **Nuevo Circo.** . . . About 70 miles west of Caracas is **MARACAY,** center of the rich coffee and sugar region. In the **Plaza de Tacarigua** you may see life-sized replicas of the most interesting pieces of sculpture of the aborigines of the country. This was the city of the firm dictator of

the early 20th century, Juan Vicente Gómez. It was he who beautified the city with broad boulevards, a great bull ring (Sevillian style) and the **Hotel Jardín,** where he used to give sumptuous banquets. Aptly named the "garden spot" of the country, the city is bordered by beautiful **Lake Valencia** on the south and the **Las Delicias** hills on the north. . . . Further to the west is **VALENCIA,** a city perfumed by the scent of lemon and orange blooms. Rambling houses, with iron-studded doors and grilled windows, built around cool patios, present a forbidding aspect to the narrow streets which stem from flower-filled plazas. Many of the country's wealthy maintain homes here. The **Battlefield of Carabobo** is but a short drive from the town. Here the patriot army commanded by Bolívar broke forever the Spanish hold on Venezuela. . . . To the north of Valencia is **PUERTO CABELLO,** second most important port of the country. The town is built on a protected harbor in which the water is so quiet it is said that a ship can be moored by a hair (cabello) — hence the name. Its ancient fortresses will remind one of the days when protection was needed against the pirates of the Spanish Main. Another place in the vicinity is **Playa Gañango,** a beautiful beach where famous deep-purple grapes the size of wild cherries grow in abundance. . . . Southwest from the port city is the thriving agricultural center of **BARQUISI-METO.** Great producer of pineapples, sugar cane and sisal, it has risen to become the third city of the Republic. . . . **MARA-**

Avenida Bolivar, a $300,000,000, Rockefeller-Center-style project in Caracas
Hamilton Wright

A remarkable picture — the result of nine tries — of amazing Angel Falls, in Sir Conan Doyle's "Lost World," in Venezuela

Hamilton Wright

CAIBO is the second city of the country and today is synonymous with oil. This lazy, sprawling, sun-baked city, with its contrasting Spanish colonial and Indian quarters, has been transformed in four decades into a thriving metropolis complete with Rockefeller supermarkets, Sears Roebuck stores and American-type hotels. This "City of Palms" contains excellent beaches along the picturesque lakeside. Here one may see the light fishing skiffs of local construction, manned by fishermen softly singing Creole songs. On the other side of Lake Maracaibo are the oil derricks which have brought so much wealth to Venezuela. One of the phenomena of the area is the intermittent silent lightning seen over the Catumbo River, far to the south. . . . A trip to the eastern section of the country to visit the city of CIUDAD BOLIVAR is worth while. Capital of the largest state in Venezuela, it is located 200 miles up the **Orinoco River** on the narrows of that great waterway. This busy port was founded in 1532 and originally was called **Angostura**, home of the famous bitters. Later the name was changed to honor the country's national hero. River boats, dugout canoes paddled by Indians from the interior and shallow draft steamers from the **Río Apure** are always seen along the waterfront. In the center of the city, facing the **Plaza Bolívar** the Congress of Angostura met to proclaim the Republic of Gran Colombia and elect Bolívar president. The **Alemeda**, the main thoroughfare of the city, is shored against the river by a huge, thick wall, at the end of which stands an old Spanish castle, now used as a warehouse for products of the region. Directly across the river and connected by a ferry is **SOLEDAD**, starting point for all places north of the Orinoco River. . . . Two excursions will prove exciting to lovers of the unusual. The first is a trip by air to view the world's highest waterfall, **Angel Falls**. The more daring may try a trip to the foot of the falls by jeep. The other excursion is a trip to **MARGARITA ISLAND**. Known as the "Isle of Pearls," it is one of 70 that make up the state of Nueva Esparta. This is the center of the pearl industry. History has it that Columbus brought Queen Isabella a necklace of Margarita pearls when he returned from his third voyage. Also located here is the **Cueva del Bufón** (Clown's Cave) where pirates were supposed to have hidden their treasure. None has yet been found!

Colombia

THE LAND OF EL DORADO

Everyone has heard of the pot of gold at the end of the rainbow. The lure of easily-acquired riches was particularly strong in the 16th century when Spanish explorers of Colombia's wild terrain were spurred to superhuman efforts by the legend of El Dorado (the Gilded Man). The legend has to do with an Indian chief living high in the Andes who made a practice of propitiating the gods by covering his entire body with powdered gold and washing it off in the waters of a crater lake, into which precious jewels were also cast as sacrificial offerings. Even today attempts have been made to find the half-billion dollars worth of treasure which supposedly lies at the bottom of Lake Guatavita. But the early explorers, in their vain search for this wealth, overlooked the real treasures of Colombia. Today the country is the principal source of the world's emeralds; her rivers and mines abound in gold, platinum and silver; her forests hold large supplies of rubber, dyewoods, hardwoods and balsam and her soil nurtures the wild orchid. Indeed, one cannot begin to measure Colombia's treasures without also including her magnificent scenic beauty, her romantic history and her proud culture.

COLOMBIAN MEALS

You will find a wide variety of good foods in Colombia ranging from delectable native dishes to sophisticated foreign fare. Baked bananas are a standard dish. Native fruit such as *nisperos* or *granadillas* (passion fruit) are a real treat. Colombian tamales are always tasty, made of corn meal, meat, vegetables and seasoning. Native dishes are usually highly spiced, but delicious. No meal is ever complete unless it is topped off by an aromatic demitasse of Colombian's excellent coffee.

CITIES AND SIGHTS

BARRANQUILLA (pop. 300,000) is the gateway to Colombia. If your hobby happens to be fishing, then Barranquilla is the right place to go. Great schools of fish feed at the mouth of the **Magdalena River** as it sweeps out into the **Bocas de Cenizas** (Mouths of Ashes). The **Pradomar Beach Club** at Puerto Colombia will arrange for the hire of fishing launches. . . . West of Barranquilla is the walled city of **CARTAGENA**. Any tour of the city should begin with the massive walls. Within the city you may visit the **Church of San Pedro Claver**, named for the gentle father who, back in slave trading days, devoted his life to caring for the slaves brought to Cartagena. Outside the walls is the **Fortress of San Felipe Barajas**, once the strongest fortress in the New World, which defended the city against the repeated attacks of the freebooters who sailed the Spanish Main. Nearby are the ruins of the **Convent of Santa Cruz de la Popa** with its charming image of the Virgin, famous in Cartagena's legends. Here on February 2nd each year a procession of townsfolk carry lighted candles up the hill to say prayers to the Blessed Mother. . . . For many years the main means of transportation within Colombia was the Magdalena River. Even today flat-bottomed paddlewheelers ply up and down its shores. Wide stretches of jungle alternate with open country and alligators are a common sight, sunning themselves on the sand bars. Monkeys chatter in the trees and birds of brilliant plumage fly through the green foilage. Here fishermen wield their huge nets from boats in midstream in the same manner that has been practiced for generations. . . . **MEDELLIN** (360,000), second city in size, is delightful for its mild climate and its facilities for gracious living. A favorite resort for tourists, its streets are overhung with trees and bordered by beautiful mansions and gardens. The massive **Metropolitan Cathedral** on the **Parque Bolívar** is said to be the largest all-brick church in the world. A short drive from the city will bring you past the impressive fincas (country estates) where you see coffee of the finest quality being picked and behold the orchid garden with its mass of fragile, exotic flowers. . . . Lying almost exactly in the center of the republic is **BOGOTA** (650,000), capital of Colombia. Old Bogotá centers around **Plaza Bolívar**. Still retaining its colonial appearance, this section of narrow streets and overhanging balconies runs from the south to the east of the main plaza. Within this area is one of the finest of the city's colonial mansions, the **Palacio de San Carlos**, home of Bolívar when he was president of Gran Colombia. To the north and west is the modern section. Here you may visit the **Banco de la República** to see the **Museum of Gold** where 5,000 hand-wrought gold and silver articles evidence the high degree of craftsmanship of the Colombian Indian. Bogotá's richest church, the Church of San Francisco, is adorned with lavish gold altars of breath-taking splendor. Overlooking Parque de la Independencia is the stunning modern building of the National Library. Following the winding road above Parque, you arrive at the gates of the Quinta de Bolívar, the quiet country home of the Great Liberator. The house has been made into a museum of Boliviana and the spacious gardens are kept as they were when he lived here. Nearby is the amphitheater

valley. There is a legend which relates how the image returned mysteriously to the original valley several times until a priest painted trees, flowers and birds on the altar to make the Virgin feel at home. Here, also, is the birthplace of one of Colombia's greatest authors, Jorge Isaacs. His romantic novel, *Maria*, is a masterpiece of Colombian literature, and through it the beauty of the Cauca Valley has gained world-wide fame. . . . One hundred miles south of Cali is the historic city of POPAYAN. Here there are many churches, as well as monasteries and cloisters, of classic Spanish architecture. The Church of San

Drowsy, noontime conversation at a plaza cafe in Ambalema, Colombia
Standard Oil of N. J.

called Media Torta (Half Cake) which is filled every Sunday morning with people who come to watch programs of folk music and dancing. On the northwestern edge of town is University City, a splendid group of buildings which house the National University. . . . Southwest of Bogotá is CALI, a charming city full of friendly people famous for their zest for living and their fondness of sports. Cali's churches are particularly beautiful and reflect the religious nature of the inhabitants. The Church of La Merced contains a large stone image of the Virgin de los Remedios (Healing Virgin) which is reputed to have been found already sculptured in a nearby

Francisco is especially famed for its carved pulpit and celebrated bell whose resonant tones have been called the "Voice of Popayán." From this picturesque city the visitor looks up to the snowclad summit of the Puracé. Popayán prides itself as being the "cradle of great men." No less than seven presidents, besides many great prelates, scientists and artists, number among her sons. Settled by many noble Spanish families, coats of arms may still be seen over the doorways of many of the city's fine old mansions. The University of Cauca contains a priceless collection of sheepskin parchment books in its extensive library.

Ecuador and Peru

AT THE EQUATOR AND BELOW

Ecuador, a country that straddles the equator, is a land of interest and surprises. Here you will learn that the best "Panama" hats are made not in Panama, but in Ecuador around Jipijapa; that the kapoc in pillows comes from Ecuador's giant ceiba trees; that model airplanes are made of Ecuadoran balsa, the world's lightest wood. Streets "paved" with cocoa beans spread in the sun to dry and Indians dyed from head to foot with flaming red stain are some of the surprises that will make a trip to Ecuador unforgettable. . . . Peru, also, is a country of great surprises and interest. It is culturally the oldest of the South American nations. For centuries it was the leading political power on the continent, first as the center of the Incan Empire and later as Spain's foremost viceroyalty in America. Here you will see throngs of Indians gather at the capital to celebrate Christian holidays in a manner reminiscent of Incan worship. You will learn that an important industry is the production of guano, a natural fertilizer, deposited by sea birds, and so vital to the country that no visitors are allowed to trespass upon the "bird sanctuaries" where it is produced. The odd, the unique and the picturesque all await the visitor who makes the trip to Ecuador or Peru.

RIVALRY AND INTRIGUE

The area of both Peru and Ecuador once formed part of the vast Incan Empire. Divided between two brothers, Huáscar and Atahualpa, a struggle ensued for control of the entire empire, in the course of which Huáscar was killed. This civil unrest greatly aided the Spanish conquest. Led by Francisco Pizarro, the Spanish forces met those of Atahualpa in what is now Peru. When the great Incan refused to acknowledge the supremacy of the Spanish king and the Christian religion, Pizarro ordered his men to fire upon the Incan warriors and Atahualpa was taken prisoner. Although the Emperor paid a tremendous ransom in gold and silver for his release, he was charged by the Spaniards with various crimes and put to death. With its leader dead, the Empire crumbled under the fierce onslaught of the Spaniards. After Pizarro's triumph, expeditions were sent southward to explore other regions. Ironically, Pizarro was slain by his own men.

MEALS FROM TWO COUNTRIES

Ecuador has many native dishes that may please the gourmet. Try *locro*, a soup made of potatoes, or *llapingacho*, a cheese and potato cake which, when decorated with a fried egg, is called *llapingacho montado* or "with a rider." Corn on the cob is called *choclo*, corn meal mush, one of Ecuador's staple foods, is *mote*. Guayaquil can provide you with *serviche*, a sea-food platter you will long remember. . . . While in Peru sample *anticuchos*, deliciously barbecued beef heart. *Picadillo a la criolla* is a Creole hash made as only Peruvians can. For sea food, try *tortillas de camarones* (shrimp omelet) or *escabeche*, the country's typical fish platter.

THE LAND OF THE EQUATOR

Of increasing tourist interest in Ecuador is GUAYAQUIL (262,624). Here "chocolate-paved streets," where brown beans of cacao are laid to dry on the roads, present one of the most unusual sights in the world. The city's main boulevard is the **Malecón Simón Bolívar**. Crossing the city is **Avenida 9 de Octubre**. On or near these two thoroughfares you will find the principal public buildings and stores of the city. The many shops here and in the Public Market offer a fascinating array of handicrafts. At the southern end of the Malecón is the statue of the Indian chieftan and his wife, **Guayas and Quil**, who were supposed to have commited suicide when the Spaniards invaded their country. A good starting point for sightseeing is **La Rotonda**. Here a colonnade partially encircles the famous **Statue of Generals Bolívar and San Martín**, whose epochal meeting took place on this spot in 1822. Be sure to see the **sorcerer's pole**, a carved totem pole, located at the central arcade of the **City Hall**. It is one of the most prized relics in South America. . . . Westward, on the coast, is SALINAS, noted for its fine bathing and excellent fishing. **Santa Elena Bay** provides unequaled faciilties for surf bathing. Fishing for black marlin, swordfish or sailfish is exciting sport from April to December. Here visitors may indulge in the intriguing pastime of hunting treasure in the form of Spanish pesos and doubloons which are still washed up on the beach from sunken Spanish galleons by the "Easter Tides" in springtime. . . . PLAYAS, 60 miles from Guayaquil, is an-

The baroque Cathedral in Quito, "most perfectly preserved Spanish colonial city in the Americas"
Hamilton Wright

other favorite resort. . . . One of the most exciting rail journeys in the world is that from Guayaquil to Quito where the train climbs a zigzag course, gaining 11,000 feet in about 100 miles, over the Andes. On the way the train stops in **RIOBAMBA**, noted for its weekly fair when the Indians bring their intriguing wares. From here the train passes through the Avenue of Volcanoes and down into the valley to **AMBATO**, the garden city of Ecuador and a fascinating market town. Nearby is Cotopaxi, the highest active volcano in the world. Throughout the trip the scenery is breathtakingly beautiful. Llamas and exotic birds and flowers and red-ponchoed shepherds brighten the landscape. . . . To the north lies **QUITO** (212,873), the capital. Nearly everything in the city exudes an air of antiquity — magnificent old churches, sleepy little plazas basking in the sun and narrow cobbled streets lined with graceful arcades. Begin your tour of the city early in the morning and you will see the rosy sunlight reflected on glistening snow-capped mountains. You will see also the Indians dressed in brilliantly colored ponchos, still chattering the ancient Quechua tongue as they trudge down from the hills with their market wares, bearing the weight of their burdens by a strap slung across their foreheads. Heart of the city is the **Plaza Independencia**, dominated by the stately **Cathedral** with gray-stone porticos and green-tile cupolas. Wander down **Calle de la Ronda**, one of the oldest streets in the city, past **Santo Domingo Square**, the principal shopping district and on to **Parque Alemeda** where you will find the oldest **astronomical observatory** in South America. Largest of Quito's churches is the **Church of San Francisco**, occupying a full block on the plaza of the same name. It is built on the exact spot where Atahualpa's palace once stood. A strikingly massive edifice, this church is built of stone, with two great bell towers crowning its Renaissance façade. Among its many treasures is a group of statues of the Virgin Mary and the twelve apostles carved by a humble Indian named Roughface. . . . About ten miles from Quito is the **Equator Line**. The granite monument which marks it was erected in 1924 to commemorate a survey taken to measure the arc of the meridian. Here you may stand astride the famous line with one foot in the Northern Hemisphere and the other in the Southern. . . . South of Quito is the lovely Los Chillos Valley with its large colonial haciendas, lush and beautiful trees and flowers and mineral springs. In this beautiful setting is the Quito Country Club. . . . West of Quito is the village of **SANTO DOMINGO DE LOS COLORADOS**, home of the fabulous Colorado Indians. Believing the color of blood to be a protection against evil spirits, the men of this tribe paint themselves from head to toe with a brilliant red dye; they wear their hair plastered down in a stiff fringe resembling a helmet rather than hair.

PERUVIAN JOURNEY

Capital and most important city of **PERU** is historic **LIMA** (520,528) "city of the kings." Situated on the Rimac River, it is the center of Peru's political and social life. Originally the center of town, the Plaza de Armas is surrounded by the City Hall and other official buildings. On the west side of the Plaza is Lima's **Cathedral**. Here lies the mummified body of Francisco

Pizarro, enclosed in a glass-paneled case behind which a stone mural depicts his exploits and life. Early Lima gloried in churches and so it is that churches are encountered everywhere. Most interesting perhaps is the **Church of San Francisco** with its mural of tiles and its marvelous architecture executed in authentic Renaissance style. Equally famous is the **Church of San Agustin** whose superlative façade reflects the luxury of Lima's colonial past. Nearby is the **Palacio de Torre-Tagle**, the finest example of colonial architecture in the country with its balconies, massive doorways and carved lions, all echoing the Lima of the viceroys. It is now Peru's Foreign Office. Today the **Plaza de San Martín** marks Lima's center about which are clustered the city's theaters, public buildings, hotels and restaurants. The shopping section is located nearby on **Jirón Union**. While in the city you will want to visit the **University of San Marcos**, oldest in the Americas and originally governed by the Dominican Order. Here, also, is located the **Pantheon of the Heroes**, containing the tombs of the most outstanding men of Peruvian history. To visit the interesting suburb of San Lázaros you will cross the old stone bridge over the Rimac River, built by a famous Marquis in the 17th century and one of Lima's most durable landmarks. . . . Interesting excursions around Lima include the beautiful suburbs of **Miraflores**, the busy port of **Callao** where you can enjoy the sun and the sea on the large beautiful beaches of **La Punta**, and a trip to **Pachacamac** to see the Incan ruins. . . . **AREQUIPA**, second city of Peru, nestles at the foot of majestic, snow-capped El Misti. Quaint old buildings and ancient churches here are constructed of a pearly white volcanic material and the streets are filled with Indians in gaily colored dress, laden llamas ambling side by side with modern automobiles and street cars, making this busy commercial town most picturesque. There are many local items for sale in the markets, including leather articles, pottery, native textiles and llama wool rugs and throws. . . . High in the Andes on the shore of beautiful Lake Titicaca is **PUNO**, from where boats cross the lake to Bolivia. The ancient city of **CUSCO** is located in south-central Peru at an elevation of 11,024 feet. This city justly deserves its title of "the Archaeological Capital of South America." Throughout the city are found the ruins of Incan temples, fortresses, palaces and other structures. On a hill overlooking Cusco from the north is the **fortress** of Sacsahuaman, an excellent example of Incan architecture. Near the **Plaza de Armas**, the principal square of the city, is the site of the **Temple of the Sun**, the Incan house of worship. A short distance from the city are the **fortress of Ollantaitambo** and the ruins of the city of **Machu Pichu**. The latter, for centuries unknown to the Spaniards, was only discovered by archaeologists in 1911. A magnificent ancient stronghold, it has become one of the wonders of the continent. . . . Of uncommon interest to tourists is the town of **HUANCAYO**, southeast of Lima. Its picturesque architecture, temperate climate and fascinating Sunday market, largely attended by Indians from surrounding areas, attract many visitors. It is probably the most unusual market in Peru.

Proud, haughty llamas, with supplies for the trail
Pan American Union

Brazil

COLOSSUS OF THE SOUTH

The fourth country in the world in terms of continuous territory, Brazil is also the largest country in the world with a Latin culture. Brazil is unique both culturally and ethnically, for its peoples during the last four centuries have produced a culture and nationality in which are blended the Portuguese heritage with its Celtic, Nordic and Moorish strains. The folkways of the Negro and the Indian, the European elements from Italy, Spain, France and Germany; all these influences have combined to create the Brazilian of today. His country is a land of exuberant vegetation, of golden beaches fringed with silvery breakers, of quiet gardens and throbbing waterfalls. But Brazil is also a land of the future. Its rivers hold the restless power of twenty million horses, and its mountains provide an inexhaustible treasure-chest of resources which pump the lifeblood of industry into the country's thriving wonders — the longest river in the world, its two waterfalls higher than Niagara, its unrivaled harbor of Rio — all of which justify Brazil as being a land of spectacle and splendor.

FOOD A LA BRESILIEN

It will prove to be fun to seek out restaurants which specialize in native Brazilian dishes. Try *feijoada completa* (black beans and meat cooked in a sauce flavored with herbs and onions), *vatapá* (usually fish or shrimp cooked in a sauce of peanuts, palm oil and cocoanut milk), or the many *picadinhos* (hashes served in a variety of ways with wonderful, piquant sauces). Brazilian cookery is at its best in Bahia, where Creole specialties of African and Portuguese origin are unsurpassed. Many of Brazil's tropical fruits may be delightful to you: *fruta do conde* (custard apple), *mamão* (papaya) and mangoes. In addition to the popular *cafézinhos* and chocolate, there are many refreshing drinks prepared from the cocoanut, *guaraná* berry or fruits.

WHERE FOOTBALL IS SOCCER

Futból (soccer) is the most popular sport in Brazil and can be watched all over the country. Horseracing and auto racing are major sports in Rio. Don't fail to visit the huge Maracanã Stadium in this city, the largest in the world. Brazil is a fisherman's paradise — lakes, rivers and the Atlantic abound in endless varieties. Game is abundant, both large and small; big-game hunters go to Mato Grosso for jaguar, puma, tapir, wild pig, ostriches, crocodiles and giant stork. Facilities for golf, tennis, horseback riding and water sports are found at all leading resorts.

CITIES AND SIGHTS

RIO DE JANEIRO (pop. 2,335,931) is a city of natural wonders and nature has been her architect. Most impressive are the peaks of great mountains which thrust themselves skyward from the surrounding waters of the bay. One of these is Pão de Açucar (Sugar Loaf), sentinel in granite at the entrance to Guanabara Bay. Another is the Corcovado (Hunchback) from whose heights the Statue of Christ the Redeemer, a hymn in concrete, seems to be giving a perpetual blessing to the city below. To the north rise the Organ Mountains, in pipelike formation. From its well-planned central zone Rio's suburbs sprawl outward and upward over wooded mountain ridges and wind through narrow chasms and around the bays and beaches. The architectural beauty of the city, its innumerable parks and plazas and miles of scenic drives are the result of years of scientific city-planning. The city's main thoroughfare is Avenida Rio Branco. Walking up this broad, tree-shaded avenue, with its patterned mosaic sidewalks, one is struck by the advanced modern design of its imposing buildings. Rua do Ouvidor, one of the principal shopping streets, is lined with fashionable shops and jewelry stores displaying Brazil's wealth of gems. At the end of Avenido Rio Branco is the Monroe Palace, seat of the Brazilian Senate. Turning south at the end of this avenue the scenic beach drive, Avenida Beira-Mar, begins at Paris Plaza and follows the sinuous curve of beaches among which is the famed, crescent-shaped Copacabana with its beach promenade of black and white mosaic. Near the beginning of the drive you may turn off and visit the Lapa district, reminiscent of Paris' Montmartre, with its cafés, cabarets and night clubs. Continuing along the sea front is the parklike Gloria Section, with fine hotels, residences and the Cardinal's Palace. Aristocratic Paysandú Street, guarded by stately rows of royal palms, ends at Guanabara Palace, former official

COPACABANA

HIGHLIGHT MAP OF
RIO DE JANEIRO
BRAZIL

MAP SHOWS MAJOR STREETS

1. João Caetano Thea.
2. Polytechnic School
3. São Francisco Ch.
4. Lyceum
5. National Library
6. Min. of Educ. & Health
7. Braz. Press Ass'n
8. Serrador Thea.
9. Chamb. of Deputies
   (Tiradentes Pal.)
10. Sta. Luzia Church
11. Supreme Court
12. Min. of Finance
13. Min. of Labor, Ind.
    & Commerce
14. U. S. Embassy
Pr.= Praça (square, park)

© C. S. HAMMOND & Co., N. Y.

230

residence of the President and now the City Hall. While touring around **Botafogo Bay** you will come to a point of land called **Morro da Urca.** Towering above this is the gigantic dome of **Sugar Loaf Mountain.** A great thrill will be the ascent to the summit (1,200 feet) by cable car made in two stages from the station at **Praia Vermelha.** The panoramic sight here will be unforgettable. Beyond the beaches you may take the interesting **Circuit of Gávea,** skirting **Lagôa Rodrigo de Freitas,** a large lagoon. On the shore is the race track of the **Jockey Club,** scene of the national sweepstakes and the famous automobile races held in June. Driving along **Avenida Niemeyer,** which cuts into thick forests, you will come to various golf courses and polo fields; thence into **Tijuca forest** with its crystal waterfalls, the **Emperors' Table** and other numerous beauty spots.

Rio is the cultural as well as the political capital of the country. Especially worthwhile is the impressive **National Museum,** occupying the former imperial palace, set in the midst of a lovely park, the **Quinta da Bôa Vista.** Here, too, is located the **Zoological Garden** with its marvelous collection of multicolored Brazilian birds. Of interest to music-lovers is the **Municipal Theater** which enjoys a brilliant opera season from May through August, and where the famed Toscanini first won acclaim as a conductor. Rio has over 200 churches all noteworthy for their richly decorated interiors. Among these is **Our Lady of Penha** which is famous for its 365 steps and annual religious festival in October. But Rio is more than scenery, marble and cement. The traveler who spends the four days before Lent in Rio will never forget the Carnival celebration which literally sweeps the people off their feet in a wave of indescribable merrymaking, masquerading and pageantry to the continuous accompaniment of the Samba — and all without benefit of hard liquors, the sale of which is banned during the festivities. During the remaining 361 days the **Cariocas** (natives of Rio) indulge in countless diversions from the **cafézinhos** (little cups of black coffee) they sip throughout the day in shaded sidewalk cafés to the daily lottery which entices the entire population to play through the ever-present posters which advise the public with the slogan *"Fique Rico"* ("Get Rich"). . . . The trip from Rio to

PETROPOLIS is an exhilarating experience and affords a magnificent view of Rio harbor. Once in the town the cobblestone streets and mountain streams which wind through the town like man-made canals will put the tourist in mind of Switzerland without snow. Here you will find the **Palace of Dom Pedro II,** the **Rio Negro Palace** and the **Pantheon of the Sovereigns** where rest the remains of the Emperor and his wife. The **Hotel Quitandinha** is a complete resort in itself. An enormous edifice of Norman-Swiss architecture, it has the **Organ Mountains** for background and, in the foreground, a large artificial lake. . . . A short distance from Petrópolis by car is the delightful resort of **TERESOPOLIS,** named after the wife of Emperor Dom Pedro. At a higher altitude, this twin resort spreads over many valleys and has the needle-pointed peaks, the **Finger of God,** dominating every view. . . . Further to the north is the mountainous state of **MINAS GERAIS** (General Mines). This was the land of Brazil's "Wild West" in the days of the **bandeirantes** (adventurers) and the "gold rush" of the 1690's. One of its chief cities is **OURO PRETO,** the museum city of colonial art and architecture still preserving its 18th-century mansions of mining magnates. At the height of its golden era Ouro Prêto's wealth was fabulous, and lest the Portuguese Crown use it up, the townspeople magnificently embellished their churches, though not their homes. The city's churches are all in exquisite 18th-century style, most notable of which is the **Igreja de São Francesco de Assis.** Also of interest is the church of **Santa Ifigenia,** founded by an African chieftain. . . . The first of Brazil's planned cities, **BELO HORIZONTE** (346,207) derives its name from the "beautiful horizon" formed by the Curral d'el Rei mountain range. Filled with modern skyscrapers and ultramodern buildings, this city truly symbolizes the new Brazil. . . . North are **LAGOA SANTA** and **CORDISBURGO,** both of great anthropological interest because of the discovery of the "Lagoa Santa Man" in one of the numerous caverns located here. . . . **DIAMANTINA,** 200 miles from Belo Horizonte, is the center of the diamond-mining region. The mines have yielded millions of carats since the 18th century, including the Getulio Vargas diamond weighing 726 carats and the third largest ever discovered. . . . Southwest of Belo Horizonte is the pleasure resort of POCOS DE CALDOS with its many hot sulphur springs and Brazil's most fashionable watering place. . . . Located further north on the coast is BAHIA (Salvador) (395,593). This is the city "with something different," full of color and movement, set amidst the blended fragrance of coffee, cacao, church incense and tropical

this territory in the 17th century. Of particular interest is the Church of St. Francis of Assisi, built in pure 18th-century style and noted for its "Golden Chapel," rich altars, carved rosewood furnishings and pictorial tiles imported from Portugal. Several bridges, notably the Bôa Vista, constructed of wrought iron, lead to a section rich in historical interest. Highlight of a pleasant excursion is a trip to

Rio de Janeiro is a city of warm, modern, fashionable beaches like Copacabana Beach

T. Janer Company

blooms. A place of majestic churches, of art and learning implanted by the Jesuits, it is also flavored by the primitive folklore of Africa — preserved in the music, dances and voodoo rituals of present-day descendants of Sudanese slaves. Baiana negresses skillfully balance fruit-filled baskets on their heads as they move gracefully through the streets. Some of the most beautiful churches are located near old colonial mansions, and a trip through Baixa do Sapateiro, named in honor of shoemakers, will make the past come alive again. . . . Further up the coast is RECIFE (522,466), the "Venice of Brazil." The reefs of coral which enclose the harbor gave the city its name. Here ruins of old Dutch forts, such as the one of Buraco, attest to the Dutch occupation of

OLINDA, suburb of the city, where you will see the Monastery of São Francisco with its carved rosewood sacristy and the Fort of St. Francis, popularly called the "Cheese Fort." Along the coastline it is interesting to watch fishermen launch their _jangadas_, whose red, blue and green sails dot the harbor. But before leaving be sure to taste the delicious pineapples for which the area is famous. . . . At the top of Brazil is BELEM (230,181) capital of the state of PARA. Although 60 miles below the equator the city is not oppressively hot. Huge mango trees spread a canopy of shade over the streets and the numerous sidewalk cafés. Here tourists may charter a boat to MARAJO ISLAND. During the rainy season, native hunters lasso and harpoon man-eating crocodiles and alligators which

The fragrant, provocative market on Bahia's waterfront
Brazilian Gov. Trade Bureau

infest the waters. . . . If you have the wanderlust and yearn to see a different world, take a trip up the Amazon to MANAUS (110,678). To glimpse only a' part of the Amazon is the experience of a lifetime. This is the land of backwoodsmen and rubber-gatherers whose huts dot the clearings on higher land. Here you can see the flight of herons, parrots and salmon-pink birds, accented by vivid splashes of color from tropical plants. When one reaches Manaus it is a surprise to find an attractive and modern city. Once the rubber capital of the world, it remains the commercial center of the Amazon Valley. Dominating the city is the Opera House, built by the rubber barons at an astonishing cost, and decorated with objects of art from Europe. . . . Returning to Rio again and moving southward one comes to the great city of SAO PAULO (2,041,716), "the Chicago of Brazil." This is a city of gardens, parks and handsome buildings. The business section is known as the Triângulo (Triangle) and contains banks and important business houses. The most fashionable shopping street is Rua Barão de Itopetininga. On the outskirts of the city is Ipiranga Hill where Dom Pedro I proclaimed Brazil's independence with the immortal cry of "Independence or Death." A fascinating place to visit is Butantán Institute, six miles from the center of the city. Better known as the "Snake

Farm," this unique institution is engaged in developing antisnakebite serums as part of its broad scientific research. The city's many churches include ancient and interesting ones such as Santo Antonio, where, it is said, girls pray for husbands. The Municipal Stadium has an ampitheater which seats 80,000 spectators and can put on a show with over 10,000 participants (a new and larger stadium is to be built in the future). . . . A trip to SANTOS (201,739) is worth while via the fine modern highway of Via Anchieta which links São Paulo with the coffee port. It is from these docks in Santos that the world's coffee cups are filled. No one should leave this region without a trip to a coffee fazenda. . . . Typical of the extreme south of Brazil is the state of RIO GRANDE DO SUL. Here the valiant figure of the gaucho (cowboy) still dominates the land. Picturesque in baggy trousers tucked in tooled-leather boots with silver spurs together with poncho, broad-brimmed hat and indispensable sheath knife, they relax with harmonicas and guitars while they sing and dance the chimarrita, a distinctive part of Brazil's folklore. . . . Worth a special trip is a visit to the crowning glory of Brazil's natural wonders, Iguassú Falls, where the Iguassú River plunges over an escarpment in the form of a two-and-one-half-mile crescent, bathed in rainbow hues, to a gorge 230 feet below.

Bolivia

COUNTRY OF ANCIENT CULTURE

Bolivia offers the visitor the opportunity of discovering one of the most fascinating yet little-known countries of the Americas. Here you can see life as it was lived centuries ago. You can gaze upon ruins which some archaeologists have estimated to be over 10,000 years old, or you may vacation on the shores of Lake Titicaca, sacred lake of the Incas, which is shrouded in pre-historic Indian legends. Nowhere else in the world will you see such colorful Indian festivals and witness such strange rites with their mixture of the pagan and the Christian. Here, too, you can watch primitive dances and hear plaintiff songs sung in an ancient language accompanied by weird music played on instruments that were old when the Spaniard came. Once within the country you will become acquainted with the haughty llama, Bolivia's beast of burden, who refuses to carry a load exceeding a certain weight. Only after a visit to this land will you come under the magical spell which only Bolivia knows how to cast.

BOLIVIAN COOKERY

Many native dishes may be sampled in Bolivia. Try *lla-uchitas,* a Bolivian tidbit somewhat like a filled cookie. They are easier to eat than to pronounce! Another popular dish is *empanadas de queso,* or cheese turnovers, fried in hot fat. *Salteñas Bolivianas* are delicious turnovers made with meat.

BEFORE AND AFTER PIZARRO

Around 600 A. D. the civilized Aymará Indians lived at the southern end of Lake Titicaca. About 600 years later the Incas, highly civilized themselves, conquered the region and incorporated the Aymarás into their empire. Within a few hundred years the Spanish conqueror, Francisco Pizarro, began his conquest of the Inca Empire. The Indians would not submit, however, to the exploitation by the Spaniards. Twice during the 17th century there were native uprisings. Once the city of La Paz was besieged by Indians who tried to force the town into submission by damming a river and then exploding the dam so as to flood the settlement, a technique they had learned during their enslaved labor in the silver mines. But the Spanish had come to stay, and with their tight hold on the country the Indians'

courage was transformed into stoic passivity. Although the Indian's physical resistance was subdued, his cultural spirit was never wholly conquered by the impact of Spanish domination. Even today he may still be seen playing his ancient *zampona* at a fiesta, or dancing the traditional *sicuri* while wearing his gigantic ostrich feather headdress. Such is the strength of the customs that emanate from his dim and remote past.

TOURING BOLIVIA

The naming of the city of LA PAZ (pop. 350,000) commemorated the end of a long warfare between Francisco Pizarro and Diego Almagro, two rival conquerors. (La Paz means peace.) Today the city is the administrative capital of the country. Of interest in the city is Santo Domingo Church where native plant forms are sculptured around the pillars of the entrance. The Cathedral located here was begun in 1835 and has only recently been finished. The Prado in the southern section is a wide avenue with flower beds in the center and spacious walks. Nearby is El Monticulo Park, known for its fine view of the city and the surrounding mountains. If you want an idea of what a colonial nobleman's house looked like, visit the former residence of the Marquis of Villaverde with its armorial bearings over the door. In the Miraflores district, east of the capital, is the stadium built to accommodate 50,000 people; international soccer matches are played here every year. A common sight around La Paz and its suburbs is the Aymará Indian, wearing his woolen, peaked cap with long ear flaps, a homespun poncho and sandals. The Aymará woman wears her black hair divided into two braids, and on top of her head is set a round, felt "derby.". . . A short distance from La Paz lies Lake Titicaca with Mt. Illampu in the distance. The Islands of the Sun and Moon (Titicaca and Coati) and other parts of the lake's basin abound in Incan and pre-Incan remains. The visitor wishing a glimpse of Indian ways of life may hire a balsa, or native fishing craft, constructed of weeds lashed together to form a boat. If you like trout fishing, you may get the trout of your life in the waters of the lake. The average catch is around 25 pounds; the record is 36½ pounds. . . . A short distance away is

In Viacha, Bolivia, you may purchase your souvenirs from the picturesque Indians without leaving the train

Rob. Gerstmann

COPACABANA. The first week in August this town is thronged with pilgrims who come to worship at the renowned shrine known as the **Virgin of the Lake**. . . . Three hours from La Paz is the village of TIAHUANACU, rich in archaeological lore. It is believed that the ruined city is the work of the Aymará Indians. Here stands the monolithic gateway or **Portal of the Sun** with its puzzling symbols. Also located here are the **ruins of the Palace of Kalassaya**, covered by ancient silence. The Aymará civilization, which flourished here 1300 years ago, presents one of the most baffling mysteries in South American archaeology. . . . Although the government has its headquarters in La Paz, the legal and official capital is SUCRE, the "garden of Bolivia." Interesting to visit are the **Cathedral**, with its jewelled statue of the Virgin of Guadelupe, and the **Government Palace** on Plaza 25 de Mayo. Once a "stop-over" for the Spanish conquistadores traveling between Lima and Buenos Aires, the city retains a lordly and aristocratic air, preserving many of its Castillian traditions and customs as well as its fine colonial buildings. . . . To the northwest of Sucre is the mining city of **ORURO**. Here are found Bolivia's famous "devil dancers" wearing their awesome masks with horns as they perform during the pre-Lenten carnival season. . . . South of Oruro is POTOSI, Bolivia's important tin center. The name of the city has become a word in the Spanish language synonymous with untold wealth. The principal public buildings are the **Casa de Moneda**, or mint, built for coining silver from adjacent mines and the old **cabildo** or town hall built in the 16th century. While here, one should visit the quaint colonial **Church of San Benito**. Near the town is the fabulous **Cerro Rico** (Rich Hill) from which two billion dollars worth of silver has been taken since it was first opened by the Spaniards. . . . If hunting is your sport, then you will want to visit **SANTA CRUZ.** Here you can experience life in the tropical jungles and still enjoy modern comforts — even if a bit on the rustic side. Tigers, panthers and deer inhabit the area around this town. If you do not care for big game hunting, you can conveniently buy a tiger skin to take back home. No one need know you didn't bag it yourself.

Paraguay

"PLACE OF THE GREAT RIVER"

Towering palms, delicate orchids and ever-present orange trees will not be the only sights that the visitor will encounter in this rural, inland country lodged between the two giants of the continent. It is also a land where the golden-skinned salmon is caught, where trees grow so hard they are called *quebrachos* (ax-breakers), where the people sip their tea from gourds and where one may observe Indian women contentedly smoking big black cigars. It is a land where the old Indian tongue, Guaraní is still the language of the "man in the street," and where milk is delivered to your doorstep on a burro. Exquisite lace, so fragile it is referred to as "spider web" cloth, is the secret art of the Paraguayan women whose skillful hands perform a seeming feat of magic. Such a panorama of the colorful and curious awaits the visitor who enters the borders of Paraguay.

PARAGUAYAN FOOD

The tourist should certainly sample *sopa Paraguaya,* a delicious corn cake, as well as *albóndigas con chipá guazú,* a combination of meat balls and corn pie. If you have a sweet tooth try *cocereva* (candied grapefruit). No trip to Paraguay is complete unless you have tried the aromatic *yerba maté,* a drink which has made Paraguay famous.

CAPITAL AND COUNTRYSIDE

Capital and most important city is ASUNCION (pop. 204,085), river port and commercial center of the country. The wide streets and regular blocks give the city a distinctive charm, especially after a downpour, when the cobblestones take on a shiny black appearance. Orange trees line the broad avenues and buildings have courtyards filled with magnolia, jasmine and rose plants. The spirit of Paraguayan life will be captured in one of the several markets of the town. Outside such places oxen rest from dragging the loaded carts and gray donkeys with hobbled feet stand blinking in the sun. Inside is a scene of cheerful confusion: Servant girls mill around with their baskets, trying to outbid or at least outshout each other. Squatting stolidly on the ground by their wares are the merchants, mostly women who have ridden in from the country sidesaddle on the little donkeys waiting outside. With ruffled skirts and blouses, their heads wound in long black shawls, they await their customers, speaking Guaraní with their neighbors and now and then sipping maté from a gourd. A visitor may wander through the crowd looking for samples of the exquisite *ñandutí* lace; this fabuolus product, of which there are over a hundred and twenty varieties, is woven in patterns bearing such poetic names as "flower of the bewitching thistle," "monkey-eyelash" and "flower of the wild guayaba tree." Of course the majority of marketgoers come to buy fruit, vegetables, fish and meat. The visitor who cannot wait for his food may enjoy his meal on the spot if he is patient enough to sit on a bench and wait for a tasty stew while it is being prepared over the coal fires. Having had an intimate glimpse of everyday life in the capital, you will want to visit some of the sites of the town. Impressive buildings are the **Congressional Palace,** designed in severe Spanish colonial style, and the **Government Palace** nearby, which was modeled by an Italian architect in Renaissance style. Across the street from the latter is the **Cathedral** with its two square bell towers and imposing arcades. The clock on one of the towers is the city's official timepiece. The most prominent church in Asunción is **La Encarnación,** reminiscent of the Milan cathedral. Also of interest is the **Oratory of the Virgin of Asunción,** modeled after Les Invalides in Paris and containing the remains of Paraguay's paternal despot, Carlos Antonio López, and his son. The visitor will enjoy a trip to some of the city's fine parks. Standing on the highest part of the city is **Parque Antonio López.** From here spreads out a panorama of town, bay and river. The sun, when it sets beyond the distant reaches of the marshy, wooded **Chaco,** is an unforgettable sight. Another lovely park occupies the former **estate of Bernadino Cabellero,** one of Paraguay's heroes. Here the visitor may see plantings of coffee and yerba maté and of lapacho, a tree with a purple or pink flower, which yields a particularly hard wood. . . . The countryside around the capital is ideally adapted for horseback riding and visitors say an orange never tastes so delicious as when plucked from a roadside tree and eaten, still warm from the sunshine, in the

Paraguayans weaving baskets for market

Pan American Union

saddle. Continuing on horseback one sees cattle grazing in the fields or standing in quiet little streams. Crossing a brook the horse may stop halfway, facing upstream to drink, while a vulture looks on morosely from a fallen tree. Women are seen along the roads enveloped in black shawls with donkeys laden with oranges or maté. One may have a baby in her arms while holding a black umbrella. Another may be trying to lessen the rigors of a trip to market by smoking a large cigar. . . . Four miles from Asunción is the suburb of TRINI-DAD. Here the estate of the former dictator López has been converted into a **Botanical Garden** which, because of its wide variety of plants, is one of the finest in the Americas. Extending over an area covering more than two square miles, it encloses bays, lagoons, virgin forests and the sloping hills of a nine-hole golf course, Roman and Japanese landscaped gardens, pergolas overgrown with roses and jasmine and examples of Paraguayan wildlife,

both animal and vegetable, are all found here. . . . Not far from the capital is the town of **CAPIATA.** Here the church is thought to be the work of the Jesuits. It has fine bells, delicately carved altars and a renowned, life-sized **figure of Christ on the Cross.** . . . . The town of ITAUGUA, on the same road, is given over to the making of ñandutí lace. Here even the old women and little children carry their frames with them and work as they walk. . . . A pleasant excursion is one to SAN BERNARDINO, about 35 miles from Asunción. Located on the shores of Lake Ypacaray, it is Paraguay's most popular resort and health center, equipped with a country club and fine hotels. . . . Travelers to Paraguay should also make a point to admire the wildlife of the Chaco with its many brilliant birds by taking a motor launch up the **Pilcomayo River.** The round trip can be made from Asunción in one day and is well worth the extra time it takes.

Uruguay

"RIVER OF THE PAINTED BIRDS"

La República Oriental del Uruguay was so named in the colonial days because of its situation on the east bank of the River Uruguay, which in turn was named by the Guarani Indians, who once inhabited this region. Rolling grain fields, orchards and pastures are richly carpeted with intense green contrasting with black, newly turned earth. A belt of sandy lowlands extends southward down the Atlantic seaboard from the Brazilian frontier to the Río de la Plata estuary. Thus, the country is noted for its beautiful pastoral

scenery, its many fine beach resorts and its capital, Montevideo, one of the most modern cities in the world. It is the smallest republic in South America but it is one of the most advanced, politically and socially, in the world. A true welfare state, Uruguay has rightly been called the "social laboratory of the Americas." Its bountiful natural resources, its advanced social and political organization and the liberality of its laws have become well-known far beyond its frontiers and tiny Uruguay occupies an honored place among the American nations.

CULTURE

While indigenous influences played a great part in the cultural development of many Latin American nations, such was not the case in Uruguay. The foundations of Uruguayan culture were laid during the colonial era with strong emphasis on the contributions of the mother country, Spain. In the centuries that followed, the culture of Uruguay became more generally European in expression. Contemporary Uruguayan culture is a national culture that has developed from the native creativeness of the Uruguayan people. It is national in the sense that it expresses the character of the Uruguayan people but cosmopolitan in that it is not limited in scope or bound by traditionalism.

GOOD LIVING

There are few places where such abundance and variety may be found as in Uruguay. Excellent European and Creole dishes, sea food and good native wines are served. Steaks and grills of fine flavor cut from beef grazed on natural pasture are essential dishes. Vegetables and fruits also have excellent flavor, such as lettuce, peaches, apples, pears and really delightful tangerines, to mention only a few. The Uruguayan string beans and *pastel de carne* (Uruguayan meat pie) are two especially popular dishes.

BANDA ORIENTAL

Capital of Uruguay and one of the great cities of the continent is MONTEVIDEO (708,233), an active, hospitable, friendly, industrial and cultural city. When Magellan's ships sailed into the Río de la Plata in 1520, a lookout, on seeing El Cerro, the low mountain across the bay from the modern city, shouted, "I see a mountain!" or as it is in Portuguese, "*Monte vide eu!*" and thus the city was named. In December, 1726, Bruno Mauricio de Zabala, Governor of Buenos Aires, set up a Spanish colony on the small peninsula that projects into the Río de la Plata and even today this old section of the city retains its colonial atmosphere. There are, however, three distinct, well-defined districts: the Ciudad Vieja (Old City), commercial and financial center; the Ciudad Nueva (New City) and, finally, the residential district. Center of the Old City is the Plaza Constitución, the city's original square, on Sarandí Street, which with Avenida 18 de Julio, is a principal thoroughfare. Bordering the plaza are two of Montevideo's oldest and most interesting structures, the Cathedral and the Palacio del Cabildo (City Hall), whose severe lines suggest the dignity of colonial times. Also in the downtown section is the Plaza Independencia, the social center, in which is an heroic monument by Zanelli of General José Artigas, Uruguay's national hero — one of the many fine sculptures in the capital. Not far from this plaza is the Teatro Solís, one of the finest and largest theaters in South America, in which the great dramatic and operatic artists of the world appear. A symphonic center of first rank, Montevideo inaugurated its famous orchestra of the Servicio Oficial de Difusión Radio Eléctrica (SODRE), Official Broadcasting Service, in 1931. In the New City, spreading out from the peninsula, most of the modern architectural development has taken place. Special attention is reserved for the Legislative Palace, a magnificent structure where the General Assembly meets. The lower part of the building is of gray granite, while the two upper floors provide a color contrast of rose marble crowned by several symbolic groups and decorative motifs. Very impressive are the modern lines of the Hospital de Clínicas, near Parque José Batlle y Ordóñez. A unique feature of this park is one of the country's best-loved monuments, the life-sized bronze group, El Monumento a la Carreta (The Cart), by the noted sculptor José Belloni, commemorating the Uruguayan pioneers. This group demonstrates an unusual and interesting treatment of a public monument; it is not set on a raised pedestal but follows the contour of the ground. Thousands of fans jam the Estadio Centenario (Centenary Stadium), also in this park, to watch the game of soccer — the country's number one sport. In this district, too, is the National University, one of America's top-ranking institutions of higher learning. The numerous gardens throughout the city are one of its most striking features. The Prado, Montevideo's oldest and most beautiful park and a popular rendezvous, is a vast expanse of glades, gardens and lakes traversed by a picturesque little stream, containing a wonderful rose garden of some eight hundred varieties, which has given to the metropolis the name of the "City of Roses." Parque Rodó contains the Gran Teatro Municipal de Verano (Open-Air Summer Theater), the National Museum of Fine Arts, with works by living artists, and Ramírez Beach, most popular urban beach. At the end of summer, Montevideo explodes into Carnival, when the city is full of noise and fun, with a great parade, gay popular dances and small stages, called "Tablados," set up in neighborhood squares and featuring local talent. In the fall comes Semana Criolla (Creole Week), with a rodeo, barbecues and entertainment by the "Sociedad Criolla," consisting of traditional songs, dances and games. Largely because of its salubrious climate, but also because of the fine natural facilities for bathing, Montevideo has become one of the most popular summer resorts on the continent. Some of the world's finest beaches fringe the coast. Pocitos, adjoining the capital, is one of the most popular, while the social favorite is Carrasco Beach, with one of the largest beaches on the Uruguayan coast. . . . The well-known artistocratic residential resort of PUNTA DEL ESTE, on the Atlantic east of Montevideo, is the gathering place of the swankiest cosmopolitan smart set and goal of sport fishermen. There are two beaches, Las Delicias and San Rafael, and boats take fishermen either to Gorriti Island for silver porgies or trolling nearby for bonitos and bluefish. A most colorful pageantry is offered on rocky Isla de Lobos (Seal Island), permanent refuge for thousands of seals. . . . Northeast of here is ROCHA on Rocha's Lake, when great shoals of black sea drum, white bass, silversides, bluefish and pompanos come in.

Not far from the Brazilian border is the marvelous artificial forest of Santa Teresa National Park, including a large number of exotic trees from different parts of the world. At the center of the park is starshaped Santa Teresa Fortress, begun in the eighteenth century by the Portuguese, completed by the Spaniards who won it in battle and restored by the Uruguayan government. Erosion has produced some odd effects on the land near this historic fortress. . . . West from Montevideo is MERCEDES, standing on the south bank of the Rio Negro, thirty miles above its junction with Rio Uruguay. It is one of the cleanest and neatest cities of the interior — where hilly plains stretch endlessly into the distance — a favored health resort and a picturesque center for yachting and fishing, especially for dorados, surubies, a kind of deep-water catfish, and the tararira. . . . Third city of the republic is SALTO, farther up the Uruguay. There is some wine production and large-scale beef farming here, but these industries are minor compared to the great orange and tangerine groves surrounding the city, givig it the title of "City of Oranges." Above Salto the river runs between high banks, with many rapids, and a favorite excursion is by launch to one of these, the Salto Chico. Another favorite is the trip to the picturesque, majestic waterfall of Salto Grande, making this an important fishing center also, since dorados, mendoles and the giant dientudos continually climb the waterfall, a curious, fascinating spectacle.

This castlelike building in Montevideo's beautiful Rodo Park houses the children's library of Maria Stagnero de Munar

Pan American Union

Chile

THE LONG AND SLENDER COUNTRY

A spectacular display of wonderful scenery awaits the visitor to Chile. From the great chameleonlike desert in the north to the frigid reaches of the south, it is unsurpassed for its infinite variety of eye-filling beauty. The great fishing grounds off the scalloped coast of northern Chile, the towering snow-capped mountains, magnificent lakes and glacier-fringed fiords of the central region, and the internationally famous Viña del Mar, the luxurious playground city of the coast, are but a few of the vacation features offered by the varied terrain of Chile. Twenty-six hundred miles in length from the borderline of Peru to the cold, bleak Tierra del Fuego in the Antarctic, it is in no place more than 221 miles wide. Yet traversing this narrow strip of land are two great mountain ranges topped by the highest peaks in the world next to the Himalayas. The Chileans have often been called the "Yankees" of South America for their enterprise and self-reliance and for their ready sense of humor.

In no other country will you find such a delightful blending of Anglo-Saxon names: Bernardo O'Higgins, Arturo Prat, Augustín Edwards, Vicuña Mackenna — all great Chileans with whom you will become familiar as you journey through the country.

SEA FOOD, MEAT AND WINE

Beef and fowl are excellent, but the fish and shellfish are superlative. Besides lobster from Robinson Crusoe's Island, tender oysters, crab and shrimp, there are many foods not found in other countries. *Cochayuyo* (seaweed) is very popular. *Erizos* (sea urchins), *locos* and *ostiones* (shellfish and conger eel) are only a few of the many delicacies to tempt you. The native dishes include *empanadas* (meatfilled cakes), *pastel de choclo* (a combination of corn, meat, chicken and vegetables baked in a clay bowl) and *cazuela* (a stew with chicken, corn, vegetables and rice). The Chilean wines are world-famous; their excellence is partly due to being properly aged in vaults long before they appear on the market. *Pisco*, a colorless grape brandy, is very popular. It is customary in Chile to take tea at around 5 P. M.; the dinner hour is usually around 9.

FROM DESERT TO ICEBERGS

One of the principal ports in the northern third of Chile is ARICA in the region of the Atacama desert. Here an international railway begins it tortuous trip across valleys, dangerous curves and steep inclines to Bolivia. Within the city a spectacle of note is the great cliff of El Morro, rising 600 feet out of the ocean and the site of a memorable battle of the War of the Pacific. The church of San Marcos here was built by the same man who constructed the world-famous tower in Paris, Alexander Gustave Eiffel. A strange sight to see is the old American ship, the S. S. Wateree, lying high and dry a mile from town in the Atacama desert, swept there by a tidal wave in 1868. . . . A little further south is the town of IQUIQUE from whose shore line extends the best deep-sea fishing waters in the world, waters which abound in swordfish, needlefish, yellowfin tuna and striped marlin. In the center of the city is Plaza Arturo Prat, named for Chile's great naval hero. . . . Moving on through ANTOFAGASTA, great copper and nitrate center of Chile, and through some smaller cities, one comes to the capital, SANTIAGO. Winding across the city is the Mapocho River. One of its arms, which dried up when the river was walled, has been converted into a wide boulevard known as Avenida Bernardo O'Higgins but popularly called the Alameda. This thoroughfare is Chile's "hall of fame" because of the many great statues which are found along its shady walks. You may begin a tour of the city by climbing Cerro Santa Lucía, a little hill rising from the center of town like a castle in the air. In one shady corner, near the small museum of folk art and primitive arms, stands a statue of Pedro de Valdivia pensively overlooking the city which he founded in 1541. At the foot of Cerro Santa Lucía, and facing Avenida Bernardo O'Higgins, are the National Archives and the National Library. The library contains one of the finest historical collections in the world and is said to be the largest in South America. Adjoining the library is the Museum of Natural History where you will find interesting records of the colonial era, the war of independence and a fine collection of archaeological relics. Further along the Alemeda, a large open space forms **Plaza Bulnes** and **Plaza Libertad**. This area is known as the **Barrio Cívico**, where an imposing group of buildings houses the capital's civic and administrative offices. One block behind Plaza Libertad is the presidential residence where, every morning, the colorful and ceremonial changing of the Presidential Guard takes place. Between the Alemeda and the Mapocho River is the main business district which centers around the **Plaza de Armas**. Branching out from the Plaza are crowded one-way streets where you will find department stores, luxurious hotels, bookstores and newspaper offices. To the southeast of the Alemeda is the **Cousiño Park** section, centering around the city's popular playground and athletic field. Not far away is the **Club Hípico race track** —one of the finest in South America. If you have time, wander through the **General Cemetery** on La Paz Avenue under the century-old cypress trees. The many monuments to Chile's heroes will add to your knowledge of this country's illustrious past. Few cities have as many art exhibits as this one. Exhibits may be seen at the galleries of the **Fine Arts Museum** and the salons of the **Bank of Chile**. . . . There are a number of resorts near Santiago offering facilities for sports or relaxation. **FARELLONES**, high in the Andes, and **LA PARVA**, a new ski center, are popular with skiing enthusiasts and provide some of the best skiing accommodations in the world. . . . If at all possible try to visit a *fundo* or farm in the great **Central Valley**

of Chile. Here you will see the Chilean *huasos* (cowboys) perform thrilling feats at their rodeos. Dressed in colorful sombreros, wide-brimmed hats, and wearing fringed leggings, they are justly famed for their excellent riding ability. . . . Northwest of Santiago is the "Pearl of the Pacific," **VALPARAISO**. The starting point in the port section is **Plaza Sotomayor**, dominated by another statue of Arturo Prat, naval hero of Iquique. This port once saw the "Golden Hind" of Sir Francis Drake while he was waging war against the Spaniards and was where Admiral Farragut first saw sea action as a cadet of fourteen aboard the U. S. Frigate Essex. On the south of the plaza is the Intendencia, Palace of the Governor of Valparaíso, a stately building of French architecture. Three blocks below O'Higgins Plaza, palm-bordered **Avenida Brasil** runs parallel to **Avenida Pedro Montt**. The central market, a gay and colorful affair, is on Avenida Brasil. Here you will find the **British Arch** commemorating the centenary of Chilean independence; a **statue of Lord Cochrane**, the British naval officer who built up the Chilean navy; and a **statue of William Wheelwright**, the North American who did much to develop transportation in Chile. A short drive along **Avenida Altamurano** takes you around **Punta de Angeles**, with its lighthouse, to the sheltered beach of **Las Torpederas**. Beautiful flowers spill over the rocky shore line including masses of geraniums and poppies said to have been planted there by an American from California. . . . Show place of the

Rodeos are as popular—and just as exciting—in Chile as in our own West

Pan American Union

241

The world-renowned Christ of
the Andes
Pan American Union

nation, and major attraction on the coast
of Chile for tourists, is **VINA DEL MAR,**
six miles northeast of Valparaíso. The
South American "Cote d'Azure," Viña del
Mar is famous for its dazzling beaches
of fine, white sand, white sand washed
by waters cooled by the Humboldt Cur-
rent; for its fine even climate and luxurious
hotels and for its sumptuous **Casino Municipal** surrounded by terraces and gardens.
The city is especially lovely when the
jacaranda trees are in bloom, and when
the fragrance of roses, honeysuckle, oleanders and wisteria mingles with the fresh
sea air. There are facilities for all kinds
of sports here. Horse racing during January
and March at the **Valparaíso Sporting
Club** is one of the most popular events
of the season. International polo matches
are attended by the cream of society, as
are the exciting yacht races. . . . You can
visit the very island on which Defoe based
his immortal story when you are in Chile,
for it lies 360 miles due west of Valparaíso
in the **Archipelago Juan Fernández** and
may be reached during the tourist season
(November to March). The island, often
called **Robinson Crusoe Island,** is covered
with vegetation quite different from that
of the mainland and is permeated with
the sweet odor of sandalwood. This island
and the others of the group are believed
to be the remains of a large coastal island
or of a lost continent. Long the haunt of
English and Dutch buccaneers who plied
the coast, they are famous for the excellent sea food found in the waters offshore.
The only settlement on the islands is San

Juan Bautista on Más a Tierra. It lies at
the foot of a large hill overlooking Cumberland Bay. This spot is known as Selkirk's Lookout, for it was here that Alexander Selkirk, the marooned British sailor,
kept his lonely vigil for signs of an ap-
proaching ship. . . . An interesting excursion from the capital is a trip to **PORTIL-
LO,** Chile's most famous winter resort. Its
ski grounds, over 9000 feet high in the
Andes, attract professional skiers from all
over the world. . . . From Portillo a day's
trip takes you to the magnificent statue of
Christ of the Andes. Twenty-six feet high,
the imposing figure stands on a granite
column surmounted by a globe on which
the continents are set in bronze. The following words are engraved on its base:
"Sooner shall the mountains crumble into
dust than the Argentines and Chileans
break the peace to which they have
pledged themselves at the feet of Christ
the Redeemer." . . . To the far south is
PUERTO MONTT, where big three-
masted whaling vessels, steamers and
freighters lie at harbor. It is from here
that ships follow the Southern Cross,
which hangs in the sky like a brilliant
lantern, until it seems as though they
could go no further as they penetrate the
Antarctic region. Here the newer cities
of **AYSEN** and **PUNTA ARENAS** are to
be found. The former is situated near
Laguna de San Rafael, one of the nation's
wonders. Surrounding the lake are great
forests and three spectacular glaciers, one
of which reaches the icy waters of the
lagoon only to crumble into small icebergs.

Argentina

A LAND OF CONTRASTS

Argentina provides the traveler with every conceivable type of enjoyment. One may ski or fish in the Andes, golf in the Córdoba Sierras or swim in the ocean at one of the seacoast resorts. If it's a gay, fashionable holiday or a vacation of opera, symphony and art the tourist is seeking, all hopes will be realized in Argentina's up-to-date capital, glamorous Buenos Aires.

PAST AND PRESENT

Although the famed *gaucho* — that nomadic plainsman, untamed, like the wild horses and cattle he hunted—has passed into folklore, the romance of Argentina's past may still be recaptured in the beautiful homes, churches and public buildings of intricate old Spanish architecture in the colonial cities or in the primitive Indian country of the northwest. Besides the Indians of the northwest, whose remote, simple life is unchanged from that of hundreds of years ago, the most colorful Argentinians are the modern cowboys— still called gauchos—of the pampas, who preserve the typical costumes of their proud, romantic predecessors: baggy *bombachas*, short boots and black sombreros. Like their American counterpart, they are magnificent riders and ropers, and their lonely, haunting songs, in a rhythm matching the gait of their horses, are sung as they ride the wide, grassy plains.

EAT, DRINK AND BE MERRY

Argentina is noted for its fine meat dishes, especially those featuring the different cuts of *bife* (beefsteak). Their delicious charcoal-broiled steaks, chicken or lamb roasted on a spit and *parrillada*, a mixed grille of liver, kidneys, etc., are obtainable in any part of the country. The barbecue is the Argentine's favorite form of entertainment. Sea-food specialties include Chilean lobster, large shrimps and a sea-food chowder. Typical Creole dishes prepared in country style are *asado con cuero*, lamb or beef barbecued in the hide, and *puchero*, a glorified stew prepared in Spanish style. No visitor should fail to try *mate*, the national tea, or omit the excellent Argentine wines and cheeses. Argentine cooks do not try to overpower the flavor of their delicious beef and lamb and although their Creole dishes are deliciously spiced, they are not overly so.

ROUND AND ABOUT THE COUNTRY

The largest city in Latin America and the gateway to the pampas, BUENOS AIRES (pop. 4,272,337) is the nation's commercial and industrial as well as its political and cultural capital. Since its greatest growth took place during the second half of the last century and the beginning of this century, it is very modern and cosmopolitan. Chief point of orientation for sightseeing is the Plaza de Mayo, the heart of the city with the historic Cabildo (Town Hall), where the independence movement was initiated; the pink-hued La Casa Rosada (Government Palace), the official residence of the President, noted for its statuary and rich hall furnishings, and the Cathedral, containing the tomb of "The Liberator," General José de San Martín. The Avenida de Mayo leads to the Palacio del Congreso (Congress Hall), seat of the legislature. North of the plaza is the shopping, theater and commercial district, including the famous Calle Florida, the city's most fashionable shopping street, and Calle Corrientes, street of theaters, restaurants (serving especially fine steaks, the national specialty, and *carbonada criolla*, meat stew with rice, a specialty of Buenos Aires), cafés and night life, with buildings that are monumental specimens of modern architecture. South of the Plaza de Mayo is the old San Telmo section—a quiet, picturesque corner of colonial landmarks like the churches of San Ignacio de Loyola, almost unchanged since colonial days, and Santo Domingo, well-known in Argentine history, and the Casa de Liniers. Paseo Colón will take you to the waterfront and the industrial section, predominantly Italian, called the Boca, having a life of its own by day and by night with its sea-food and Italian restaurants frequented by sailors and workingmen, its Bohemian corner and popular art center. The Balneario Municipal (Municipal Bathing Beach) is the city's playground and resort area during the bathing season running from December through March. North of the commercial district is the show section of the capital, including first the National Museum of Fine Arts; the Cemetery of Recoleta, containing vaults of every possible style of architecture, and beautiful Palermo Park, famous for its Rosedal

HIGHLIGHT MAP OF
BUENOS AIRES
ARGENTINA

1 Alvear Palace H.
2 Castelar H.
3 City H.
4 Claridge H.
5 H. Continental
6 H. Crillon
7 Gran Hotel Argentino
8 Gran Hotel España
9 Gran Hotel San Miguel
10 Grand H.
11 Grand Hotel Roi
12 Grand Hotel Royal
13 Lancaster H.
14 H. Nogaró
15 H. Phoenix
16 Plaza H.
17 Richmond H.

© C. S. HAMMOND & Co., N. Y.

MAP SHOWS MAJOR STREETS

(rose garden), **Zoological Gardens,** a number of exclusive sports clubs (among them clubs for polo; soccer, the national game, and *pato,* a sort of basketball played on horseback) and the **Hipódromo Argentino,** with its internationally known Palermo race track; and beyond that, the residential section, **Belgrano,** distinguished by its cobblestone streets and tiled sidewalks, aristocratic mansions and parklike setting. A score of museums and libraries center around the **University of Buenos Aires**; the **National Museum of Fine Arts**; the important **Natural History Museum**; the **Teatro Colón,** one of the world's great opera houses, having its own National Symphony Orchestra, opera and ballet companies, and the **Mitre Museum** or **Casa Mitre,** former home of the country's first president, with quiet patios and *salas* typical of the colonial era. . . . Thirty-five miles south of Buenos Aires, on the Río de la Plata, **LA PLATA** (Ciudad Eva Peron) (207,031) is the center of the meat-packing industry (tours are conducted through the plants) and a main port. It is also famous for its schools for women. It was geometrically planned as a model city and is unique with its handsome public buildings, wide streets and modern improvements. The **Museum** is outstanding for its rich collection of fossils of prehistoric animals. . . . Still further south along the coast is **MAR DEL PLATA** (pop. 114,729), called the "Pearl of the Atlantic" and queen of Argentina's ocean resorts, summer playground of the country's "smart set" and internationally famous for its luxurious casino. The sea food served here is excellent. Its five miles of beaches include fashionable **Playa Grande,** with its private clubs and extensive estates; **Parque Camet,** with its attractive golf course and polo grounds, and **Bristol Beach,** with the fabulous **casino,** which can accommodate up to 20,000 persons, including one huge room where more than 65 tables can play at one time, and featuring also a gymnasium and ice-skating rink. Preceding the season, which begins the end of December, is the annual "Spring Week" of sports tournaments and activities held the first part of November. . . . Southwest of Buenos Aires is the important tourist center of **TANDIL** (32,309). Built on hills and set among hills, it is a quiet, pleasant resort with fine views of sierra scenery and clear, refreshing air. . . . The

quaint town of **SAN CARLOS DE BARILOCHE** is the principal center for visiting **Nahuel Huapí National Park,** most popular of the seven national parks extending along the Chilean border in the Andean Lake region. Among the many attractions in the park are famed **Lake Nahuel Huapí**; beautiful **Lake Traful,** a fisherman's paradise; **Isla Victoria,** a must for nature lovers with its rare and interesting species of flora and fauna, and **Cerro Catedral,** where thrilling international skiing competitions are held. This region is the mecca for Argentine ski enthusiasts. . . . North of Buenos Aires, up the Paraná River, is **ROSARIO** (pop. 467,937), the second city of Argentina. It is, like Buenos Aires, a modern, well-planned city with attractive public squares, excellent boulevards and wide streets. . . . Up the Paraná is the beautiful colonial city of **SANTA FE** (pop. 168,791), one of the country's oldest and richest in historical and architectural interest. It was in its **Cabildo (Town Hall)** that the Constitution of 1853 was adopted, with the delegates taking their oath of allegiance upon the crucifix preserved in the famous church of San Francisco. Santa Fe is a university city, but it also has theaters and a race course. Most of its best buildings are in the eastern section, grouped around two plazas: the **Plaza Mayo,** including the **Casa de Gobierno,** begun in 1660, and the **Plaza San Martín,** whose buildings are of modern origin. . . . When you reach **POSADAS** (pop. 37,588), on the Alto Paraná River, you are in Misiones Territory—a remote arm of forested lowland which, before the coming of the Jesuits in 1617, was the home of the Guarani Indians. Not far from Posadas are thirty ruins of old Jesuit missions and no one should fail to see those at **San Ignacio Miní,** which at its height of prosperity in 1713, contained 4,356 people. . . . From **PUERTO IGUAZU** you may drive to the **Iguazú Falls,** one of the great sights of South America. Here the Iguazú River thunders over a double-horseshoe escarpment more than two miles wide to a narrow gorge 230 feet below. Among the 275 separate cataracts are projecting ledges carpeted with tropical growth. The town itself, at a height of 200 feet above the river, affords a magnificent view of the Iguazú . . . **CORDOBA** (pop. 369,886), surrounded by mountains known as the "Argentine Switzerland," is

The stark, lonely grandeur of the ski and mountaineering area in Nahuel Haupi National Park

Herbert Kirchhoff

Argentina's all-year-round vacationland. This city, geographically in the center of the country, was a religious and intellectual center for more than two centuries. For this reason it has been called the Argentine Rome or "learned city." The Universidad Mayor de San Carlos, founded in 1613, was the first in the country and one of the first in America. Many of the colonial buildings, with the graceful portals, carved wooden balconies and wrought-iron grilles for which Córdoba is famous making them reminiscent of old Spain, are still standing in the section around the Plaza San Martín, including the Cathedral, one of America's finest examples of Spanish colonial architecture; the house of Viceroy Sobremente, constructed in 1700 and now a museum; the church of La Merced, famous for its hand-carved colonial pulpit and candelabras, and the impressive colonial mansion of the Allende family. Another enjoyable spot is the beautiful Parque Sarmiento, with its zoo, waterfall and fine views of the city. The Sierras of Córdoba attract many visitors from the city who wish to swim, ride, shoot or golf. Among the most popular and attractive resorts near Córdoba are Capilla del Monte with its curious rock formations and spectacular gorges; Jesús María; Mina Clavero, a charming town noted for its natural waters, and Alta Gracia, one of the country's most popular summer and winter resorts. The whole province of Córdoba is famous for its pastries called alfajores. . . . The southern terminus of the old Inca Empire is the city of TUCUMAN (pop. 194,166). In this city, on Plaza Belgrano in 1812, a decisive victory over the royalists was won by patriot forces, and in 1816, at the Casa Histórica, the Congress of the United Provinces of Río de la Plata drafted and proclaimed Argentina's declaration of independence. At Villa Nogues, up the mountainside, are fine buildings of European style, summer homes of the well-to-do residents. . . . From here the Pan American Highway follows the ancient route of the Incas to Cuzco, Peru, through ROSARIO DE LA FRONTERA, a popular resort; tradition-steeped SALTA; JUJUY, with its famous Tumas de los Reyes (Baths of the Kings), and the remote Indian villages along the route. . . . On the route from Buenos Aires to Chile, at the foothills of the Andes, is the historic city of MENDOZA (pop. 97,496), center of the nation's thriving wine and fruit industry. It was from here that José de San Martín set out with his Army of the Andes to cross the cordillera and help to liberate first Chile and then Peru, and today an astonishing monument to him crowns the Cerro de la Gloria, a hill in one of the public parks. Visitors will also enjoy visits to the sun-drenched vineyards and the large wineries. Grapes from Mendoza Province are among the finest in the world and each year, in March or early April, the city holds a gay harvest festival known as the Fiesta de la Vendimia. The Moyano Museum of Natural History is known for its collection of Argentine plants and animals. . . . PUENTE DEL INCA, west of Mendoza, is named for the extraordinary natural bridge, one of the marvels of South America, spanning the Mendoza River. This is also a resort noted for its thermal springs and mineral waters and for its superb ski courses. From here excursions may be taken to the base of Mt. Aconcagua (23,000 feet), the loftiest peak in the Western Hemisphere, and to the statue of Christ the Redeemer, the "Christ of the Andes," marking the frontier between Argentina and Chile and symbolizing eternal peace between them.

Alaska

FROM TOTEM TO TUNDRA

Comprising the northwest peninsula of North America, two geologically related archipelagos and numerous off-lying islands, Alaska covers an area of 586,400 square miles, indented by numerous coastal waterways, incised by several mountain ranges and crowned by the loftiest summit in North America, Mt. McKinley. Popularly known as America's last frontier, Alaska is quickly becoming, through the development of communications spurred by the defense necessities of World War II, America's first playground. Since it is richly endowed in face and fortune, the territory still intrigues, beckoning everyone from the scientist probing the secrets of the earth to the sightseer scanning the scapes of land and sea. From the native village of the Aleut on the southeast island chain to the Eskimo igloo on the fringe of the Arctic Circle, Alaska is an avenue of adventure.

FLORA

Alaskan bean vines may not grow as high as a Jack's beanstalk, but cabbages do weigh as much as fifty pounds, cucumbers and carrots extend the length of a man's forearm and strawberries grow almost as large as our tomatoes. The long hours of sunshine, in this land where the summer nights never really become dark, and the fertile black soil account for the phenomenal size of the vegetables and flowers, some of whih grow as high as nine feet. Alaska's official flower, the forget-me-not, and colorful alpine flowers, in many shades of bright red, burnt orange, blue and golden yellow, spread over the tundra. A soft, mushy, mossy terrain with strange, stunted trees, the tundra appears from a distance like a dark, reddish-brown carpet. A few feet under the tundra is the famous permafrost earth that normally never thaws because of the very few summer days staying above freezing. In Alaska's early days, many a minor disaster occurred when the heat from the sourdoughs' homes thawed the permafrost underneath them and the foundations buckled as the ground softened.

AND FAUNA

Alaska is notable for big-game hunting and sport fishing, since the game is still plentiful even near the settlements and the streams still bulge with fish. Biggest challenge of all is the rugged Kodiak bear, which sometimes weighs as much as 2,000 pounds, with a pelt thirteen feet six inches long, but the black bear, moose (the Kenai moose is the biggest in the world), caribou, elk, deer, smaller game and birds also offer exciting hunting. Alaska still abounds with shaggy white mountain goat and mountain sheep, although few hunters have the patience and agility required to stalk them. Greyling, Mackinaw, rainbow, steelhead, eastern brook, cutthroat, Dolly Varden trout all compete with the noted salmon for the fishermen's interest.

THE INDISPENSABLE MAN

Air transportation plays the leading role today in Alaska's economy, and Alaska is truly air-minded: it leads the world in per capita flying! Besides the many flights to the United States, flying is big business within the territory, too. Daring bush pilots are the only contact many people in the interior have with centers of civilization and supply, and through them the settlers obtain their food, clothing, medicines and other necessities, along with other items like cows and even complete prefabricated homes, as well as newspapers and mail. The landing fields and float-plane bases in Anchorage and Fairbanks are busy terminals during the snow-free months, with planes constantly taking off as others land, with no lessening of activity during the winter months, when the wheels or pontoons are replaced by skis. Also for the hunter, fisherman and even the sightseer, the bush pilot is the man of the hour, because the very best locations are usually far from roads or railroads, and without him the Alaskan visit would be far less exciting or unusual. Only by air can the people in Alaska get completely off the beaten path, to see all of this Great Land.

LAST FRONTIER

KETCHIKAN is the first port of call for northbound steamers and a scheduled stop on the daily flights to and from Juneau. The "Salmon Capital of the World," the city is the home of a mighty fishing fleet. Situated on Revillagigedo Island, Ketchikan is in a setting of natural beauty, where the hunter, fisherman or camper can be guided to a choice of sites for his sport. During August and September salmon can be seen fighting their way up the falls of

Ketchikan Creek. Nearby is Saxman Indian Village and the thirty-eight-acre Old Kasaan National Monument, with totem poles, grave houses, monuments and parts of the original framework of an abandoned Haida Indian village. . . . WRANGELL, north of Ketchikan, is the second oldest town in southeastern Alaska. Port of call for all steamship lines, its excellent land-locked harbor is practically ice-free the year round. Rich in tradition, picturesque Wrangell, founded in 1833 by Russians on an old Indian settlement, has become historically famous for its totem poles. Located near the mouth of the Stikine River, it was, at the turn of the century, the embarkation point of prospectors setting out for the Yukon gold fields and is now an outfitting point for hunting and fishing trips into popular Cassiar country. . . . Located on the north end of the Wrangell Narrows is PETERSBURG, "the peaceful city." One of the territory's important fishing, canning and food-processing centers, it is a town with a bright industrial future. Some of the world's most beautiful mink coats come from this section, where pelts raised on surrounding farms command the highest prices of any Alaskan section. Its most scenic attraction is nearby LaConte Glacier, from which thousands of icebergs fall annually into LaConte Bay, originally called Hutli (Thunder) by the Stikine Indians because of the crashing roar of falling icebergs. From here the Baird and Patterson Glaciers can also be seen. . . . Sprawling along placid Gastineau Channel is JUNEAU, capital of Alaska. Situated in a mountainous setting, crested by Mount Juneau, the capital resembles a typical American city. Its six-story Capitol Building houses the U. S. District Court, post

office, Territorial Museum and other governmental departments. It is an important sea and air port of entry, enjoying a continuous flow of trade. The first white settlement founded in Alaska under the the American flag, dating back to 1880 when gold was discovered in nearby Silver Bow, Juneau gained financial strength and stability from mining, fishing and lumber industries. Urban though it may be, it is still a sportsman's paradise, since its mountains, valleys and waters are the habitat of big game, birds and fish, all adequately protected by governmental game laws. At Hasselborg Lake, seventy miles away, is a hunting lodge maintained by the Forest Service, with many adjoining moderate-size lakes that are virtually virgin fishing grounds. Not far from the city is Douglas, "city of homes," and one of the oldest communities in southeastern Alaska. . . . Once called the "Paris of the New World," SITKA was the capital of Alaska during the days of Russian administration. Reminiscent of that era is the Greek Russian Orthodox Church, standing in the center of the city. The timbers of its central towers were salvaged from a Russian warship wrecked on Kruzof Island and among its treasures are priceless icons, rich carvings and religious art. Nearby is Castle Hill, historically significant because it was here that the United States and Russia signed the transfer title to Alaska. A 200-bed tuberculosis sanitorium and a large vocational school are among the city's most recent developments. . . . Situated on Kodiak Island, "Alaska's Sunshine Island," is the thriving city of KODIAK, apex of the world's largest fishing banks and home of the renowned Kodiak bear, the world's largest carnivore. A wealthy city, Kodiak is on its way to becoming the commercial

Some of Juneau's large salmon-fishing fleet, a part of the principal commercial enterprise in Alaska

Alaska Development Board
Photo by Greany

Severe Isanotski and Round
Top Peaks on Unimak, one of
the Aleutian Islands
Official Photo., U. S. Navy

center of the entire North Pacific. It is now the site of American Army and Navy bases. Opposite Kodiak Island is **Katmai National Monument**, site of 7,500-foot **Mt. Katmai**, which in 1912 staged one of the greatest volcanic eruptions of this century. Located here, too, is the **Valley of Ten Thousand Smokes**, where jets of steam rise from the earth's crevices. . . . ANCHORAGE, located on the shores of Cook Inlet and protected by the Chugach Range, Talkeetna Mountains and the Alaska Range, is the territory's largest and fastest growing city. It is the hub of an "aviation life line" stretching to the furthermost Aleutians, a main stop for Great Circle Flights to the Orient and a jumping-off point for flights to Nome and Bristol Bay. A major northern defense center, it is the site of **Fort Richardson** and **Elmendorf Air Force Base**. It is also the headquarters of the Alaska Railroad, to which the city owes its beginning in 1915 and its rich industrial life. On what has been described as one of the most scenic rail trips in the world, this railroad services farmers, fishermen and vacationists of the **Kenai Peninsula**, residents of the rich **Matanuska Valley** agricultural area, the **Bristol Bay** fishing region and the coal, gold and platinum districts of the north. Proud of its national and municipal achievements, Anchorage has a modern **Federal Building**, fireproof and earthquakeproof schools and fourteen churches, including Alaska's oldest Greek Russian Orthodox Church in the **Russian village** on Kuskokwim River. Approximately 150 miles from Anchorage is **Mt. McKinley**, the highest mountain in North America, and the scenic site of **Mt. McKinley National Park**. Within the park are 91 miles of road for saddle horses, pack trains and seasoned guides leaving from **Camp Eielson** and **Wonder Lake**. Thirty-four species of animals and 112 kinds of birds

live within the park's confines. The second highest tides in the world — second only to those of the Bay of Fundy—occur in vividly named **Turnagain Bay**, near Anchorage, where the tide actually comes in as a massive wall of water. From Anchorage special summer flights are made to the colorful **Pribilof Islands**, in the Bering Sea, to observe the colonies of the famous Alaska seals. . . . The "Golden Heart of Alaska," FAIRBANKS is situated deep within the interior in the center of a vast gold-mining district, the **Tanana Valley**. At the back door of this modern town is a region of unlimited mineral resources, including the potentially wealthy **Barrow Oil Fields**, covering an estimated 70,000 square miles, and since it is the terminus of the Alaska Railroad and the Alaska Highway, Fairbanks is the logical shipping center for these fields. It is also a chief departure point for flights to Nome, Barrow, Wiseman and the vast interior regions and during the summer months, tourist **flights to the Arctic Circle** leave from here. It is a hunting region for caribou, moose, bear and other big game, as well as a fisherman's paradise. America's northernmost university, the **University of Alaska**, is just outside the town, and it also claims the northernmost golf and country club in the world. . . . NOME, the famed gold-rush town of 1900, is situated on the shores of the Bering Sea. Today it is a modern town with governmental offices, several churches, excellent schools and active civic organizations, although still the main supply center for a rich mining district. Eskimo ivory carving and needlecraft are growing industries, as is the reindeer industry supplying much food and clothing. From its romantic past can be seen a few of the **old buildings** erected during the gold-rush days and two huge **gold dredges** still operate within driving distance from the town.

Canada

FAVORITE NORTHERN VACATIONLAND

Canada, with its beautiful scenery, its rivers, lakes and seashore, its opportunities for sport of every kind has long been a favorite vacationland with its neighbors to the south. OTTAWA (202,-045), a capital of stately dignity and pleasant homes, is situated in a beautiful setting at the meeting of the Rideau and Ottawa Rivers. The Italian-Gothic Parliament Buildings, housing the Senate and House of Commons, include a Peace Tower with carillon and a Memorial Chamber honoring Canadians who died in World War I. Other interesting public buildings are the Confederation Building; the Justice Building, headquarters of the Royal Canadian Mounted Police; the Supreme Court Building and the National Art Gallery, with an excellent collection of works by Canadian artists. Of the many churches, two outstanding ones are the Basilica of Notre Dame (Roman Catholic) and Christ Church Cathedral (Anglican). The Central Canada Exhibition, noted for its exhibits of agriculture, livestock and industry, is held here annually in Landsdowne Park. The city also is prominent in the winter sports of skiing, skating and hockey.

THE MARITIME PROVINCES AND NEWFOUNDLAND

The hunting of moose, deer and game birds, fishing for trout and salmon, sailing, canoeing, swimming in lakes and ocean, horse racing, tennis and golf for years have lured sportsmen to NEW BRUNS-WICK, while the many historical sites and beautiful scenery delight students and photographers. Samuel de Champlain and Sieur de Monts first viewed New Brunswick's mighty river — the Saint John — in 1604, when they saw it tumbling into the Bay of Fundy over its eleven-foot drop. Here at half tide, vessels may enter the river for a few minutes, until the rising tide forces ocean waters into the river channel and the falls flow upstream, producing the famous Reversing Falls, one of the natural phenomena of the continent. But New Brunswick has other rivers equally important and famous, including the Mirimachi, thoroughfare of the lumberman, where the sportsman may fish for salmon and trout; the Restigouche, the salmon river attracting fishermen from all over eastern Canada and the United States;

the Tobique, also the home of salmon and trout, draining a country rich with moose and deer; the Tantramar, celebrated in Canadian literature and history, and the Peticodiac, famed for another natural curiosity: the tidal bore. Here the high tides of the Bay of Fundy force a tidal wave over the river which may be seen as far up the river as Moncton, some thirty-six miles away. At the mouth of this river, the rugged cliffs of Cape Hopewell are carved by the water into fantastic shapes and Albert County, on the western shore, is considered one of the fine hunting areas. . . . FREDERICTON, on the Saint John River, was designated as capital by Sir Thomas Carleton on what is now St. Anne's Point when London established the province of New Brunswick in 1734. The present site of the city was hewn out of the wilderness by Loyalists fleeing the American Revolution. It is also the center of the Handicraft Division of the New Brunswick Department of Industry and Reconstruction, attracting hundreds of visitors each year. With the laying of the cornerstone of Christ Church Cathedral in 1845 began the erection of the first new cathedral foundation on British soil since the Norman Conquest. The buildings now occupying Parliament Square were erected in 1880, soon after the disastrous fire which destroyed Old Province Hall. On the square are the Assembly Chamber, containing portraits of King George III and Queen Charlotte executed by Sir Joshua Reynolds; the library, featuring a copy of the Domesday Book as well as one of the two complete sets of the Audubon bird paintings now in existence, purchased from Louis Philippe of France, and the Old Government House, long the official residence of the governor, now the barracks and district headquarters of the Royal Canadian Mounted Police. The oldest university building in Canada is the Arts Building of the University of New Brunswick, built in 1828, which in recent years has enjoyed the patronage of the Rt. Hon. Lord Beaverbrook. Another institution of note in Fredericton is the Provincial Normal School, established in 1847. The Fredericton Exhibition Grounds, scene of the annual exhibition of agricultural products and harness racing, are internationally well known. . . .

All dressed for the Gaelic Mod and Highland Gathering held each summer on Cape Breton

Canadian Gov. Trav. Bur.

SAINT JOHN, city of the seven hills, at the mouth of the river whose name it bears, holds the distinction of the first city to be incorporated in British America, having received its charter in 1785. While the modern city is of Loyalist origin, it was the site of the fort of La Tour, fur trader of the seventeenth century, and scene of many a battle of fur-trade rivalry. Among its churches two stand out as especially worthy of note: Trinity Church, the first building of the Church of England, opened on Christmas Day in 1791, displaying among its treasures the communion service sent by George III and one of the six royal coats of arms of the Hanoverian Dynasty rescued from the American Colonies, and Old Stone Church, built in 1824 from stone quarried in Bristol, England, displaying the colors of the Third New Brunswick Medium Brigade, Royal Canadian Artillery, founded in 1793, the second oldest artillery militia unit to be organized in the Empire outside the British Isles. The Court House, dating from 1830, has a spiral stone staircase unsupported by pillar or post, and the New Brunswick Museum preserves the historical records of the province. In the city's harbor is the largest dry dock in the British Commonwealth. Visiting golfers will enjoy the excellent courses at the Westfield Golf and Country Club and the Riverside Golf and Country Club. . . . ST. ANDREWS, in the extreme southwest, is a fashionable summer resort. Of historical interest is the old blockhouse. . . . East of Saint John, MOSS GLEN is the home of the famous Dykelands Pottery of Kjeld and Erica Deichmann. . . . Near the Fundy coast and New Brunswick's National Park is the industrial city of MONCTON, where visitors may see the tidal bore and the magnetic hill. . . . SACKVILLE, home of Mt. Allison University, also includes Fort Beausejour, with its museum. . . . On Northumberland Strait, sheltered from the cold waters of the Gulf of St. Lawrence by Prince Edward Island, are the villages of COCAGNE, BUCTOUCHE and RICHIBUCTO, combining sea bathing and scenic beauty with such excellent native sea foods as oysters, clams and lobsters. . . . At ST. LOUIS DE KENT is an exact reproduction of the celebrated shrine of Notre Dame de Lourdes, while at ROGERSVILLE is a Trappist Monastery of unique interest. . . . In the extreme northeast are SHIPPIGAN and CARAQUET, commercial fishing towns where the traditional blessing of the fleet is a colorful event. . . . The BAIE DE CHALEUR, discovered by Jacques Cartier, offers beautiful beaches and resorts, with the added attractions of salmon fishing in the Restigouche and deep-sea fishing offshore. . . . CHARLOTTETOWN, capital of Prince Edward Island and its largest community, has been called the birthplace of Canada, and rightly so, for here in the Old Provincial Building in 1864 twenty-six representatives of Prince Edward Island, New Brunswick, Nova Scotia, Ontario and Quebec first discussed union. The furnishings of the Confederation Chamber remain exactly as they were when the historic meeting took place. One of many charming residences of the city is Government House, the official residence, erected in 1834. Two institutions of higher learning are located here: St. Dunstan's University and Prince of Wales College, while the Island Regional Library is the center of the excellent library service available to all schools in the Province. St. Dunstan's

Basilica, the Soldiers Monument and Fort Edward Battery, guarding Charlottetown's fine harbor, are other points of interest. The Provincial Exhibition and Old Home Week, held annually in August, offers agricultural and other competitive exhibits, horse racing, vaudeville and midway fun. . . . SUMMERSIDE, second largest town, surrounded by typically beautiful scenery, is the center of the oyster industry. . . . Malpeque Bay, home of "the world's most perfect oysters," is also the home — on Lennox Island — of the modern Micmacs, the original inhabitants of Prince Edward Island. At Malpeque once stood the Council House of the Micmacs. . . . The Green Gables Country around AVONLEA, where the actual Green Gables is located, has been made famous by L. M. Montgomery and her books about *Anne of Green Gables.* . . . Nearby is CAVENDISH, with its fine beach and the Green Gables Golf Course, one of the most beautiful in Canada. . . . At Cape Traverse near PORT BORDEN is the island Pottery and Painting Studio of Miss Mary Allison Doull, where hundreds of tourists come yearly. . . . Sometimes called "the beginning of America," NOVA SCOTIA is the site of the oldest settlement north of the Gulf of Mexico. Many attractions are offered to the tourist: swimming, bathing, sailing, tennis, golf, hockey and other sports, carnivals and festivals. Its numerous historical sites, too, are well worth a visit. But possibly the most popular of all recreations, however, are the hunting and the fishing. Moose, deer, muskrat, mink and raccoon abound, while woodcock find here the best cover in the world. Other fowl available are Wilson's snipe, duck of various species, ruffed grouse and Hungarian partridge. Deep-sea fishing off the Nova Scotian coast is of particular interest to the sportsman, since these waters provide some of the best tuna fishing in the world. In fact, the annual International Tuna Cup Match is held at Wedgeport in September. Swordfish, halibut, pollock, mackerel, striped bass and cod may also be caught, and the network of lakes and streams throughout the Atlantic peninsula and Cape Breton Island offer speckled trout, striped bass and salmon. Some of the famous salmon rivers are the Margaree in Cape Breton, the Annapolis, Mersey, Medway, Lahave and St. Mary's. . . . There are three National Historic Parks in the Province: the FORTRESS OF LOUISBOURG, once termed the "Dunkirk of America," on Cape Breton Island, site of the fortress built by the French to protect the entrance of the St. Lawrence River; the restored PORT ROYAL at Lower Granville, erected on the original site of the Port Royal Habitation, built in 1605 by Sieur de Monts and Champlain and destroyed in 1613; FORT ANNE at Annapolis Royal, a combination of both French and English fortifications, since it changed hands seven times during the struggle between the French and English for the control of Canada. A large building erected at Fort Anne in 1797 holds a museum of historic exhibits and a fine library. . . . Memorial Park at GRAND PRE, scene of Evangeline, includes the old French willows, Evangeline's well and the chapel, all surrounded by lovely flower gardens. The ancient village church, once known as the Church of the Covenanters, is surrounded by old graves and has old box pews and a high pulpit. In the distance is beautiful Blomidon Mountain with its famed Look-off. . . . CAPE BRETON HIGHLAND NATIONAL PARK, in one of the outstanding scenic regions of North America, has a rugged and picturesque coastline, indented by deep bays and inlets providing excellent harbors. Inland lie the beautiful Bras d'Or Lakes, where at Baddeck begins the Cabot Trail, continuing through scenery reminiscent of the Highland country of Scotland, to Ingonish and then on down the coast, where steep hills rise to a height of 1400 feet. Large herds of caribou, white-tailed deer, moose and bear may be seen, along with the small game of the region. Except for high interior barrens, the whole area is well-forested and particularly beautiful in the fall. Recreation in the park includes bathing, boating, fishing, golf, lawn bowling, tennis, hiking, horseback riding and motoring. At Baddeck, too, is Alexander Graham Bell's home, Beinn Breagh (Beautiful Hill), and here, in 1909, took place the first airplane flight in the British Empire. . . . Because many people of Scottish and French descent live on Cape Breton, their cultures have been preserved over the years. Each summer they hold the Gaelic Mod and Highland Gathering, with contests in piping, Highland dancing and Gaelic singing, varied leg sports exhibitions, old fiddler contests and massed reels.

The people are friendly and hospitable and welcome visitors into their homes. Handicrafts of the region include the making of rugs, tartans and pottery. At **ENGLISHTOWN** is the grave of Angus MacAskill, the Cape Breton giant who stood seven feet nine inches tall and weighed 425 pounds. . . . **HALIFAX**, capital city of Nova Scotia, is situated on the hills surrounding its harbor, one of the finest on the Atlantic seaboard. This lovely city is rich in historic sites, parks and other points of interest, including St. Paul's, the oldest Protestant church in Canada; **Point Pleasant Park** with the **Martello Tower**; the **Public Gardens**, unexcelled on the continent; the **Old Town Clock**; **Province House**, a Georgian masterpiece of architecture; **Memorial Tower** in Point Pleasant Park, commemorating the first Elective Assembly of the Dominion; **Citadel Hill**, with its old barracks and squat buildings, from which a magnificent view may be had over the harbor, and **Dalhousie University**. Halifax has been closely knit with the finest traditions of the British army and navy, having nurtured several of its admirals. Wolfe, stopping here on the way to the siege of Louisbourg, entertained forty-seven friends at famous "Great Pontac" inn; when he was Prince William Henry, William IV of England stayed at Halifax and the Duke of Kent, also stationed here, was responsible for the Martello Tower. Ships of all nations dock at **Bedford Basin**, in the Halifax harbor, gathering place for vessels of war and trade throughout the centuries, giving the city a cosmopolitan air. The city was the site of the first hockey game played on the first skating rink in Canada and also had the first tennis court. The tradition of sport is still alive and to these two may be added golf and all types of aquatic sports. Nova Scotia's **Junior Bengal Lancers** make a colorful and thrilling display at various shows like the **Royal Winter Fair**. . . . **DIGBY** is a well-known summer resort overlooking Annapolis Basin where all types of sport may be enjoyed. . . . A cool and healthful summer resort, **YARMOUTH**, on the south coast, is a headquarters for deep-sea fishing and beautiful drives. . . . **SHELBURNE**, shipbuilding town on the east coast, is known as the "birthplace of yachts," where the *Malay*, winner of the Bermuda Trophy, and the *Halegonian*, winner of the Havana

Trophy, were built. Donald McKay, one of the most famous builders of wooden ships, learned his trade in the shipyards of this city. At the entrance to the harbor is **McNutt's Island**, with one of the oldest lighthouses in Nova Scotia, the **Cape Roseway Light**. . . . **LUNENBURG**, further north on the coast, is the home of the greatest deep-sea fishing fleet in America, including the *Bluenose*, undefeated champion of the North Atlantic fishing fleets and winner of four International Schooner Races. . . . Situated on a fine north-shore harbor, **PICTOU** is headquarters for the lobster industry of this region. The annual summer **Lobster Festival** is unique. . . . **KENTVILLE**, in the Annapolis Valley, is the scene of the **Apple Blossom Festival**, accompanied by folk dancing and singing. . . . At **WINDSOR** is the **Haliburton Memorial**, elegant home of Sam Slick's creator, Judge Thomas Chandler Haliburton, regarded as the father of American humor. . . . **TRURO**, hub of Nova Scotia, offers a wide range of entertainment, including hunting, fishing and golf, particularly at Victoria Park, a magnificent natural playground. . . . Latest of the provinces to join the Confederation of Canada, **NEWFOUNDLAND** became the tenth province in April, 1949. Besides having an old and interesting history, it has long been famed as a vacation spot for sportsmen. To the visitor it offers many attractions, not the least of which is the temperate and equable climate. However, the sportsman comes here principally for the fishing and hunting, because the lakes provide trout and the rivers provide salmon and sea trout, while moose and caribou are plentiful in the forests, small game, such as rabbits and partridge, abound in all districts and species of salt-water birds are found along the coast. In the **Labrador** area, too — included in the government of Newfoundland — moose, bear, caribou, deer, wolves, otter, mink and seals are plentiful. Work in wood, leather, wool and ceramics, the cutting of labradorite, a many-hued stone from Labrador, are among the handicrafts offered for sale to the tourist. . . . One of the oldest cities in the New World, **ST. JOHN'S**, the capital of Newfoundland, has had a romantic history. First a rendezvous for fishermen of many nations, it began to take on the characteristics of a commercial center in 1547, though still retaining much of its old-world atmosphere.... **CORNER BROOK,** at the mouth of the Humber on the west coast, is the second city of Newfoundland and center of the pulp and paper industry, while **BELL ISLAND** is the great iron-mining center. ... The original French settlement was at **PLACENTIA,** in Placentia Bay.

QUEBEC

From Quebec went forth the explorers, traders, missionaries and voyagers, who helped to open up the inner regions of this vast continent. Since these original settlers were from France, the visitor feels as though he had stepped into a foreign land, upon seeing, for example, the wayside shrines, ox carts, outdoor ovens and other quaint reminders of Old France. Largest of the provinces, it is an all-year paradise for the vacationer. Fishing and hunting are popular attractions, for the streams and lakes abound in trout, bass and pike, while the **Restigouche River** in eastern Quebec is internationally famous for its salmon fishing. Canoe trips can be taken on the network of fresh-water lakes and streams and steamer trips on the St. Lawrence and the **Saguenay.** A well-known motor trip is the one around the Gaspé Peninsula, where rugged scenery of cliffs and ocean combine with quaint fishing villages and such natural wonders as **Percé Rock** and **Bonaventure Island,** seabird sanctuary. Quebec has seven provincial parks, possibly the two best known being the **Shickshock Mountains** of the Gaspé area and **Laurentide Park,** famous for its golf courses, fishing, hunting and canoeing facilities, in addition to its attraction as a winter-sports center. There are two national historic parks in Quebec. One of them is **Fort Lennox,** the well-preserved remains of one of the largest fortresses constructed in Canada during the last two centuries. Situated on the Richelieu River, that ancient war and trade route to the south, this fort, first built by the French, changed hands frequently during the various wars. Its final fall to the British in 1760 was the prelude to the fall of Montreal and finally, all of Canada. The other historic park is restored **Fort Chambly,** one of several forts constructed on the Richelieu River to protect the French settlers from Iroquois raids. When the first fort, built of wood, was destroyed by fire, it was rebuilt of stone. It, too, fell to the English in 1760. Captured by the Americans during the American Revolution, it was evacuated and burned. An interesting museum is maintained here.... Called the "Gibraltar of America," **QUEBEC,** the capital city, sits perched on its high rock, looking up and down the St. Lawrence and dreaming of its past, for it was the center and bastion of New France. Here came the governors and intendants and the regiments of soldiers to protect the colony and from here went the settlers of Montreal and Three Rivers. It is a city of remembrance, with its quaint houses, narrow, winding streets, old market places, where the visitor may wander on foot or ride in that curious two-wheeled vehicle called a *caleche*. Among the most important historic sites are the **Ursuline Convent and Chapel,** where votive lamps have been burning continuously through three centuries; **Hotel-Dieu Hospital,** with interesting exhibits of antique silver and other treasures; the **Plains of Abraham,** including the **monument to Wolfe and Montcalm;** the **Citadel** and battlements, **City Gates** and **Martello Towers,** all part of the city's de-

Ski shop at Ste. Adele, one of the many popular resorts in the Laurentians
Canadian Gov. Trav. Bur.

fenses; Quebec Seminary and Laval University; Basilica of Notre Dame, oldest church in the city; the Church of Notre-Dames-des-Victoires, with its exquisite woodwork and valuable paintings; the Cathedral of the Holy Trinity (Anglican); the Chapel of the Franciscans (White Sisters), where there is a magnificent display of fine needlework; the stately Parliament House; City Hall, on the site of Canada's first school, and the Provincial Museum, with its interesting exhibits. The Lower Town, at the water's edge, is also fascinating. The famed Chateau Frontenac is only one of many hotels offering fine entertainment and good food, with a French and French-Canadian cuisine. All the traditional summer sports may be enjoyed in the city and its environs, while in the winter skiing, skating, curling and sleigh riding take their place. The trip to Sainte-

miracle-working Frere Andre, and the Wax Museum. The stores of the city offer the cream of Quebec handicrafts, imported fine china, woolens and glassware. From Montreal cruises may be taken to the lower St. Lawrence, where the history of old Quebec unfolds before your eyes, and up the Saguenay, and motor trips to the Laurentians through quiet and ancient settlements of quaint houses. . . . In THREE RIVERS, once a great fur-trading center where the Indians came every summer, but now noted for its great pulp and paper industry, are very ancient buildings almost in the shadow of huge woodpiles.

ONTARIO

In the early days, this province was part of the vast fur empire of the French. The Hurons, principal nation with whom the French traded, had their villages on the shores of Georgian Bay in a district

Young explorers paddle the waters of Georgian Bay Islands National Park in Ontario

Canadian Gov. Trav. Bur.

Anne de Beaupré, world-famous shrine of healing, winds through old French farmlands and villages and past the beautiful Montmorency Falls, dropping over a cliff twice the height of Niagara. . . . MONTREAL (1,021,520), metropolis of Canada, is a young-old city, for although dating from the seventeenth century, it is a more modern city than Quebec. Towering over the buildings is Mont-Royal, with its great Cross, around which the city is built, both on an island beside the St. Lawrence River. Attractions include Notre Dame Church; St. James' Cathedral; the old Place Royale, where *voyageurs* were hired to go out in search of furs; the Chateau de Ramezay, now a museum; McGill University, with the stern beauty of its Scottish baronial architecture; the modern buildings of the University of Montreal; the Oratory of St. Joseph, now the tomb of

known as Huronia. As is then to be expected, it is rich in historic sites — records of the struggles to form an empire and to convert the Indian to Christianity. All Indians in this region now live on the Indian Reserves and almost none of them is Huron. The fur trade through the years remained an important industry, however, and trading posts were established, some of them on the sites of present cities and towns. The visitor to Ontario, whatever his tastes in recreation, will find ample opportunity to gratify them. There are major fishing regions, such as Muskoka Lake, the Georgian Bay—Bruce Peninsula area, with Manitoulin Island in the bay, Kawartha Lakes and Algonquin Park in Central Ontario, where trout — rainbow, lake and brown — bass, pickerel and the Great Northern pike may be found; Lake Nipissing, one of the best pickerel lakes

MONTREAL, CANADA
BUSINESS CENTER

To Stadium
DE BULLION
General Hospital
ST. GABRIEL
(37) To Jacques Cartier
Bridge & Quebec
To Victoria Pier
Chamber of Commerce
ST. DOMINIQUE
JEAN BAPTISTE
BLVD.
ST. LAWRENCE
Themis Bldg.
LaPresse
CLARK
Le Canada
Aldred Bldg.
Duluth Bldg.
Church of St. John the Evangelist
ST. URBAIN
Power Bldg.
Tramways Bldg.
Notre Dame Church
(2) To Quebec
BENOIT
COTE
Place D'Armes
Transportation Bldg.
C.P.R. Bldg.
Montreal Star
ST. FRANCOIS XAVIER
ONTARIO
ST. GEORGE
CHENNEVILLE
ST. GEORGE
NICHOLAS
Coristine Bldg.
To Outremont
The Herald
ANDERSON
Ins. Exch. Bldg.
Board of Trade Bldg.
Customs House
NORMAND
SHERBROOKE
CONCORD
MAYOR
BLEURY
Imperial Thea.
College Ste. Marie
Belgo Bldg.
BLEURY
Reed Bldg.
Royal Bank Bldg.
Shaughnessy Bldg.
St. Patrick's Church
Bank of Toronto Bldg.
McGill McGill Bldg.
LONGUEUIL
KING
St. James United Church
ST. ALEXANDER
Alexander Bldg.
Princess Thea.
C.I.L. Bldg.
Canada S.S. Lines
Victoria Square
ST. HENRY
QUEEN
City Councillors
Orpheum Thea.
BEAVER HALL HILL
PRINCE
AYLMER
Phillips
Canada Cement Bldg.
Shawinigan Bldg.
Railway Exch. Bldg.
DUKE
Royal Victoria College
Morgan's
UNION
Square
New Birks' Bldg.
Royal Auto Club
Bell Tel. Bldg.
OTTAWA
Christ Church Cathedral
UNIVERSITY
BELMONT
Eaton's
VICTORIA
Palace Thea.
International Aviation Bldg.
RUTLAND RY.
McGill University
Confederation Bldg.
McGILL
COLLEGE
Central Station
Queen (C.N.R.)
ST. DAVID
INSPECTOR
Capitol Thea.
Elizabeth Hotel (Site)
St. James Cathedral
The Gazette
Chaboillez Square
MANSFIELD
Simpsons
METCALFE
Sun Life Bldg.
Tourist Bureau
ST. CECILE
CATHEDRAL
Post Office
COLBORNE
(3)(7)(9)
Sheraton
Mt. Royal Hotel
Hermes Bldg.
Dominion Square
Dominion Sq. Bldg.
St. George's Ch. (Anglican)
WINDSOR
Bonaventure Station (C.N.R.)
Queen's Hotel
To New York & Victoria Bridge
PEEL
M.A.A.A.
Drummond Bldg.
Windsor Hotel
MURRAY
STANLEY
Castle Bldg.
Y.M.C.A.
Hotel Laurentien
Windsor Station C.P.R.
ELEANOR
(3)(7)(9)
Berkeley Hotel
Drummond Medical Bldg.
Ritz-Carlton Hotel
DRUMMOND
Hotel De La Salle
Bus. Terminal
ST. FELIX
MOUNTAIN
MOUNTAIN
Ogilvy's
CRESCENT
AQUEDUCT
GUY
Art Gallery
Y.W.C.A.
Empire Life Bldg.
BISHOP
VERSAILLES
NOTRE DAME
Church of St. James the Apostle
C.B.C.
OVER DALE
ARGYLE
LUSIGNAN
MACKAY
Keefer Bldg.
York Thea.
Her Majesty's Thea.
GUY
Medical Arts Bldg.
GUY
SHERBROOKE
PIERCE
Richmond Square
RICHMOND
To Airport, Westmount, Ottawa & Laurentians
ST. LUKE
ST. MATTHEW
DORCHESTER
D. & H. RY.
ST. ANTOINE
SEIGNEURS
ST. JAMES
ST. MARTIN
ST. MARK
FORT ST.
CHATHAM
LINCOLN
CHOMEDEY
TUPPER
SEYMOUR
HOPE
SUSSEX
RICHMOND
FULFORD
CANNING
Seville Thea.
(2) To Toronto
CLOSSE
Forum
ESSEX
Western Hosp.
ATWATER
N.Y.C.R.R.
COURSOL
BLAKE
QUESNEL
DOMINION
ALBERT
DELISLE
OVINET
(1) University Tower Bldg.
(2) Loew's Thea.
© C. S. Hammond & Co., N.Y.

in Canada, with bass, muskie, trout and pike plentiful in the rest of northern Ontario; the region around Hudson Bay and northwestern Ontario, lying along the northern shores of Lake Superior and the Manitoba border, including the beautiful Lake of the Woods. In most of these regions the hunter will be pleased to find deer and moose in quantity and smaller game in abundance. . . . Other attractions Ontario offers to the visitor are bathing, swimming, boating, camping, picnicking and hiking in the national parks. **Point Pelee National Park** in the southwest offers the study of trees and flowers, small game and birds. The park's marshes give food and shelter to thousands of migrating waterfowl. . . . **Georgian Islands National Park** is rich in history, for it was here the Hurons had their villages and traces of those Indians and the missions may be found. Beausoleil Island was for years the home of the Ojibwa or Chippewa Indians. Interesting caves and rock pillars, formed by erosion of limestone cliffs, from which small trees and shrubs sprout, gave to Flowerpot Island its name. . . . St. Lawrence National Park is located in the "Thousand Islands Region" — one of the most picturesque regions of the North American continent—and thirteen of these islands have been set aside as a park. Here the government has provided wharves, pavilions and beach facilities for the vacationer. . . . **Fort Wellington at Prescott**, on the St. Lawrence, a fortification of the War of 1812, is now a historic park. Although never besieged during that war, it figured in later incidents of the nineteenth century. Particularly interesting are the blockhouse and the caponier, or listening post, outside the fortification, which was reached through a subterranean passage. . . . **Fort Malden** at Amherstburg, another historic park, was constructed on the banks of the Detroit River between 1797-1799. For the next forty years it was one of the principal frontier posts and figured in the War of 1812. The government maintains an interesting museum at this site. . . . **TORONTO** (675,754) — Indian for "The Meeting Place" — is the provincial capital and the commercial, industrial and cultural metropolis of central Canada, a city of great wealth with beautiful residential districts. Some of the most interesting places are the **monument in Exhibition Park**, marking the site of Fort

Rouille, first recorded white settlement established by the French; the oldest civil clock, topping St. Lawrence Market, once City Hall; the old lighthouse on Fleet Street, which marked the harbor entrance for nearly a hundred years; the blockhouses of Fort York, with bullet scars of the War of 1812; the memorial to Zebulon Pike, of Pike's Peak fame, who died when a magazine blew up; Holy Trinity Church, more than a century old; the memorials to **Queen Victoria** and to **Robert Raikes**, the founder of Sunday Schools, in Queen Park; the memorial plaque commemorating the invention of standard time, in the Sons of England Building; **Colburne Lodge** in **High Park**, the home of John G. Howard, Esq., who bequeathed many acres of park land to the city; unique **Casa Loma**, home of Sir Henry Mill Pellat, nineteenth century financial king, a spectacular stone castle with secret stairways, wine cellars, elegant rooms; the **Parliament Buildings** and **Supreme Court**; the **University of Toronto**; **David Dunlop Observatory**; **Royal Ontario Museum**, and the **Art Gallery**. The open-air Shakespearean Festival and the Canadian National Exhibition, with its many exhibits, are held in Toronto each year. . . . Once the capital of united Upper and Lower Canada, **KINGSTON** is a town of historic interest. Founded by the Empire Loyalists in 1783, the **first mill** and the **first newspaper** in the province were started here. It is also the home of **Queens College**. **Fort Henry** was one of the strongest fortifications in Canada after Quebec and Halifax. . . . **HAMILTON**, a transportation center on Lake Ontario, has one of the finest landlocked harbors on the Great Lakes and one of the most modern Canadian **art galleries**. . . . **SAULT STE. MARIE**, a large manufacturing city, is also a site of much historical interest. . . . **STRATFORD** is the home of the Stratford Shakespearean Festival.

THE PRAIRIE PROVINCES

Manitoba, Sasketchewan and Alberta form the innermost part of Canada. They have physical features in common: their plains — the great grain bowl of the country — rivers, lakes and scenic beauty and in the two westernmost provinces, the foothills and peaks of the Rocky Mountains. **MANITOBA** offers excellent hunting for moose, caribou, deer and small game; fishing for trout, pike and rock bass; canoeing; camping and hiking. **Whiteshell**

Unexcelled Hunting and fishing lure the sportsman to the Prairie Provinces

Canadian Gov. Trav. Bur.

Provincial Park, located in the eastern part, studded with two hundred lakes and rivers, has facilities for swimming, boating and fishing. Here the vacationer may explore the **Land of the Granite Cliffs**, which rise steeply from the water, covered with forests of poplar, birch and tamarack, interspersed with picnic grounds shaded by clumps of pine.... In **Riding Mountain National Park**, in midwestern Manitoba, the visitor finds all the fishing, motoring, hiking and riding he could wish. Big game such as elk, deer, moose, bear and wolf, as well as small game, make the hunter happy. Waterfowl such as duck, swan and geese abound. There is an exhibition herd of buffalo, that former rover of the plains. . . . The Trout Festival is held in northern waters, while in Hudson Bay white whale is hunted. **The International Peace Garden**, in southern Manitoba, is of interest. WINNIPEG (235,710), founded by Lord Selkirk's colony of the Red River Valley, is the capital of the province. The classic beauty of the **Manitoba Legislature Building**, with the famous **Gold Boy** atop the dome, is one of the city's chief attractions, while the **Civic Auditorium**, with its museum and art gallery; the **Cenotaph**; the city's first **post office**; the gate to old **Fort Garry** and the many churches are other points of interest. The music festival, annual **Canoe Club Regatta** and **Red River Exhibition** are events attracting many visitors annually. The **trip** up **Lake Winnipeg** by steamer is interesting and beautiful. . . . **THE PAS**, the gateway to the north, holds the Trappers Festival, attended by Indians and trappers from all over the north country. Near here is the **Nelson River**, one of the famous trout-fishing areas of the world. . . . FLIN FLON, noted

for its mines of copper, zinc, gold, silver, cadmium and salinium, has an interesting history. . . . The wheat city of BRANDON, in the south, is noted for its **Provincial Fair**, with livestock and other interesting exhibits. . . . SASKATCHEWAN is the middle Prairie Province. Within it are four regions: the open plains of the south and going northward, the parklands, commercial forest lands, lands of rivers, lakes and streams and in the northeast, the "Land of the Little Sticks." In the south lies the great grain-growing region, reclaimed from the wild grasses and buffalo of early days. In **Prince Albert National Park**, in a vast region of rocks, woods and water at almost the exact geographical center of Saskatchewan, the recreational facilities are practically unlimited, with thousands of crystal lakes tied together by little rivers, providing hundreds of miles for canoe trips. Along the shores of **Lakes Waskesiu, Kingsmere** and **Crean** are fine beaches for swimmers, while sport fish abound in their waters. The forests contain various species of big and small game, with a small herd of buffalo brought from Alberta. On **Lake Lavallee** are the pelican rookeries, one of the quaint birds of the north. Golf, tennis, hiking and riding are popular diversions provided by park authorities. At **Montreal Lake** is a trading post of the Hudson's Bay Company and Cree Indian reserve. Two other parks, **Cypress Hills** and **Moose Jaw**, provide similar recreation. . . . REGINA, the capital, has its white-walled, dark-domed **Legislative Building** rising amid man-planted trees. . . . PRINCE ALBERT, fourth largest city, is the gateway to both the commercial forest region and the "Land of the Little Sticks," a sub-Arctic territory merging into the Northwest Territories. . . . ALBERTA, the Foothills Province, is the most westerly of the Prairie Provinces, named for the wife of the Governor-General of Canada, Her Royal Highness, Princess Louise Caroline Alberta. Of greatest interest to the visitor are the scores of lakes and streams affording sport to the angler. Here he may fish for several varieties of trout, including the Loch Leven, found nowhere else in western Canada. The game, overflowing from the national parks where it is protected, includes elk, grizzly, black and brown bear, caribou, deer, antelope, Rocky Mountain sheep, goat, cougar and wolf. In the autumn, when the birds fly south, duck and goose are also popular. . . . It is in the national parks that Alberta's scenery can be most admired. Banff National Park is the oldest and second largest of Canada's national playgrounds. Its mountain peaks pierce the sky; its beautiful valleys with their green forests and lakes delight the visitor. The vast Columbia Ice-Field, at the northern end of the park, is a remnant of the ice age. Here also are the resorts at Banff and Lake Louise with their hotels, Banff Springs and Chateau Lake Louise, of international fame. Other points of interest include Cascades Rock Garden; the government museum near Bow River Bridge, with its exhibits of the flora, fauna and geology of the region; the hot mineral springs, equal to any on the continent, and Moraine Lake, in the Valley of the Ten Peaks. In the park there is varied entertainment for the visitor, including hiking, riding, swimming, climbing, boating, tennis, golf, skiing and fishing. . . . On the highway to Jasper National Park is seen the Athabaska Glacier, largest to issue from the Columbia Ice-Field. Through Jasper, largest of the seven parks in the mountains of western Canada, on the Athabaska Trail, passed the explorers and fur traders of history. As a matter of fact, the park owes its name to Jasper House, a fur-trading post of the North West Company. Within its borders are many beautiful lakes, among them Lac Beauvert, with its jade-green waters, Medicine Lake, Pyramid Lake and Maligne Lake. Maligne Canyon is a remarkable example of erosion and the waters of Miette Hot Springs, having a wide reputation for their medicinal qualities, are the hottest in the Rockies. At Jasper Park Lodge is one of the finest golf courses on the continent. The wildlife sanctuary, one of the largest, provides a home for big and small game of the mountains. . . . The "Bad Lands" of the Red Deer Valley wonderfully illustrate the effects of the erosion of wind and rain on rock. . . . Set apart primarily as a wildlife reserve, first in the country to be so designated, Elk Island National Park is the home of Canada's national herd of plains buffalo. Purchased from two Montana ranchers, it is one of the relatively few existent herds of this almost extinct animal. Elk Island Park contains numerous elk and is also one of the most important bird sanctuaries in western Canada. . . . The Waterton Lakes National Park, another charming playground, adjoins Glacier National Park in Montana, forming with it the Waterton-Glacier International Peace Park. At the head of the valleys are cirques forming mountain lakes, while the beautiful coloring of the rock is one of the park's outstanding features, with outcroppings of reddish shales darkening to wine and purple, green and gold. Boating on Upper Waterton Lake is a fine way to view the spectacular scenery. Excellent fishing is available in the lakes and streams, where several varieties of trout and whitefish are found. There is golf on the park course, horseback riding over mountain trails to the various lakes and motoring on the excellent highways. The wildlife sanctuary contains many species of big and small game like Rocky Mountain sheep, black bear, elk, deer, Rocky Mountain goat, beaver and squirrel. . . . Alberta's capital city, EDMONTON, is the focal point of the mining and fur-producing regions of the Arctic and an agricultural distributing center. Its airport is the hub of traffic to Alaska and northern Canada from southern Canada and the United States. . . . CALGARY, in the center of fertile ranching lands, is the scene of an annual roundup, the famous Calgary Stampede.

BRITISH COLUMBIA, THE YUKON AND NORTHWEST TERRITORIES

Separated by the Rocky Mountains from the rest of Canada, BRITISH COLUMBIA is almost a country by itself, providing striking scenery, an excellent climate and four beautiful national parks, where camping, boating, swimming, canoeing, climbing, cycling, hiking, riding over mountain trails, fishing and winter sports may be enjoyed. Kootenay, divided

by the valleys of the Vermilion and Kootenay Rivers, includes the **Radium Hot
Springs,** the **"Iron Gates"** at Sinclair Canyon, **Marble Canyon,** the **"Paint Pots"** and
an **iceberg lake. Yoho,** an Indian word
meaning "It is wonderful," is noted for the
Yoho and **Kicking Horse valleys; Seven
Sisters, Bridal Veil** and **Twin Falls; Daly
Glacier;** the **Natural Bridge** over **Kicking
Horse River;** interesting peaks and beautiful lakes. **Glacier** comprises a magnificent
alpine region of immense peaks, many of
them 10,000 feet, ice-fields, glaciers —
Illecillewaet Glacier is the largest — deep
canyons and foaming streams. One of the
most primitive of the Canadian national
parks, it is of special interest to the mountaineer and nature lover. Therefore, **Mount
Revelstoke,** on an alpine plateau near the
junction of the Columbia and Illecillewaet
Rivers, including meadows dotted with
small lakes, is an all-season playground,
offering skiing as a winter sport. From
Lookout Station, a vast panorama spreads
for miles. One of its natural phenomena is
the **Ice Box,** a great cleft in the rock strata
containing ice and snow even in midsum-
mer. **Kamloops** is a town, not a park, but
it is also a region famous for its trout fishing, skiing and hunting. The region of the
north is a beautiful but rugged country
offering excellent sport in hunting and fishing, while seventy-mile-long **Lake Okana-**

gan, on the Washington border in the south,
is another vacation paradise. . . . The capital of the province is **VICTORIA,** on Vancouver Island, a quiet, regal city with
shaded curved streets, stately homes and
vivid gardens. The gray-stone Parliament
Buildings overlook the inner harbor and
the cathedral rises from the calm seclusion
of the Bishop's Close. Famed Beacon Hill
Park affords vistas of the Olympic and
coast ranges and roads in all directions
lead to good fishing. In the shops may be
found fine china, woolens and linens of
international reputation, while its hostel-
ries provide excellent food and entertainment. . . . **VANCOUVER** (344,833) on a
fine harbor, is British Columbia's metropolis. Its shops are excellent; the sheltered
waters of English Bay are fringed with fine
beaches, and hunting, fishing and exploring excursions, golf, tennis, riding and
bowling are easily available throughout the
year. Chinatown makes a fascinating tour
and no visit is complete without a trip to
the great, natural Stanley Park forming
one side of the harbor entrance. . . . The
YUKON and the **NORTHWEST TERRI-
TORIES** are Canada's Arctic regions and
as such do not hold much appeal to the
average vacationist although the Yukon
is familiar to most through stories of the
gold rush of the 1800's and the poems of
Robert Service.

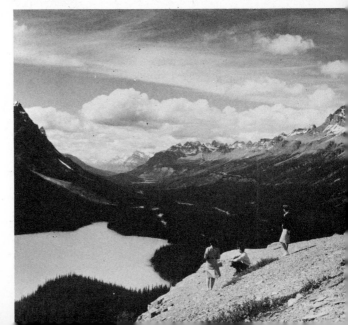

Scenic grandeur in the
Canadian Rockies
Canadian Gov. Trav. Bur.

Mexico

ADVENTURING IN MEXICO

When the Spaniards first landed on the unexplored Mexican coast they found a fabulous country and called it New Spain. Visitors today will still find Mexico a fabulous country, whether they be tourists or scholars, businessmen or artists. Mexico is truly all things to all people. Here ancient ruins exist in close proximity to modern, progressive cities. Lakes, forests and imposing volcanoes present scenes of unmatched beauty. Wonderful churches and cathedrals vie with one another for the supremacy of Mexico's landscape. And most interesting of áll are the people whose customs and dialects vary from place to place. Especially interesting is the Indian population, many of whom still speak the ancient Mayan or Aztec tongue and live much the same way as their renowned ancestors did. Whatever the visitor's interests are, he may be sure of bearing away with him some treasured memory from this land of old and new.

THE EAGLE AND THE SERPENT

Legend says that in 1325 the Aztecs, searching for a place to settle, came to a lake. Here they saw an eagle perched on the stem of a native cactus, which was growing out of a rock. The eagle held a serpent in its talons. Taking this as a good omen, the Aztecs founded their capital here — Tenochtitlán, site of present-day Mexico City. Less than two centuries later the famed Spanish conqueror, Hernán Cortés, landed and subjected the entire region in about two years. From the time of this conquest to the establishment of independence Mexico was governed as the Viceroyalty of New Spain. After nearly three hundred years of Spanish control, the Mexicans first anounced their desire for freedom in 1810, when a Mexican priest, Miguel Hidalgo, declared independence with the rallying cry of "El Grito de Dolores." After Hidalgo's defeat and execution, the patriotic cause was taken up by José María Morelos, and the Declaration of Independence was formerly signed in 1813. Later in the century Benito Juaréz, who became president in 1858, forcibly opposed the setting up of a French Empire in Mexico under the puppet-ruler Maximilian. After much guerilla warfare, Maximilian was captured and shot by Mexican soldiers and the Empire came to an end.

MEXICAN MEALS

Mexican *tortillas* and tamales are famous as typical native foods, but while in Mexico you will want to try some of the other dishes whose renown has been confined to the borders of the country. A savory dish is *pollo en estofado* or Mexican stewed chicken made with cinnamon, olives and other seasoning. Another tasty dish is *cembollos rellenos* (stuffed onions) which will easily prove to be a meal in themselves. If you like salads, try *ensalada de guacamole,* a delicious mixture of eggs, tomatoes, olives and avocados. While in Mexico you may want to sample *penuche,* a type of delicious candy. Wines are plentiful and good. Tequila is an alcoholic drink made from the maguey plant and is known as the national drink of Mexico.

INTERESTING CITIES OF MEXICO

MEXICO CITY (2,233,914), the capital, is a modern metropolis which has sprung from the ancient center of the Aztec Empire. The Spanish conqueror Cortés had the main square of the city constructed on the central plaza of the Aztecs. Known today as **Plaza de la Constitución,** it is popularly referred to as the Zócalo. On the east side of this plaza is the **National Palace,** now containing various government offices, but once the site of Cortés' residence. Above the central portal of the Palace hangs the **Liberty Bell** rung by the patriotic priest Hidalgo in 1810. Every year on the night of September 15 crowds swarm into the plaza to hear the President ring the bell and give the celebrated *Grito de Dolores* from the balcony. **The National Museum,** on the northeast corner of the Zócalo, has an extensive collection of Indian handicraft and relics. The most prized item is the Aztec calendar stone weighing over twenty-four tons and testifying to the scientific attainments of Aztec culture. To the east of the Museum is the **National Institute of Fine Arts,** with its valuable collection of church paintings including such masters as Murillo, Zurbarán and Rubens. Also in the Zócalo quarter is the **School of Medicine,** interesting because it was originally constructed as the headquarters of the Holy Office of the Inquisition, where the cells of its victims may still be seen. Also noteworthy is the **Palace**

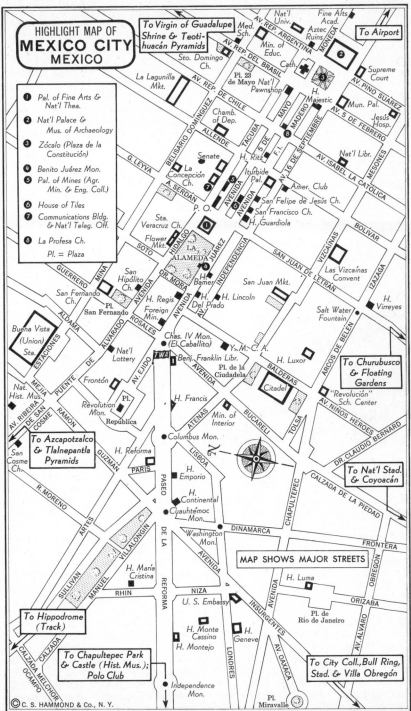

HIGHLIGHT MAP OF
MEXICO CITY
MEXICO

1. Pal. of Fine Arts &
   Nat'l Thea.
2. Nat'l Palace &
   Mus. of Archaeology
3. Zócalo (Plaza de la
   Constitución)
4. Benito Juárez Mon.
5. Pal. of Mines (Agr.
   Min. & Eng. Coll.)
6. House of Tiles
7. Communications Bldg.
   & Nat'l Teleg. Off.
8. La Profesa Ch.
   Pl. = Plaza

To Virgin of Guadalupe
Shrine & Teoti-
huacán Pyramids

To Airport

To Churubusco
& Floating
Gardens

To Azcapotzalco
& Tlalnepantla
Pyramids

To Nat'l Stad.
& Coyoacán

To Hippodrome
(Track)

MAP SHOWS MAJOR STREETS

To Chapultepec Park
& Castle (Hist. Mus.);
Polo Club

To City Coll., Bull Ring,
Stad. & Villa Obregón

© C. S. HAMMOND & Co., N. Y.

of Fine Arts, a large ornate building executed in white marble with yellow domes. Its great weight pressing upon the spongy lake bed of the city has caused the building to sink six feet. Mexico City's main boulevard is the **Paseo de la Reforma.** This walk is interrupted at intervals by circles or *glorietas,* adorned with monuments and flowers. At the end of the walk is **Chapultepec Park.** It was on the hill in the center of the park that the great Aztec Emperor,

northeast of the capital is the pre-Aztec city of **SAN JUAN TEOTIHUACAN.** At the center of this ancient spot rises the **Pyramid of the Sun,** nearly 220 feet high, ruins of a residence of an ancient dignitary revealing halls, stairways, a chapel and altar. Pottery, jade ornaments, weapons, and human masks made of nephrite may be seen on display in the **regional museum** nearby. . . . The religious center of Mexico is the **Shrine of the Virgin Guadalupe,** four

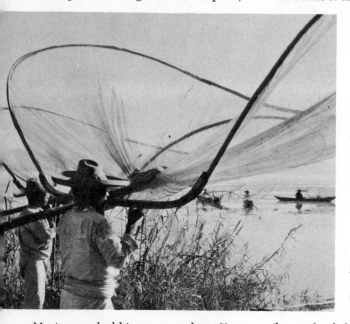

These are Mexican fish nets, not huge, gossamer-winged dragonflies
Pan American Union

Montezuma, had his summer palace. **Chapultepec Castle** was begun here in 1783 and later used as a residence by the ill-fated Emperor Maximilian and his wife. Located within many public buildings throughout Mexico City are the forceful murals of such world-famous Mexican painters as Rivera and Orozco. The latter has done an impressive mural on the walls of Chapultepec Castle. . . . Fifteen miles from the center of the capital is **XOCH-IMILCO** and its wonderful "floating gardens." Visitors may hire flower-decorated boats and drift along the canals of this "Venice of Mexico." The islands here were originally Aztec settlements constructed on floating rafts of twigs and reeds, covered with earth and planted with gardens. Later, as the waters of the lake went down, the plants took root so that the islands were held fast. . . . A short distance

miles north of the capital. According to legend, the Virgin appeared to an Indian boy and told him to gather roses from a barren hill. The boy obeyed and carried the miraculous blossoms to the bishop in his cloak. When the mantle was opened a portrait of the Virgin was discovered upon the cloth of the Indian boy's garment. This portrait, framed in gold, is set above the altar in the church erected in honor of the official patroness of the Mexican people. . . . About 80 miles south of Mexico City is **PUEBLA.** Laid out by the Spaniards in 1531, it is the most characteristically Spanish city of the Republic, often called "the royal seat of the Spanish Empire," for from its beginning it has clung to Spanish tradition. Keeping an eternal vigil over the **Valley of Puebla** is **Popocatépetl** (Smoking Mountain), famous in Mexican legend and song. Interesting to

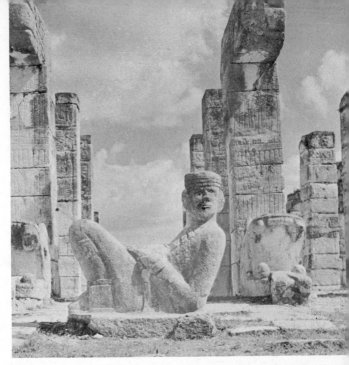

Unusual statue of Chac-Mool among the impressive Mayan ruins at Chichen Itza in Mexico
Pan American Union

visit in the city is the **Church of San Francisco** with its graceful towers and glazed tile. The famous **Chapel of Our Lady of the Rosary** nearby is one of the finest examples of ultra-baroque in the world. One of the most refreshing spots in Puebla is the **Agua Ozul**, a huge outdoor swimming pool fed by natural warm sulphur springs. In this town the national costume of Mexico originated, the "china poblana." Legend says that a Chinese princess, arriving in Mexico, adopted the native dress and further enhanced it by embroidering it with colored glass. . . . One of Mexico's most beautiful resorts is **ACAPULCO**, on the Pacific coast. Here fishermen may glory in the abundance of sailfish and marlin. Glass-bottom boats offer the tourist a marvelous opportunity to study the magnificent underwater life. Not only can you swim in the blue waters, but also water ski and sail to your heart's content along the fabulous beaches. While here, it is thrilling to witness the courageous diving feats of the young boys who perilously dive from a high cliff into an exceptionally narrow channel below. . . . Northeast of Acapulco is the quiet town of **OAXACA** with its colonial homes and green-stone buildings. The lovely **Church of Santo Domingo** is supposed to be one of the finest of its type in the Americas.

Commanding a beautiful view of the city is the **Cerro del Fortín**, a site at which lovely rites recalling those of the ancient goddess of harvest are held every year. This hillside is topped by a massive bronze **Statue of Benito Juárez**, the Oaxacan Indian who rose to be president of the Republic. If time permits, an excursion to the surrounding areas should not be overlooked, including one to **MITLA** to see the Zapotecan ruins known as the "City of the Dead." Another interesting trip is to **Monte Alban** where the fabulous tombs of the past may be seen. . . . North of Oaxaca is the bustling port city of **VERACRUZ**. Here there are beaches so wide and sand packed so hard that automobiles may travel along them for miles. The warm climate and unexcelled coastline provide excellent facilities for surf bathing or just basking in the sun. Here you may sample the famous regional drink made from coconut or guanábana. Offshore is the island of **Sacrificios** where a famous pirate allowed his rebellious captives to die of starvation. Not far from Veracruz is **Boca del Río**, famous for its delicacies prepared with shrimp, oysters and crab meat. From this port city deep-sea fishing is a popular attraction which constantly lures fishermen who come from all parts of the world to try their luck.

Guatemala

TRADITIONAL HOME OF "PAXIL"

The Indian Garden of Eden, Guatemala maintains the charm of bygone days. Two-thirds of the population are descendants of the ancient Mayan civilization and still tread the same fertile valleys and tree-clad mountains beloved of their forebears. These proud people maintain their ancient customs, language and their gorgeous costumes. Their fascinating, colorful native life and the many ancient Mayan ruins comprise the main tourist attraction of the country. Of course, the land itself, largely mountainous, is of great beauty with numerous lofty volcanoes, sweet-smelling pine woods, dense forests, turquoise-blue lakes and fertile plateaus. And wherever you go in Guatemala, you will hear in the background the tinkling music of the marimba playing folk tunes.

GLORIES OF COLONIAL SPAIN

Then there is the modern, cosmopolitan society of the Spanish Guatemaltecans, many of whose forefathers were among the brave band of three hundred who placed the country under Spanish domain in 1524. In the cities still stand many fine examples of colonial Spanish architecture, and in many cases, as in Antigua, buildings leveled by earthquakes have been rebuilt in the same grand style.

ABOUT FOOD

Continental foods of excellent variety and quality, especially Italian and Spanish, are served in the larger places. You will certainly want to try some of the local specialties, such as *Gallo en chicha* (chicken in a very special sauce), the Guatemalan version of *enchiladas* and *tamales*, and several of the many concoctions made from bananas or plantains. As in all tropical countries the variety of exotic fruits is infinite.

IN THE CAPITAL

In 1776, the year of our War of Inpendence, GUATEMALA CITY (283,100) was founded as capital of Guatemala. Built on a high plateau, in an ideal climate, it is a clean and attractive city with gleaming modern buildings standing shoulder to shoulder with stately old colonial ones. Parque Central, a park bright with flowers, forms the hub of the city. Facing it is the National Palace, the official seat of government. Its arched courtyards, fountain-fed patios, murals and magnifi-

cent mahogany-paneled reception rooms are open to the public. Other notable buildings include the University, the National Archeological Museum, the beautiful colonial cathedral and the little chapel atop the Cerro del Carmen, from where there is a fine view of the surrounding green hills and volcanoes. In Minerva Park is a unique relief map of the country. Elevated platforms allow one to look down and get a bird's-eye view of the country. The market here is especially exciting with a lavish display of fruits, flowers and native handicraft. Golf, polo and tennis are popular in the capital and there are excellent facilities for sailing, swimming, fishing and other sports within easy reach.

ROUND AND ABOUT THE COUNTRY

A short drive from the capital, via lovely Lake Amatitlán, is the fascinating resort town of ANTIGUA at the foot of Aqua volcano. Capital until 1774, when it was almost leveled by an earthquake, it preserves many interesting ruins. Around them the city has been rebuilt entirely in the old Spanish style, with pastel-hued houses fronting on narrow cobbled streets and the whole framed against a backdrop of blue-green volcanoes. The Palace of the Captains, the University, several monasteries and convents are among the restored buildings of interest. . . . A trip to the HIGHLANDS is absolutely essential, for here are the majestic mountains, the deep sheltered valleys and gorges, the scented pines, the land of the Mayans. In the midst of this splendor lies Lake Atitlán, probably the world's most beautiful mountain lake. . . . PANAJACHEL, on the northern shore of the lake is a luxurious resort. From here launches carry you to the primitive Indian villages which line the 70-mile shore line of the lake. Each village has distinctly different characteristics in dress, customs and handicrafts, and one never tires of observing their unique ways of life. . . . North of Atitlán, high in the mountains, is CHICHICASTENANGO, most famous of Guatemalan resorts. Market days, Thursdays and Sundays, are absolutely amazing and are the reason for "Chichi's" popularity. Squealing pigs, strutting turkeys, hand-loomed textiles, beautiful pottery, exotic fruits and colorfully clad Indians overflow the market place. Special rites are performed at

Some natives in Guatemala travel with these cacaxtes on their backs, holding not only what they have for sale, but everything necessary for days on the road

Consulate Gen., Guatemala

the old church of **Santo Tomás** and the scent of flowers and incense and the sound of marimba music fill the air. . . . From **QUEZALTENANGO**, second city of the country and itself a picturesque city, may be taken many interesting excursions, down into the **coffee plantations** of the warm coastal lands, or up into the cool **Cuchumatanes Mountains**. . . . In these mountains, near **HUEHUETENANGO** are the **ruins of Zaculeu**, outstanding relics of the Mayan civilization. . . . To the north of the capital, **COBAN** is a charming old town famous for its **shadow-work textiles** and **silverwork**, particularly the Cobán **wedding chains**. . . . Further north, in the real jungle country of orchids and chicle

trees, **FLORES** is a fascinating town built on an island in the middle of beautiful Lake Petén-Itza. Nearby are the ruins of Tayasal. . . . On the Caribbean coast, **PUERTO BARRIOS**, chief port of the country, offers unsurpassed **deep-sea fishing**. . . . From here a trip across Lake Izabal and down the Río Dulce to **LIVINGSTON** will take you through lush tropical forest and give you a glimpse of the great variety of exotic wildlife and vegetation that grows along the coast. You might even sight a **Quetzal**, that brilliantly-plumaged, long-tailed bird whose traditional love of liberty caused it to be adopted, appropriately, as the national bird of Guatemala.

Honduras

HOW DEEP IS THE OCEAN

Honduras, the largest of the Central American Republics, is an enigmatic country, fascinating to travelers and explorers, and an often-used setting for tellers of intriguing tales. Columbus, alleged to be the first white man to see the country, named it *Honduras,* the Spanish word meaning "depths." Although historians claim the explorer chose this appellation because of the deep waters found offshore, Columbus, viewing its towering mountains, could have sensed the mysteries churning within the canyons of the land. Bordering on the Caribbean Sea and on both the Atlantic and Pacific Oceans, this 59,000-square-mile country, is the most mountainous of the Central American Republics. Cut by the Central American Cordillera from northwest to southeast, Honduras is crowned with an infinity of irregular crests, between which are extensive, fertile valleys and plateaus. Ringed with the golden banana plantations and the green jungles of the southeast, Honduras is a kaleidoscopic delight to the visitor.

AT FIRST GLANCE

Sightseeing in this country of changing contours, bordering on Guatemala, El Salvador and Nicaragua, reveals that its history is as colorful as its topography. Indian and Spanish names disclose the origin of towns and cities. Its architectural chronicle is carved in the stone ruins of its Mayan dwellers, the ornate, romantic façades of its Spanish conquerors and in the uncluttered, modern structures of its now progressive, mestizio population.

WHAT'S COOKING?

The menus of its hotels and restaurants include many native dishes. Typical among them are tortillas (flat corn cakes), enchiladas (tasty meats or vegetables rolled in tortillas), tamale pie (tamal and chile), *tapado* (a stew of smoked beef, vegetables and coconut milk) and *mondongo* (made of tripe and beef knuckles). Honduran tropical fruits include mangoes, papayas, *annonas, zapotes,* granadillas, pineapples, avocados and bananas.

WHAT YOU WILL SEE

TEGUCIGALPA, the capital and chief comercial city of Honduras, is situated on a plateau 3200 feet above sea-level against a background of wooded mountains. Its name allegedly derives from the Indian for "silver hills"; extensive silver and gold mining is carried on in the nearby hills. The city really comprises two towns: low-lying Comayagüela and Tegucigalpa proper, with the Choluteca River between. Two masonry bridges connect the two sections. Tegucigalpa is quite hilly and at several points streets of stairs connect one level with another; its pastel stucco houses and white public buildings stand out brightly against the verdant background of mountains. Comayagüela, resting at the foot of the mountains, is level and broad. Here is located the National University and the National School of Fine Arts, the center of contemporary Honduran art. Tegucigalpa's main square is **Parque Morazán,** named for the nineteenth-century national hero, where are located the **Cathedral,** the beautiful **Palace of the Central District,** built of Honduran marble and hardwoods, and the **National Museum,** housing four divisions dedicated to archaeology, history, natural history and national products. Within walking distance are the **Presidential Palace,** the **House of Congress** and other government buildings and churches. Along the river is **Concordia Park,** where you can see replicas of striking monuments in the Mayan ruins of Copán. Climb up to the **Paseo La Leona,** the beautiful tree-lined promenade, 700 feet above the city, on the steep slope of **El Picacho.** At the top of this mountain is the city's reservoir, around which is built the three-and-a-half acre **Park of the United Nations,** from where one can see the fiesta of colors in the city below. Many of the city's modern, palatial residences are built on El Picacho's terraces and the paths leading to them are lined with orchid-festooned pines and flowery terraces. . . . SAN JUANCITO, 20 miles northeast of the capital, is the site of the Rosario silver and gold mines; the $2,000,000 worth of silver and gold taken out annually is transported by mule trains down the hills to Tegucigalpa. The mines are reached by a thrilling mountain road which winds tortuously through some of the most glorious scenery in the country. . . . The second largest city in the Republic is SAN PEDRO SUIA, the center of the banana and sugar-growing industries. A briskly modern city, it is in close proximity to the Mayan ruins of Travesia and to La Lima, headquarters of the United Fruit Company. . . . About a three-hour drive from Tegucigalpa over the winding, steep mountainside takes you to **COMAYAGUA**, once the capital of the Republic, in a rich, agricultural valley. Now a small, quiet, provincial town, it has preserved its colonial air in elaborate churches and low houses. Its three-hundred-year old **cathedral** contains priceless Old-World relics and paintings, including a solid silver tabernacle and candelabra which were gifts of Philip IV of Spain and Murillo's "Martyrdom of St. Bartholomew." . . . Beyond **Siguatepeque Mountain** is sparkling **Lake Yojoa**, one of the beauty spots of the Central American cordillera. Serene among pine-covered mountains, Yojoa is an ideal camping, fishing and hunting site. . . . West of this lake region is **SANTA ROSA DE COPAN**, largest city in the north of the country and the center of the prosperous mining and cattle-raising district, as well as the site of the tobacco, coffee and straw-hat industries. . . . Not far from here, near the border of Guatemala, are the ruins of **COPAN**, the second largest city of the old Mayan Empire and the probable cultural center of the whole region. One of the most representative sites of baroque Mayan art in the hemisphere, Copan is now the center of Honduras' pre-Columbian art studies. Here you will see the spacious courts, temples, palaces and stairways of the ancient city. There are many examples of the remarkable stone carving of the Mayas, huge heads of animals, representations of gods and hieroglyphs. . . . Traveling east from

Copan one comes to the Caribbean Coast cities of Honduras: **La Ceiba, Tela, Puerto Cortés** and **Trujillo**, the principal ports of the north coast and the heart of its export life, nourished by the wealth of its bananas, mahogany, gold, silver, coconuts and coffee. All the ports on the northern coast are connected with Tegucigalpa by air and to the principal banana producing centers by railroad. . . . **ROATAN** is the Honduran port of entry and capital of the fabulous **Bay Islands**. Lying 10 to 40 miles north of the Caribbean coast, these **Islas de la Bahía**, as they are known locally, consist of three large islands, **Roatan, Utila** and **Guanaja**. Often referred to as an earthly paradise, they are covered with lush forests, mahogany and fig trees and coconut palms. Many of the islanders are British by ancestry, consequently English is the language spoken with greatest fluency. Their secluded beaches are wonderful for swimming, fishing and exploring. Nearby is **PORT ROYAL**, famed in buccaneer days. Strategically situated in the emerald-green foothills on the eastern end of Roatan, it is the site of an old buccaneer town, tumbled-down forts and a real pirate's cave. The largest community on **Guanaja**, christened the "Isle of Pines" by Columbus, is built almost entirely over water; here one finds all manner of delicious crustaceans, turtles and small fish. . . . If Honduras' Pacific coast is preferred for exploration one can spend many pleasant hours in **San Lorenzo** on the Gulf of Fonseca or the verdant **Amapala** on **Tigre Island**.

Splendid replicas of the Mayan civilization at Concordia Park, Tegucigalpa
Philip Gendreau

El Salvador

LOVELY TO LOOK AT

Comparable in size to the state of Maryland, the garden republic of El Salvador is a traveler's treasure house. Covering the lower slopes of the Central American cordillera, it is landscaped with verdant mountains, active volcanoes, crater lakes, green forests, tropical valleys and beaches washed by the blue Pacific. Though the smallest of the Central American republics, El Salvador is the most densely populated, with natives living in hinterland villages and urbanites in modern cities. Its natural and cultural contrasts offer a maximum of sightseeing with a minimum of traveling and diversity of activity in a choice of climates.

THROUGH THE HOURGLASS

A tour of the cities and towns of this small, oblong-shaped country wedged between Guatemala and Honduras is a journey through the present and a pilgrimage into the past. Ancient ruins clinch El Salvador's claim to the great pre-Hispanic civilizations of the Mayans, Toltecs and Aztecs; many cathedrals and opulent homes reflect the Spanish influence and its latest buildings reveal the economic strides and comparative political stability of the twentieth-century republic.

BE THEIR GUEST

Typical Salvadorean dishes have corn *tortillas* as a base and show kinship to those of Mexico and other Central American countries. Lake and river fish are varied and tropical fruits are many. Native fruits are mangoes, papayas, annonas, guanabas, zapotes, granadillas, as well as pineapples, avocados and bananas.

THE INSIDE STORY

Called the most progressive city in Central America, SAN SALVADOR (pop. 160,380), the capital, is situated in the Valle de las Hamacas (Valley of the Hammocks) at the foot of the San Salvador Volcano. The valley's name suggests the numerous earthquakes that have shaken the city, the effects of which are indicated by its modern rather than colonial appearance. San Salvador is laid out in the form of a cross, with four spacious avenues meeting at its center. Plaza Bolívar, formerly called Parque Barrios, is the city's principal square and the site of its National Palace. Other buildings of major importance in the area are the National University, the Archbishop's Palace, the National Treasury and the Presidential Mansion. The oldest church is the church of La Merced, one of the few buildings not destroyed by the earthquakes. In its tower is the bell which the famed Father Delgado rang in 1811 to proclaim the country's independence from Spanish rule. The National Museum houses an interesting collection of jade and pottery relics from the Mayan ruins. Five miles outside the city stands the famed National Stadium, built especially for the Central American Olympic Games in 1935, now used for baseball and soccer. Akin to its historical and religious atmosphere are El Salvador's many holidays and fiestas. Of prominent significance is the one honoring the patron saint of the republic, El Salvador del Mundo (The Saviour of the World). Booths are set up in the main plaza, where handicrafts from all parts of the country are sold, allegorical floats are paraded through the streets and Indians perform traditional native dances. . . .

West of San Salvador is SANTA TECLA, or NUEVO SAN SALVADOR, founded two years after the 1854 earthquake. Situated in an idyllic valley, Santa Tecla's mild, healthful climate attracts many wealthy plantation owners and prominent families. Above the town stand the laboratories of the Coffee Growers' Association of El Salvador, where all phases of coffee growing are studied. Higher, on the road to the San Salvador Volcano, live the mountain flower gardeners who sell in the capital's market places. Early in the morning the women may be seen descending the steep roads dressed in their native costumes, carrying their blossoms to market in baskets balanced on their heads. . . . At the very rim of the San Salvador crater is a popular resort, EL BOQUERON. Commanding a spacious view in every direction, it is an artist's and photographer's paradise. From El Boqueron can be seen Lake Ilopango, San Salvador's playground. Towered by the 6,000-foot volcano of San Vicente, the lake's shores are dotted with vacation homes, hotels and Indian fishing villages. . . . Northeast of the lake is one of the country's most beautiful spas, LA TOMA. . . . North of the lake is COJUTEPEQUE, an old sixteenth-century town which has twice been the capital of

Steaming Izalco — most exciting of El Salvador's many active volcanoes—mirrored in lovely Balneario Atecozol, near San Salvador

Secty. of Info., El Salvador

the republic. Annually, on August 29, Indians come from near and far to the Cojutepeque fair to trade their native handicrafts. . . . Still further north is ILOBASCO, where most of the Salvadorean dolls are made. During the Christmas season the open-air stalls in San Salvador's markets are filled with these tiny dolls, some as small as a grain of rice, representing the Wise Men, shepherds, angels and the Christ Child. Besides dolls, the Ilobascans make **pottery** of every kind. Since all of its inhabitants work in clay, many of El Salvador's well-known sculptors have been Ilobascans. . . . Unlike most of the other cities of the country, SAN VICENTE, to the east, has endeavored to preserve its historical old buildings, making it a jewel of Spanish colonial architecture. . . . SANTA ANA, west of San Salvador and second only to it as a business center, lies in a large and fertile valley almost surrounded by a gigantic amphitheater of mountains. Its cathedral is one of El Salvador's finest examples of Spanish Gothic. Near the Santa Ana Volcano is Lake Coatepeque, whose musical name means "Eye of the Sea." Famous for its mineral waters, the lake is known as "the Vichy of Central America." Completely hemmed in by wooded hills, this rustic weekend resort has excellent facilities for bathing, fishing and sailing. The other nearby lake, Guija, is especially interesting to archaeologists because of the ancient ruins along its shores and on its islands. . . . ACAJUTLA is the most popular seashore resort in El Salvador and the port serving the western and central regions of the republic. The stretch of coast between Acajutla and La Libertad is the famous Balsam Coast. Here grows the special variety of balsam tree from which is extracted the valuable medicine and perfume base, "balsam of Peru." . . . Lying at the foot of the active Izalco Volcano, IZALCO is really two towns — one Indian, the other ladino (mixed Indian and Spanish) — merged into one, with each retaining its distinctive characteristics. The natives of this town and the nearby Indian villages retain the dress and customs of olden times, and many still speak their Indian language. The most interesting geographical feature, however, is the volcano. Besides the most active in Central America, it is — with the exception of two others in Mexico — the most recently formed as well. Because the flames of its regular eruptions can be seen nightly at sea, the natives have given it the appropriate title of "Lighthouse of the Pacific."

Nicaragua

THE CRADLE OF A POET

The Republic of Nicaragua, bathed by the waters of the Caribbean and the Pacific, is the largest of the Central American republics. It is a land of lakes, dormant volcanoes and tropical jungle. Through her ports have passed such men as Francis Drake and John Hawkins on their way to sack wealthy Granada. Two centuries later came Admiral Nelson, heading an unsuccessful naval expedition. Finally the famous "forty-niners" arrived, walking unmindfully over the deposits of gold in Nicaragua, on their way to seek the precious metal in California. Today one hears English spoken in the Caribbean ports of Nicaragua by descendants of British settlers and Jamaican Negroes, both of which became the first permanent colonists. But above all, Nicaragua is the land of Rubén Darío, the world-renowned poet whose lyric verse comes readily to the tongues of all Spanish-speaking peoples. Nicaragua bore him and now forever holds him. Through his verse he sang of the odd, the beautiful, the true, and created rare and delicate music from the words of the Spanish tongue.

NATIVE FOOD

A typical dish which you should try is Nicaraguan hot tamales known as *naca-tamales* and deliciously cooked in banana leaves. Try *tiste,* the national beverage, made of foamy chocolate served in a carved gourd. Excellent beer is made in Managua.

COLUMBUS STOPPED HERE

Columbus sailed along the coast of Nicaragua on his last voyage in 1502. He had met heavy seas along the Honduran coast and when he found calm waters at the cape he named it Cabo Gracias a Dios (Cape Thanks To God), as it is stilled called. Spanish conquerors sent from Panama under Gil González Dávila arrived in 1519. They were received by an Indian tribe that lived around Lake Nicaragua. The chief of this tribe, Nicarao, consented to be baptized and ordered his subjects to be baptized as well. It was from him, it is believed, that the country came to be known as Nicaragua. Much of Nicaragua's colonial history is a story of warfare between the wild Mosquito Indians of the Atlantic Coast and the Spanish colonials of the Pacific side and of pirate depredations and of struggles with the British settlers who maintained a strong foothold on the east coast until the end of the nineteenth century. Also running through Nicaragua's past is the question of an interoceanic canal. Since the time of the country's first settlements, Spain's rivals in the New World sought to gain control of her strategic waterway between east and west. A Nicaraguan canal is still an idea which may yet become a reality.

AROUND THE COUNTRY

MANAGUA (110,000), capital of the country, differs from all other Latin American capitals in that it has not been built around a single main plaza. The principal park, **Parque Central,** in spite of its name is on the northern edge of the town close to **Lake Managua.** It is interesting to observe the life of this tropical city by strolling along the downtown streets and walking along the palm-lined **Malecón** overlooking the lake. Across the street from the Parque Central is **Parque Darío** containing an artistic monument to her greatest son and immortal poet. At the base of the Statue of Rubén Darío is the gondola of Poetry which bears the goddess of Fame proclaiming the glory of the poet to the four winds. A block from **Avenida Roosevelt** (named to commemorate the late president's sixtieth birthday) on **Calle Central** is the large public market with its vast array of agricultural products, native foods and handicrafts. Among the cultural institutions you will want to visit are the **University of Nicaragua** and the **National Museum.** In the southwestern section of the capital, in El Cauce Park, are the **Huellas de Acahualinga.** These are footprints of human beings and animals which are probably the very earliest trace of man yet discovered in Central America. South of the city is the **Campo de Marte** a large parade ground which contains the country's fine military academy. Not far beyond is the **President's Palace** done in Moorish style and looking down over the expanse of the capital. Beyond is the new residential section of **Las Piedrecitas** with its beautiful gardens and terraces. Here a magnificent view may be had of **Lake Asososca, Lake Managua** and **Lake Jiloá** with the old volcano, **Momotombo,** in the distance. . . . **TIPITAPA** is a spa on Lake Managua about 14 miles from the capital.

This spot promises to become the most important resort in the country. The Tipitapa water is hot and sulphurous and has become a favorite watering place. If you enjoy fish dinners, by all means take advantage of Tipitapa's restaurants. Freshly-caught fish from Lake Managua are roasted and served in a variety of ways. . . . About 50 miles from Managua is the beautiful city of LEON. This city cherishes its tradition of learning and culture and has the distinction of being the boyhood home and resting place of Rubén Darío. Be sure to visit the 18th century Cathedral, completed after a century of construction and one of

Rock), a cave in which, according to an old story, two lovers once hid and were devoured by a tiger. . . . Southeast of the capital lies GRANADA on the edge of Lake Nicaragua. This was the wealthy city of colonial times that was so often sacked by English, Dutch and French pirates. Still clinging to its traditional ways, it is a leisurely old town full of old-world charm and simplicity. Of interest here is the 16th century Church of San Francisco built to serve as both church and fortress. It was here that Hernando de Soto was once imprisoned and where Bartolomé de las Casas preached his sermons condemn-

Managua's enticing market
Nat'l Tourist Board, Nic.

the largest in Latin America. Here the remains of Nicaragua's poet rest in an impressive tomb. Other interesting colonial buildings are the Palacio Episcopal and the Instituto Nacional, the latter occupying an ancient monastery. Walking along León's cobbled streets you will admire the typical houses of Spanish architecture, built around a central patio and roofed with red tiles. Still used in the streets are yokes of oxen drawing high-wheeled carts just as they appeared in colonial days. . . . If possible, take a short trip to the seaside resort of PONELOYA where you will find beautiful, broad beaches, colorful sunsets and the Peña del Tigre (Tiger

ing the excesses of the Spaniards against the native Indians. Other sites of importance are the Governor's House, dating from 1708, and the Central American School on the lake shore with its valuable collection of prehistoric Indian idols. . . . If you are a sportsman, try some deep-sea fishing off CORINTO on the Pacific side, and off BLUEFIELDS (named after the pirate, Blewfeldt) on the Caribbean coast. Lake Nicaragua offers the experience of fishing for shark and tarpon in fresh water. Big game such as jaguars will be found in the jungles of the interior; wild boar, deer and smaller game are to be found on the Pacific side.

Costa Rica

LAND OF TRANQUILITY

Costa Rica is a beautiful and enchanting country and her delightful climate, natural beauties and unique atmosphere of serene joy and calm endear her to the hearts of all visitors. Hospitality is the keynote of this "Land of Eternal Spring" and whether you are in search of a restful vacation just admiring the lovely scenery or more exciting diversions, you will be warmly welcomed.

BOOKSHOPS AND FESTIVALS

Costa Ricans, predominantly of Spanish origin, are a happy people, very fond of music, dancing and sports. There is great merrymaking during the annual carnivals in San José during December and January, at which time one can see bullfights a la Costa Rica — the bull is never killed. The high degree of culture is attested to by the preponderant number of bookshops. As a matter of fact, Costa Rica reportedly has more per square mile than any other country. The Spanish touch is apparent in the cooking, and native dishes, especially in San José, are deliciously prepared. Be sure to try their specialities, such as *palmito* or *pejivalle* (fruits of palm trees used in a variety of dishes), *gallo pinto* (rice and beans) or *paella* (deliciously flavored rice, meat and vegetables). Although well-seasoned, the food is not too spicy and can be enjoyed by all. Of course, in the larger hotels and restaurants the cuisine is international. Don't fail to sample and perhaps take home some of the famous national liquors, especially *crema de nance* and *crema de cafe*.

THE HAPPY CAPITAL

In the heart of the central plateau lies SAN JOSE, the "Happy Capital," one of the most attractive cities of Central America, with broad, clean streets and beautiful gardens at every turn. The architecture is an attractive mixture of traditional Spanish and modern. Make a point of visiting the National Theater, a really magnificent edifice with marble balconies and carvings. Its foyer decorated in gold and adorned with Venetian plate mirrors is awe-inspiring. The National Museum, a converted fortress built around a landscaped quadrangle, features rare old pottery and well-planned special exhibits. Visit the Zoo, the Country Club, the Metropolitan Cathedral, Legislative Assembly, the Union Club, principal social center of the country, and make a tour of the national liquor factory where you can sample the delicious crema de nance. In the heart of the city is the Parque Central, a beautiful park with mosaic sidewalks and many huge tropical trees. Make a point of taking a drive along the Paseo Colon. One of the three main arteries of the city, it is a wide modern parkway flanked with magnificent chalets and mansions. At the National Stadium are played all the important soccer (football) and other outdoor-sports matches. Visit the National University, one of the finest in Latin America. Another must is a visit to the famous orchid exhibit in the La Mil Flor garden.

ROUND AND ABOUT THE COUNTRY

The central plateau, where the great majority of people live, is a very picturesque land with charming little villages, extensive coffee plantations and magnificent scenery. . . . LA CATALINA, only thirty minutes by car from the capital, is a lovely mountain resort, a bit of Switzerland, transported, where one can enjoy horseback riding, swimming, hunting and mountain climbing. . . . HEREDIA, six miles from San José, is the center of the coffee industry. It is reminiscent of cities in southern Spain with its church towers, red roofs, grated windows and its flower gardens surrounded by white adobe walls. Visit one of the numerous plantations in the area. . . . Westward is ALAJUELA, a resort town and the sugar capital. It is famous for its flowers and for its market days on which you will see the best examples of these quaint little hand-painted ox carts still in use in the rural areas. . . . Near Alajuela is the Ojo de Agua, a picturesque swimming pool fed by cascades from numerous springs in the vicinity. . . . North of Alajuela is the volcano Poas, 9,000 feet high. Its crater, largest in the world, encloses a vast sulphur lake from which intermittently erupts a geyser 2,000 feet high. . . . Southeast of San José is historic CARTAGO, the first city founded by the Spaniards and formerly capital of the country. Here is still preserved the atmosphere of the colonial period. The Basilica of our Lady of the Angels is a favorite national shrine. On Sundays the market is most colorful and one can buy earthenware and leather and wood

273

Brilliant, colorful costumes
and oxcart of Costa Rica
Nat'l Tour. Board, C, Rica

articles from the country folk who bring their wares in their little carts. . . . East of Cartago is the beautiful OROSI or EN-CHANTED VALLEY through which runs the tumultous Revantazón River. The valley can be explored by car or horseback and at the far side, across the mountains, is the famous Orosi cataract which falls from a height of 300 feet over the crest of a mountain. Also in the valley is the Church of Orosi, an old Spanish mission which preserves important relics and artistic treasures. . . . Nearby are the famous ruins of UMARRAS, site of another Spanish mission. . . . Northeast of San José, IRAZU VOLCANO, towers 11,300 feet high. One can drive clear up to the mouth of the crater and the panoramic view from the top is breathtaking. On a clear day can be seen both the Atlantic and the Pacific. . . . Coastal towns are in real tropical climate and do not enjoy the ideal year round weather of the central plateau. However, between January and March PUNTARENAS is an ideal resort for swimming and fishing. . . . From LI-MON, the busy port, the railroad carries you through the most gorgeous scenery of the country. As the train climbs from sea level to over 5,000 feet where it crosses the Continental Divide, one gets an un-ending procession of exciting views.

Orosi's charming old mission
Pan American Union

Panama and the Canal Zone

LAND OF THE POLLERA

Panama is typically Latin and the architecture, national customs and the beautiful costumes are reminiscent of Old Spain and the early "conquistadores." The land is one of many contrasts in scenery, people, customs and costumes. From the cosmopolitan cities near the Canal Zone to Chiriqui Highlands in the west or the Darien region in the east one passes through picturesque villages where ox carts or horses are the standard transportation, quaint coastal fishing villages and beautiful mountain scenery. Of particular interest is the Panamanian Carnival which takes place annually during the four days before Ash Wednesday. Then the Montunos or country people troop to Panama City and the streets are gay with celebrants, the women attired in their beautiful *pollero*, the extravagant, bouffant dress worn on festive occasions when dancing the national folk dance, the "Tamborito."

GASTRONOMICALLY SPEAKING

There is a great variety of dishes and native drinks and both hotel and restaurant food is excellent. Be sure to try some of the typical and delicious Panamanian dishes like *puerco con patacones* (pork with deep-fried banana slices), *sancocho* (thick soup with chicken and vegetables) or treat yourself to an *empanada* (tasty little pies stuffed with meat, fish or chicken).

HISTORIC PANAMA CITY

Is built near the site of the original city sacked by Morgan the Pirate in 1671. Architecturally the city is Spanish with an admixture of modern. Narrow streets open onto great plazas planted with lovely flowers and tall palms. As in most Panamanian towns, the houses, built of concrete or stone, inevitably have grillwork balconies and are built around a patio. Culturally the city has a cosmopolitan air because of the continual stream of visitors from other lands that throng the narrow streets, gay cafés and fascinating shops. Central Avenue is the shopping center and its many shops and bazaars are filled with a galaxy of souvenirs and gifts from practically every country in the world. Among the many churches in the city, the most interesting include the twin-towered cathedral, San Francisco, San José with its magnificent Golden Altar which was formerly in Old Panama and was ingeniously saved by a monk who camouflaged it with black paint so Morgan and his pirates would ignore it, and Santo Domingo with its incredible flat arch made entirely of brick and mortar and with no internal support. Other points to see include Bolivar Plaza with its monument to the great Liberator, the very impressive President's Palace with lovely patios and tame egrets wandering about, and the native market, always very busy and very colorful. On the waterfront stands a great monument to the French and their struggle to build the canal. The promenade here, Las Bovedas affords a magnificent view of the bay. One can visit the dungeons in the nearby Palace of Justice.

ROUND ABOUT THE COUNTRY

A sightseeing highlight is a tour of the ruins of Old Panama, one of the great historical landmarks of the Americas. Here it was that all the gold and treasures from the fabulous land of Peru were stored awaiting transshipment to Spain. It was a flourishing trade center until, at its peak, it was attacked and reduced to smoking ruins by Morgan in 1671. On the way to the ruins you pass through the lovely suburbs of Panama and the ever-popular dog track and race track. At the boundary of the old city still stands the famous King's Bridge. . . . On the Atlantic side of the Isthmus is the "Gold Coast" and COLON, a veritable melting pot of all nations, and one of the world's greatest commercial centers. Colon's Front Street far surpasses even Central Avenue in the capital for its amazing variety of wares from the world over. Night life here is absolutely "frenzaic," with every conceivable type of entertainment, food and drink. Points of interest in the city include the beautiful Hotel Washington with its lovely lawns and large swimming pool, the cathedral, the magnificent statue to Columbus, the Stranger's Club and Colon's magnificent Municipal Building and Plaza. . . . From either Colon or Panama one crosses freely into the CANAL ZONE. On the Atlantic side one can visit CRISTOBAL with its palm-shaded avenues, clean modern buildings and air of efficiency, a direct contrast to its cosmopolitan twin city, Colon. The docks and the residential section are the chief tourist attractions. Near here one

This gay carnival float in Panama City features pretty girls dressed in their elegant polleros

Pan American Union

can visit the **Gatun Locks, Mount Hope, Silver City** and the various U. S. Army bases, including **Fort Davis**. . . . On the Pacific side **BALBOA** is the administrative center for the canal. The Administrative Building contains an interesting museum and excellent murals depicting scenes from the building of the canal. Be sure to visit the **Orchid Gardens**. . . . Adjacent to Balboa is **ANCON**, of interest because of its tropical housing project. . . . Other places of interest nearby are the U.S. Army posts and Naval bases, **Miraflores Locks, Pedro Miguel Locks** and the experimental tropical gardens at Summit. . . . On the way to **Madden Dam** you cross **Las Cruces Trail**, a part of the old stone highway to Old Panama. This is in the heart of the **Jungle Preserve**, a fascinating area of dense tropical growth. . . . **PORTOBELO**, northeast of Colon, is now just a small native village but it contains interesting ruins of the Spanish city that flourished here until it was sacked by Morgan in

1668. . . . From here the route leads to the **SAN BLAS ISLANDS**, the incredibly beautiful emerald islands where the San Blas Indians still live in primitive fashion according to their ancient tribal laws and customs. . . . The **CENTRAL PROVINCES** of Panama comprise an area of rolling plains, dotted with tiny thatched adobe "ranchos" and colorful towns and villages. The costumes of the natives are especially attractive and one can find many treasures among the native handicrafts. . . . In Panama Bay is **TABOGA**, Island of Flowers, an ideal resort with excellent fishing and swimming. . . . For those whose interests incline toward hunting, fishing and the outdoor life, the **CHIRIQUI HIGHLANDS** offer the best in hunting and **trout fishing**. This is the sugar and coffee country and the hills and slopes of the towering volcanic peaks abound in a great variety of **birds** and wild game. Trout streams at the base of 11,000-foot **El Volcan** offer unexcelled rainbow and native trout fishing.

San Blas Indians

Flatau—from
Pan American Union

Bermuda

POETIC ISLANDS

A graceful string of coral islands set in the bluest sea, the radiant beauty of semitropical foliage, sweeping pink sandy beaches, sailing craft gliding in and out of sheltered harbors and a beaming sun showering down golden hours — this is Bermuda, oldest British colony, situated due east from North Carolina, home of the glorious, fragrant Bermuda Easter lily, of colonial formality and ceremony, of unique, pastel-tinted cottages, of gaily costumed, dancing "Gombeys" — the ultimate in pleasure and health resorts, about which one famous resident has written: "You'd think that Nature lavish'd here/ Her purest wave, her softest skies,/To make a heaven for love to sigh in,/For bards to live and saints to die in!" — Tom Moore.

BERMUDA LOBSTER

The Bermuda lobster is one of the most cherished local dishes. It resembles a large crawfish and can be broiled or boiled, or served as lobster thermidor or Newburg. Cassava pie is the *pièce de résistance* of Christmas dinner and beloved by Bermudians, who wouldn't think of Christmas without it. The root of the cassava plant is used to make a thick, sweetish pie crust, covering cubes of cooked pork and chicken. Sweet potato-pudding, not like the United States sweet potato pie, is the Bermuda dish for Guy Fawkes Day, November 5, while salt cod and bananas is the traditional Sunday breakfast dish. In addition to the well-known vegetables, be sure to try such local triumphs as pawpaws and cristophenes.

ISLAND HOPPING

HAMILTON, capital of Bermuda, is the cultural and shopping center as well. Front Street, where the liners and freighters dock, Queen Street and Reid Street form the shopping center, and every visitor should take some time browsing through shops along here. Bermuda and Bermudians have established a distinguished record in sailing circles the world over and the magnificent Royal Bermuda Yacht Club, the patriarch of Bermuda racing and the most exclusive club in the colony, has an impressive location on Albuoy's Point, an attractive park on Hamilton Harbour. The Colonial Parliament and the Supreme Court both meet in Sessions House, with its famous clock tower. Tourists enjoy the spirited debates of the Parliament, the oldest in the world except for those of England and Iceland, and the sessions of the wigged and very British court. Another landmark is the majestic Cathedral, built of native stone, but with liberal use of stone imported from Scotland, Normandy, Nova Scotia and Indiana as well. The library is in Par-la-ville, a fine old house whose gardens, dating from the middle of the nineteenth century when this was the home of William Perot, are among the loveliest in the colony. The Bermuda Historical Society Museum has interesting collections of old furniture, china and silver, mementos of Bermuda history and oil paintings of early settlers. The beautiful Government House, residence of the Governor, and Admiralty House near Spanish Point, residence of the ranking British admiral, are open to tourists several times a year. The center of tennis activity — a popular, year-round sport — is the Bermuda Tennis Stadium, a few minutes' walk from Front Street. From Hamilton, an excursion may be taken to the Sea Gardens, the coral reef encircling Bermuda, to watch the strange coral formations and varicolored fish from the glass-bottomed boats ... At the far eastern end of the colony is quaint ST. GEORGE, the oldest settlement and the capital until 1815. Venerable St. Peter's Church, probably the site of the oldest Anglican church in the Western Hemisphere, has communion silver valued at $250,000, a cedar altar so old it looks like mahogany and a gallery where the slaves used to sit. The beautiful little park, Somers Garden, is where the heart of Sir George Somers, leader of the company to first set foot on Bermuda, is buried, although his nephew took his body back to England. On Old Maid's Lane, the street where poet Tom Moore lived while in Bermuda, is an entrance to famous St. George Hotel ... Take the delightful ferry trip across St. George's Harbour to ST. DAVID'S ISLAND, to see the unusual St. David's Islanders, an interesting mixture of American Indian, Negro and Irish ancestry, and to visit the lighthouse, from which there is a wonderful view ... There are a number of points of interest around HAR-

Perfumed fields of exquisite, creamy Easter lilies grow all over Bermuda
Bermuda News Bureau

RINGTON SOUND, west of St. George's Island, including several beautiful caves where the stalagmites and stalactites have assumed many lovely and spectacular effects, with **Crystal Cave** and **Leamington Cave** the most popular; **Tucker's Town,** where many wealthy Americans and Britishers have their homes and the location of the world-famous golf course at the **Mid-Ocean Club**; the **Lili Perfume Factory,** which visitors may tour; the deep natural fish pool at **Devil's Hole** and the **Bermuda Government Aquarium,** with probably the finest collection of tropical marine fish in the world, and the adjoining **Government Museum** . . . The entire **SOUTH SHORE** of Paget, Warwick and Southampton is dotted with many magnificent pink-coral beaches, Bermuda's greatest attraction, including the small deserted coves and the

formal facilities like **Elbow Beach Surf Club, Breakers Club, The Reefs** and **Princess Beach Club.** During the spring, the oleanders along the South Road make the view of the breaking surf even more beautiful and many tourists prefer to take the trip along here by carriage . . . Also in **SOUTHAMPTON** is **Gibb's Hill Lighthouse,** producing one of the best views of the islands you can find — dramatic in daytime, romantic by moonlight. . . . **Somerset Bridge,** in **SANDYS,** connecting the main island with Somerset Island, with a draw just large enough for a sailboat mast to pass, is said to be the smallest drawbridge in the world. About a quarter of a mile from here are the **Cathedral Rocks,** where the coral cliff has been worn by the ocean until it resembles Gothic architecture.

The Bahamas

VACATIONER'S HIDEAWAY

One-time haven of adventurers, buccaneers and blockade-runners, and now one of the world's most celebrated international playgrounds are the Bahama Islands, just east and southeast of Florida. Here life is deep-rooted in gracious, leisurely Old World traditions — charming background for an excitingly different vacation in a vast island paradise of exotic ever-blooming flowers and year-round beauty on land and sea. There is a very special quality of softness to the Bahamas, meeting place of the world's elite — in the pastel pinks and yellows of old houses, in the velvety sands of the beaches, in the very air itself.

ABOUT FOOD

Specialties of the Bahamas cuisine are the conch salads, with lettuce, tomatoes, peppers and onions, and conch fritters. Of course, the fish dishes are delectable and Nassau is especially noted for its fine sea foods. One of the unusual sea-food favorites is green turtle pie. In addition to these, Bahamians use coconuts and pineapples — their own, which, although small, are deliciously tender and juicy — in a variety of ways.

NASSAU, ETC.

NASSAU, the capital of the Bahamas, on the island of **NEW PROVIDENCE,** is characterized by its wealth of historic charm, modern sophistication and tropical atmosphere. Here, where the international set play, pirates once held sway. Throughout Nassau — and, indeed, the entire Bahamas — you'll find thrilling reminders of the swashbuckling seventeenth-century existence. Here, for instance, is rugged **Fort Charlotte**, still commanding the approaches to the harbor. The **Queen's Staircase**, with sixty-six bricked treads cut in the solid rock, said to be the work of slaves, leads to the back of another old fort, **Fort Fincastle**. The first glimpse of this charming colonial capital after disembarking from the ship at Prince George's Wharf will be the view of the beautifully proportioned **post office, House of Assembly** and other government buildings at busy Rawson Square in the heart of downtown Nassau. The wharf, itself, is another charming part of the city, where eager native boys dive for coins tossed into the water. The picturesque **markets** scattered along the wharves, including the informal open-air native market in Rawson Square, are well worth visiting. A trip through Nassau's busy harbor to the **Sea Gardens** is one that should not be missed. Through the glass bottom of the boat may be seen an underwater panorama of exotic and gaily colored fish, darting among feathery sea plumes, pastel-colored fans and weird formations of coral. There's nothing more relaxing or more typically Bahamian than another kind of ride, in a fringed-topped carriage, past quaint Bay Street shops, through an avenue of royal palms and past the beautiful homes of Bahamians and winter visitors, where gardens of bougainvillaea, hibiscus, frangipani and passion flower overflow pink walls. Another short ride — this time on another boat — from Prince George's Wharf to Hog Island brings you to **Paradise Beach**, Nassau's most famous. On all the soft sands and crystal-clear Bahamian waters, like the magnificent beaches at **Fort Montagu**,

the **Bahamas Beach Club, Rose Island** and others, you will enjoy the world's finest sea bathing and sailing. The bay is superb for water skiing, and the Bahamian waters offer a thrilling challenge to the fisherman to match wits with amberjack, kingfish, bonito, tuna, marlin, tarpon, bonefish and other scrappy fighters. You can also enjoy golf at the smart **Bahamas Country Club**, tennis on championship courses, horse racing at **Hobby Horse Hall** and polo matches at **Clifford Park** ... **HARBOUR ISLAND**, at the northern tip of Eleuthera, with its secluded beaches, provides an ideal setting for those who want a quiet vacation. One of the oldest settled islands, as well as one of the most popular, it has always been noted for its seamen and ships. On the ocean side is the famous **Pink Beach**, one of the Bahamas loveliest ... The largest island, **ANDROS** was once a pirate rendezvous. Since it is low, swampy and cut through by mangrove-bordered creeks, there is good duck shooting here and for years it has been the breeding place of flamingos. ... The quaint, three-hundred-year-old villages and superb beaches on **ELEUTHERA** make it the best-known and most populous island after New Providence ... To **BIMINI** came the pirates of one century and the rum-runners and the bootleggers of a later date. And nowadays come the greatest big-game fishermen of the world, seeking blue marlin, white marlin, giant tuna and many other varieties. Here also is the legendary **"Fountain of Youth"** which Ponce de Leon sought ... **LITTLE EXUMA** and **GREAT EXUMA** are parts of a chain of numerous cays, noted for their beauty. Because there are several good harbors, this is a favorite of the Bahamas with yachtsmen ... Most southerly and third largest of the Bahamas, **INAGUA** has wild horses, the largest flamingo rookery in the colony, duckshooting and great salt ponds.

A slow, quiet afternoon on delightful Bay Street
Nassau-Bahamas Dev. Bd.

British West Indies

IN A PLACID SEA

If you are looking for some place to spend a quiet, lazy vacation of swimming, fishing, sailing or just picnicking on a wide beach under a bright tropical sun, then by all means go to the British West Indies, where the landscape is magnificent, life is easy and the pace slow. For a vacation spot that is really off the beaten path, go to the Windward or Leeward Islands, or if you prefer a little more popular place, try Barbados, "the Riviera of the Caribbean," or fascinating, cosmopolitan Trinidad. Wherever you choose, among this alluring variety of gorgeous tropic isles, you will return rested and refreshed.

TROPICAL CUISINE

Fish is often plentiful and very good on all these islands. Flying fish is the specialty of Barbados, and a fresh-water dish served in Trinidad called the cascadou or cascadura has a remarkable flavor and is excellent stuffed. The legend on the island is that anyone who eats the cascadura returns to Trinidad to end his days. Other Trinidad specialties include bean-size oysters, pastelles made of meat and cornflour dough, crab meat served in the shell and called crab backs, crab matete (crab meat and farine), chicken pilau, pepper-pot, pigeon peas and rice, and the indescribable king and queen of "Creole" soups — sans coche and calaloo. Highly seasoned curries, toti and other Indian dishes should be sampled with caution. Game in season is occasionally served at one or two restaurants; such specialties include venison, lappe (greatest of all delicacies), quenk (wild pig), tattoo (armadillo) and wild duck. Fish also abound in Tobago, but there are no shrimps and oysters as in Trinidad. However, there is the conch, a Creole delicacy, which is best "soused," and there is "Jack" fish that is not found in Trinidad.

TROPICAL DRINKS

Rum is the national drink on all the islands in the British West Indies. Barbados planters punches and rum punches are famous, and so are the fresh lime squashes and gin slings. The green swizzle is a Trinidad specialty made from Carypton (an Angostura product). Less extensively used but worth trying are poncha crema, sorrel cocktail, soursop punch and granadilla punch.

LAND OF THE FLYING FISH

"Warm, favoured lands that never know the biting northern cold, where endless summer ever reigns with glories manifold." This is BARBADOS, the Caribbean Island lying farthest east. The most English of the West Indian Islands, both in scenery and in the character and habits of its inhabitants, it has in consequence received the affectionate sobriquet of "Little England." However, the abiding charms of Barbados are the sunshine and the sea which encircles this tropical isle with a belt of the deepest blue. BRIDGETOWN is a busy port, a blend of the old and the new, with narrow, winding streets and byways with quaint names giving it a picturesque atmosphere. Bathsheba, a seaside resort on the east coast with fine stretches of beach, is where the flying fish fleet returns usually at about two in the afternoon. In this area the hills run nearer to the coast, and the scenery is more rugged and picturesque than in any other part of the island. Hackleton's Cliff, at an altitude of approximately 1,000 feet, commands a splendid view of this coastal region. There is fine bathing, too, and sea fishing for barracuda, dolphin, king fish and flying fish at the Barbados Aquatic Club, Paradise Beach, Crane, Hastings, Worthing, Freshwater Bay and other places. A magnificent mansion with very fine old ceilings is Sam Lord's Castle, built about 1820 for Samuel Hall Lord, one of Barbados' most colorful figures of the early nineteenth century. Carved in the side of the cliff at Gun Hill by a British soldier in 1868 is an excellent stone sculpture of a lion. Cherry Tree Hill, reached by a double avenue of old mahogany trees, commands a delightful view overlooking the Scotland valley.

LAND OF THE CALYPSO

African rhythms, Hindu temples, Moslem mosques — British in character, Latin in disposition, cosmopolitan in appearance. This is amazing TRINIDAD. The population of this southernmost island in the Caribbean is basically Negro, but the mixture of races is unique in the Western Hemisphere. Men and women in Indian dress are seen everywhere. Their Moslem mosques and Hindu temples are but one part of the motley architecture which includes patios and tiled roofs reminiscent of the Spanish and Portuguese and iron grilles of the French. There are several thousand Chinese as well. The capital is **PORT OF SPAIN** (92,793), described authoritatively as the cleanest and healthiest city in the West Indies. One of the wonders of the world is Pitch Lake, 114 acres of asphalt, glamorized in fantastic stories and legends. Popular shore excursions are drives along the Saddle, a road built by American Seabees during World War II, through the grapefruit orchards, cocoa estates and bamboo groves of Santa Cruz valley, and the North Coast Road, 1,000 feet above the blue Caribbean, with a sweeping view of of about 100 miles. Maracas Bay is Trinidad's popular picnic beach, while others almost equally popular are at Toco, Manzanilla, Mayaro and Balandra, a perfect half-mile-long crescent. Shop for bargains in British goods and French perfumes on Frederick Street and Marine Square and for filigree jewelry and Oriental treasures in the Hindu bazaars. There are periodical activities, such as the ancient Carnival or Mardi Gras, famous for its spontaneity and brilliant costumes, on Monday and Tuesday preceding Ash Wednesday, the calypso season for some weeks prior to this and the Moslem festival of Hosein, some of these festivals featuring such spectacles as the colorful, exotic West Indian dancers and the steelbands, consisting of converted oil drums and biscuit tins, which originated in Trinidad. The legends of the aboriginal Caribs are still associated with the Santa Rosa fete held in Arima at the end of August. Racing, the favorite sport, is held in June and December at the track in Queen's Park Savannah—where you can also see the candlewood trees and the silk-cotton trees, otherwise known as saba or kapok trees. Local sportsmen are keen

on underwater and deep-sea fishing, duck shooting in the swamps and hunting small game in the forests.

UNSPOILED, TROPICAL EDEN

TOBAGO'S coastline is deeply indented, girdled by sun-baked beaches and coconut groves, and the scenery is undescribably beautiful, from the coral shore of the southwestern lowlands to the loveliness of volcanic hills and valleys in the north and east. The pattern of life is simple, woven in soft tones of informality and ease; sea bathing, horseback riding through coconut estates, tennis, deep-sea fishing and hiking are the main recreations. Robinson Crusoe Hotel, within fifteen minutes walk of **SCARBOROUGH**, the main town, is noted for its delicious "Creole" dishes and Castle Cove Beach Hotel specializes in Chinese dishes. Off the northeast coast is Bird of Paradise Island, an experience for sightseers, a mecca for naturalists, for here is the only place in the world outside of New Guinea where these unique birds exist in the wild state. Go out by boat to the wondrous coral sea gardens on Buccoo Reef, off the southwest shore, said to rank with the world's finest exhibitions of marine life. Walk on the reef through lanes of living coral, waist deep in calm water; then, with diving mask in place, look under water on an incredible, brilliant marine world.

VOLCANIC ISLES

The four colonies making up the **WINDWARD ISLANDS** form part of the chain of islands known as the Lesser Antilles. The islands are volcanic in origin and the more sheltered coasts are fringed by reefs. **GRENADA**, "Spice Island of the West," whose capital is **ST. GEORGE'S**, is the most southerly and the most populous of the group. It is very picturesque, with volcanic mountains and a great many

Concealed English Harbour on Antigua, an attractive, natural harbor and famous yachting center known locally as "Nelson's Harbour"
British Information Services

St. Kitts workers return home by bullock cart after the day's cane cutting
British Information Services

streams and springs, and breathtaking landscapes thrill the sightseer at every turn. A well-known landmark is **Grand Etang**, a lake formed in the crater of an extinct volcano on the top of a mountain ridge. Easily the best in the island chain and accounted by travelers to rival any in the world, lovely **Grand Anse Beach** is unforgettable. Against a background of waving coconut palms lie about two miles of sparkling white sand with water crystal clear and deep. Begun by the French in 1780 and completed by the British in 1794, **Richmond Hill**, with its forts and barracks, commands a lovely view of the town and harbor of St. George's. . . . The island of **ST. LUCIA** is very mountainous, with forest-clad volcanic cones rising sheer out of the sea on the west coast and sulphurous springs nearby. The capital is **CASTRIES**, where there are a number of comfortable hotels. Excellent sea bathing can be had in many places round the island. . . . The most striking feature of mountainous and densely wooded **ST. VINCENT** is the volcano, **Soufriere** (4,048 feet), on the northern shore, which was active as recently as 1902. Here, too, sea bathing is unexcelled all year round, while the island is also a naturalist's paradise because of its many specimens of magnificent sea birds. The town of **KINGSTOWN** is the capital of St. Vincent. . . . The most northerly island of the group is **DOMINICA**, having a continuous range of mountains running the whole length of the island. The soil is volcanic and there are several soltafaras, hot streams and an awe-inspiring **boiling lake**. Domi-

nica's capital of **ROSEAU** is the largest town in these islands.

HISTORICALLY RICH

The British colony of the **LEEWARD ISLANDS** is divided into four presidencies. The western part of the island of **ANTIGUA**, one of the presidencies, is composed of volcanic rocks, while the remainder consists of plains just above sea level on which sugar cane is widely grown. **English Harbour** is the site of an old naval dockyard where Lord Nelson once had his headquarters. **Barbuda**, a dependency of Antigua, is a flat coral island with a large lagoon on the west. There is deer, duck and pigeon shooting on Barbuda and excellent fishing and bathing round the coast. . . . **ST. CHRISTOPHER**, generally known as **ST. KITTS**, is of volcanic origin and very mountainous, and **NEVIS** resembles it in general characteristics. St. Kitts is known for that remarkable old fortress called **Brimstone Hill**, famous during the eighteenth century as the "Gibraltar of the West Indies." On Nevis, hot mineral springs with valuable medicinal properties, which made the island a fashionable health resort in the eighteenth century, are found near **CHARLESTOWN**, the town where Alexander Hamilton was born. There is good bathing and sea fishing on both these islands and a limited amount of shooting when migratory birds visit them from July to September. . . . Also of volcanic origin, **MONTSERRAT** has rugged forested hills. Sea bathing is good, and picnics on the beaches, boating and fishing can be arranged.

Cuba

FIRST COLONY

Lying off the Florida Keys, Cuba is a traditional vacationland for visiting Americans. For excellent swimming, exciting deep-sea fishing or just relaxing in the bright sunshine, no place surpasses it. In addition, there is Havana — beautiful, gay, sophisticated Havana — with its modern conveniences, urban enjoyments and bright festival air. And for a glimpse of the old life, when Cuba was the first colony in the New World, there are the mellowed churches, venerable palaces and imposing fortresses still standing in every part of this sunshine island. Truly, the modern visitor of today can well agree with Christopher Columbus when he wrote: "This land is the most beautiful that eyes have ever seen."

ABOUT FOOD

Cuba has many delectable typical dishes, of which these are the specialties: *arroz con pollo* (rice and chicken), *cangrejos moros* (Moorish crabs), *congri* (rice with black beans), filet of Pargo, *picadillo* (Cuban version of beef hash), hot tamales, avocado salad.

THE CAPITAL

HAVANA (659,883), on the northwest coast, is the capital and largest city in Cuba. A modern, cosmopolitan city, with wide boulevards and buildings of ultramodern architecture, it has yet retained all the interesting aspects and charms of colonial times. Facing the Plaza de Armas, around which the original city was founded in 1519 at the western end of the channel, are a number of old buildings: El Templete, a small chapel in Tuscany style, built in 1828 to commemorate the first mass and first city council held on that site; La Fuerza Castle, second oldest fort in the New World, begun in 1538 and now the National Library; Lieutenant-Governor's Palace, today the seat of the Supreme Court, and City Hall, which for centuries was the home of the island's Spanish governor-general, both fine examples of colonial architecture. Morro Castle, famous fort across the channel at the entrance to Havana harbor, constructed in 1589-1597 and containing many interesting and exciting relics of the past, and across from it, La Punta Fortress, built in 1589, recall exciting episodes, pirate attacks and the short war with

England. Not far west, quaint, old Cathedral Square has been restored to its original glory. Columbus Cathedral, for which the square is named and an excellent example of Spanish baroque, contains a wealth of treasures in gold, silver and precious stones, paintings and gorgeous vestments. On either side and opposite the Cathedral are colonial mansions that once were the homes of Cuba's nobility. The colonial structure of perhaps the greatest architectural value is San Francisco Convent, dating from the 16th century. In the patio of Santa Clara Convent, used for offices now, are still to be seen the 300-year-old section of a street with three of the original houses, including the first market, bathhouse and village pump. Adjoining the old colonial city rises modern Havana—vast, beautiful and sumptuous. A handsome structure combining various architectural styles, the Presidential Palace contains beautiful paintings by leading Cuban artists. However, the remarkable feature of this palace is the glass tiled dome. The National Capitol is impressive for its sumptuous decorations, noble proportions and rich materials like marble, stone, gilt, bronze, precious woods. Central Park is the starting point of Havana's night life and on the east side of the park is Centro Asturiano, with its beautiful ballroom, all-marble stairs and tiled bar. Another night spot is Casino Nacional, a lavishly fitted palace with gorgeous interior decorations and at its entrance, a fountain of graceful nymphs that is famous as a fine work of art. In the upper part of the Paseo de Martí (Prado Boulevard), a gay, historical boulevard called the "Champs Elysées" of Havana, are the open-air cafés where orchestras feature typical native music. For those interested in sports, there are all kinds of games to be seen, including boxing matches, dog shows and others at the magnificent Sports Palace; horse racing at the outstanding Oriental Park Hippodrome; jai-alai, probably the speediest game in the world, at Frontón Jai-Alai and Frontón Havana-Madrid; and many others like polo, baseball and sailing. La Concha Beach, in Marianao, is the most popular in the neighborhood. On the cultural side, there are concerts by the Philharmonic Orchestra of Havana and other world-famous artists at the **Auditorium Theater.** Magnificent residences border the avenues, such as the **Avenida de los Presidentes,** in the aristocratic section of **Vedado** and particularly along **First** and **Fifth Avenues** in the wealthy, exclusive section of **Miramar.** Other points of interest are the **University of Havana** and **"Jesús de Miramar" Church,** the largest church in Cuba, considered a model of Roman architecture and enriched with imposing murals. The **Carnival,** which takes place in Havana during the Lenten season, is a unique, fascinating spectacle. The special feature is the parade of *"Comparsas,"* based on the tradi-

Casas River ... West of Havana is **PINAR DEL RIO,** from where visits can be made to spectacular **Viñales Valley,** the loveliest in Cuba, popularized by painters and photographers, and the tobacco fields of **Vuelta Abajo,** where the world's best tobacco is grown ... **MATANZAS,** east of Havana, has been called the "Cuban Athens," because of its social and cultural refinement. Facing an enchanting bay, with a marvelous scenic background of sloping hills, the serene grandeur of the **Yumurí Valley** and the banks of the Canimar River, it also has nearby the wondrous **Bellamar Caves,** whose crystallizations pro-

A quaint, cobblestoned street in ancient Trinidad, with buildings over 300 years old
Cuban Tourist Commission

tional slave celebration of their one day of freedom granted every year. Each *Comparsa* includes numerous men and women descendants of the same tribe, gorgeously attired in velvet and satin of vivid colors, set off by sparkling jewels. The men leading the group carry *farolas* (tissue paper lanterns) and the dancers and singers execute intricate steps to the accompaniment of the incessant conga beat. The Carnival Pageants are made up of decorated floats, riders on handsomely caparisoned steeds and clowns and comic giant figures on foot. Excursions can be made to sugar mills like **Central Toledo** in Marianao, **Central Hershey and others.**

ROUND ABOUT THE COUNTRY

The **ISLE OF PINES,** off Cuba's southern coast, is called "Treasure Island," since it is believed to be the locale of Stevenson's immortal novel. A pirate rendezvous in bygone days, it is today a popular vacation area because of its healthful climate; extensive beaches, like **Bibijagua Beach** with its black sand; tropical vegetation; abundance of hunting and fishing; and fine boating, especially on the **Las**

duce an incomparably beautiful gamut of colors ... A famous beach, distinguished and cosmopolitan, **VARADERO BEACH** is renowned for its brilliantly blue waters and silvery white sands. Visitors may tour the **Jose Arechabala, S. A. Industries,** an important liquor and candy factory ... **SAN MIGUEL DE LOS BANOS,** frequently called the "Vichy of America," is a few miles away. Located among picturesque mountains, it has five mineral-water springs ... Yachting is the main attraction at the shipping port of **CIENFUEGOS,** called the "Pearl of the South." Each year it is the scene of the Inter-Club Rowing Races. Historic Jagua Castle and Hanabanilla Falls, the most beautiful in Cuba, are located here ... The wealthiest storehouse of fishes and variety of species in Cuba is in **CAIBARIEN,** on the north shore, and the richest fishery of all is **Los Ensenachos Key.** On the nights of the 24th and 25th of December, the famous *Parrandas de Noche Buena* festival takes place ... In **SANCTI SPIRITUS** the original narrow streets and architecture, denoting the Moorish influence, still prevail, casting a singularly attractive appearance of ancient beauty, so much so that most of it has been reproduced on canvas by noted painters. Facing the Plaza Mayor is the church, containing a charming "Chapel of The Rosary," and the Museum has numerous historical treasures . . . TRINIDAD, on the south coast, has preserved, as none other in the New World, its colonial atmosphere and charm of the past. Recommended especially are the ancient palaces of the Iznagas, Canteros and Borrells and the Conde de Brunet. Several old families, such as the Torrados, Frías and Palacios, possess wonderful collections of antique works of art. Especially Trinitarian are the "parrandas" composed of a group of young men who parade the streets at night, with violin and guitars, intoning songs beneath the grilled windows of the young ladies. . . . The first metropolis of Cuba, SANTIAGO DE CUBA (118,266) is now second only to Havana in importance. It was in this vicinity that the principal events of the Spanish-American-Cuban War took place, now commemorated by landmarks and monuments at famous San Juan Hill. Very interesting and pleasant excursions can be made within the bay of Santiago and along the seacoast. An imposing panoramic view can be seen from Puerto Boniato. The peculiar feature of their *Gran Semana Santiaguera* Carnival, held in July, consists in having the residents, as well as the paraders, appear in fancy disguise.

Jamaica

MEMORABLE ISLE

Jamaica is an island of legends, the intermingling of many old races, the modern accent of fabulously chic visitors. In this loveliest of islands is found not only scenic beauty, but also an ideal climate throughout the year, excellent sport facilities, a restful environment, friendly native people and the hospitable social life of the largest British colony in the West Indies. Jamaicans say that anyone who has been to their island must return again. Perhaps they are right—for visitors nostalgically remember that great houses still survive from old planter days, the natives sing pensive ditties, orchids hang from trees and the rum is the best in the world.

FOOD

The fish is superlative, the bananas grow large and are colored by a pretty pastel palette and here is an *embarras de choix* of vegetables. You can pluck oysters fastened to the roots of mangrove trees under water.

FAMOUS, FASHIONABLE RESORTS

The main metropolitan area of Jamaica is the capital, KINGSTON (pop. 109,056). Among its many attractions is the sprawling Institute of Jamaica, with its library, museum, history gallery, lecture hall and vivarium. Besides shopping in the stores with attractive prices, visit the perfume factory and one of the bottling and blending plants of the famous Jamaica rums. Near this commercial area is the largest open-air native market in the West Indies. There are excellent facilities for sportsmen, including deep-sea fishing, especially for marlin; riding in the delightful mountains; golfing on courses like the smart Liguanea Club, in the foothills of the Blue Mountains; yachting at the Royal Jamaica Yacht Club and exciting polo, besides racing, on one of the world's most picturesque polo fields at renowned Knutsford Park, the "Ascot of the Caribbean," where the brilliant Racing Carnival is celebrated in December and January. Nearby are the ruins of Port Royal, once the "wickedest place on earth," in its brawling heyday an opulent rendezvous of seventeenth-century pirates and buccaneers. At suburban St. Andrew are the Hope Botanical Gardens, with their wealth of tropical plants, trees, orchids and bougainvillaea. An amazing, winding drive of several miles through the Blue Mountains will take you to Newcastle and its exciting panoramic view of Kingston and its harbor. . . . The north coast, around the sleepy little fishing village of OCHO RIOS, is noted for its excellent hotels and guest houses, its unexcelled facilities for water sports, like Roaring River Beach, and golf at the Upton Country Club. Fern Gully is a cool and narrow canyon of breathtaking beauty, in which one motors between awesome phalanxes of giant ferns and other exotic vegetation. . . . On the northwest coast, MONTEGO BAY, with its amazingly clear sea water, is internationally known as the fashionable center

Jamaica's Blue Mountains—
and they are blue—provide a
scenic backdrop for the Hope
Botanic Gardens near Kingston

Jamaica Developm't Board

of the Caribbean. It is praised for its many excellent beaches, including the celebrated "Doctor's Cave" or "White Sands" Beach, said to be the world's finest. Many picturesque sugar-cane and coconut plantations are located nearby. . . . Near the old town of **FALMOUTH,** east of Montego, is **Good Hope Ranch,** surrounded by coconut groves and banana plantations visible for several miles, a fine example of the old great houses of the West Indies. Visitors should take the horseback ride from the ranch through the weird and legendary Cockpit Country. An unforgettable experience is the boat trip out into Oyster Bay and the brilliant **phosphorous lagoon,** one of the most concentrated in the world, where the movement of a fish or a hand in the water creates vivid streaks of light like liquid fire. . . . In the central highlands are the popular resorts of **CHRISTIANA** and **MANDEVILLE,** "the English village," with its serene atmosphere and rather British appearance, complete with village green. Pleasant drives take visitors

to the excellent bathing beaches and deep-sea fishing facilities of the south coast and the alligator hunting and river fishing on the Black and Cabaritta Rivers. . . . At nearby **LACOVIA** is the famous "Bamboo Avenue," whose gracefully intertwined bamboo trees form a two-mile continuous natural archway. . . . On the northeast coast, an area noted for the almost unreal beauty and brilliance of its tropical flowers, plants and trees, is lovely **PORT ANTONIO,** a center for swimming and deep-sea fishing. For the exhilarating and unique experience of "river rafting," embark on a bamboo raft guided by a native pilot over a sinuously curving stretch of gentle rapids on the Rio Grande. The mysterious **Blue Lagoon,** of "unfathomable" depth, is world-famous because of its intensely blue water. . . . The Jamaican dependencies, the **CAYMAN ISLANDS,** consisting of **Grand Cayman, Cayman Brac** and **Little Cayman,** are becoming increasingly popular as tourist resorts.

Haiti

UNIQUE REPUBLIC

The Hispaniola of the Spanish, the Saint-Domingue of the French has become Haiti, where whistles of the master's whip are no longer heard, where life is gentle and pleasing in the shade of mysterious mountains. The western part of the island of Hispaniola, it is, next to the United States, the second oldest independent state and the only French-speaking republic in the Western Hemisphere, with a potential prosperity far in excess of other lands of equal area. Americans will love this fascinating little republic for the special qualities making it really unique — the independence of the people, their intrigu-

ing, unusual cultural heritage and their exceedingly interesting and checkered history. Creole dances and songs, a past full of eventful memories, an atmosphere still saturated with shadows of those who belong to history, what more can be desired in this outstanding spot of extraordinary charm.

CULTURAL TRADITION

The unique combination of cultural traditions found in present-day Haiti is typified in the country's unofficial language — Creole. This tongue — the only one that has been created spontaneously in the Western Hemisphere — is based on the Norman French of the sixteenth-and-seventeenth-century buccaneers. From the island's native Indians it borrowed the names of fauna and flora and many objects of everyday life; other words, as well as a tendency toward a simple syntax, were contributed by English privateers; the Spaniards of the Caribbean region supplied a large number of nouns, adjectives, pronouns and auxiliary verbs, as well as certain subtler characteristics of speech; the Negroes contributed to the suppression of the "r's" and gave the language its accent, modulation and tone.

OLD RECIPES

Dine on flaming lobster *Sauce Ti malice* or turkey prepared with shrimp according to a recipe that comes down from the buccaneers. Try the Haitian version of a boiled chicken dinner, known as *Bouillon Poulet*. Other specialties include *Black Rice* — studded with tiny mushrooms known as *Djon-Djon*.

FASCINATING CULTURE AND HISTORY

PORT-AU-PRINCE (142,840), the capital, is an orderly city of wide streets, green parks and a mixture of French colonial and modern architecture. There are two main plazas: the Champs de Mars, a combination park, military field and recreation center, and the Place de l'Indépendance, laid out in gardens of tropical flowers surrounding the tomb of the great heroes Dessalines and Pétion, who forged the republic. Public buildings of interest include the beautiful, domed "Casa Blanca," the presidential palace, containing the famous hall of busts; the French-influenced Treasury and the very modern Postal Palace. Since Haiti, of all the Caribbean islands, has developed the only distinctive art culture, those interested in this unique aspect of the tiny republic should visit the Centre d'Art, where primitive paintings and some sculpture of young Haitians are shown. Another fascinating cultural characteristic is the fact that the dances and songs of present day differ little from those of the slave period and have preserved the rhythmic qualities and beauty of African folk art. Performances are given by the Troupe Folklorique Nationale at the open-air Theatre de Verdure, by the bay, and by courtyard gatherings of natives presenting the original voodoo dances under the spell of the sacred drums. Many rare documents and relics are on display in the Museum, among them the famous diamond crown of Emperor Soul-

ouque, who ruled the country a century ago. Toussaint Louverture, the former slave who rose in the ranks to general in the French army, is memorialized by a monument in the public garden built in honor of this "greatest black man of the world," who freed the Haitians from slavery in 1804. An entirely different scene is viewed by taking the glass-bottom boat to Sand Cay, the most spectacular coral reef and tropical marine garden in the bay. The underwater islands teem with lobsters, and those who wish may go spear fishing. Hunters will be delighted by Lakes Saumatre, Azuey, Miragoane and Les Eaux Gaillees, where the variety of wild ducks is the richest in the West Indies. Another favorite amusement is the weekly cockfights. The most exciting and exotic of all Haitian festivals is the three-day, pre-Lenten Mardi Gras. A traditional carnival made up by the people themselves, the ceremonies are full of symbolism and magic . . . In the mountains behind Port-au-Prince, known as the Haitian "Alps," is PETIONVILLE, full of fanciful decorated villas. From here you may see the thatch-roofed native houses and peasant women walking gracefully along the road to market with basketsfull of fruit and vegetables skilfully balanced on their heads. Dine and dance at Haiti's best night club, the "Cabane Choucoune." . . . Farther up the mountains are the famous year-round resorts of KENSCOFF and FURCY . . . Southeast is the cool FORET DES PINS. Unique in the Caribbean, it covers 150,000 acres where one can find strawberries, green parrots and, if you are lucky, the rare "L'oiseau musicien" singing his three mysterious notes . . . On the southern peninsula is the historic port of JACMEL, where the streets are like stairways, with famous, coconut-shaded Carrefour Raymond, most beautiful of Haiti's beaches . . . From SAINT MARC on the northern peninsula you may visit the enchanting island called Ile de la Gonâve, a paradise for nature lovers and fishermen. According to legend, it was here that the Lost Dauphin, Louis XVII, was hidden and died . . . Historic CAP-HAITIEN, on the north coast, was the wealthy colonial capital and still retains some of its earlier aspect, with its balconied houses and short, narrow streets. Dating from that period are the centennial Cathedral and the Justinian Hospital. When Napoleon sent his brother-in-law, General Leclerc, to quell the rebellion, his beautiful sister established there her luxurious court and the ruins of **Pauline Bonaparte's regal palace** still are on view. After the successful revolt, Henri Christophe, the fabulous revolutionary personality and former slave who inspired Eugene O'Neill's *Emperor Jones*, proclaimed himself King Henri I. On top of a mountain peak 3000 feet above sea level, he built the grim, majestic, impregnable fortress, **Citadelle La-** ferriére, a spectacular masterpiece of architecture designed by Henri Besse, a local engineer. Completed in 1817 with the help of 200,000 conscripted former slaves, out of which 20,000 lost their lives, it was here, in 1820, that King Henri committed suicide by shooting himself with a golden bullet. At the foot of the mountain lie the ruins of his pleasure palace, **Sans-Souci,** modeled on the royal chateau of Saint-Cloud near Paris, where the king lived with a fantastic nobility created by him.

Ruins of King Henri I's fabulous Sans Souci Palace at Cap Haitien
Philip Gendreau

Dominican Republic

LAND OF DISCOVERY

This tiny country, the first of the New World to be sighted by Christopher Columbus, is being discovered all over again, this time by her North American neighbors, as an ideal place to spend a blissful holiday playing on magnificent beaches and in tropical-blue waters and gay night spots. The eastern part of the island of Hispaniola, the Dominican Republic is well-known for its spectacular, ultramodern hotels, casinos and night clubs, providing every conceivable convenience to enhance an already luxurious life in this Caribbean tourist's delight.

DOMINICAN DISHES

The usual cuisine is Creole or American, with these favorite Dominican dishes: *arroz con pollo* (chicken and rice); plantains cooked with wine and spices or sliced and fried like potato chips; *salcocho,* a stew made of local vegetables and different kinds of meats; *pastelitos,* pastries filled with meat, fish or preserves; roast pig; *pinonate,* a confection of cocoanut and milk, and *rosquetes,* a pastry made with oranges, guayaba, cherries and papaya. They also serve excellent beers and rums.

THE OLD AND THE NEW

Founded by Bartholomew Columbus, brother of the discoverer, as Santo Domingo in 1496, **CIUDAD TRUJILLO** (181,553), the oldest city in the Western Hemisphere, is today a modern, progressive, clean metropolis. No other city in America has the distinction of having been the starting point of so many discoverers and conquerers, since here lived Cortez, Pizzaro, Velazquez, Alonso de Ojeda, Juan de Esquivel, Ponce de Leon, Balboa, De Soto and many others. And of all the islands and countries in the Caribbean,

Ultramodern Medical School of the University of Santo Domingo, in Ciudad Trujillo, the oldest university in America, founded in 1538

Dom. Rep. Tourist Office

the Dominican Republic has more of its history colored with the exploits and legends of Columbus than any other. Naturally, therefore, there are many of the aged buildings still standing here. Foremost of these is the **Primate Cathedral of America (Santa Maria la Menor)**, the oldest cathedral in the New World, built about 1523. Here, amid a fabulous array of silver and gold ornaments, jewelry and art treasures, including the crowns of Ferdinand and Isabella and a silver carillon made by Benvenuto Cellini, the remains of Columbus lie in state within an awe-inspiring marble monument. Overlooking the harbor stand the moldering ruins of the **Palace of Alcazar**, built in 1510 for Diego, the discoverer's son. Not far from the sea are the ruins of **San Nicolas de Bari**, the first hospital in the Americas, built in 1503, with its exquisite arches and columns. Of interest, too, to every citizen of every country in this New World, is the new **Columbus Lighthouse**, the largest man-made monument in the world, and also the **Columbus Ceiba**, the tree to which he chained his ships. Since most of the city was destroyed by a hurricane in 1930, many of the buildings are ultramodern and especially interesting are the beautiful new homes, the luxurious up-to-date hotels and the brand-new campus at the **University of Santo Domingo**, the oldest university in this hemisphere. In contrast to these man-made buildings are such natural marvels as the nearby **caverns**, with Indian carvings, going deep into the rock and surrounding a virtual sunken tropical Garden of Eden. Visits to **Haina Sugar Mill**, where the natural cane is processed into the sweet white crystals, or to one of the breweries are interesting observations.

Colorful peasants still vend their wares in the **Mercado Modelo**, a model market unique in Latin America, and along the **Calle Conde**, principal shopping street, wonderful hand-wrought curios await the shopper. Ciudad Trujillo also maintains an ambitious cultural program, including regular concerts by the **National Symphony Orchestra**. At delightful "Perla Antillana" Park gay crowds gather to watch exciting horse races and polo matches, and a new stadium furnishes the most modern facilities for soccer, baseball, football and outdoor pageants . . . **BOCA CHICA**, on the south coast east of Ciudad Trujillo, is the unsurpassable water-sports resort. Fishing for tarpon, marlin, sailfish, snook, bonefish, wahoo and many other thrilling species and water skiing in the shelter of the coral reef are especially popular. This town is also famous for the delicious sea food served there. Nearby, a mangrove island has been transformed into an interesting tropical **aquarium, aviary** and **zoo** . . . The most famous seaside resort on the north coast is **SOSUA** . . . Nestling on the fragrant, pine-clad slopes of the central mountains are the two most fashionable resorts of the interior, **JARABACOA** and **CONSTANZA**, where especially fine horseback riding is available. Usually unheard of in the tropics, fine apples, pears and grapes are grown in the vicinity of Jarabacoa, while the mountain air of Constanza is constantly scented with the roses and carnations cultivated there . . . A good base for exploring the north coast of the island, the part where Columbus first landed, is **SANTIAGO**, north of the mountain resorts . . . Worth seeing, too, are the colorful flamingos at **ENRIQUILLO LAKE**, 135 feet below sea level.

Puerto Rico

CROSSROADS OF THE CARIBBEAN

Roughly rectangular, Puerto Rico is the smallest and easternmost of the four islands known as the Greater Antilles. About one-hundred miles long and thirty-five miles wide, this island is three-quarters mountainous. Puerto Rico is, in fact, a mountain crest, volcanic in action. The Atlantic side of the island is rimmed with a coastal plain eight to thirteen miles in width, while the plain on the Caribbean side narrows from eight to two miles. This contrast in topography creates colorful resorts throughout the entire island, offering a wide choice in vacation activity, but not in climate. The ever-prevailing trade-winds bequeath it a mildness comparable to New England's late spring and early summer. Ever since World War II, Puerto Rico's personality has acquired a new vitality. Emerging from that world conflict as the strategic center of the United States' Caribbean defenses, Puerto Rico decided to change its submerged economic personality. The administrators of this courageous plan, "Operation Bootstrap," have been so successful in attracting American investors to improve tourist facilities that Puerto Rico's natural beauty has been complemented by the best in hotels, resort developments and communications.

CUISINE CUE.

Hotels feature many popular American dishes as well as Puerto Rican specialties. Among the latter is *lechon asado* (barbecued pig), native as the hot dog is to the U.S.A., and *arroz compollo*. Bananas are served in a variety of ways, each more tasty than the last. While all types of liquors and wines are available, the island's light rum is an international favorite. Popular, too, is Puerto Rican coffee, as a demitasse or *con leche* (with milk).

AROUND THE ISLAND

The capital and metropolis of Puerto Rico is SAN JUAN. The city proper is situated on an islet, two and one half miles long by one half mile wide, and connected to the mainland by three bridges leading to Santurce. Founded in 1519 by Ponce de León, San Juan is the oldest city flying the American flag, and nowhere on American soil is there such a concentration of ancient and historic buildings. In its infancy San Juan was protected by a ring of walls — "Casco" — meaning shell. The term is still used in reference to the old, walled part of the city, which still retains much of its colonial charm. The architecture is Spanish with some adaptations to adjust to the tropical climate, principally heat-proof massive walls, shutters, high ceilings and immense doors. Except for the installation of electric lights, many of the narrow, crowded streets have undergone little change through the centuries. Here are the monuments of its early struggles: La Fortaleza, San Juan's first fort built in 1533, and now the residence of the governors of the island; San Juan Gate, where the early governors landed from Spain amid much pageantry; Casa Blanca, built in 1523 as a fortress residence for the family of Ponce de León, and which was owned by them for two centuries. Well-restored and beautifully terraced, it is now the residence of the commanding officer of the Antilles Forces of the U. S. Army. In this old section of the city is the Cathedral of San Juan Bautista, originally built of wood and thatch in 1519. The burial place of Ponce de León and rebuilt many times, the Cathedral has survived storm, enemy and earthquake. Close by is the Church of San José, housing old-world religious treasures. . . . Standing in close proximity to this old section of the city and facing San Juan Bay is the United States Customhouse. Erected in 1931, it is called the most beautiful customhouse in America. Constructed of reinforced concrete, its plain rose-colored walls are topped by a clay-tile roof of Spanish Renaissance style. Its two interior courtyards are surrounded by arcaded galleries and are the setting for lily pools and varicolored tropical plants. . . . Continuing toward the Bay one comes to the Arsenal, the Royal Navy Yard during Spanish Days and from which the Spanish troops sailed in 1898 at the end of the Spanish American War. It now serves as office for the Insular Department of Labor and other governmental agencies. . . . Perhaps the most beautiful spot in San Juan is El Morro, for centuries Puerto Rico's chief defense. Known originally as Castillo de San Felipe del Morro, this fortress was started in 1539 and situated on the rocky headland of the harbor facing the Atlantic Ocean. Rich in defensive history, its surrounding green, rolling fields are today part of the military reservation of Fort Brooke. . . . Ever since its foundation, San Juan has been the center of Puerto Rico's governmental, intellectual, commercial and financial activities. On its main thoroughfare, **Avenida Ponce de León,** may be seen the **Insular Capitol,** the seat of the Government and the Island Supreme Court. The entire exterior of this handsome structure is executed in white Georgia marble, while the materials used for interior decoration include both American Tennessee and Italian marbles. Also situated on the main thoroughfare is the **School of Tropical Medicine,** a three-story building of pure Spanish Renaissance style. Laid out in quadrangle fashion around a spacious Spanish patio, it joins the Insular Capitol grounds, overlooks the rolling Atlantic and houses the University Hospital. Opened in 1926 the School of Tropical Medicine is operated co-operatively by the University of Puerto Rico and Columbia University of New York. . . . Outgrowing its islet some forty years ago, San Juan leaped the Condado Lagoon and overflowed into the section now known as **SANTURCE,** which is subdivided into the **Condado** and **Miramar sections.** The Condado section is purely residential and contains some of the recently built luxurious hotels, including the Caribe Hilton. Miramar, also residential, includes a progressive business center and practically everything that can be bought in San Juan can now be purchased in Santurce. . . . The second largest city of Puerto Rico and the largest on its southern coast is **PONCE,** with the world's most photographed fire

station. In addition to its fine residental sections blooming with tropical flowers, Ponce has gardenlike plazas, first-class hotels, restaurants, theaters, modern stores and a large public market. Its streets are wide and its atmosphere is South American. . . . The third largest city is **MAYAGUEZ,** center of the famous needlework industry. Situated at the foot of the Cordillera Central, Mayaguez overlooks **Mona Passage** which separates Puerto Rico from Santo Domingo. Distinctly Spanish in character and customs, this city is the site of **Farragut School,** the first educational institution erected under American sovereignty. In the outskirts is the **Orchid Museum** featuring over 1500 varieties.

Your visit should certainly include a visit to **El Yunque,** the beautiful, lush tropical rain forest where you can swim in the beautiful mountain-top swimming pool fed by the purest spring water. . . . Another fascinating excursion is to **Phosphorescent Bay** and the quaint fishing village of **Parguera;** the water of the bay glows in the moonlight and tiny organisms in the water twinkle like diamonds. . . . Wherever you go you will be enchanted with the magnificence of the tropical growth. Palm-fringed beaches offer delightful swimming; landscaped rural and mountain roads display a variety of lovely trees, waving fields of sugar cane, pineapples and coffee, here and there highlighted with brilliant flowers, including the red poinsettia and the African tulip trees. Visit a pineapple plantation or a coffee finca.

San Juan Harbor at night is
a sparkling fairyland
Puerto Rico Government

Virgin Islands

PIRATES' HIDEOUT

That hardy explorer, Christopher Columbus, made a second voyage, in 1493, to the New World he had visited the year before. This time he cruised around the islands in the eastern Caribbean Sea. He saw they were lush and beautiful, and looking for fresh water, landed on an island he called Santa Cruz (Holy Cross), which the French during their occupancy translated to Saint Croix. Carib and Arawak Indians, who inhabited the islands, fiercely resented invasion by these strangers; they fought hard for their rights, but without success. The group we now know as **THE VIRGIN ISLANDS** was claimed for Spain by Columbus, but people from other lands were among early colonizers, all looking for the fabulous riches supposed to be found in a fabulous land. The sugar industry did later bring great wealth to many planters, but with the decline of that industry much of the islands' prosperity disappeared. Pirates and buccaneers found the hidden coves and bays a useful hiding place for the wealth they gathered on the high seas, and almost every island has its tales of buried treasure. The setting of Robert Louis Stevenson's *Treasure Island* is believed to be in the Virgin group.

The Virgin Islands are dormant volcanic peaks, but only a few are considered important. Most are bare reefs and uninhabited islets. Of the 100 islands, more than half are a territory of the United States, purchased from Denmark in 1917; the rest are part of the British Leeward Islands Colony. As a group they are becoming widely known for their beauty, quaint charm and healthful climate. A measure of prosperity is returning to some of the islands in development of the tourist business.

THE BRITISH VIRGIN ISLANDS

Somewhat off the tourist path are the islands of the British group. **TORTOLA** is about twelve miles long and three miles wide, with lovely mountain scenery, a fine harbor and inviting beaches. **ROAD-TOWN**, the capital of the colony is located here. It is a yachting center, but unless you arrive in your own yacht, you can only reach the island by motor launch from St. Thomas — a two-hour trip. There are few guest houses on Tortola and, as they are small, reservations are advisable. All water sports are available and beach picnics most enjoyable. An especially attractive beach is on the northern side of the island at **Cane Garden Bay**; to reach it you travel by donkey or horseback. Here you may visit a 200-year-old **rum distillery**. Should you desire to sample some fine old rum on the premises, it will be served to you in calabash shells, but if you wish to buy some to take away with you, you must have your own bottles. ... **ANEGADA** and **VIRGIN GORDA** are each about ten miles long. The former is a low-lying island, the most northerly one of the Lesser Antilles, and the latter is beautiful with forested mountains and brilliant foliage. The shallow waters offshore are ideal for spear fishing.

THE VIRGIN ISLANDS OF THE UNITED STATES

Having begun to attract visitors from other lands less than ten years ago, it is only in that short time that catering to tourists has become big business. However, efforts are being made to keep the beauty and charming atmosphere of colonial days. On the island of **ST. THOMAS, CHARLOTTE AMALIE**, the capital of the territory, has become a famous tourist resort, although retaining much of the color of its Dutch and Danish days. Many old mansions, built by sugar barons and rum distillers — left vacant and neglected for many years — have been restored and are now attractive homes of permanent residents. Some of the old estates are fine guest houses, with beautiful views from their terraces and gorgeous flowers in their gardens. Many homes of recent construction have been designed to blend with the old. The ideal climate of St. Thomas, combined with the available comforts of modern living, are bringing a growing number of permanent residents. In Charlotte Amalie you will find several old **churches** of architectural interest; **Fort Christian**, built in the seventeenth century, overlooking the **Emancipation Gardens**; a **Danish Cemetery**, where old stones tell some of the history of the island; **Market Square**, where farmers bring their products from their fields on donkeys; a 200-year-old hand-carved Italian marble **Wishing Well** near the square and many attractive **shops** on tree-shaded streets or occupying old warehouses of buccaneer days. Stop at **Government House** to sign the visitors' book and note the murals on the grand staircase. . . . CARENGE is the "Frenchtown" of St. Thomas, where live descendants of refugees who came to the island from Saint Barthelemy, fleeing the slave riots of the early 1700's. . . . In a drive around the island, a main point of interest is the tower on the top of Bluebeard's Castle, from which you get a magnificent view of Charlotte Amalie and its beautiful harbor. The tower was built and fortified in the seventeenth century, but the castle has been restored and is now a fine hotel. Another point from which a wonderful view may be obtained is Rosendahl Hill, looking across Drake Channel to the British Virgin Islands. Along the shores of Magen's Bay, on the north side of the island, archaeologists have found traces of an unknown civilization. There is a very beautiful beach here, once the site of an

wish — stop at any island for a swim or sightseeing — and be sure of a warm welcome. Spring and summer are the best seasons for cruising or touring, as rates are lower, the waters are clear and usually calm and the trade winds keep you cool and comfortable. . . . Carnival time on St. Thomas is also in the spring, sometimes lasting a week. It is a gay time indeed — parades with huge floats, native bands, dancing in the streets, masked balls and hospitality the keynote. . . . The island of ST. JOHN has not quite caught up with the pace of a modern tourist resort, although it is expected to reach that status when proposed plans for future development are carried out. CANEEL BAY is the nucleus around which a model village will be built, retaining as much as practicable its primitive atmosphere. There will be several beautiful beaches and a protected

Swimming is the most poular sport in lovely St. Thomas
Philip Gendreau

Indian village. . . . To the tourist looking for gaiety during the evening hours, St. Thomas can furnish a variety of entertainment. There are hotels and night clubs of the luxury type and those catering to modest purses, where as a background to an excellent dinner, you can listen to calypso singers, native music played by native bands who make their own instruments, or you can dance to the music of modern orchestras. A moonlight sail or swim are also pleasant diversions. For the daylight hours there are golf, tennis, swimming, "snorkeling" (exploring the wonders of the underwater world with a mask and a breathing tube called a "snorkel") or just lazing on the beach. The clear waters around the islands make a trip in a glass-bottom boat one of interesting pleasure. All types of vessels are available and a cruise around all the islands should be a a must. You are free to go wherever you

yacht anchorage. Proposals have been made to have the island of St. John declared a national park. Caneel Bay has some ruins dating back to 1773, when plantation owners and their families were besieged by Negro slaves until rescued by French troops. African Negroes in large numbers were brought to the islands in the early years of the eighteenth century and sold as slaves to the sugar planters. Substantial numbers of their descendants still live on the islands and still carry on some of the customs and traditions of their ancestors. . . . TRUNK BAY is well worth visiting not alone for its beauty, but for the glimpse it will give you of the lavishness of the past, when you visit what is left of the great mansions built by prosperous plantation owners in the seventeenth and eighteenth centuries. . . . A north trail leading to CORAL BAY is a real part of the island's early days, for it looks today as it did when the Indians were the only ones to use it. . . . St. John's island has its share of pirate legends centering around Bluebeard, Henry Morgan and Edward Teach (Blackbeard). . . . ST. CROIX — beautiful, charming, peaceful, a wonderful contrast to the turbulence of the early days after white men came to the island. Spanish, Dutch, French, English and Danes each took possession of the island at various periods, usually by force. Denmark had the longest rule, although not continuous, until acquired, through purchase, by the United States. St. Croix's scenery is varied — a rocky coastline, fields of sugar cane, gorgeous flowers and forested mountains. Outdoor and water sports, gracious hospitality, a leisurely social life and a comfortable year-round climate make a delightful change from the usual busy pace of modern centers. . . . In CHRISTIANSTED you find the architecture and charm of a seventeenth-century town. The peaked-roofed houses, beautiful archways, patios and gardens

filled with lovely flowers and shrubs make Christiansted a most colorful town; it well deserved to be designated a National Historic Site and became officially so in 1952. . . . FREDERIKSTED also has beautiful old homes with graceful balconies and gardens brilliant with tropical foliage. Tours are conducted through some of the old estates. . . . SALT RIVER has changed little since Columbus landed there in 1493. A museum contains an interesting collection of Carib and Arawak Indian relics. In Government House you will see early Danish furniture — some originals, some reproductions. The hardware store where Alexander Hamilton clerked as a young man is still in business. Hamilton was born on Nevis, but came to live with relatives on St. Croix after he was orphaned; the house in which he lived is now a hotel. You can also visit old forts, old abandoned sugar mills and ruins of manor houses on plantation estates. Some of the stone windmills on these plantations have been remodeled into attractive homes.

French West Indies

TOUCH OF FRANCE IN THE CARIBBEAN

Once France's vast empire in the New World stretched from ocean to ocean, covering over half of North America, all of Hispaniola and most of the Greater Antilles in the Caribbean. Now the only piece still left are these islands and French Guiana in South America. Of all the Caribbean islands, these French-speaking people have the closest ties with the homeland, actually being departments of the continental country. So, for the flavor and atmosphere of France, combined with the usual splendid Caribbean climate and fine water sports, and gorgeous tropical scenery as well, take the short trip down to the French West Indies, fairyland isles of happiness and gaiety. You'll find laughter in the hearts of its friendly people and rhythm in their souls.

FRENCH FOOD, TOO

In the excellent restaurants, the visitor can eat as he wishes, either in incomparable French style or in the Creole, which is a good deal more spicy and highly flavored. In any case, the local cooking is a gourmet's delight. At Pointe-a-Pitre, Guadeloupe, and Fort-de-France, Martin-

ique, the market is very well supplied with the specialties of the island: yams, Carib cabbage, sweet potatoes and delicious tropical fruits, pineapple, mangoes, corrosols, sapodillas, bananas, breadfruit. The delicious French wines are sold, also. The favorite cocktail on Martinique is Martinique punch, made up of $\frac{1}{3}$ sugar syrup and $\frac{2}{3}$ rum and served with a squeeze of green lemon.

Guadeloupe

FAMOUS COAST LINE

Guadeloupe is famed for the beauty of its shores: deep inlets on the west, rosy sands on the north, white beaches on Grande-Terre and jagged cliffs at the Pointe des Châteaux. Actually consisting of two islands separated by a salt river (Rivière Salée) four miles long, Guadeloupe proper is of volcanic origin and very mountainous, whereas Grande-Terre, the section to the east, is relatively low and composed mainly of coral and limestone. The old historic capital, BASSE-TERRE, lies at the foot of La Soufrière at the ex-

An ocean liner steams gracefully into Fort de France's tropic port

Screen Traveler, Gendreau

treme southwest of the main island. For
those who like climbing and mountain
walks, there are exciting explorations in
the thick forests (Victor Hugo Trail, Mer-
wart Trail). Access to the highland forests
can also be had by the traces, or rides,
from Pointe Noire to Sofaïa or La Boucan
and from Petit Bourg to Bouillante. Such
excursions lead through dense forest and
along torrential mountain rivers, lined by
graceful bamboo trees. Among the splendid scenery, that seen during the classical
excursion to La Soufrière is especially fine.
All the enjoyments of the sea are to be had
for the asking: yachting, sea bathing, fishing and submarine fishing, with wonderful catches among the fairylike grottoes of
the sea bed. Excellent nearby beaches are
those of black, ferruginous sands at Ban-
anier and Grande-Anse at Trois-Rivières.
Hot springs of all kinds abound on Guadeloupe, with the thermal center at Dolé.
Those at Bouillante, another popular spa,
bubble out of the sea itself. The most unusual attraction of all is the "Valley of the
Ancient Caribs" at Trois Rivières, an exhibition of Carib Indian art (the Roche
Graves Pre-Colombiennes), like the unique
sculptured rocks associated with age-old
legends. No visitor should leave Guadeloupe without seeing, too, the beautiful islands of Les Saintes, offering, in their road-
stead of limpid waters, in the calm and
mildness of their scenery, an epitome of all
the grace of the Antilles. . . . Foremost city
of Guadeloupe is POINTE-A-PITRE on the
island of Grande-Terre, a sugar and rum
export center considered as one of the saf-
est as well as one of the most picturesque of
West Indian harbors. There are excellent
restaurants specializing in French and
Creole cuisine, especially La Pergola-du-
Gosier, famous with gourmets for many
years. Nearby beaches are of surprising
variety, with some of white coral sands, as
Gosier, Sainte-Anne, Saint-François, Moule
and Port-Louis, and others of honey-colored sands, like Cluny and the Grande
Anse at Deshaies. The hot springs at La
Ravine-Chaude—only half an hour's drive
away—and Sofaïa enjoy a well-established
and merited reputation. . . . The dependencies of St. Martin, whose sovereignty is divided between France and the Netherlands, St. Barthélemy, better known as St.
Barts, and Marie-Galante are good centers,
too, for fishing, swimming, sailing and
horseback riding.

Martinique

"LAND OF FLOWERS"

That is what the Carib Indians called
the island of Martinique. Others have been
enchanted with it, too, for instance the
magnificent painter, Paul Gauguin, who
wrote, "Nature is so rich, the climate so
warm, though lightened with cool breezes,
that I cannot describe to you how enthusiastic I feel." The surface of the island is
hilly, mountainous and covered with exuberant vegetation; the flowers are brilliant, the fruits splendid, while the colorful towns lie at the head of picturesque
creeks and on the flanks of mornes or
knolls. There's a strong and fascinating
flavor of French colonialism in Martinique
that visitors never forget. In the capital
city of FORT-DE-FRANCE the small cafés,

sidewalk bookstores and multihued dress of the French-speaking inhabitants create a continental atmosphere reminiscent of far-off Paris. The **Salon Martiniquais** and the **School of Applied Arts** show interesting works by local painters and sculptors, as well as some from France and foreign countries, and the latter also has folklore and archaeological displays. The Empress Josephine was born at **Trois Ilets** and a beautiful marble statue to her memory graces the capital's "savanna" or park. Rising from the waters of the southwest coast is **Diamond Rock**, a natural phenomenon, commissioned a British ship in the eighteenth century, which for ten years successfully held off the French forces, but now stands guard over the lovely beach lying opposite. Beyond the picturesque fishing villages on the shore north of Fort-de-France are the ruins of St. **Pierre**, once the Paris, now the Pompeii of the New

World. Here, in May, 1902, the former gay capital was wiped out by the eruption of nearby Mt. Pelée. Out of almost 30,000 inhabitants, only one man survived — a prisoner in an underground dungeon. At the southeast corner of the island is **Savane des Petrifications**, one of the four petrified forests in the world. Sailing and boating— in fact, all nautical sports — are much in favor, and excellent regattas are organized by the **Yacht Club**, which plays an important part in the life of the island. Fish are plentiful in the rivers and off the shore, with tuna most sought after and esteemed. Migratory birds also abound at the change of seasons, while in the wooded mountains the wild pigeon are excellent. Cock fighting ranks high among the sports of the islanders — the season lasting from June to December — while fights between mongooses and snakes sometimes are arranged for the tourist.

Quaint scene along a calm river at Fort de France
Screen Traveler, Gendreau

Curaçao

WOODEN SHOE SAMBA

Thirty-eight miles northeast of Venezuela lies **CURACAO**, busiest port in the Caribbean, and most important of the six islands forming the Netherlands West Indies or Netherlands Antilles. An autonomous part of the Kingdom of the Netherlands, these Antilles are divided into two groups, the Leeward or ABC group comprising Aruba, Bonaire and Curaçao, and the Windward Isles of St. Maarten, Saba, and St. Eustatius. Curaçao, with its 115,000 inhabitants and covering an area of 173 square miles, is the largest and the seat of the central government of the Netherlands Antilles. Like a tulip dropped

among tropical bougainvillaea, Curaçao is Dutch in character and seems incongruous amid the Spanish-cultured countries of the Caribbean.

APERITIF

Her people being a mixture of many different nationalities, Curaçao's menu is international. Each of its leading hotels specializes in one type of cuisine. Regardless of its specialty one will be able to get the island's most famous product, the orange-flavored liqueur, Curaçao.

TOUR DU JOUR

WILLEMSTAD, situated on its landlocked, clover-shaped harbor, the city is bisected by St. Anna Bay which flows into the busy Schottegat Basin, both of which are sufficiently deep to accommodate large cargo vessels and ocean liners. Barring entrance to the harbor in the heart of the city is the floating causeway known as Queen Emma. Supported by a string of pontoons, this bridge of boats is towed parallel to the quay by a steam launch whenever a vessel enters or leaves the harbor. Equally as quaint are the brightly painted red, green, yellow, pink and blue houses and buildings that line both sides of the channel. The oldest quarter of the city is called the Punda. The two principal streets of this section are Heerenstraat and Breedestraat, where are located the city's leading shops, banks and offices. Other points of interest are the Governor's House at Fort Amsterdam and the Legislative Council and Court of Justice with statues of former Queen Wilhelmina

skippers of Caribbean schooners bring their wares from the South American mainland and sell them directly from ship to customer. . . . Pietermaai and Scharloo are the residential sections of the city, and well worth seeing for their ornate and colorful Dutch architecture. . . . The section of the city on the west side of the bay is called Otrabanda, a combination of residential and business areas. Here one finds the famed Curaçao Museum, a government-restored example of old Dutch architecture. It houses many valuable antiques, valuable paintings and furniture of the colonial period. Here one also may see exhibits of Curaçao's recent industrial and economic history. In its spacious gardens are found specimens of all trees and plants growing on the island. . . . East of the city on the bay-studded southern coast is the internationally famous Caracas Bay

Part of Willemstad's floating market, where skippers sell foodstuff from neighboring islands right from schooner to customer
Neth. W. I. Tourist Com.

and Peter Stuyvesant, who was Governor of Curaçao from 1643 to 1661. (It was through Governor Stuyvesant that Curaçao became linked with New Amsterdam, the present city of New York, when he became its governor in 1646.) . . . In Punda also is Mikve Israel Synagogue, built in 1732, and said to be the oldest synagogue in the Western Hemisphere. . . . Magnificently located on top of Ararat Hill overlooking Willemstad is the F. D. Roosevelt House, the official residence of the Consul General of the U. S. in the Netherlands West Indies. This superb building was presented to the United States by the people of Curaçao in 1950 in recognition of the beneficial cooperation between the two countries during the last war. . . . Before leaving for other sections of the island a tourist will certainly enjoy visiting the colorful Native Schooner Market where

where the larger cruise ships stop for refueling. (So close to the shallow oil fields of Venezuela, Curaçao has become the home of the world's second largest refinery.) Nearby is Spanish Water Bay with its popular Boca Beach, the haven of water-sport enthusiasts. . . . The most famous beach resort on the island is Piscadera Bay, to the west of Willemstad. Originally built as a recreation center for the Royal Dutch Shell Company, it has been enlarged on a luxurious scale to accommodate visitors to Curaçao's shores. . . . Unlike the southern coast with its many bays, the northern coast is cliff-lined and crowned with St. Christoffel Hill, 1,230 feet high. The mountain range is composed of limestone, a famous formation of which is Boca Tabla, or Devil's Mouth Grotto, pounded by the trade-wind driven surf.

The United States

Pacific Coast States

Think of any type of vacation you can, then think of the Pacific Coast states Stretching over 1,200 miles from Mexico to Canada, with a 2,730 mile coastline, coast ranges, valleys, towering mountains, deserts, lakes, rivers, giant cities, hidden coastal villages — it's all here and much more. A vacation to this vast, diverse playground which offers the utmost in recreational facilities and accommodations is a vacation never to be forgotten.

CALIFORNIA

No matter how exacting your specifications, they can be met, for California is blessed by nature in many ways. An equable climate, the health-giving sun of the southern California deserts in winter, the curative properties of her mineral springs, a thousand mile shore line bathed by the blue Pacific and ranges of majestic snow-capped mountains are to mention but a few. A land rich in historical landmarks from the early Spanish missions to the glamorous days of the "Gold Rush" to the present time — California is, indeed, a vacationist's paradise.

LOS ANGELES (1,970,358), on the coast of southern California, is the third largest city in the country. It is one of the fastest-growing big cities in the world, and already is the world's largest city in area. The coming of the railroad, the discovery of oil, the orange-grove boom, motion pictures and the air-age boom — all have contributed to the most phenomenal civic growth in the history of the world. In downtown Los Angeles see the Civic Center and Plaza. Old Mission Church, on the Plaza, is the city's oldest and most historic building. By contrast the nearby City Hall, gleaming white, towers 32 stories. Visit the tower of the City Hall to see all of downtown and commercial Los Angeles. Nearby, Pershing Square is the nearest thing you will find to a general business center. If you wish an Old Mexico atmosphere, walk along Olvera Street. Here, you will find authentic and imported Mexican handicrafts and restaurants with wandering musicians. Avila Adobe is here. If your taste is Oriental visit China City, with its many curio shops and teahouses, or Chinatown, with its mystery-story air.

A drive down Wilshire Boulevard, which leads toward the west, ending at the sea about 20 miles away, takes you past the Brown Derby, the Cocoanut Grove, perhaps the world's most famous night spot, La Brea Tar Pits, remains of prehistoric monsters, through BEVERLY HILLS, where more Hollywood notables live than anywhere else, through WESTWOOD VILLAGE to SANTA MONICA on the Pacific Ocean, the most famous of the many beaches in the Los Angeles area. Visit the Palisades Park and Municipal Pier here. Also, the Will Rogers State Park, site of Will Roger's Ranch. A few miles up the coast is the famed MALIBU BEACH. HOLLYWOOD, the city's most famous district, lies northwest of downtown Los Angeles. Its main streets are Sunset Boulevard and famed Hollywood Boulevard. The intersection of Hollywood and Vine is its main center. Some of the tourist high spots in Hollywood include: Grauman's Chinese Theater, where you can compare your footprints to those of your favorite star; Don the Beachomber Restaurant, world famous for exotic setting and Oriental food; Café de Paris, sidewalk café; Tom Breneman's; and numerous major movie studios. Griffith Park, lying just to the north of Hollywood proper, is the city's biggest playground. It has a zoo, a Greek theater, an observatory, a planetarium, a miniature railway, miles of bridle paths, hiking trails and playfields of all types. Along Sunset Boulevard, just before it enters Beverly Hills, is a spectacularly notable stretch called the Strip with the gayest, most colorful and fashionable restaurants and night clubs—the most famous is Ciro's. Other major tourist attractions include: Biltmore Bowl, scene of the annual Academy Award Dinner; Hollywood Bowl — with its summer evening symphonies under the stars, and its famed Easter Sunrise Services; Pasadena Playhouse, one of America's most famous experimental theaters; Pilgrimage Theater, open-air amphitheater which stages annual passion play; Theater Mart with *The Drunkard*, old-time melodrama — longest running play in the U. S. — Biltmore Theater and Philharmonic, with their opera and legitimate stage plays. Due south of the center of Los Angeles is SAN PEDRO HARBOR, the world's biggest and busiest man-made harbor. Just west of San Pedro is LONG BEACH with its famous Rainbow Pier, enclosing a 32-acre lagoon, and Signal Hill, one of the great oil producing areas of the West Coast. Forest Lawn Memorial Park, a burial ground which ranks as a major sightseeing attraction, is northeast of the city proper in GLENDALE. Just east of the city is PASADENA, noted for its Rose Bowl, and superb Huntington Library and Art Gallery in the suburb of SAN MARINO just to the south. A little further south is San Gabriel Mission. A visit through one of the major movie studios in CULVER CITY or BURBANK is a top tourist attraction. Be sure to visit Disneyland, a recently added children's "wonderland come to life." Twenty-five miles east of Los Angeles is POMONA, where the Los Angeles County Fair, largest in the nation, is held annually in late September. The San Fernando Valley lies to the northwest of downtown Los Angeles. The nearby mountains offer excellent winter sports. Baseball, football, fights, wrestling and midget-car racing are found at the following stadia and arenas: Olympic Stadium; Pan Pacific Auditorium; Memorial Coliseum — home field for U.C.L.A., U.S.C. and the Los Angeles Rams football teams. If interested in horse racing, go to the spectacular Santa Anita Track at Arcadia or the Hollywood Park. There are 26 universities or colleges in the Los Angeles area. They include: University of California at Los Angeles (U.C.L.A.) in Westwood Village, University of Southern California on University Avenue, California Institute of Technology at Pasadena. Santa Catalina Island, called the "Magic Isle," is a scenic mountain rising out of the Pacific Ocean 25 miles off the southern California coast. It is renowned for its deep-sea game fishing, and through glass-bottomed boats may be viewed the wonders of fantastic submarine gardens. . . . To the south of Los Angeles is the SAN DIEGO-CORONADO area which includes San Diego Bay and the surrounding territory. In and around San Diego, the birthplace of California history, are many interesting and unusual places. San Diego is the center of extensive Navy activities. Here, is Balboa Park, one of the show places of the world; Torrey Pines Park; the marriage place of Ramona, famous in song, story and on the screen; Mission San Diego de Alcala, founded in 1769, first of the 21 missions that stretch northward along the coast on the famous California Mission Trails; numerous beaches and beach cities — CORONADO, LA JOLLA, MISSION BEACH, Silver Strand Beach Park and Point Loma. Below the Mexican border, just a few miles away is colorful TIJUANA. The famous fresh-water fishing lakes of San Diego County, Lakes Hodges, Wohlford, San Vincente, Henshaw and Cuyamaca, are reached via the ESCONDIDO gateway. Palomar Observatory, with the world's greatest telescope, and Palomar Mountain State Park are reached out of OCEANSIDE and Escondido. Lake Elsinore, with its hot mineral springs, is the "Scenic Health Resort of California." To the south and to the east are a number of other fine mineral springs. Mt. San Jacinto Recreational Area, a summer and winter resort area, is a favorite with teachers and music lovers because of its permanent music and other cultural facilities. It is the gateway by trail to the summit of Mt. San Jacinto. At the summit is Mt. San Jacinto State Park, surrounded by a vast wilderness area. At the foot of the mountain to the east nestles PALM SPRINGS and other desert resort centers. The Palms to Pines Highway circles the mountain from the desert side. Between BEAUMONT and San Jacinto are a number of fine mineral springs. . . . Northwest of here, and to the east of Los Angeles lie the San Bernardino Mountains. Here, you will find Lake Arrowhead and Big Bear Lake Resorts, situated among the pines of the San Bernardino National Forest. Year-round recreation facilities of all types are available at both resort communities. Along and adjacent to the "Rim of the World Drive," from Lake Arrowhead to Big Bear Lake, are many other resort communities, including BLUE JAY, RUNNING SPRINGS, GREEN VALLEY LAKE and SNOW VALLEY. Some of the finest facilities and snow conditions for winter sports during the winter months are found in this region. . . . North along the coast from Los Angeles you come to the Santa Barbara area. SANTA BARBARA, nestling between the mountains and the sea, owes much of its charm to its old Spanish atmosphere — rich in heritage and flavor of the "Days of the Dons"—Mission Santa Barbara, "Queen

California's favorite sport—
sea or sun bathing—at Alligator Head in La Jolla
All Year Club, So. Calif.

of the Missions," the Court House and other buildings of Spanish architecture and numerous historic adobes. Old Spanish Day Fiesta, in which the entire community participates, is held annually at the full moon in August. The Botanic Garden and Museum of Art and Natural History are of particular interest. The smooth sandy beaches and aquatic sports in the harbor are the chief recreational attractions. . . . To the north is the Los Padres National Forest with numerous recreational areas and the Sespe Game Preserve. Continuing north, the PISMO BEACH area includes many beach resort communities. You will enjoy year-round camping facilities, excellent surf fishing and clam digging for the famous Pismo clam. A few miles to the north is the Mission San Luis Obispo de Tolosa. . . . In southeastern California and extending into Lower California and Mexico is the Colorado Desert. Included in the desert area are Imperial Valley and Coachella Valley, noted for its date gardens. Both are famous irrigated agriculture areas. Located here, also, is the Salton Sea. In the northern part of the Colorado Desert is Palm Springs. To the west of Palm Springs is the Joshua Tree National Monument, rich in desert vegetation and wildlife. Nearby is the oasis of Twentynine Palms, a health resort. North of the Colorado Desert extends the great Mojave Desert. Here you will find many dude ranches and the health resorts of BARSTOW, VICTORVILLE and MOJAVE. To the north and bordering the Nevada state line is Death Valley National Monument. Here you can see the greatest contrasts in altitude, scenery, coloring, mineral and chemical formations of any place in the United States. Here is the lowest point in the United States, 280 feet below sea level.

Death Valley's history, starting with the Gold Rush of 1849, is as fascinating as its weird and colorful scenery. . . . INYO-MONO playgrounds, including Owens Valley, Mammoth Lakes, June Lake and Mono Lake, is an outstanding recreational region stretching along the eastern slope of the Sierra Nevada for more than 200 miles. It is a section of beauty and mystery, of purple mountain ranges, golden desert spaces, tumbling streams and hundreds of gemlike lakes in stately surroundings of crag and pine — a section whose historical storehouses are filled with a wealth of pioneer lore and Indian legend. To the west the Sierra Nevada reach their greatest height. Mt. Whitney, with an altitude of 14,495 feet, is the highest point in continental United States and in sharp contrast Death Valley, to the east, is the lowest. Mono Lake, 6,420 feet above sea level, the "Dead Sea of America," contains no living thing except a species of shrimp. The entire Inyo-Mono region is famous for its trout fishing. Here, too, is the habitat of the golden trout. . . . The San Joaquin Region, with its fertile valleys, foothills and rugged mountains, is another one of the finest of the state's recreational areas. Hundreds of crystal-clear, gemlike lakes dot the vast reaches of the Sierra, and it is in this region that practically all the remaining stands of the Sierra redwoods, the *Sequoia gigantea*, are found. In the southern section of the region are Red Rock Canyon of scenic interest, the Kern River Canyon and the recreation centers at Hart Memorial Park, Mt. Breckenridge and Mt. Frazier. North of BAKERSFIELD are California Hot Springs and Camp Nelson. From the valley is reached Kings Canyon, Sequoia and Yosemite National Parks, Millerton Lake National Recreation

Area and the recreation areas of the Sequoia, Sierra and Stanislaus National Forests. Sequoia National Park was created for the preservation of its vast groves of "big trees," the *Sequoia gigantea*. The General Sherman Tree, largest and oldest of all living things, rises to a height of 272 feet, has a diameter over 36 feet and is estimated to be between three and four thousand years old. Directly north, Kings Canyon National Park has some of the wildest and most beautiful scenery in the United States — massive peaks, glacier cirques and lake-covered plateaus 10,000 to 14,000 feet above sea level — "Wild as the Himalayas," a region of superlative unspoiled mountain wilderness. Millerton Lake National Recreation Area is the result of one of the huge construction projects of the Central Valley Project. Waters of the lake are backed up by Friant Dam. Along the 43 miles of lake shore line are beautiful wooded areas. Yosemite National Park lies to the west of Lake Mono. Glacier-carved Yosemite Valley, with its towering cliffs of sheerest granite, is so massive and high that it is difficult to appreciate the scale on which they were sculptured. Here, you can see the world's highest waterfalls, glacier-polished domes, mountain lakes and flower-strewn meadows. High Sierra panoramas are awe-inspiring. The Mariposa Grove of Big Trees and Glacier Point are renowned features. Ski Lodge at Badger Pass is a major snow-sports area. A short distance southeast of Yosemite is the Devil Postpile National Monument. It consists of peculiar vertical and curved basaltic columns 60 feet high and ranks with the famous Giant's Causeway of Ireland.

SAN FRANCISCO (775,357), a strikingly situated cosmopolitan city on the coast, is an important port and second largest financial center in the country. First founded in 1776 by Spanish settlers as a fort and a mission (the Mission Dolores is still there), it became United States property in 1846 during the war with Mexico. Two years later gold was discovered in California and almost immediately the settlement of San Francisco, with its great natural harbor, became one of the important places in the world. It became the trading center and financial base for the gold seekers and the place where they spent incredible fortunes made in the mines. The gold rush and the period of lawlessness which followed saw the rise of the Barbary Coast and organizations of vigilantes to fight crime and corruption. In 1906 a disastrous earthquake, followed by an even more destructive fire, lay the city in ruins, but rebuilding was rapid and by 1915 the city celebrated the opening of the Panama Canal with the Panama-Pacific Exposition. Few cities anywhere offer a wider range of sightseeing and diversion than San Francisco. Civic Center has a cluster of handsome public buildings around a plaza filling about ten square blocks. The buildings around the plaza include a Federal Office Building, a State Building, the Public Library, City Hall, Municipal Auditorium, Opera House (where the founding sessions of the United Nations were held in 1945) and a War Memorial. Chinatown is the biggest and by far the most interesting Chinese neighborhood outside the Orient. Visit it slowly and on foot. There is a Chinese temple and a Mandarin theater, both of which can be visited. Telegraph Hill, in the midst of the Latin Quarter, has the Coit Memorial Tower where you can get a wonderful panorama of the harbor. Fisherman's Wharf with its wonderful confusion of net wonders, swaying boats, steaming crab cookers, and fine restaurants is typically San Franciscan. Strolling along the Embarcadero that girdles the waterfront and seeing the ships and sailors of every nation is like a quick trip around the world. Visit the Presidio, U. S. reservation, where you can see the old adobe Officers' Club, first building erected in San Francisco, and bronze cannons 250 years old. Golden Gate Bridge is the city's most spectacular single sight. It is the longest and highest single-span bridge in the world. Cliff House and Seal Rocks, an historic scenic point and restaurant, is at the extreme northwest point of the peninsula. In the sea offshore is a cluster of rocks, home of a colony of sportive sea lions (not seals at all). Golden Gate Park is one of San Francisco's most famous show places and one of the largest and most beautiful parks in the entire world. Included here are the De Young Memorial Museum, the city's largest art museum, the Academy of Science, one of the oldest natural history and scientific centers in the West, and the Steinhart Aquarium. Nob Hill, one of the city's most famous and steepest hills, still has standing some of the mansions built by the gold, silver and railroad kings. The **Top-o-the Mark,** probably the world's most spectacular cocktail lounge, on the roof of the Mark Hopkins Hotel, commands a superb view of the city and harbor. **Twin Peaks,** in the center of town, is another excellent vantage point. **San Francsico-Oakland Bay Bridge** leads east across the bay from the downtown area to Oakland. It is often called the world's longest bridge (8½ miles to Oakland). Actually, it is not one but several bridges, linked together with foundations on bay islands. An interesting visit can be made to the **Wild West Museum** of the Wells-Fargo Bank in the Nevada Building, where you can see relics of the vigilantes, the Barbary Coast, a stagecoach which crossed the Sierra Nevada and the original gold spike of the world's first transcontinental railway. A view of **Treasure Island,** Navy training and air base, and **Alcatraz Island,** site of United States penitentiary, both in San Francisco Bay, are of interest to the tourist. A must on everyone's list is a ride on the famous little relic of bygone days, the **cable car,** with its clanging bells symbolic of fun-loving San Francisco. . . . San Francisco is a convenient base for trips into adjacent areas. These include an easy trip to **Muir Woods** and the great redwood grove just beyond Golden Gate Bridge to the north. . . . An exploration of the chain of towns across the bay to the east includes: **OAKLAND** where you can see **Lake Merritt,** a salt-water lake in the heart of the city, **Lakeside Park** with its Children's Fairyland, **Snow Museum** and the **Municipal Rose Gardens.** Regional parks adjoining Oakland include **Redwood, Round Top** and **Lake Temescal.** Other places of interest are **ALAMEDA** with the

Alameda Naval Air Station; **BERKELEY,** home of the University of California and the **Golden Gate Fields Track** for horse racing; **RICHMOND,** major sea-port. A trip down to **PALO ALTO,** home of Stanford University, takes you through a chain of handsome suburban communities which include **SAN BRUNO** and **SAN MATEO.** A trip southward to the **Monterey Peninsula,** termed the "Circle of Enchantment," takes you to a world-famed playground, with the nationally known **Pebble Beach** and other golf courses, and numerous recreational facilities. Historically, old **MONTEREY** was the capital of California under three flags and the birthplace of the state's constitution. Several state historic monuments and numerous adobes are reminders of this era. Today, Monterey typifies the spirit of the Riviera of the Pacific. The picturesque commercial fishing fleet; **Point Lobos State Park; Pacific Grove** and the **Hopkins Marine Station; Carmel-by-the Sea,** with its artist colony; **Mission San Carlos Borromeo de Carmelo,** where rests Junipero Serra, father of the missions, and **Pfeiffer-Big Sur State Park,** all add to the visitors' interest in this area. . . . The Santa Cruz Mountain Area, with redwood-covered mountains dotted with summer homes and resorts, is a favorite playground of the San Francisco Bay region. Here are located the **Big Basin Redwood State Park** and the county-owned **Felton Grove of Big Trees.** Ocean bathing, pier and deep-sea fishing at **SANTA CRUZ** add to the attractions. . . . The **Mother Lode Country** is a reminder of the discovery of gold and the "Gold Rush" which followed. Starting at Mariposa in the south, State Highway 49 traverses the Mother Lode to **GRASS VALLEY, NEVADA CITY** and to **SATT-**

Mount Hood provides a regal background to Portland, "City of Roses"
Oregon State Hwy. Com.

LEY on the north. Ghost towns and historical markers are reminders of that glamorous era and make it easy to follow the paths of those pioneers. Near PLACER-VILLE is COLOMA where gold was discovered in 1848.

SACRAMENTO (137,572), capital of California, lies in the southern part of the immensely fertile Sacramento Valley. Here is Sutter's Fort Historical Monument and many other historical points of interest. . . . North of San Francisco, SONOMA, lying in the Sonoma Valley, the "Valley of the Moon" made famous by Jack London, is the site of the last of the 21 California missions, Mission San Francisco de Solano. . . . The Redwood Empire (*Sequoia sempervirens*) embraces that part of California in a 10- to 30-mile-wide belt starting across the bay north from San Francisco and extending northward along the coast to Oregon. Resorts of all types are found throughout the region along with many of the beach, lagoon and redwood state parks. Near DYERVILLE, 33 miles south of EUREKA, is the world's tallest tree, Founder's Tree (364 feet). The streams of the region afford some of the state's finest fishing for trout, steelhead and salmon. A forest of petrified giant redwoods, natural steam geysers and the heart of California's light-wine industry are among the many attractions of the region. . . . The region around Clear Lake has been aptly termed "The Switzerland of America." The lake is the largest body of fresh water lying wholly within the state. Its elevation is 1,350 feet, with volcanic mountains that rise to a height of 4,000 feet surrounding it. Boating is excellent and the usual recreational activities are available. . . . The Lake Tahoe region lies within three national forests: the Tahoe and Eldorado in California and the Toiyabe in Nevada. It is one of the state's most popular playgrounds. (See description under Nevada). Donner Pass, one of the country's most outstanding snow-sports areas in winter, lies northwest of the lake. The Feather River and Yuba River region is a region of rivers and streams of jewel-like lakes and gorgeous scenery. Mines and ghost towns, reminders of the gold rush, abound. LA PORTE and JOHNS-VILLE are the birthplaces of skiing in the United States. . . . Lying between Siena City and the Feather River is the Lakes Basin Recreational Area, where, within a radius of a few miles, are some 35 lakes which afford excellent fishing. . . . In Lassen Volcanic National Park stands Mt. Lassen, the most recently active volcano in continental United States. The last eruption occurred in 1915, the scars of which still remain. Volcanic activity is evidenced by geysers, bubbling mud pots, a boiling lake, hot and cold mineral springs, Cinder Cone, a mountain of volcanic ash, and others. . . . Mt. Shasta marks the conjunction of the Coast Range with the Sierra Nevada. It is 14,161 feet in height, rises a sheer 10,000 feet above its surrounding ranges and its snow-covered summit is visible for more than 100 miles from valley highways. It is the center of an outstanding recreational area. Shasta Lake and Shasta Dam are in this region, as are Castle Crags and Burney Falls State Parks. . . . The Trinity Alps is a region of rugged mountains, rushing streams and lakes. Most of it can be characterized as primitive or wilderness, accessible only by hiking or packing in. It is a paradise for the fisherman and the hunter. . . . If you are looking for a dude or guest ranch vacation, California has a large number. They are located in all sections of the state — in the mountains, valleys, foothills and along the coast. One of the many things which makes the state so interesting to the visitor is California's love of a fiesta. Approximately one thousand such colorful and entertaining celebrations are held throughout the year in all sections of the state. Special foods in southern California include: pink beans (frijoles) simmered, then fried with cheese; Japanese sukeyaki; barbecued spareribs; fresh fruit and vegetable salads. In San Francisco and the northwest: Columbia salmon; smoked salmon; jerked salmon; abalone steak; Dungeness crab; croppino; Oriental foods and teas.

OREGON

Nature endowed Oregon with fertile valleys, great mountains, snow-capped peaks, vast sweeps of forests, an ocean to make her climate perfect, rivers and lakes fed by mountain snows and valley rains. She filled her woods with game, her streams with fish. This was the glittering paradise that started the covered wagons rolling westward with their cry "On to Oregon!" The paradise that the pioneer found is yours today in a visit to Oregon. Fishing, hunting, skiing, boating, swimming, mountain climbing, horseback trips, golf — these are only a few of the pleasures at your choice.

You've never seen beaches quite like the Oregon beaches, for here mountain, forest and ocean meet. Spurs of the Coast Range, heavily wooded, come down as a great drop curtain for the stage of hard, clean sands. Each beach has its legend — the forgotten treasure of early Spanish or Russian ships, the mountain-high shell-mounds of the Indians and relics of the earlier peoples. Southernmost are the popular BRANDON and COOS BAY sections. Northward there are WALDPORT on the Alsea River, the picturesque old fishing town of NEWPORT on Yaquina Bay and the famed Tillamook beaches. Northernmost are the Clatsop beaches — CANNON BEACH, a 12-mile strand, ideal for horseback riding and bicycling, and SEASIDE, where the End of the Trail Monument marks the conclusion of the Lewis and Clark expedition in 1805. A pleasure unique is the hunt for agates which are found in profusion in the sands after each high tide around AGATE BEACH. At the mouth of the Columbia River, near ASTORIA, horses are used to haul in the great salmon seines, sometimes as long as 2,000 feet. . . . PORTLAND (373,629), the Pacific Northwest's "City of Roses," straddles the Willamette River, on the south bank of the Columbia River about 75 miles east of the Pacific Ocean. With Mt. Hood in the background, it is one of our most photogenic cities. Spanning the Willamette River is St. Johns Bridge, cathedral-like in appearance, and listed by many as one of the seven most beautiful bridges in the world. The Sanctuary of Our Sorrowful Mother, the world's outstanding memorial to universal motherhood, is a mecca for nearly a half million pilgrims

and visitors annually. Sacajawea, the "Bird Woman" credited with leading the Lewis and Clark expedition to the Pacific Northwest, is one of the many statues and fountains to enjoy in Portland. Visit the colorful International Rose Test and Sunken Rose Gardens. Lambert Gardens, consisting of ten gardens of unparalleled beauty, is a paradise of flowers from April until late in the fall. Forestry Building, world's largest log cabin, houses the Gallery of Trees, where you can get a complete picture of the forests products industry. . . . South of Portland lies the Willamette Valley, one of the richest agricultural areas in the world, between the Coast and Cascade Ranges. SALEM, capital of Oregon, is in the middle valley. The University of Oregon is at EUGENE, and Oregon State College is at CORVALLIS. Willamette University, at Salem, founded in 1842, is the oldest American educational institution west of the Missouri River. BREITENBUSH SPRINGS is a resort with some fifty mineral hot springs. . . . One of the world's most scenic drives, the Columbia River Highway takes you eastward from Portland through the great gorge the river has cut in the Cascade Mountains. The Vista House at CROWN POINT, 750 feet above the river, is among many lookout points You pass Multnomah Falls which drops 620 feet down the wall of Columbia gorge in a misty recess of green moss and delicate ferns, and 10 more spectacular waterfalls in the next 11 miles. In the gorge visit Bonnerville Dam and its ingenious fish ladders which lead around the dam and enable the salmon migrating upstream to by-pass the obstacle. After the town of HOOD RIVER you approach THE DALLES, where the Columbia rushes through an eight-mile narrow channel. . . . The entire Cascade Mountain Range from one

The wild Rogue River is the only means of transportation through Hells Gate canyon in southeastern Oregon
Oregon State Hwy. Com.

end of Oregon to the other is dotted with lakes set like jewels in the timbered mountains. **Crater Lake**, one of the true wonders of the world, is a great body of water 2,000 feet deep and six miles across set in the crater of a once gigantic volcano 8,000 feet high in the Cascades of southern Oregon. It has been set aside in **Crater Lake National Park** for the enjoyment of the tourist. Its water is of an indescribable blue, mirroring the trees and mountains around the lake's great rim. Visitors may enjoy the scenic values of Crater Lake in winter amid a fantasy of snowy splendor. Just to the north is **Diamond Lake**, one of Oregon's premier rainbow-trout waters.... The **Oregon Caves** or **Marble Halls**, southwest of Crater Lake near the California state line are famous for their Ghost Chamber, King's Palace and Dante's Inferno rooms. Continuing northward in the Cascades from Crater Lake are **Three Sisters** and **Mt. Jefferson**, beauty spots that are uniquely their own. . . . Just a short distance east of Portland is the most famous of Oregon's alpine playgrounds, **Mt. Hood**, where the government has erected **Timberline Lodge** at the 6,000-foot level above Government Camp. For magnificent views of Mt. Hood and the Cascade Range, ride the Skiway from Government Camp to Timberline Lodge — a treetop trip on the world's largest and longest (3.1 miles) tramway. . . . To one who loves wide open spaces and solitude, central and southeastern Oregon offer everything. On the dry plateau near **JOHN DAY**, the **John Day Fossil Beds State Park** permits a glance into the early eras of the earth. Fossils have been unearthed there of huge mastodons and miniature horses, of giant sloths and saber-toothed tigers. In this area are **Hart Mountain Antelope Refuge** and **Malheur Migratory Bird Refuge**. **Owyhee Canyon**, in extreme southeastern Oregon, is a chasm of stark, grim, rugged beauty. . . . The **Wallowa** and **Blue Mountains** area of northeastern Oregon is another tourist playground. The **Anthony Lakes** in the Blue Mountains are a choice summer and winter playground in the **BAKER-LA GRANDE** area. **Wallowa Lake** is the heart of this area. Lying at the edge of the Wallowas, along the Idaho state line is the **Grand Canyon on the Snake River**, deeper than the Grand Canyon of Arizona. . . . Northwest of the Blue Mountains is

PENDLETON, where every September it is host to the Pendleton Round-Up, a three day rodeo and Indian ceremonial which is one of the gayest and most colorful pageants of the northwest. . . . Clams, giant crabs, sea bass and perch, cod, sole, salmon and halibut provide epicurean treats which make Oregon famous for its sea-food dishes.

WASHINGTON

Washington, the "Evergeen State," which a little more than a century ago was part of the Oregon Territory, is an ideal vacation spot. Here, you will find America's coolest summer climate, magnificent scenery, mountains, verdant forest, ocean beaches, lakes, rivers, unrivaled recreational facilities and modern cities and towns. It's cool, it's green, it's great — in Washington state.

SEATTLE (467,591), metropolis of the Northwest, gateway to Alaska and the Orient, is situated on Puget Sound along Elliot Bay. It is a city of changing vistas broken by hills and numerous water routes. The snowy ridges of the Olympics may be seen to the west and the blue-green Cascades, dominated by **Mt. Rainier**, are visible to the southeast and east. It is the second largest fur market in the country, has one of the largest aircraft factories in the world and as a result of development of western Canadian oil resources, is becoming a big refining center. The **Waterfront** has long been an important area of activity and today still retains much of its earlier picturesque features. Along here you will find curio shops, fish and oyster booths and ship chandlers. Also in downtown Seattle see **Ye Olde Curiosity Shop**, where you will find curiosities from the lands of the seven seas; **Live Fish Aquarium**, with its performing seal and "Pat," the octopus; **Totem Pole**, Alaska Indians' family tree carved from a cedar log 60 feet long; **Smith Tower**, for a wide view of city, harbor and mountains. Within the city limits other tourists' attractions include: **Seattle Art Museum**; **University of Washington**; **University of Washington Arboretum**, which has 2,000 trees and shrubs from all parts of the world; **Civic Auditorium**; **Lake Washington Floating Bridge**, a four-lane highway across Lake Washington, built on huge pontoons and the largest floating structure in the world; **Lake Washington Canal and Locks**, exceeded in size in America only by those

The dazzling winter snow in Mount Baker National Forest produces this skiers' heaven
Wash. State Adv. Com.

of the Panama Canal; **Showboat Theater**, constructed as a replica of the old river showboats and **Penthouse Theater**. Cycling around Green Lake in the heart of metropolitan Seattle is a favorite for tourists. Two state parks near Seattle are popular: **Saltwater State Park** and **Twanoh State Park** across from Bremerton. . . . From Seattle a number of interesting side-trips may be taken. North of Seattle and east of **BELLINGHAM** in the Cascade Range lies **Mt. Baker**, elevation 10,750 feet. At the 4,000 foot level is **Mt. Baker Lodge and Resort**, a haven for skiers as the snow remains all year round. **LYNDEN**, near the Canadian border, is a bit of Holland in Washington. Dutch customs and language are still cultivated there. . . . Directly west of Seattle, across Elliot Bay on the Kitsap Peninsula, lies the thriving community of **BREMERTON** and the home of the **Puget Sound Navy Yard**, second largest in the United States. **Puget Sound**, famous for its fighting salmon, also offers visitors fine salt-water swimming beaches and excellent boating facilities. . . . Surrounded by the azure waters of Puget Sound are the **San Juan Islands**, an enchanting paradise for the nature-loving pleasure seeker. These islands offer an ever-changing panorama of wooded slopes, hidden bays, narrow inlets and distant mountain peaks. **San Juan Island, Orcas Island** and **Lopez Island** are the three largest of the group and have modern tourist resorts of every type. Located on San Juan Island, **FRIDAY HARBOR** has the **University of Washington's Oceanographic Laboratory**. . . . The Olympic Peninsula, on which is located the Olympic National Park, is one of the last frontier areas in the United States. In the northeastern section **Deer Park** offers

a magnificent panorama of **Juan de Fuca Strait** and **Vancouver Island**. **Olympic National Park**, dominating the center of the peninsula, is a unique wilderness of coniferous rain forest, wildlife, alpine-flower meadows, glaciers and trout-filled lakes and streams, set in one of the most rugged mountain masses in the entire country, the **Olympic Mountains**. Surrounded by this fortresslike stronghold is **Mount Olympus**, 7,923 feet high, quite similar to the one in Greece. An interesting trip is the 364 mile Olympic Loop through the foothills that offers such attractions as a 50-mile ride along the beautiful **Hood Canal**, a visit to the little city of **PORT ANGELES** with its famous salmon and crab grounds, and a view of crystal-clear **Lake Crescent**, which lies in the shadow of **Mount Storm King** in the northern end of the park. The wettest winter climate in the continental United States prevails on the west side of the park. Here, an extraordinary junglelike forest growth has developed with giant conifers reaching 200 feet or more into the sky, mosses softly carpeting the forest floor and upholstering tree trunks and fallen trees, with draperies hanging from the branches — all permeated with a misty green light. This belt stretches from sea level to a height of about 5,000 feet. . . . South of the park is **LONG BEACH** on the Pacific Ocean, with more than 28 miles of sandy beach where visitors can drive cars or ride horseback on a firm surface or just relax comfortably in the sunshine. . . . About 20 miles south of Seattle lies **TACOMA** (143,673) lumber capital of the world and a busy industrial and commercial city and port. West of Tacoma is **SHELTON**, a logging town, where the daily speech is spiced with lumberjack expressions. . . . About 30 miles southeast of Tacoma lies the vast mountain forest playground **Mount Rainier National Park,** "the mountain the Indians called God," a mecca for sight-seers, camera enthusiasts, mountain climbers, fishermen and skiers. **Mount Rainier,** located on the western edge of the Cascade crest line, towers to a height of 14,408 feet and its glacial systems, which conceal all but the more rugged crags and ridges, are greater than those of the Swiss Alps. Set in a parklike paradise of flower-carpeted mountain meadows, giant forest, glacial rivers and cascading waterfalls it is a never-to-be-forgotten sight of awe-inspiring beauty. Mt. Rainier presents a difficult climb over ridges of crumbling lava and pumice and along inclined and deeply crevassed ice fields and glaciers. Saddle-horse trips will take you to the points of greatest scenic interest throughout the park. For those who have the time to spare, a week's pack trip over the Wonderland Trail is a unique experience of primitive and beautiful nature. The trail completely encircles the mountain. Relatively good trout fishing may be enjoyed in park lakes and streams. Situated on the north side of Mt. Rainier is **Paradise Valley,** said by some to be the greatest single scenic attraction in the entire Pacific Northwest. Nearby you can see the great **Nisqually Glacier,** the famous **Silver Forest** and the beautiful **Narada Falls** dropping 168 feet to the **Paradise River Canyon.** Farther south **Spirit Lake,** backed by **Mt. St. Helen,** is another scenic area. Throughout the Cascades you will find snow-capped mountain peaks and sparkling lakes, each offering its own scenic beauty to the tourist. Snoqualmie Pass is a spectacular stretch of road drilled through rock tunnels and hewn into canyon walls; it is a spot of record snowfalls—up to 400 inches a year. Twenty-five miles east of **ELLENSBURG** is the **Gingko Petrified State Forest.** To the north is **WENATCHEE,** the world's apple capital. . . . SPOKANE (161,721), a great trading center, is the hub of the "Inland Empire." **Spokane Falls** is a never-to-be-forgotten sight, particularly in the spring and early summer. The falls are beautifully illuminated during the period of high water. In the city is located **Gonzaga University.** Spokane is the center of a superlative land of lakes and dashing trout streams. Within a circle of 50 miles surrounding the city are 76 mountain lakes. Summer homes, cabins and camps nestling on forest-bordered lake shores, in glens and shaded woods, and on rocky cliffs, offer comfortable accommodations. Northeast of the city a scenic drive leads to the top of **Mt. Spokane.** . . . Spokane is the nearest large city and the main gateway to **Grand Coulee Dam.** Here you will thrill to the sight of man's greatest handiwork. Five hundred feet high, the biggest concrete structure ever raised on earth, the dam impounds the waters of the mighty Columbia River, forming **Lake Roosevelt,** 151 miles long, which extends to Canada on the north and provides a man-made navigable waterway and water playground. . . . South of here, at the bend of the Columbia River, near **PASCO,** the **Hanford Atomic Energy Plant** is one of the largest nuclear (fission projects. . . . Baked salmon, goeducks, large native clams, Olympic pan roasts and an oyster-catchup mixture on toast are favorite specialties.

Mount Shuksan's snow-capped, jagged peaks are reflected in a clear, cold lake in Mount Baker National Forest

Wash. State Adv. Com.

Rocky Mountain States

The Rocky Mountain states encompass the huge mountainous area that divides the continent. This is the land of snow-capped peaks, dark canyons and battlemented mesas. The mountains, called the Rockies, are actually a vast system of various ranges, each one different in detail or structure, each one of ever-changing hue and color depending on the time of year and time of day. They provide unlimited recreational activities, whether it be hunting or fishing, skiing down snow-covered slopes or just enjoying the majestic mountains and valleys. Added to this mountaintop land are an exhilarating climate and dramatic historic associations — the saga of the westward movement, the Lewis and Clark Expedition, the Oregon and Mormon Trails, frontier forts and mining boom towns, Indian wars and cattle wars. The Indians have changed a great deal since the time when they valiantly defended their homeland but you can always find an ancient chief (not always really a chief) willing to pose in full regalia for a picture while his grandsons are off going to school or earning a living in the contemporary fashion. The latest newcomers and perhaps the ones most perfectly at home in the mountain valleys are the Basque sheepherders who tend their flocks on mountain pastures. Whether you come to enjoy the scenic wonders and wilderness of the national parks, the Western atmosphere of thrilling rodeos and dude ranches or the pleasures of a modern resort, you will find the Rocky Mountain states a treasure chest of things to do and see.

COLORADO

The Rocky Mountains in Colorado begin where the High Plains leave off. There is no chance of missing them as you travel west for they loom up on the horizon as a seemingly solid barrier to the Far West. At the foot of the mountain wall is the capital city of DENVER, base of operations for vacationists and travelers who visit the mountaintop state. The city itself is a pleasant one; its mile-high elevation gives it an invigorating climate, ideal in summer and winter. Denver's park system not only includes expansive landscaped areas in the downtown section but also comprises part of the Rocky Mountains, fifteen miles west of the city. Some 25,000 acres of canyons, mountain trout streams, lakes and recreational areas are included in the Denver Mountain Parks. A visit to the parks might include a drive to the summit of Mount Evans on the highest auto road in the country, a stop at Buffalo Bill's (William Cody) grave on top of Lookout Mountain and possibly a summer concert at Red Rocks Amphitheater, a colorful outdoor arena among dramatic sandstone formations. For downtown sights, there is the neo-Greek Civic Center, with various government buildings like the handsome City and County Building, which faces the gold-domed State Capitol from across a broad esplanade. Other places of interest nearby are the United States Mint, which coins a good portion of the nation's money; the Denver Art Museum (in the City and County Building) and the Colorado State Historical Museum. . . . CENTRAL CITY, thirty miles west of Denver, is the scene for the Central City Play Festival, a major attraction in the West. The old mining town's Opera House has been rehabilitated from the dim past in order to stage dramas and operas with outstanding stars from the East. . . . About 65 miles northwest of Denver is Rocky Mountain National Park, 405 square miles of mountain splendor, glacial lakes, rugged peaks, flower-bright upland meadows and a variety of wildlife. The park is one of the country's largest and best mountain playgrounds, with over 65 peaks with elevations above 10,000 feet. ESTES PARK is a resort town at the entrance to the park. . . . For ski facilities Berthoud Pass and Arapahoe Basin lead a long list of popular ski areas, all within 100 miles of Denver. You will, of course, find numerous ski centers throughout the Colorado Rockies, slopes for both novice and expert, ski jumps, single and double chair lifts that carry you silently to the tips of breath-taking mountain peaks. ASPEN and STEAMBOAT SPRINGS are two other outstanding Colorado ski centers with facilities and winter carnivals. . . . South from Denver, COLORADO SPRINGS is noted both as a resort town and a health center. Fabulous resort hotels like the Broadmoor have an ideal location with the Rockies as a backdrop. . . . It is not far to MANITOU SPRINGS, where you can take the cog railway to the summit of Pike's Peak, the 14,110-foot moun-

Rocky Mountain States

tain that was the goal for wagons heading west to the Colorado goldfields. An automobile road also climbs the high peak for a vista that is hard to surpass. Within easy driving distance is the **Royal Gorge** of the Arkansas, a mighty chasm gouged in solid granite. A highway bridge spans the gorge 1,053 feet above the river and an incline railway descends at an angle of 45 degrees to the bottom of the canyon. Also of scenic interest, a few miles west of Colorado Springs, is the **Garden of the Gods**, a natural park with grostesque shapes in red sandstone, particularly striking in the morning or evening sun. . . . To the south near **ALAMOSA** is **Great Sand Dunes National Monument**, a vast expanse of sand covering an area of sixty square miles. The dunes rise in knife-edged slopes and peaks sometimes 1,500 feet high. . . . To the west a delightful drive through the San Juan Forest and Wolf Creek Pass will take you to **DURANGO**, center of one of the most scenic regions of the state. Further west in the southwest corner of the state, **Mesa Verde National Park** includes thousands of acres of canyons and mesalands set aside for the preservation of many ancient cliff dwellings and surface pueblos. The mesa itself rises a sheer 2,000 feet from the floor of Montezuma Valley. The most spectacular Indian dwellings are found along the walls of the deep canyons left exactly as they were when deserted in the thirteenth century. The National Park Service has an extensive program of talks and guided tours which give an accurate picture of the lives of the prehistoric inhabitants. . . . To the north, the **Black Canyon of the Gunnison National Monument** includes eleven miles of the most picturesque portion of the fifty-mile gorge. GUNNISON is the headquarters for the famed trout streams of central Colorado. . . . **Colorado National Monument** is a half-hour's drive west of **GRAND JUNCTION**. The 18,000-acre area is seamed with canyons honeycombed with caves and unusual rock formations. . . . In the northwestern part of the state Colorado shares with Utah **Dinosaur National Monument**, a fantastic land only partly explored as yet, with rich fossil beds of prehistoric animals. To complete the circuit of the state you can recross the continental divide in the north over the scenic highway U.S. 40 to make the return trip to Denver.

WYOMING

CHEYENNE (31,935), capital of Wyoming, is probably the first stop for travelers entering the state from the southeast. The name always conjures up images of Indian attacks, bad men in gunfights, vigilantes and cattle wars, for the city has always been closely allied with the Old West. The spirit of those rip-roaring days is recaptured in the **Cheyenne Frontier Days Celebration**. It is held in the last week of July and is undoubtedly one of the best shows of its kind. . . . To the north **Fort Laramie National Monument** preserves the remains of old Fort Laramie, one of the most important posts when westward was the course of empire. Built in 1834, it offered protection and furnished supplies to trail-blazing fur traders and the immigrant trains which followed. It also served as a station for the Pony Express and as a military base in the conquest of the Plains Indians. A number of buildings have been restored to their appearance just before the fort was abandoned by the Army. . . . The trading center of CASPER, to the northwest, has several points of interest nearby. The **Casper Mountains** are both a scenic area and a winter-sports playground. To the north, the **Teapot Dome oil fields** recall to mind the national scandal of the 1920's. To the west, **Hell's Half Acre** is a great depression filled with deep caverns, pits, spires, towers and other architectural effects. Pioneers using the Oregon and Mormon Trails left a "register of the desert" by carving their names on **Independence Rock**, to the southwest of Casper. . . . In western Wyoming the mountains of the Grand Tetons are rightfully called the "Alps of America." At **Grand Teton National Park** the mountain chain is at its scenic best. There are no foothills to soften the bold peaks which rise almost vertically 7,000 feet above a comparatively flat valley floor. The range borders the west side of **Jackson Hole**, an excellent place to view the mountain scenery, especially when mirrored in the depths of Jenny and Jackson Lakes. The log-cabin church at **MOOSE** frames a view of the Tetons in its altar window, an appropriate altarpiece for the mountain church. The Teton range includes twenty peaks over 10,000 feet, the highest being **Grand Teton**, which reaches a height of 13,766 feet. There are higher mountains in the world but few offer as great a challenge to moun-

Dudes watch the branding
activities on a Wyoming
ranch at fall roundup time
Focus Ranch, Wyoming
Com. & Ind. Commission

tain climbers. Knifelike ridges, Matter-horns and polished rock walls carved by the glaciers entice mountain climbers from all over the world. You don't have to be an expert, however, to enjoy the mountains. Less arduous trails lead along the glacial lakes or to the mountaintop glaciers. Horseback and foot trails provide occasional glimpses of elk, big-horn sheep and moose, as well as the more common small-game animals. Dude ranches and lodges in the park area and near JACKSON supply accommodations for extended visits. . . . **Yellowstone National Park**, in the northwest corner of Wyoming, is nature's greatest variety show. Here in a hissing arena geysers, hot springs and boiling pools spout and spray, performing nature's own "spectacular" amid the rugged Rockies. Large geysers like the well-known **Old Faithful** throw tons of water several hundred feet into the air while growling pools and roaring mud volcanoes perform supporting roles. The colors of the terraces formed by springs and geysers vary from sparkling shades of pink and red to tans and yellows. If there were no geysers or other hot-water phenomena Yellowstone Park would still warrant national park status. One reason would be the **Grand Canyon of the Yellowstone River** with the **Great Falls**, a thundering cataract that drops 300 feet — twice that of Niagara — in a dazzling water display. The park area is also primitive; it remains as nearly as possible as nature executed it. Uncut forests spread over a vast area providing a home for elk, deer, antelope and bears who have become as famous as the geysers. Lakes and streams are stocked for trout fishing. . . . **CODY**, to the east of Yellowstone, was founded by Col. William

F. Cody, known more widely as Buffalo Bill. The town's big rodeo and stampede is held the first week in July. . . . Mention should be made of a unique feature of northeast Wyoming — **Devil's Tower National Monument**. This great tower rising 1,200 feet above the plains has the appearance of a gigantic tree stump, even to the barklike outer surface of fluted volcanic rock. A close inspection is worth while for anyone entering or leaving the Black Hills.

MONTANA

When the Lewis and Clark Expedition of 1805 and '06 traversed what is now the State of Montana, they found mile after mile of rolling plains and soaring mountains, hundreds of still lakes and clear streams — a vast land inhabited only by the Indians. Fur trappers and miners followed in later years but for a long time the Indians ruled the plains. Their last victory in striving to keep their lands was the **Battle of the Little Big Horn River**, near **HARDIN**, where General Custer and 300 troops met disaster. The Indian cause was lost, however, for the weight of the U. S. Army soon scattered the Indians. . . . **MILES CITY** is the center for the vast livestock ranches sprawled over eastern Montana. To the north is the Missouri River on which the Lewis and Clark Expedition traveled. They would not recognize one section of the river, however, for the **Fort Peck Dam** has created a large man-made lake that serves both as an irrigation project and as a recreational lake. Nor would they have realized what great oil wealth lay beneath the surface of **Williston Basin** to the east. . . . Western Montana is dominated by the Rocky Mountains, the site for the mineral wealth that makes Montana "the treasure state."

BUTTE, in the south, is known as "the richest hill on earth," for beneath the city itself are 2,000 miles of tunnels where copper ore is mined. . . . The ore is shipped to ANACONDA, 26 miles away, for processing. The gigantic smokestack of the Washoe Smelter is the world's largest. East of Butte, Lewis and Clark Cavern State Park offers guided tours of limestone caves, while to the south the old mining town of VIRGINIA CITY has been restored as the "Williamsburg of the West." . . . Throughout the mountainland of western Montana dude ranches flourish. Whether you spend a vacation at one of the ranches especially set up for visitors or at one of the operating stock ranches, you will enjoy the outdoor life amid unforgettable scenery. There is plenty of opportunity for horseback trips, overnight camping and a chance to see how a cattle ranch is run. In addition to normal dude activities, almost every Montana ranch boasts excellent trout fishing in nearby streams and lakes. Those visitors who like hunting will enjoy a fall trip when the mountain dude ranches offer pack trips to big-game country for elk, moose, deer, antelope and even grizzly bear. . . . For lake resort pleasure Flathead Lake, near POLSON, is the largest fresh-water lake west of the Mississippi; it offers fishing, boating and camping facilities. . . . Located in northernmost Montana, astride the continental divide, is Glacier National Park. The vast park contains more than sixty glaciers and 200 beautiful lakes. The peaks are alpine in character, shaped by glaciers much larger than those visible now. Cataracts and cascades fall from "hanging valleys" to collect in sparkling lakes like Lakes McDonald and St. Mary. The spectacular Going-to-the-Sun Highway, which crosses the main ridge at Logan Pass, provides a good view of the mountain scenery but for a closer view of the glaciers and a better appreciation of the wilderness, a trip on foot or by horseback over some of the 1,000 miles of trails is recommended. Glacier National Park continues as Waterton Lakes National Park on the Canadian side, a symbol of the friendship of the two nations. For an illuminating picture of the life of Plains Indians a trip to the Museum of the Plains Indians at BROWNING cannot be too strongly recommended. Exhibits of Indian lore, history and art are some of the finest to be seen. Genuine Indian handicraft may also be purchased at the same building. . . . The best skiing facilities of northwest Montana are located on snow fields around WHITEFISH, on the western border of Glacier Park.

IDAHO

Idaho is probably the most varied of the Rocky Mountain states. It has mountains to be sure — some 22 separate ranges rising to elevations as high as 12,000 feet — but it has also rivers that foam white in their fury to race through bottomless canyons, weird lava flows and extinct volcanoes, vast forests and rolling wheatlands. . . . The Panhandle of northern Idaho is a region of lovely lakes and great evergreen forests. Near SANDPOINT, Lake Pend Oreille is not only a scenic delight but also ideal for fishing for prize landlocked salmon and Kamloops rainbow trout. Hunting in the nearby mountains is considered excellent. Along with Lake Pend Oreille, Priest Lake to the north and Coeur d'Alene to the south make up "the big three" of resort lakes of Idaho. . . . East of Coeur d'Alene is the silver, lead and zinc mining region; guided tours of the Sunshine Mine at KELLOGG are available. . . . South from Coeur d'Alene U. S. Highway 95 descends 2,000 feet to LEWISTON in a series of spirals offering excellent scenic views. . . . The deepest gorge in America is the Grand Canyon of the Snake River extending along the Idaho-Oregon border. The average depth of this chasm is 5,500 feet but at Hell's Canyon the canyon bottom is almost lost from sight; it measures a depth of 7,900 feet at a point near Hat Point. But unlike the Grand Canyon of the Colorado, the gorge is very narrow — less than 100 feet in some places. A panoramic view of this chasm can be had at Kinney Point near CUPRUM. For a closer view, boat trips to the northern end of the canyon from Lewiston are available. Another "white water" canyon has been formed by the Salmon River, a tributary of the Snake River. Accessible scenic portions of the Salmon Canyon may be reached from CHALLIS. . . . In southern Idaho the capital city of BOISE was founded during the gold-mining rush of 1862. Nearby Arrowrock Dam, one of the highest irrigation dams in the world, is part of a vast irrigation system that brings water to the fertile Snake River basin. . . . East of Boise, in the rugged alpine-like Sawtooth

Mountains is the famous **Sun Valley** resort, one of the most popular of western ski centers and one which has done much to promote winter sports in general all over America. There are a number of ski runs ranging from beginners' slopes to the difficult slopes of **Baldy Mountain**. Facilities are excellent — whether it is a ski lift to take you up to the top of a run or a nice warm lodge at the bottom. Swimming in an outdoor warm-water pool, dog sledding, sleighing and ice skating are some of the sports to be enjoyed. The mountains of the Sawtooth Range are pleasant at any time of the year, however, and are at their spectacular best around **Mount Hyndman** (12,078 feet). . . . Until such time when space travel is more than a remote possibility a trip to the moon can be enjoyed in facsimile version by visiting **Craters of the Moon National Monument** near ARCO, for here indeed is another world of desolate wonder, with cinder buttes, lava flows and strange pock-marked terrain. This moon-like area was the scene of volcanic activity off and on during geologic history, the latest being about 500 years ago. Lava flows spread out in billowy waves, iridescent and glossy as seen in formations like the **Blue Dragon**. Other curious features are the lava bombs, masses of molten lava which were thrown into the air and hardened on the way down, and tree molds where the lava cooled around trees that were in the path of the lava flow. . . . To the south, between the cities of **TWIN FALLS** and **JEROME**, the **Rim to Rim Bridge** spans the Snake River, offering a vast panorama of the fertile Magic Valley country. The nearby falls of the Snake River, **Twin Falls and Shoshone Falls**, are somewhat reduced in their splendor due to irrigation projects but during the spring they regain their power; the flood-swollen waters plunge 212 feet at Shoshone Falls.

UTAH

Nature was in a lavish mood when she ladled out to Utah a wealth of scenic wonders. But scenic beauty was not the sole concern of early Utah settlers. It took men of vision, ingenuity and leadership to create a civilization in such an apparently hostile land. It is always a pleasure to come into **SALT LAKE CITY** (181,121) from the mountain pass or from across the salt plains. That in 1847 there was nothing but an arid valley seems hard to believe. Yet such it was when Brigham Young, the Mormon leader, decided to build a new Zion. First-time visitors to Salt Lake City will enjoy the wide streets, clean atmosphere and wonderful setting. The city's great attraction is **Temple Square**, the center of Mormonism, or the Church of the Latter-Day Saints, as it is called. The six-spired **Mormon Temple** is closed to the non-Mormons but the interesting **Tabernacle** building next to it can be visited and the famed organ and choral recitals enjoyed. Not far from Temple Square is the **State Capitol**, overlooking the entire valley. **Great Salt Lake**, to the west of the city, is one of America's largest lakes. More notable is its salt content — six to eight times saltier than the ocean's. Bathing in this briny sea is an aquatic experience; you can float with ease but find swimming difficult. **Promontory Point**, nearby, was the place where the two sections of the first continental railroad were joined with the ceremony of driving the golden spike. To the west of the lake, the **Bonneville Salt Flats** are known for the world's fastest automobile speed runs. . . .

Three bull elk and a youngster browse in a Montana valley

Montana Highway Photo

Also of interest near Salt Lake City are the open-pit copper mines at **BINGHAM CANYON**. . . . The **Wasatch Mountains** of northern Utah provide excellent alpine terrain for skiing and outdoor recreation. Canyons such as the 1,000-foot deep **Ogden Canyon** traverse the north-south range. **OGDEN** has the popular **Ogden Snow Basin** as a ski center, while the slopes of **Alta, Brighton and Ecker's Hill** are favorite haunts of Salt Lake City skiers. . . . For scenic drives do not miss the **Alpine Scenic Loop**, near **PROVO**, which leads to **Timpanogos Cave National Monument**. . . . In southern Utah the mountains give way to plateau country where nature displays her brightest colors and most awe-inspiring rock formations. Beginning in the southwest the first great national park is **Bryce Canyon National Park**. It is not a canyon in the usual sense but rather a

by way of **Mt. Carmel Highway**. The highway parallels the canyon wall, passes through a mile-long tunnel which is pierced with huge windows that look out on a scene of awe-inspiring beauty. The cliffs and monuments soar to heights over 3,000 feet and are especially impressive when seen from below. The names of the features are often taken from religious text — the **Three Patriarchs, Angel's Landing** and the **Great White Throne** — and are in keeping with their actual appearance. . . . Less accessible but no less impressive are the national monuments of southeastern Utah. U. S. Highway 160 leads south from **CRESCENT CITY** past **Arches National Monument**, a series of wind-and-sand-eroded arches and windows. A side road near the movie-location town of **MOAB** leads to breathtaking views of the Colorado River at **Dead Horse Point** and

Thrilling wild country in the Lost River Range, near Mackay, Idaho

Standard Oil Co. of N.J.

series of amphitheaters a thousand feet deep, covered with a bewildering assortment of stone pinnacles, towers and spires alive with glowing colors. Scenic drives amid spruce, aspen and pine traverse the park, and trails lead along the rim and descend to the bottom of the canyon for a closer view of the strange rock sentinels. . . . To the west, near **CEDAR CITY**, is **Cedar Breaks National Monument**, a vast bowl of eroded sandstone. Here you will see a labyrinth of ridges and magnificent architectural forms, tinted in all the colors of the spectrum. The cliffs are white and orange at the top, breaking into deep rose and coral further down. Other shades of chocolate, yellow and purple are visible depending on the light and shadow. . . . Further south is **Zion National Park**, a realm of majestic stone temples and cathedrals in a 2,000-foot gorge. You can enter

Grand View Point. . . . Further southwest of **BLANDING** are several prehistoric cliff dwellings and three natural bridges within a six mile radius. It takes a little hiking to reach them but they are well worth the exertion. South from Blanding the road becomes more rugged while the scenery increases in dramatic quality. This section is **Monument Valley**. From out of the level red plain rise huge monoliths and skyscraping needles of rock, like towering sentinels of the desert. **Rainbow Bridge National Monument**, the world's largest natural bridge and perhaps the least accessible of America's wonders, is near the Arizona border. Horseback trips from **MEXICAN HAT** in Utah or Rainbow Lodge in Arizona do reach the monument, however, and both the adventure of the trip and the beauty of the colossal arch reward those who brave the desert.

The Southwest

The Southwest, land of enchantment and contrast, possesses an ever-changing panorama of vast mesa and towering mountains; of forested retreat and cactus-guarded desert. Wind and water have carved giant forms from a media of colored sandstones and shales. Here also is a cultural crossroad with three civilizations blending into a distinctive way of life — Indian, Spanish and English. Settlements range from modern metropolitan centers, touched by the romance of the Conquistadores and the vigor of the frontier, to sprawling cow towns and Indian pueblos where Hopi and Zuñi have lived for centuries amid what appears to be a barren land. Besides the scenic wonders and historic places of interest, there is lots to see and do. There are Indian ceremonials where tribal dancers in resplendent costume perform primitive dancers, thrilling rodeos and local festivals either of Spanish or Old West origin. Resort centers with dude ranches or more luxurious guest ranches provide varied entertainment with horseback trips and outdoor life, while the bigger cities offer more sophisticated pleasures. Ski slopes on the mountains of Nevada and northern Arizona are only a few hours drive from warm, sun-drenched valleys. You will want to bring back some of the authentic handicraft items; Navajo rugs and blankets, Hopi and Zuñi inlaid jewelry, Hopi Kachina dolls, Indian pottery and beadwork. There are also Mexican hand-tooled leather work, and southwest apparel that is both comfortable and distinctive. Don't miss the pleasures of an outdoor barbecue or overlook sampling Indian and Mexican foods.

NEW MEXICO

First visited by white man in the expeditions of Spanish explorers seeking the Seven Cities of Cibolá. They did not find the cities of gold but they did establish a vast empire for Spain. SANTA FE, capital of the state, was the seat of government for this empire ten years before the landing of the Pilgrims. The Palace of Governors, erected in 1610, served the royal governors and their successors for three centuries. The low adobe structure has been restored to its original appearance. Santa Fe's churches are excellent examples of Spanish-American ecclesiastical art and architecture, with the Mission of San Miguel de Santa Fe probably the most interesting. The Museum of Navajo Ceremonial Art contains a complete collection of Navajo sand paintings. . . . TAOS, seventy miles to the north, is actually three separate villages — the old Indian pueblo of San Geronimo de Taos dating from the 16th century, the farming section, Ranchos de Taos, with the massive-walled Mission of St. Francis of Assisi, and the artist colony of Don Fernando de Taos. . . . In northwest New Mexico are several ruins of ancient Indian civilizations which reached their zenith around 1100 A. D. The Indian villages contained terraced buildings with as many as 1,200 rooms. The larger and more impressive are to be seen at Pueblo Bonita in Chaco Canyon National Monument and Aztec Ruins National Monument. Complex masonry walls and underground ceremonial chambers or kivas built by Stone-Age architects and masons remind visitors of the similar ancient ruins in Egypt and Asia Minor. . . . ALBUQUERQUE, southwest of Santa Fe, is one of the fastest growing cities of the Southwest. The Old Town of early Albuquerque, founded in 1706, displays the characteristic traits of the Spanish settlements with flat-footed adobe buildings. The pueblo architecture of the University of New Mexico in the new city is in keeping with that early style. From Albuquerque it is only a short drive to reach neighboring Indian pueblos of Jemez, Zia, Laguna and others. At the Acoma Pueblo, 60 miles west of the city, 1000-odd members of the Acoma tribe live atop the 357-foot sandstone tableland reached only by foot trail. The Indians were fierce in defending their homeland against the Spanish, yet aided the padres in building the imposing Church of San Esteban Rey atop the mesa. All the materials for the church and burial grounds had to be carried on the backs of the Indians up the steep rock-cut trail. . . . Further west Highway 66 leads to the city of GALLUP where the Inter-Tribal Indian Ceremonial is held every year in mid-August. The colorful ceremonial brings thousands of Indians from all over the southwest to display their native dances: The Taos perform the Hoop, Deer and Horsetail Dances; the Hopis, the Butterfly Dances; Zuñi, the Eagle Dance, and so on during the

An endless, rippling river of
White Sands in New Mexico
New Mexico State
Tourist Bureau

four-day festival. Parades, an all-Indian rodeo and riding contests round out the program. Indian artisans display the finest specimens of pottery, silver jewelry, weaving and other handicrafts. You may watch Navajo artists making sand paintings, a strange ritual art in which different colored sands are arranged in stylized paintings. . . . To the south of Gallup is El Moro or Inscription Rock, a sandstone mesa where interesting footnotes to history have been recorded. Travelers beginning with Don Juan Onate, returning from the Gulf of California in 1605, have left their inscriptions on the rock. . . . In southern New Mexico near ALAMOGORDO is White Sands National Monument. The shifting sands create an endless pattern of rippling beauty as far as the eye can see. The sands are actually deposits of gypsum piled into great dunes, ranging from 10 to 60 feet high. . . . To the southeast is one of the most impressive sights of the region — Carlsbad Caverns. Here in bottomless passageways is a weird kingdom which took nature 60 million years to fashion. The main corridor of the caverns is immense but it does not prepare the visitors for the beauty of the chambers beyond. These chambers — the Green Lake Room, King's Palace and Queen's Chamber—are unparalleled in their splendor. Stone draperies give a truly regal touch to the rooms. In the Big Room, the largest open space found underground anywhere in the world, are intricate formations; giant pinnacles reach up to meet their mirrored image hanging from the ceiling; "lily-pads" of stone grow from pools of water. Delicate tints of minerals in the rocks add to the spectacle. Another attraction of Carlsbad Caverns is to stand watch in the

summer evening as millions of bats swarm from the entrance arch, spiral upward and disappear for a night's foraging. At dawn they return to a cavern not open to the public, to hang upside down deep within the earth.

ARIZONA

The nation's youngest state has an invaluable resource in her sunny, dry climate. It has made Arizona a new-found vacationland. TUCSON, major city of Southern Arizona, is popular with winter visitors who come to enjoy the exhilarating winter climate. Adobe buildings with flowered patios, reminiscent of the days when Tucson was a Spanish town, still grace parts of the town but the atmosphere is more closely allied to the American West. The annual celebration is the Fiesta de los Vaqueros, one of the top events of the championship rodeo circuit. The University of Arizona is famous for its work in archaeology and anthropology. About seven miles south of the city is San Xavier Mission, a particularly distinguished example of mission art and architecture with a carved façade, twin towers supported by flying buttresses and a richly decorated interior. An attraction near Tucson is Saguaro National Monument, seventeen miles east of the city. The tract covers a weird leafless forest of fluted giant cacti, the saguaro. Here the amazing desert giants grow in grotesque shapes above typical Sonoran desert vegetation surrounded by the scarred and furrowed slopes of three mountain ranges. Spectacular at any season, the forest is especially beautiful in May when the towering columns are crowned with creamy-white blossoms which later turn to brilliant scarlet, edible fruits. . . . TOMBSTONE, southeast of

Tucson, was one of the wildest mining towns of the West in the 1880's. Rich silver strikes like those at Lucky Cuss and Good-enough Mines attracted miners from all over. Along with them came the gamblers, dance-hall girls, gunmen and other questionable persons who wished to join in the spoils. After a decade of boom, Tombstone became almost a ghost town when flooding ended mine operations. Today the town is curious as a relic of the roaring West. Points of interest are the **Bird Cage Theater**, former variety theater, gambling establishment and bar, now a museum and restaurant, and **Boothill Graveyard,** where notorious gunmen were buried, as the name implies, "with their boots on." . . . The capital of Arizona, **PHOENIX,** lies in the center of the fertile Salt River Valley. The name of the city is appropriate, for like the legendary phoenix bird it rose from the ashes of an ancient city. The warm, sunny climate makes Phoenix a popular winter resort area and also a rich agricultural center. Vacationists come to enjoy the desert and mountain country, staying either at one of the more luxurious inns complete with swimming pools and elegant furnishings, or at one of the more modest dude ranches where the accent is on a more rugged outdoor life. During the winter season there are a succession of local celebrations — a championship rodeo in February, the Fiesta del Sol in March and the Pioneer Reunion in April. An interesting side trip from Phoenix is the scenic drive along the **Apache Trail,** State Highway 88, following the winding Salt River, with deep chasms and man-made lakes. . . . To the north is **FLAGSTAFF,** hub of the many marvels of Northern Arizona. The city not only meets the needs of travelers but also the Hopi and Navajo Indians from nearby reservations. The normal influx of vistors is swelled during the **Indian Pow Wow** every July 4th when 20 tribal nations from seven states gather for parades and ceremonial dances. The exhibit of Indian art in the **Museum of Northern Arizona** and **Lowell Observatory** are additional local attractions. About 15 miles northwest of the city, the **Arizona Snow Bowl** in the high San Francisco Peaks can offer seasonal skiing with a ski-tow, trails and ski-lodge. For the sights around Flagstaff the list is both long and varied. Beginning in the south there is what many persons consider the most

beautiful canyon in Arizona — **Oak Creek Canyon.** Not as well known as Grand Canyon, it is still a magnificent spectacle; you can drive through it on Highway 89A following the winding creek past green forests set against 2000-foot red-stone canyon walls. You will pass scenery that you may recognize, for many movies have been filmed here. Special features are **Tuzigoot National Monument,** an ancient Indian pueblo, and nearby **Montezuma Castle,** a well-preserved adobe ruin perched high in a canyon wall. Closer to Flagstaff to the southeast are the **Walnut Canyon Cliff Dwellings** and **Meteor Crater** where an interplanetary missile crashed into the earth, leaving a mile-wide crater. A drive to the north will bring you to **Sunset Crater National Monument,** a 1000-foot-high volcanic cinder cone whose pock-marked summit is tinted with hues of dull red and orange. Further north are the **Wupatki Ruins** which date from the 12th century. Here, too, is the celebrated **Painted Desert,** a magnificent stretch of escarpments, mesas, flat buttes and dunes, all delicately shaded by nature in pastel colors. It is best seen in the early morning light when the formations come to life as the sun rises in the east. The desert actually covers some 300 miles of northeast Arizona so they may be seen at other vantage points. The **Petrified Forest,** just east of **HOL-BROOK,** combines the natural wonders of the world's largest group of petrified wood along with the fantastic landscape of the Painted Desert. . . . Nothing you have read or heard will quite prepare you for the spectacle of the **Grand Canyon.** This titanic gorge, 4 to 18 miles wide and over 200 miles long, has been carved by the mighty Colorado River. Standing on the **South Rim** as the sun comes up one sees the distant caps of the opposite rim take shape and become alive with color. Later, as the sun rises mountains emerge from the purple gloom of the canyon. Throughout the day the changing light causes the whole panorama to slowly alter, giving varying impressions, each succeeding one different than the last. Views alone are not all there is to the Grand Canyon. There is the interesting story of how it all came about: the millions of years of building that created the plateau and the slow unrelenting erosion — the cutting of the tremendous chasms which still goes on. Fascinating, also, is the history of the dis-

Fantastic, altar-shaped rocks
in Monument Valley
Arizona Highways

covery by the Spanish and the story of
the first trip down the roaring Colorado
made by Major J. W. Powell and his party.
No trip to the Canyon is complete without
a journey to the bottom of the gorge. As
you descend on muleback over **Bright
Angel** or **Kaibab Trail** the chapters of
geologic history unfold until you reach
the turbulent river. You can cross the
gorge to the North Rim for an overnight
stay, returning the next day. . . . Of a
smaller scale but no less impressive is the
Canyon de Chelly National Monument in
the Indian country of northeast Arizona.
The canyon contains a number of cliff
dwellings, located in natural crevices, high
in smooth, massive, red-sand-stone canyon
walls. **White House Ruins** is particularly
impressive, set like a jewel in the sculptured, brilliantly colored rock wall.

NEVADA

Predominantly a mining state in high,
sunny land of the Great Basin region,
her history and development can be read
in the discovery of rich veins of gold,
silver and copper which created boom
towns overnight. But one of the richest
strikes to enliven the interest of the nation
is not in silver and gold but in legalized
gambling. **LAS VEGAS** is presently undergoing the biggest boom that Nevada has
seen since the silver strikes of Comstock
Lode. Gambling exists elsewhere in the
state but not done up in such a bright
package. Swank million-dollar hotel establishments like the Desert Inn and the
Sands, the Sahara and Flamingo line a
section called "the Strip," on the outskirts

of town. Both "the Strip" and downtown
area offer the best in big-time entertainers from Broadway, Hollywood and
television, along with deluxe accommodations and fine foods, in addition to high-
stake gambling. The idea of combining
hotel, night club and gambling casino all
into one is not new, for the old mining
boom towns had such establishments in
cruder versions. The appeal is the same,
however, and there is no place in America
quite like it. It is a 24-hour festival, exciting and brightly lit, capturing the fancy
of blasé Hollywood stars and gray-haired
retired schoolteachers alike. . . . Only 30
miles from Las Vegas is **Hoover Dam**, an
engineering marvel that harnesses the
mighty Colorado River. You can drive
along the crest of the giant dam as well
as visit the powerhouses at the base which
supply electricity for three states. Lake
Mead is a consequence of Hoover Dam.
The Colorado bulges out behind the concrete structure to form a broad expanse of
water 113 miles long, providing excellent
recreational facilities as well as water for
the parched soils of the desert. To the
west of Lake Mead in the **Valley of Fire
State Park** red sandstones have been wind-
whipped and honeycombed into fantastic
shapes and near animal-like forms. For
those visiting the Las Vegas area who
prefer mountain terrain there is the
Charleston Peak area with an 11,910-foot
peak, 35 miles west of the city. Ski slopes
attract visitors during the winter and high
recreation grounds offer respite from the
noonday desert sun in the summer. . . .

To reach western Nevada, you will have to traverse basin country marked by a series of north-south jagged mountain ranges. In between are valleys where herds of white-faced cattle graze on open ranges like the 25,000-acre-spread of Bing Crosby's near **ELKO**. Other times the open country is almost desert, barren except for sagebrush and mesquite. The Las Vegas Bombing and Gunnery Range in southeast Nevada is in country like this. Here in a large restricted area, the Atomic Energy Commission carries out nuclear experiments. . . . In the southwest corner of Nevada are grouped a number of points of interest. **RENO** regards itself as "the

in the '70's the town had no equal in the West for making millionaires and for making pleasure. Bret Harte and Mark Twain once worked for the town's newspaper; their later stories are often based on the wild doings of this fabulous city now almost a ghost town. Still standing are **Pipers Opera House** where audiences acclaimed Edwin Booth and Sarah Bernhardt; the **Bucket of Blood Saloon** and the **Crystal Bar**, survivors from over 100 saloons of more prosperous days. . . . North of Reno the turquoise-blue **Lake Pyramid** lies in a desert-mountain setting. The lake takes its name from the 475-foot tufa rock pyramid that juts out of the deep-blue

Nature provides her most inspiring setting for spectacular, man-made Hoover Dam.
TWA-Trans World Airlines

Biggest Little City in the World." It is little in population, numbering around 33,000 even if you count those temporary citizens awaiting divorce decrees. It does have a big-city atmosphere, however. Like Las Vegas, its brightly lighted downtown section is jammed with gambling casinos and night clubs. In the daylight the city reveals itself as a neat, clean city with parks along the Truckee River and an excellent school in the **University of Nevada**. Just 20 miles from Reno is historic **VIRGINIA CITY**, site of the richest silver strike ever made in the world — the famed Comstock Lode. Almost a billion dollars in precious metals were mined before the lode was virtually exhausted. At its zenith

waters. **Anaho Island** is a bird sanctuary for thousands of pelicans, sea gulls and cormorants. Nevada's second largest lake, **Lake Tahoe**, is shared with California. It is south of Reno in the eastern Sierra Nevada Mountains and is one of the most beautiful. Deep blue in color, it is surrounded on all sides by snow-capped peaks and evergreen forests. A scenic drive encircles the lake and a number of uncrowded resort centers like **TAHOE CITY** and **MEEKS BAY** dot the shore. Both sides of the lake are popular with skiers. Double chair-lifts at Squaw Valley in California and at **Reno Ski Bowl** in Nevada carry snow enthusiasts to high altitudes where the snow lasts for half the year.

West North Central States

The states included in this section are a part of the world's richest larder — one vast productive area capable of feeding the nation and peoples in other lands as well. Travelers crossing the agriculture belt will find broad fields, blue skies with white scudding clouds bringing a promise of needed rain, red barns and white farm houses in seas of tall corn and ripening wheat. To the west and north the corn fields give way to wheat and then the drier range land where cattle graze. Even the larger cities have their roots in the soil; most of the talk is about crops, weather, the price of cattle, for their lives depend on the prosperity of the farms. This rich country was bought from the French under the Louisiana Purchase in 1803. The Americans didn't even know what they bought so they sent an expedition under Lewis and Clark to explore the country. Their journey up the Missouri and over the Rockies to the West Coast is a New World saga. Here, forested hill regions, such as the Ozarks and Black Hills, provide ample rugged country of scenic beauty. Flat-topped mesa and buttes in warm colors relieve the monotony of the plains. The northern wilderness and lake country, especially in Minnesota, provide virgin country, excellent for fishing and hunting and outdoor activities. The history is tied closely to the development of the West.

Regional foods include dishes that early settlers and frontier men lived on; Dakota and Buffalo steak, country hams, fried catfish, hoe cakes (cornmeal), Minnesota wildfowl with wild rice, Squaw dish (omelet with bacon, eggs and corn), venison shoulder and Buffalo berry jelly.

MISSOURI

The crossroads city of **ST. LOUIS** (856,796) lies along the crescent-shaped bend in the Mississippi River just south of the junction of the Missouri River. It was named in honor of the French Monarch, Louis IX. The river town began as a fur-trading post in 1763 and has grown into one of the leading cities of the nation. The old city on the banks of the river is being developed under federal government auspices and includes **The Old Rock House**, the city's oldest building. A few blocks away is the **Old Cathedral**, a yellowed limestone edifice over 100 years old on the site of the first church in St. Louis.

The **Old Courthouse**, nearby, has a slave block in one entrance. Opposite the Union Station is the fountain, "**The Meeting of the Waters**", by Carl Milles. The most important recreational and cultural center for the city is 1400-acre **Forest Park**, west of the downtown area. It includes, in addition to the usual recreational facilities, the **Jefferson Memorial**, with Jefferson manuscripts and relics, and Charles Lindbergh's trophies. The St. Louis Zoo, also in the park, has a notable feature in the Chimpanzee Circus. Cultural attractions in Forest Park are the **Art Museum**, one of America's finest, with a wide collection of paintings and other art work and the **Municipal Opera Theater**, outdoor amphitheater which holds nightly summer performances. Shaw's Garden on the south side of town, is both unique and internationally famous, has remarkable plant exhibits ranging from water lilies and rare orchids to cactus and plant curiosities that are Botanic freaks. At the Anheuser-Busch Breweries, to the east, one can see the age-old process of brewing beer in its most up-to-date fashion and sample the final product. Mississippi River cruises are available aboard one of the regular packet steamers or on the modern streamlined excursion steamer the S.S. Admiral. . . . Perhaps not as famous as St. Louis but well-known to all readers of "Tom Sawyer" by Mark Twain is the Mississippi river town of **HANNIBAL**. Mark Twain's boyhood home is still there along with the white-washed fence, Becky Thatcher's house and other landmarks which appear in Twain's writing. . . . **COLUMBIA**, in the Daniel Boone country west of St. Louis, is the seat of the **University of Missouri**, known for its School of Journalism. . . . **JEFFERSON CITY** in central Missouri is located on the bluffs above the Missouri River, providing a splendid setting for the **State Capitol**. The walls of the House lounge are decorated with farm murals by Thomas Hart Benton. . . . Southwest from here is the dragon-shaped **Lake of the Ozarks**, created by the damming of the Osage River. Whole towns were submerged in the waters of the new lake making a weird lake bottom for fishermen and swimmers. The lake with its many coves and turns has a shore line of over a thousand miles so there is ample room for the vacationists. The **Ozark Hills**

South Dakota's enchanted
Badlands
Standard Oil Co. of N.J.

region which covers southwest Missouri and parts of neighboring states are famous for their scenic beauty of gentle rolling hills and rugged rock promentories above clear streams, of redbud and dogwood trees along quiet country roads. Fishing is excellent; an Ozark specialty is float fishing on James, White and other rivers. Lake Taneycomo and Bull Shoals Lake are noted for fishing and water sports. . . . On the eastern edge of the Ozarks, the Big Springs country is another attraction. Here tremendous volumes of water pour forth from moss-covered rocks. One of the longest, in Big Springs State Park near VANBUREN, flows at a rate of over half a billion gallons per day. The Ozark area is populated with hill folk who are descendants of Scotch-English pioneers from the East. They have preserved many of the slowly dying folk crafts and customs; their Saturday night square dances are in the old traditions with untiring "callers" and "fiddlers," and are not encumbered with electric guitars or Brooklyn cowboys. . . . In western Missouri KANSAS CITY (456,-622) used to be a wild outfitting post for wagon trains heading west over the Santa Fe and Oregon Trails. Today it is a key transportation center, the gateway to the West and Southwest for 12 trunk-line railroads, Trans World Airlines and five other major airlines. It is also a leading livestock and grain market as is evident from massive grain elevators and sprawling stockyards on the edge of the city; the annual stock shows draw thousands of exhibitors and spectators. Swope Park, third largest municipal playground in the nation, con-

tains the outdoor Starlight Theater, where nightly summer musicals are given, a zoo, golf courses and other recreation facilities. William Rockhill Nelson Art Gallery is a handsome building housing an excellent Chinese art collection. Opposite Union Station, with its great 8-story-high lobby, stands Liberty War Memorial which affords a wide view of the city from its tall shaft; a museum of war relics is housed in the base of the building. Country Club District is one of the beauty spots of the city; it is a model for city planning with inviting homes, apartment houses and an unusual shopping center. Kansas City has its own philharmonic orchestra and recently acquired a major-league baseball team, the Athletics. . . . ST. JOSEPH to the north was the starting point for the Pony Express Riders in the early days of the West.

KANSAS

Although Kansas may be without the rugged grandeur of mountain ranges or thrilling seascapes it does possess a pastoral beauty that can be just as enthralling – golden wheat fields stretching as far as the eye can see, the vast apple orchards of northeast Kansas in full bloom and tall grain elevators and silos serving as skyscrapers above the checkerboard pattern of the fields. The whirring harvester combines moving across the fields of ripened wheat are fascinating to watch. Visitors interested in history will find reminders of the days when the state was called "Bleeding Kansas," the scene of undeclared civil war over the slavery question. Kansas was also a part of the Wild West when differences of opinion were too often settled by the quickest draw.

In eastern Kansas, LEAVENWORTH, originally a frontier post to protect wagon trains, is now the U. S. Army's largest military post. A Command and General Staff School is maintained here as well as a federal penitentiary. To the south, KANSAS CITY (129,553) (often confused with Kansas City, Missouri) is a major stockyard center. Tours of the meat packing plants are available. . . . At TOPEKA, further west, the State Capitol is famous for the John Steuart Curry murals of abolitionist John Brown. In Gage Park are two attractions, the Reinisch Gardens and the Old Settlers Memorial Cabin. . . . John Brown lived at OSAWATOMIE to the south. The simple home, now part of a state park, served as a station on the "Underground Railway" for fugitive slaves. . . . ABILENE was once a roaring cowboy town, the northern terminus of the cattle drives over the Chisholm Trail. Today it is best known as the boyhood home of President Eisenhower. The Eisenhower house has been set aside as a museum. West of Abilene, the area around SALINA and MINNEAPOLIS, are several weird rock foundations. . . . Lake Kanopolis in central Kansas is one of several artificial lakes created by damming the rivers of Kansas, thus making up for nature's omissions. . . . DODGE CITY in the western part of the state was once the cowboy capital of the world. The stories and legends of its wilder days have given yeoman service to the "Westerns" of Hollywood. Boothill near the City Hall was once the burial ground for victims of gun fights. Burials were often quick and unceremonious, the deceased was interred wrapped in a blanket, his boots still on.

NEBRASKA

In the early pioneer days of the nation the principal route of the westward movement was across Nebraska to the passes in the Rocky Mountains. Through the great Platte River Valley passed Astorian fur traders seeking the pelts of the northwest. Later the settlers moved along this route following the Mormon and Oregon Trails. With the passage of the Homestead Act of 1863, giving free land to those who would work it, the land boom was on. Today Homestead National Monument, near BEATRICE in southeast Nebraska, encloses the 160-acre claim of Union soldier Daniel Freeman. Some of the original buildings have been restored. . . . An important stop for wagoneers heading west in those early days was the town of OMAHA on the Missouri River. The Union Pacific Museum commemorates the first transcontinental railroad which commenced from that city. Also in Omaha is the Joslyn Memorial, a beautiful marble building housing notable exhibits of folk art and paintings. . . . About ten miles west of Omaha is Father Flanagan's Boy's Town, a novel social undertaking for homeless boys. The project which covers 1200 acres is actually an incorporated village complete with post office, shops and farms, most of which are managed by the boys themselves. . . . The skyline of LINCOLN, to the southwest is dominated by the white stone shaft of the modern State Capitol Building. The 400-foot buttressed tower, a pleasing departure from conventional capitol buildings, is crowned with a gold glazed-tile dome and bronze statue of the Sower, symbol of the plains. In the wing of the building the State Historical Museum includes Indian and pioneer relics and a large gun collection. On the University of Nebraska campus is located the Nebraska State Museum. Two collections make this museum of interest to visitors. The Art Collection contains a good cross-section of paintings of American artists. The second is the Hall of Elephants in the science section, where there is a large collection of fossil and mounted elephants, including a large mammoth. . . . At HASTINGS, further west, the House of Yesterday is a museum for Western Americana: early vehicles, weapons and pioneer furnishings. . . . In western Nebraska Scotts Bluff National Monument is a landmark of the great plains. It is a huge sandstone tableland towering above the Oregon Trail. A paved road leads to the summit which offers a sweeping view of the North Platte Valley. A museum at the Administration headquarters illuminates the history of the region with paintings and dioramas of buffalo hunting and the westward migration.

SOUTH DAKOTA

The Black Hills of western South Dakota are under-valued by the name. In reality they are mountains, highest in the United States east of the Rockies. From the surrounding prairies and plains they appear black against the distant skyline, which on closer approach turns to purple and soon to the deep green of pine and spruce which clothe them. In the southern part of the Black Hills, **Wind Cave National Park** is noted for the beautiful box-formed crystals of calcite left in the caves when the limestone rock dissolved. The largest herd of American Bison on the continent roams in **Custer State Park**. Further north, in the heart of the Black Hills, **Needles Highway** winds past granite monoliths hundreds of feet high. A popular attraction of the Black Hills is the **Mount Rushmore National Memorial** where the faces of Washington, Jefferson, Theodore Roosevelt and Lincoln have been carved into the side of a granite mountain. The scale of this monumental sculpture by Gutzon Borglum is in the proportions of a man 465 feet tall. The work of blasting away thousands of tons of granite took 14 years. Black Hills' city of **LEAD**, one of the original old gold-rush towns, is the site of the **Homestake Mine**, the nation's principal source for the precious metal. Guided tours of the surface workings in the summer show how tons of ore are processed for a few ounces of gold. Nearby **DEADWOOD**, wild-West town of truth and dime-novel fiction — once claimed as residents such heroes as Wild Bill Hickock and Calamity Jane. These colorful figures of the West have long been dead, buried in the cemetery on the hill above town, but they are remembered in the "Days of '76" celebration held in Deadwood. At **SPEARFISH** the famed **Black Hills Passion Play** presents the immortal story of the last days of Christ. On the east of the Hills, at

RAPID CITY, the South Dakota School of Mines has an excellent Geology Museum displaying giant fishes and reptiles from the prehistoric sea that once covered the Dakotas. On a hill outside of town are huge stone statues of antediluvian monsters. An Indian Museum and Range Days rodeo are other attractions. . . . The **Badlands National Monument** 60 miles east of the Black Hills are a startling contrast to the cool forest, sparkling streams of the Hills. Desolate, arid, eerie — almost devoid of vegetation the Badlands cover a wasteland of 640,000 acres. In early morning or late afternoon jagged peaks, turrets, spires and steep canyons of colored ocean sediments create an unbelievable world that well could be Dante's *Inferno*.

NORTH DAKOTA

The **Badlands** of western North Dakota, not to be confused with those in South Dakota, consist of numerous flat-topped buttes and mesas cut by erosion into fantastic shapes. The best scenic views of the Badlands can be seen at **Theodore Roosevelt National Memorial Park**, with a north unit near **WATFORD CITY** and a south unit which includes a petrified forest at **MEDORA**. Teddy Roosevelt came to the area for his health and once operated the **Elkhorn Ranch** north of Medora. Also in Medora is the **De Mores Historic Site**, a 28-room chateau museum of a French nobleman who made a fortune in cattle during the time of Roosevelt. . . . **BISMARCK**, in the center of the state, has for its **State Capitol Building** a tall modern structure that is a relief from the usual imitation of the national capitol. The state's **Historical Society Museum** has a fine col-

A hushed, snow-blanketed wheat farm, with shelter belt, in the Red River Valley near Hatton, North Dakota
Standard Oil Co. of N.J.

lection of relics of the early pioneer days. Nearby **Fort Lincoln State Park** in **MAN-DAN** is the site of the old infantry and cavalry posts from where Gen. Custer left to meet the Sioux in his "last stand" at Little Big Horn; the old fort has been reconstructed along with several Indian earth lodges. To the south, **Standing Rock Indian Reservation** includes the site of Sitting Bull's grave at **FORT YATES**. . . . Upstream from Bismarck, on the Missouri River, U. S. Army Engineers are completing **Garrison Dam**, the largest earth-filled dam in the world. . . . On the Canadian boundary the **International Peace Gardens** commemorate a hundred years of peace between the United States and Canada. Near the Peace Gardens are **Souris National Migratory Bird Refuge**, to the west, and **Turtle Mountain Indian Reservation**, to the east. The Sun Dance performed by Chippewa Indians attracts visitors every June. . . . **Devils Lake**, the state's largest, is a recreational center with water sports, camping and picnic grounds.

MINNESOTA

The 10,000 sparkling blue lakes and towering pine forests make Minnesota a vacation paradise for sportsmen and vacationists that is hard to surpass. Legend has it that the thousands of lakes were caused by the footprints of Paul Bunyan, giant lumberman whose exploits are a fascinating part of American folklore. At **BEM-IDJI**, fishing and hunting center, the **Paul Bunyan Water Carnival** celebrates the end of the summer season. Giant statues of Bunyan and his blue ox "Babe" stand on the town lake shore. **BRAINERD**, to the south, also claims Paul Bunyan as a native product and holds an annual colorful pageant in his name. . . . **Itasca State Park**, southwest of Bemidji, is a pleasant vacation spot with lakes, outdoor recreational facilities, plenty of wild life and the source of the Mississippi River. . . . The gigantic, awe-inspiring open-pit iron mines near **HIBBING** are interesting to visit. The nation's largest iron-ore deposits, the three ranges Mesabi, Vermilion and Cuyana, send a continuous stream of loaded freight trains to the ore ports on Lake Superior. . . . A large part of the northeast Minnesota forest has been set aside in the **Superior National Forest**. Canoe trips through this wilderness prove to be a rewarding experience for modern-day "voyageurs," properly outfitted to meet the demands of days of paddling and portage over miles of uninhabited country. Canoe trips start from towns on the north shore of Lake Superior, Hovland, Grand Marais and Tofte, or inland at Tower or Ely. Detailed information and maps can be obtained from forest and travel organizations at Duluth. The **North Shore Drive** from Duluth to the Canadian border is a scenic highway where on one side are the horizon blue waters of Lake Superior with low silhouetted ore boats and fishing craft. High on the other side towers the forests of **Misquah Hills** through which tumble countless streams. . . . **DULUTH** serves as the gateway to the vacation country of northeast Minnesota but is economically more important as a transshipment point for grain and iron ore. The **Aerial Lift Bridge** spanning the ship-canal entrance to Duluth Harbor is an attraction, along with loading operations on the piers. . . . Minneapolis and St. Paul, Minnesota's twin cities to the south, are friendly rivals on the Mississippi River. Both cities have pleasant residential areas among crystal lakes, numerous parks and tree-lined boulevards. **ST. PAUL** (311,349) has a slight advantage as the State Capital. Key attractions are the **Capitol**, **Como Park** and **Indian God of Peace** statue in City Hall. The nine-day **Winter Carnival** held every year is climaxed by a firework display on the ramparts of a medieval ice castle built in Como Park. . . . **MINNEAPOLIS** (521,-718) has in the way of scenic views the "**Grand Rounds**," 61 miles of boulevards encircling the city, **Minnehaha Falls** and the **Falls of St. Anthony**. The city's cultural attractions are extensive: the **Walker Art Galleries**, emphasizing modern art; **Minneapolis Institute of Art**, with a well-balanced collection of traditional art, and the **University of Minnesota Art Gallery**. Northrup Auditorium is the concert hall for the **Minneapolis Symphony Orchestra**, one of the five top-most symphony orchestras in the nation. In July the famous Aquatennial takes over the city with colorful parades, water shows and Mardi Gras atmosphere. . . . Northeast of the Twin Cities the St. Croix River threads its way through striking rock cliffs at the **Dalles of the St. Croix**. Further south is another scenic part of Minnesota that has become famous through the poem of Longfellow — that part of the Mississippi called "Hiawatha Valley." The famous **Mayo Clinic**, known the world over for medical research and treatment facilities, is at **ROCHESTER** in southeast Minnesota.

IOWA

This land of plenty is a state which although predominantly agricultural is not without points of interest. In eastern Iowa, near **MC GREGOR**, there are scenic river bluff views and lotus-filled bayous. The **Pikes Peak** area has colored sand cliffs and several Indian effigy mounds. There are many Iowa State Parks which provide camping and fishing facilities along stocked streams and lakes. East of **CEDAR**

shops of German design are of interest. German-style foods such as hearth-baked breads, Amana smoked hams and kuchen or coffeecake are a specialty. . . . Along the highways near **TAMA** one can purchase Indian handicrafts such as bead work and basket work skillfully made by Sac and Fox Indians from the nearby reservations. **DES MOINES** in the center of the state is the state capital and perhaps the farm capital of the nation. The **Iowa State Fair** held here is one of the world's premier agricultural expositions. Farmers from Iowa and neighboring states bring in

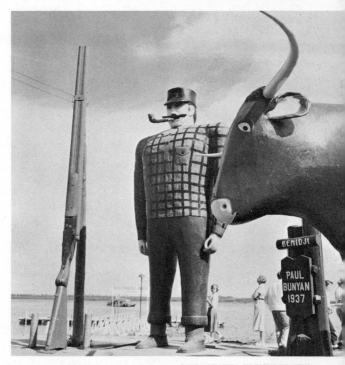

This statue of Paul Bunyan and Babe, his Blue Ox, stands on the shore of Lake Bemidji, for Minnesotans claim the legendary lumberman as a native son

Minnesota Department of Business Development

RAPIDS is **Palisades-Kepler Park** with limestone cliffs along the Cedar River. . . . To the west of Cedar Rapids are the **Amana Villages,** established by a religious sect of German immigrants in 1855. The original settlement was a communal enterprise and remained so for about 70 years. The seven villages are now organized in a joint stock corporation with less stringent rules over its members. The products of the villages include wool blankets and furniture of early-American design, noted for their craftsmanship, farm products and refrigerators. The quaint homes and craft

their prize livestock of powerful horses, prima donna steers and giant hogs, and agricultural products of grains, fruits and oversize vegetables; the womenfolk compete for honors in delicious baked goods, jams and preserves. The huge midway of rides and thrills adds a carnival flavor to the proceedings. . . . **Drake University** at Des Moines holds the **Drake Relays,** a national track event. . . . In northeast Iowa are the lake resorts of **Spirit Lake** and **Okoboji Lakes** offering the usual summer sports of swimming, boating, golf and fishing.

East North Central States

The five states that cover this part of the Mid-West, east of the Mississippi and north of the Ohio Rivers, once made up the Northwest Territory, the first step in the expansion from the 13 original states. Long before white men settled here, however, the Indians had utilized the open country for the growing of Indian corn and had hunted game in the forests. The first white visitors were the French explorers followed by the *voyageurs* who came to barter the trinkets of civilization for priceless furs. The English who arrived later to dispute French possession of the fur country were closely followed by a large group of settlers who came from east of the Appalachians, to clear farmlands, build lumber mills and found towns. With the opening of the **Erie Canal** in 1825 the water route to the **Great Lakes** was complete. Immigrants poured westward to the agricultural lands of Ohio, Indiana and Illinois. Loggers came to cut the virgin timber of Michigan and Wisconsin. Finally, in modern times, the pioneers of the automobile industry chose this site to erect the mile-long assembly plants and giant steel mills that have transformed cities like Detroit into major industrial centers.

Visitors will find different kinds of scenery in this region. The Great Lakes give a maritime flavor to the states bordering their shores. In the northern woods and lake country are well-known vacation spots, and while the rich agricultural prairies to the south do not offer the "spectacular vistas" usually described in guide books, they are, nevertheless, impressive to one unfamiliar with the huge rolling farms of the Corn Belt. In late summer the rural and state fairs provide an excellent opportunity to see the agricultural bounty of the land.

For regional specialties in food the accent is both on quality and quantity, for skimping is frowned upon in this land of plenty. So be prepared for local provender in man-sized portions. State specialties are planked Michigan whitefish, Great Lakes perch, fried Michigan smelts, Wisconsin roast goose stuffed with apples and Indiana chicken pot pies. German and other European dishes are special treats to visitors to those communities which have retained an Old-World character. Kassler Rippchen

(smoked rib chop) with Sauerkraut, blood sausage and jellied pigs feet are a few of the dishes available. Special mention should be made of Wisconsin's non-processed cheeses, such as cave-cured natural Cheddars, Camembert, Swiss and Blue.

ILLINOIS

CHICAGO is young as cities go, yet its growth has been phenomenal. It is now the nation's second largest city, with a population of over 3½ million. Originally a small portage town chartered in 1833, the city has become the world's greatest transportation center, the nation's chief market for grain and livestock, and at present its number one convention city. The devastating Chicago Fire of 1871 scarcely interrupted the city's early expansion. The Old Water Tower and the legend of Mrs. O'Leary's cow kicking over a lantern are the only remnants of the older city, for rebuilding proceeded promptly in steel and stone instead of wood. The first skyscraper in the nation rose in the new city. Today the lake front is lined with tall buildings in a striking setting of parks, white beaches and the waters of **Lake Michigan.** The stretch north of the Chicago River is particularly impressive with apartment houses, big hotels and the landmarks of the **Tribune Tower, Palmolive Building** and old "Gothic" **Water Tower.** The center of the downtown section of Chicago is the area called the **"Loop,"** the heart of the city where rapid-transit lines circle (actually loop, hence the name) about the financial and commercial buildings. East of the Loop, in Grant Park, is the **Chicago Institute,** housing one of the world's best collections of 19th- and 20th-century paintings and water colors. Works by El Greco, Goya and Rembrandt are among those displayed. The Institute is also a leading art school of the Middle West. To the north is the famous department store, Marshall Field's, one of the few big stores which maintain regular sightseeing tours for visitors. The showpiece of the building is a dome made of millions of pieces of Tiffany glass. North of the Chicago River (it was made to run backwards for navigation) is the **Merchandise Mart,** a behemoth of a building housing display rooms and offices for busy Chicago mer-

Indianapolis Speedway—site
of the world's greatest auto
races
TWA-Trans World Airlines

chandising firms. **Lincoln Park,** on the northern part of Lake Shore Drive, is an extensive park offering many recreational activities. It includes a **Zoo** of TV fame, golf course, skeet club, beaches, bridle paths and scenic drives. South of the Loop, the **Chicago Board of Trade** rises 44 stories and is topped by a massive statue of the goddess Ceres, an appropriate symbol, since the building houses the world's largest grain market. Here one may witness the buying and selling in the "wheat pit." Actually there is a different pit for each type of grain, which is bought and sold by rapid and mysterious signals. For scientific museums Chicago offers three outstanding institutions, all located on the south side of Grant Park: the **Chicago Museum of Natural History,** the **Shedd Aquarium** and the **Adler Planetarium.** Further south, Michigan Avenue leads to the **University of Chicago,** whose campus covers 100 acres. Most of the buildings are of English Gothic architecture; the **Rockefeller Memorial Chapel** is one of the more notable buildings and houses the world's largest carillon. The University's athletic field, Stagg Field, is an atomic-age landmark; beneath one of its stands (marked by a tablet) the first controlled nuclear chain reaction of atomic energy was demonstrated during World War II. South and southwest are two widely scattered points of special interest: the **Union Stockyards,** center of the meat-packing industry, and **Brookfield Zoo,** officially the Chicago Zoological Gardens, with a fine natural-habitat exhibit of animals.

For the theater and night life, Chicago has regular shows sent out from New York and a long list of supper and night clubs. **Randolph Street** in the Loop area is Chicago's counterpart of New York's Broadway. Nationally known orchestras and entertainers may be found at the big hotels and night clubs scattered throughout the Loop area and near the North Side. Chicago-style Jazz music is undergoing a rebirth at some of the clubs. For those who prefer classical music there are two centers: the **Civic Opera House** and **Orchestra Hall,** both near the Loop. In the way of spectator sports, Chicago offers professional baseball with two major league teams, pro football, hockey, horse racing at five tracks and many amateur sports with several local colleges competing. Programs for all such entertainment are announced in the daily papers.

For regional foods Chicago is best known for its steaks and roasts. Chicago porterhouse or T-bone steak served with home-fried potatoes is a specialty. Fine international cuisine is available at the big hotels and many of the recommended restaurants.

South from Chicago the Illinois River cuts through **Starved Rock State Park,** an area of great scenic beauty: bluffs, gorges and rock formations that were the backdrop for an interesting history of Indians and French explorers. Marquette and Joliet erected a fort here in 1682. The name comes from the legend of a group of Illinois Indians who suffered starvation rather than surrender to a warring band of Iroquois. . . . In northwest Illinois, at **GALENA** in 1860, lived a former Army captain and unsuccessful businessman named Ulysses S. Grant. At the end of the Civil War, Grant returned to Galena a famous general. The pleasant brick home, presented to him by the local citizens, is now preserved as a State Memorial. . . . **Black Hawk State Park,** near **MOLINE,** marks the hunting grounds of the Sac and Fox Indian tribes. Chief Black Hawk, born and raised here, led the Indians in the war against the white settlers that blazed over western Illinois and southern Wisconsin in the 1830's. The **Hauberg Collection** of Indian relics is located at Black

Hawk Watchtower, the highest point in the park. . . . SPRINGFIELD, the State Capital, is well-known as a Lincoln shrine. Lincoln came to Springfield in 1837 as a backwoodsman, with few earthly possessions and with some experience as a member of the State Legislature. Establishing himself in law practice in the new State Capital, he married and became a prominent citizen. In the unpretentious white frame house on Jackson Street, Lincoln and his family spent 17 happy years. The building and furnishings remain today just as they were when Lincoln received the Republican Notification Committee. After Lincoln's assassination, his body was returned in state to Springfield. The Lincoln Tomb, marked by a tall marble shaft, is in Oak Ridge Cemetery. . . . Twenty miles northwest of Springfield is the reconstructed village of New Salem where Lincoln lived his formative years. On the banks of the Sangamon River stand the pioneer cabins, the general store where Lincoln worked, the cooperage, tavern and gristmill. Each building is furnished with authentic heirlooms of the period. Reconstruction was facilitated by the fact that New Salem did not prosper but became a ghost town shortly after Lincoln left, remaining undisturbed until it was rebuilt. . . . Southwest of Springfield, at the junction of the Illinois and Mississippi Rivers, are the wooded hills of Pere Marquette State Park, largest in the state. . . . In southern Illinois, Giant City Park receives its name from the high vertical blocks of stone which are arranged in a street-like pattern to resemble the handiwork of some giant race.

INDIANA

The "Hoosier State," as Indiana is often called, has a homey quality that is one of the state's main assets. Except for the hilly southern part, the state is mostly level prairie country punctuated by occasional low ridges. The physical scenery is restful, in keeping with the natural friendliness of the people. The expression, "grass roots American," usually reserved for use by political orators, can perhaps be best used to characterize the agricultural country of Indiana. . . . In southwest Indiana, at NEW HARMONY on the banks of the Wabash River, an agricultural community was founded in 1814. The Settlement differed from others in that it practiced celibacy and outlawed private property. The set-

tlers were Germans, religious followers of George Rapp, and their colony flourished for ten years. The lands were then sold to the Scottish socialist Robert Owen, who planned a more permanent colony based on communal living without religious overtones. The colony failed but it did establish a reputation for education and for granting equal rights to women. A few relics of these early experiments are to be found in New Harmony. A Golden Rain Festival held every June attracts visitors. . . . To the east, the Nancy Hank's Lincoln Memorial at LINCOLN CITY includes the grave of Lincoln's mother and the log cabin of Lincoln's boyhood. Further east is the village of SANTA CLAUS where it is Christmas all year round; the post office handles many thousands of letters to keep alive the legend of St. Nicholas. A candy castle and toy village are a delight to youngsters. . . . VINCENNES, territorial capital of Indiana and the oldest city in the state, was an important frontier outpost. It was named after the French nobleman Sieur de Vincennes who built the post fort. The French were succeeded by the British and finally by the Americans under George Rogers Clark. The George Rogers Clark Memorial, a Greek-Doric temple, has been erected at the site of the old fort in honor of Clark's achievements. A souvenir of Vincennes territorial capital days remains in the Old Territorial Legislative Hall. The plain exterior and simple country-made furniture reflect the pioneer days. . . . Indiana has its own resort and health spas with three mineral springs at FRENCH LICK, 45 miles east of Vincennes. . . . INDIANAPOLIS is internationally known for the Memorial Day racing classic — the 500-mile race at the Indianapolis Motor Speedway. This grueling race not only provides the thrill of high-speed racing but also acts as a testing ground for new auto improvements; innovations such as balloon tires, rear-vision mirrors and four-wheel brakes were first introduced here. Other attractions in the capital city are the Scottish Rites Cathedral, World War Memorial Plaza and the James Whitcomb Riley Home. . . . In northwest Indiana the large iron and steel works at GARY provide guided tours. One cannot help but be impressed by the giant blast furnaces, towering smokestacks and harbor activity of this industrial area. Indiana Dunes State Park, to the east, is a lake shore vacation spot matching Cape Cod for windswept sand dunes and natural scenery. . . . SOUTH BEND, 30 miles east, is an industrial city famous as the seat of the University of Notre Dame.

OHIO

Once a pioneer state of the Northwest Territory, Ohio is now part of the great industrial heartland of the United States. One of the wooden forts which protected the early settlements has been reconstructed at FORT RECOVERY on the Indiana state line. The fort was originally built by General Anthony Wayne in 1793. . . . At DAYTON, in western Ohio, the Wright Brothers produced the first successful airplane. The U. S. Air Force aeronautical laboratories, at Wright Field, have continued to give Dayton a prominent position in airplane development. Also of interest in Dayton are the Dayton Art Institute, with specialties in Italian and Oriental art work, and Deeds Carillon in Dayton Carillon Park. East of Dayton, at YELLOW SPRINGS, Antioch College is an outstanding school for progressive education where academic study is alternated with practical experience. . . . COLUMBUS, the state capital, is also the seat of Ohio State University, a leading institution of higher learning in the Mid-West. The Ohio State Museum, located on the campus, contains various collections dealing with Ohio history. . . . South of Columbus, near CHILLICOTHE, the Mound City Group National Monument preserves interesting remnants of an age-old Indian civilization. A three-foot embankment encloses a group of 23 burial mounds containing altars and human remains. Little is known of the prehistoric Indians who once inhabited the area. The most impressive of the many Indian mounds in the area is that of Serpent Mound, southwest of Chillicothe. Built of

earth, it curls like an enormous snake for 1300 feet. Its exact purpose is unknown. . . . For recreational facilities, the Hocking Parks, east of Columbus, offer pleasant hiking, camping and picnicking facilities among streams, waterfalls and hardwood forests. . . . The first white settlement in Ohio was founded in eastern Ohio in 1772 at Schoenbrunn Village, now NEW PHIL-ADELPHIA. The settlement has been authentically restored to appear as it did 175 years ago as a Moravian mission colony. MARIETTA, further south on the Ohio, was the first settlement to survive and become a permanent city. . . . AKRON, part of industrial Ohio, is the nation's rubber capital, processing about 40 per cent of the world's raw rubber supply. The International Soap-box Derby held every August at Dayton is the climax of soap-box racing held throughout the country for boys under twelve. . . . On the shores of Lake Erie is CLEVELAND, Ohio's largest city, an iron and steel center and key port for much of the Great Lakes shipping. For an over-all view of the city, visit the Terminal Tower on Public Square. Modern parkways encircling the metropolitan area provide a pleasant motor tour of the harbor, nine city parks and the lake front. At The Mall, in the downtown section, are the Cleveland Museum of Art, the Municipal Stadium and Severance Hall, home of the Cleveland Symphony Orchestra. Cleveland's many national groups unite each year to hold an annual festival of flower displays, folk music and native dancing at Cultural Gardens in Rockefeller Park. . . . At the western end of Lake Erie, Marblehead Peninsula and Lake Erie Islands are popular summer vacation spots. Perry's Victory National Monument on South Bass Island commemorates the naval battle fought off Put-In-Bay during the War of

Mighty Chicago, hub of the nation
TWA-Trans World Airlines

1812. Further west, **TOLEDO'S Museum of Art** has one of the world's best collections of ancient and modern glass along with other art treasures.

MICHIGAN

The State of Michigan is known throughout the world as the producer of that chrome-plated symbol of modern civilization, the automobile. For a look at the production techniques of the modern automotive industry, a visit to **DETROIT** is highly recommended. In a behind-the-scenes tour of any one of the large auto-making corporations one can watch autos take shape as they move along the assembly line. At peak production a glistening new car rolls off under its own power every 20 seconds. Best known of the large assembly lines is probably the **Ford River Rouge Plant** in **DEARBORN**, part of the industrial Detroit area. Tours start at the Fort Rotunda where displays tell the story of the automotive industry. In contrast to the ultramodern features of the Rotunda, pages from an early American book of history are unfolded in the calm and peaceful atmosphere of **Greenfield Village**. An old windmill, a blacksmith shop, replicas of the homes of Stephen Foster, Noah Webster and William McGuffey are reminders of the days when life was a lot simpler than today. Only horsedrawn carriages roll down the streets past the Wright Brothers Cycle Shop where the airplane was born, and past Menlo Park where Thomas Edison gave meaning to electricity. **Edison Institute Museum** contains fascinating collections of early Americana with displays ranging from the silverware of Paul Revere to the trimotored airplane that carried Rear Admiral Byrd across the South Pole in 1928. Among other sights in Detroit are the **Detroit Institute of Arts** and the **Detroit Public Library**, facing one another on Woodward Avenue. **Belle Isle Park**, located in the Detroit River between the U. S. and Canada, is a popular recreation area with picnic grounds, drives, sport events and summer concerts. . . . The cultural center of **Cranbrook**, 20 miles north of Detroit, is made up of six institutions including the well-known **Academy of Arts**. The impressive buildings and grounds include a fountain designed by the late Carl Milles, noted Swedish sculptor. . . . **ANN ARBOR**, west of Detroit, is the seat of the **University of Michigan**, a leading university of the Mid-West. A visit to the campus in the fall would not be complete without witnessing a big-time college football game in **Michigan Stadium**, the largest college-owned stadium in the world. . . . **EAST LANSING** is the home of Michigan's second largest college, **Michigan State University**, with a campus of modern buildings and spacious grounds. . . . The **Furniture Museum** in **GRAND RAPIDS** attracts travelers interested in interior decoration; on display are fine examples of period furniture produced by native craftsmen. . . . May is the time of the **Tulip Festival** at **HOLLAND**, southwest of Grand Rapids. Wooden shoes complete the colorful Dutch costumes worn by local citizens, 90 per cent of whom are of Dutch descent. A scrubbing of Eighth Street marks the beginning of a four-day festival featuring parades, folk dances and huge flower exhibits.

Michigan's 11,000 lakes and its long shore line bordering four of the Great Lakes make the state a water wonderland that is popular with swimmers, fishermen, boating and nature enthusiasts. Inland, sparkling streams such as the Sturgeon, Muskegon and Au Sable echo through cool shaded forests. In the western part of the lower peninsula, the area around Traverse Bay is a popular resort land. **TRAVERSE CITY** is the center of this country of water-skiing, lake-trout trolling and other sports. The **National Cherry Festival**, held when the bay region orchards are brilliant with blossoms, attracts large numbers of visitors annually. . . . The **National Music Camp** at **INTERLOCHEN**, southwest of Traverse City, is host to more than a thousand music students from all over the country. Numerous concerts in country surroundings make up the summer program. . . . For a snow holiday Michigan offers a wide variety of winter sports including ice fishing on the Great Lakes, ice skating at the many rinks and lakes, and skiing on snow-covered slopes. In the lower peninsula no one area holds a dominant position as *the* winter sports center. The possible exception to this may be **CADILLAC**, where the Caberfae skiing facilities are outstanding. . . . In the straits of Mackinac, separating the two peninsulas of Michigan, lies the pleasant, historic island of **Mackinac**. This island resort, which has flown the flags of three nations, was important in the War of 1812 as a fortress and later as the headquarters of John Jacob Astor in the booming fur-trade days. Today the island is a scenic attraction noted for the tree-lined bluffs with huge summer homes — some dating from the gay nineties. Splendid formal gardens and long verandas are special features of the famous **Grand Hotel.** . . . Visitors to the Soo Canal at SAULT STE. MARIE find the passage of the long ore boats through the locks a fascinating experience. Annually, more tonnage passes through this canal than through the Panama and Suez Canals combined. . . . To the west of Sault Ste. Marie, in the wilds of the upper peninsula, the **Tahquamenon Falls** are well worth visiting. The falls are reached by excursion boats from the mouth of the Tahquamenon River or by combination railway and boat tour from SOO JUNCTION. . . . The upper peninsula recreation area centers around MARQUETTE. Good fishing waters provide a variety of species from wall-eyed pike to trout and perch; hunting includes both large and small game with deer and bear as the big prizes. . . . IRON MOUNTAIN on the Wisconsin state line offers to snow enthusiasts two toboggan slides along with ski tows and lodge facilities. . . . **Isle Royal** in Lake Superior is a National Park of untouched wilderness. Since no cars or wheeled vehicles of any sort are allowed on the island, visitors, touring the 44-mile-long island, must follow the trails on foot. The island's beauty lies in the mixed forests of birches and evergreens, the deep fjord-like bays and harbors. Moose as well as coyote, mink, beaver and rabbits are among the fauna of this island sanctuary.

WISCONSIN

The northern gateway to Wisconsin's vast reservoir of recreational areas is SUPERIOR. The city shares an extensive harbor with its "twin," DULUTH, Minnesota. The tall grain elevators and massive iron-ore loading piers give testimony to the great wealth of the region. . . . **Pattison State Park,** ten miles south of Superior, has Wisconsin's highest falls in **Big Manitou Falls** with a sheer drop of 165 feet. . . . Located offshore from BAYFIELD, the **Apostle Islands** are known for their fine fishing waters and scenic red cliffs. . . . Northern Wisconsin lake and woods country is such a large vacationland that detailed descriptions of each fishing and resort location is impossible.

RHINELANDER is a center for the lake district known for its record-size muskellunge fish. WAUSAU, to the south, in the more mountainous country of the **Rib Mountain State Park,** can offer stimulating snow sports of skiing and tobogganing as well as the usual summer fare. . . . GREEN BAY was the site of Wisconsin's first settlement of French fur traders who arrived in 1634. The **Neville Museum** has special exhibits of this early history. The **Roi-Porlier-Tank Cottage** in Tank Park is Wisconsin's oldest standing house. . . . In southern Wisconsin where the Wisconsin River has eroded a channel through the sandstone bedrock are the **Wisconsin Dells,** a scenic attraction capitalizing on the water-sculptured rock formations. Sight-seeing can be done at both the Lower and Upper Dells on foot or in a more leisurely way aboard sightseeing boats. . . . Further south, near BARABOO, the blue waters of **Devils Lake** are surrounded by quartzite bluffs that climb to heights of 600 feet. The whole area is rich in geologic history — the glacier age leaving its trademarks of glacial striae and tumbled rocks. . . . MADISON, Wisconsin's capital, is ideally located on the isthmus between lakes Monona and Mendotta. The **University of Wisconsin** shares the spotlight with the State Capitol to give Madison a lively cultural and intellectual life. The nearby tree-lined lakes give urban Madison a country resort flavor. Picnickers and bathers need not travel far to reach sparkling lakes and shady groves. . . . Wisconsin was settled by immigrants from Europe so that it is not surprising to find various communities retaining an Old-World character. Southwest of Madison is NEW GLARUS, a Swiss settlement famous for cheese and laces and to the west, MINERAL POINT, a mining town, predominantly Cornish. MILWAUKEE, on Lake Michigan, has many Swiss and Germans, expert brewers, hence the famous Milwaukee beers. Milwaukee has other points of interest beside the breweries, however. It has a magnificent lake front, many fine parks, a zoo and two art galleries. The Milwaukee Symphony Orchestra is world famous. . . . To the south is RACINE, where the functional **Johnson Wax Building** will interest students of modern architecture. It was designed by Wisconsin-born Frank Lloyd Wright, pioneer of modern architects.

South Central States

The four states of this section do not form a homogeneous region; in fact, each state is usually quite distinct from its neighbors. Louisiana is French-speaking, bayou country; Arkansas, predominantly mountainous; Oklahoma, Indian territory of the Great Plains, and Texas — well, Texas is different from any place in the world.

LOUISIANA

NEW ORLEANS (570,445), one of the romantic cities of the United States, has always been an exciting place. As the key to the great Mississippi Valley, it has flourished under French, Spanish and American flags. Whether in steamboat era, jazz age or in booming modern commercial days, it has continually attracted visitors looking for something different. The **French Quarter,** or Vieux Carré, is only part of New Orleans but for visitors it has the greatest attraction. The best way to see it is on foot. You walk along narrow streets lined with old shops, cafés and quaint buildings with overhanging iron-trellised balconies. You may wander among buildings with two centuries of romantic history; watch painters trying to capture on canvas the Old World charm of the buildings or take refreshment in a courtyard restaurant bright with flowers and shaded by banana or palm trees. The heart of this quarter is **Jackson Square,** formerly Place d'Armes, where the flag of the United States was first raised over the land of the Louisiana Purchase. The formal ceremony took place nearby in a room in the **Cabildo,** the ancient Spanish government building now a museum. Flanking Jackson Square are the two beautiful block-long **Pontalba Buildings,** excellent examples of Creole architecture and the first American apartment houses. Also on the square is **St. Louis Cathedral,** originally a Spanish provincial church in brick and stucco built in 1794 but now somewhat altered from many changes over the years. The **Old Absinthe House** on Bourbon Street is famous as the one-time headquarters of the pirate Lafitte. The **French Market** with its open displays of fruits, vegetables and other provisions is a traditional New Orleans haunt for early risers and late merrymakers desiring café-au-lait and fresh doughnuts. The **Garden District,** a small area between St. Charles Ave.

and the river, contains ante-bellum mansions with broad verandas, white columns and cast-iron railings almost hidden by palms, live oaks and magnolias. A visit to New Orleans would not be complete without wandering along Bourbon Street at night — festive crowds spill over the sidewalks into the already congested streets and jazz music drifts out from bars and night clubs. This is just a sample of what all of New Orleans is like at **Mardi Gras** time. The pre-Lenten bacchanal begins in late December or early January with masked balls, dances, parties and other festivals. The carnival spirit grows in intensity to break forth in unrestrained enthusiasm with a week of mammoth street parades illuminated at night by flambeaux, dancing and merrymaking climaxing on Mardi Gras Day, Shrove Tuesday, when the Lord of Misrule reigns over the city. Two other New Orleans events are the New Year's Day football classic at the **Sugar Bowl** and a **Spring Fiesta** with garden tours of homes in the Vieux Carré and Garden District. **Lake Pontchartrain** serves as a water-sports playland for the New Orleans area.

New Orleans' high position in the gastronomic world is based on her reputation for Creole cooking, a happy combination of French and Spanish cuisine, plus Negro and Choctaw Indian influences. Creole dishes spiced by piquant herbs are especially inspired in the preparation of the plentiful Louisiana sea foods: shrimp, oysters, crabs, crayfish and pompano. Jambalaya (rice cooked with crab meat, shrimp, ham and sausage), bouillabaisse, Pompano en Papilote are but a few of the more famous dishes. The luxurious restaurant features the spectacle of flaming dishes like crepes suzettes, cherries jubilee and café brûlot. . . . **BATON ROUGE,** Louisiana's capital city, northwest of New Orleans, is marked by the tall capitol building, one of the most impressive in the country. The observation tower offers a splendid panorama of the city and the meandering Mississippi River. Baton Rouge is in the heart of the magnolia country. The heavy fragrance of the snow-white blossoms fills the air from April to June. . . . North of Baton Rouge, near **ST. FRANCISVILLE,** are several ante-bellum homes that are reminiscent of the

The dark, serene beauty of bayou country in Chicot State Park, at Ville Platte, Louisiana

Louisiana State Pub. Photo

Old South. Set in beautiful landscape grounds and gardens these mansions are often masterpieces of design, furnished in the finest European originals. Two of the outstanding homes are **Afton Villa** and **Greenwood**, north of St. Francisville. . . . In the intricate network of bayous west of Baton Rouge is the alluring Acadia land, the home of the descendants of French peasants expelled by the English from Nova Scotia. The Acadians found refuge in the quiet bayou country of French-speaking Louisiana, took up homes, have multiplied and now are an integral part of the tropical bayou country. Their curious patois of French and English, their customs and handicrafts have been preserved for the span of two centuries. The story of the Acadians is familiar to most Amercians through Longfellow's epic poem *Evangeline,* the story of two lovers separated in the banishment. The couple had their real life counterparts in Emmeline Labiche and Louis Arceneaux. Their reunion on the banks of Bayou Teche, contrary to the poem, did not end happily, however. Louis had by that time despaired of finding his love again and had taken another wife. **Evangeline Memorial State Park,** near **ST. MARTINVILLE,** is the locale of the Evangeline story. No finer setting could have been chosen than this shadowy land of deep green and soft grays, where sunlight glances with a golden touch·on stately age-old live oaks and tranquil depths of bayous. . . . South of St. Martinville, **NEW IBERIA** has a fine plantation manor, **The Shadows.** At nearby **AVERY ISLAND** the **McIllhenny Mansion** and **Jungle Gardens** attract visitors in the spring. The island among the salt marshes produces not only rock salt and

peppers for the famous McIllhenny tobacco sauce but is also a snowy egret sanctuary. Other wildlife refuges in the marshy coast of Louisiana such as **Sabine Migratory Waterfowl Refuge** provide a semitropical haven for millions of heron, Canadian geese and wild ducks. Fishing for tarpon and other deep-sea fish is a big-time sport for several coastal centers, **LAKE CHARLES, MORGAN CITY** and others. Inland fishing and hunting for all parts of Louisiana is excellent. . . . **ALEXANDRIA** in central Louisiana is the headquarters for **Kisatchie National Forest,** a natureland of bayous surrounded by forests of virgin pine, cypresses and moss-hung oaks. . . . **SHREVEPORT** plays host to the citizenry from all over for a spring festival "Holiday in Dixie" which includes rodeos, parades and exhibits saluting the advent of spring. The State Fair held here in the fall is also a big event.

ARKANSAS

The green and golden hills of Arkansas begin where the plains country of the Mississippi Valley leaves off. Two separate mountain systems provide Arkansas with unlimited outdoor recreational opportunities with scenic panoramas from 2000-foot peaks, tumbling mountain streams where small mouth bass lie waiting to rise to the bright colors of the angler's fly, and miles of hiking trails in pine-clad mountains. The **Ouachita Mountains** of central Arkansas are popular with fishermen and campers desiring the quiet wilderness of the forested hills. **Petit Jean State Park,** near **MORRILTON,** is just one of the many mountain retreats where scenic beauty is likely to make the sportsman forget his goal of a prize catch. At the edge of the expansive Ouachita National

Forest is the resort and health spa of **Hot Springs National Park**. The health-giving mineral waters were first enjoyed by white men in the expedition of Hernando de Soto but the value of the mineral baths had been known to Indians long before the coming of the Spaniards. In 1832 the U. S. Government established the springs as a national park, the first such park in the nation. Today a visitor can enjoy a single or series of baths at one of the elegant hotel establishments or at one of the spick-and-span government bathhouses. The resort also has round-the-clock entertainment ranging from mountain climbing on foot or on horseback, to the sophisticated pleasure of night clubs. Top-flight fishing and all kinds of water sports can be enjoyed on nearby **Lakes Hamilton, Catherine** and **Ouachita**. In passing, mention should be made of the nation's only diamond mine located to the southwest near **MURFREESBORO**. The admission price allows the visitor to try his luck in finding a rough diamond in the open crater. . . . **LITTLE ROCK**, state capital, has the distinction of owning three capitol buildings. The **Territorial Capitol**, now restored, was constructed in 1820 from hand-hewn oak logs and cypress siding; the reconstruction project includes several frontier homes complete with gardens and furnishings of the period. The **Old State House** is an ante-bellum building of classic design, considered one of the finest in the country. The present **Capitol** is of Arkansas white marble and is known for its photomural rotunda and the mineral and historical exhibits housed in the building. . . . To the southeast in the rice-growing Grand Prairie country, **STUTTGART** is well-known as a duck hunting center. The fall migration of enormous flocks of wild ducks brings about a corresponding gathering of duck hunters at the public shooting grounds. . . . In northern Arkansas are the Ozark Mountains, the second mountain system of the state. The southern continuation of the Ozark hills gives Arkansas some of the same scenic grandeur that is described in the Missouri section. **EUREKA SPRINGS** is a center for this rugged mountain country, rich in springs, caverns, lovely glens and waterfalls. Handicraft items such as wood carvings, quilts and hooked rugs are popular with tourists who visit this hillside town. Arkansas also shares with Missouri the wide waters of Bull Shoals Lake and Norfolk Lake, although the giant dams are actually in Arkansas. **BELLA VISTA** in the northwest corner of the state is a popular resort town with giant springs and underground caverns. The town's **Wonderland Cave** includes a night club in one of the larger caverns. **FORT SMITH**, to the south, located between both the Ouachita and Ozark Mountains, was once a frontier post, now a commercial and industrial center. Part of the old fort of 1818 still stands as a museum. The annual Arkansas-Oklahoma Rodeo held here is an outstanding event.

OKLAHOMA

The "Sooner State" as it is called was originally reserved for the Indian tribes displaced by the westward movement. Pressure for homestead lands, however, forced the government to open up the rich lands of the Cherokee Strip for white settlement. At noon on April 22, 1889, as the signal guns went off a great mass of homeseekers in wagons, on horseback and on foot rushed to stake out land claims. Some of the more anxious settlers had previously slipped into the territory unobserved and staked choice claims, thus earning for themselves the name "Sooners," a term which eventually became the state sobriquet. Today most of the Oklahoma rolling plains are devoted to agriculture, either crops or cattle, but some of the lands have produced another richer yield in black gold — petroleum. Some of the richest oil wells were on lands formerly held by Osage Indians who have become rich through royalties they received from oil production on their land. Most of Oklahoma's Indians, except for older generations, live in much the same way as the white people, go to public schools and colleges, work on farms or in the oil fields or, as in some cases, go on to high offices in the state and nation. One of Oklahoma's most famous citizens was part Cherokee Indian. He was the homespun philosopher and humorist, Will Rogers. At **CLAREMORE** in northeast Oklahoma, the state has built the **Will Rogers Memorial** as the burial place for one of the best-loved Americans. The stone building that houses Rogers' personal possessions stands on the hill where he had planned to build a ranch house for his retirement. . . . To the southwest, the modern city of **TULSA** considers itself the oil capital of the world. It appears

Picturesque natural land formations are the feature of Buffalo River State Park in northern Arkansas
Arkansas Resources and Development Commission

to be true when one sees the extensive refineries and oil fields that surround the city. The biennial International Petroleum Products Exposition held here would tend to reinforce the impression. But of more interest to visitors will be the **Philbrook Art Center**, a private mansion now a museum, and **Gilcrease Foundation** where excellent examples of Indian art and paintings of the Old West by Remington and Russell are displayed. An extensive collection of books, manuscripts and letters on art and history of the region supplement the art works of the Gilcrease museum. ... OKLAHOMA CITY (243,504) in the center of the state is the capital and a strange one it is, for beneath the city is one of the largest oil pools in the nation. Oil rigs erected to tap this rich deposit have appeared on the lawns of private homes and even on the grounds facing the Greek temple front of the State Capitol. ... To the south near SULPHUR, **Platt National Park** is an attraction with over thirty large mineral springs which, like those at Hot Springs, Arkansas, are under federal government supervision. The curative waters, which in some cases spout forth as artesian wells, combine with mountain streams, cliffs and bluffs and scenic drives lined with wild flowers to make the park one of the state s most pleasant vacation spots. ... Further south are two Oklahoma lakes also popular with vacationists, **Lake Murray**, near ARDMORE and **Lake Texoma**, to the east. ... A drive through **Wichita Mountain Wildlife Refuge** in the western part of the state will yield sights of herds of buffalo and Texas longhorns grazing by the roadside.

TEXAS

This mighty empire of the Southwest sprawls across the map of the United States taking up a vast territory. It is a land of rolling plains, sleepy rivers, rugged mountains and wide gulf beaches. It is also a land of superlatives — largest in size, greatest producer of oil, cotton, livestock and so on *ad infinitum*. Texans are famous for elaborating the virtues and history of their state so that it is difficult to separate fact from fiction. Texas has been under six flags and its life still bears the imprint of Spanish and Mexican history. The land is studded with old Franciscan missions, forts and battlefields that tell the history of early settlements and the fight for independence. ... AMARILLO is the center for the high plains country of the Texas Panhandle, once desolate range land, now prosperous with oil fields and productive farms; the annual rodeo on the 4th of July is a local attraction. ... Near CANYON to the south, **Palo Duro Canyon State Park** is located in the deepest, most rugged part of a 120-mile canyon noted for rock formations and colored walls. In western Texas, the expression "West of the Pecos" used to denote that region beyond the Pecos River which was without law. Law, of course, has now reached the area but the open country is still forbidding at times. Cactus displays grotesque angular shapes against the gray sands and isolated mountain ranges loom on the horizon which seems devoid of all habitation. At the westernmost tip of Texas, EL PASO has grown to be an important center for people who live in or visit the sun-drenched southwest. The city's international flavor is evident everywhere; in the adobe shops, filled with native hand-tooled leather goods and silver jewelry, hand-loomed Mexican rugs and pottery; in the highly spiced Mexican foods and in the ability of local citizens to speak either Spanish or English with ease. A trip across the Rio Grande to the town of JUAREZ is a must for visitors who want to get a glimpse of Old Mexico. . . . Big Bend National Park, to the southeast, is a great untamed mountain wilderness along the U-shaped bend of the Rio Grande. Driving from MARATHON to the park one first catches sight of a haze-shrouded sawtooth mass on the horizon — the Chisos Mountains which rise to over 5,000-foot 'elevation. The highway leads to a great rocky Basin surrounded by mountains such as the castlelike Casa Grande. There are improved trails from the park headquarters in the Basin to the Window on Lost Mine Peak. Or, one can hire horses to ride to the South Rim for an awe-inspiring view across the Rio Grande to Mexico. Deer and antelope are frequently seen along the trail. The Santa Elena Canyon, Hot Springs and Boquillas area, outstanding attractions of the park, provide splendid all-day motor trips from the Basin. Accommodations are limited at the lodges in the park so reservation should be made in advance during the busy summer season. Outdoor clothing is recommended and as a precautionary measure motorists should have filled gasoline tanks and food for the longer trips. . . . BROWNSVILLE on the lower Rio Grande enjoys a Mexican atmosphere like the other border towns of El Paso and Loredo. The annual Charo Days Festival held the week before Lent is a gay celebration with the Latin influence predominant. . . . Despite its modern skyline, SAN ANTONIO (408,442) is rich in historic sites. Here is the fortress-mission of the Alamo where a handful of Texans fell, including Bowie and Crockett, in battle against over 3000 Mexican troops under Santa Anna. The long, low, white Governor's Palace and La Valita, a block of early Spanish homes where native crafts are preserved, are of interest along with the San Fernando Cathedral. The landscaped banks of the winding San Antonio River are a pleasant feature of the downtown area. The Spanish missions to the south of the city are elegant symbols of the work of the San Franciscan Missionaries. Here among the cloistered arches, workrooms and walled patios they patiently instructed the Indians in various crafts and religious teachings. San Jose, the "queen of the missions," is world-renowned for its beauty of form and sculptural detail. . . . BANDERA, 50 miles northwest, is a typical town of the Old West which has become a center for dude ranches where non-Texans can enjoy rural Western life with modern comforts. . . . The larger cities of Texas are always somewhat of a shock to visitors prepared for something more in keeping with a Hollywood "Western." AUSTIN, the state capital and seat of the University of Texas, has its own inland water playground in the Highland Lake nearby. FORT WORTH, to the north, is a big livestock market for Texas. Trinity Park with the Will Rogers Memorial Coliseum and other exhibit halls is the site for the Southwestern Exposition and Fat Stock Show each year. Also in the park is a notable Botanic Garden with more than 10,000 rose bushes. DALLAS (434,462), to the east of Fort Worth, is a streamlined modern city whose wealth comes from cotton and oil. More sophisticated than other cities of the southwest, Dallas has become a style leader. The luxurious store of Nieman-Marcus rivals New York's most fashionable and expensive shops. Fair Park, where the Texas State Fair is held, is an attraction with the Hall of State, a museum of Texas history. Dallas also has a fine symphony orchestra. HOUSTON (596,163), largest Texas city, is booming with new skyscrapers, lavish stores and such flamboyant establishments as the Shamrock Hotel. The wealth of its citizens has earned the city the title of "millionaires' city." Chief visitor attraction is San Jacinto Battlefield fifteen miles east of the city. A 570-foot monument topped by a lone star commemorates the victory which won Texas her independence. An added attraction to the park is the old battleship Texas anchored in a slip of the Buffalo Bayou. . . . The city of GALVESTON is one of several resort Gulf cities which can offer seashore relaxation, deep-sea fishing and sailing. . . . Regional food specialties of Texas include a variety of Mexican dishes, chili con carne, *pollo villeno* (baked chicken with highly seasoned ground beef), tamales, *tortillas, tacos* and enchiladas. A different barbecue-sauce recipe can be had from each area.

The Southeast States

The Southland has often been pictured in fiction and the popular imagination as a large amorphous region of unreconstructed Southern colonels, cotton plantations and dull countryside. Actually the South is made up of a variety of landscapes, occupations and cultures. Each state is different in many ways. Agriculture, admittedly, is dominant but busy industrial centers have been built to process the enormous reservoir of raw materials. The tobacco fields of Virginia are quite different from the newly-arrived, productive beef-cattle ranches of the Gulf States. The peoples of this land have separate histories; some are of English descent, others of French origins, each one producing a rich and varied culture. For scenic variety there are the coastal beaches, the rolling hills of the eroded Piedmont and the great mass of mountains which make up the Appalachians. There is plenty to see and do in the Southland. Historic sites are not dull ruins torn from the pages of history; the important ones often are places for creative pageants and dramas. The period costumes are not gathering dust in museums but are worn on special days by local townspeople anxious to display their heritage. For sports and recreation there is no end to the list of national and state parks with excellent facilities. Metropolitan centers provide their share of night life, carnivals and luxurious living.

For regional foods the Southland has its own specialties. Fried chicken is served in several ways, each state regarding its own recipes as the best. Hominy grits, black-eyed peas, red beans, baked hams, spoon bread and hot breads are served almost everywhere. Hog jowls and turnip greens are usually found in the mountainous areas while pecan pie and shrimp pie are Gulf State dishes. Hush puppies (flat corn-meal cakes fried in hot fat) is one of Florida's contributions along with baked pompano (often with shrimp stuffing). Sweet potato pie with two crusts originated in Georgia. Kentucky is famous for its bourbon whiskey and mint juleps while throughout the Southland native corn whiskey is made.

VIRGINIA

Mt. Vernon is familiar to every American and countless foreigners as the be-loved plantation home of the first President of the United States. A short drive from the city of Washington brings the visitor to the white columned mansion overlooking the Potomac River. The classic proportion of the 18th-century mansion stands in the midst of a manorlike village with outbuildings, guest houses, gardens and slave quarters. Here Washington lived the life he most enjoyed — that of a prosperous squire. Mt. Vernon is, of course, just one of the many 18th-century tidewater plantations. Stratford Hall further down the Potomac was the ancestral home of the Lee family, birthplace of Robert E. Lee. It is easily reached from FREDERICKS-BURG, historic town which is linked closely with the Washington family. In the vicinity of Fredericksburg are the battle-grounds of four separate important engagements of the War Between the States. . . . To the west loom the beautiful Blue Ridge Mountains. In Shenandoah National Park, Skyline Drive winds its airy way along the crest of the ridge for 100 miles. Near the southern terminus of Skyline Drive lies the pleasant town of CHAR-LOTTESVILLE, native home of Thomas Jefferson. The third President was an architect of buildings as well as nations for in his home of Monticello he built an imposing example of his artistic ability. The original buildings of the University of Virginia in Charlottesville were also designed by Jefferson. The serpentine garden walls and the classic Rotunda are notable exhibits. . . . RICHMOND on the James river is closely associated with the Civil War since, as the capital of the Confederacy, it was the prime object of the Union attack. The monuments to the leaders and soldiers of the southern cause are numerous. The former Confederate White House is now Richmond's Confederate Museum. The State Capitol, patterned after the Maison Carre at Nimes, France, is the work of Jefferson. Richmond has one of of the finest museums of the south in its Virginia Museum of Fine Arts. For a side glance of modern Richmond a visit to a tobacco company plant is recommended. . . . East of Richmond on the York Peninsula are three sites of national historic importance. WILLIAMSBURG, 18th-century capital of the Virginia colony, was the center of culture and commerce for over 80 years. As early as 1693 the College of William and Mary was chartered. Williamsburg declined after the capital was moved to Richmond in 1779 to become a quiet county seat and college town. An ambitious undertaking, however, has restored Williamsburg to its colonial grandeur. Reconstruction of destroyed structures and restoration of those still standing were carried out with strict adherence to original plans and details wherever possible. The story of this restoration is fascinating in itself. For this story as well as the history of Williamsburg, the official orientation center provides films and literature. In the restored area are the Governor's Palace, the dignified Capitol, several taverns, craft houses and many fine homes. Authentic atmosphere is attained by dressing the guides in costume and providing meals in the 18th century manner. . . . Nearby JAMESTOWN was the site of the first permanent English settlement in America. The ivy-clad brick ruins of the Old Church are the sole remnant of Jamestown remaining above ground. The area is part of Colonial National Park. YORKTOWN, the third historic site, is east of Williamsburg on the bluffs overlooking York River. Here at Yorktown the American and French armies conducted the final siege which established American Independence. The fortifications, Yorktown Custom House and several other historic houses are worth visiting.

Not all of Virginia is history. Virginia seashore resorts contribute their share of entertainment. VIRGINIA BEACH, a dozen miles from the busy Navy port of NORFOLK, is a popular ocean spot.

NORTH CAROLINA

The Midsouth vacationland spans a variety of landscapes ranging from the coastal dunes to the mountains of the west. Roanoke Island, one of the chain of islands that are strung along the coast of North Carolina, is an historic site. It was here that the first English attempt to found a colony in America ended in tragedy and mystery. In 1587, at Fort Raleigh a group of 117 colonists under the leadership of John White prepared a settlement following an abortive previous attempt. Virginia Dare, first child of English parentage, was born in the colony that same year. Shortly after White returned to England for supplies. His return was delayed until 1591 and by then the colony had completely disappeared. To this day no explanation can be found as to the fate of those first colonists. The fort and building have been restored as a national monument and in an open-air theater nearby The Lost Colony pageant is performed. On the mountainous sand dunes of Kitty Hawk a second, more modern event took place. Here the Wright brothers achieved fame in the first successful flying machine. The Wright Memorial Monument commemorates their flight with a pylon of granite. . . . South of these two sites a modern highway leads along the narrow offshore islands to Cape Hatteras, long synonomous with storms and ship hulks. New navigation aids, however, have reduced the danger. This virgin stretch of sand is to be preserved as a National Seashore with new

Raleigh Tavern, famous gathering place of patriots during the Revolutionary era, at Williamsburg

Virginia State C. of Com.

improvements making it more accessible yet retaining the distinctiveness of the old shore. . . . Inland, the tobacco lands rise gently to the industrial Piedmont Plateau. At the edge of the Piedmont are the cluster cities of **RALEIGH, DURHAM** and **CHAPEL HILL.** Within twenty-five miles of each other, these towns contain the capitol of the state, at Raleigh, the state's biggest colleges and important manufacturing plants. **Duke University,** dominated by the **University Chapel's** high Gothic tower, is located at Durham. The **University of North Carolina,** at Chapel Hill, has an exceptionally fine campus. The state capital of Raleigh has two places of interest that reflect the modern South. The **State Fair Arena** is an immense modern structure composed of two parabolic arches from which a saddle-shaped roof is suspended. Evidence of the atomic age may be found in the **Nuclear Reactor** on the campus of the State College. The building is open to the public for demonstrations of atomic processes. . . . To the west **WINSTON-SALEM** is the best place for visitors to see tobacco auctioned and cigarettes made by modern machinery. . . . The Southern Appalachian Mountains which stretch across western North Carolina have only recently been made accessible to visitors. This beautiful area of mountain forest has been the homeland of the mountain people who have lived apart for many generations. Their plain and simple life is rich in folklore, music and handicrafts. The mountains are crossed by a **Blue Ridge Parkway,** a splendid drive through hardwood forests and wild flowers, especially colorful in the spring with rhododendron, laurel and azalea blooming along the roadside. In the fall the gold and scarlet of the leaves cover the slopes in a flamelike mantle. **Mt. Mitchel** is just one of the many peaks above 6,000 feet which give an alpine character to the landscape of the Blue Ridge. At **ASHEVILLE** in the midst of mountain gardens is the fabulous **Vanderbilt Palace of Biltmore.** Too big for its inheritors, it is now open to the public. . . . **The Great Smoky Mountains,** the southern end of the Appalachians, receive their name from the smokelike mist which rises from the thick forests. This whole area is largely virgin timberland, forming a green sanctuary of untold splendor. This was the land of the Cherokees, the most intelligent and advanced of all Indian tribes. The descendants of those Cherokees who were able to avoid the forced move to Oklahoma live on the Qualla Reservation; their handicrafts of baskets, rugs and wooden articles are sought by tourists.

SOUTH CAROLINA

South Carolina's biggest attraction is the beautiful harbor city of **CHARLESTON.** Here is the picturesque and romantic South at its best. Historic monuments combine with old mansions and nearby tropical gardens to attract visitors from far and wide. The gardens outside of Charleston are the big attraction in the spring months. **Cypress Gardens** offer paddle-boat tours along waterways arched over with moss-hung trees. **Middleton Gardens** are more formal in their beauty with statuary suggesting the gardens of Versailles. **Magnolia Gardens** with 25 acres of azaleas and camellias are nearby. . . . In Charleston the old houses of the Battery area are attractive with their light pastel colors and graceful ironwork. From anywhere in the Battery section **Fort Sumter** can be seen guarding the harbor as it did in April, 1861, when the first shots of the Civil War were fired. Of the various fine churches in town St. **Michaels** has achieved extra distinction in that her church bells have crossed the Atlantic five times. **Charleston Museum** contains a fine collection of pre-Civil War antiques and artistic interiors. During the spring festival, tours are arranged for visiting some of the old mansions. Three houses, however, are open all year long: the Manigualt Mansion, the Heywood-Washington House and Pringle or Miles Brewton House.

Rice was once the staple crop of the Carolina coast so it is a traditional dish of the area, to be found combined with sea food or chicken in many pleasant ways. She-crab soup is a dish that is probably limited to the Charleston area.

GEORGIA

This largest state east of the Mississippi River has a variety of landscape. The Blue Ridge and Smoky Mountains extend into the northeast section of the state providing breath-taking vistas, turbulent trout streams, lakes in a pleasant summer vacationland. Further south, **ATLANTA,** in the fabled *Gone With The Wind* country, is an historic city. The Cyclorama, one of the largest paintings in the world, records the Battle of Atlanta.

Skimming the mountain crests on the Blue Ridge Parkway, near Grandfather Mountain in North Carolina
North Carolina News Bur.

. . . On the coast of Georgia near the Carolina boundary is the city of SAVAN-NAH. The town was laid out in a classic pattern by General Oglethorpe in 1733. Some of the old residences reflect the Roman pattern of the streets by their Classical Revival architecture. The Telfair House is a good example of this style. It houses the Telfair Academy of Arts and Sciences, one of the finest art museums in the South. Savannah resembles Charleston in many ways. Gardens with magnolia trees and flaming azaleas, old mansions and the waterfront areas are often compared with those of Charleston. Factor's Row is the interesting waterfront portion of Savannah. . . . From Savannah to Florida the Georgia mainland is separated from the sea by a series of islands called the "Golden Isles." These flat, secluded islands are covered with the trees of the Southland, live oaks, magnolias and cedars, while the waters are warmed by the southern sun. Tyler Island is the favorite beach resort of Savannah. Here on the clean white sands are held oyster roasts, a local specialty. The oysters are roasted in a small oven or pit, removed from the shells when done and dipped in a savory sauce before eating. Of the islands further south only Sea Island and nearby St. Simons Island are open to the public. Both are pleasant resorts for the sand and sun enthusiasts. . . . The Okefenokee, a vast swamp covering 660 square miles, extends across southern Georgia into Florida. Most of the primeval swamp is a National Wildlife Refuge. It is accessible from several places, however. Boat trips from FOLKSTON, FARGO or WAYCROSS penetrate the maze of trees

and untamed wilderness. The number and variety of wildlife is endless: bears and alligators of the more exciting species as well as the graceful egret and heron.

FLORIDA

Florida adds a chapter to history that recalls the explorations of Spanish conquistadores, the search for a mythical Fountain of Youth, and the colorful days of the Spanish Main. ST. AUGUSTINE played an important part in that history, beginning with the landing there of Ponce de Leon in 1513. The ancient buildings of this oldest city in the United States still preserve a part of Old Spain in their overhanging balconies, grilled windows and walled patios. The Oldest House in the United States is St. Augustine's most famous building. It is a two story building of wood and coquina (a local limestone) with low ceilings, hand-hewed beams and large fireplaces reminiscent of the Middle Ages. The Old Spanish Treasury is another interesting building with a patio of rare plants along with the rare furnishings of the interiors. The Cathedral of St. Augustine is in the style of the Spanish Missions that are usually found in the southwest United States . . . Near St. Augustine on Anastasia Island, the Alligator Farm with some 6,000 specimens is a local curiosity. On the same island can be seen the Coquina Quarries which have furnished the shell rock for St. Augustine's buildings since 1600. . . . Further south are the Marine Studios of Marineland an outstanding attraction of the coast. Here one can watch at close range the activities of giant sharks, porpoises, sawfish and other marine life. The high spot of a visit is at feeding time when the porpoises perform for their meals. . . . In central Florida ORLANDO has become a winter resort in addition to being a fine residential city. Stately live oaks and palms grace the parks and boulevards and subtropical plants blossom in lush gardens. Cypress Gardens near WINTER HAVEN have become the show place of the many gardens of Florida, receiving national attention with movie and magazine acclaiming her beautiful gardens. The still waters of the lagoon reflect the beauty of the azaleas, camellias and gardenias. Water-ski shows have been added to the natural scenery as an additional attraction. . . . A few miles to the south near LAKE WALES is Bok Tower, an imposing structure housing one of the finest carillons in the world. The tower itself is a thing of beauty. Built of steel and faced with coquina rock from Florida's coast and Georgia marble, it rises 230 feet above Mountain Lake Sanctuary. . . . The fabulous "Gold Coast" of Florida is an example of man's improving nature. The excellent climate, white sandy beaches and warm waters of the Gulf Stream were gifts of nature, but enterprising men have added the royal palm trees, gardens, lavish homes and hotels. PALM BEACH is the fashionable resort center of the coast. Here are the lavish estates of the wealthy, luxurious hotels, exotic shops and art studios. The Royal Palm Way with its double row of stately palms is impressive. Further south Greater MIAMI is a newer resort center, attracting the big names of the entertainment and business worlds. MIAMI BEACH is unique with hundreds of waterfront hotels, each with its own beach, swimming pool, cabanas and sun deck. For those who have had enough sunbathing there are sightseeing boats which cruise among the islands and lush estates of Biscayne Bay. Fishing boats are available for the more active vacationers. Night-club life is gay and lively with big-time entertainers. In Hialeah Park, the race track is well-known for its beauty as well as the impressive bets placed there. . . . South of the lively resort center of Miami, highway US 1 leads to the Florida Keys. The highway connects a chain of islands that stretches out into the Gulf of Mexico for 100 miles. KEY WEST at the end of the chain is a picturesque "Caribbean" city that once prospered on ill-fated ships that grounded on the outlying reefs. . . . Also

in southern Florida is Everglades National Park, a vast wilderness of swamp and hammocks filled with all sorts of wildlife, including alligators, bears, giant turtles, heron and egrets. Trails such as Anhinga and Gumbo Limbo lead into the wilderness for a short distance so that visitors may observe the wildlife at close range. . . . The west coast of Florida has its share of vacationlands. Attractive SARASOTA is the winter quarters for the Ringling Brothers, Barnum and Bailey Circus. The price of admission will allow a visitor to wander around the grounds where the acts for the spring tour are being rehearsed. The Ringling Museum of Art, established by John Ringling, contains one of the world's best collections of baroque paintings; it includes works by Titian and Tintoretto, Raphael and Rembrandt and many others. The Ringling Residence overlooking Sarasota Bay is a magnificent mansion set in well-kept grounds. As a reminder of the source of the wealth that enabled Ringling to collect works of art there is the Circus Museum. Here are displayed the retired parade wagons in all their splendor, along with other interesting circusiana, including scale models, old lithographs and posters. . . . At TARPON SPRINGS may be seen a demonstration of sponge fishing. The celebration marking the return of the sponge fleet at Eastertime is a colorful affair to witness. Music and a festive crowd of friends and relatives line the docks to greet the brightly painted boats as they arrive.

ALABAMA

This state is not without its own seasonal celebrations. Mardi Gras time in MOBILE is a big event with parade floats, masked balls and generally a good time for all. This carnival originated in Mobile and not in New Orleans as one might believe. The city itself has lots of fine old homes with French and Spanish touch still remaining in the lacelike ironwork. For flowers, the Azalea Trail starting at Bienville Square has few equals, with 17 miles of streets blazing with flowers and numerous gardens along the route opened to the public. To the south of Mobile, the Bellingrath Gardens are another top flower attraction covering some 800 acres. . . . The mansions of Alabama are of course interesting. The coastal region is notable for the wrought-iron work of the Gulf style while the fine homes found in the interior are usually Greek Revival style. **Magnolia Grove** in GREENSBORO is a fine example of one of the ancestral homes done in this style. . . . For a glimpse at the new Southland a visit to BIRMINGHAM, "the Pittsburgh of the South," should dispel any preconceived opinion of the South as being purely agricultural.

MISSISSIPPI

On Mississippi's Gulf Coast, the present shore road that follows what used to be the Spanish Trail is now a pleasant marine drive through resort towns and colorful ports with shrimp-boat fleets. . . . The names of the Gulf cities of BILOXI and PASCAGOULA are taken from the Indian tribes that once made their homes there. The beaches seem endless; white sands glisten against a background of flowers and moss-draped oaks. The calm waters between the shore and the low islands are popular fishing grounds; the migratory fish pour through the channel passes in consecutive waves. Near Biloxi, **Beauvoir,** the home of Jefferson Davis, has been restored to its former condition. PASS CHRISTIAN is one of the more beautiful of the Gulf resort towns with many stately homes fronted by classic white pillars. . . . NATCHEZ on the Mississippi River was perhaps the first to display her ante-bellum homes to visitors as an annual event. Today the **Natchez Pilgrimage** is almost a national institution. In March the show places of the South, **Rosalie, Dunleith** and **Stanton Hall** among many others, are opened to the public. These mansions are furnished and decorated with a lavishness unmatched in the South. Carrara marble mantles, enormous mirrors from France,

giant ballrooms paneled in rich woods, along with many other fine treasures, make a tour of the homes an impressive event. Period costumes and a Confederate Ball help to awaken a feeling of Natchez's heritage. . . . North of Natchez the city of VICKSBURG rests on the high bluffs above the river. In the Civil War this important river town was put under concentrated attack by Union Armies under General Grant. The long seige and final surrender are remembered in the **Vicksburg National Military Park,** well marked to present a clear picture of the struggle for the city. The **U. S. Waterways Experiment Station,** also in Vicksburg, contains a model of the Mississippi River System used for research in problems of drainage and flood control.

TENNESSEE

The Mississippi River country is quite different from the mountain country of eastern Tennessee. At MEMPHIS King Cotton rules in the world's largest cotton market. The **Memphis Cotton Carnival** held in May is an annual affair. At NASHVILLE, the State Capitol of Greek architecture stands on a hill which commands a splendid view of the city and surrounding country. **Fort Nashborough,** the frontier post which grew into the city of Nashville, has been authentically reconstructed. In Centennial Park there is a full-sized replica of the **Parthenon** of Athens. . . . A few miles northeast of Nashville is Andrew Jackson's home, the Hermitage. Jackson built the present mansion while President; the furnishings remain as they were in the days of "Old Hickory." The general and his wife are

Nicknamed "Big Mama," the largest steamboat to operate on the Mississippi is now anchored permanently at Vicksburg

Mississippi Agr. & Ind. Bd.

The old Kentucky home at Bardstown where Stephen Collins Foster wrote many of his famous melodies
Ky. Dept. of Conservation

buried here. . . . Norris Dam, near KNOX-VILLE, has become a tourist attraction, both for the impressive structure and for the large resort lake created by the dam. Nearby OAK RIDGE is a new city whose significance in the atomic age is known everywhere. The Museum has exhibits explaining atomic energy.

KENTUCKY

Of the many wonders of the world. Mammoth Cave has continued to attract visitors consistently. The caves contain miles of passageways at different levels with underground waterways, falls and a lake. The lowest level, Echo River is an interesting world of strange inhabitants, blind fish and transparent crayfish. The rock formations, of course, have been given fancy names but nevertheless are impressive; the so-called Frozen Niagara is noteworthy. . . . Lincoln's Birthplace Memorial stands near HODGENVILLE. A stone monument encloses a simple cabin that is said to be the birthplace of Lincoln. . . . The Bluegrass Country of Kentucky around LEXINGTON is the land of the world's finest thoroughbred race horses. Here may be found the famous stud farms with their velvety pastures, well-kept barns and, of course, horses — the young playful foals, mares and handsome stallions. The great annual event of racing circles is the Derby at LOUIS-VILLE'S Churchill Downs. People from all over the world attend this classic of horse racing. . . . In eastern Kentucky the Cumberland Gap forms the historic gateway to the West, through the forested Cumberland Mountains. A toll road climbs Pinnacle Mountain for a breath-taking view.

WEST VIRGINIA

The mountain state of the East. The scenic Allegheny Highland covers a million and half acres of park, forests and vacation retreats. On the western boundary formed by the Ohio River is HUNTING-TON, the state's largest city, noted for its parks, churches and residential district. . . . At CHARLESTON, to the east, the gold-domed Capitol Building is an impressive sight. . . . Southeast of the capital a new turnpike provides an unparalleled scenic drive through West Virginia's rugged mountains. At the terminus of the route is WHITE SULPHUR SPRINGS with the fabulous hostelry of Greenbrier. This has been a popular resort since antebellum days and still retains many of the customs and traditions of the Old South. . . . Northeast from White Sulphur Springs to Maryland stretches the Monongehela National Forest, an uncrowded recreation area of clear mountain streams and forest-clad mountains. ELKINS, the forest headquarters city, presents an annual pageant, the Forest Festival. Smoke Hole Caverns, limestone caves found near PETERSBURG, and Seneca Rock near MOUTH OF SENECA are two popular attractions. Seneca Rock consists of glistening white sandstone which rises spectacularly in towers over 1,000 feet high. . . . CHARLES TOWN, in the eastern panhandle, was founded by Charles Washington, a brother of the nation's first President. It is a charming city with many fine old homes built and lived in by close relatives of Washington. The most famous of those that have been restored is Harewood. East of Charles Town lies historic HARPERS FERRY where in 1859 Abolitionist John Brown made his daring raid on the Federal Arsenal. The enginehouse which served Brown as a fort is now a museum.

Middle Atlantic States

The Middle Atlantic States offer travelers the unique combination of great urban areas of unlimited cultural and entertainment facilities, along with wide expanses of rural and often completely wild country. The beaches lining the great coastal plain and the lakes and streams of the Appalachian upland offer countless resorts for outdoor recreation; many of these vacationlands are only a short distance away from the metropolitan areas. The large cities of the East, like New York, Philadelphia and Washington entertain a year-round stream of guests. Historic landmarks abound in this area particularly those shrines dating from Colonial and Revolutionary times. An airline flight across the Middle Atlantic States traverses in minutes the same terrain that weary Continental and Civil War soldiers marched, fought and died over. The ribbons of rivers seen from the plane were the early highways that opened up the interior westward beyond the Appalachians.

NEW YORK

NEW YORK has been called capital of the world for just about everything, finance, shipping, culture and now with the United Nations located here, it has the added distinction of being the world's political capital. The staggering statistics on New York's 8,000,000 people, hundreds of miles of streets and utility arteries, schools, churches, etc., are apt to overwhelm the visitor. Accepting the fact that New York is big, the best over-all picture of the city can be obtained by either a steamer tour around the island or by a trip to the observation tower of the Empire State Building. . . . New York has not, of course, always been a giant of a city. It had its humble beginnings as a small Dutch settlement at the southern tip of Manhattan. The site of that settlement is now overgrown with the towers of the financial district. Wall Street takes its name from the protective wall built by the Dutch. Battery Park, on the very tip of the island, is a good place to begin a tour of the city. It offers a fine view of the busy harbor and contains one of the city's oldest landmarks, Castle Clinton, once a fort, later an exhibition hall where Jenny Lind made her American debut. From the Battery ferry boats leave hourly for the Statue of Liberty on Bedloe's Island. The monu-

mental figure has been a symbol of freedom for two generations. The giant ferries that shuttle to Staten Island from the Battery provide an inexpensive and pleasant way to view the city sky line and harbor. . . . North of Battery Park, in the canyons of the financial district, is the famous Trinity Church. The present church was built in 1846 but the parish itself is New York's oldest (founded in 1697). The churchyard, which is real estate worth about $500 a square foot, has some of the city's oldest graves, Alexander Hamilton's and Robert Fulton's among the more famous. . . . For a brief look at the activities of the nearby investment houses a visit to the galleries of the New York Stock Exchange on Broad Street is recommended. Also in the downtown area are: the Federal Hall Memorial, site of Washington's inaugural; Fraunces Tavern, an authentic colonial building; and Chase Manhattan Bank, where money of all ages is on display. . . . North on Broadway at City Hall Park are found St. Pauls Chapel, the oldest church in the city, and City Hall, considered an architectural masterpiece by many. . . . East of City Hall Park is New York's oldest and most famous big river span, Brooklyn Bridge. The twenty-year history of the construction and the interesting tales that are connected with the bridge form a saga by itself. North of the bridge is the Lower East Side with many nations represented in its crowded tenements. The area is changing, however, as the various districts lose their distinctive national characteristics with American-born generations growing up and housing developments replacing the more dilapidated sections. Chinatown is still a big sightseers attraction but actually there is little to see there. An authentic Chinese dinner, however, may be had at one of the recommended restaurants, making a trip worth while. Greenwich Village, about a mile north of City Hall, was once a residential suburb, later a literary and art center. It is now a place to live for many professional and career workers, students, would-be artists and hangers-on. It has some attractive old houses both quaint and handsome, some notable restaurants and night clubs and an outdoor art show that attracts wide interest. Heart of the area is Washington Square with a few

NEW YORK CITY
MIDTOWN AREA

Theatres

1 Alvin		**25** Mark Hellinger	
2 Astor		**26** Martin Beck	
3 Belasco		**27** Mayfair	
5 Booth		**28** Morosco	
6 Broadhurst		**29** National	
7 Broadway		**30** N.Y.City Center	
8 Capitol		**31** Palace	
11 Coronet		**32** Paramount	
12 Cort		**35** Playhouse	
14 E. Barrymore		**34** Plymouth	
15 48th St.		**34** Radio City	
16 46th St.		Music Hall	
17 Fulton		**36** Roxy	
17 Globe		**37** Royale	
19 Golden		**38** St. James	
18 Henry Miller		**39** Shubert	
20 Imperial		**41** The Music Box	
21 Loew's State		**42** Victoria	
22 Longacre		**40** Warner	
24 Lyceum		**43** Winter Garden	
23 Majestic		**44** Ziegfeld	

TWA OFFICES

1st Av. & 38th St.
80 E. 42nd St.
460 W. 42nd St.
Sheraton-Astor Hotel
624 Fifth Av.
630 Fifth Av.
Hotel Statler
67 Broad St.
120 Broadway
380 Madison Av.
200 Livingston St.
(Brooklyn)

© C. S. HAMMOND & Co., N.Y.

remaining old buildings on the north side. New York University has its downtown campus here. Little Italy to the south of the square is also in a period of change with whole blocks marked for razing to make way for new building plans. . . . For shoppers, real or window variety, 34th Street and Fifth Avenue offer the biggest department stores and the swankiest shops. **Empire State Building** at the intersection of 34th Street and Fifth Avenue, already the world's highest structure, has been boosted to even greater heights with the addition of a television tower. The top is now 1,472 feet above the street. On Fifth Avenue at 42nd Street behind protective lions is the **New York Public Library.** Besides housing one of the greatest book collections the library offers concerts, lectures and exhibits. . . . The newest attraction in New York is the **United Nations Headquarters.** The striking modern buildings are set in a handsome landscaped plaza along the East River from 42nd to 48th Streets. The Secretariat building, a majestic slab of marble and glass, towers above the curved walls and low dome of the General Assembly building. The interiors of the buildings are as bold and interesting as the exteriors. The visitors' main entrance is through the General Assembly building where trained guides are available for special tours. The UN Bookshop has on sale various handicraft items from member nations that make fine souvenirs. . . . Due west on 42nd Street is **Times Square,** entertainment center of New York, with motion-picture houses, theaters, restaurants and hotels. Bright and gaudy and somewhat cheapened by shooting galleries and souvenir stands the area is impressive at night when the giant signs and trick displays compete with each other in a blaze of neon pyrotechnics. On the side streets are the "legitimate theaters," as they are known in New York. Here are staged the musical and dramatic shows. Best guide to any of the entertainment features of New York is a daily newspaper, *Cue* magazine or *New Yorker* magazine. **Rockefeller Center** fills the area between 48th and 51st Streets, Fifth and Sixth Avenues with the world's biggest and most striking group of business buildings. It houses offices for more than a thousand firms, a major radio and television network and one of the largest and most elaborate theaters, **Radio City Music Hall.** A walk through the floral displays on the Promenade leads to the outdoor skating rink on the Lower Plaza. Guided tours of the buildings and NBC studios are well worth while. Opposite Rockefeller Center on Fifth Avenue is **St. Patricks Cathedral,** seat of the Roman Catholic Archdiocese of New York. The graceful towers of the French Gothic church are patterned after the spires of Cologne Cathedral. For museums New York probably has no equal, there being museums for just about every interest. The more famous are: the **Museum of Natural History** on Central Park West, which includes the Hayden Planetarium; **Metropolitan Museum of Art** across the Park, one of the great art galleries of the world, and **Museum of Modern Art** on West 53rd Street off Fifth Avenue. **Central Park** is a resort in itself with a small zoo, lakes, skating rink, a carousel and some fine landscaped areas. . . . In northern Manhattan on the west side at Morningside Heights are found a group of buildings and institutions which are famous. They include Columbia University, Cathedral of St. John the Divine, Riverside Church and Grant's Tomb. Spanning the Hudson at 178th Street is the **George Washington Bridge,** second to the San Francisco Golden Gate Bridge in size. The impressive structure carries 25 million vehicles a year in eight lanes. **The Cloisters** in Fort Tryon Park to the north is one of New York's most unusual exhibits. It is a museum set on a wooded knoll above the river. The building incorporates within a modern structure parts of several medieval monasteries. The prize collection of medieval art and relics together with the superb setting overlooking the Hudson make the Cloisters a must for visitors. . . . **Coney Island,** at the southwestern tip of Long Island, about fifteen miles from Manhattan and easily reached by subway, is the city's popular ocean beach as well as a huge amusement park with every facility for beguilement and fun. On a hot Sunday afternoon the Coney Island Beach will draw a million or more visitors, which, while making the beach difficult for bathing, is a sight worth seeing in itself. **Bronx Zoo** also on the outskirts of the city can be reached by subway. The collection of animals is the world's largest with almost every known one represented. As many as possible are shown in their natural habitat.

New York offers unlimited events in the sports world with three major league baseball teams, a professional football team and numerous top-flight college athletic teams. Whatever sport one wishes, be it boxing, soccer, basketball, boccie or cricket, New York probably has it.

No city in the world has more good restaurants of varied type than New York. For international cuisine there is a long list of foreign restaurants in the Classified Telephone Directory. New York has few local specialties but many international dishes have become standard menu items in restaurants. Sea foods are popular and plentiful, for New York serves as a distribution point for the East.

LONG ISLAND is the maritime province of New York State, reaching 125 miles into the Atlantic. At the western end are the populated boroughs of Queens and Brooklyn. Further out on the island the congestion diminishes gradually, becoming suburban and eventually rural in eastern Suffolk County. The Atlantic side of the island is a series of long sandy beaches ideal for salt-water bathing. Atlantic Beach, Long Beach, Jones Beach, Fire Island, the Hamptons and Montauk are noted for their bathing facilities. **Jones Beach** has added to its fine facilities a huge Marine Theater for lavish spectaculars and water shows. Long Island Sound is a large yachting center. Pleasure craft and fishing boats sail from the many fine harbors. Salt water fishermen, whether they be the big-game variety, surf casters or patrons of the party boats, find plenty of opportunities to try their skill.

SAG HARBOR, once a whaling center, has an interesting whaling museum and one of the most beautiful churches in America, **Old Whalers Church**. Long Island has more 18th century windmills standing than any other section of the country. The **Hook Mill** at **EASTHAMPTON** is still able to grind flour with its old wooden machinery. . . . The island is famous for its sea food and also its farm products; Long Island ducklings are a specialty.

One of the great rivers of the world, the **Hudson** has been well-known to generations of travelers for the beauty of its scenery. This mighty river begins at a small lake in the Adirondacks and flows south, gathering strength and momentum to carve its way through the mountains. The southern terminus is below the rampartlike **Palisades**, beyond lower New York Bay for it continues ninety miles on into the Atlantic as a great underwater canyon. Ever since white man came to these shores, the river has played an important role in the lives of the settlers. Dutch names of river towns recall the days when the Hudson was part of the Holland Empire. During the Revolution the defense of the Hudson Valley became a vital necessity if the new nation was to survive. The mansions and castles that line the valley are landmarks of more peaceful times. . . . At **TARRYTOWN** is Washington Irving's home **Sunnyside**, a curious mansion with crow-step gables and ornate cupolas giving a gingerbread appearance. **NORTH TARRYTOWN** has Philipse Castle, a restored 17th-century manor house, with heirloom furnishings and work buildings. . . . **Bear Mountain State Park** on the west side of the Hudson is a popular recreation area that can be reached by pleasant excursion steamer from New York. Further north the **Storm King Highway**,

This log fort at Syracuse is a reproduction of Fort St. Marie de Gannentaha, built here by French settlers in 1656

New York State Dept. of Commerce

one of the most spectacular highways, follows the highlands above the river, the road in places perching on a narrow ledge cut in the mountains. West Point on the plateau overlooking the river is a colorful setting for the U.S. Military Academy, training ground for future generals. A visit to the Point on a Saturday in the fall is a memorable occasion with a stirring full-dress parade of the corps of cadets prior to an Army football game at Michie Stadium. . . . NEWBURGH and BEACON, across the river from each other are two historic sites. Washington had his headquarters at Hasbrouck House in Newburgh. Beacon on the east shore was named for the signal fires that warned Revolutionary troops of the movements of the British. An inclined railway climbs the steep slopes of Mt. Beacon. To the north is POUGHKEEPSIE, formerly the site of a classic in boat racing. Vassar College on the east side of the city is one of the foremost women's colleges of the country. . . . HYDE PARK, north of Poughkeepsie, was the ancestral home of President Franklin D. Roosevelt. The President's grave in the rose garden, the home and a special library housing the many papers, books and other interesting belongings of the President are maintained as a national historic site. Nearby is the Vanderbilt Mansion, an impressive 19th-century estate now open to the public.

West of the Hudson beyond KINGSTON are the haze-shrouded Catskill Mountains, a rural vacationland for metropolitans. The popularity of this region has created hundreds of lavish hotels featuring entertainment from metropolitan theaters and night clubs. WOODSTOCK is noted for its art colony and summer theater. Throughout this land of legend are many old stone houses antedating the Revolution. Noteworthy are those at HURLEY and NEW PALTZ. . . . ALBANY, capital of the Empire State, was originally a Dutch trading post. Colonial buildings such as the Schuyler Mansion in Albany and Fort Crailo in RENSSELAER provide a glimpse of the nostalgic past of this region. Three prominent buildings in the Capitol Hill area of Albany are the chateaulike State House, the State Education Building and the Alfred E. Smith State Office Building. . . . West of Albany, near COBLESKILL, Howe Caverns, the caves of the northeast, give visitors an opportunity to sightsee underground. Nearby COOPERSTOWN is a village of museums. The State Historical Association is located here along with Baseball's Hall of Fame, commemorating the birthplace of America's national sport. A third attraction is the Farmers Museum with early agricultural tools and gadgets and a complete re-created rural town. . . . North of Albany the Saratoga-Lake George region, now a quiet scenic area, was the wilderness background for the bloody campaigns of upper New York State. The Battleground of Saratoga, now a National Historic Park, was the scene of the defeat of Burgoyne's British Army, a turning point in the Revolution. SARATOGA SPRINGS is famed for its mineral waters, its horse racing and its old hotels. On elm-shaded Union Avenue the outdated hotels with endless verandas recall the spacious grandeur of the post-Civil War period when Saratoga was the social and sporting center of the North.

The Adirondack Mountains, New York's rugged mountain area, is famous for its beautiful wild scenery — its clear lakes, tumbling streams and waterfalls, its trails and purple-tinted peaks. On the eastern fringe of this wilderness is Lake Champlain and Lake George. Between the two lakes lies the reconstructed Fort Ticonderoga, important during the French and Indians Wars and the Revolution. Near Lake Champlain is Ausable Chasm, an impressive gorge which may be viewed from the galleries cut in the rock walls or from boats sent through the "flume." For a thrilling view of the Adirondack area the peak of Mt. Whiteface can be reached by automobile from WILMINGTON. Lake Placid is just one of the many lake resorts. It has become prominent as a winter resort center, often is called the St. Moritz of America. . . . The Thousand Islands and St. Lawrence still retain the irresistible beauty that thrilled French explorers a few hundred years ago. Les Mille Isles, more than 1,700 gems set in azure-hued expanse of the St. Lawrence River, attract travelers from all parts of the world. Some of the islands are just points of rock; others are large enough for whole villages. Tour boats ply among the unspoiled islands and visit places like Boldt Castle in Alexandria Bay, a landmark from the time when island residents were limited to millionaires. The view from International Bridge is outstanding.

Washington's Headquarters in Morristown National Historic Park, where the Continental Commander spent two heartbreaking wartime winters

N. J. Dept. of Conservation

South of Lake Ontario are located the **Finger Lakes** of New York State. On the gentle slopes of the low-lying hills are grown the grapes for New York State wines. Every September the quiet countryside at **Lower Seneca Lake** is broken by the roar of sports-car motors in the Grand Prix of America, **WATKINS GLEN** sports-car race. . . . **Niagara Falls**, mighty cataract between Lakes Erie and Ontario, have been equalled and surpassed in height by many falls but none has ever matched the majesty of the thundering waters of Niagara. The constant roar of the falling water, the clouds of mist rising upward, the frantic fury of the **Whirlpool Rapids** make an awesome spectacle. From **Goat Island** elevators take visitors down to the **Cave of the Winds** at the base of the falls. The boat trip on the "Maid of the Mist" is another way to get a close view of the falls.

NEW JERSEY

Almost legendary is the fascination of the **New Jersey shore**. The 125-mile-long shore from Sandy Hook to Cape May is an inviting stretch of white, surf-washed sand. Surf bathing is the seashore number one activity but promenading and enjoying the attractions of the boardwalk is a close second. Amusement parks, big movie houses and steel piers featuring name bands and variety acts compete for the patronage of the vacationists. . . . The centers of this resort life are **LONG BRANCH** and **ASBURY PARK** in the north, **ATLANTIC CITY** further south and **WILDWOOD** on Cape May. **ATLANTIC CITY** is a big convention city; the Miss America contest held here is an annual September pageant. **CAPE MAY**

on the south has a somewhat quieter atmosphere reminiscent of New England. At Cape May, on the undeveloped stretches of shore line, the sea-bird colonies of terns, heron and sandpipers have laid claim to the wind-swept beaches and dunes. Salt-water fishing is a big attraction along the whole coast. . . . New Jersey's important part in the Revolutionary War is marked by a number of historic sites. At **MORRISTOWN** Washington and his ragged army spent two winters. The stately **Ford Mansion** served as Washington's headquarters. Three miles from Morristown at **Jockey Hollow** the main army was encamped. Of interest here are the reconstructed barracks and hospital.

Southwest of the industrial lowland of New Jersey is the beautiful university town of **PRINCETON**. Points of interest are the **Princeton Battlefield**, old **Nassau Hall**, famed in song and story, and **Nassau Inn** which was originally built in 1756 and has been serving Princeton men for 200 years. At **TRENTON** 12 miles away Washington surprised Hessian troops after crossing the Delaware during a bitter snowstorm. The **Old Barracks** in Trenton which housed Hessian soldiers is one of the finest specimens of colonial barracks.

PENNSYLVANIA

PHILADELPHIA (2,071,605), the birthplace of the nation, is an industrial giant that William Penn would never recognize as the "greene countrie towne" he laid out in 1681. Besides being one of the great ports of the world, the City of Brotherly Love has grown to become a center of insurance and banking. Curtis Publishing Company, one of the oldest publishing enterprises (Benjamin Franklin started it in 1730) has grown to be one of the largest in the magazine field. . . . Within the bustling modern metropolis is the old city of Penn and Franklin — the city where a new nation was founded. On **Independence Square** is the classic Georgian building **Independence Hall**, scene of the signing of the Declaration of Independence. In the same building eleven years later the Constitution was written. In the main corridor of Independence Hall stands the **Liberty Bell**, symbol of freedom for the new nation. A block from Independence Square stands **Carpenter Hall**, the meeting place for the first Continental Congress. Other historic buildings nearby are **Christ Church**, where leaders of the Revolution worshiped, and charming **Betsy Ross House** where, according to tradition, the Stars and Stripes were born. In the new city of Philadelphia the broad tree-shaded Benjamin Franklin Parkway leads from City Hall northwest to the **Philadelphia Museum of Art** containing a priceless collection. Behind the museum is Fairmount Park with a zoo, old mansions and some 3,500 acres of park. . . . The **University of Pennsylvania**, west of the Schuylkill, has a large campus with some notable buildings. The archaeological collection at the university is probably the world's best. . . . At Logan Circle on Benjamin Franklin Parkway there is a group of cultural buildings that includes the **Franklin Memorial Institute** and the **Free Library**.

Philadelphia has always been an important town for sport events, with some national classics such as the Army-Navy football game.

Traditional Philadelphia foods are scrapple and pepper pot and snapper soups. Philadelphia ice cream is rated as the best by experts and Philadelphia cream cheese has become a national food. . . . West of Philadelphia, beyond the famous "Main Line" residential area, lies one of America's great historic shrines, **Valley Forge**. A large state park encloses the breastworks and reconstructed huts where the ragged Continental Army encamped during the winters of 1777-8. The rural stone house where Washington conferred with his generals Lafayette, Pulaski and von Steuben has been preserved intact.

In rural eastern Pennsylvania lies the **Pennsylvania German** country. Often called Pennsylvania Dutch these hard-working people who tend the rich lands around **ALLENTOWN**, **READING** and **LANCASTER** are widely known for their picturesque speech, well-kept farms with immense red barns painted with decorative hex symbols, their devotion to religion and avoidance of the evils of modern living. The Amish have come to typify the various religious groups of the Pennsylvania Dutch with their traditional garb of black. Others in the plain sects are the Mennonites, the Moravians and Dunkards. Traditional foods of the Pennsylvania Dutch make a long list of dishes as easy to eat as they are hard to pronounce. To name a few there are schnitz-und-knepp (dried apples, smoked ham, dumplings), lebkuchen, Schwenkfelden bread, Mennonite toast fried in deep fat, seven sweets and seven sours, and shoo-fly pie. . . . In northeast Pennsylvania are the **Poconos**, a resort country of hills, lakes and generally lots of outdoors. **Mt. Pocono** is in the center of an increasingly popular ski region. Near **STROUDSBURG** the Delaware River cuts through the Kittatinny range to form the impressive **Delaware Water Gap**. . . . In central Pennsylvania are a series of parallel mountains that form a part of the great Appalachian chain. The great mountain-making forces produced Pennsylvania's great coal deposits. The anthracite fields around **WILKES-BARRE** while not exactly a tourist area are interesting to see especially if a tour is made of one of the huge colleries where the coal is processed. . . . The state capital of **HARRISBURG** is on the Susquehanna River in central Pennsylvania. The large impressive capitol building enjoys a prominent site overlooking the river. South of Harrisburg in the attractive farmland country of southern Pennsylvania is **GETTYSBURG**. Outside the limits of this crossroads town two great armies, Union and Confederate, clashed in a battle that was to continue for three bloody days. At the close of this terrible struggle with tremendous losses on both sides the Confederate Army withdrew, ending the invasion of the North and the hopes of victory for the South. The battlefield is now a National Military Park. . . . **PITTSBURGH** (676,806) is Pennsylvania's second greatest city. The valleys of the bituminous coal region have become the world's greatest iron and steel center. The city is located at the triangle of land where two rivers join to form the mighty

Ohio River. At the apex of this triangle Fort Pitt was located. The **Blockhouse,** part of the original frontier fort, remains standing in the new Point Park development, a part of Pittsburgh's ambitious building program. Several modern buildings of the great face-lifting project have already been completed. **Greater Pittsburgh Airport,** included in the scheme, was created by slicing off the top of a mountain. The **Oakland Civic Center,** east of the triangle, contains a remarkable assortment of scientific and cultural buildings. Here is the University of Pittsburgh's **Cathedral of Learning,** a skyscraper college; **Mellon** and **Carnegie Institutes** and the **Stephen Foster Memorial.**

DELAWARE

Although Delaware is the second smallest state of the Union, there is much

ing still in use. Both Dover and New Castle have birthday celebrations when historic old homes are open to public view. . . . The industrial city of **WILMINGTON,** home of the DuPont firm, holds a colorful religious festival, the "Big Quarterly," on the last Sunday in August; feasting and religious service continuing for the greater part of the day.

MARYLAND

Maryland is divided by the broad waters of Chesapeake Bay to form two separate and distinct regions. Western Maryland is characterized by the mountains of the Appalachians. The southern boundary is marked by the Potomac River which winds its way through the hills, past **HARPERS FERRY** and **CUMBERLAND.** The river never achieved the great hopes of Washington and other investors who

A charming farm in western Pennsylvania, near Somerset
Standard Oil Co. of N.J.

to see and do in this old colonial state. The beaches of **Rehoboth** and **Bethany** are well-known to vacationists from neighboring cities of Philadelphia, Washington and Baltimore. The warm waters of the coast and inland bays are not the only attraction, however. The early settlements which passed through successive Swedish, Dutch and English rule have preserved many pre-Revolutionary homes and administrative buildings. The Dutch settled at **LEWES** many years before the landing of the Pilgrims at Plymouth. The Zwaanendael Museum replica of the Dutch town hall at Hoorn, Holland, commemorates that first settlement. **NEW CASTLE,** state capital until 1777, has some excellent examples of Georgian architecture including **Read House.** At **DOVER,** Delaware State House is the nation's second oldest capitol build-

saw it as a commercial waterway for the interior. It was important, however, in the struggles of the Civil War. Only twice were the Confederates able to cross the river in force. The first ended in the bloody engagement at **ANTIETAM** and the second in the already mentioned Gettysburg. . . . The eastern shore is a rich agricultural area with many estates and plenty of ocean beaches. **OCEAN CITY** is popular with Washingtonians escaping the summer heat of the capital. The whole bay area is a fisherman's paradise. Here is the watery home of the oysters, crabs and finfish that grace the dinner tables of the East. At the head of Chesapeake Bay is **BALTIMORE** (pop. 949,748), an "in-between" city since it is close to Philadelphia and Washington. But notwithstanding this geographical proximity Baltimore has

Monument commemorating the first landing of the Swedes, in Christina Park, Wilmington

TWA-Trans World Airlines

a proud history and important facilities of its own. The principal sights are widely scattered. **Johns Hopkins University**, on the north side of town, is world-renowned for its medical school and hospital. Overlooking the busy harbor of the city is **Fort McHenry**. The defense of the fort during the British bombardment in the War of 1812 inspired Francis Scott Key to write the national anthem. The **Transportation Museum** has an interesting collection of locomotives from the most ancient vintage steam engines to the latest diesels. Baltimore has a tradition for fine foods, especially sea foods and pastries. Soft-shell crabs and pan-roasted oysters head the list of popular dishes. Diamondback terrapin stew and Maryland chicken fried in salt pork fat and served in hot cream are two regional favorites. . . . Also on Chesapeake Bay, south of Baltimore, is ANNAPOLIS, state capital and home of the U.S. Naval Academy. In visiting the academy do not overlook the town itself, with the **State House** and several colonial homes of interest.

WASHINGTON, D. C.

WASHINGTON (802,178), capital of the nation, has been acclaimed one of the most beautiful and cosmopolitan cities in the world. Wide tree-lined avenues and green parks serve to set off the impressive government buildings. Since it is a city where government is the big business, there are no industries to mar the sky line or to laden the air with the soot that blights so many metropolitan cities. Washington was the first great world capital that was built from a carefully made master plan. Although the plans of engineer Pierre Charles L'Enfant have not always been followed, the city has come to fulfill the dreams of its creators. . . . Most visitors wish to see first the **Capitol**, the home of the Legislative Branch of the Government. It stands in spacious grounds on the crest of a hill dominating the entire city. The great dome awash with lights at nighttime is an impressive sight. A visit to the galleries of the Senate and House of Representatives may prove somewhat disappointing in that much of the work of Congress is done not on the floor but in the committee rooms and in the nearby office buildings reached by miniature subway. . . . To the east, the **Library of Congress** with its ornate architecture houses the world's greatest collection of books. It has some notable exhibits of rare books and presidential papers. Next to the library is the **Supreme Court** building. Relatively new, it is built of dazzling white marble with a stately columned portico; it is regarded by many as the finest building in Washington. The courtroom is open to the public when the court is in session. . . . On the mall west of the Capitol is the **National Gallery of Art**, rapidly becoming one of the world's great galleries. The building itself is a showpiece; the fountain and dark marble columns in the rotunda are especially striking. On the other side of the mall is the **Smithsonian Institution**, a scattered group of buildings housing Lindbergh's plane, the "Spirit of St. Louis," besides a thousand and one other relics, inventions and curiosities. North of the mall between Constitution and Pennsylvania Avenues is the **Federal Triangle**. It is the longest, most expensive

WASHINGTON, D.C.
BUSINESS CENTER

1. American Security & Trust Co.
2. Equitable Bldg.
3. Jul. Garfinckle & Co. Dept. Store
4. National Savings & Trust Co.
5. Riggs National Bank
6. A.S.N. Assn.
7. Shoreham Bldg.
8. Southern Bldg.
9. Trans-Lux Theater
10. Union Trust Bldg.
11. Washington Bldg.
12. Woodward Bldg.

TWA OFFICES
Statler Hotel
Willard Hotel
716 14th St.

© C. S. Hammond & Co., N.Y.

and impressive collection of government buildings anywhere. They include the Departments of Commerce, Labor and Justice. At the Department of Justice, the FBI provides an unusual public tour every half hour through its crime detection labs and exhibits. The **Archives Building**, also in this group, has on display America's great historic documents including the Constitution, the Declaration of Independence and the Bill of Rights. . . . The **White House** on Pennsylvania Avenue is the home of the President. The dignified mansion set in beautifully kept grounds has recently been completely remodeled. A number of the stately rooms on the first floor are open to the public at specified hours. . . . At the western end of the mall is **Washington Monument**, a severe marble shaft rising 555 feet into the air. An elevator takes visitors to the observation windows at the top. Directly south of the Washington Monument, on the east shore of the Tidal Basin, setting for Washington's famed Japanese cherry trees, is the **Jefferson Memorial**. The monument is in circular pantheon form, a design favored by Jefferson in his home, Monticello, in Charlottesville, Virginia. Within the memorial is a towering statue of Jefferson with significant quotations of Jefferson carved on the walls. Completing the axis of the mall is the **Lincoln Memorial**. The stately building overlooks the Arlington Memorial Bridge spanning the Potomac River. Inside the memorial is the colossal seated statue of Lincoln by Daniel Chester French and on the walls are the noble words of Lincoln's Gettysburg Address and Second Inaugural Address. . . . The Arlington Memorial Bridge leads directly to the Arlington National Cemetery on the Virginia side of the Potomac. It is the largest and most famous of all national burying grounds, covering over 400 acres. Its most famous grave is the **Tomb of the Unknown Soldier**, guarded day and night by sentries. . . . Southeast of the cemetery is the **Pentagon** the Defense Department's huge office building. . . . Northwest of the downtown area, across Rock Creek Park, is Georgetown, the fashionable residential quarter of the city. It has some fine colonial and Georgian mansions among which is Dumbarton Oaks, famous for its Byzantine art collection and many fine gardens.

Washington offers excellent park facilities. **Rock Creek Park** is a rugged, rambling park of unusual beauty. Its best known feature is the Washington Zoo. On the old **Chesapeake and Ohio Canal**, the National Park service provides a canal boat tour along the Maryland side of the Potomac River. **Embassy Row** on Massachusetts Avenue is another sightseeing attraction with many of the foreign embassies and legations. Also on Massachusetts Avenue may be found the new **Islamic Center** and **Washington Cathedral**, a large Gothic structure still under construction. . . . Washington has its share of Broadway shows, either prior to their New York run or afterwards.

The round, symmetrical lines of the inspiring Jefferson Memorial, in Washington, are complemented by the sharp, towering shaft of the Washington Monument

TWA-Trans World Airlines

LAND OF AMERICAN FREEDOM

New England, birthplace of American freedom, offers a unique variety of attractions to the visitor. Proud possessor of some of the finest scenic wonders in the world, it can boast of picturesque towns, rugged sea coasts, rolling green hills, wide river valleys and granite mountains. Historic landmarks abound to remind the visitor of New England's heritage. Here the protests against the unjust rule of England broke out into open revolt. The old fishing ports retain their charm and rural towns with village greens and white churches have not changed like their industrial neighbors. Summer theaters and art colonies seem to thrive in New England. Fishing and hunting facilities are excellent and sailing on the coastal waters is a popular pastime. Summer camps abound throughout the region. Although the six New England states share a common history and are alike in many ways, they preserve separate local characteristics that mark their accents and ways of life. Everywhere, however, the visitor is welcome, for this land has long entertained summer and winter guests.

ABOUT FOOD

Regional dishes of New England make up a long list of tempting foods. Sea food is probably the most famous with Maine lobster, clam chowder, codfish cakes, and clams steamed on hot rocks in a traditional New England clambake. Other local dishes are: New England boiled dinner, baked beans and brown bread, hot cakes with maple syrup, pumpkin pie with Vermont cheese, New Hampshire deep-dish blueberry pie and real country cider.

BOSTON

Historic capital of the Commonwealth of Massachusetts, Boston (801,444) is a combination of the old and the new. Wide avenues leading into the city disappear into narrow crooked streets that follow the same winding path as the old colonial lanes. Modern buildings tower above graceful spires of colonial churches and quiet burial grounds are to be found in the shadows of office buildings. A walking tour of the historic sites of the downtown area is recommended. Start with the State House on Beacon Street; the gold-domed building, designed by Bulfinch, houses the Senate and Hall of Representatives. Of interest inside are the hall of flags and other historical souvenirs such as the Sacred Cod hanging in the Hall of Representatives. Below the State House is the Boston Common, the popular city park which began as a community cow pasture. At the Old Granary Burial Grounds on Tremont Street are the graves of such famous Americans as Paul Revere, Samuel Adams and John Hancock. Old South Meeting House at the corner of Milk and Washington Streets was once the meeting hall for fervent revolutionary patriots. Nearby, Paul Revere had his shop, and Benjamin Franklin learned the printing trade just around the corner. The Old State House, built in 1713 for representatives of the Crown, still retains the royal emblem of the Lion and the Unicorn. The building now houses an interesting historical and marine museum. Nearby Faneuil Hall, called the "Cradle of Liberty," was the scene of violent protests against the British. Paul Revere's House on North Square has been restored and furnished as it was in the days of Revere. North Church with its steeple rebuilt for the second time was the lookout from which the British approach was signalled to the patriots in Charlestown.

To return to the center of the city, the Public Gardens' ordered flower beds and popular swan boats provide a pleasant place to rest a while. North of the State House is the Beacon Hill area, long the home of many famous Boston families. Further north along the Charles River lies the Esplanade, a mile-long park where summer band concerts are held. In the Copley Square area can be found Trinity Church, a fine Romanesque building and the John Hancock Life Insurance Building, a landmark in the more modern style with an observation tower giving a fine view of the city and harbor. Also on the square is Boston Public Library, one of the world's best. Further west are the Christian Science Church and Publishing House. The Mother Church is a large edifice of Italian Renaissance architecture with a dome which rises 200 feet to mark the Boston skyline. The adjacent publishing house issues church publications including the *Christian Science Monitor* and can be visited during the summer. Symphony Hall, home of the Boston Symphony Or-

Tioga Towers at Marblehead
Mass. Dev. & Ind. Com.

chestra and Boston "Pops" Orchestra, is on Huntington Avenue. On the same avenue may be found the **Museum of Fine Arts** which has an impressive collection of art and some exceptionally fine colonial rooms. The Boston area is a center of education; the number of institutions of higher learning is impressive. Most well-known, of course, are **Harvard University** and **Massachusetts Institute of Technology.** They are located across the Charles River in Cambridge. **Harvard,** the oldest university in the country, has a fine campus, combining the old in the historic "yard" and the new in the more recent houses fronting the Charles River. The **Agassiz Museum** at Harvard houses the world's finest collection of glass flowers. Massachusetts Institute of Technology, better known as **MIT,** is America's leading engineering school. Just east of Harvard, the MIT campus has some unusual exhibits plus some impressive new buildings of modern architecture. Further east in the **Charlestown** area is the **Bunker Hill Monument,** an austere obelisk marking the low hill (actually Breed's Hill) where British troops met the determined opposition of Americans in the famous Battle of Bunker Hill. **Boston Navy Yard,** nearby at the junction of the Charles and Mystic Rivers, has been an active naval establishment for 150 years; on display is the naval **frigate Constitution,** immortalized as "Old Ironsides." Also in Cambridge, near Harvard, the **Longfellow House** on Brattle Street is just one of the many colonial buildings of interest. Built in 1759 this house served as Washington's headquarters early in the

war and later as the home of the poet Longfellow.

Boston has a world-wide reputation for its fine foods, especially those New England dishes such as clam chowder, boiled dinners and sea food of all sorts. Of local origin are Boston cream pie, brown bread and baked beans and Parker House rolls; the latter originated by the chef of the Parker House Hotel.

Sporting events are constantly being held with both college and professional teams competing for national rankings in baseball, football, basketball and hockey.

For the theatergoer the area south of the Common boasts of many theaters where Broadway shows appear following their New York run.

MASSACHUSETTS' ATTRACTIONS

North of Boston is the city of SALEM where the witchcraft trials took place in 1692. The buildings that remain from these early dark days include the Court House, the Witch House and the reconstructed jail. From the more glorious days of the Clipper Ships when Salem was a famous shipping center there are the many old captains' homes on Chestnut Street. **Salem Maritime National Historic Site** preserves the old Custom House, Derby Wharf and Derby House. Also in Salem is Hawthorne's **House of the Seven Gables.** . . . On CAPE ANN is the old fishing port of GLOUCESTER with narrow streets and miles of colorful wharves where boats in from the Grand Banks unload tons of fish. . . . In a wide area around Boston are found the industrial cities of New England: Lawrence, Lowell, Worcester, Waltham and Manchester. These busy cities are interspaced with many small, New England towns complete with tidy village greens and white churches, towns like LEXINGTON and CONCORD where the first engagements occurred between British troops and American Minute Men. On the Lexington Green the first volleys of the war were fired as a small number of Minute Men under Capt. John Parker opposed the British marching on Concord. Dispersed by the British, the Americans fought a second battle that same day at the bridge at Concord, ending with the complete rout of seasoned British troops. LEXINGTON today is a quiet town whose main activity centers around the 7:15 commuter train to Boston. . . . CONCORD added to her colonial history by becoming an important literary center. Emerson, Thoreau and Hawthorne all lived here; the sleepy pond of Walden is only a short distance away.

On lovely **Buzzards Bay** in Massachusetts, **New Bedford** was once the most important whaling port in the world. The whaling days passed with the discovery of petroleum but their reminders are present in an interesting **whaling museum** on Johnny Cake Hill and the **seaman's chapel** made famous in Melville's *Moby Dick.* . . . A pleasant boat trip takes visitors from New Bedford to the islands of **Martha's Vineyard** and **Nantucket** and to **Woods Hole** on Cape Cod. Nantucket and Martha's Vineyard, once important as whaling centers, now attract visitors as summer resorts. Much · of the old charm of the seafaring towns remains to be enjoyed along with the fine beaches and good fishing waters. . . . CAPE COD, long a summer playground, is marked by sand dunes and beaches whose dazzling whiteness is relieved by green marshlands and blue tidal inlets. Small resort towns dot the long arm of the cape. The larger summer colonies are at HYANNIS and PROVINCETOWN. At DENNIS there is the **Cape Playhouse**, one of the more successful summer theatres with big name stars. SANDWICH once produced the famous Sandwich colored glass. A collection of this now rare and valuable glass may be seen at the town's historical society. Summer theaters and artists' colonies abound but despite the unavoidable commercialism there is still plenty of natural beauty to enjoy. . . . Across Cape Cod Bay from Provincetown is PLYMOUTH, site of the first permanent colony of the Pilgrims. Plymouth Rock where the Pilgrims first stepped ashore is now protected with a granite monument. Nearby has been built a full-size replica of a pilgrim house. A Pilgrim Trail directs the visitor to the places of historic interest throughout the town. During the month of August and at Thanksgiving time local citizens dressed in Pilgrim attire re-enact the scene of the Pilgrims' going to church.

NEW HAMPSHIRE AND MAINE

The coastline of New Hampshire has only one seaport, PORTSMOUTH. Here there are many reminders of its colonial past in fine old houses and narrow winding streets. A protective harbor shelters many pleasure craft as well as the ships of the U.S. Navy. . . . Just beyond the narrow bit of coast claimed by New Hampshire is MAINE, almost as large as the rest of the New England states combined. The famous rugged coastline of Maine has its southern beginnings in a subdued coastal strip of sandy beaches such as that of OLD ORCHARD. . . . At PORTLAND further north, the shore line becomes more dramatic, where unprotected headlands bear the attack of the seas while the long-fingered bays offer calm and safety. A steamboat from Portland takes visitors around Casco Bay, stopping at the many resort islands. A short way inland from Portland is Sebago Lake, popular resort area for children and adult camps. . . . Northeast from Portland the indented coast presents a succession of resort communities with summer theaters, art colonies and old sailing ship cruises. In all these coastal towns Maine lobster and other sea food fresh from the sea is at its best. . . . On one of the long peninsulas jutting out into the ocean is BOOTHBAY HARBOR, a pleasan old seaport with a quiet harbor. . . . At ACADIA NATIONAL PARK on Mt. Desert Island, there is an inspiring combination of ocean and mountain scenery. Here the granite cliffs have been undermined at the base by the pounding surf, leaving caves in some places. Mt. Cadillac, accessible by car, presents a fine view of the harbor and islands. Trails, roads and sea cruises have helped to make this magnificent region one of the finest vacation spots in the East. The center of the island's social life here is BAR HARBOR. . . . Inland, a journey up the Penobscot River

Entrancing little cog railway on Mount Washington in New Hampshire

N. H. Plan. & Dev. Com.
Photo, D. B. Grundy

leads to the lumber center of **BANGOR** and **OLD TOWN**, site of the Old Town canoe factory (open to visitors). . . . The many lakes of Maine are the last remains of the great ice sheet that once covered the area. Those lakes closer to the metropolitan areas are sites of popular summer camps, where movies and ice cream are only as far as a drive to a nearby town. . . . In the northern woods, however, lakes are set among the trackless forests and provide ample solitude and unblemished wilderness for nature lovers or sportsmen. From **Moosehead Lake** north to the Canadian border there are no roads; only the waterways of the Alagash, St. John and other rivers penetrate the endless . forests. . . . Northeast of Moosehead is **Mt. Katahdin** in **BAXTER STATE PARK,** one of America's great fish and game preserves. Katahdin is Maine's highest peak and marks the beginning of the **Appalachian Mountain Trail,** over which hikers may go as far south as Georgia if ambitious enough. . . . In northeast Maine, along the Canadian boundary, is the large agricultural country of Aroostook, producer of Maine's great potato crop. Twenty communities take part each summer in a **Potato Blossom Festival** to celebrate the coming harvest. . . . In the Blue Mountains of western Maine are the sprawling **Rangeley Lakes,** long famous for their trout and landlocked salmon. Not only fishermen come here, however, for there are opportunities for the other outdoor sports of horseback riding, hiking, etc. In wintertime the **Blue Mountains** are a popular skiing region.

In northern **NEW HAMPSHIRE** the **White Mountains** rival Maine's scenic wonders. The beauty of New Hampshire lies in her granite peaks, rushing mountain streams, endless wooded hills, well-kept valley farms and neat villages. Each summer thousands visit the areas to view the mountain passes of **Franconia Notch** and **Crawford Notch**; the **Flume,** a 700-foot sluiceway through granite cliffs; **Old Man of the Mountain,** the stern profile of man, carved by nature, and **Lost River Reservation,** a series of caverns and giant potholes carved by an ancient glacial stream. Towering above this enticing country is **Mt. Washington.** The windy summit of New England's highest mountain is reached by a quaint cog railway, from near Bretton Woods on the west or by hairpin road from Pinkham Notch on the east side. With the arrival of the winter snow this whole area becomes a great winter sports land. The slopes around **BERLIN** and **NORTH CONWAY** offer excellent ski facilities for both novice and·expert skier alike. . . . The area south of the White Mountains is not without its own attractions. The Connecticut and Merrimac Rivers, many small lakes and the giant Lake Winnipesaukee provide ample recreational facilities. Winnipesaukee with hundreds of islands, bays, and coves is one of New England's loveliest lakes. Boats make daily circuit of the lake during the summer. Water sports are a popular attraction at **The Weirs.** . . . At **HANOVER, Dartmouth College** breaks out from the academic world each February to put on a popular Winter Carnival, featuring skiing and skating exhibitions and ice sculptures.

AROUND VERMONT

In **VERMONT** the Green Mountains reach from Canada to Massachusetts in a long never-ending chain of forested hills overlooking quiet towns and valley farms.

The **Long Trail** which follows the ridges of the Green Mountains throughout their length provides hikers with a well-marked trail with numerous shelters and camp-sites. In the north the slopes of Mt. Mans-field have made **STOWE** a skiers' haven with deep snow, excellent trails, lifts and tows and pleasant inns and lodges. . . Nearby **Smugglers Notch** was once used by smugglers bringing goods from Canada. At **BURLINGTON**, on Lake Champlain, the University of Vermont is located. From the campus there is a fine view of the lake, with the Adirondacks as a backdrop. **MONTPELIER**, the state capital, is set in the narrow Winooski River Valley. The handsome granite State House is topped by a gold dome. There are a number of inter-esting historical items to be seen in the building proper as well as in the annex housing the Vermont Historical Society.

Nearby **BARRE** is the center of the granite industry. Visitors should take time to visit the quarries and interesting finish-ing shops here at the granite center of Barre or around **RUTLAND**, to the south, where marble is extracted from deep with-in the ground. At **PROCTOR** on exhibit are specimens of fine stone work. South of Rutland is **MANCHESTER**, a well-known winter and summer resort and golf-ing center. Further south is the historic area around **BENNINGTON**. This is the homeland of Ethan Allen and his follow-ers, the "Green Mountain Boys," whose exploits against the British are famous. The plans for the capture of Fort Ticon-deroga were laid in the Catamount Tavern in Bennington. The important Battle of Bennington is commemorated by a tall monument. In the town itself there are many colonial buildings including the **First Congregational Church**, one of New England's finest churches, and Walloom-sac Inn, used continuously since 1764. . . . East of Bennington is the recently opened ski area of **WILMINGTON**.

THE BERKSHIRES

In western **MASSACHUSETTS**, the Berkshire Hills offer miles of scenic motor roads, hiking and skiing trails and dozens of lakes for summer sports. **TANGLE-WOOD** in the pleasant town of Lenox, is the permanent home of the **Berkshire Mu-sic Festival** with the Boston Symphony performing under the foremost conductors. Nearby are two other cultural attractions, Berkshire Playhouse at **STOCKBRIDGE**

and the **Jacob's Pillow Dance Festival** at **LEE**. . . . As the Connecticut River valley winds its way through southern New Eng-land, the quiet of the fertile valley of farms and tobacco sheds is interrupted by the activity of several large industrial cities. **SPRINGFIELD**, center of the fire-arms industry, has an interesting **armory** with displays of old and new weapons.

CONNECTICUT

In western **CONNECTICUT** the roll-ing Litchfield hills, a part of the Berkshire range, are a pleasant rural vacationland. Of the many charming small towns of the area, **LITCHFIELD** is outstanding for its street of 18th century mansions. . . . Hart-ford, to the east, has an impressive sky line of tall insurance buildings. Of interest besides the **State Capitol** are the **Mark Twain** home and the **Colt Museum** for firearms. . . . At Danbury, near New York State, the annual fair in October is a big attraction of the East. Close to New York City are the suburban communities of **GREENWICH, STAMFORD** and **DARIEN** with many fine old homes along with the new housing developments that have sprung up to meet the demand for pleasant country living. Further east along the Sound, **WESTPORT** has become a flourish-ing art colony with many top-notch artists and writers. The **Westport Summer Play-house** draws upon New York talent for its shows. **BRIDGEPORT**, one of the larger industrial centers which occupy the deep tidal river inlets has a beautiful beach at **Seaside Park** and **The P. T. Barnum Mu-seum** of circus life. . . . To the east, **STRATFORD** sponsors a Shakespeare drama festival. . . . In **NEW HAVEN** the Yale University Campus is interesting. The entire southern boundary on Long Island Sound is lined with pleasant sum-mer resort towns, with excellent bathing and yachting facilities. The smaller bays swarm with dinghies and small-class sail-boats while on open waters the prize sailing yachts prepare for ocean cruises. . . . Of the many pleasant Connecticut towns with their elm-arched streets and old homes, it is possible to name only a few. East of New Haven, **MADISON**'s village green is lined with early-American homes; the **Nathaniel Allis House** contains a museum of colonial period furnishings. **OLD SAY-BROOK**, at the mouth of the Connecticut River, and **NIANTIC** are just two of the older seaports that have become popular summer resorts. **NEW LONDON**, once a home port for whaling ships, now shelters the gray hulls of U. S. Navy submarines. The U.S. **Coast Guard Academy** is located here as well as the Connecticut College for Women, noted for its **Summer School of Dance** which specializes in modern dance. . . . To the east of New London **MYSTIC**, a small trim maritime community, earned world renown for the first clipper ships built there. The **Marine Historical Museum** is a treasure house of ship models, figureheads and sailing gear. Among the outdoor exhibits are the whaling ship *Charles W. Morgan* and the square rigger *Joseph Conrad*.

Revolution and the War of 1812. In the old port city may be seen colonial mansions and city buildings such as the **Old Colony House** and the **Old City Hall** of 1761. Along the shore drives outside of town are found the fabulous mansions that made Newport the resort center for the socially prominent families of New York at the turn of the 19th century; the palatial homes of the so-called "400" can best be seen on "Ocean Drive." **The Breakers**, the Vanderbilt mansion, is open to the public. Newport sport attractions are the tennis matches held in August and the June deep-water sailing classic to Bermuda and Annapolis in alternate years. The new-

A magical, "old-fashioned" New England winter
Standard Oil Co. of N.J.

RHODE ISLAND

The smallest state of the Union is highly industrialized but not without the charm of a colonial past and many fine recreational areas. Sailing and fishing are popular sports in the Narragansett Bay waters. The principal places of interest are on the shores of the bay. At **WICKFORD**, on the west side of the bay may be found St. Pauls Episcopal Church built in 1707. In nearby **EXETER** the South County Museum contains exhibits of colonial crafts and Americana. The resort island of **Jamestown**, to the south, boasts a colonial windmill. **NEWPORT** across the bay (reached by ferries from Jamestown) is perhaps unique in America for its varied history and activities. In early American times it was successively a colonial seaport, then a center for naval activities during the

est phenomenon to come to Newport is a summer **Jazz Festival** featuring the top names in Dixie-Land and modern jazz. . . . **PROVIDENCE**, the state capital, is particularly interesting around **Brown University**. The campus is attractive as well as the fine old residences of Providence's more wealthy citizens. The **First Baptist Church** organized by Roger Williams is one of the city's finer buildings; also the place of Brown commencements since 1775. **Roger Williams Park** has spacious grounds with rose gardens, drives and an outdoor amphitheater for special events. . . . Block Island, 25 miles south of Narragansett Bay, offers some outstanding tuna and swordfish fishing waters on the Atlantic. Ferry service is available from the mainland at **NARRAGANSETT** and New London.

COUNTRY	CLIMATE	CUSTOMS AND ENTRY REQUISITES	TIPPING	MONEY	WATER	HOTELS	WHAT TO BUY
ALASKA	In southeastern Alaska, there is no great variation between summer and winter temperatures and near sea level the yearly average is mild. However, precipitation is heavy but decreases rapidly going inland. On the peninsula, temperature variation is definitely pronounced, the temperature sometimes falling as low as 70° below in winter and rising to 90° above in summer. Only the Arctic coast can be categorized as frozen waste.	No passport for U.S. citizens, but proof of citizenship may be required. Naturalized citizens must present citizenship papers, while resident aliens should obtain re-entry permit from nearest U.S. Immigration Office.	Same as U.S.	Same as U. S.	Perfectly safe.	There are fewer hotels per city than in U.S., so reservations have to be made in advance. In some of the interior recreation areas, lodges are available. While hotel rates run the same as U.S., prices of meals are 10% to 50% higher.	Hematite, or "black diamond," jewelry; Eskimo ivory carvings, baleen basketry, models (boats, harpoons, sleds, masks), grass basketry and skin sewing; moosehide moccasins, gloves, vests, beaded skin work, birch-bark basketry, split-willow basketry of the interior Indians; wood carvings, especially of totems, masks and potlatch bowls, skin sewing, spruce-root and cedar-bark basketry, Chilkat blankets of the southeastern Alaska Indians.
ALGERIA	From October to June, the coast has a mild Mediterranean climate comparable to that of the French Riviera, the mountains have a rather severe, snowy climate, while the Saharian regions are dry with no bad weather.	Passport, certificate of vaccination against smallpox. Personal effects admitted duty free.	Same as in France.	$1=349 francs, 1c =3.5 francs.	Usually safe and bottled water is available.	Comfortable hotels are all over, including many at the seaside resorts, the mountain resorts and the spas.	Handwoven carpets of designs handed down through the years, sweetmeat, brass trays, jewelry, pottery and leather work.
ARGENTINA	Much like U.S., except reversed seasons. Southern and Andean section cool even in summer.	Passport; good health certificate from doctor stating freedom from contagious diseases; certificate of good conduct from local police. May bring in all articles for personal use.	Bellhops, etc., 1 peso per service. Waiters, 10% extra. Cabdrivers, 25%. In general, tip as in U.S. with peso equivalent to quarter.	1c=20 centavos, 5c =70 centavos, $1 =14 pesos, $2 = 27.30 pesos, 100 centavos=peso.	Bottled water advised.	Excellent accommodations in cities and resorts.	Mate gourds with silver bombillas; leather goods; native handicrafts made from wool and fur; gaucho paraphernalia; vicuna ponchos; rugs, house slippers and bedspreads of guanaco fur.
AUSTRALIA	Much of Australia resembles California, but in reverse, with no great extremes of temperature. The north has monsoonal weather and Tasmania is rainy and misty. Inland is desert.	Passport; visa; vaccination certificate; evidence of sufficient funds. May bring in all personal effects free.	Same as in U.S.	1 pound=$2.24, 20 shillings=1 pound, 12 pennies=1 shilling.	Perfectly safe.	Excellent accommodations.	Woolen fabrics, crocodile handbags and shoes, opals, etc.
AUSTRIA	Has a temperate subalpine climate. Never gets extremely hot, is seldom piercingly cold and except in small areas, for brief periods, is rarely humid.	Passport. Personal articles admitted free.	Bellhops, 1 schilling per bag plus liberal tip. Waiters, 15%. Cabdrivers, 10%.	$1 = 26 schillings, 1 schilling = less than 4c.	Perfectly safe and very tasty throughout the country.	Excellent Hotels in cities and resorts.	Glassware; folk costumes, especially in Salzburg; wooden articles; guns; textiles; skiing equipment.

COUNTRY	CLIMATE	CUSTOMS AND ENTRY REQUISITES	TIPPING	MONEY	WATER	HOTELS	WHAT TO BUY
BAHAMAS	Visitors go sea bathing thruout the winter and in the summer, sea breezes allay the sultriness common to so many southern resorts. The mean average temperature ranges from about 80° in July, Aug. and Sept. to about 67° in Feb.	Citizenship identification.	Waiters, 10% - 15%. Bellboys, a shilling or two. Cabdrivers, slightly more than 15%. When in doubt, tip as at home.	U.S. dollars are accepted generally.	Pure in Nassau. Elsewhere the boiling of water is still a necessary precaution.	Accommodations in Nassau are expanding, but reservations should be made during the season.	Textiles; leather goods; china; perfumes; wines; silver; crystal; native crafts like bags, mats, sandals and hats woven from palm strips or sisal, and novelty jewelry made from sea shells, fish scales and coral.
BARBADOS, B.W.I.	Barbados is the healthiest of the West Indian Islands. There is little variation in temperature, its range being generally from 69° F. to 90°F. Constant consecutive days of rain seldom occur.	Passport. Used clothing and certain bona fide personal effects, like jewelry and used sport requisites, admitted duty free.	10-15% unless included on bill.	British West Indian dollar—58c, $1 = $1.69 B.W.I.	An excellent water supply, obtained from a subterranean reservoir of fresh water and streams.	Numerous hotels, residential clubs and guest houses throughout the island.	Rum, handicrafts, pottery, "sea-island cotton."
BELGIAN CONGO, BRITISH EAST AFRICA AND RHODESIA	Over such an immense territory, climatic conditions will vary considerably, but this large area enjoys a pleasant climate throughout the year. Certain periods are more favorable, nature being generally at its best between mid-October and mid-April.	Passport, visa, police registration upon arrival, vaccinations against smallpox and yellow fever. Before leaving, it is suggested that you consult your doctor as to what type of preventive you should use against malaria.	10 - 12% in hotels and restaurants. 10 francs for incidental services.	In the Belgian Congo: $1 = 50 francs, 1c = 50 centimes. In British East Africa: $1 = 7 shillings, 1c = 1 pence, $2.80 = 1 pound, $3 = 1 pound, 1 shilling.	Safe.	It is not always possible to secure accommodations with private bath in Africa, and reservations should be made in advance.	Ivory and wood carvings and other native handicrafts.
BELGIUM	Temperature is not extreme at any season. Best months, however, are May — Sept.	Passport, smallpox vaccination.	Bellhops, hotels add 12% - 15% service charge. Waiters, small charge if service charge of 12% - 15% is added; if not, tip 12% - 15%. Cabdrivers, 15% - 25%.	$1 = 50 Belgian francs, 5c = 2.5 Belgian francs, 1 franc = 100 centimes, 1c = 50 centimes.	Perfectly safe.	Good accommodations all over but make reservations.	Laces; various objects in wood from Spa; crystal; Flemish earthenware; stoneware vases; sporting goods; wooden toys; ceramics; shoes; cakes and biscuits.
BERMUDA	The annual average temperature is 70.7°, with summer temperatures from about mid-April to Dec. and spring-like temperatures from about mid-November to May. There is no rainy season.	Proof of U.S. citizenship.	Same as U.S.	United States currency is readily accepted. Bermuda pound = $2.82.	Perfectly safe—but don't waste it.	There are numerous fine hotels and guest houses, but make reservations first, especially in spring and summer. Bermuda's hotels are noted for their good food, service and social life.	Liquor-in-bond; cashmere or Shetland sweaters; woolens; leather goods; china and silver; perfume; fishing tackle; English pipes and pipe tobacco; locally made cedar boxes.
BOLIVIA	Climate varies in the different regions: The plateau region is clear and cold; the eastern region is generally hot and humid, as are the tropical lowlands.	Passport. You may bring in items for personal use; there is a limit on tobacco.	10 - 15% is the general practice.	The Boliviano is the unit of currency. Its value fluctuates greatly; at present $1.00 = 192 bolivianos.	Bottled water recommended.	Hotels in large cities are usually filled. Best to have a reservation.	Vicuña and alpaca fur garments, hand-woven rugs, pottery jugs, idols, carved stone, wooden figurines, wood and copper images of saints, silver jewelry.

COUNTRY	CLIMATE	CUSTOMS AND ENTRY REQUISITES	TIPPING	MONEY	WATER	HOTELS	WHAT TO BUY
BRAZIL	The Amazon basin is characterized by high temperatures and humid atmospheric conditions. The northeastern states are warm but dry. The southern and central coastal regions have a more agreeable climate, being somewhat cooler and benefiting from a moderate but adequate rainfall.	Passport, visa, health certificate, letter proving you have sufficient funds for maintenance. Personal effects, including camera and cigarettes, admitted free.	Bellhops, 5 to 10 cruzeiros per bag. Waiters, 10%-20%. Cabdrivers, 10%.	$1 = 60 cruzeiros, 5c = 3 cruzeiros, 1c = 60 centavos.	Bottled water advised, except in the larger hotels and restaurants and in the bigger towns.	Very good accommodations in Rio and some interior towns have surprisingly good accommodations, although most of them are equal to the second-class hotels in Rio.	Antiques; wood carvings; hand-made lingerie and blouses; Portuguese silver; precious and semi-precious stones, including topazes, amethysts and aquamarines; leather goods, including alligator handbags.
BURMA	Hot February to May; rainy May to November, cool November to February.	Passport, visa, health certificate, smallpox vaccination. Limits on tobacco and alcoholic beverages brought in.	Check locally for practice.	1 kyat=6c.	Bottled water recommended.	Fair accommodations in the capital, but have reservations.	Gold and silver articles; teak and ivory carvings; precious stones, woven textiles.
CEYLON	For a tropical country, the climate of Ceylon is comparatively healthy. There is a well-marked season of the year known as the "hot" season, generally March to May, when conditions are best described as "sticky." During the cool season, roughly November to February, the nights are cool.	Passport, visa. Wearing apparel and personal effects, including 100 cigarettes, exempt from duty.	Check with your hotel manager for local practice.	$1=4.74 Ceylon rupees, 1 rupee=21c.	Perfectly safe in Colombo, Kandy and other larger cities.	Advisable to make reservations.	Pottery; basketware; hand-woven textiles and mats; precious and semi-precious stones, including sapphires, rubies, aquamarines, topazes, spinels, garnets, zircons and moonstones; tea; cinnamon; lacquerware; lace work; silverware; brassware; ivory; woodwork.
CHILE	In the north the temperature maintains a steady average of from 70° to 80°. The central valley is pleasant but becomes colder in the winter months. The south is rainy except from December to March, when it is clear and warm.	Passport, health certificate, smallpox vaccination.	Bellhops, 10 pesos. Waiters, 12%-20%. Cabdrivers, not tipped.	$1=110 pesos.	Bottled water advised.	Facilities are excellent.	Long-napped rugs and ponchos made by descendents of Araucanian Indians; pure-wool blankets, belts and scarves, and musical instruments made of chestnut wood, from the islands of Chiloé; fine leatherwork; carved wooden figures; terra cotta ware; copperware.
COLOMBIA	The lowlands bordering the Atlantic and Pacific have perpetual summer; the intermediate area enjoys perpetual spring and the higher regions enjoy perpetual winter.	Tourist card and smallpox vaccination certificate.	Same as in the U. S.	1 peso = 39c; the peso is divided into 100 centavos.	Safe in large cities; bottled water recommended elsewhere.	Excellent in large cities. Check reservations in smaller places.	Hats, shoes and bags woven of native fiber; articles of alligator skin, tortoise shell and mother-of-pearl; silver, wood and leather products; drawn linen; Indian rugs and blankets; figurines sculptured from crude rubber and tinted.

COUNTRY	CLIMATE	CUSTOMS AND ENTRY REQUISITES	TIPPING	MONEY	WATER	HOTELS	WHAT TO BUY
COSTA RICA	Ideal climate year round, but at its best November to April. Central plateau averages around 70°. Slightly cooler in mountains (sweater and coat necessary) and rather warmer on the coasts. Rainy season between April and November.	Passport and visa. May bring in all articles for personal use. Limits on tobacco and liquor.	About the same as in U.S.	$1.00 = 5.6 colons. 1 colon = about 18c. More favorable on free exchange market.	Tap water in the cities is safe.	Hotels are plentiful, clean and serve good food. There are also innumerable private homes and boarding houses who welcome guests.	Hand painted miniatures of the traditional ox carts. Native crafts—wood, leather, fabric and earthenware articles. Embroidered and painted women's skirts and blouses. Handmade jewelry, new and antique.
CUBA	Due to the subtropical position and insular condition, Cuba enjoys a delightful climate, constantly refreshed by the trade winds and land breezes.	Proof of U.S. citizenship, tourist card. Free entry of regular baggage.	Same as in U.S.	$1 = peso, 1 peso = 100 centavos.	Bottle water recommended.	Comfortable accommodations can be found at every place mentioned, and almost anywhere else on the island.	Liquor, especially rum; leather goods; shoes; cigars and cigarettes.
CURAÇAO	The annual average temperature is 81 degrees, varying from 78 in January to 87 in September. November and December are the rainy months.	U. S. citizens need only birth certificate or naturalization certificate if naturalized citizens.	10 to 15% as in the U. S.	1 guilder = 53c. The guilder is divided into 100 cents.	Perfectly safe.	There are a number of good hotels moderately priced.	Curaçao's shopping center is an international market. Sold across its fabulous counters are articles gathered from all over the world.
CYPRUS	In summer it is hot and dry on the plains, damp and hot on the seashore and on the hills inland equable and invigorating. The winter is mild and cool season is from October to March.	Check with your travel agent.	10 - 15% included in bill.	Same as Great Britain.	Safe.	Accommodation is available in all the principal towns.	
DENMARK	Despite Denmark's northerly location, its climate is pleasant and comfortable, thanks to the warm influence of the Gulf Stream. Summer temperatures are much like late spring in the United States.	Passport.	Bellhops, .75 to 1 krone per day. Waiters, 15%. Cabdrivers, 10% to 15%.	15c = krone, 1 krone = 100 öre.	Perfectly safe.	Good hotels in all price classes are available. It's important to have reservations in advance, especially in Copenhagen.	Fine silver, steelware, porcelain, furniture, textiles and many handmade articles for the home.
DOMINICAN REPUBLIC	Average is 77°, with only four to five degrees of difference between summer and winter.	Tourist card.	10 - 15% unless included in bill.	1 peso = $1, 100 centavos = $1.	Safe water supply everywhere.	Government completed last year a vast new program of hotel construction in the various resort areas.	Sisal and mahogany articles, native handicrafts, tortoise-shell or amber ornaments; paintings; needlework.
ECUADOR	The highland region enjoys a temperate climate all year. The rainy season is from November to May, the dry season from July to November. Coastal regions range from cool to hot with wet and dry seasons opposite from those of the highlands.	Tourist card from Ecuadorian consulate.	10-15%. Tip 1 sucre for incidental services.	1 sucre = 6c. The sucre is divided into 100 centavos.	Bottled water recommended.	Excellent accommodations may be had in all large cities.	Woolen rugs, blankets, ponchos, shawls, suit material resembling fine English tweed made by the Otavalo Indians, "Panama hats" from Jipijapa, willow baskets, hand-carved articles of vegetable ivory from the Tagua palm, dolls in native dress and Indian souvenirs.

COUNTRY	CLIMATE	CUSTOMS AND ENTRY REQUISITES	TIPPING	MONEY	WATER	HOTELS	WHAT TO BUY
EGYPT	Spring, fall and winter are seasons of warm weather with few rainy days. Summers, though, are hot with low humidity.	Passport; visa; registration at police station within three days after arrival. Personal effects including foodstuffs, alcoholic beverages and tobacco for own use, admitted free.	Porters, 2 piastres per piece of luggage or service. Waiters, 20% if no service charge, otherwise 10%. Cabdrivers not generally tipped.	$1 = 34.8 piastres, 100 piastres = Egyptian Pound, 1 piastre = 10 milliems (mills).	Safe.	Advisable to make reservations.	Wooden objects encrusted with ivory and ebony; copper plates encrusted with different metals; Egyptian perfumes; brocades and hand embroideries; precious stones; leather goods; pottery; cotton cloth; carpets. Silver and gold filigree jewelry.
EL SALVADOR	Comfortably warm; particularly pleasant during the summer months of November to April. On its many plateaus and hills the average temperature is 75, while the coastal areas are warmer. Its rainy season is from April to November.	Passport, visa. No plants or fruits may be brought in. To the U. S. without permission from the Dept. of Agriculture.	10% is generally acceptable.	Monetary unit is the colon, equal to 40c in U.S. currency.	Bottled water advised.	Many hotels and boarding houses throughout the country, especially in San Salvador.	Pottery llobascon dolls; Isalcon gourd bowls; Panchimalcon textiles; hand-made leather shoes and bags; blankets; rugs; table-cloths; hammocks, bags and sandals woven from sisal fiber; decorative baskets.
FIJI ISLANDS	In northern and western areas, most rain falls between December and March. Temperatures seldom go above 90° or fall below 60°; the cool season from April to September can be delightful.	Passport. Personal effects, including 200 cigarettes and 1 quart of liquor, admitted free.	10% is generally acceptable.	$2.50 = 1 Fijian pound, 1 Fijian pound = 20 shillings, 1 shilling = 12 pence.	Perfectly safe at Suva, Tavua and other large settlements.	There are good hotels at all the resorts, but reservations should be made, especially during the cool season from April to September.	Masi, or tapa cloth, a bark cloth made from the paper mulberry tree and stenciled with intricate patterns in dyes made from clays and tree sap; and other native handicrafts.
FINLAND	The climate of southern Finland corresponds to that of Maine. The warmest month is July, with temperatures well up in the high 70's and low 80's.	Passport; visa. All personal effects including cameras, are duty free.	Service charges are added to bill in hotels and restaurants. Cabdrivers do not expect tips.	$1 = 340 Finnmarks, 1 Finnmark = 100 pennies.	Excellent.	Modern hotels and tourist inns have been built all over the country, and even the most faraway reaches are conveniently accessible.	Wood products and carvings, pottery, glassware, fabrics.
FRANCE	Much like the U.S. except the extremes of hot and cold are not as great. Paris, lovely in any season, is best in spring and fall. Winter in Paris means summer in the Riviera.	Passport; visa only if stay is longer than 3 months. May bring in all articles for personal use. Limits on tobacco and liquor.	Hotel bills and restaurant checks usually include tip. Check, and if not give 12-15%. Tip bellboys 100 francs per service. Tip wine steward personally. Taxi drivers, 20% (fares much less than U.S.; they increase after 11 P.M.). Hat check and washroom attendants, as in the U. S. Porters, 50 francs per bag.	$1.00 = 350 francs. Use 100 francs as our quarter for tipping, etc.	Tap water in Paris is good. Varies in other parts, but bottle water is excellent and inexpensive. Some famous brands, Perrier, Vichy, Evien, Vittel.	Paris offers countless hotels and pensions to suit any pocketbook. However, if you go in spring or summer, have a reservation. The same is true of seacoast resorts and of the Riviera in winter. Regional inns are good and plentiful.	Women's fashions of course. Gloves, handmade lingerie, belts, artificial flowers and other accessories. Men's ties, scarves and handkerchiefs. Perfume and jewelry (real and costume). Fine china, ceramics, glassware and bric-a-brac. Paintings and engravings. Wines, liqueurs, and brandies. A smart umbrella and perhaps a French poodle.

COUNTRY	CLIMATE	CUSTOMS AND ENTRY REQUISITES	TIPPING	MONEY	WATER	HOTELS	WHAT TO BUY
GERMANY	Germany is cooler in the summer, but not quite so cold in the winter as the northern United States. Snowfall is heavy only in the Alps, in northern Germany and on the higher slopes of the mountain ranges in the central part.	Passport. Personal effects duty free. May take out $400 in gifts. An equal amount may be taken in and out in transit.	Bellhops, 20 pfennigs per service. Waiters, 5% - 15% more, despite service charge of 10%. Cabdrivers, 15%.	$1=4.20 Deutsche Marks. 1 Mark=24c. 100 pfennigs=1 Mark. 1c=.04 pfennigs. 50c=2.10 pfennigs.	All cities and towns now have pure drinking water. Only in the smallest of villages which might still have wells or pumps is it necessary to be careful in drinking the water.	It is advisable to reserve your rooms in advance, both to make sure that you get a room at all and to make sure you get the kind you want.	Cameras and binoculars; chinaware, including the Hummel ceramic figurines, especially Hanau silver; steelware, especially Solingen steel; toys, especially toy trains; Bavarian costumes, including the leather shorts; antiques, with Berlin the best place to buy them; handmade cuckoo clocks and 400-day clocks from the Black Forest; leather goods; gadgets; jewelry, especially garnets.
GREAT BRITAIN	London and the south much like San Francisco though more changeable and damper. (Summer average 70°; winter, 45°). Northern England and Scotland are slightly colder. Even in summer a light coat is needed and suits and sweaters come in handy.	Passport. You may bring all articles for personal use. Restrictions on tobacco and liquor.	Some hotels add 10 - 15% to the bill. If they don't, divide tip accordingly among those serving you. Tip same percentage in restaurants. 10% of a pound is two shillings. Tip taxi drivers sixpence or ninepence if fare is under five shillings, a shilling if fare is more. A shilling is sufficient for porters carrying a bag to your taxi.	1 pound = $2.80. 1 shilling = 14c (20 shillings to a pound) (12 pennies to a shilling).	Perfectly safe.	London has many excellent hotels to suit any taste or budget. Country inns and hotels are equally good, though you may not find a private bath in most of them.	For men there is the best in every type of wearing apparel including shoes. Woolens (sweaters, scarves, socks and yarn goods). Men's pipes and umbrellas. Raincoats for men and women. Antique silver, fine china, porcelain and glass. Irish linen. Leather goods. Gin and Scotch Whiskey.
GREECE	Spring and autumn are the best seasons for visiting Greece; the climate during these seasons is mild and temperate. Even during the winter months there is plenty of sun, while in summer, though the days are hot, the nights are always reasonably cool.	Passport. Used personal articles admitted free, and up to $300 value of new articles.	Bellhops, 5 drachmas for a lot of luggage. Waiters, 15% service charge is added. Cabdrivers, ½ - 1 drachma.	$1 = 30 drachmas.	Safe.	Athens, Thessaloniki, Corfu and Rhodes and certain other towns and health resorts are well-provided with up-to-date hotel accommodations, although visitors are advised to reserve accommodations in advance of their arrival.	Local wines; hand-woven materials, including embroideries; silversmith's ware, like cigarette cases or peasant ornaments; carved woodwork, like walking sticks, boxes or chests; glassware; hand-woven tapestries.
GUADELOUPE	There are two seasons: the carême, relatively cool and dry, from January to April, and the hivernage, warmer and wetter, from July to Oct. Generally speaking, the climate is mild and healthy.	Passport, smallpox vaccination.	Bellhops, 100 francs per vice charge, tip 12%-15%. Cabdrivers, 20%. service. Waiters, if no ser-	Legal currency is the French franc. $1=349 francs, $2=698 francs, 1c=3.5 francs.	Sterilized.	Excellent and comfortable hotels. Write well in advance for the dependencies.	Dolls dressed in Creole costume; "armed fish" stuffed and "saintois" hats with a fetching curve.

COUNTRY	CLIMATE	CUSTOMS AND ENTRY REQUISITES	TIPPING	MONEY	WATER	HOTELS	WHAT TO BUY
GUATEMALA	Ideal climate year round, but at its best November to April. Plateau surrounding the capital averages about 60°. 8 - 9 degrees cooler in mountains and about 8-9 degrees warmer on tropical coasts. Rainy season May to October.	Tourist card obtainable from Guatemalan Consulate or travel agent and vaccination certificate less than a year old. Limits on tobacco and liquor but may bring all articles for personal use.	About the same as in the U.S.	$1.00 = 1 quetzal. The quetzal is subdivided into 100 cents as ours.	Guatemala City water is good. Water elsewhere should be boiled. Typhoid injections a good idea.	Hotels in Guatemala City and in Highland resorts are good and serve fine meals. Pensions, at less cost, are also available in the city.	Hand-woven fabrics are incomparably fine and colorful. Women's skirts and shadow-work blouses. Silver jewelry and ornaments. Pottery, woven baskets and mats. Decorative masks and dolls in native dress. Sandals for men and women and hand-tooled shoulder bags.
HAITI	Warm and equable. In the chief cities, the yearly range is from 70° to 85°F., with a slight variation between seasons. Mountain heights are considerably cooler, sometimes even subject to frost. Normally, rain comes from April through June and during October and November.	Health certificate, smallpox vaccination, round-trip ticket, tourist card.	10 - 15% unless included in bill.	Gourde=20c. U. S. currency is legal tender.	Safe in Port-au-Prince, Jacmel and Petionville. Should be boiled elsewhere.	Good hotels, in every price range.	Mahogany, tortoise - shell and sisal articles; Barbacourt Rhum; creole earrings; silver bracelets; French perfumes; embroidered fabrics; Haitian carpets; Haitian paintings and hand painted articles; Haitian records.
HAWAII	Pleasant all year, much like our spring with no real rainy season.	No passport for U.S. citizens.	Same as the U. S.	Same as the U.S.	Perfectly safe.	Excellent hotels on main islands.	Jewelry, dolls, hand-woven articles, hula skirts and Oriental novelties.
HONDURAS	Varies with altitude, and has two distinct climatic zones: hot lowlands and cool highlands. In the mountain valleys the average temperature is 73 degrees. The average temperature in the coastal lowlands is 88 degrees.	Tourist Card, birth certificate, smallpox vaccination certificate.	About the same as in U.S.	Honduran monetary unit is the lempira, stabilized in 1952 at 49½c United States money.	Bottle water recommended.	Adequate in largest cities, must have reservations.	"Panama" hats, straw rugs, alligator skin articles, native earthenware, hand-woven crafts from the Indian territory and pieces of old Spanish, colonial silver.
HONG KONG	It is sub-tropical and governed to a large extent by the monsoons, the winter being normally cool and dry and the summer hot and humid. The summer is the rainy season. From July to October Hong Kong is most liable to be affected by typhoons.	Passport, visa, registration at U.S. Consulate. Personal effects admitted free.	Tipping at most places is about 10% of the bill.	$1=5.7 Hong Kong dollars.	Safe.	Hong Kong has a number of first-class hotels. To avoid disappointment, it would be wise to make reservations.	Dolls, pincushions; wastepaper baskets; camphorwood chests, carved furniture; ivoryware; silks; embroideries; linen and cotton goods; pewter and tinware; brass trays; embroidered footware; Japanese porcelainware decorated in Hong Kong; cork pictures; tea.

COUNTRY	CLIMATE	CUSTOMS AND ENTRY REQUISITES	TIPPING	MONEY	WATER	HOTELS	WHAT TO BUY
INDIA	The winter months (November-March) are extremely pleasant throughout India, although in the northern part, it is at times very cold. The summer (April-June) is generally hot. The monsoon, or rainy season, extends from July to September.	Passport, visa, registration upon arrival, yellow fever vaccination. Advised to have vaccinations against small-pox and cholera, also. Personal effects, not including radios and firearms, admitted free.	Hotels and rest houses generally do not include service charges in their bills. When no such charge is shown, tip approximately 10% of the bill. It is not customary to tip taxi drivers.	21c=1 rupee, 1 rupee=16 annas, $1 = 4 rupees, 12 annas.	Safe in the larger cities. In the smaller towns, it should be boiled.	All principal cities have good hotels run on Western style. Advised to reserve accommodation well in advance during the tourist season.	Leather and reptile-skin handbags; carved sandalwood and ivory articles; brass bowls; ornamental plates worked in silver; wooden toys; fancy wicker baskets; soft fine mats; Ellore carpets; embroidered linen; brocades of Banaras and Murshidabad; jewelry of Delhi and Jaipur; glass bangles of Firozabad; silks; lace; embroidered slippers; articles made from horn; copper ware; lacquer work.
INDONESIA	Although the sun is always hot at midday, it is cool in the early morning and in the evenings. Humidity is high even in the dry season.	Passport and visa. No restrictions on items for personal use. Limits on tobacco.	10-15% unless included in your bill.	The rupiah=9c.	Bottle water recommended.	Hotel accommodations are adequate in the largest cities.	Fine pottery, gold and silver ornaments from Bali; woven and plaited cigarette cases, purses and rattan products from Makassar; baked and hand-painted figurines from Surakarta; batik, leather goods and polished horn goods from Djokjakarta; brass gongs from Semarang.
IRAN	The country falls in the Temperate Zone. Teheran and the Caspian area have mild winters and hot summers. However, in summer the humidity is low and the nights cool, making conditions fairly comfortable.	Passport and visa.	10% is generally acceptable.	$1.00=80-100 rials. The value fluctuates greatly.	Bottle water recommended.	Hotel accommodations are adequate in the largest cities.	Carpets, rugs, embroideries and brocades; silver filigree, metalwork, lacquered ware, jewelry. Intriguing native handicrafts of all kinds abound in the bazaars.
IRAQ	Iraq is characterized by a hot summer and a mild winter. Summer begins in May and lasts until October. Winter, the rainy season, lasts from November to April.	Passport, visa. It is advisable to take every precaution against malaria. Personal effects admitted free.	Check with your hotel manager for local practice.	Iraqi dinar = $2.80 Iraqi dinar = 1,000 fils.	Bottled water advised.	Facilities adequate in largest cities.	Silverware, native handicrafts.
IRELAND	Slightly cooler than Great Britain with smaller range between summer and winter. There are frequent local showers, so take a raincoat.	Passport. No restrictions on items for personal use. Restrictions on tobacco and liquor.	Hotels usually add 10% service charge. 10-15% in restaurants. Tip sixpence for incidental services. Taxi drivers get a shilling for short trips, 10% for long ones.	Same as Great Britain.	Perfectly safe.	There are excellent hotels throughout the country, though a private bath is the exception rather than the rule.	Tweeds, linen and lace. Waterford glass, Belleck china and Arklow pottery. A good briar pipe. Irish whiskey. Craft souvenirs.

COUNTRY	CLIMATE	CUSTOMS AND ENTRY REQUISITES	TIPPING	MONEY	WATER	HOTELS	WHAT TO BUY
ISRAEL	Similar to that of southern California. Summer is warm and moist in the Coastal Plain, warm and dry in the hill regions, with cool nights. In the Hills of Galilee it is even cooler, while seaside resorts are favored by a cool Mediterranean breeze. Autumn and spring are comfortably warm.	Passport, visa, smallpox vaccination. Duty free on personal effects and used traveler's accessories, like cameras and portable radios, and other articles not exceeding $112 in value.	Not generally practiced. Service charge of 10% is added in restaurants and hotels. Additional tipping at individual's discretion.	$1==1.8 Lira or Israel pounds. I Israel pound == 1000 prutot (sing: pruta.)	Absolutely safe.	Advised to book hotel accommodations well in advance, particularly in Tel Aviv during the summer season and in Tiberias during the winter season.	Silver jewelry and other articles; gold and silver embroidered costume blouses, scarves and handbags; hand-wrought brass and copper pots, trays and vases; Persian carpets; articles and figurines of olive wood; vases and hand-painted tiles of Negev clay.
ITALY	You can pick your climate at almost any time of year, from sub-tropical south to the cool mountain regions. Rome is generally mild year round with cool evenings even during the hot spell from May to Sept.	Passport. No visa. May bring in all articles for personal use. Limits on tobacco and liquor.	In Italy everyone gets tipped, regardless of whether or not there is a service charge on your bill. Ten per cent is normal. 50 to 100 lire per service, depending upon circumstances is expected. Taxis at night get 150 lire in addition to normal fare.	$1.00—625 lire. 100 lire==16c. Use 150 lire (24c) like our quarter.	The water is good and safe to drink in Italy. Excellent bottle water is sold, also.	You will always find well-equipped, comfortable hotels but you will always need advance reservations.	Florentine leather, straw and silver articles; Venetian glass; cameos in Naples; silk in Como; Men's hats (Borsalino or Panizza); men's ties; gloves, lingerie, blouses and scarves; lace, linen, brocades; lipstick cases, zippo lighter cases and an elegant umbrella.
JAMAICA, B.W.I.	Tropical. No violent fluctuations of temperature. In the highest mountain resorts the temperature varies between 40° and 50°. Principal rainy time is September, October and May.	Return ticket. Advisable to have inoculation against yellow fever.	Waiters, 10% - 15%. Cab-drivers, slightly more than 15%.	British money used. 1 pound==$2.80, ½ crown==35c, 1 florin == 28c, 1 schilling == 14c, sixpence == 7c.	Pure in Kingston and other chief towns. Should be boiled in country districts.	Very many hotels and guest houses, with some very luxurious ones. Be sure to get reservations November to March.	Jamaica rum, perfumes, cashmere sweaters, linens, silverware, china, fine jewelry, crystal, leather goods, imported liquors.
JAPAN	With the exception of Hokkaido, the northernmost of the Japanese islands, the country has about the same climate as that of the middle belt of the U.S. or the central and southern parts of Europe.	Passport, visa, return ticket, money to cover expenses of visit. No duty on personal effects.	Bellhops, 100 yen per service. Waiters, 10% - 20%. Cabdrivers, tip not generally expected, but for a long or expensive trip 100 yen is convenient.	$1 == 360 yen, 100 yen==30c, 5 yen== 1½c.	Perfectly safe.	Well-equipped Western-style hotels are found in the large cities and leading tourist resorts and there are a large number of Japanese-style inns thruout the country.	Silks; pearls and pottery; porcelain and lacquer ware; dolls of all varieties; masks; lanterns and fans; bamboo ware; wood-block prints; art objects in silver, bronze, crystal, coral and ivory; tortoise-shell ware; hand-made paper; rush and straw products; cameras and binoculars.
JORDAN	Hot and dry in summer; winters are cool with heavy rainfall, except in the desert.	Passport and visa. Personal effects duty free but no firearms, radios or phonographs allowed. Restrictions on tobacco.	Check with your hotel manager for local practice.	1 dinar == $2.80. The dinar is divided into 1,000 fils.	Bottle water recommended.	Adequate accommodations in tourist centers.	Native handicrafts, including pottery, lovely jewelry, embroideries, hand-wrought silver.
LEBANON, see SYRIA and LEBANON							

COUNTRY	CLIMATE	CUSTOMS AND ENTRY REQUISITES	TIPPING	MONEY	WATER	HOTELS	WHAT TO BUY
LEEWARD ISLANDS, B.W.I.	Usually dry and fairly healthy. The mean temperature is about 80°. The hot season is from May to October and the rainy season from August to January. Antigua, however, is subject to drought.	Return ticket.	10 - 15% unless included in bill.	Same as Barbados.	Care must be taken with drinking water, which must be boiled.	There are comfortable hotels on Antigua and St. Kitts. There is only one hotel on Montserrat, although some private families will take boarders, and none on Barbuda.	Rum; native handicrafts.
LUXEMBOURG	Considerable variations in weather conditions, although never rigorous. Conditions are usually mild and healthful.	Passport. Articles for personal use admitted free.	Same as Belgium.	$1=50 Luxembourg francs, 5c = 2.5 francs, 100 centimes = 1 franc.	Perfectly safe.	Good accommodations available everywhere. Important reductions are granted during the periods between Easter and Whitsun, after Whitsun until the first of July and from the first of September.	Moselle wine, Luxembourg beer, black-currant wine, cottage industries.
MARTINIQUE	Cool and showery from December to March, warm and dry from April to July and hot with torrential downpours from July to November.	Passport, return passage, smallpox vaccination. No duty on personal effects.	Same as Guadeloupe.	Same as Guadeloupe.	Safe.	Accommodations are limited but comfortable.	French perfumes, rum and native handicrafts.
MEXICO	There are two seasons in Mexico - wet and dry. The wet season extends from June to October, the dry from November to May. Temperature varies with location, ranging from tropical to cool temperate.	Tourist card from Mexican consulate.	Same as in the U. S. Use a peso as a quarter for incidental services. Taxi drivers are not tipped.	1 peso = 8c.	Bottle water recommended in most parts of Mexico.	There are numerous hotel and tourist courts in Mexico ranging from moderate to expensive. Hotels in Mexico City are usually crowded and reservations should be made in advance.	Glazed ceramic-ware, silver jewelry, colorful serapes, tooled leather, glassware, carved and painted wooden masks, lacquered bowls and trays, retablos or religious picture drawings, basketware.
MOROCCO	In summer the temperature is high in eastern and southern Morocco. The coast is cooler but the atmosphere is damp. In winter the temperature is agreeable throughout Morocco, so the best time to visit the country is from the end of October to the end of May.	Passport, no vaccination required during epidemics. Used clothing and personal effects, including typewriter, admitted free.	10 - 15% unless included in bill.	$1=349 francs, 1c = 3.5 francs.	Usually safe, but bottled water is available.	Morocco has every kind of hotel accommodations, but visitors are advised to make reservations in hotels in the main towns, especially for Christmas, New Year and Easter.	Corded, crocheted caps; fine leather work, especially from Fès; silver jewelry from Tiznit; Safi glazed pottery; embroidery from Fès, Meknes and Rabat; rugs and carpets from Casablanca, Marrakech, Rabat and Sale; copper work from Casablanca, Fès and Marrakech; thuya wood inlaid with citron wood and ebony from Mogador; wood carvings from Rabat and Sale.
NETHERLANDS	As a rule, there is no excessive heat in summer nor extreme cold in winter, although during most of the year it is advisable to take both a raincoat and sweater. Rainfall is lowest between February and May.	Passport. Personal goods, including sports equipment, admitted free.	Bellhops, 30 cents for first piece of luggage and 20c for each remaining piece. Waiters, small change additional to 15% service charge on bill. Cabdrivers, 10%, but no less than 25c.	$1 = 3.80 guilders, rijksdaalder = 2.50 guilders, gulden=1 guilder.	Perfectly safe.	Advisable to book rooms as long as possible in advance, especially in the large cities at Christmas, during the bulb season and in March and September.	Tulip bulbs, chocolate, Hague toffees, cheese from Edam and Gouda, Holland gin, liqueurs, dolls in traditional Dutch costume, silverware, wooden shoes, Delft porcelain, diamonds, earthenware and tiles.

COUNTRY	CLIMATE	CUSTOMS AND ENTRY REQUISITES	TIPPING	MONEY	WATER	HOTELS	WHAT TO BUY
NEW ZEALAND	The main islands lie in a location in the Southern Hemisphere corresponding with the latitude of Italy in the Northern. Although the extreme north is sub-tropical, the hottest days are experienced in the south, where a more extensive landmass induces a wider range of temperatures. However, the differences between summer and winter are not great throughout most of the country, which can easily claim to have an equable and pleasant climate.	Passport. Personal effects, including firearms and cameras, admitted free.	Bellhops, shilling or two for each service. Waiters, 10%-20%. Cabdrivers, slightly more than 15%.	1 New Zealand pound = $2.80, 20 shillings = 1 pound, 12 pence = 1 shilling.	Perfectly safe.	Hotels are comfortable and pleasing, with reasonable rates. Busiest season is from middle of December to April, so reservations should be made early for this time.	Dolls dressed in native Maori costumes and Maori pois; jewelry made of the highly polished, blue-green paua, a large shell-fish; Maori ornaments and weapons carved from "greenstone," a type of jade; jewelry fashioned from the quaint "tiki"; wood-carvings, many inlaid with paua shell; objects made from the gum of the kauri tree.
NICARAGUA	Nicaragua has two seasons, wet and dry. The dry season is from November to April, the wet from May to October. The Atlantic side has frequent showers even in the dry season. The climate varies from warm to hot.	Tourist Card from Nicaraguan consulate, health certificate, smallpox vaccination certificate.	10-15%.	The official unit of currency is the cordoba, five of which equal one U.S. dollar. $1.00 = 5 cordobas.	Bottle water recommended.	Fine hotels with good accommodations are to be found in all of the larger towns and resort areas. Reservations should be made in advance regarding the latter.	Articles of alligator and snakeskin; wrought gold and silver filigree jewelry; mats, purses and shopping bags of woven straw; hammocks made by Indian women of Masaya; hand-tooled leather goods.
NORWAY	Thanks to the Gulf Stream, the mean temperature is 30-40 degrees higher than in other places equally far north. In the eastern valleys the climate is as warm as on the Continent, and along the west coast pleasantly mild.	Passport. Personal effects admitted free.	Hotels and restaurants add service charge.	$1 = 7.12 kroner.	Excellent.	Norwegian hotels are spotlessly clean and comfortable. They vary, of course, in size, but prices are very reasonable.	Gold and silverware; enamelware; pewter; brightly colored woolens; ski equipment; furs; handcarved wooden articles; Lillehammer pipes.
PAKISTAN	In West Pakistan desert heat, mountain cold and Riviera-like temperatures can be found. In contrast, East Pakistan's climate is tropical: warm and humid with heavy monsoon rainfall.	Passport, visa. Advisable to have inoculations for cholera, smallpox, typhus and yellow fever. Bona fide baggage is exempt from duty.	10% is generally acceptable.	1 rupee = 30.203c, 1 rupee = 16 annas.	While piped water throughout Pakistan is absolutely pure, it is advisable to boil other water.	A number of good hotels will be found in most of the leading cities such as Karachi, Lahore and Peshawar. At other places rest houses are available.	Sports equipment from Sialkot; cutlery from Wazirabad; leather work, ornate pottery from Multan; carpets; goldthreaded footwear and headgear; blankets; richly embroidered silks and muslins; inlaid metal work; wood carvings; inlaid woodwork; filigree work in gold and silver; ivory carvings.

COUNTRY	CLIMATE	CUSTOMS AND ENTRY REQUISITES	TIPPING	MONEY	WATER	HOTELS	WHAT TO BUY
PANAMA	Warm days and cool nights. Yearly average around 80° in day dropping 10° to 15° at night. Best in dry season, December to April. And no flies or mosquitoes.	Tourist card and vaccination certificate.	Slightly less than in the U.S. except a little more in swanky clubs.	$1.00 = 1 balboa.	Excellent.	Many fine hotels with good food. Advance reservation is obligatory.	Panama hats, native jewelry, pottery and wooden bowls; Trembleques (hair ornaments made in fanciful shapes); hand woven materials and Panamanian alligator skin products. Everything from French perfume to Chinese silks is sold here and if one is a cagy shopper, many bargains can be had.
PARAGUAY	Weather ranges from cool to hot. Summer can be extremely hot, lasting from December through February. Rest of year varies from warm to cool, with June, the coolest month.	Passport and visa.	A little less than in the U. S.	The guarani = 6c.	Bottle water recommended.	Good accommodations in the capital and its suburbs.	Woven blankets; curious stones, weapons, feather headdresses and necklaces of puma teeth from the tribes of the Chaco region; leather valises; palm leaf hats; fine lace.
PERU	The climate is variable according to region. The coast and flatlands generally warm and dry. In the highlands the climate ranges from cool to warm. The Humboldt current moderates temperature but causes fogs in the winter months.	Passport; no visa unless stay exceeds 48 hours. No restrictions on articles brought in.	Hotels and restaurants add 10% to bill. Waiters get 5% extra. Tip 1 sol for incidental services.	1 sol = 7c. The sol is divided into 100 centavos.	Bottle water recommended.	Accommodations are good in the large cities, but have a reservation.	Silver articles, hand-woven materials, ceramics, Indian handicrafts, leather articles, jackets and coats lined with llama wool, dolls in native dress.
PHILIPPINES	Dry and hot March to July; rainy July to November. Mildly tropical November to March.	Passport, visa, 3 passport pictures, smallpox vaccination; unexpired visa for next country. Personal effects admitted free.	Same as in the U.S.	$1.00 = 2 pesos.	Safe.	First class in larger cities.	Igorot wood carvings; Baguio silver filigree; pina cloth; jusi and cotton table sets; reptile-skin articles; embroideries; straw hats; native weavings; Manila cigars.
PORTUGAL	Portugal has little or no spring or fall change-over. Temperatures vary from a minimum in the winter of 38° to a high of 98° in summer. Generally, December through March it is usually rainy in Lisbon and in the north, with the southern plains having moderate rainfall during the same season.	Passport, with visa only required for visit to Azores. Personal effects, including liquor, food, camera and 400 cigarettes, admitted free.	Bellhops, 5 escudos per bag and 1½-2½ escudos per service. Waiters, 12%-15% if no service charge is included. 5%-10% if one is included. Cabdrivers, 10%-15%.	$1 = 28.5 escudos, 5c =1.5 escudas, 1c =30 centavos.	Good in Lisbon, Estoril and Porto, but bottled water is suggested for other parts, since it varies.	Good, clean accommodations in all cities, but advance reservations are advisable.	Hand embroidery; ceramics; porcelain; cork products; watches and jewelry; dolls; men's hand-made shirts; hand-made lace; hand-made dining room suites of oak and mahogany.

COUNTRY	CLIMATE	CUSTOMS AND ENTRY REQUISITES	TIPPING	MONEY	WATER	HOTELS	WHAT TO BUY
PUERTO RICO	Average annual temperature is about 76 degrees, being slightly cooler in the mountains than on the coastal plains. Cooling Trade Winds eliminate humidity and there is no rag weed pollen.	No entry requirements; proof of nationality required for re-entry to the U. S.	Same as in the U. S.	U. S. currency.	Perfectly safe.	Excellent accommodations.	Among native handicrafts, characteristic is the pelisse or string rug. Basketwork, hats, grass rugs, carved wood novelties, tortoise shell and coconut pins, buckles and buttons, shell articles. Famous for needlework. Import items.
SALVADOR, see EL SALVADOR							
SAUDI ARABIA	Generally hot and humid; rainy season November to May.	Passport and visa.	Check with your hotel manager for local practice.	1 rial = about 28c.	Bottle water recommended.	Adequate but have reservations.	Jewelry, woven textiles, metal articles, leather goods.
SINGAPORE	Singapore lies in the tropical zone and is warm and moist with little seasonal change, although the months from October to February are slightly cooler.	Passport, visa, registration within thirty days or exit permits. Bona fide personal effects, including 50 cigarettes, admitted free.	Same as in U. S.	$1 = 3.05 Malayan dollars, 33c = 1 Malayan dollar.	Safe.	There are many first-class hotels, but reservations should be made.	Since Singapore is a free port, the shops are well-stocked with goods from all over the world and there is no purchase tax. Tourists specialties are; pewter goods, sarongs, modern silverwork, jewelry and other Malay handiwork.
SPAIN	Throughout Spain, it is generally warm during July and August, although the nights are cool enough to sleep. However, climatic changes are sometimes rapid. Best months for good weather are April, May, September and October, but the year-round climate is never too extreme to enjoy one's trip.	Passport. Personal effects, including cameras, film and 2 cartons of cigarettes, admitted free.	Bellhops, 3 pesetas per bag or 1 peseta per service. Waiters, 7%-10%, since a service charge is added. Cabdrivers, 1 or 2 pesetas.	$1 = 40 pesetas, 5c = 2 pesetas, 1c = 45 centimos.	Drinking water is good in Madrid. In small towns, especially in the south, bottled water is recommended.	Rates are exceptionally reasonable, but be sure to have reservations in advance.	Leather goods, including hand-made shoes; and ladies' handbags; fans; gloves; woolen goods; ceramics; antiques; rugs and tapestries; hand embroidery; Mallorca glassware; mantillas, shawls, and handkerchiefs; iron-grill work; bullfight; costume and capes; dolls; costume jewelry.
SWEDEN	Despite the northerly location, the climate is temperate, thanks to the proximity of the Gulf Stream. In central Sweden, it is quite similar to that of New England.	Passport. Personal items not intended for commercial purposes are duty free.	Waiters, 10% minimum. Bellhops, 50 ore per bag, 25 ore per service. Cabdrivers, 10%.	20c = 1 krona, 1 krona = 100 ore.	Excellent.	Hotel accommodations are on the whole satisfactory, although a room shortage has developed, especially in major cities. Make reservations well in advance.	Exquisite glassware and ceramics, fine silver, stainless steel tableware, textiles and furniture are the favorites.

COUNTRY	CLIMATE	CUSTOMS AND ENTRY REQUISITES	TIPPING	MONEY	WATER	HOTELS	WHAT TO BUY
SWITZERLAND	Temperatures range about the same as in the northern U.S., but not quite as extreme and with low humidity. Best weather is from May through September and December through March. The southern part of Switzerland has sub-tropical vegetation and like California, has a year-round climate.	Passport, smallpox vaccination. Used personal effects, including cameras, admitted free.	10% - 15% is general rule. When tip is included in bill, it is not necessary to give more unless service has been exceptional.	$1 = 4.30 Swiss francs, 23c=Swiss franc.	Perfectly safe.	The Swiss have been called "a nation of hotelkeepers". Their inns, noted for immaculate cleanliness and homey comfort, are governed by codes of fair and hospitable treatment of travelers dating back centuries. Excellent accommodation is available, but make reservations.	Swiss watches and cuckoo clocks; textiles; embroideries; sporting goods; small precision instruments, like cameras, binoculars, drawing instruments; typewriters; Swiss linen stationery; wood-carvings, including music boxes; antiques; cheese; chocolate; antiques; native handicrafts.
SYRIA and LEBANON	Winter is generally mild with only a few cold days and spring and autumn are very pleasant. In mid-summer the temperature rises during the day but drops off after sunset.	Passport, visa, smallpox vaccination, report to the Department of Public Security on arrival. Personal effects, including 200 cigarettes, admitted free.	15% if service charge is not included in your bill.	Syrian pound = 27.8c, 3.7 pounds = $1, 1 pound = 100 piastros. Lebanese pound = 28c, 3.6 pounds = $1.	Safe in Damascus and Beirut, but bottle water recommended.	Good accommodations in larger cities.	Damascus brocade; cotton cloth; silk; glassware; leather work; wood inlay work; brassware.
THAILAND	Generally warm and moist. Rainy season June to November.	Passport and typhoid and smallpox vaccination certificate. No firearms, radios or phonographs allowed.	10-15% where not included in bill.	The tical or baht is the monetary unit; it fluctuates in value, usually worth about 5-7c.	Bottle water recommended.	Adequate in the large cities, but have reservations.	Silver articles, jewelry, hand-woven textiles; teakwood items and locally-made novelties.
TRINIDAD & TOBAGO, B.W.I.	Tropical. Average annual temperature: 84°F. by day, 74° by night. Dry season is from January to May; wet season from June to December.	Round-trip ticket. Personal effects admitted free.	10 - 15% unless included in bill.	Same as in Barbados.	Pure and safe at all times in Port of Spain and Scarborough; advisable to boil it in other districts.	A number of good, well-equipped hotels and guest houses in both Trinidad and Tobago, but most of them are in Port of Spain and Scarborough.	Angostura bitters and rum; native handicrafts; French perfumes; filigree jewelry and oriental treasures from Hindu bazaars, especially "cascadure" bracelets in silver.
TUNISIA	The coastal regions have a climate very similar to southern California, with cool, rainy winters and warm summers. The climate of the desert area has blazing, hot mid-days and cold nights.	Passport. Personal effects admitted free.	10 - 15% unless included in bill.	$1=349 francs, 1c =3.5 francs.	Usually safe, but bottled water is available.	Comfortable hotels all over.	Native handcrafts.
TURKEY	The Istanbul region enjoys approximately the same conditions as those of New England. In the central Anatolian plateau around Ankara, you encounter the same severe winters and hot summers as in the Middle West. The Adana district in the south is very much like the southern states.	Passport, visa.	Both at hotels and restaurants, a 10% charge for tips is added to all bills, but additional tipping of 5% to 10% is also customary. Cabdrivers, 20% - 25%.	$1 = 2.80 Turkish Lira, or Turkish Pound 1 lira = 100 kurush.	Safe, in the biggest cities, bottled water suggested in country.	Good accommodations in prominent cities like Ankara, Istanbul and Izmir, but make reservations. In smaller towns accommodation is only adequate.	Turkish carpets; silver ornaments; hand-embroidered lingerie; leather goods; fabrics of Bursa silk; Turkish pottery; hand-carved meerschaum. (Export of precious metals and every kind of jewelry is prohibited.)

COUNTRY	CLIMATE	CUSTOMS AND ENTRY REQUISITES	TIPPING	MONEY	WATER	HOTELS	WHAT TO BUY
UNION OF SOUTH AFRICA	There are no real extremes and climate is pleasant year around. During the summer months, December to February, the days are quite warm but there is little humidity.	Passport and visa.	About the same as in the U.S.	Same as Great Britain.	Perfectly safe.	Excellent accommodations throughout the country.	Native handicrafts: fine beaded articles of the Ndebeles, lovely wood carvings of the Zulus, beaded sandalwood dolls of the Basutos. Natives expect you to bargain and respond favorably to native words.
URUGUAY	Uruguay is blessed with a benign climate the year round. Coolest month is June, with an average temperature of 50° and the warmest is January, when the average is 74°. The rainfall is evenly distributed throughout the year.	Passport, smallpox vaccination certificate. Personal effects, including sports equipment and typewriters admitted free.	Bellhops, 20-50 centésimos per bag and 25 centésimos per service. Waiters, leave something more even though restaurants add minimum service charge of 17% and as much as 10% additional. Cabdrivers, 25-50 centésimos.	Peso — $.5263. 100 centésimos = 1 peso.	Outside Montevideo, bottled water is recommended.	There are many hotels comparable in comfort and service to first-class North American hotels. Reservation should be made.	Leather goods, Uruguayan wines, woolen textiles, furniture, bottles and glassware, paper and paper articles, candy and enameled ware.
VENEZUELA	Climate ranges from tropical in lowlands to temperate in highlands, with extreme cold in higher altitudes. Dry season is November to May; rainy season is May to November.	Tourist card, proof of citizenship and smallpox and health certificate.	15% in restaurants and night clubs. Use 1 bolivar as our quarter for incidental services.	$1.00 = 3.32 bolivars. 30c = 1 bolivar. The bolivar is divided into 100 centimos.	Bottle water recommended.	You will find excellent hotels in Caracas and the larger cities. Best to have reservations.	Oro Cochano jewelry (exquisitely wrought flowers of nugget gold brightened with dew-drop pearls). Tortoise shell and horn articles. Mother-of-pear articles; carved hardwood boxes and chests. Delicate lace and fine embroidery. Straw hats and sandals. Leather and alligator skin articles.
VIRGIN ISLANDS	Mildly tropical; cool trade winds in summer with no extremes in temperature. Hurricane season August through October.	No passport if arriving in U.S. islands from U.S. or Puerto Rico. Return ticket necessary to enter British islands.	10% is customary and most hotels and guest homes add it to your bill.	U.S. currency. See Barbados for British islands.	Bottle water recommended. Otherwise, see that the water is boiled.	Good hotels on larger islands. Guest houses on all islands are well-run.	Jewelry, silver, liquor, bay rum, wines, cigarettes, perfumes, dolls, linens, bone china, local handicrafts, needlework.
WINDWARD ISLANDS, B.W.I.	The prevailing trade winds provide a good climate with little variation in temperature. Rainfall varies.	No passport or visa.	10-15% unless included in bill.	Same as Barbados.	Should be boiled	Good accommodations but have reservations.	

FROM/TO	Azores	Baghdad	Berlin	Bombay	Buenos Aires	Callao	Cairo	Cape Town	Chicago	Istanbul	Guam	Honolulu	Juneau	London	Los Angeles
Azores.........	....	3906	2148	5930	5385	4825	3325	5670	3305	2880	8985	7421	4715	1562	5034
Baghdad........	3906	....	2040	2022	8215	8618	785	4923	6490	1085	6380	8445	6180	2568	7695
Berlin.........	2148	2040	....	3947	7411	6937	1823	5949	4458	1068	7158	7384	4638	575	5849
Bombay.........	5930	2022	3947	....	9380	10530	2698	5133	8144	3043	4831	8172	6992	4526	8810
Buenos Aires....	5385	8215	7411	9380	....	1982	7428	4332	5598	7638	10516	7653	7964	6919	6148
Callao.........	4825	8618	6937	10530	1982	....	7870	6195	3765	7666	9760	5993	5806	6376	4155
Cairo..........	3325	785	1823	2698	7428	7870	....	4476	6231	780	7175	8925	6352	2218	7675
Cape Town......	5670	4923	5949	5133	4332	6195	4476	....	8551	5210	8918	11655	10382	5975	10165
Chicago........	3305	6490	4458	8144	5598	3765	6231	8551	....	5530	7510	4315	2310	4015	1741
Istanbul.......	2880	1085	1068	3043	7638	7666	780	5210	5530	....	7015	8200	5665	1540	6895
Guam...........	8985	6380	7158	4831	10516	9760	7175	8918	7510	7015	....	3896	5225	7605	6255
Honolulu.......	7421	8445	7384	8172	7653	5993	8925	11655	4315	8200	3896	....	2825	7320	2620
Juneau.........	4715	6180	4638	6992	7964	5806	6352	10382	2310	5665	5225	2825	....	4496	1835
London.........	1562	2568	575	4526	6919	6376	2218	5975	4015	1540	7605	7320	4496	....	5496
Los Angeles....	5034	7695	5849	8810	6148	4155	7675	10165	1741	6895	6255	2620	1835	5496	....
Melbourne......	12190	8150	9992	6140	7336	8196	8720	6510	9837	9189	3497	5581	8162	10590	8098
Mexico City....	4584	8155	6119	9818	4609	2619	7807	8620	1690	7160	7690	3846	3210	5605	1445
Montreal.......	2548	5814	3776	7582	5619	3954	5502	7975	750	4825	7840	4992	2647	3370	2468
New Orleans....	3718	7212	5182	8952	4902	2990	6862	8390	827	6220	7895	4305	2860	4656	1695
New York.......	2604	6066	4026	7875	5295	3633	5701	7845	727	5060	8115	5051	2874	3500	2466
Panama.........	3918	7807	5902	9832	3319	1450	7230	7090	2320	6797	9220	5347	4456	5310	3025
Paris..........	1617	2385	540	4391	6891	6455	2020	5762	4219	1390	7675	7525	4700	210	5711
Rio de Janeiro..	4312	7012	6246	8438	1230	2400	6242	3850	5320	6420	11710	8400	7611	5747	6330
San Francisco...	5114	7521	5744	8523	6487	4500	7554	10340	1875	6770	5952	2407	1530	5440	345
Santiago.......	5718	8876	7842	10127	731	1548	8100	5080	5325	8230	9946	6935	7320	7275	5595
Seattle........	4720	6848	5121	7830	6956	4964	6915	10305	1753	6124	5785	2707	870	4850	961
Shanghai.......	7324	4468	5323	3219	12295	10760	5290	8179	7155	5084	1945	5009	4968	5841	6598
Singapore......	8338	4443	6226	2425	9940	11700	5152	6025	9475	5440	2990	6874	7375	6818	8955
Tokyo..........	7370	5242	5623	4247	11601	9740	6005	9234	6410	5649	1596	3940	4117	6050	5600
Wellington.....	11475	9782	11384	7752	6341	6696	10360	7149	8465	10790	4206	4676	7501	11790	6806

FROM/TO	Melbourne	Mexico City	Montreal	New Orleans	New York	Panama	Paris	Rio de Janeiro	San Francisco	Santiago	Seattle	Shanghai	Singapore	Tokyo	Wellington
Azores.........	12190	4584	2548	3718	2604	3918	1617	4312	5114	5718	4720	7324	8338	7370	11475
Baghdad........	8150	8155	5814	7212	6066	7807	2385	7012	7521	8876	6848	4468	4443	5242	9782
Berlin.........	9992	6119	3776	5182	4026	5902	540	6246	5744	7842	5121	5323	6226	5623	11384
Bombay.........	6140	9818	7582	8952	7875	9832	4391	8438	8523	10127	7830	3219	2425	4247	7752
Buenos Aires....	7336	4609	5619	4902	5295	3319	6891	1230	6487	731	6956	12295	9940	11601	6341
Callao.........	8196	2619	3954	2990	3633	1450	6455	2400	4500	1548	4964	10760	11700	9740	6696
Cairo..........	8720	7807	5502	6862	5701	7230	2020	6242	7554	8100	6915	5290	5152	6005	10360
Cape Town......	6510	8620	7975	8390	7845	7090	5732	3850	10340	5080	10305	8179	6025	9234	7149
Chicago........	9837	1690	750	827	727	2320	4219	5320	1875	5325	1753	7155	9475	6410	8465
Istanbul.......	9189	7160	4825	6220	5060	6797	1390	6420	6770	8230	6124	5084	5440	5649	10790
Guam...........	3497	7690	7840	7895	8115	9220	7675	11710	5952	9946	5785	1945	2990	1596	4206
Honolulu.......	5581	3846	4992	4305	5051	5347	7525	8400	2407	6935	2707	5009	6874	3940	4676
Juneau.........	8162	3210	2647	2860	2874	4456	4700	7611	1530	7320	870	4968	7375	4117	7501
London.........	10590	5605	3370	4656	3500	5310	210	5747	5440	7275	4850	5841	6818	6050	11790
Los Angeles....	8098	1445	2468	1695	2466	3025	5711	6330	345	5595	961	6598	8955	5600	6806
Melbourne......	....	8599	10553	9455	10541	9211	10500	8340	7970	7130	8330	4967	3768	5172	1655
Mexico City....	8599	....	2247	940	2110	1532	5800	4810	1870	4122	2339	8120	10495	7190	7003
Montreal.......	10553	2247	....	1390	340	2545	3490	5110	2557	5461	2309	7141	9280	6546	9206
New Orleans....	9455	940	1390	....	1161	1600	4846	4798	1960	4553	2137	7830	10255	6993	7950
New York.......	10541	2110	340	1161	....	2211	3600	4810	2606	5134	2440	7460	9617	6846	9067
Panama.........	9211	1532	2545	1600	2211	....	5440	3311	3349	3000	3680	9430	11800	8560	7580
Paris..........	10500	5800	3490	4846	3600	5440	....	5710	5680	7300	5080	5855	6730	6132	11865
Rio de Janeiro..	8340	4810	5110	4798	4810	3311	5710	....	6655	1852	6945	11510	9875	11600	7510
San Francisco...	7970	1870	2557	1960	2606	3349	5680	6655	....	5960	692	6245	8440	5250	6800
Santiago.......	7130	4122	5461	4553	5134	3000	7300	1852	5960	....	6466	11850	10270	10850	5925
Seattle........	8330	2339	2309	2137	2440	3680	5080	6945	692	6466	....	5780	8200	4863	7310
Shanghai.......	4967	8120	7141	7830	7460	9430	5855	11510	6245	11850	5780	....	2395	1095	6080
Singapore......	3768	10495	9280	10255	9617	11800	6730	9875	8440	10270	8200	2395	....	3350	5360
Tokyo..........	5172	7190	6546	6993	6846	8560	6132	11600	5250	10850	4863	1095	3350	....	5730
Wellington.....	1655	7003	9206	7950	9067	7580	11865	7510	6800	5925	7310	6080	5360	5730	....

Index

Index

Index

Index

MAJOR AIRLINES
OF THE
United States

TWA Trans World Airlines Routes ————
Interchange with other Airlines ══════
Other Airlines ·················
Copyright by C.S. HAMMOND & Co., N.Y.